Cassell

Dictionary
of Christianity

Cassell

Dictionary
of Christianity

EDITED BY J.C. COOPER

CASSELL
London and Washington

Cassell
Wellington House, 125 Strand, London WC2R 0BB
PO Box 605, Herndon, VA 20172, USA

First published 1996
Paperback edition 1997

British Library Cataloguing in Publication Data
A catalogue record for this book is available from the British Library.

ISBN 0-304-33623-8

Front cover illustration: *The Protection of the Holy Virgin.*
Novgorod School, late 15th century.
Courtesy of The Temple Gallery, London

Back cover illustration: detail from *The Mother of God Enthroned.*
Cretan School, late 15th–early 16th century.
Courtesy of The Benaki Museum, Athens.

Typeset by Falcon Oast Graphic Art
Printed and bound in Great Britain by
Biddles Ltd, Guildford and King's Lynn

Contents

Preface

The present volume is based on the Christian references taken from Brewer's *Dictionary of Phrase and Fable*, and is, therefore, mainly a tribute to Dr Brewer's erudition, his wide-ranging interests and his ability to extract and present the essential matter of his subject.

Since Christianity was only a part of the whole work, references to it were necessarily condensed. It is, thus, a work of expansion which is now presented. Only a limited number of saints could be included in *Phrase and Fable*, and so it is in this subject that the main expansion occurs. Even then, limitation has to be exercised; the sheer bulk of the material available imposes strict selection. Any country, or indeed many a county, can present a book of its own saints, as could such names as John, Peter, Felix, Mary or Margaret. As an illustration, there are some 300 saints of the name of Colman in Ireland; the martyrology of the one county of Donegal alone names ninety-six. Hence the aim has been to make a selection which covers a wide spectrum of saints and martyrs of different eras, countries and character, and to include some of the interest and charm of the more singular legends derived from literature, myth, and folklore such as would have appealed to Dr Brewer.

Early Christianity, simple in nature, grew rapidly more complex in the course of its contacts with other cultures and traditions, and this process has continued over the centuries, giving rise to divisions and schisms, which divided Eastern and Western Catholicism and culminated in the Reformation and the birth of Protestantism. There was then a proliferation of sects and denominations, a process which continues today. Also, just as early Christianity met, and came to terms with, Hellenic culture in the Apologists, so it has been adapted to, and influenced by, other beliefs, customs, myths, legends and folklore through the ages. For example, there is the marriage between imported Catholicism and the native Amerindian tribal culture, and the fusion of Catholic and Protestant persuasions with African and Caribbean beliefs. This has resulted in an ever-growing number of branch-churches and sects, as is evident in the great number of churches now registered with the World Council of Churches. Here, again, selection must be made.

Since Brewer's time there has been a notable development in ecumenical movements, leading to a fuller communication between the Eastern and Western divisions in the Catholic Church. There has also been a marked increase of interest in, and membership of, the Eastern Orthodox Church in the West, which now plays an important part in the ecumenical movement. Here, also, the rebirth of the Orthodox Church in Russia since the fall of Communism must be taken into consideration. These factors have made it appropriate to include more of the Eastern rites and dogmas, and the lives of their outstanding saints. For example, St George, reduced to the status of a local cult in the Roman calendar revision in 1969, continues to hold a very important position in the calendar of the Orthodox Catholic Church, where he is the most venerated of the saints and the one most often portrayed in icons.

In the immense diversity of Christianity today, it has also been impossible to include all the sects, fringe movements, institutions and methods of worship. In Dr Brewer's own words, it is 'wholly impossible to exhaust the subject'.

Acknowledgements

The publishers gratefully acknowledge the permission of the World Council of Churches, Geneva, to reproduce the list of member churches found in the World Council of Churches article.

Cross-references

These are indicated in the text by the use of SMALL CAPITALS unless *q.v.* is used.

NOTE

All biblical references are to the *Authorized Version* unless otherwise stated. Entries concerning liturgical customs of the Church of England refer to those associated with the *Book of Common Prayer*. Ecclesiastical usages are those of the Church of England except where otherwise indicated.

Abbreviations

AV	Authorized Version	L.Lat.	Late Latin
BB	Blessed (*pl.*)	*Mal.*	Malachi
Bl.	Blessed (*sing.*)	*Matt.*	Matthew
BVM	Blessed Virgin Mary	M.E.	Middle English
c.	*circa* (about)	Med.	Mediaeval
Chr.	Chronicles	Med. Lat.	Mediaeval Latin
Col.	Colossians	*Mic.*	Micah
Cor.	Corinthians	MM	Martyrs
cp.	compare	MS.	manuscript
d.	died	MSS.	manuscripts
Dan.	Daniel	Mt	Mount
Deut.	Deuteronomy	*Neh.*	Nehemiah
Dr	Doctor	NT	New Testament
Dut.	Dutch	*Num.*	Numbers
Eccles.	Ecclesiastes	*Obad.*	Obadiah
e.g.	*exempli gratia* (for example)	O.E.	Old English
Eph.	Ephesians	O.Fr.	Old French
etc.	*et cetera* (and so on)	O.H. Ger.	Old High German
Exod.	Exodus	OT	Old Testament
Ezek.	Ezekiel	*Pet.*	Peter
f.d.	feast day	*Phil.*	Philippians
fl.	*floruit* (flourished)	*Philem.*	Philemon
Fr.	French	*pl.*	plural
Gal.	Galatians	Port.	Portuguese
Gen.	Genesis	*Prov.*	Proverbs
Ger.	German	*Ps.*	Psalms
Gr	Greek	*q.v.*	*quod vide* (which see)
Hab.	Habakkuk	*Rev.*	Revelation
Hag.	Haggai	*Rom.*	Romans
Heb.	Hebrew	Russ.	Russian
Heb.	Hebrews	*Sam.*	Samuel
Hos.	Hosea	SJ	Society of Jesus (Jesuit)
i.e.	*id est* (that is)	S. of S.	Song of Solomon
Isa.	Isaiah	Sp.	Spanish
Ital.	Italian	SS	Saints
Jas.	James	St	Saint
Jer.	Jeremiah	*Thess.*	Thessalonians
Josh.	Joshua	*Tim.*	Timothy
Jud.	Judges	USA	United States of America
Kgs.	Kings	*viz.*	*videlicet* (namely)
Lam.	Lamentations	*Zech.*	Zechariah
Lat.	Latin	*Zeph.*	Zephaniah
Lev.	Leviticus		

A

Aaron, and Julius c. 304, f.d. 1 July). Saints of whom little is known. They were Roman–British, probably Roman soldiers, martyred under the Diocletian persecution. They were killed at Caerleon-upon-Usk where several churches are dedicated to them. It is, however, doubtful whether the Diocletian persecution reached Britain.

Abaddon. The angel of the bottomless pit (*Rev.* ix, 11), from Heb. *abad*, he perished. Milton used the name for the pit itself.

Abbé. Originally the title of the abbot of a monastery, but now a general title of respect given to secular clergy in France.

Abbess. The woman superior of a convent or nunnery, originally applied to those following the RULE of St BENEDICT. It is now necessary for a nun to be professed for ten years and to be over forty years of age before being elected to the office.

Abbot (Syriac *Abba,* father, Lat. *abbas*). In the Western Catholic church it is the title of the superior of the community of an abbey or large monastery of the orders of the BENEDICTINES, CISTERCIANS and CANONS REGULAR.

Abecedarian. A teacher or learner of the A B C or rudiments. Also an Anabaptist sect, the ZWICKAU PROPHETS, founded in 1520. Led by Nicholas Stork, a weaver, they relied on direct inspiration from God, rejecting all learning as a hindrance.

Abecedarian Hymns. Hymns the lines or divisions of which begin with the letters of the alphabet in regular succession. In Hebrew the 119th Psalm is abecedarian.

Abelard and Héloïse. Peter Abelard (1079–1142), eminent scholar, theologian and philosopher, studied under William of Champeaux and Anselm, and founded an internationally famous school of theology in Paris. At the age of thirty-six he became tutor to Héloïse, the beautiful and accomplished seventeen-year-old niece of Canon Fulbert of Notre Dame. They fell in love, a son was born and they were secretly married, but Héloïse soon disavowed the marriage that she might not hinder Abelard's preferment. Fulbert, enraged at her husband's seeming connivance, caused him to be emasculated. Abelard entered the monastery of St Denis. Héloïse became a nun. Abelard continued his highly controversial teaching and later founded another school near Nogent-sur-Seine called PARACLETE, which, after his departure to take charge of the Abbey of St Gildas in Brittany, was given to a sisterhood under Héloïse. His stormy career ended in 1142 and Héloïse was laid by his side in 1164. Their remains were transferred from Paraclete and re-buried in the Pere Lachaise cemetery (Paris) in 1817.

Abelites, Abelians, or **Abelonians.** A Christian sect of the 4th century living in North Africa, mentioned by St AUGUSTINE. They married but remained virgin, as they affirmed Abel did, since no children of his are mentioned in the SCRIPTURES. Children were adopted to maintain the sect.

Abjuration. The formal renunciation by heretics, apostates or schismatics of their erroneous beliefs in order to be absolved from excommunication and re-admitted to the CATHOLIC CHURCH

Ablutions. The cleansing, or washing, or purification of the body, or hands, or hands and face, or of sacred vessels, generally with water, before rituals or certain religious ceremonies.

Abomination of Desolation. Probably refers to some statue set up in the Temple by heathens or the Romans and is mentioned in *Daniel* 9, 10, 11, and *Matthew* 24:15. The subject is very obscure.

Abraham, St, and his niece **Mary** (6th cent., f.d. 16 March, Greek 29 October). Born of a wealthy family near Edessa, Abraham left his marriage feast to become a desert monk after giving away all his goods to the poor, except bare necessities. Asked by the bishop of Edessa to convert the local pagan population, Abraham became a priest and preached to the people, suffering much persecution but ultimately converting them by his example. He then returned to his desert cell. Legend says that his niece Mary was placed in his charge and that he reared her in piety until she was twenty, when she was seduced by a renegade monk and left with him to see the world. She became a prostitute but Abraham rescued her after two years, disguising himself as an army officer in need of her services but persuading her to return to a life of holiness, in which she developed powers of healing. Their story has been used as a theme in literature and drama.

Abraham's bosom. The repose of the happy in death:

The sons of Edward sleep in Abraham's bosom.
SHAKESPEARE *Richard III*, IV, iii

The allusion is to the ancient custom of allowing a dear friend to recline on one's bosom (*Luke* 16:22), as did John on the bosom of Jesus.

There is no leaping from Delilah's lap into Abraham's bosom. Those who live and die in notorious sin must not expect to go to HEAVEN at death.

Absolution (Lat. *absolvers,* to set free). The forgiveness and release of a penitent from the guilt of sins committed. In the CATHOLIC CHURCH it is the remission of sin and its consequences granted, after confession, by a priest.

Abyssinian Christians. A branch of the Coptic Church. See COPTS.

Acca, St (d. *c.* 740, f.d. 6 August and 20 October). A Benedictine monk, a disciple of St Bosa and later of St WILFRID with whom he journeyed abroad and whom he was said to have succeeded as abbot of Hexham. He was bishop of Hexham from 709–32 and was ultimately buried at the cathedral. Acca was an expert singer, a great collector of relics and a notable scholar whose theological library was mentioned by BEDE who dedicated works to Acca.

Aceldama. The Aramaic for the 'field of Blood' figuratively used for any place of great slaughter. It was the POTTER'S FIELD near Jerusalem bought to bury strangers in (*see Matt.* xxvii, 7, 8 and *Acts* i: 18, 19), and was used by Christians during the CRUSADES and as late as the 17th century.

Acephalites (Gr. *akephale,* without a head). A name given to various schismatical Christian bodies, principally to (i) those MONOPHYSITES who rejected the authority of Peter Mongus, Bishop of Alexandria, in 482, and were later absorbed by the JACOBITES; (2) those NESTORIANS rejecting patriarchal condemnation of Nestorius in 431; (3) priests rejecting episcopal authority or bishops that of their metropolitans; (4) a group of English levellers in the reign of

Henry I, who acknowledged no leader.

The name is also given to various legendary headless monsters.

Acolyte. A person who assists the priest at Mass; in the CATHOLIC CHURCH, the highest of the four minor orders, whose duty is to carry the incense, light the candles and generally serve the priest. Acolytes can also be laymen.

Action Sermon. In the Scottish PRESBYTERIAN Church the sermon sometimes preached before administering the Communion.

Adalbert of Prague, St (d. 997, f.d. 23 April). Called the Apostle of Prussia, he was born into Bohemian nobility and was under thirty years of age when appointed bishop of Prague. He founded the BENEDICTINE Abbey of Brevnov, but met with political opposition, was exiled and went to ROME. He was a friend of Otto III and attempted to convert the Magyars. He returned to Prague but, after a second expulsion, undertook a mission to Pomerania and the Baltic coast. According to tradition he was martyred at Königsberg. His cult became widespread among the Magyars and Slavs, also in Germany, Poland and at Kiev.

Adam. For the Bible story of Adam, see *Genesis* i–v.

The curse of Adam. The necessity of working for a living. 'In the sweat of thy face shalt thou eat bread, till thou return unto the ground' (*Gen.* ii, 19). In the story of the Creation, Adam and Eve were driven from the Garden of EDEN for disobedience, and God cursed the earth, which had hitherto borne only plants 'pleasant to the sight and good for food' (*Gen.* ii, 9) so that it now put forth 'thorns also and thistles' (*Gen.* iii, 18).

Adaman, Adoman, or **Eunar,** St (624–704, f.d. 23 September). Born in Co. Donegal, he entered a monastery there, then went on a mission to Northumbria. He became a monk at Iona, following his kinsman St COLUMBA, and under the direction of Abbot Seghine whom he succeeded as ruler. He was famous as a writer, his chief work being his life of St Columba; he was also noted for his efforts to convert the Easter calculation from the Celtic to the Roman usage and for the Andaman Law which exempted women from taking part in warfare and insisted that they, children and the clergy should be treated as non-combatants.

Adamites. The name given to various heretical sects, possibly of misguided ascetics, who practised nudity and rejected marriage. Such were the 2nd-century Adamites in North Africa, but similar ideas, leading to licentiousness, were revived in Europe by the *Brethren and Sisters of the Free Spirit* in the 13th century; the BEGHARDS in France, Germany and the Netherlands; and the PICARDS of Bohemia in the 14th and 15th centuries, etc. Adamites are mentioned in James Shirley's comedy *Hyde Park* (II, iv) (1632) and in the *Guardian,* No. 134 (1713).

Adelaide, St (*c.* 931–99, f.d. 16 December). First married to King Lothair of Italy, and then the second wife of Otto the Great, she was crowned Empress by Pope John XII. After the death of Otto she suffered political and family troubles, being rejected by her son Otto II, and his wife, and by her grandson Otto III. She founded a convent at Seltz in Alsace where she died; she was noted for her generosity and was called 'a marvel of beauty and goodness'.

Adhelm, St. *See* ALDHELM, ST.

Adiaphorists (Gr. indifferent). Moderate Lutherans, followers of Melanchthon, who accepted the Interim of Leipzig (1548) on ceremonies indifferent (i.e. neither sanctioned nor forbidden by the Scriptures), causing controversy among the Lutherans, which substantially ended in 1555.

Adoption controversy. Elipand, Archbishop of Toledo, and Felix Bishop of Urgel (in the 8th century), maintained that Christ in his human nature was the son of God by adoption only (*Rom.* viii, 29), though in his pre-existing state he was the 'begotten Son of God' in the ordinary Catholic acceptation. The **adoptionists** were condemned by the Council of Frankfurt in 794.

Adrian. Adrian IV, cp. Hadrian. Born Nicholas Breakspear, at Abbots Langley, and becoming a monk in France, then abbot of St Rufus, near Arles, he was the only Englishman to become a pope.
Adrian of Canterbury, St (d. 709, f.d. 9 January). An African monk who was abbot of a monastery near Naples. He was offered the archbishopric of Canterbury by Pope Vitalian, which he declined, suggesting Theodore, a Greek monk, in his place. The Pope then persuaded Adrian to accompany Theodore as an adviser. Adrian became head of the abbey of SS Peter and Paul, later St AUGUSTINE's and was responsible for establishing a school which became famous for its wide range of subjects which included Greek, Latin, Roman law, astronomy, theology and poetry. Many notable scholars, abbots and prelates received their education there. Adrian died in 709 and when his body was translated with others in 1091, it was found incorrupt. Miracles were recorded in which the saint helped scholars when they were at odds with authority.

Adulterous Bible. *See* BIBLE. SOME SPECIALLY NAMED EDITIONS.

Advent (Lat. *adventus,* arrival). The four weeks before CHRISTMAS, beginning on St ANDREW's Day (30 November), or the Sunday nearest to it, commemorating the first and second coming of Christ; the first to redeem, and the second to judge the world.
Advent Sunday. The first Sunday in Advent, the beginning of the Church Year, except in the Greek Church where it begins on St MARTIN's Day (11 November).
Adventists. Those who expect a second coming of Christ on earth as imminent. They originated in the USA as MILLERITES. *See* MILLENARIANS (see under MILLENNIUM); SEVENTH-DAY ADVENTISTS.

Adversary, The. SATAN or the DEVIL (from I *Peter* v, 8).

Adversity Hume. Joseph Hume (1777–1855) was so called through his forebodings of national disaster in the mid-1820s.

Advocate. The Devil's Advocate. A carping or adverse critic, from *Advocatus Diaboli* (Devil's Advocate). In the ROMAN CATHOLIC CHURCH, the popular name given to the Promoter of the Faith whose duty it is to promote vigorously the arguments against a proposed BEATIFICATION or CANONIZATION. The supporter was (until 1983) called *Advocatus Dei* (God's Advocate).

Advowson (Lat. *advocatio,* a summoning). The right of presentation to a church BENEFICE. Thus named because the patron was the advocate or defender of the living and of the claims of his candidate. The different advowsons are:
Advowson appendant. When the right of presentation belongs to and passes with the manor whose owner originally built, or endowed, the church.
Advowson collative. When the BISHOP himself is patron; presentation, admission, and institution are replaced by collation.
Advowson donative. When the patron (usually the Crown) donated the benefice without the bishop's playing any part in its disposal. These became presentative after 1898.
Advowson in gross. One which has been sold and become legally separated from the manor.
Advowson presentative. Where the patron presents the clerk to the BISHOP, who must institute the nominee unless there are legal or ecclesiastical grounds for refusal.
The transfer and sale of advowsons is now subject to restrictions.

Aedilburgh, St. *See* ETHELBURGA.

Aethelthryth, St. *See* ETHELDREDA.

Aelred or Ailred, St (1109–1167, f.d. 12 January, 3 March). Born at Hexham, the son and grandson of priests, he entered the service of King DAVID OF SCOTLAND. At twenty-four he became a monk at Rievaulx and later was abbot of a newly-founded monastery at Revesby, in Lincolnshire, but after four years returned to Rievaulx. Under his rule the monastery increased greatly in numbers and reputation. In spite of great physical pain he travelled widely, visiting other CISTERCIAN houses in England, Scotland and France. He was a man of energy, yet gentle and sympathetic and both practised and wrote of friendship, one of his works being *On Spiritual Friendship*; he was known as the Pattern of True Friendship.

Affusion. The baptism of a believer by pouring water upon the person as distinct from sprinkling (aspersion), or dipping (immersion).

Agape. A love-feast (Gr. *agape,* love). The early Christians held a love-feast in conjunction with the Lord's Supper when the rich provided food for the poor. Eventually they became a scandal and were condemned by the Council of Carthage, 397.

Agatha, St (f.d. 5 February). Was tortured and murdered at Catania in Sicily, possibly during the Decian persecution of 250–3. She is sometimes represented holding a salver containing her severed breasts, and the shears or pincers with which she was mutilated. She is invoked against volcanic eruptions, probably Etna, and, by extension, fire. Her veil, which she once used to deflect a flow of lava from engulfing Catania, was kept as a relic in the Duomo at Florence and was reputed to extinguish fire. She is also the patron saint of bell-founders and is invoked against diseases of the breast.

Agnes, St (d. *c.* 304, f.d. 21 January). The patron saint of young virgins, possibly martyred in the Diocletian persecution at the age of 13. There are various unreliable and conflicting accounts on the manner of her death; some say she was burnt at the stake and others that she was beheaded or stabbed. She vowed that her body was consecrated to Christ and rejected all her suitors. Upon St Agnes's night, says Aubrey in his *Miscellanies* (1696), you take a row of pins, and pull out every one, one after another. Saying a PATERNOSTER stick a pin in your sleeve, and you will dream of him or her you shall marry. In Keats' *The Eve of St Agnes,* we are told:

how upon St Agnes' Eve,
Young virgins might have visions of delight,
And soft adorings from their loves receive
Upon the honey'd middle of the night,
If ceremonies due they did aright;
As, supperless to bed they must retire.

The 'Golden Legend' version of her story is similar to that of LUCY. When she refused either to marry, or to worship the Roman gods, she was sent to a brothel, led naked through the streets, but her hair grew miraculously to cover her completely. In the brothel an angel covered her with a brilliant light, making her invisible. She is portrayed as only twelve or thirteen years of age when she was martyred. In one account she was burned, but the flames killed her executioners instead. She was then either beheaded or killed by being stabbed in the throat. In art she is accompanied by a lamb, or half-burned faggots, with a protecting angel, or with a sword. She is the patron saint of Purity.

Agnes of Montepulciano, St (1268–1317, f.d. 20 April). A DOMINICAN nun, said to have been appointed abbess at a very early age—one tradition says fifteen—and later founded the convent at Montepulciano. She had visions of Christ, the MADONNA and ANGELS, and when she was installed as abbess a shower of heavenly MANNA descended on the ALTAR. Her body remained incorrupt and her tomb was a place of pilgrimage.

Agnoetae (Gr. α, not; *gignoskein,* to know). (1) Certain 4th-century Eunomian heretics, who maintained that God was not completely omniscient.
(2) A group of 6th-century MONOPHYSITES, who maintained that Christ, by the limitations of his human nature, had incomplete knowledge of both present and future.

Agnostic (Gr. *a,* not; *gignoskein,* to know). A term coined by T. H. Huxley in 1869 (with allusion to St PAUL's mention of an altar 'To the Unknown God' in *Acts* xvii, 23) to indicate the mental attitude of those who withhold their assent from whatever is incapable of proof, e.g. the existence of God, a First Cause, etc. An agnostic simply says 'I do not know'. *See* THEIST.

Agnus. Agnus Bell. *See* AGNUS DEI.
Agnus Dei (Lat. Lamb of God). (1) A title of Jesus; (2) the figure of a lamb bearing a cross or flag, the symbol of Christ; (3) the cake of wax or dough bearing this imprint, distributed by the POPE on the Sunday after EASTER—a relic of the ancient custom of distributing the wax of the Paschal candle, which was stamped with the lamb; (4) that part of the MASS introduced by the ringing of the *Agnus bell,* beginning with the words, *Agnus Dei, qui tollis peccata mundi*

(O Lamb of God, that takest away the sins of the world); also part of the *Gloria* in the English Communion service.

Agonistics. A group of roving DONATISTS in Africa in the early 4th century. The name means 'Champions' (of Christ). They committed acts of violence and were called *Circumcellions* by the Catholics because they wandered among the dwellings of the peasants (*circum cellas*).

Agrapha (Gr. not written). Sayings attributed to Christ, though not included in the GOSPELS, e.g. the 'Logia', a collection of the sayings of Jesus from papyri discovered in Egypt in 1897–1907 at the ruins of Oxyrhynchus.

Aidan, St (d. 651, f.d. 31 August). A monk of Iona who was chosen in 635 in answer to King Oswald's request to spread and rekindle Christianity in Northumbria. He established a monastery on the island of Lindisfarne (HOLY ISLAND) and founded many churches and schools on the mainland. He died at Bamburgh.

Aidan (Maedoc or **Ferns), St** (*c.* 626, f.d. 31 January). An Irishman of Connacht who founded monasteries at Ferns (of which he became the first bishop) Drumland and Rossinver. There are few historical facts about his life but many legends of his generosity, kindness and obedience. He is credited with prodigious feats such as travelling to ROME and back in twenty-four hours and undertaking an austerity of seven years during which he existed on only barley bread and water.

Ailbe, St (d. 527, f.d. 12 September). Said to have been born to a slave girl in Ireland but suckled by a she-wolf which he was later able to befriend. He travelled as a preacher and is reputed to have founded the see of Embry or Imlech, of which he became the first bishop. When he retired he went to the mythical Land of Promise.

Aisle (Lat. *ala,* a wing). The side division of a Church, flanking the NAVE, TRANSEPT and CHANCEL; the lateral division of a Gothic church. In churches in England there are usually two aisles to the north and south of the nave. Some churches have only one aisle. The term is now used incorrectly to apply to the passage-ways between PEWS.

Alb. The white linen vestment worn under the COPE, CHASUBLE or DALMATIC by a priest celebrating the EUCHARIST; it has long sleeves and reaches to the feet.

Alban, St (d. *c.* 305, f.d. 22 June, in the Church of England 17 June). Britain's first martyr, beheaded at Verulamium during the Diocletian persecution, for harbouring a Christian priest. The monastery of St Albans was built by Offa in 795 on the spot where he died. The story is given in the works of GILDAS. Like many other SAINTS he is sometimes represented carrying his head in his hands to signify death by beheading.

Alberic, St (d. 1109, f.d. 26 January). At first a HERMIT and a BENEDICTINE, Alberic, with companions, moved to Molesme as a community, but following disputes he, with St ROBERT OF MOLESME and St Stephen HARDING, an Englishman, founded a monastery at Cîteaux from which developed the CISTERCIAN order, based on a regime of poverty and simplicity and the use of LAY BROTHERS. Robert became the first abbot, but he returned to Molesme and Alberic then took his place. At his death Stephen became his successor, saying he had lost 'a father, a guide and a fellow-soldier in the Lord'.

Albert the Great. Albertus Magnus (*c.* 1206–80, f.d. 15 November), Albert of Cologne, famous DOMINICAN scholastic philosopher, also called *doctor universalis.* He was placed by Dante among the lovers of wisdom. Born of a noble family in Swabia, he became a Dominican at Padua, then joined the recently-founded Order of Preachers. He taught at Cologne where St THOMAS AQUINAS was a student. In 1260 Albert was appointed bishop of Ratisbon but resigned after two years to return to teaching and his writing, which covered a vast range of subjects from the theological, ethical, biblical and metaphysical, to the scientific. He was largely responsible for the combination of Aristotelian philosophy and Christian theology which was the basis of SCHOLASTICISM. Although beatified in 1622 Albert was not canonized until 1931, when Pope Pius XI enrolled him among the DOCTORS OF THE CHURCH. He became the patron saint of students of natural science.

Albigenses. A common name for various 12th- and 13th-century MANICHAEAN sects in southern France and northern Italy; so called from the city of Albi in Languedoc; where their persecution began. Violent opponents of the CATHOLIC CHURCH, they were subjected to a crusade by Innocent III in 1208 and they were finally exterminated by the end of the 14th century. They were also called Cathari and Bulgarians.

Alcantara, Order of. A military and religious order, developing from the 12th-century order of St Julian de Pereiro, founded to combat the Moors in Spain, and following the CISTERCIAN rule. Charged with the defence of Alcantara since the early 13th century, it became a lay order in the mid-16th century and a civil and military decoration after 1875.

Alcuin (*c*. 735–804, Beatified). Born of a noble Yorkshire family, he was noted as a scholar who founded schools and became educational adviser to Charlemagne. He rectified many abuses in the Church and reformed the LITURGY. Alcuin returned to England as ambassador to King Offa, but went back to the court of Charlemagne and was appointed abbot of St MARTIN of TOURS. He wrote in defence of the orthodox doctrine of the TRINITY and opposed ADOPTIONISM.

Aldhelm, or Adhelm, St (639–709, f.d. 25 May, 3 October). Born in Wessex and brought up under St ADRIAN and St THEODORE at Canterbury and later at Malmesbury, where he became abbot and where he was ultimately buried, he was also appointed bishop of Sherborne by his kinsman King Ina, or Ine. He had a reputation as both a notable scholar and a humorist and versifier, singing and reading the GOSPELS in public and attracting people to church by his singing while accompanying himself on the harp. His writings in Latin were widely read and he was said to be the father of Anglo-Latin poetry. Aldhelm visited ROME and founded monasteries. The promontory of St Alban's Head, in Dorset, should be St Aldhelm's Head.

Alexander, St (4th cent., f.d. 26 February). Patriarch of Alexandria, he was responsible for the excommunication of Arius. He attended the General Council of NICAEA in 325 which finally condemned the ARIANS.
Alexander Acoemetus, St (*c*. 430, f.d. 15 January). Of Asian origin, he travelled extensively in Asia Minor, performing miracles, converting Syrians and robbers and founding monasteries. Finally settling at Gomon, on the Bosphorus, with his monks, he divided them into six CHOIRS to sing the DIVINE OFFICE continually night and day, from which they were called the 'Sleepless Ones' and Alexander was given his name.
Alexander Nevski, St (1219–63, f.d. 23 November, 23 May, 30 August). A prince of Novgorod, Vladimir and Kiev, he was called Nevski following his victory over the Swedes at the river Neva. He defeated the TEUTONIC KNIGHTS, then met the threat of the Tartars by negotiation and intercession. He was an excellent ruler of the people and greatly venerated. Shortly before his death he became a monk, dying at the monastery of Vladimir-Kljazma where he was buried and which became a centre of his cult. He was canonized in 1381 by the metropolitan of Kiev and All Russia. After Russian resistance to the Nazi invasion in the Second World War an Order of Alexander

Nevski was instituted. A film of his life was made in 1938, with music by Prokofiev.

Alexis, St (f.d. 17 July) Patron saint of hermits and beggars. According to the story in the Gesta Romanorum (*Tale* XV) he lived on his father's estate as a hermit until he died, but was never recognized. He had left his wife at the church and retired to Edessa for eighteen years before returning to his father's house and living on alms. He is depicted as a beggar with a bowl or as a poor pilgrim and is venerated in hospitals and houses for the poor.

Alfwold, St (d. 1058, f.d. 25 March). A monk of Winchester, appointed bishop of Sherborne. He visited Durham, being particularly devoted to St CUTHBERT, and he also greatly venerated St SWITHUN. When he quarrelled with Godwin of Wessex the earl was smitten with a disease which could not be cured until the saint intervened miraculously. Alfwold was noted for his simple and austere life.

Alien priory. A priory which was dependent upon a monastery in a foreign country.

Alipy, St (d. *c*. 1114). Regarded as the father of Russian iconography, he painted as a child under Greek masters, and then became a monk and was ordained into the priesthood. He collaborated with St GREGORY.

Alkmund, St (d. *c*. 800, f.d. 19 March). Of the royal house of Northumbria, he was exiled for some years among the Picts. He was said to have been martyred, but it is uncertain where or when. He was buried at Lilleshut and his body was translated later to Derby where he became the patron saint of the town.

All Hallows. All-Hallows' Day. All Saints' Day (1 November), 'hallows' being the Old English *halig,* a holy (man), a saint. Pope Boniface IV converted the Pantheon at Rome into a Christian church, dedicated to all the martyrs, in 610. The festival of All Saints, originally held on 1 May, was changed to 1 November in 834.
All-Hallows' Eve or **Hallowe'en** (31 October), also called 'Nutcrack Night' and 'Holy Eve', is associated with many ancient customs including bobbing for apples, cracking nuts (mentioned in *The Vicar of Wakefield*), finding one's lover by various rites, etc. Burns portrays the Scottish customs in his poem *Hallowe'en,* and Scottish tradition says that those born on HALLOWEEN have the gift of second sight.
All-Hallows Summer. Another name for St Martin's Summer or an Indian summer, so called because it set in about All-Hallows; similarly there is a St Luke's Summer (from 18 October).

Farewell, thou latter spring! farewell, All-hallown Summer!

(SHAKESPEARE: *Henry IV, Part I*, I, ii)

All Saints. *See* ALL HALLOWS.

All Souls' Day (2 November). The day which Roman Catholics devote to prayer and alms-giving on behalf of the faithful departed. According to tradition, a pilgrim returning from the HOLY LAND took refuge on a rocky island during a storm. There he met a hermit, who told him that among the cliffs was an opening to the infernal regions, through which flames ascended, and where the groans of the tor-mented were distinctly audible. The pilgrim told Odilo, abbot of Cluny, who appointed the day following (2 November 998) to be set apart for the benefit of those souls in PURGATORY.

Allen, St. *See* ELIAN THE PILGRIM, st.

Almedha, St (6th cent., f.d. 1 August). Reputedly the daughter of Brychan, King of Garthmathrin, Wales; she was martyred by Saxons near Brecknock.

Almond, St John (*c.* 1577–1612, f.d. 25 October). Born at Allerton, Lancashire, and educated in Ireland and at ROME, he became a doctor of divinity and gained a reputation for learning and as a preacher. He was imprisoned in England, was released, but was again preach-ing at large in 1609 and was once more impris-oned in Newgate, accused of being a priest. Although the accusation was not proved he was hanged at Tyburn. He was canonized in 1970 by Pope Paul VI as one of the FORTY MARTYRS OF ENGLAND AND WALES.

Almonry. The place where the almoner resides. In monasteries, one-tenth of the income was distributed to the poor by the almoner. *Almonry* is from the Lat. *eleemosynarium,* a place for alms but the word became confused with AMBRY, thus 'Ambry Close' in Westminster used to be called 'Almonry Close'.

The place wherein this chapel or almshouse stands was called the 'Elemosinary' or Almonry, now cor-rupted into Ambrey, for that the almis of the Abbey are there distributed to the poor.

(STOW: *Survey of London* (1598))

Alms (OE *aelmysse,* ultimately from Lat. *eleemosina* from Gr. *eleemosyne,* compassion), gifts to the poor. It is a singular word which, like riches (from Fr. *richesse*), has by usage become plural. In the BIBLE, we have '(he) asked an alms' Acts 3:3), but Dryden gives us 'alms are but the vehicles of prayer' (*The Hind and the Panther,* iii, 106), 1687.

Alombrados. *See* ALUMBRADO; ILLUMINATI.

Alpha. 'I am Alpha and Omega, the first and the last' (*Rev.* i, II). *Alpha* (A) is the first and *Omega* (Ω) the last letter of the Greek alphabet. *See* TAU. The phrase is used in connection with Christ as the beginning and the end, the first and last of Christianity. The two letters to-gether were used on early Christian monu-ments, tombstones and on coins. They appeared widely in art.

Alphege, St (*c.* 953–1012, f.d. 19 April). Also called Elphege, Aelfheagh or Anlaf, he retired to a monastery in Gloucestershire and later to a hermitage near Bath. He was reluctantly appointed bishop of Winchester at the insis-tence of St DUNSTAN, and during his twenty-year episcopacy his generosity was such that it was said that there were no beggars in his diocese, while he personally maintained the austerities of his monastic days. In 1006 he was made Archbishop of Canterbury in recognition of his great abilities. When the Danes raided the city Alphege remonstrated with them for their cru-elty and refused to pay a ransom; he was taken prisoner then brutally murdered. He was buried in St Paul's Cathedral, but when Canute became king he translated the body to Canterbury with great honour.

Alphonsus Liguori, St (1696–1787, f.d. 2 August, now 1 August). Of a noble Neapolitan family he was educated as a barrister but for-sook the law to become a priest, a notable preacher and a missionary, especially in rural districts. He founded the Congregation of the Holy Redeemer, the REDEMPTIONISTS, but the order was torn by rivalries and dissensions and was split by an error on the part of Alphonsus who signed a document he had not studied and which excluded him from his own community: it was not united again until after his death. He was appointed bishop of Sant' Agata dei Goti but resigned through ill health. He wrote many theological works, the best known being *Moral Theology* and the *Glories of Mary,* and his polemics against the severities of the JANSENISTS. He was proclaimed a DOCTOR of the Church in 1871, when his feast day, formerly 2 August, became 1 August. After his death the Redemptionists spread widely. He was one of the saints said to have the power of BILOCATION.

Altar (Lat. *altus,* high). The block or table used for religious sacrifice. In many Christian churches the term is applied to the Communion Table.
Led to the altar. Married, said of a woman, who as a bride is led up to the altar-rail, where marriages are solemnized.

Alternative Services Book. *See* BOOK OF COMMON PRAYER.

Alumbrado (Sp. illuminated, enlightened). A perfectionist; so called from a Spanish sect claiming special 'illumination', which arose in 1575. *See* ILLUMINATI.

Amalricians. *See* BRETHREN OF THE FREE SPIRIT.

Amandus, St (*c.* 584–679, f.d. 6 February). He lived as a hermit in a cell at Bourges for fifteen years, then set out on extensive missionary journeys in Flanders and among the Slavs of the Danube region. He was consecrated bishop without a definite see. Later he was said to have been appointed bishop of Maastricht, though this is disputed. He rebuked King Dagobert for licentiousness and his use of force. Amandus founded several monasteries and was abbot of Elnon, retiring there and dying at the age of ninety after having written his testament.

Ambo. A small pulpit or reading desk placed in the CHOIR, used in the early Church for the liturgical parts of the service.

Ambrose, St (*c.* 340–97, f.d. 7 December, 4 April). He became BISHOP of Milan in 374. He was noted for the penance he imposed on the Eastern Emperor Theodosius, for the massacre of the Thessalonians; also for his victory over the ARIANS at the synod of Aquileia (381), and for his organization of church music. The *Ambrosian Chant* was used until the GREGORIAN CHANT became the basis of church music two centuries later. His emblems are (1) a beehive, in allusion to the legend that a swarm of bees settled on his mouth when he was lying in his cradle—a favourable omen; (2) a scourge, by which he expelled the Arians from Italy.
Ambrosian Library, founded in Milan (1609) by Cardinal Borromeo, Archbishop of Milan, and named in honour of St Ambrose. Its famous collection of manuscripts includes a 4th-century codex of Homer, the earliest known.

Ambry (Lat. *armarium*, cupboard, chest). A cupboard, wall-press, or locker. In church a closed recess for keeping books, vestments, sacramental plates, consecrated oil, etc. There are several variant forms such as *aumbry, awmry, almery,* etc., the latter leading to confusion with ALMONRY.

Amen. Used by Christians at the end of a prayer; it is an expression of assent, meaning 'so be it'; derived from the ancient Hebrew liturgy.
Amen Corner, at the west end of PATERNOSTER ROW, London, was where the monks finished the PATERNOSTER, on CORPUS CHRISTI Day, as they went in procession to St Paul's Cathedral.

They began in *Paternoster* Row with the *Lord's Prayer* in Latin, which was continued to the end of the street; then said *Amen* at the corner of the Row; on turning down *Ave Maria* Lane, commenced chanting the *Hail Mary*! then, crossing Ludgate entered *Creed* Lane chanting the CREDO. Paternoster Row, Amen Corner and much of Ave Maria Lane were destroyed in an air raid on 28 December 1940.

Amice. An oblong white linen vestment worn by the priest when officiating at MASS.

Aminadab. A QUAKER. The Scripture name has a double *m,* but in old comedies, where the character represents a Quaker, the name has generally only one. Obadiah was also used to signify a Quaker and Rachel a Quakeress.

Amish, The. Followers of Jakob Ammann; a strictly conservative sect which separated from the MENNONITES in the late 17th century. They first appeared in Pennsylvania in *c.* 1714 and settlements in other parts of America followed. They are conspicuous for their colourful customs, industry, and frugality. They still use the German language, wear old-fashioned dress and beards without moustaches, use hooks and eyes instead of buttons, and employ horse-drawn vehicles.

Amulet (Lat. *amuletum,* a charm). Something worn, usually round the neck, as a preventive charm. The word was formerly connected with the Arabic *himalah,* the name given to the cord that secured the Koran to the person. The early Christians used to wear amulets called ICHTHYS.

Anastasia, St. A Roman matron said to have been beheaded with St Basilissa for having buried the bodies of St PETER and St PAUL.

Anathema. A denunciation or curse. A Greek word meaning 'a thing set up or hung up', an offering to the gods. Thus Gordius hung up his yoke and beam; the shipwrecked hung up their wet clothes; retired workmen hung up their tools, cripples their crutches, etc. Later it came to mean a thing devoted to evil since animals offered up were destined for death.

In the Catholic and Calvinistic churches it became a more extreme form of denunciation than EXCOMMUNICATION.

Anchor. In Christian symbolism the anchor is the sign of hope, in allusion to *Hebrews* vi, 19, 'Hope we have as an anchor of the soul'. It also symbolizes security. In art it is an attribute of Pope CLEMENT I who was said to have been tied to an anchor and cast into the sea (1st century); and St Nicholas of Bari, the patron saint of sailors.

Anchorite (Gr. *anachorites,* one who retires). A recluse or hermit who withdraws from the world for religious reasons but does not join an order or community.

Anchoress. A female hermit.

Ancient of Days. A scriptural name given to God (*Dan.* vii, 9).

Andrew, St (d. *c.* 70, f.d. 30 November). He was a fisherman and brother of St PETER, depicted in Christian art as an old man with long white hair and beard, holding the Gospel in his right hand, and leaning on a St Andrew's cross. It is said that he was crucified in Patrae on a *crux decussata* (*see* CROSS). He is also the patron saint of Russia and Scotland. *See* RULE, st.; CONSTANTINE'S CROSS *under* CROSS.

Andrew of Crete, St (*c.* 660–740, f.d. 4 July). Also called 'of Jerusalem', having been a monk there. He went to Constantinople in 685 and was ordained deacon and put in charge of both a childrens' orphanage and a home for old men. Later he was appointed archbishop of Gortyna, in Crete, and was famous as a preacher and liturgical poet, writing many HYMNS and introducing a form of composition called 'kanons', which were incorporated into the Byzantine LITURGY, some of which are still sung. Andrew died on the island of Lesbos.

Angel. In post-canonical and apocalyptic literature angels are grouped in varying orders. The commonly used hierarchy of nine orders is that popularized by the Pseudo-Areopagite or Pseudo-Dionysius (early 5th century) in his *De Hierarchia Celesti,* which arranges them in three triads:

(1) Seraphim, Cherubim, and Thrones in the first circle.
(2) Dominions, Virtues, and Powers in the second circle.
(3) Principalities, Archangels, and Angels in the third circle.

The names are taken from the *Old Testament* and *Ephesians* i, 21 and *Colossians* i, 16.

The seven holy angels are MICHAEL, GABRIEL, RAPHAEL, URIEL, Chamuel, Jophiel and Zadkiel. Michael and Gabriel are mentioned in the BIBLE, Raphael in the APOCRYPHA and all appear in Enoch (viii, 2).

Milton in *Paradise Lost,* Bk. I, 392, gives a list of the fallen angels.

Angel of the Schools. St Thomas Aquinas. *See* ANGELIC DOCTOR.

Angela Merici, St (1474–1540, f.d. 31 May). Born in Lombardy and orphaned at an early age, Angela joined the Franciscan TERTIARIES and, with others, devoted herself to educating poor girls. After a pilgrimage to the HOLY LAND and ROME, she and her companions bound themselves to devote the rest of their lives to the education of girls under the patronage of St URSULA who was patroness of mediaeval universities and was venerated as a leader of women. This was the foundation of the URSULINES, the first teaching order of women. At first no vows were taken, no habit worn, and the order was not enclosed. In 1544 Pope Paul III issued a BULL confirming the Company of St Ursula. Angela Merici was canonized in 1807.

Angelic. Angelic Brothers, or **Gichtelians.** A separatist sect founded in Holland in the latter part of the 17th century by the German mystic Johann Gichtel (1638–1710).

Angelic Doctor. Thomas Aquinas (*c.* 1225–74) was so called, probably because of the purity and excellence of his teaching. His exposition of the most recondite problems of theology and philosophy was judged to be the fruit of almost more than human intelligence and in 1879 Pope Leo XIII directed that the teachings of Aquinas should be the basis of theology. His *Summa Theologica* is the culmination of SCHOLASTICISM. *See* DUMB OX.

Angelic Hymn, The. The hymn beginning with *Glory to God in the highest* (Luke 2:14), so called because the former part of it was sung by the angel host that appeared to the shepherds of Bethlehem.

Angelic Salutation, The. The AVE MARIA.

Angelus, The. A Roman Catholic devotion in honour of the Annunciation. It begins with the words *Angelus Domini nuntiavit Mariae.* It is recited thrice daily, usually at 6 a.m., noon, and 6 p.m. at the sound of the *Angelus* bell.

Angles. Non Angli, sed angeli (Not Angles, but angels). The legend is that when Pope GREGORY THE GREAT (590–604) saw some fair-complexioned youths in the slave-market he asked whence they had come. He was told that they were Angles and also heathen. 'Not Angles, but angels' was his comment and on becoming Pope he sent St AUGUSTINE to effect their conversion.

Anglican. In America means 'English' (sometimes with no ecclesiastical implications).

…suitable abodes for country gentlemen, in the strictly Anglican sense of the expression.
C. E. CASON: *Culture in the South*

In England it is used in connexion with the CHURCH OF ENGLAND.

Anglo-Catholic. *See* HIGH CHURCH.

Animals. Animals in Christian Art. Some

animals are appropriated to certain saints: as the calf or ox to St LUKE; the cock to St PETER; the eagle to St JOHN the Divine; the lion to St MARK and St JEROME; the raven to St BENEDICT, etc. *See* SYMBOLS OF SAINTS *under* SAINT.

Animals in Heaven. According to Muslim legend the following ten animals have been allowed to enter paradise: Jonah's whale; Solomon's ant; the ram caught by ABRAHAM and sacrificed instead of Isaac; the lapwing of Balkis; the camel of the prophet Saleh; Balaam's ass; the ox of Moses; the dog Kratim of the Seven Sleepers; Al Borak, Muhammad's steed; and Noah's dove.

Animals in symbolism.

The lamb, the pelican, and the unicorn, are symbols of Christ.

The dragon, serpent, and swine, symbolize Satan and his crew. The ant symbolizes frugality and prevision; ape, uncleanness, malice, lust, and cunning; ass, stupidity; bantam cock, pluckiness, priggishness; bat, blindness; bear, ill-temper, uncouthness; bee, industry; beetle, blindness; bull, strength, straight-forwardness; bulldog, pertinacity; butterfly, sportiveness, living in pleasure; calf, lumpishness, cowardice; camel, submission; cat, deceit; cicada, poetry; cock, vigilance, overbearing insolence; crocodile, hypocrisy; crow, longevity; cuckoo, cuckoldom; dog, fidelity, dirty habits; dove, innocence, harmlessness; duck, deceit (Fr. *canard,* a hoax); eagle, majesty, inspiration; elephant, sagacity, ponderosity; fly, feebleness, insignificance; fox, cunning, artifice; frog and toad, inspiration; goat, lasciviousness; goose, conceit, folly; grasshopper, old age; gull, gullibility; hare, timidity; hawk, rapacity, penetration; hen, maternal care; hog, impurity; horse, speed, grace; jackdaw, vain assumption, empty conceit; jay, senseless chatter; kitten, playfulness; lamb, innocence, sacrifice; lark, cheerfulness; leopard, sin; lion, noble courage; lynx, suspicious vigilance; magpie, garrulity; mole, blindness, obtuseness; monkey, tricks; mule, obstinacy; nightingale, forlornness; ostrich, stupidity; owl, wisdom; ox, patience, strength, pride; parrot, mocking verbosity; peacock, pride; pig, obstinacy, dirtiness, gluttony; pigeon, cowardice (pigeon-livered); puppy, conceit; rabbit, fecundity; raven, ill-luck; robin redbreast, confiding trust; serpent, wisdom; sheep, silliness, timidity; sparrow, lasciviousness; spider, wiliness; stag, cuckoldom; swan, grace; tiger, ferocity; tortoise, chastity; turkey cock, official insolence; turtledove, conjugal fidelity; vulture, rapine; wolf, cruelty, ferocity; worm, cringing; etc.

Ann, Mother. Ann Lee (1736–84), the founder and spiritual mother of the American sect of SHAKERS.

Annates. (Lat. *annus,* a year), also called FIRST-FRUITS. Payments to the POPE, on the appointment of a BISHOP or other ecclesiastic, of a year's income of the SEE or BENEFICE. In England these payments were finally stopped in 1534 and transferred to the Crown.

Anne, Ann, or **Anna, St** (f.d. 26 July). Traditionally the mother of the VIRGIN MARY by JOACHIM, a man of Galilee, though nothing is actually known of her beyond the account in the apocryphal *Protoevangelium of James.* After twenty childless years Mary was born and at three years of age was dedicated to the Temple, after which the parents died. The story has affinities with that of Hannah and Samuel in the OLD TESTAMENT. St Anne is particularly venerated in the Eastern ORTHODOX Church. One legend says that her body was found in France, at the time of Charlemagne, by a dumb boy who suddenly exclaimed: 'There lies the body of Anne, mother of the Blessed Virgin.' Relics are found in many churches. In art the Virgin is depicted placing a CANDLE in the hand of the dying Anne, with Christ giving his blessing.

Annihilationism. A belief held by some Christians that the wicked do not go to Hell but are annihilated at death, the SOUL dying with the body.

Anno Domini (Lat.). In the Year of our Lord; i.e. in the year after the Nativity; or AD. This system of dating was introduced by the monk Dionysius Exiguus who lived in the first half of the 6th century. *Anno Domini* is also used colloquially as a synonym for old age, e.g. 'Anno Domini is his complaint.'

Annunciation, The Feast of the. 25 March, also called LADY DAY, on which the angel GABRIEL announced to the Virgin MARY that she would be the mother of the MESSIAH (*Luke* i, 26–38).

Order of the Annunciation. An Italian order of military knights thus named from 1518, but founded by Amadeus VI, count of Savoy, in 1362 as the *Order of the Collar,* from its badge, a silver collar bearing devices in honour of the Virgin.

Sisters of the Annunciation. *See* FRANCISCANS.

Anointing. Blessed or consecrated oil is used in the CATHOLIC CHURCH in the ceremonies of anointing at BAPTISM, CONFIRMATION and EXTREME UNCTION. The early Church 'anointed with prayer' in spiritual healing, a practice revived in modern times.

Anselm, St (*c.* 1033–1109, f.d. 21 April). A Churchman, born near Aosta, in Piedmont, he was educated at the abbey of Bec, in Normandy, where he later became abbot and made Bec the centre of European scholarship. In 1093 he was appointed to the archbishopric of Canterbury, somewhat against his will, and opposed the English kings on the question of the rights of Papal Investiture. A final compromise was reached, giving the King the right to temporal investiture, with the spiritual for the Church. He was also involved with the Council of Bari on the subject of the FILIOQUE dispute among the Greek bishops of south Italy, being able to settle their doubts. Anselm was buried at Canterbury and was canonized in 1494. He is regarded as the founder of scholastic theology and in 1720 was named a DOCTOR OF THE CHURCH. His chief works were *Cur Deus Homo*, *Proslogion* and the *Monologian*.

Anskar, St (801–65, f.d. 3 February). Born of a noble family near Amiens, he became a monk, then carried out extensive missionary work in Denmark and Sweden. He was appointed first bishop of Hamburg, then archbishop of both Hamburg and Bremen, being given jurisdiction over Denmark, Norway and Sweden. He lived an austere and devout life, worked for the poor, founded schools and tried to combat the Viking slave trade. Many miracles were attributed to him, but he said that he would ask for one miracle only, that God would make him a good man. He is the patron saint of Denmark.

Anthem. A piece of choral music sung in Church, the words being taken from the SCRIPTURES. The word is derived from 'antiphon', and anthems are often sung antiphonically.

Anthony. Anthony the Great, St (*c.* 250–356, f.d. 17 January). The patron saint of herdsmen and hermit of Upper Egypt; also the father of Christian monasticism. The story of his temptations by the devil was a popular subject in literature and art.
Anthony of Padua, St (1195–1231, f.d. 13 June). Rigorous follower of St FRANCIS of Assisi and famous preacher. He was canonized in 1232 by Pope Gregory IX. He was one of the saints said to have the power of BILOCATION.
St Anthony's Cross. The TAU cross, T, called a lace.
St Anthony's fire. In mediaeval times a pestilential disease, so called from the belief that those who sought the intercession of St Anthony recovered from this epidemic or sacred fire. It was commonly supposed to be erysipelas (Gr. red skin) or the rose (from its colour) but in fact the disease was ergotism, a poisoning due to eating rye bread with fungal infection. *Cp.* st VITUS'S DANCE *under* VITUS.
St Anthony's pig. A pet pig, the smallest of the litter, also called the TANTONY PIG.

Antichrist, or the Man of Sin, due to appear at the end of time, is mentioned in the *Epistles of St John* (I, ii, 18, 22) and is derived from

Hebrew teachings. The belief that the arrival of Antichrist was to precede the second advent is chiefly founded on II *Thess.* ii, 1–12, and *Rev.* xiii. In the early Christian Church the Roman Empire and its rulers were frequently referred to as Antichrist and later the title was bestowed upon the Emperor Frederick II and various Popes. With the REFORMATION the PROTESTANT conception of the papacy as Antichrist became widespread and its later use is largely as an abusive term and it has been applied even to Napoleon and William II of Germany. The Mohammedans have a legend that Christ will slay the Antichrist at the gate of the Church at Lydda, in Palestine. *See also* NUMBER OF THE BEAST.

Antinomian (Gr. *antinomos,* exempt from the law). One who believes that Christians are not bound to observe the 'law of God', but 'may continue in sin that grace may abound'. The term was first applied to John Agricola by Martin Luther, and was given to a sect that appeared in Germany about 1535. It was put forward as an excuse for immorality by extremist sects from early Christian times and appeared in England during the Commonwealth period.

Anti-pope. A usurping or rival pontiff set up in opposition to one canonically elected. Of the thirty-nine anti-popes, those residing at Avignon during the Great SCHISM (1378–1417) are perhaps best known. When John XXIII (a schismatic) summoned the Council of Constance (1414) to end the schism, there were three rival popes. John and Benedict XIII were deposed as schismatics, Gregory XIII resigned and a new pope, Martin V, was elected in 1417.

Antonius of Florence, St (1389–1459, f.d. 10 May). Born in Florence, he became a Dominican Friar and was made prior of various houses. He was consulted by ROME, especially on CANON LAW. He founded the famous SYLVESTRINE convent of San Marco and the college of St Martin, and was made archbishop of Florence. Antonius lived a life of poverty for himself and generosity to others, especially to the poor and those affected by the plague and earthquakes; he was both a character of outstanding excellence and a notable writer and administrator.

Anxious seat, To be on the. To be in a state of apprehension or suspense. A metaphor derived from American revivalist meetings where the penitents' bench was popularly known as the *anxious bench.*

Apocalypse. A prophetic writing or revelation of mysteries, especially that which is concerned with the end of the world. In Christianity it is applied in particular to the NEW TESTAMENT book of Revelation. Apocalyptic writings are also frequent in the OLD TESTAMENT.

Four Horsemen of the Apocalypse. *See under* FOUR.

Apocalyptic Number. The mysterious number 666 (*Rev.* xiii, 15). *See* NUMBER OF THE BEAST.

Apocrypha (Gr. *apokruptein,* to hide away); hence the meaning 'withheld from general circulation' (for various reasons), and therefore coming to be regarded as of doubtful origin, false or spurious. In the early 5th century JEROME was responsible for its inappropriate application to the non-canonical books of the Old Testament found in the SEPTUAGINT and VULGATE and not usually included in PROTESTANT Bibles. In the preface to the Apocrypha in the 1539 Bible the explanation that the books are so called 'because they were wont to be read not openly' is untenable. The Apocrypha was included in the AUTHORIZED VERSION (see under BIBLE, THE ENGLISH) of 1611. The Apocrypha proper consists of:

> I and II Esdras, Tobit, Judith, additions to Esther, Wisdom of Solomon, Ecclesiasticus, Baruch, part of the Epistle of Jeremiah, the SONG OF THE THREE HOLY CHILDREN, the History of Susanna, Bel and the Dragon, the Prayer of Manasses, I and II Maccabees.

Apart from other Old Testament Apocryphal books there are numerous New Testament Apocryphal Gospels, Acts and Teachings of the APOSTLES, Epistles and Apocalypses. *See* The ACTS OF PILATE *under* PILATE; PROTEVANGELIUM; PSEUDEPIGRAPHA.

Apocryphal. Applied to a story or anecdote, especially one concerning a celebrity or well-known individual to indicate that it is in character but fictitious. *See* APOCRYPHA.

Apollinarians. A heretical 4th-century sect, followers of Apollinaris, Bishop of Laodicea, a vigorous opponent of Arianism. They denied that Christ had a human soul and asserted that the *Logos* supplied its place. This heresy was condemned at the Council of Constantinople (381) and subsequently.

Apollonia, St (*c.* 249, f.d. 9 February). Although in art she is depicted as a young woman, she was an aged deaconess martyred at Alexandria by a mob. Her teeth were knocked out and she was threatened with being burnt alive if she did not renounce her faith. She then said prayers, leapt into the flames and perished. In art she is represented holding pincers grasping a tooth. She is invoked against toothache and is the patron saint of dentists.

Apollonius the Apologist, St (*c.* 185, f.d. 18 April). As a senator of ROME Apollonius was converted to Christianity and wrote against the PHRYGIAN heresy. Under the tyrant Commodus he was martyred, having his legs broken and being beheaded. He was regarded as one of the most outstanding of the early Christian APOLOGISTS.

Apologist (Gr. *apologeisthai,* to speak in defence). The apologists were a body of writers whose chief work was the defence of Christianity against criticisms and charges by the opponents of the Faith. The general trend of their work was within the structure of the philosophical traditions of Greece, but also emphasized the importance of the OLD TESTAMENT Scriptures and prophecy and argued that Christianity could be seen as the fulfilment of earlier thought, both Greek and Hebrew, having common ground with other traditions. Among them were JUSTIN MARTYR, ORIGEN, St AUGUSTINE and THOMAS AQUINAS. In modern times apologists are concerned with defending the faith from attacks resulting from scientific and historical discoveries and developments, and philosophical and ethical criticisms.

Apostasy. The public abandonment of religious faith, particularly of Christianity in CATHOLIC usage.

Apostate, The. JULIAN, the Roman Emperor (*c.* 331–63). So called because he forsook the Christian faith for paganism, which he sought to promote after his accession (361).

Apostles. The word *apostle* (Gr. *apostolos,* envoy, messenger, one sent) was especially applied to the Twelve Disciples of Christ as those sent forth to preach the gospel. They are named in *Matthew* x, 1–4; *Mark* iii, 14–19; *Luke* vi, 13–16; and *Acts* i, 13. The original list comprises PETER, ANDREW, JAMES and JOHN (the sons of Zebedee), PHILIP, BARTHOLOMEW, THOMAS, MATTHEW, James (the son of Alphaeus), Judas or JUDE, SIMON and JUDAS Iscariot. The Gospels of *St Matthew* and *St Mark* give Thaddaeus in place of Jude, and the Gospel of *St John* (xxi, 1–2) has Nathanael, who by some has been identified with Bartholomew. James the Less has also been identified, somewhat dubiously, with James, the son of Alphaeus. MATTHIAS and PAUL were subsequent additions. The badges or symbols of the fourteen apostles (i.e. the original twelve with Matthias and Paul) are as follows:

> Andrew, *an ×-shaped cross* because he was crucified on one.
> Bartholomew, *a knife,* because he was flayed with a knife.

James the Great, *a scallop shell, a pilgrim's staff,* or *a gourd bottle,* because he is the patron saint of pilgrims.

James the Less, *a fuller's pole,* because he was killed by a blow on the head with a pole, dealt him by Simeon the fuller.

John, *a cup with a winged serpent flying out of it,* in allusion to the tradition about Aristodemos, priest of Diana, who challenged John to drink a cup of poison. John made the sign of a cross on the cup, Satan like a dragon flew from it, and John then drank the cup which was quite innocuous.

Judas Iscariot, *a bag,* because he 'had the bag and bare what was put therein' *(John* vii, 6).

Jude, *a club,* because he was martyred with a club.

Matthew, *a hatchet* or *halberd* because he was slain at Nadabar with a halberd.

Matthias, *a battleaxe,* because he was first stoned, and then beheaded with a battle axe.

Paul, *a sword,* because his head was cut off with a sword. The convent of La Lisla in Spain boasts of possessing the very instrument.

Peter, *a bunch of keys,* because Christ gave him 'the keys of the kingdom of heaven'. *A cock,* because he went out and wept bitterly when he heard the cock crow *(Matt.* xxvi, 75).

Philip, *a long staff surmounted with a cross,* because he suffered death by being suspended by the neck from a tall pillar.

Simon, a *saw,* because he was sawn to death, according to tradition.

Thomas, *a lance,* because he was pierced through the body, at Mylapore, with a lance.

According to tradition:

Andrew lies buried at Amalfi (Naples).

Bartholomew, at Rome, in the church of Bartholomew, on the Tiber Island.

James the Great was buried at St Jago de Compostella, in Spain.

James the Less, at Rome, in the church of SS Philip and James.

John, at Ephesus.

Jude, at Rome.

Matthew, at Salerno (Naples).

Matthias, at Rome, in the church of St Peter.

Paul, at Rome, in the church of S. Paolo fuori le Mura.

Peter, at Rome, in the church of St Peter.

Philip, at Rome.

Simon or Simeon, at Rome.

Thomas, at Ortona (Naples). (? Madras).

The supposed remains of Mark the Evangelist were buried at Venice, about 800.

Luke the Evangelist is said to have been buried at Padua.

See EVANGELISTS; SYMBOLS OF SAINTS *under* SAINT.

Apostles of

Abyssinians, St Frumentius *(c.* 300–*c.* 360).

Alps, Felix Neff (1798–1829).

Andalusia, Juan de Avila (1500–1569).

Ardennes, St Hubert (d. 727).

Armenians, Gregory the Illuminator *(c.* 257–*c.* 337).

Brazil, José de Anchieta, Jesuit missionary (1533–1597).

English, St Augustine (d. 604); St George (d. *c.* 300).

Free Trade, Richard Cobden (1804–1865).

French, St Denis (? 3rd century).

Frisians, St Willibrod *(c.* 657–738).

Gauls, St Irenaeus *(c.* 130–*c.* 200); St Martin of Tours *(c.* 316–400).

Gentiles, St Paul (d. 67).

Germany, St Boniface (680–754).

Highlanders, St Columba (521–597).

Hungary, St Stephen (975–1038), the Apostle King.

Indians (American), Bartolomé de Las Casas (1474–1566); John Eliot (1604–1690).

Indies (East), St Francis Xavier (1506–1552).

Infidelity, Voltaire (1694–1778).

Ireland, St Patrick *(c.* 389–461).

North, St Ansgar or Anscarius (801–865), missionary to Scandinavia; Bernard Gilpin (1517–1583), Archdeacon of Durham, evangelist of the Scottish border.

Peru, Alonso de Barcena, Jesuit, missionary (1528–1598).

Picts, St Ninian (? 5th century).

Rome, St Philip Neri (1515–1595) for his good works there. (See ORATORIANS).

Scottish Reformers, John Knox (1505–1572).

Slavs, St Cyril (827–869).

Spain, St James the Great (d. 44).

The Sword, Mohammad *(c.* 570–632).

Temperance, Father Mathew (1790–1856).

Wales, St David *(c.* 500–*c.* 600).

Yorkshire, Paulinus, Archbishop of York (d. 644).

Prince of the Apostles. St PETER *(Matt.* xvi, 18, 19).

Apostle spoons. Silver spoons having the figure of one of the APOSTLES at the top of the handle, formerly given at christenings. Sometimes twelve spoons, representing the twelve apostles; sometimes four, representing the four EVANGELISTS; and sometimes only one was presented. Occasionally a set occurs, containing in addition the 'Master Spoon' and the 'Lady Spoon'.

Apostles' Creed. A Christian creed supposed to be an epitome of doctrine taught by the apostles. It was received into the Latin Church, in its present form, in the 11th century, but a formula somewhat like it existed in the 2nd century. Items were added in the 4th and 5th centuries, and verbal alterations much later. *See* ATHANASIAN CREED (under ATHANASIUS); NICENE CREED.

Apostolic Brethren or **Apostolici.** A SECT

founded in Lombardy on early Christian lines of a celibate, communistic community; there were also Spiritual Sisters. The founder, Gerhard Sagarelli of Parma, was burned as a HERETIC in 1300. After his death Dolcino of Novara continued the tradition and held out against the power of Pope Boniface VIII for two years before being captured, tortured and executed.

Apostolic Delegate. One representing the POPE in a country which maintains no regular diplomatic relations with the HOLY SEE.

Apostolic Fathers. Christian writers born in the 1st century supposedly in contact with the original APOSTLES. Polycarp, the last of the Apostolic Fathers, born about 69, was believed to be the disciple of St John the Apostle. Clement of Rome died *c.* 101, Ignatius *c.* 120, and Polycarp *c.* 155. Others are Barnabas, Hermas (author of *The Shepherd*) and Papias (a bishop of Hierapolis, mentioned by Eusebius).

Apostolic Majesty. A title borne by the Emperor of Austria, as King of Hungary, first conferred by Pope Sylvester II on King Stephen of Hungary in 1001.

Apostolic Nuncio. A legate or representative sent by the POPE as an ambassador to a government or court.

Apostolic Succession. The doctrine that the mission given to the APOSTLES by Christ (*Matt.* xxviii, 19) must extend to their legitimate successors in an unbroken line. Thus the only valid ministry is that of clergy ordained by properly consecrated BISHOPS.

Apparel. One meaning of this word used to be 'ornament' or 'embellishment', especially applied to orphreys, the embroidered borders of ecclesiastical vestments, and in particular to the ornamental parts of the alb, at the lower edge and at the wrists.

> The albe should be made with apparels worked in silk or gold, embroidered with ornaments.
>
> PUGIN: *Glossary of Ecclesiastical Ornament* (1844)

Apple. There is no mention of an apple in the Bible story of Eve's temptation. She took 'the fruit of the tree which is in the midst of the garden' (*Gen.* iii, 3).

Apple-john. An apple so called from its being mature about St JOHN THE BAPTIST'S Day, 24 June. The French call it *Pomme de Saint Jean.* We are told that apple-johns will keep for two years, and are best when shrivelled.

> I am withered like an old apple-john.
>
> SHAKESPEARE: *Henry IV, Part I,* III, iii

Incorrectly called *Apples of King John,* other probable names are *Deus Ans, Dusand, Dewsum, Jewsum* and *Pomme de Fer.*

Apples of Paradise, according to tradition, had a bite on one side, to commemorate the bite given by Eve.

Apse (Gr. *hapsis,* a loop). A semicircular recess at the east end of the church, especially in Gothic churches. In early churches the apse contained the bishop's throne.

Arabians. An obscure Arabian Christian sect of the 3rd century who maintained that the soul dies with the body but rejoins the body on the last day. This heresy was overcome by ORIGEN (*c.* 185–*c.* 254).

Arbor Judae. *See* JUDAS TREE.

Archangel. In Christian story the title is usually given to MICHAEL, the chief opponent of SATAN and his angels, and to GABRIEL, RAPHAEL, URIEL, Chamuel, Jophiel and Zadkiel. *See* ANGEL.

According to the Koran, there are four archangels; Gabriel, the angel of revelations, who writes down the divine decrees; Michael, the champion, who fights the battle of faith; Azrael, the angel of death; and Israfel, who is commissioned to sound the trumpet of the resurrection.

Archbishop. The chief bishop of the Church, having a certain authority and taking precedence over the other bishops in his ecclesiastical province: a Metropolitan of the ORTHODOX CHURCH directly below a PATRIARCH.

Archbishop Parker's Table. *See under* TABLE.

Archdeacon. Originally an ordained dignitary of the Church who supervised the deacons. In the ROMAN CATHOLIC CHURCH the office is titular, where he is an honorary official. In the ORTHODOX CHURCH an archdeacon is often a deacon, not an ordained priest, and is more an administrative officer. In the CHURCH OF ENGLAND there are archdeacons in each diocese, they are appointed by the bishop and have been in orders for at least six years; they visit parishes, admit churchwardens and present candidates for ordination.

Arches, Court of. The ecclesiastical court of appeal for the province of Canterbury, which was anciently held in the church of St Mary-le-Bow (*Beata Maria de Arcubus,* St Mary of the Arches), Cheapside, London.

Archimandrite. In the Eastern ORTHODOX CHURCH the archimandrite is an abbot who is the head of a large monastery or who supervises several monasteries; it is an honorary title. Bishops are often chosen from among them.

Archontics. A 2nd-century GNOSTIC sect attributing the Creation to God's agents or *archons* (Gr. *archon,* a chief magistrate or ruler).

Arians. The followers of Arius, a presbyter of the Church of Alexandria in the 4th century. He maintained (1) that the Father and Son are distinct beings; (2) that the Son, though divine, is not equal to the Father; (3) that the Son had a state of existence prior to His appearance on earth, but not from eternity; (4) that the MESSIAH was not a real man, but a divine being in a veil of flesh. The heresy was condemned by the Council of Nicaea (325), which upheld the orthodox view of Athanasius that the Son was 'of the same substance' with the Father.

Ariel. A Hebrew name signifying 'lion of God'. In *Isaiah* xxix, 1–7, it is applied to Jerusalem; in astronomy a satellite of Uranus; in demonology and literature, the name of a spirit. Thus Ariel is one of the seven angelic 'princes' in Heywood's *Hierarchie of the Blessed Angels* (1635); one of the rebel angels in Milton's *Paradise Lost*, VI, 371 (1667).

Arild or **Alkeld, St** (date unknown, f.d. 20 July). A virgin, said to have been beheaded because she would not yield to the tyrant Muncius. Her relics were later enshrined in Gloucester Abbey and became famous for many miracles. Churches were dedicated to her and she is depicted in the Gloucester East Window and on the Lady altar REREDOS.

Armageddon. The name given in the Apocalypse (*Rev.* xvi, 16) to the site of the last great 'battle of that great day of God almighty' between the forces of good and evil. Hence any great battle or scene of slaughter.

Armel, St (d. *c.* 552, f.d. 16 August). Said to have been born in Wales, he became a monk then left with others for Brittany where he founded two monasteries. His cult spread in both France and England; in the latter it was promoted by King Henry VII who believed Armel's intercession had saved him from shipwreck off the coast of Brittany. There were statues of the saint in Westminster Abbey and at Canterbury. In art he is depicted as leading a dragon with a STOLE round its neck. He was patron of several hospitals and was invoked against headaches, rheumatism, gout, colic and fever.

Arminians. Followers of Jacobus Hermansen or Arminius (1560–1609), anti-Calvinist theologian and professor at Leiden. They asserted that God bestows forgiveness and eternal life on all who repent and believe; that he wills all men to be saved and that his predestination is founded on his foreknowledge. His Dutch followers came to be called 'Remonstrants' after their 'remonstrance' of 1610 embodying their five points of difference from orthodox Calvinism. In England the name was applied to the supporters of William Laud, Archbishop of Canterbury (1633–1645).

Arm-shrines. In the Middle Ages bodily relics of saints were often put in metal containers modelled on the shape of the contents. Arm-shrines were normally cylinders of silver ending in the shape of a hand. Head-shrines were called *Chefs*.

Arnulf of Metz, St (d. 643, f.d. 18 July). Born in Lorraine, he was appointed chancellor to King Dagobert who gave him the bishopric of Metz which he left later to become a monk, first living as a HERMIT in the Vosges mountains, then entering the monastery at Remiremont, where he died.

Arrowsmith, St Edmund (1585–1628, f.d. 25 October). Born at Haydock, in Lancashire, the son of a yeoman farmer, he was first educated by a priest then went to the English College at Douai. After being ordained priest he returned to Lancashire and carried out a mission of fearless teaching which led to his arrest. He was examined by the bishop of Chester but was released. Later he became a JESUIT. He was denounced by a man whose morals he had censured and was again arrested, this time he was tried at Lancaster Assizes, was found guilty and sentenced to death. He was kept in chains for two days without food or water but, still refusing to recant, was executed. A relic of his at the Church of St OSWALD at Ashton-in-Makerfield was said to have been responsible for miraculous cures. He was canonized in 1970 by Pope Paul VI as one of the FORTY MARTYRS OF ENGLAND AND WALES.

Arsenius the Great, St (4th cent., f.d. formerly 8 May, now 21 May). Probably born in ROME, he later lived in Constantinople at the court of the Emperor Theodosius, possibly as tutor to his two sons. Arsenius was a noted scholar but, hearing a divine call, went to the Egyptian desert, first to Scetis, then to Canapius and to Troe, near Memphis. He was famed for his love of silence and for his saying: 'I have been sorry for having spoken but never for having kept my tongue.' He was also a man of great humility. He is particularly venerated in the Russian ORTHODOX CHURCH.

Asaph. In the Bible, a famous musician in David's time (I *Chron.* xvi, 5 and xxv, 1, 2). He is supposed to be the founder of the hereditary choir of *b'ne Asaph* in the Second Temple (*Ezra* iii, 10, 11 and *Neh.* vii, 44). *Psalms* 50 and 73–83 are ascribed to Asaph.

St Asaph. A 6th-century Welsh saint, abbot and first Welsh bishop of the see of Llanelwy which came to be called St Asaph in the 12th century.

Ascension Day, or **Holy Thursday** (*q.v.*). The day set apart by the Christian Churches to commemorate the ascent of Christ from earth to HEAVEN. It is the fortieth day after EASTER. *See* BOUNDS, BEATING THE.

Asceticism. Self-denial, discipline and the renunciation of physical pleasure, using pain and discomfort to 'mortify the flesh'. Practised in monasticism and by HERMITS and ANCHORITES or by individuals.

Ash. Ash Wednesday. The first day of LENT, so called from the Roman Catholic custom of sprinkling on the heads of penitents the consecrated ashes of palms remaining from the previous PALM SUNDAY. The custom is of uncertain date but is commonly held to have been introduced by GREGORY THE GREAT (Pope 590–604).
Ashes to ashes, dust to dust. A phrase from the English burial service, used sometimes to denote total finality. It is founded on scriptural texts such as 'dust thou art, and unto dust thou shalt return' (*Gen.* iii, 19), and 'I will bring thee to ashes upon the earth in the sight of all them that behold thee' (*Ezek.* xxvii, 18).

> Ashes to ashes and dust to dust,
> If God won't have him the Devil must.

Asperges. The ceremony of sprinkling the ALTAR and the CONGREGATION with holy water before High MASS; the aspergillum is a small brush or rod with a perforated metal bulb at the end. In art the aspergillum is associated with EXORCISM.
Aspersion. Sprinkling with holy water; BAPTISM by sprinkling.

Ass. According to tradition the dark stripe running down the back of an ass, crossed by another at the shoulders, was the cross communicated to the creature when Christ rode on the back of an ass in His triumphant entry into Jerusalem.
Feast of asses. *See under* FOOL.
Asses that carry the mysteries (*asini portant mysteria*). A classical knock at the Roman clergy. The allusion is to the custom of employing asses to carry the *cista* which contained the sacred symbols, when processions were made through the streets (Warburton: *Divine Legation,* ii, 4).

Assemblies of God. A PROTESTANT fundamentalist movement in Britain, the Commonwealth and the United States; its followers maintain the infallibility of the BIBLE, the Second Coming of Christ and the MILLENNIUM and the eternal damnation of sinners. Adult BAPTISM is practised by total immersion and there is spiritual healing.

Assumption, Feast of the. 15 August, celebrated in the ROMAN CATHOLIC CHURCH to commemorate the death of the Virgin MARY and the assumption of her body into HEAVEN when it was reunited to her soul. It can be traced back to the 6th century and in 1950 Pope Pius XII declared that the Corporal Assumption was thenceforth a dogma of the Church.
Assumptionists. A Roman Catholic association under the name of the *Augustinians of the Assumption,* founded by the Abbé Emanuel d'Alzon in France in 1843. Its chief work was in education and missions to the Near East. It was suppressed in France in 1900, but many of the monks migrated to England. The *Ladies of the Assumption,* an associated order, is largely involved in the education of girls.

Assyrian Church. A SECT which survived for centuries in Assyria in the middle of an Islamic district and having offshoots in Iraq, Iran, Syria, Russia and the United States; it claims to be neither Roman nor Orthodox Catholic, but has a PATRIARCH at its head.

Athanasius, St (*c.* 298–373, f.d. 2 May). Bishop of Alexandria and a DOCTOR OF THE CHURCH, legend says that the solemnity with which Athanasius played the part of a bishop in a children's game as a small boy, prompted the aged bishop of Alexandria to take the boy into his household where, in due course, he was made his archdeacon. He later accompanied the bishop to the Council of NICAEA. When Alexander died in 328, Athanasius succeeded him as bishop. His life's work became his fierce struggle against the ARIAN heresy. False accusations were made against him to the Emperor CONSTANTINE and Athanasius was exiled five times and was said to have hidden in various places in Europe and the Egyptian desert. He was reputed to have composed the ATHANASIAN CREED while concealed in a cave at Trèves in Gaul. He was finally reinstated as bishop of Alexandria in 366. He was a prolific writer, his best known work being *Oration Against the Arians.*
Athanasian Creed. One of the three creeds accepted by the Roman and Anglican churches; so called because it embodies the opinions of Athanasius. It has been said to be neither a CREED nor written by Athanasius, but was associated with his name from the 7th century and embodies his opinions respecting the TRINITY. It is often referred to as the *Quicunque Vult,* from its opening words. It is one of the three creeds accepted by CATHOLIC and PROTESTANT CHURCHES. The ORTHODOX CHURCH accepts its Athanasian authorship but rejects the FILIOQUE doctrine, suggesting that it is a later addition. *See* APOSTLES' CREED; NICENE CREED.

Atheism (Gr. without God). The denial of a belief in the existence of God. Early Christians were called atheists by Greeks and Romans since they denied their gods. *See also* THEIST.

Atheists. During World War II Father W. T. Cummings, an American army chaplain in Bataan, in a sermon used the phrase 'there are no atheists in foxholes', meaning that no one can deny the existence of God in the face of imminent death.

Athos. The peninsula on the Macedonian coast is occupied by a Basilian monastic community of the ORTHODOX CHURCH, consisting of some 3000 monks and lay brothers. The region is mountainous with a peak of white marble over 6000 feet high. The Mount Athos monastery was built between 967 and 1545. Legend says that it was on Athos that St Anthoni, founder of the Cave Monastery at Kiev, was blessed and given instructions for his work in Russia. Athos occupied a place of importance for the Slavs, serving as a bridge between the Orthodox churches of Russia, the Balkans and Byzantium. There are sanctuaries, hermitages and farms and a magnificent library attached to the settlement. Nothing of the feminine gender is allowed within the area.

Atonement (at-one-ment). Reconciliation, expiation, making amends. In Christian usage the *Atonement* denotes the reconciliation of God and man through the life, sufferings and crucifixion of Jesus Christ. It presupposes man's alienation from God through sin.

Audrey, St. *See* ETHELDREDA.

Augsburg Confession. The historical confession of faith compiled by MELANCHTHON in consultation with Luther and presented to Charles V at the Diet of Augsburg in 1530.

Augustine. Augustine, St (354–430, f.d. 28 August). Bishop of Hippo, DOCTOR OF THE CHURCH, and the greatest of the Latin fathers. He was baptized in 387 after an earlier life of self-indulgence and in due course (396) became Bishop of Hippo in N. Africa. Distinguished by his zealous opposition to the heresies of his time and by his prolific writings, his best-known works are his *Confessions* and *De Civitate Dei* (the City of God).

Augustine Erlendsson, St. *See* EYSTEIN.

Augustine of Canterbury, St (d. 604, f.d. 26 May, 13 September). APOSTLE of the English and first Archbishop of Canterbury. He was sent from ROME by POPE Gregory the Great with a band of 40 monks to convert the English. They first landed on the Isle of Thanet, gained the support of King Aethelbert of Kent and established themselves at Canterbury in 597 when Aethelbert was baptized. Differences with the older British Church became apparent before Augustine's death.

Augustine, The Second. THOMAS AQUINAS, the ANGELIC DOCTOR.

Augustinian Canons. Regular CANONS who adopted the Rule of St Augustine in the 11th century. Also called **Austin Canons,** their first house in England was established at Colchester between 1093 and 1099. They took religious vows like the monks but made clerical and parochial duties their predominant obligation.

Augustinian, or **Austin Friars,** also called Augustinian Hermits from whom they were formed (1243–56). The fourth of the MENDICANT ORDERS, they first came to England in 1248.

Auld Hornie. After the establishment of Christianity, the heathen deities were degraded by the Church into fallen angels; and Pan, with his horns, crooked nose, goat's beard, pointed ears, and goat's feet, was transformed to his Satanic majesty, and called Old Horny.

> O thou, whatever title suit thee,
> Auld Hornie, Satan, Nick, or Clootie.
> BURANS

The Auld Kirk. The CHURCH OF SCOTLAND.

Aumbry. *See* AMBRY.

Aureole (Fr. through Lat. *aura,* air). A luminous radiance surrounding the whole figure in paintings of the Saviour and sometimes of the SAINTS. Du Cange (1610–1688) informs us that the aureole of nuns is white, of martyrs red, and of doctors green. See HALO; NIMBUS; VESICA PISCIS.

Austell, St (7th cent., f.d. 28 June). A monk from South Wales who settled in Cornwall and founded a church in the town named after him. He was a disciple of St MEEN and was reputed to be his godson; their parishes adjoin in Cornwall and both saints were buried in the same tomb.

Authorized Version, The. *See* BIBLE, THE ENGLISH.

Autocephalous. A term used in the Eastern ORTHODOX CHURCH for the self-governing system which appoints its own bishops but remains in dependence on the PATRIARCH.

Auto da fé (Port. an act of faith). The ceremonial procedure of the Spanish INQUISITION when sentences against heretics were read. Persistent HERETICS were subsequently delivered to the secular arm for punishment. The reason why their victims were *burnt* was because inquisitors were forbidden to 'shed blood'; a tergiversation based on the axiom of the ROMAN CATHOLIC CHURCH, *Ecclesia non novit sanguinem* (The Church is untainted with blood).

Ave. Latin for 'Hail!'

Ave Maria (Lat. Hail, Mary!). The first two words of the Latin prayer to the Virgin MARY used in the ROMAN CATHOLIC CHURCH. (*See* Luke: 28.) The phrase is applied to the smaller beads of a ROSARY, the larger ones being termed PATERNOSTERS.

Avignon Popes. In 1309 Pope Clement V (1305–1314), a Gascon, under pressure from Philip the Fair of France, transferred the papal court to Avignon, where it remained until 1377. This Babylonian captivity weakened the papacy and led to the Great SCHISM.

Other Avignon popes were:

John XXII	1316–34	Innocent VI	1352–62
Benedict XII	1334–42	Urban V	1362–70
Clement VI	1342–52	Gregory XI	1370–78

Azazel. In *Leviticus* xvi, 7–8, we read that Aaron, as an atonement, 'shall cast lots' on two goats 'one lot for the Lord, and the other lot for the scapegoat' (Azazel). Milton uses the name for the standardbearer of the rebel angels (*Paradise Lost*, I, 534).

Azymites (Gr. not leavened). The Eastern ORTHODOX CHURCH uses leavened bread for the SACRAMENT, believing this to be in accordance with the tradition of Christ and the APOSTLES. They use the term 'azymites' as a reproach to the ROMAN CATHOLIC CHURCH who use unleavened bread.

B

BC. In dating, an abbreviation for 'Before Christ', before the Christian era.

Babel. A perfect Babel. A thorough confusion. 'A Babel of sounds', a confused uproar and hubbub. The allusion is to the confusion of tongues at Babel (*Gen.* xi).

Babylon. The whore of Babylon. A PURITAN epithet for the ROMAN CATHOLIC CHURCH. The allusion is to *Revelation* xvii–xix (*cp.* SCARLET WOMAN), where Babylon stands for Rome, the embodiment of luxury, vice, splendour, tyranny and all that the early Church held was against the spirit of Christ.

Baca, The Valley of. An unidentified place mentioned in *Psalm* lxxxiv,6, meaning the 'Valley of Weeping', and so translated in the Revised Version of the BIBLE.

Baithen, St (d. 600, f.d. 9 June). He succeeded St COLUMBA as abbot of Iona and ruled there for four years. He was reputed to be extremely holy; while reaping he held one hand up in adoration while reaping with the other. Churches are named after him in East Lothian and Berwickshire.

Balaam. A misleading prophet or ally as Balaam was in *Numbers* xxii–xxiv.
Balaamite. One who makes a profession of religion for profit or gain, as did Balaam.

Balm (Fr. *baume,* a contraction of balsam). An aromatic, resinous gum exuded from certain trees and used in perfumery and medicine.
Is there no balm in Gilead? (*Jeremiah* viii, 22). Is there no remedy, no consolation? 'Balm' here is the Geneva Bible's translation of the Heb. *sori*, which probably means 'mastic', the resin yielded by the mastic tree, *Pistacia lentiscus.* In Wyclif's Bible the word is translated 'gumme' and in Coverdale's 'triacle'. (*See* BIBLE, THE ENGLISH; TREACLE BIBLE *under* BIBLE, SOME SPECIALLY NAMED EDITIONS.

The gold–coloured resin now known as 'Balm of Gilead' is that from *Balamodendron gileadense.*

Balthazar. One of the three kings of COLOGNE. See MAGI.

Bamberg Bible, The. *See* BIBLE, SOME SPECIALLY NAMED EDITIONS.

Bampton Lectures. Founded by the Rev. John Bampton, minor CANON of Salisbury, who, in 1751, left £120 per annum to the University of Oxford, to pay for eight divinity lectures on given subjects to be preached yearly at Great St Mary's and for their subsequent publication. Only MAs of Oxford and Cambridge are eligible as lecturers and the same person may not be chosen twice. First given in 1780, the lectures by Dr Hampden in 1832 aroused great controversy in theological circles. *Cp.* HULSEAN LECTURES.

Banbury Cross of nursery rhyme fame was removed by the PURITANS as a heathenish memorial in 1646. Another CROSS was erected on the site in 1858.

Bands. Clerical bands are a relic of the ancient *amice,* a square linen tippet tied about the neck of priests during the saying of MASS. Disused by ANGLICAN clergy in the late 19th century, they have partially come back into fashion of late and are also worn by PRESBYTERIAN ministers and continental clergy.

Banners in churches. These are suspended as thank offerings to God. Those in St George's Chapel, Windsor, Henry VII's Chapel, Westminster, etc., are to indicate that the knight whose banner is hung up avows himself devoted to God's service.

Banns of Marriage. The publication in the parish church for three successive Sundays of an intended marriage. It is made after the second lesson of the Morning Service, or of Evening Service (if there be no Morning Service). The word is from the same root as *ban.* The custom was pre-Christian but was adopted and ratified at the Synod of Westminster in 1200 and the LATERAN COUNCIL in 1215. The announcement provides an opportunity for a statement of objection or of impediments, and this is known as forbidding the banns.

Baptism. This SACRAMENT of the Christian Church dates back in one form or another to pre-apostolic times. In most Christian

Churches the ceremony marks admission to the Church, it symbolizes initiation and the washing away of sin; it is frequently accompanied by Christening or naming. Baptism can be by ASPERSION (see under ASPERGES) (Church of England and most Free Churches); by AFFUSION (Roman Catholic); by total IMMERSION (Orthodox Catholic and Baptists), the rite being in the name of the TRINITY. The Russian Orthodox Church holds an especially solemn baptism on the eve of EPIPHANY and on 6 January, the actual first day. At the end of the ceremony the consecrated water is divided among the congregation to sprinkle around the house.

Baptism for the dead was a kind of vicarious baptism of a living person for the sake of one dead. An heretical and superstitious custom referred to in I *Corinthians* xv, 29.

Baptism of blood. Martyrdom for the sake of Christ which supplied the place of the sacrament if the martyr was unbaptized.

Baptism of desire is the grace or virtue of baptism acquired by one who earnestly desires baptism by water but dies before receiving it.

Baptism of fire is really martyrdom, but usually means experiencing the fire of battle for the first time.

Baptists. English Baptists are of 16th-century origin. Their first independent church, however, was founded from a group of separatists under John Smythe at Amsterdam in 1609, from whence an offshoot returned to London in 1612 to form the General Baptists. Their Arminianism (*see* ARMINIANS) led to the growth of the Strict, Particular, or Calvinistic Baptists in the 1630s. In the 18th century many General Baptists became UNITARIANS and the more orthodox formed the New Connection in 1770. The Baptist Union (1832) eventually led to closer co-operation and the Particular Baptists joined forces with the New Connection in 1891. Church government is congregational and baptism (by total immersion) is only for believers. *Cp.* BARROWISTS; BROWNISTS; CONGREGATIONALISTS; PRESBYTERIANS.

Baptist Missionary Society. Founded in 1792 at Kettering, Northamptonshire, it sent its first missionary to India in 1793. It works also in Africa, China and Jamaica.

Baptistry. A sacred building, formerly separate from the church and circular in shape, in which baptisms took place; now connected with the church.

Barbara, St. Virgin and martyr (*c.* 4th century, f.d. 4 December). Her father, a fanatical heathen, delivered her up to Martian, governor of Nicomedia, for being a Christian. After she had been subjected to the most cruel tortures, her unnatural father was about to strike off her head, when a lightning flash laid him dead at

her feet. Hence she is invoked against lightning and is the patron saint of arsenals and artillery.

Barbatus or **Barbat, St** (7th cent, f.d. 19 February). As Bishop of Benevento he was noted for his opposition to the superstitions of the people who venerated a golden viper and a sacred tree. He had the serpent melted down and made into a chalice or PATEN and cut down the tree. He was an opponent of the MONOTHELITES. In art he is depicted with a golden viper under his foot and an axe in his hand.

Barcochebah, or **Barcochebas.** In Hebrew means 'Son of a star'. One Simeon, a heroic Jewish leader against the Romans, who is reputed to have claimed to be the 'Star out of Jacob' mentioned in *Numbers* xxiv, 17, was so called. He took Jerusalem in 132 and was acclaimed by some as the MESSIAH. He was overwhelmed and slain by the forces of Julius Severus in 135.

Barefooted. Certain FRIARS and nuns (some of whom wear sandals instead of shoes), especially the reformed section of the CARMELITES (White Friars) founded by St TERESA in the 16th century, known as the *Discalced Carmelites* (Lat. *calceus,* a shoe). The practice is defended by the command of our Lord to His disciples 'Carry neither purse, nor scrip, nor shoes' (*Luke* x, 4). The Jews and Romans used to put off their shoes in mourning and public calamities, by way of humiliation.

Barlaam and Josaphat. An Indian romance telling how Barlaam, an ascetic of the desert of Sinai, converted Josaphat, a Hindu prince, to Christianity. Probably translated into Greek by the 6th century, and put into its final form by St John of Damascus, a Syrian monk of the 8th century, in part it corresponds closely with the legendary story of Buddha's youth. It became a widely popular mediaeval romance.

Barnabas. St Barnabas's Day, 11 June. St Barnabas was a fellow-labourer of St PAUL. His symbol is a rake, because 11 June is the time of hay-harvest. Tradition says he founded a church at Antioch and was martyred at ROME. The 'Epistle of Barnabas', included in the Codex Sinaiticus, is attributed to him.

Barnabites. An order of regular clerks of St PAUL, recognized by Clement VII in 1533. Probably so called from the Church of St Barnabas in Milan which became their centre.

Barnaby Bright. An old provincial name for St BARNABAS'S Day (11 June). Before the reform of the CALENDAR it was the longest day, hence the jingle in *Ray's Collection of Proverbs*—

Barnaby bright Barnaby bright!
The longest day and the shortest night.

Barnaby Lecturers. In the University of Cambridge, four lecturers elected annually on St BARNABAS'S Day, to lecture on mathematics, philosophy, rhetoric and logic.

Barr, Barry, St. *See* FINBAR.

Barrowists. In the reign of Elizabeth I, PURITAN followers of Henry Barrow, holding CONGREGA-TIONALIST (see under CONGREGATION) views similar to the BROWNISTS.

Bartholomew, St (f.d. 24 August). The symbol of this SAINT is a knife, in allusion to the knife with which he was flayed alive, reputedly in AD 44. He is named as an APOSTLE in the SYNOPTIC GOSPELS, but is said to have been the Nathaniel mentioned in John 1:45 and 21:2. Little is known about him but tradition says he was apostle of India and Arabia, and he was reputed to have been flayed alive by the order of an Armenian prince. There are relics of him in various churches and monasteries and numerous churches are dedicated to him. He is depicted in art as a man in the prime of life, with black hair and bushy beard, either holding the knife or carrying the skin of a man with a face attached. He is the patron saint of tanners and workers in skins. His day has many weather predictions associated with it, but the best known is: 'All the tears that St SWITHIN can cry, St Barthelmy's mantle will wipe dry.' It foretells the weather up to MICHAELMAS, on September 29.

Bartholomew Fair. A FAIR opened annually at Smithfield on St Bartholomew's Day, from 1133 to 1752; after the reform of the CALENDAR it began on 3 September. It was removed to Islington in 1840 and was last held in 1855. One of the great national fairs dealing in cloth, livestock, etc., accompanied by a variety of amusements and entertainments, it long held its place as a centre of London life. The PURITANS failed to suppress it. Ben Jonson's *Bartholomew Fair*, a comedy of manners, was first acted in 1614.

> Here's that will challenge all the fairs,
> Come buy my nuts and damsons and Burgamy pears!
> Here's the *Woman of Babylon, the Devil and the Pope.*
> And here's the little girl just going on the rope!
> *Here's Dives and Lazarus,* and the *World's Creation;*
> Here's the Tall Dutchwoman, the like's not in the nation.
> Here is the booths where the high Dutch maid is,
> Here are the bears that dance like any ladies;
> Tat, tat, tat, tat, says little penny trumpet;
> Here's Jacob Hall, that does so jump it, jump it;
> Sound trumpet, sound, for silver spoon and fork.
> Come, here's your dainty pig and pork!
> *Wit and Drollery* (1682)

Bartholomew, Massare of St. The slaughter of the French HUGUENOTS begun on St Bartholomew's Day, 24 August 1572, in Paris and the provinces, at the instigation of Catherine de' Medici, mother of Charles IX. Probably some 50,000 people perished.

Bartholomew of Farne, St (d. 1193, f.d. 24 June). Originally named Tosti or Tostig, he was a native of Whitby. He changed his name to William to avoid local ridicule, but was probably of Scandinavian origin. He went to Norway and was ordained there, then returned to England to become a monk at Durham. There he adopted the name of Bartholomew. Following the example of St CUTHBERT he retired to Farne Island as a hermit, but there were many disagreements with other hermits owing to his difficult character. He was said to be a careful cultivator of his plot, a keen angler, and to have kept a pet bird. He died and was buried on the island. He had a reputation as a worker of miracles.

Bartholomites. An Armenian community of monks who left Egypt under persecution in 1296 and established themselves at Genoa where they built themselves a church dedicated to St Bartholomew. They spread through Italy, at first using the Armenian LITURGY and the Rule of St BASIL, but later adopted the Rule of St AUGUSTINE and the Roman Liturgy.

Basil of Ancyra, St (d. 680, f.d. 30 January). A priest who was noted for his opposition to the ARIAN heresy. He was martyred under Julian at the time of the revival of paganism. He was hanged by the wrists and ankles and his flesh gradually torn with rakes and was finally thrown on red-hot iron spikes.

Basil. Basil the Great, St (*c.* 329–79, f.d. 14 June). Born at Caesarea in Cappodocia of a wealthy, distinguished and pious family, Basil was one of the most noted of the FATHERS OF THE CHURCH and an opponent of ARIANism. As a bishop he built hospitals, churches and food-distribution centres. He was appointed archbishop of Caesarea in 370. Some of his relics are at Bruges. In Greek Orthodox art he is represented with a long beard and moustache and a broad, high forehead. He wrote many theological works which gave rise to a LITURGY still in use. He is one of the Three Holy Hierarchs of the Eastern Church, with JOHN CHRYSOSTOM and GREGORY OF NAZIANZUS and was a great influence on St BENEDICT in establishing the RULE in monasticism.

Basilian Monks. A monastic order founded by St Basil *c.* 360 whose rule became the basis of monasticism in the Greek and Russian churches.

Basilica (Gr. *basilikos,* royal). Originally a royal palace, but afterwards (in ROME) a large building with nave, aisles, and an apse at one end used as a court of justice and for public meetings. Some were adapted by the early Christians and many churches were modelled on them. Constantine built the great basilicas of St PETER (rebuilt in the 16th century), St PAUL, and St John Lateran.

Bassendyne Bible. *See* BIBLE, THE ENGLISH.

Baur, Ferdinand Christian (1792–1860). A German PROTESTANT theologian, teaching at Tübingen University and founding the Tübingen School of HIGHER CRITICISM. He arrived at the conclusion that most of the NEW TESTAMENT was written in the second century.

Bead. From OE *-bed* (in *gebed*), a prayer. 'Bead' thus originally meant 'a prayer'; but as prayers were 'told' (i.e. account was kept of them) on a PATERNOSTER, the word came to be transferred to the small globular object which, threaded on a string, made up the paternoster or ROSARY.
Beadsman, or **Bedesman.** Properly, one who prays; hence an inmate of an Almshouse, since most of these charities, under the terms of their foundation, required the inmates to pray for the soul of the founder. *See* BEAD.

Beadle. One whose duty it is to bid or cite persons to appear in a court; also a church servant, whose duty it was to bid parishioners to attend the VESTRY and to execute its orders. The word is ultimately from the Old High Ger. *Bitel,* one who asks, but it came to us from the O.Fr. *badel,* a herald.

Beatific Vision. The sight of God, or of the blessed in the realms of HEAVEN, especially that granted to the SOUL at the instant of death. *See Isaiah* vi, 1–3 and *Acts* vii, 55, 56.

Beatification. In the ROMAN CATHOLIC CHURCH this is a solemn act by which a deceased person is formally declared by the POPE to be one of the blessed departed and therefore a proper subject for a MASS and OFFICE in his honour, generally with some local restriction. Beatification is usually, though not necessarily, a step to CANONIZATION.

Beatitude. Blessedness, perfect felicity.
The Beatitudes are the eight blessings pronounced by Our Lord at the opening of the Sermon on the Mount (*Matt.* v, 3–11).
Beatus. The first stage in CANONIZATION in the CATHOLIC CHURCH is BEATIFICATION and a beatified person is called 'beatus', blessed. The beatified may be venerated in many ways and are given the title 'Blessed'; it is usually followed by canonization.

Becket, Thomas. *See* THOMAS OF CANTERBURY.

Bede, The Venerable (*c.* 673–735). Also called the *English* DOCTOR. This most renowned of early English scholars became a monk at Jarrow and devoted his life to religion and learning. His industry, output and range were remarkable, but he is probably best known for his *Ecclesiastical History of the English People,* a work of unusual merit and value, which has led him to be called the *Father of English History.* His book is a major source of information to the year 731. The title 'venerable' is by one tradition assigned to an angelic hand; it is certainly not due to great age as is often thought.

Beelzebub. Other forms are *Beelzebul, Baalzebub.* Baalzebub was the god of Ekron (II *Kings* i, 3), and the meaning is obscure although it has been popularly held to mean 'lord of flies'. In any event it was probably a derisory title. The most likely explanation so far is that Baalzebul means 'lord of the lofty dwelling' and refers to the Syrian Baal. This was altered to Baalzebub by the Jews, as the former title seemed only proper to Jahweh. To the Jews he came to be the chief representative of the false gods. In *Matthew* xii, 24, he is referred to as 'the prince of the devils' and similarly in *Mark* iii, 22, and *Luke* xi, 15. Hence Milton places him next in rank to SATAN.

> One next himself in power, and next in crime,
> Long after known in Palestine, and named
> Beelzebub.
> *Paradise Lost,* I, 79

Bega or **Bee, St** (7th cent., f.d. 6 September). An Irish nun, said to have been the daughter of an Irish king and asked in marriage by the son of the King of Norway, but she had vowed to devote her life to God. To escape marriage she was conveyed across the Irish Sea by a miraculous bracelet, given by an angel, and seated on a clod of earth. She landed on the Cumbrian coast at a place now named St Bee's. Her bracelet, marked with a cross, was kept at her hermitage and became an object of veneration. She was fed by the birds of the sea. Later, at the advice of St OSWALD, King of Northumbria, she became a nun and received the VEIL from St AIDAN. Her shrine became a monastery. She was also venerated in Northumbria. She was said to have worked for the poor and oppressed, but her story is wrapped in obscurity and conflicting legends.

Begging Friars. *See* MENDICANT ORDERS.

Beghards. Monastic fraternities which first arose in the Low Countries in the late 12th century, named after Lambert le Bègue, a priest of Liège, who also founded the BÉGUINES. They took no vows and were free to leave the society at will. In the 17th century, those who survived Papal persecution joined the TERTIARIES of the FRANCISCANS. The word *beggar* possibly derives from beghards. Le Bègue means 'the stammerer'. *Cp*. LOLLARDS; ORATORIANS.

Béguines. A sisterhood founded in the late 12th century by Lambert le Bègue (*see* BEGHARDS). They were free to quit the cloister and to marry, and formerly flourished in the Low Countries, Germany, France, Switzerland and Italy. There are still communities in Belgium.

Behmenists. A sect of theosophical mystics, called after their founder Jacob BÖHME. Jane Leade founded a Behmenist sect in England in 1607 called the Philadelphists.

Belfry. Originally a movable tower used in sieges from which the attackers threw missiles. (O.Fr. *berfrei*. Mid. High Ger. *Bercfrit,* a place of safety. Thence a watch-tower, beacon or alarm bell-tower.) Thus a church bell tower is called a belfry not because bells are hung in it.

Belial (Heb.). In Old Testament usage it has the meaning of worthlessness, wickedness, but later it is used as a proper noun in the sense of the wicked one.

> What concord hath Christ with Belial?
> II *Corinthians* vi, 15

Milton thus uses it as a proper name:

> Belial came last—than whom a spirit more lewd
> Fell not from heaven, or more gross to love
> Vice for itself.
> *Paradise Lost* I, 490

Sons of Belial. Lawless, worthless, rebellious people.

> Now the sons of Eli were sons of Belial; they knew not the Lord.
> I *Samuel* ii, 12

Bell, book, and candle. The popular phrase for ceremonial EXCOMMUNICATON in the ROMAN CATHOLIC CHURCH. After pronouncing sentence the officiating cleric closes his book, quenches the candle by throwing it to the ground and tolls the bell as for one who has died. The book symbolizes the book of life, the candle that the soul is removed from the sight of God as the candle from the sight of man. Hence, **in spite of bell, book and candle** signifies in spite of all opposition the Christian hierarchy can offer.

Passing bell. The hallowed bell which used to be rung when persons were *in extremis,* to scare away evil spirits which might be lurking ready to snatch the SOUL while *passing* from the body. A secondary object was to announce to the neighbourhood that all good Christians might pray for the safe passage of the soul into PARADISE. The bell rung at a funeral is sometimes improperly called the 'passing bell'.

Tolling the bell for church. The 'churchgoing bell' as Cowper called it (*Verses by Alexander Selkirk*) was in pre-Reformation days rung as an Ave Bell to invite worshippers to a preparatory prayer to the Virgin.

Beloved Disciple. St JOHN (*John* xiii, 23).

Beloved Physician. St LUKE (*Colossians* iv, 14).

Bema (Gr. *bema,* a platform). In the Eastern ORTHODOX CHURCH, the enclosure containing the ALTAR, raised above the level of the NAVE and shut off by the ICONOSTASIS.

Bendy, Old. The DEVIL; who is willing to bend to anyone's inclination.

Benedicite (Lat.). 'Bless you', or 'may you be blessed'. In the first sense it is the opening word of many old graces; hence a grace or a blessing. The second sense accounts for its use as an expression of astonishment.

> The god of love, A benedicite,
> How myghty and how great a lord is he!
> CHAUCER: *Knight's Tale,* 927

Benedict. Benedict, St (480–543, f.d. 21 March). Born in Nursia, of a patrician Roman family, Benedict renounced family and fortune and retired to a cave, living there as a hermit for three years. He attracted disciples and at their request he took over a neighbouring monastery, but his rule was too severe and the monks tried to poison him. He retired again, lived in a cave for thirty-five years, then went to MONTE CASSINO and built two oratories which became the basis of his famous monastery and the BENEDICTINE Rule based on obedience and hard work, both physical and mental. The Benedictine is the oldest monastic order in the Western Church. In art St Benedict is depicted with his fingers to his lips, enjoining silence, and with his Rule in his hand, or with the first words of the Rule coming from his mouth: *Ausculta, O fili.* Other emblems are a scourge, a thorn, or rose bush at his side or a broken goblet in his hand. He is also portrayed with his sister, St SCHOLASTICA, a nun in black habit.

Benedictines. Monks who follow the rule of St Benedict of Nursia (*c.* 480–*c* 553), also known as the 'Black Monks'. Monte Cassino became their chief centre and they were renowned for their learning. Apart from their religious exercises, the monks were to be employed in study, teaching and manual labour. The Benedictines were a great civilizing influence in western Europe. St Benedict's sister Scholastica is regarded as the founder of the Benedictine nuns.

Benedictine. A liqueur still made on the site of the Benedictine abbey at Fécamp based on the original early 16th-century recipe of Brother Vincelli.

Benedict of Aniane, St (750–821, f.d. 11 February). As a young nobleman at the court of CHARLEMAGNE he became cup-bearer to Pepin and Charlemagne but left at the age of twenty-three to become a monk at St Seine. He was asked to become abbot but refused and became a hermit instead, on his family's estate at Aniane, where he was joined by others living the same austere life. He founded monasteries and his life work was monastic reform and the restoration of the Rule of St BENEDICT of Nursia.

Benedict Biscop, or **Benet, St** (c. 628–90, f.d. 12 January). Of Northumbrian, Anglo-Saxon nobility, he was in the service of King Oswy until, at the age of twenty-five, he became a monk, taking the name of Benedict. He was founder and first abbot of Wearmouth, also founding the monastery of Jarrow, both on the BENEDICTINE Rule. He made several journeys to ROME and did much for the Church and the arts in northern England in bringing back with him books, pictures, coloured images, painters and mosaic-workers, stone-masons and glass workers. Among the books was the famous CODEX Amiatinus. He also brought a monk from Rome, who had been precentor of St PETER's to teach his monks music.

Benediction. A short service in the CATHOLIC CHURCH of certain canticles and antiphons after which the priest makes the sign of the cross over the congregation with the HOST. A benediction is also a formal prayer of blessing in Christian worship and is called the Pax or Peace. 'Good-bye' is an abbreviation of the blessing 'God be with you'.

Benedictus (Lat. blessed). The hymn of thanksgiving of Zacharius on the birth of his son JOHN THE BAPTIST (*Luke* i, 68–70). The prayer at the MASS beginning with the word 'Benedictus', following the Sanctus; also a CANTICLE in the BOOK OF COMMON PRAYER.

Benefice. Under the Romans certain grants of land made to veteran soldiers were called *beneficia*, and in early feudal times an estate held for life, in return for military service, was called a *benefice*. The term came to be applied to the possessions of the Church held by individuals as a recompense for their services. Hence a church 'living'. In the CHURCH OF ENGLAND the term is used for the living of a priest in charge of a parish as distinct from bishoprics, deaneries and other cathedral and ecclesiastical offices.

Benefit of Clergy. Formerly, the privilege enjoyed by the English clergy of trial in an ecclesiastical court, where punishments were less harsh than in the secular courts, and where bishops could not impose the death penalty. A clerk came to be identified with one who could read the NECK VERSE. By an Act of Henry IV's reign, no woman was to suffer death for circumstances in which a man could 'plead his clergy', and a blind man could avoid the rope if able to speak Latin 'congruously'. Benefit of clergy was steadily curtailed from the time of Henry VII and by the end of the 17th century most of the serious crimes were excluded, but it was not totally abolished until 1827.

Benen or **Benigus, St** (d. *c.* 466, f.d. 9 November). Of the race of Oillil Olom, he was St PATRICK's psalm-singer and said to be his best-loved disciple. While young he joined Patrick and later succeeded him as chief bishop of the Irish Church. He founded a monastery at Drumlease and evangelized Clare and Kerry and is patron of Connacht.

Benezet of Avignon, St (*c.* 1163–84, f.d. 14 April). Known as the Bridge-builder, he began life as a shepherd-boy at Hermillon, in France. He went to Avignon where he had a vision of a bridge over the Rhone. When the bishop refused to accept the vision Benezet and companions started to build the bridge and won the bishop's support. The work was not completed until some years after the saint's death, and a chapel was built on it, in which the coffin was placed. Part of the bridge was destroyed by flood in 1669 but the coffin was saved and the body was found incorrupt and was translated to Avignon Cathedral, and later to Saint Didier. Benezet is the patron saint of bridge-builders and of the town of Avignon.

Benjamin. The pet, the youngest; in allusion to Benjamin, the youngest son of Jacob (*Gen.* xxxv, 18). Also (in early and mid-19th century), an overcoat, so called from a tailor of this name, and rendered popular by its association with JOSEPH's 'coat of many colours'.

Benjamin's mess. The largest share. The allusion is to the banquet given by Joseph, viceroy of Egypt, to his brethren. 'Benjamin's mess was five times so much as any of theirs' (*Gen.* xliii, 34).

Benjamin tree. A tree of the Styrax family that yields benzoin, of which the name is a corruption. Friar's Balsam or Jesuit's Drops is compounded from its juice.

Taste, smell; I assure you, sir, pure benjamin, the only spirited scent that ever awaked a Neapolitan nostril.

BEN JONSON: *Cynthia's Revels*, V, ii

Bereans. Followers of the Rev. John Barclay (1734–1798), who seceded from the Scottish kirk in 1773. They held that all we know of God is from the Bible alone; that all the *Psalms* refer to Christ; that assurance is the proof of faith; that unbelief is the unforgivable sin, etc. They took their name from the Bereans mentioned in *Acts* xvii, 10, 11, who 'received the Word with all readiness of mind, and searched the Scriptures daily'.

Bernadette, St (1844–79, f.d. 10 April). Bernadette Soubirous was born at Lourdes of a poor peasant family. She experienced visions of the Virgin Mary who appeared to her in the grotto of Massabielle, predicting that a spring would rise from the grotto floor. When the spring appeared it was reported to have healing properties and a church was built on the rock. Both church and spring became an international centre of pilgrimage. Bernadette entered a nunnery at Nevers at the age of twenty, there she nursed the wounded of the Franco–Prussian war. She died of tuberculosis, confirming her visions on her deathbed. She was canonized in 1933.

Bernard. Bernard, St (1090–1153, f.d. 20 August). Abbot of Clairvaux. Renowned for his wisdom and abilities, he did much to promote the growth of the Cistercian Order, and exercised great influence in Church matters. He was nicknamed the 'MELLIFLUOUS DOCTOR', with a beehive as an emblem, in allusion to his 'honeyed words'—this he shares with St AMBROSE. The hive also represents the monastic life. Like other DOCTORS OF THE CHURCH he may be depicted with a pen and book but he is also famous for his writings which include his Letters, Sermons, Commentaries and Treatises, particularly that on 'The Love of God'. In art he is usually represented as a young man, wearing the white habit of his Order, holding a pastoral staff; he may also be accompanied by a dragon, symbolizing the suppression of heresy.

Bernard of Menthon or Aosta, St (d. 1081, f.d. 28 May). Little is known of his early life except that he became a priest and was said to have been an archdeacon, then a canon of the cathedral of Aosta. In this capacity he was responsible for the alpine region, now named after him as the Great and Little St Bernard Passes, and he set himself to overcome the fierce banditti who preyed on the travellers. He built rest-houses and, on the summit, on the site of an old pagan temple, he founded a church and a house for AUGUSTINIAN CANONS Regular whose special care was the safety and rescue of Alpine travellers. The famous breed of dogs, established there later, was named after him. He is patron saint of Alpinists in particular and mountaineers in general.

Bernardino of Siena, St (1380–1444, f.d. 20 May). Known as the 'Peoples' Preacher', Bernardino at first devoted himself to work in hospitals and the care of plague victims of Siena. He also nursed his aunt, who had reared him after he was orphaned, when she was bedridden. After her death he joined the FRANCISCANS and became a noted preacher, travelling widely and preaching to large crowds in the open air. He used a mixture of the serious and humorous, but constantly inveighed against usury, witchcraft, gambling and the political strife among the cities. He extended and reformed the Franciscan Order and founded schools of theology, maintaining that ignorance was as dangerous as riches. He was falsely accused of heresy but was vindicated. In his preaching Bernardino stressed the name of JESUS and displayed a plaque with the letters IHS surrounded by rays, so that in art he is represented as a small man, with blazing eyes, dressed in the habit of a MINORITE, with this symbol on his breast. He is also depicted with three MITRES of the bishoprics he refused and sometimes there is a trumpet to signify his preaching powers. His tomb is at Aquila, where he died, and was famous for miracles.

Bertha, St (d. 725, f.d. 4 July). Daughter of Count Rigobert, born at the palace in the reign of Clovis II, she married and had five daughters. After the death of her husband she founded a convent at Blangy and became its first abbess, remaining there until her death.

Bertilla Boscardin, St (1888–1922, f.d. 20 October). Anna Francesca Boscardin was a simple peasant girl who joined the Sisters of St Dorothy at Vicenza as a kitchen-maid and after three years became a nurse in a children's ward. In World War I she showed great courage and care for her patients during air raids, attracting much admiration, but her Superior failed to appreciate her qualities and relegated her to the laundry until a higher authority saw the position and placed her in charge of a children's isolation ward. Never in good health, she died as a result of a serious operation in 1922. Her simple, dedicated and holy life had made a great impression on her contemporaries and she was canonized in 1961. Miracles of healing were attributed to her.

Bertram, St Luis (1526–81, f.d. 9 October). A DOMINICAN priest, ordained by St Thomas of Villanova, he was a noted preacher and counsellor. St TERESA OF AVILA was amongst those who sought his advice. He went to Latin America as a missionary, having considerable success, first on the mainland, then in the Leeward, Virgin and Windward Islands. He deplored the cruelty of the Spanish invaders.

He was said to be responsible for miracles and had the gift of prophecy and the gift of tongues. He is the patron saint of Colombia.

Bestiaries, or **Bestials.** Books which had a great vogue between the 11th and 14th centuries, describing the supposed habits and peculiarities of animals both real and fabled, with much legendary lore and moral symbolism. They were founded on the *Physiologi* of earlier centuries and those in English were mostly translations of continental originals. Among the most popular were those of Philippe de Thaun, Guillaume le Clerc, and Richard de Fournival's satirical *Bestiaire d'Amour* (*c.* 1250).

> The unicorn represents Jesus Christ, who took on him our nature in the virgin's womb, was betrayed to the Jews, and delivered into the hands of Pontius Pilate. Its one horn signifies the Gospel truth, that Christ is one with the Father, etc.
>
> GUILLAUME: Le Bestiaire Divin

Bethel (Heb. house of God). A hallowed place where God is worshipped (see *Genesis* xxviii, 18, 19). The name has frequently been given to Nonconformist chapels, especially in Wales, and also to religious meeting houses for seamen. They were sometimes referred to, somewhat disparagingly, by ANGLICANS as *little Bethels*.

> And God said unto Jacob, Arise, go up to Beth-el, and dwell there: and make there an altar unto God...
>
> *Genesis* xxv, 1

Bethlehem. A small town five miles south of JERUSALEM; the reputed place of the birth of JESUS Christ and of King David. The Church of the Nativity stands on the assumed site and is divided into sections for the use of Latin, Roman, Greek or Eastern Orthodox and Armenian worship. It is an important place of pilgrimage.

Bethlehemites. (1) A monastic order existing at Cambridge in 1257. Members wore a red star on the breast in memory of the Star of Bethlehem. (2) A short-lived military order instituted by Pius II in 1459 against the Turks. (3) A religious society for tending the sick, founded in Guatemala, *c.* 1659, by Pierre de Bethencourt, a native of the Canaries. Innocent XI approved of the order in 1687. (4) Followers of John Hus, from the fact that he used to preach in the church of Bethlehem in Prague.

Beuno, St (6th cent., f.d. 21 April). A Welsh saint, often regarded as the most important of the saints of North Wales where he travelled extensively, founding churches; he also founded a monastery at Clynnog Fawr which became the centre of his work and where he died and was buried. A stone ORATORY was erected over his tomb. His relics were later translated to Eglwys y Bedd and miracles occurred there and at his holy well where sick children were bathed and kept overnight at his tomb. Cattle and sheep prospered after being taken to his tomb and there were many legends of miracles of the usual type. He was uncle to St WINIFRED, and when a chieftain's son struck off her head St Beuno restored it to her shoulders and brought her back to life.

Bible. The word is derived from the Greek *Ta Biblia* through mediaeval Latin and means *The Books. See* APOCRYPHA; DEAD SEA SCROLLS; NEW TESTAMENT; OLD TESTAMENT; PENTATEUCH; PSALMS; PSEUDEPIGRAPHA; 'Q'; SEPTUAGINT; VULGATE.

Bible, The English. The principal versions in chronological order are:

Wyclif's Bible. The name given to two translations of the VULGATE. The earlier one completed *c.* 1384 is the first complete English Bible, although there were renderings of parts of the Scriptures from Anglo-Saxon times. Wyclif may have translated parts of it and one of his circle, Nicholas of Hereford, is known to have participated. The second and improved version, probably written between 1395 and 1397, is considered to owe much to John Purvey, a LOLLARD scholar. As a whole it remained unprinted until a monumental edition of both versions, prepared by Forshall and Madden, appeared in 1850.

Tyndale's Bible. This consists of the New Testament printed at Cologne in 1525 (Revisions 1534 and 1535); the PENTATEUCH, printed at Marburg, 1530; the Book of Jonah, 1531; Epistles of the Old Testament (after the Use of Salisbury), 1534; and a MS. translation of the Old Testament to the end of Chronicles, which was afterwards used in MATTHEW'S BIBLE. His work was chiefly based on Greek originals, while making use of the Greek and Latin versions of the New Testament by Erasmus, Luther's Bible, and the VULGATE. His work fixed the language and style of subsequent English versions which were more often revisions of his work rather than independent translations.

Coverdale's Bible. This first printed edition of a complete English Bible appeared in 1535, translated 'out of Douche (German) and Latyn', by Miles Coverdale. It was based on Luther, the ZÜRICH BIBLE, the VULGATE, the Latin version of Pagninus, and Tyndale. The first edition was probably printed at Zürich, the second was printed by Nicolson at Southwark in 1537 (the first Bible printed in England). See BUG BIBLE *under* BIBLE, SOME SPECIALLY NAMED EDITIONS.

Matthew's Bible. Printed in Antwerp in 1537 as the translation of Thomas Matthew, most probably an alias, for self-preservation, of John Rogers, an assistant of Tyndale. It is essentially made up from the work of Tyndale and Coverdale. Like Coverdale's third edition it appeared under the King's licence, but was soon superseded by the GREAT BIBLE. It is important as a basis of the approved editions which culminated in the AUTHORIZED VERSION. *See* BUG BIBLE UNDER *under* BIBLE, SOME SPECIALLY NAMED EDITIONS.

Taverner's Bible. A revision of MATTHEW'S BIBLE by Richard Taverner printed in 1539. It had little influence on subsequent translations, but is notable for its idiomatic English.

The Great Bible. Published by Grafton and Whitchurch in 1539 as an authorized Bible sponsored by Cranmer and Cromwell, being a revision by Coverdale substantially based on MATTHEW'S BIBLE. It went through seven editions and it was made compulsory for all parish churches to possess a copy. See CRANMER'S BIBLE, CROMWELL'S BIBLE.

Cromwell's Bible. The GREAT BIBLE of 1539. The title-page includes a portrait of Thomas Cromwell, under whose direction the Bible was commissioned.

Cranmer's Bible. The name given to the 1540 edition of the GREAT BIBLE. It and later issues contained a prologue by Cranmer, and, on the woodcut title-page by Holbein, Henry VIII is shown seated handing copies to Cranmer and Cromwell. Its Psalter is still incorporated in the BOOK OF COMMON PRAYER.

The Geneva Bible. An important revision in the development of the English Bible, undertaken by English exiles in Geneva during the Marian persecutions, first published in 1560; largely the work of William Whittingham, assisted by Anthony Gilby and Thomas Sampson. Whittingham had previously (1557) published a translation of the New Testament. Based on the GREAT BIBLE, MATTHEW'S BIBLE, etc., it was the first English Bible to be printed in roman type instead of black letter, in quarto size, and the first in which the chapters were divided into verses (on the model of Robert Stephen's Greek–Latin Testament of 1537). It was immensely popular; from 1560 to 1616 no year passed without a new edition. *See* BREECHES BIBLE, GOOSE BIBLE, PLACEMAKER'S BIBLE *under* BIBLE, SOME SPECIALLY NAMED EDITIONS.

The Bishops' Bible. A revision of the GREAT BIBLE to counter the growing popularity of the GENEVA BIBLE. Organized by Archbishop Matthew Parker, it appeared in 1568 and a number of the abler bishops took part in the work. It reached its 18th edition by 1602 and was the basis of the AUTHORIZED VERSION. *See* TREACLE BIBLE *under* BIBLE, SOME SPECIALLY NAMED EDITIONS.

Matthew Parker's Bible. The BISHOPS' BIBLE.

The Douai Bible. A translation of the VULGATE by English Roman Catholics. The New Testament was published at the English College at Rheims in 1582, the Old Testament at Douai in 1609; hence called the **Rheims and Douai version.** *See* ROSIN BIBLE *under* BIBLE, SOME SPECIALLY NAMED EDITIONS.

The Authorized Version. This version, still in general use in England, was produced by some 47 scholars, working at the command of King James I, and was a by-product of the HAMPTON COURT CONFERENCE. Begun in 1607 and published in 1611, it was based on the BISHOPS' BIBLE, but Tyndale's, Matthew's, Coverdale's and the Geneva Bibles were followed where they gave more accurate renderings. Since 1984 published as the *Authorized King James Version.*

King James's Bible. The AUTHORIZED VERSION.

The Revised Version. This revision of the AUTHORIZED VERSION resulted from a resolution passed by Houses of Convocation in 1870. It was the work of two companies of English scholars, with American co-operators. The New Testament appeared in 1881, the Old Testament in 1885, and the APOCRYPHA in 1895.

The American Standard Version (1901). Essentially a modification of the Revised Version of 1881 to meet American preferences.

The New Testament in Modern Speech (1903). A new translation from the Greek by R. F. Weymouth.

Moffat's Translation. A revised edition of the Bible by James Moffat (NT, 1913; OT, 1924; complete edition, 1935).

Knox Version. A new Roman Catholic translation of the VULGATE by Monsignor R. A. Knox. The NT was authorized in 1945, the OT (for private use only) in 1949.

The Revised Standard Version. The work of American scholars issued between 1946 and 1952. It was to embody the results of modern scholarship 'and to be in the diction of the simple classic English style of the King James version'. The APOCRYPHA was published in 1957.

The New Testament in Modern English. A translation by J. B. Phillips aiming at clarity of expression, first published in 1958 with a revised version in 1973.

The New English Bible. A translation into contemporary English first proposed by the CHURCH OF SCOTLAND and directed by a joint committee of the PROTESTANT Churches of Great Britain and Ireland. The NT appeared in 1961 and the translations of the OT and the APOCRYPHA were finished in 1966. The complete bible was published in 1970. The 1989 edition was revised to eliminate 'sexist language' such as *man, sons, brothers,* etc.

The Jerusalem Bible. A new translation of the Bible, prepared from the ancient originals by Roman Catholic scholars, largely in contemporary English. First published in 1966, it derives its notes and introduction from the French *La Bible de Jérusalem* produced under the editorship of Père Roland de Vaux in 1956. Yahweh replaces the traditional JEHOVAH.

The Revised Standard Version Common Bible. Published in 1973, based on both the Protestant and Roman Catholic (1966) editions of the REVISED STANDARD VERSION, and intended for interdenominational use. It has been accepted by the PROTESTANT churches generally as well as by the ROMAN CATHOLIC and Eastern CHURCHES.

The Good News Bible: Today's English Version. An illustrated version, produced by the American Bible Society, designed to be easily understood, including by those whose first language is not English. The NT was published in 1966 and the complete Bible in 1976. It follows the traditional numbering of chapter and verse.

The New International Version. A new translation, the work of an Anglo–American team seeking to present a modernized version in good English. First published by the New York Bible Society in 1978 followed by a British edition in 1979.

Many other individually produced translations have appeared over the years.

Bible, Some specially named editions.
The Adulterous Bible. The WICKED BIBLE.
The Affinity Bible, of 1923, which contains a table of affinity with the error, 'A man may not marry his grandmother's wife.'
The Bad Bible. A printing of 1653 with a deliberate perversion of *Acts* vi, 6, whereby the ordination of deacons was ascribed to the disciples and not to the apostles.
Bassendyne Bible. The first edition of the Bible printed in Scotland; the NT was published in 1576, followed by the whole Bible in 1579.
The Bear Bible. The Spanish Protestant version printed at Basle in 1569; so called because the woodcut device on the title-page is of a bear.
Bedell's Bible. An Irish translation of the Old Testament carried out under the direction of Bishop William Bedell (1571–1642). The Irish NT was published in 1601.
The Breeches Bible. The popular name for the GENEVA BIBLE (*see under* BIBLE, THE ENGLISH) because in it *Genesis* iii, 7, was rendered, 'and they sowed figge-tree leaves together, and made themselves breeches.' It is also given in the then unprinted Wyclif MS. (ya swiden ye levis of a fige tree and madin brechis), and also in the translation of the PENTATEUCH printed in Caxton's edition of Voragine's *Golden Legend* (1483).
The Brothers' Bible. The KRALITZ BIBLE.
The Bug Bible. COVERDALE'S BIBLE (*see under* BIBLE, THE ENGLISH) of 1535 is so called because

Psalm xci, 5, is translated: 'Thou shalt not nede to be afrayed for eny bugges by night.' The same occurs in MATTHEW'S BIBLE (*see under* BIBLE, THE ENGLISH) and its reprints. Both the AUTHORIZED VERSION (*see under* BIBLE, THE ENGLISH) and REVISED VERSION (*see under* BIBLE, THE ENGLISH) read 'terror'.
Camel's Bible, of 1823. *Genesis* xxiv, 61, reads: 'And Rebekah arose, and her camels (for *damsels*).'
Complutensian Polyglot. Published between 1514 and 1517 at Alcalá (the ancient Complutum), near Madrid, at the expense of Cardinal Ximenes. In six folio volumes, it contains the Hebrew and Greek texts, the Septuagint, the VULGATE, and the Chaldee paraphrase of the PENTATEUCH with a Latin translation, together with Greek and Hebrew grammars and a Hebrew dictionary.
The Denial Bible. Printed at Oxford in 1792, in *Luke* xxii, 34, the name *Philip* is substituted for *Peter,* as the apostle who should deny Jesus.
The Discharge Bible. An edition of 1806 containing *discharge* for *charge* in I *Timothy* v, 21: 'I dis-charge thee before God,... that thou observe these things.'
The Ears to Ear Bible. An edition of 1810, in which *Matthew* xiii, 43, reads: 'Who hath ears to *ear*, let him hear.'
The Ferrara Bible. The first Spanish edition of the Old Testament (1553) for the use of Spanish Jews. A second edition for Christians was published in the same year.
The Fool Bible. An edition of Charles I's reign in which *Psalm* xiv, 1, reads: 'The fool hath said in his heart there is a God.' (instead of *no god*). The printers were fined £3,000 and all copies were suppressed.
The Forgotten Sins Bible, of 1638. *Luke* vii, 47, reads: 'Her sins which are many, are forgotten (instead of *forgiven*).'
The Forty-two-line Bible. The MAZARIN BIBLE.
The Goose Bible. The editions of the GENEVA BIBLE (*see under* BIBLE, THE ENGLISH) printed at Dort: the Dort press had a goose for its device.
The Gutenberg Bible. The MAZARIN BIBLE.
The He Bible. In the first of the two editions of the AUTHORIZED VERSION in 1611, known as 'the He Bible', *Ruth* iii, 15, reads: 'and he went into the city.' The other, and nearly all modern editions (except the REVISED VERSION) have 'she'. 'He' is the correct translation of the Hebrew. See BIBLE, THE ENGLISH.
The Idle Bible. An edition of 1809, in which 'the idol shepherd' (Zech. xi, 17) is printed 'the idle shepherd'. In the REVISED VERSION (*see under* BIBLE, THE ENGLISH) the translation is 'the worthless shepherd'.
The Incunabula Bible. The date on the title page reads 1495 instead of 1594. The word incunabula came to be applied to all books printed before 1500, the period when

typography was in its 'swaddling-clothes', or its beginnings.

The Indian Bible. The first complete Bible printed in America, translated into the dialect of the Indians of Massachusetts by the Rev. John Eliot and published by Samuel Green and Marmaduke Johnson in 1663.

Judas Bible, of 1611. *Matthew* xxvi, 36, reads 'Judas' instead of 'Jesus'.

The Kralitz Bible, also called the *Brothers' Bible,* was published by the United Brethren of Moravia at Kralitz, 1579–1593.

The 'Large Family' Bible. An Oxford edition of 1820 prints *Isaiah* lxvi, 9: 'Shall I bring to the birth and not cease (for *cause*) to bring forth?'

The Leda Bible. The third edition (second folio) of the BISHOPS' BIBLE (*see under* BIBLE, THE ENGLISH), published in 1572, and so called from the decoration of the initial at the Epistle to the Hebrews which is a startling and incongruous wood-cut of Jupiter visiting Leda in the guise of a swan. This and other decorations in the New Testament were from an edition of Ovid's *Metamorphoses.* Such was the protest that they were never used again.

The Leopolita Bible. A Polish translation of the VULGATE by John of Lemberg (Jan Nicz of Lwów) published at Cracow in 1561. So called from the Latin name, *Leopolis,* of his birthplace.

The Lions Bible. A bible issued in 1804 containing many printers' errors such as: *Numbers* xxv, 18, 'The murderer shall surely be put together (instead of *to death*)'; I *Kings* viii, 19, 'but thy son that shall come forth out of thy lions (for loins)'; *Galatians* v, 17, 'For the flesh lusteth after the Spirit (for *against the Spirit*)'.

The Mazarin Bible. The first known book to be printed from movable type, probably by Fust and Schöffer at Mainz, who took over most of Gutenberg's presses in 1455. This edition of the VULGATE was on sale in 1456 and owes its name to the copy discovered in the Mazarin Library in Paris in 1760. A copy of Vol. I fetched a record price of £21,000 at a London auction in 1947. It was for long credited to Gutenberg and is frequently called the **Gutenberg Bible.** It is usually known to bibliographers as the **Forty-two-line Bible** (it having 42 lines to the column) to differentiate it from the THIRTY-SIX-LINE BIBLE.

More Sea Bible, of 1641. *Revelation* xxi, 1, reads: 'and there was more sea', instead of 'no more sea'.

The Murderers' Bible. An edition of 1801 in which *Jude* 16 reads: 'These are murderers (for *murmurers*), complainers', etc.

The Old Cracow Bible. The LEOPOLITA BIBLE.

Old Latin Bible. The Latin version of the Scriptures was used by the Church prior to the VULGATE of St JEROME.

The Ostrog Bible. The first complete Slavonic edition; printed at Ostrog, Volhynia, Russia, in 1581.

Paragraph Bible. Issued by John WESLEY in 1755 as the NT arranged in paragraphs instead of verses. The entire AV was published in 1838 by the RELIGIOUS TRACT SOCIETY.

Pfister's Bible. The THIRTY-SIX-LINE BIBLE.

The Placemakers' Bible. The second edition of the GENEVA BIBLE (*see under* BIBLE, THE ENGLISH, 1562. *Matthew* v, 9, reads: 'Blessed are the placemakers (peacemakers): for they shall be called the children of God.' It has also been called the WHIG BIBLE.

Polyglot Bible. A Bible which contains the text in several languages, such as were issued in the 16th and 17th centuries, the most noted being the Complutensian Polyglot of 1522. It was printed in parallel columns of Hebrew, Greek and Latin in the OT and Greek and Latin in the NT.

The Printers' Bible. An edition of about 1702 which makes David complain that 'printers (princes) have persecuted me without a cause'. (*Ps.* cxiv, 161.)

The Proof Bible (Probe-Bibel). The revised version of the first impression of Luther's German Bible. A final revision appeared in 1892.

The Rosin Bible. The DOUAI BIBLE (*see under* BIBLE, THE ENGLISH), 1609, is so called because it has in *Jeremiah* viii, 22: 'Is there noe rosin in Galaad?' The AUTHORIZED VERSION (*see under* BIBLE, THE ENGLISH) translates the word by 'balm', but gives 'rosin' in the margin as an alternative. *Cp.* TREACLE BIBLE.

Sacy's Bible. A French translation by the Jansenist, Louis Isaac le Maistre de Sacy, director of PORT-ROYAL (1650–1679). He began his work when imprisoned in the Bastille.

Schelhorn's Bible. The THIRTY-SIX-LINE BIBLE.

The September Bible. Luther's German translation of the New Testament, published anonymously at Wittenberg in September 1522.

The She Bible. *See* HE BIBLE.

'Sin on' Bible. The first printed in Ireland was dated 1716. *John* v, 14, reads: 'sin on more', instead of 'sin no more'. The mistake was undiscovered until 8,000 copies had been printed and bound.

The Standing Fishes Bible. An edition of 1806 in which *Ezekiel* xlvii, 10, reads: 'And it shall come to pass that the fishes (fishers) shall stand upon it,' etc.

The Sting Bible of 1746. *Mark* vii, 35, 'the sting of his tongue', instead of 'string'.

The Thirty-six-line Bible. A Latin Bible of 36 lines to the column, probably printed by A. Pfister at Bamberg in 1460. It is also known as the Bamberg, and Pfister's, Bible and sometimes as Schelhorn's, as it was first described by the German bibliographer J. G. Schelhorn, in 1760.

The To-remain Bible. In a Bible printed at Cambridge in 1805 *Galatians* iv, 29, reads: 'persecuted him that was born after the spirit to remain, even so it is now.' The words 'to remain' were added in error by the compositor, the editor having answered a proofreader's query as to the comma after 'spirit', with the pencilled reply in the margin 'to remain'. The mistake was repeated in the Bible Society's first 8vo edition (1805) and their 12mo edition of 1819.

The Treacle Bible. A popular name for the BISHOPS' BIBLE (*see under* BIBLE, THE ENGLISH), 1568, because *Jeremiah* viii, 22, reads: 'is there no tryacle in Gilead, is there no phisition there?' 'Tryacle' is also given for 'balm' in *Jeremiah* xlvi, ii, and *Ezekiel* xxvii, 17. *Cp.* ROSIN BIBLE (*see under* BIBLE, THE ENGLISH). COVERDALE'S BIBLE also uses the word 'triacle'.

The Unrighteous Bible. A Cambridge printing of 1653 contains: 'know ye not that the unrighteous shall inherit the Kingdom of God?', instead of 'shall not inherit' (I *Cor.* vi, 9). Also in *Romans* vi, 13, 'neither yield ye your members as instruments of righteousness unto sin,' in place of 'unrighteousness'. This edition is also sometimes known as the WICKED BIBLE.

The Vinegar Bible. An Oxford printing of 1717 in which part of the chapter heading to *Luke* xx, reads: 'The parable of the Vinegar' (for *Vineyard*).

The Whig Bible. Another name for the PLACE-MAKERS' BIBLE. The jibe is obvious.

The Wicked Bible. So called because the word 'not' was omitted in the seventh commandment (*Exodus* xx, 14) making it, 'Thou shalt commit adultery.' It was printed by Barker and Lucas, the King's printers at Blackfriars in 1631. The fine of £300 helped to ruin the printer. It is also called the *Adulterous Bible. See* UNRIGHTEOUS BIBLE.

The Wife–hater Bible. An 1810 edition gives *Luke* xiv, 26: 'If any man come to me, and hate not his father and mother … yea, and his own wife,' instead of 'life'.

Wujek's Bible. An authorized Polish translation by the Jesuit, Jacub Wujek, printed at Cracow in 1599.

The Zürich Bible. A German version of 1530 composed of Luther's translation of the New Testament and portions of the Old, with the remainder and the APOCRYPHA by other translators.

Bible, Statistics of. The following statistics are those given in the *Introduction to the Critical Study and Knowledge of the Bible*, by Thos. Hartwell Horne, D.D., first published in 1818. They apply to the English AUTHORIZED VERSION (*see under* BIBLE, THE ENGLISH).

	OT	NT	Total
Books	39	27	66
Chapters	929	260	1,189
Verses	23,214	7,959	31,173
Words	593,493	181,253	774,746
Letters	2,728,100	838,380	3,566,480

APOCRYPHA. Books, 14; chapters, 183; verses, 6,031; words, 125,185; letters, 1,063,876.

	OT	NT
Middle book	*Proverbs*	II *Thess.*
Middle Chapter	*Job* xxix	*Rom.* xiii and xiv
Middle verse	II *Chron.* xx, 17 & 18	*Acts* xvi, 17
Shortest verse	I *Chron.* i, 25	*John* xi, 35
Shortest chapter	*Psalm* cxvii	
Longest chapter	*Psalm* cxix	

Ezra vii, 21, contains all the letters of the alphabet except j.

II *Kings* xix and *Isaiah* xxxvii are exactly alike.

The last two verses of II *Chron.* and the opening verses of *Ezra* are alike.

Ezra ii and *Nehemiah* vii are alike.

The word *and* occurs in the OT 35,543 times, and in the NT 10,684 times.

The word *Jehovah* occurs 6,855 times, and *Lord* 1,855 times.

About thirty books are mentioned in the Bible, but not included in the canon.

In addition it is noteworthy that by the end of 1965 the United Bible Societies had circulated the Scriptures in 1251 languages.

Bible. Bible-backed. Round-shouldered, like one who is always poring over a book.

Bible belt. In the USA the south central Midwest, south of the Mason Dixon line reputedly associated with puritanism and religious fundamentalism.

Bible-carrier. A scornful term for an obtrusively pious person.

Some scoffe at such as carry the scriptures with them to church, terming them in reproach Bible-carriers.

GOUGE: *Whole Armour of God* (1616), p. 318

Bible Christians. An evangelical sect founded in 1815 by William O'Bryan, a Cornish METHODIST; also called Bryanites. The movement grew steadily, beginning in the fishing and farming districts of Devon and Cornwall. They joined the United Methodist Church in 1907.

Bible-Clerk. A student at Oxford or Cambridge who formerly got pecuniary advantages for reading the Bible at chapel, etc.

Bible-puncher. A modern equivalent of BIBLE-CARRIER.

Bible Societies. PROTESTANT societies founded for the purpose of circulating copies of the

Bible either by distributing them free or selling at a low price. An early example was the Constein Bible Society at Halle, in Germany, in 1710. The British and Foreign Bible Society founded in 1804, in London, is the largest, with versions in some 800 languages. The American Bible Society followed in 1816 and there are also the National Bible Societies of Scotland and of the Netherlands. 'Gideon's International' places Bibles in hotel bedrooms. The last formed group, the United Bible Societies, was founded in 1946. The Bible now appears in 1100 different languages with an annual distribution of about 17 million volumes.

Biblia Pauperum (Lat. poor man's Bible). A misnomer coined long after the first appearance in the 1460s of these late mediaeval block books. They contain a series of NEW TESTAMENT scenes from the life of Christ, each surrounded by their OLD TESTAMENT antetypes, and with a brief text engraved in the same block below the illustration. Despite their name, the *Biblia Pauperum* can hardly have been intended for the illiterate, their iconography and text being replete with allegory and symbol, and must rather have served itinerant preachers and the lower orders of clergy. *See* SPECULUM HUMANAE SALVATIONIS.

Biblical Criticism. The term includes three main sections of criticism: (1) the LOWER CRITICISM, concerned with the text of the BIBLE; (2) HIGHER CRITICISM, treating of dates, authorship and sources; (3) Historical Criticism which deals with the actual historical matter in the Bible in the light of new and archaeological discoveries.

Biddle, John (1615–1662). Called 'the Father of English UNITARIANS', John Biddle, educated at Oxford, became a schoolmaster but was imprisoned in 1645 for having professed his disbelief in the HOLY TRINITY. His pamphlet on the Holy Ghost was publicly burned by the hangman. Biddle was banished to the Scilly Isles from 1655 to 1658. In 1662 he was again imprisoned and died in gaol, being unable to pay a fine of £100 imposed for preaching in London.

Bilocation. The appearance of a person in two distinct places at the same time; the phenomenon is reported to have occurred with various SAINTS, among them ANTHONY OF PADUA, ALPHONSUS LIGUORI, PHILIP NERI and the Curé d'Ars.

Biretta. A square cap of silk or velvet, with three ridges on top, worn by clergy of the Western Catholic Church when out of Church. That of a priest is black, a bishop's is purple and a cardinal's red, the Pope's white.

Birinus, Birin or **Berin, St** (d. 650, f.d. 3 December). Called the 'Apostle of Wessex' he had been a monk at Rome and was sent by Pope Honorius I to convert the heathen of the Midlands of Britain. He landed in Wessex and, finding the people still pagan, remained there, later being made the first bishop of Dorchester (near Oxford) by King Cynegils whom he had instructed in the Christian faith. It was said that Birinus firmly planted Christianity and consecrated many churches, among them one at Winchester. He died and was buried at Dorchester. His tomb has been recently restored, and miracles and visions were reported there.

Bishop (OE *biscop*; from Lat. *episcopus*, and Gr. *episkopos*, an overseer). One of the higher order of Christian priesthood who presides over a diocese and has powers of ordaining and confirming.

The name is given to one of the men in chess (formerly called the *archer*); to the ladybird; to a lady's bustle (sometimes called a 'stern reality'); and to a drink made by pouring red wine, such as claret or burgundy, either hot or cold, on ripe bitter oranges, the liquor being sugared and spiced to taste. Similarly a *Cardinal* is made by using *white* wine instead of *red* and a *Pope* by using *tokay*. *See also* BOY BISHOP.

The Bishops' Bible. *See* BIBLE, THE ENGLISH.

Black Canons. The AUGUSTINIANS, from their black cloaks.

Black coat. An old name for a parson.

Black Friars. The DOMINICAN Friars, from their black mantle. The London district of this name is on the site of the former Dominican monastery.

Black Genevan. A black preaching gown formerly used in many Anglican churches and still used by NONCONFORMISTS. So called from Geneva, where CALVIN preached in such a robe.

Black Mass. A sacrilegious MASS in which the DEVIL is invoked in place of God and various obscene rites performed in ridicule of the proper ceremony. It is also a REQUIEM Mass from the custom of wearing black vestments.

Black Monks. The BENEDICTINES.

Black Pope. The General of the JESUITS.

Black Rood of Scotland. The 'piece of the true cross' or ROOD, set in an ebony crucifix, which St MARGARET, wife of King Malcolm Canmore, left to the Scottish nation in 1093. It fell into English hands at the battle of Neville's Cross (1346) and was kept in Durham Cathedral until the REFORMATION when it was lost.

Blaise, Blase or **Blayse, St** (date unknown, f.d. 3 February). Said to have been bishop of Sebaste in Armenia and martyred under the

Emperor Licinius, but there is little other than legend attached to his name. There are various accounts of cures and miracles which were responsible for cults and festivals, such as bonfires on the hills, the Bradford festival held every five years, and the ceremony of the Blessing of St Blaise commemorating his healing of a boy near death with a fishbone in his throat; the cure was effected with two candles. Later, the boy's mother brought candles to the Saint when he was in prison. The legend gave rise to a ceremony of blessing throat-sufferers with two crossed candles and to the symbolism of the candle or taper in St Blaise's hand, or the candle carried before him. He healed sick animals which came to him when he was hidden in a cave to escape persecution and is invoked against diseases in both humans and animals. In art he is portrayed in bishop's robes and MITRE, holding a wool-comb with which he was said to have been tortured before being beheaded, or he may carry crossed candles; he can be surrounded by birds and beasts. Blaise is the patron saint of wool-combers.

Blake, William (1757–1827). English poet, artist and mystic. He was born in Soho, apprenticed to an engraver, and remained a professional in the art all his life. He studied art under Reynolds. All his works are highly symbolic, especially his early poems *Songs of Innocence* and *Songs of Experience*. His most noted illustrations were those of Young's 'Night Thoughts', the 'Book of Job' and Dante and other poets.

Blasphemy (Gr. *blaptein*, to damage). Written or spoken impious or contemptuous words against God, religious beliefs and things held sacred which deliberately offend or outrage believers. Laws of blasphemy against Christianity still remain on the statute book. Blasphemy is also an offence at Common Law.

Blessing. Benediction, divine favour or its invocation; frequently used in Christian services in the LITURGY, in the MASS, in CONFESSION and at the end of divine worship. *See also* BENEDICTION.

Blood. Blood represents the life principle, the soul, rejuvenation; hence blood sacrifice. Blood and wine are symbolically interchangeable and in Christian symbolism blood and water at the Crucifixion are the life of the body and the life of the spirit.
Man of Blood. Any man of violent temper. David was so called in II *Samuel* 16:7 (REVISED VERSION), and the PURITANS applied the term to Charles I.
The Field of Blood. ACELDAMA, the piece of ground purchased with the blood-money of our Saviour.

Bloody Bill, The. Better known as the Act of the SIX ARTICLES (31 Henry VIII, *c.* 14), it made the denial of TRANSUBSTANTIATION a heresy punishable by death.
Bloody Thursday. The Thursday in the first week of LENT, that is, the day after ASH WEDNESDAY, used to be so called.

Boanerges. A name given to James and John, the sons of Zebedee, because they wanted to call down 'fire from HEAVEN' to consume the Samaritans for not 'receiving' the Lord Jesus. It is said in the Bible to signify 'sons of thunder', but 'sons of tumult' would be a better rendering. (*Luke* iv, 54; *Mark* iii, 17.)

Boethius. Roman philosopher and writer (*c.* 475–*c.* 525 AD). His manuals and translations from the Greek were widely used in the Middle Ages. Both King Alfred and Chaucer translated his *De Consolatione Philosophiae*. Evidence now points to his having been a Christian.

Bogomils. A long-lasting heretical sect which sprang up in Thrace and Bulgaria in the 10th century, named after the priest Bogomil. Their heresy was a compound of Manichaeism and the errors of the Massalians, rejecting the TRINITY and the sacraments and holding that matter is evil. As a result *Bulgar* became an abusive term in the West, being identified with Bogomilism and evil practices generally. Hence the word *bugger* as a low term of abuse, etc. *See also* MANICHAEANS.

Bohemian Brethren. A religious sect formed from the HUSSITES which arose in Prague in the 15th century. They were the forerunners of the MORAVIANS.

Böhme, Boehme or **Behmen, Jacob** (1575–1624). A German mystic born near Görlitz where he became a shoemaker. He was accused of heresy after he wrote 'Aurora' and was summoned to appear at Dresden; there he successfully defended his views, but died on the way home. He wrote of the 'urgrund', the unity of all and nothing from which we rise and to which we return. He was a Lutheran and wrote theosophical treatises, winning a considerable following in Germany, Holland and England. He claimed his writings were from divine revelation.

Bollandists. JESUIT writers of the *Acta Sanctorum* or *Lives of the Saints*, the original editor being John Bolland, a Dutchman. The first two volumes giving the SAINTS commemorated in January were published in 1643. The disturbances of the French Revolution of 1789 led to cessation of the work in 1794 but the society was reconstituted in 1837. Sixty-seven volumes (from 1 Jan. to 10 Nov.) had been completed by 1967.

Bonaventure, St (1221–74, f.d. 14 July). A DOCTOR OF THE CHURCH, he was John of Fidenza, born in Tuscany. He became a FRANCISCAN monk and studied at, and helped to reform, the University of Paris. He was one of the great theological teachers of the Order, of which he was elected General in 1256; he was reputed to have been offered, but refused, the bishopric of York. Against his will he was made Cardinal and Bishop of Alba, one of the six SUFFRAGANS of Rome. He died while attending the Council of Lyons and was buried there. In 1430 his relics were enshrined, but a century later they were burnt by the HUGUENOTS. Bonaventure was known as The Seraphic Doctor on account of his fervent exhortations on such subjects as Mariolatry, celibacy, the ascetic life and the mystic union of the soul with God. In art he is usually represented with an angel communicating him, in reference to the legend that when he was too humble to draw near the ALTAR, an angel brought the SACRAMENT to him. He wears the habit of the Franciscan or full episcopal robes; he may hold a cross and chalice or book, with a cardinal's hat at his feet. His best known work is *Journey of the Soul to God*.

Boniface, St (680–754, f.d. 5th June). The APOSTLE of Germany, a West Saxon whose English name was Wynfrith. He was born in Devon, probably at Crediton, of Anglo-Saxon farming family, and was educated first at Exeter, then at a monastery at Nursling, in the Diocese of Winchester where he later became director of the school and wrote the first Latin grammar to have been compiled in England. He also wrote poems and acrostics. Letters written by, and about, him give valuable historical information and present him as a noble and lovable person. He left England for Fisia to be a missionary, but finding the times unsuitable, returned to England to Nursling where he was elected abbot but declined the office. He then went to ROME and was commissioned by Pope GREGORY II as a missionary to Germany, in Bavaria and Hesse. There he changed his name from Wynfrith to Boniface. In Bavaria he felled a pagan sacred oak to demonstrate that the pagan gods were powerless to protect it and their followers; this resulted in many conversions. Pope GREGORY III sent him the PALLIUM, making him Archbishop and giving him the power to create bishops for Germany beyond the Rhine. Later, after another visit to Rome, he was appointed archbishop of Mainz. His work was closely associated with the PAPACY and with the Emperors Carloman and Pepin the Short. When on a mission down the Rhine, at a great age, Boniface and his followers were murdered by a body of pagans. The Saint is depicted in art in a bishop's robes and MITRE, holding a book pierced by a sword.

Boniface Curitan, St (7th cent. f.d. 14 March). Said to have been a Roman who became a bishop of Ross, in Scotland, and to have converted large numbers of Picts and Scots and to have founded 150 churches. His particular life work was to establish Roman uniformity as opposed to the Celtic usage.

St Boniface's cup. An extra cup of wine; an excuse for an extra glass. Pope Boniface, we are told in the *Ebrietatis Encomium*, instituted an indulgence to those who drank his good health after grace, or the health of the POPE of the day. This probably refers to Boniface VI, an abandoned profligate, who was elected Pope by the mob in 896 and died fifteen days later. The two Saints Boniface to be Pope were Boniface I (418–22) and Boniface IV (608–15).

The Book of Books. The BIBLE; also called simply 'the Book', or 'the good Book'.

Book of Common Order. The order of worship drawn up by John KNOX in 1556, in Geneva, for PROTESTANT congregations, also known as the Order of Geneva and 'Knox's Liturgy'. It was used by Calvinists until it was replaced by the Westminster Directory in 1645.

The Book of Common Prayer. The official liturgy of the CHURCH OF ENGLAND first issued in 1549 under Cranmer. Modified in 1552, 1559, and 1604 it was revised after the Restoration and reissued in 1662. The amended Prayer Books of 1927 and 1928 were approved by Convocation but rejected by Parliament.

Since the 1960s *The Book of Common Prayer* has been increasingly displaced by alternative forms of service commonly known as Series 1, Series 2 and Series 3. The *Alternative Services Book* of 1980 contains three alternative forms of Communion Service, namely, revised versions of Series 1 and 2 (largely based on the *Book of Common Prayer*), and the more controversial Series 3 (Revised) in modern English. The other services are all in the Series 3 idiom, those for the Visitation and Communion of the Sick being dropped. None of the readings (formerly called *lessons*) is from the AUTHORIZED VERSION (*see under* BIBLE, THE ENGLISH) and perhaps more properly it should have been called 'The Replacement Service Book', although this was not supposed to be the intention.

The Book of Kells. An exceptionally fine illustrated copy of the Gospels in Latin. It is kept in the Library of Trinity College, Dublin, and probably dates from the 8th century.

The Book of Life, or of Fate. In BIBLE language, a register of the names of those who are to inherit eternal life (*Philem*. iv, 3; Rev. xx, 12).

Booth, William (1829–1912). Founder, and first

General, of the SALVATION ARMY. He was born in Nottingham but removed to London where he was a publisher's assistant. He experienced conversion at the age of sixteen and devoted his spare time to evangelical preaching and was associated with the Methodist New Connection. In 1861 he became an itinerant preacher and began to work, free of any denomination, among the poorest in the East End of London, founding, in Whitechapel, the Christian Mission which later became the Salvation Army. He married Catherine Mumford in 1855 and she became a public preacher and the 'Army Mother', initiating the ministry of women. From this marriage their children William Bramwell and Evangeline Booth both became 'Generals' in their time. Booth's *In Darkest England and the Way Out* was a manual of social reform. The Army used unconventional, revivalist methods in services and worked for all branches of down-and-outs. Booth's work was recognized by the authorities and King Edward VII was a supporter.

Boris and Gleb, SS (d. 1015, f.d. 24 July). The two Russian princes, brothers of Svyatopolk the Accursed who succeeded St VLADIMIR, were both killed by the orders of their brother to secure his position. Boris was slain with a spear and sword as he returned from an expedition against the Pechenags, and Gleb shortly after. Neither brother offered resistance to the attackers, on the grounds of Christian resignation and unwillingness to use force against an older brother. They became 'passion-bearers', those who suffer voluntarily in the name of Christ and renounce violence. They were canonized by Pope Benedict XIII and are revered in Russian Orthodox Churches. The brothers are also known by their Christian names Romanus and David in the West.

Born Again Christians. Based on the text 'Except a man be born again he cannot enter the Kingdom of Heaven,' (*John* iii, 3, from the story of Nicodemus) the Born Again Christian goes through the experience of conversion and regeneration to be reborn of the Spirit and renew the response to God. The term is applied by EVANGELISTS to one who has undergone this experience and made all future actions conform to Evangelical Christian standards.

Bosa, St (d. 705, f.d. 9 March). A monk from the monastery of St HILDA at Whitby who was appointed bishop of York in 678 by St THEODORE after St WILFRID had been expelled from Northumbria. Bosa retained the diocese except during the period of St Wilfrid's reinstatement. St ACCA was one of his disciples. Bosa was described by BEDE as a man of 'singular merit and holiness'.

Boscardin, St. *See* BERTILLA.

Bosco, John, St (1815–88, f.d. 1 January). Born in Piedmont, of a peasant family and fatherless at two years, he was reared in great poverty, his clothes having to be provided by charity when he entered a seminary. He was ordained priest in 1841 and worked among men and boys of the working class in Turin and in the slums and prisons. He also served in a refuge for girls but abandoned this to live with his mother in poverty with a group of destitute boys, establishing workshops and teaching them trades. The group increased greatly in numbers and Don Bosco expanded the boys' interests by taking them into the country and teaching them music. He founded the SALESIAN Order which is concerned with schools of all kinds, both technical and agricultural, and with ecclesiastical seminaries. The Order spread widely in the Old and New Worlds. He also founded an order for nuns, the Salesian Sisters, the Daughters of Our Lady, to carry out work on the same lines, the first Superior being Maria MAZZARELLO. Bosco gained a reputation as a skilful handler of difficult youths, as a preacher and writer, and as a visionary and worker of miracles. He was canonized in 1934.

Bosom friend. A very dear friend. Nathan says it 'lay in his bosom and was unto him as a daughter' (II *Sam*, xii, 3). St JOHN is represented in the New Testament as the 'bosom friend' of Jesus.

Bosom sermons. Sermons committed to memory and learnt by heart; not extempore or delivered from notes.

> The preaching from 'bosom sermons', or from writing, being considered a lifeless practice before the Reformation.
>
> BLUNT: *Reformation in England,* p. 179

Boste, John, St (1543–94, f.d. 25 October). Born in Cumbria and educated at Queen's College, Oxford, Boste was converted to Roman Catholicism, went to the English College at Reims and was ordained priest. He returned to the North of England and carried out an active missionary campaign, sometimes under the disguise of a liveried servant, but he was betrayed and imprisoned in the Tower of London where he suffered torture. He was sent to Durham, accused of high treason, found guilty and was hanged, drawn and quartered. He was canonized in 1970 and included among the FORTY MARTYRS OF ENGLAND AND WALES.

Botolph or **Botulf, St** (d. 680, f.d. 17 June). An obscure saint who had a considerable cult in East Anglia in the Middle Ages; he was said to have been 'of remarkable life and learning'. He founded a monastery at Icanhoh, a site which is disputed as either Boston in Lincolnshire, or Iken in Suffolk. He had been chaplain to a convent which housed two of the king's sisters. His brother, St Adulf, was a monk. The bones of the brothers were translated as relics, the head of St Botolph going to Ely and the rest being distributed between Bury St Edmunds, Thorney and Westminster. Sixty-four churches were dedicated to him in East Anglia and London.

Bottomless Pit, The. Hell is so called in *Revelation,* xx, 1. *See* ABADDON.

Bounds, Beating the. An old custom, still kept up in a few English parishes, of going round the parish boundaries on Holy Thursday or ASCENSION DAY. The schoolchildren, accompanied by the clergymen and parish officers, walked round the boundaries, which the boys struck with peeled willow wands. The boys were sometimes 'whipped'at intervals and water was sometimes poured on them from house windows 'to make them remember' the boundaries.

In Scotland beating the bounds was called *Riding the marches* (bounds), and in England the day is sometimes called *gang-day.*

Bourne, Hugh (1772–1852). Founder of the PRIMITIVE METHODISTS. The son of a farmer, Bourne undertook lay preaching among the WESLEYAN METHODISTS, but his unconventional methods and predilection for open-air meetings set him at odds with the Wesleyan leaders and he formed a committee of his own which later took the name of Primitive Methodists.

Bowels of Mercy. Compassion, sympathy. The affections were once supposed to be the outcome of certain secretions or organs, as the bile, the kidneys, the heart, the liver, the bowels, the spleen etc. Hence the word *melancholy* or 'black bile'; the Psalmist says that his *reins,* or kidneys, instructed him (*Ps.* xvi, 7), meaning his inward conviction; the *head* is the seat of understanding, the *heart* of affection and memory (hence 'learning by heart'); the *bowels* of mercy, the *spleen* of passion or anger, etc.
His bowels yearned over, upon, or **towards him.** He felt a secret affection for him.

Joseph made haste; for his bowels did yearn upon his brother.
Gen. xliii, 30; *see also* I *Kings* iii, 26

Boxing Day. *See* CHRISTMAS BOX.

Boy Bishop. St NICHOLAS of Bari was called 'the Boy Bishop' because from his cradle he manifested marvellous indications of piety.

The custom of choosing a boy from the cathedral or parish choir on his day (6 December), as a mock BISHOP, is very ancient.

It was also the custom in schools and colleges such as St Paul's, Eton, Winchester; King's College, Cambridge etc. The boy held office for three weeks and the rest of the choir were his prebendaries. If he died in office he was buried *in pontificalibus.* Probably the reference is to the boy Jesus sitting in the temple among the doctors. The custom was abolished by Henry VIII in 1541, revived in 1552, and finally abolished by Elizabeth I.

Boyle Lectures. A course of eight sermons to be delivered annually, in defence of the Christian religion; endowed by the Hon. Robert Boyle, the natural philosopher, and first given in 1692.

Brandan, St, or **Brendan.** A semi-legendary Irish saint, said to have been born at Tralee in 484. He founded the abbey of Clonfert and died in 577. The *Rule of St Brendan* was dictated to him by an angel and he is said to have presided over 3,000 monks in the various houses of his foundation.

He is best known for the mediaeval legend, widespread throughout Europe, of his seven-year voyage in search of the 'Land of the Saints', the Isle of St Brendan, reputed to be in mid-Atlantic. The very birds and beasts he encountered observed the Christian fasts and festivals. The earliest surviving version of the story is the *Navigatio Brendani* (11th century).

And we came to the isle of a saint who had
    sailed with St Brendan of yore,
He had lived ever since on the Isle and his
    winters were fifteen score.
TENNYSON: *Voyage of Maeldune*

Brandenburg Confession. A formulary of faith drawn up in the city of Brandenburg in 1610, by order of the elector, with the view of reconciling the tenets of LUTHER with those of CALVIN, and to put an end to the disputes occasioned by the AUGSBURG CONFESSION.

Brandon. An obsolete form of *brand,* a torch. *Dominica de brandonibus* (St VALENTINE's Day), when boys used to carry about *brandons* (Cupid's torches).

Brass. A church brass. A memorial brass plate engraved with details of the person commemorated. The earliest complete specimen is late 13th century in Stoke d'Abernon Church, Surrey.

Bray, Thomas (1658–1730). An ANGLICAN priest largely instrumental in founding the SPCK (Society for the Promotion of Christian Knowledge) in 1698 and later in 1701 the SPG (Society for the Propagation of the Gospel in Foreign Parts). He was rector of Sheldon, near Birmingham and was appointed to the post of

Commissary to Maryland, in North America, which he visited in 1699.

Breaches, meaning *creeks* or *small bays*, is to be found in *Judges* v, 17. Deborah, complaining of the tribes who refused to assist her in her war with Sisera, says that Asher 'abode in his breaches', that is, creeks on the seashore.

Bread. As the sustainer of life bread symbolizes God's providence. Christ is 'the bread of life' (*John* vi, 35); the 'body of Christ', (*Luke* xxii, 19). Bread and wine denote the two natures of Christ in the EUCHARIST. The ROMAN CATHOLIC and Armenian Churches use unleavened bread, while the Orthodox Catholics and NON-CONFORMISTS use leavened bread.
Breaking of bread. The EUCHARIST. In scriptural language *to break bread* is to partake of food.

> They continued... in breaking of bread, and in prayer.
>
> *Acts* ii, 42 (also 46)

Cast thy bread upon the waters; for thou shalt find it after many days (*Eccles*, xi, 1). The interpretation of this well-known passage is obscure. Perhaps the most likely meaning is 'do not be afraid to give generously without hope of immediate gain, sooner or later you will reap as you have sown.' Another common explanation is that seed cast on flooded land will take root and profit the sower when the waters recede, bread in this context meaning 'corn' or 'seed'.

Breakspear, Nicholas (*c.* 1100–59). The only English Pope. *See* ADRIAN IV.

Breeches Bible. *See* BIBLE.

Brethren in Christ. A PROTESTANT sect established by European pietists in Pennsylvania in 1862 and in Canada. Based on Biblical FUNDA-MENTALISM the sect practises triple BAPTISM by Immersion. The Holy Kiss, washing of feet, spiritual healing and pacifism are among other practices.
Brethren, or Brothers, of the Common Life. A ROMAN CATHOLIC fraternity of priests and laymen established at Deventer, in Holland, by Gerhard Groote, a missioner, and Florentinus Radewyn, a canon, about 1380. Their mission in life was to reproduce the conditions of living of the early Christians, taking vows of poverty, chastity and obedience and holding no personal property. They went into the world teaching, preaching and administering the SACRAMENTS. They also copied MSS and taught handicrafts. They were officially recognized by the Church in 1414. The fraternity declined after the REFOR-MATION and was finally suppressed under Napoleon.

Brethren of the Free Spirit. A mystical sect with pantheistic leanings which appeared in the 13th century. Its chief exponent, Almeric or Amalve of Bena, was expelled from Paris University; he appealed to the Pope, but was condemned. Known also as the Amalricas, they were accused of heresy in believing that salvation depended on the service of God in freedom of the Spirit rather than on the SACRAMENT. Many of the brothers perished at the stake.

Breviary. A book containing the ordinary and daily services of the ROMAN CATHOLIC CHURCH, which those in orders are bound to recite. It omits the EUCHARIST, which is contained in the MISSAL, and the special services (marriage, ordination, etc.), which are found in the *Ritual or Pontifical*. It is called a breviary because it is an abbreviation in the sense that it contains prayers, hymns, and lessons, etc., thus obviating the need to use a separate hymn book, and BIBLE.

Briant, St Alexander (*c.* 1556–81, f.d. 25 October). Born in Somerset and educated at Oxford, he reverted to ROMAN CATHOLICISM while at the university and went on to the ENGLISH COLLEGE at Douai. After being ordained priest he returned to England on a mission, making many converts. He was arrested and questioned as to the hiding place of the famous JESUIT, Robert Persons (who was, in fact, living next door) but, refusing to answer, he was imprisoned in the Tower where his tortures were so atrocious as to shock the people and involve the Government; his courage amazed even his torturers. He was tried at Westminster on false charges and suffered the barbarous execution of the times. Briant was canonized by Pope Paul VI, in 1970, as one of the FORTY MARTYRS OF ENGLAND AND WALES.

Brice, St (d. 444, f.d. 13 November). Educated under St MARTIN OF TOURS, Brice's character appears highly controversial as he caused considerable scandal in his way of life, being accused of various crimes, including adultery with a nun, and was exiled for seven years after having succeeded St Martin in the bishopric of Tours, some saying he owed this appointment to his birth and wealth as his life continued to be scandalous. However, in old age he appeared to be revered and remained nominally bishop of Tours for forty-seven years. His cult became widespread in Italy and England.

Bridget. Bridget, St (Bridig, Bride, Brigid) (453–523, f.d. 1 February). The second patron saint of Ireland. She became a nun renowned for her piety and founded an abbey at Kildare—the first for women in Ireland. She is the protectress of dairy workers and became popular in England as St Bride. In Ireland her cult is second only to that of St PATRICK. Accounts of her life are mainly legendary and full of miracles, many of which bear close relationship with pre-Christian Irish folklore. On one occasion, after a shower of rain, she took off her cloak and caught a sunbeam in it; it remained in this position until late at night and a nun remarked upon it, Bridget then removed the cloak and the sunbeam departed, hurrying away after the long-gone sun. Miracles included the increase of food and cows giving miraculous milk at need and bath-water being changed into beer. Her cult was also closely related to that of the VIRGIN MARY. A fire was kept burning perpetually at her shrine by the nuns of her order at Kildare, so that in art she is represented with perpetual flames, or a column of fire; she is also depicted with a cow at her feet. Bridget is the patron saint of poets, healers and blacksmiths.

Bridget of Sweden (Birgitta, or Britta) St (1303–73, f.d. 23 July, formerly 8 October). Married to a Swedish nobleman at the age of fourteen, she had eight children, among them St Catherine of Vadstena. Bridget was lady-in-waiting to Queen Blanche, wife of King Magnus II, both of whom she endeavoured to reform. After the eighth child her husband had retired to the CISTERCIAN monastery at Alvostra. When he died Bridget founded an order at Vadstena which had monks and nuns living in separate buildings but sharing a church, this was the Order of the Holy Saviour, known as the BRIDGETTINES, and the monastery became an important religious centre, Bridget having journeyed to ROME and obtained papal approval. She went from there to the HOLY LAND on a pilgrimage, returning to Rome and remaining there until her death, living austerely and working devotedly for the poor, the sick and pilgrims. She was noted as a visionary after giving advice to the Pope. Marvellous stories have been told of her childhood and life, one of her confinements having been attended by the VIRGIN MARY. She is the patron saint of Sweden. In art she is depicted in a nun's black habit with white wimple and veil, occasionally with a red band across her forehead. Her chief attribute is a candle or taper and she can carry a pilgrim's staff or a book and inkhorn to allude to her book *Revelations*.

Bridgettines or **Brigittines**. The Order of the Holy Saviour, founded by St BRIDGET OF SWEDEN in 1346 for sixty nuns and twenty-five monks who lived in separate quarters but shared a church. The original monastery was at Vadstena. Luxury was forbidden but there was no limit on obtaining books for study. All surplus income was devoted to the poor. St Bridget journeyed to ROME in 1350 and obtained papal

approval for the order. At one time its houses numbered seventy and extended to other countries. In England it continues to this day in Syon Abbey, founded by King Henry V, but the monks died out in the 20th century. St Richard REYNOLDS, one of the FORTY MARTYRS OF ENGLAND AND WALES, was a Bridgettine monk.

Bridgewater Treatises. Instituted by the Rev. Francis Howard Egerton, eighth Earl of Bridgewater. He left £8,000 to be given to the author or authors of the best treatise or treatises 'On the Power, Wisdom, and Goodness of God, as manifested in the Creation'. The money was divided between eight authors: Dr Chalmers, Dr John Kidd, Dr Whewell, Sir Charles Bell, Dr Peter Roget, Dean Buckland, the Rev. W. Kirby, and Dr William Prout. The award was made by the President of the Royal Society (Davies Gilbert) in consultation with the Archbishop of Canterbury (Dr Howley) and the Bishop of London (Dr Blomfield).

Brief. An official letter issued by the POPE and sealed with the Fisherman's Ring which bears the figure of St PETER hauling in his net; the name of the Pope appears above. A Brief is less final and deals with less important matters than a BULL.

Brioc (or Brieuc), St (6th cent., f.d. 1 May). A Celt, born in Britain, probably in Cardigan, who died in Brittany where he had founded the monastery of St Brieuc-des-Vaux. Before leaving for Brittany he had worked in Cornwall, giving his name to St Breock. He was said to be a great preacher, making many converts. His reputation for great liberality made him patron saint of purse-makers.

British Council of Churches. An ecumenical movement, founded in 1942, of three PROTESTANT bodies: the CHURCH OF ENGLAND, the CHURCH OF SCOTLAND and the FREE CHURCHES. The YMCA, the SCM and various missionary societies, aiming at church unity and eventual union, also took part in the movement.

British Israelites. An interdenominational body which claims actual descent from the Children of Israel, it includes members from Britain, the Commonwealth and the USA, maintaining that the Lost Ten Tribes, or their descendants, reached these lands and that there were Hebrew settlements in Britain even before the Captivity. These views were promulgated by John Wilson, in the last century, in his book *Our Israelitish Origin*, but they had also been held by some of the Levellers in the middle of the 17th century.

Broad Church. A group within the CHURCH OF ENGLAND favouring theological liberalism and tolerance, typified by the writers of *Essays and Reviews* (1860). The name dates from the mid-19th century and the party have certain affinities with the LATITUDINARIANS of former times. They were the forerunners of the MODERNISTS. *Cp.* HIGH CHURCH; LOW CHURCH.

Brotherhood of the New Life. *See* HARRIS, Thomas Lake.

Brothers Hospitallers. Founded on the work of St JOHN OF GOD and established first in Madrid with the help of King Philip II, the order, chiefly of laymen, worked under the Augustinian Rule but added a vow to care for the sick in hospitals. The Order spread through Europe and continues to the present time.

Brownists. Followers of Robert Browne, who established a congregational society at Norwich in 1580. Both episcopal and presbyterian organization was rejected. Browne eventually left his own society and returned to the Church. *See* INDEPENDENTS.

> I had as lief be a Brownist as a politician.
> SHAKESPEARE: *Twelfth Night*, III, ii

Bruderhof (Ger. Society of Brothers). A Christian sect founded in Germany in 1920 with beliefs similar to the MENNONITES. They came to Gloucestershire in 1937 when driven out by the Nazis, but to avoid internment in World War II left for Paraguay in 1941. They re-established themselves in Sussex in 1971. The men wear beards and dark trousers with braces, the women are simply clad with long skirts and headscarves or caps. They support themselves by making quality wooden toys in community workshops and the children first go outside the community at the secondary school stage. There are four other groups in the Eastern USA and they are linked with the Hutterian Anabaptists in the Western USA and Canada.

Bruno, St (*c.* 1032–1101, f.d. 6 October). Founder of the CARTHUSIAN Order, Bruno was born at Cologne of noble family and studied at Rheims and Cologne. He was ordained priest and made a canon. He taught theology and philosophy at Rheims, Pope Urban II being among his pupils. The simony and corruption of the archbishop Manasses, being more than he could endure, made him leave to become a monk and with six others went to find a secluded place. St HUGH, bishop of Grenoble, gave them the mountain valley of Chartreuse where Bruno founded the monastery which later became the place of the austere Carthusian Community. Pope Urban II summoned him to ROME to advise him and offered

him the archbishopric of Reggio, which Bruno refused. Instead, he founded a new settlement at La Torre, in the diocese of Squillace in Calabria, where he died. In art he is depicted contemplating a CRUCIFIX with the words 'O bonitas' issuing from his mouth; sometimes he holds an olive branch. He wears the distinctive habit of his order, the white SCAPULAR.

Bryanites. *See* BIBLE CHRISTIANS.

Brychan, St (*c.* 450, f.d. 6 April). A legendary Welsh king, not himself a saint but listed among them on account of having fathered so many of them. One legend credits him with twelve sons and twelve daughters, all saints, but another tradition says there were twenty-four sons and twenty-six daughters, while the number of his wives and concubines is equally variable. It is possible that two or more Brychans are involved. Brychan and his offspring are venerated in Brecon, Cornwall and Devon.

Buchanites. A deluded group of fanatics, appearing in the west of Scotland in the latter part of the 18th century, and named after their foundress Mrs, or Lucky, Buchan. She called herself the 'Friend Mother' claiming to be the woman mentioned in Rev. xii and maintaining that the Rev. Hugh White, a convert, was the 'man-child'.

> I never heard of ale-wife that turned preacher, except Luckie Buchan in the west.
> SCOTT: *St Ron's Well*, ch. ii

Budoc (Buoc or **Beuzec), St** (6th cent., f.d. 8 December). Venerated in Pembrokeshire, Devon, Cornwall and Brittany. A church in Oxford is dedicated to him. A legend said that his mother Azenor was falsely accused of infidelity and was thrown into the sea in a cask in which she gave birth to Budoc. Five months later they were cast up on the shore in Ireland. The child immediately asked to be baptized and this was done by the bishop of Youghal. Budoc grew up in the monastery there, his mother becoming its laundress and he its abbot. He was reputed to have crossed to Brittany, sailing across the sea in a stone trough, and to have been bishop of Dol. Many miracles are associated with his name.

Bull (Lat., *bulla*, a seal). An edict or document issued by the POPE; it is the most formal and authoritative of documents, conveying decisions on points of doctrine and matters of great importance. Bulls are written in Latin.

Bun. Hot cross buns on GOOD FRIDAY were supposed to be made of the dough kneaded for the HOST, and were marked with a cross accordingly. As they are said to keep for twelve months without turning mouldy, some persons still hang up one or more in their house as a 'charm against evil'.

> Good Friday comes this month: the old woman runs.
> With one a penny, two a penny 'hot cross buns',
> Whose virtue is, if you believe what's said,
> They'll not grow mouldy like the common bread.
> *Poor Robin's Almanack*, 1733

Bunyan, John (1628–88). Born at Elston, near Bedford, he followed his father's trade as a tinker or brazier. He was conscripted into the Parliamentary army. After a period of religious soul–searching and doubt he joined the fellowship of the BAPTISTS and became an outstanding preacher. After the Restoration he was arrested as an unlicensed preacher and was confined to Bedford gaol from 1660 to 1677. During this time he wrote 'Grace Abounding to the Chief of Sinners'. He was released on the issue of the Declaration of Indulgence, became a pastor at Bedford, then calling himself a CONGREGATIONALIST (see under CONGREGATION). Arrested again and in prison for six months, Bunyan wrote the first part of the *Pilgrim's Progress* in 1678, the second part being published in 1684/5. It was an instant success. For the last sixteen years of his life Bunyan was pastor to the Baptist chapel in Bedford. Altogether he wrote some sixty books.

Burden of Isaiah. 'The Burden of Babylon, which Isaiah the son of Amoz did see' (*Isaiah* iii, 1, etc.). Burden here is a literal translation of the Heb. *massa* (rendered in the Vulgate by *onus*), which means 'lifting up', either a burden or the voice; hence utterance, hence a prophecy announcing a calamity, or a denunciation of hardships on those to whom the burden is uttered.

Burgundofara, St. *See* FARA.

Bush Baptist. A person of dubious religious convictions.

Bush Brotherhood. An association formed to take the Christian religion to the Outback and remote cattle stations. Its members sacrifice their own personal and domestic comforts in so doing.

Bushel. To hide one's light under a bushel. To conceal one's talents; to be self-effacing and modest about one's abilities. The bushel was measured in a wooden or earthenware container, hence *under a bushel* is to hide something.

> Neither do men light a candle and put it under a bushel, but on a candlestick.
> *Matt.* v, 15

C

Cabrini, St Frances Xavier (d. 1917, f.d. 22 December). An Italian farmer's daughter, orphaned as a child, who eventually founded an Order after having been rejected by two orders on the grounds of ill health after leaving her convent school. She became a school teacher, devoting herself to the care of orphans and founding orphanages; she also founded, and received papal approval for, her 'Missionary Sisters of the Sacred Heart'. Originally intending to go to China, she was persuaded to dedicate herself to work among the Italian immigrants in the USA instead. There she founded schools and orphanages, extending her work to eight countries, with sixty-seven houses. She died of malaria in Chicago and was canonized by Pope Pius XII in 1966.

Cadoc (or **Cadocus**), **St** (6th cent., f.d. 25 September). A noted Welsh saint whose mission, according to the number of churches dedicated to him, was mainly in South Wales and Brittany where he was greatly venerated. He founded the abbey of Llancarfan. Accounts of his life are legendary rather than historical and are full of the miraculous. Said to have been the son of a robber chief in South Wales, there are many stories of his miraculous escapes from robbers. He also discovered subterranean fire (coal?). At the end of his life he was transported on a white cloud from Llancarfan to Benevento in Italy, there he was made a bishop and finally was martyred while celebrating MASS. There are two other saints of the same name, one Scottish and the other Breton, who are sometimes confused with Cadoc of Wales.

Caedmon, St (d. 680, f.d. 11 February). The earliest English poet. Little is known of him except from BEDE who preserved some of his poetry, and the hymn said to have been composed in a dream, in the *Ecclesiastical History*. Caedmon was an illiterate herdsman who in a dream 'uttered verses which he had never heard'. It was said that when in company after supper it came to his turn to sing but he left the table, being unable to do so. But one night, when he was asleep with his swine, he had a vision in which a voice told him to sing. He asked, 'What shall I sing?' and was told to sing of the Creation; this he did. He became a monk at Streamaeshalch (Whitby) under St HILDA and spent most of his time reproducing sacred poems and hymns in the vernacular in an age when few people knew Latin. He turned the knowledge imparted to him by the more learned monks into a language the people could understand. In addition to pioneering Anglo-Saxon poetry, Caedmon was a zealous monk and blameless character.

Caesarius of Arles, St (*c.* 470–542, f.d. 27 August). Son of the Count of Chalon-sur-Saône, he became a monk at Lérins; was ordained priest and appointed bishop of Arles at the age of thirty-three. He was noted as a preacher and a prelate of high principles. Later, as archbishop of Arles, he presided over four COUNCILS, including that of Orange in 529, at which he had SEMI-PELAGIANISM condemned as a HERESY. He founded a nunnery at Arles, for which he wrote a Rule, stipulated that the nuns should be literate, and gave them the right to elect their abbess. The first abbess was his sister and the nunnery was the first recorded in Gaul.

Cain. Cainites. An heretical sect of the 2nd century so named because they held that Cain was made by an almighty power and Abel by a weak one. They renounced the NEW TESTAMENT in favour of *The Gospel of Judas* which justified the false disciple and the crucifixion of Jesus, and held that the way to salvation was to give way to every lust and make a trial of everything.
To raise Cain. To 'raise the devil', to 'play hell', to make an angry fuss or noisy disturbance. Cain here is either used as an alternative to 'the DEVIL', or is a direct allusion to Cain's violent anger which drove him to kill his brother. (*See Gen.* iv, 5.)

Cajetan, St (1480–1547, f.d. 7 August). Born of a noble family at Vicenza, he was educated at Padua University and became a noted theologian, holding office at the papal court under Julius II. He was ordained and worked at ROME, Vicenza and Venice where he laboured for the sick and poor. In Naples he established pawn shops, *Monts de Piété*, to relieve the conditions of the poor, not to exploit them. With Pietro Caraffa (later Pope Paul IV) he founded the THEATINE Order to reform and train the corrupt clergy and, amoing other aims, to care for the sick and needy. The order was established at Rome but after its sacking in 1527 was moved to Naples and Cajetan became its Superior. The Englishman Thomas Godwell, bishop of St Asaph's (1555–9), was a Theatine at Naples.

Calas. The case of Jean Calas. A celebrated case in French history. Jean Calas (1698–1762), a HUGUENOT cloth-merchant of Toulouse, was tortured, broken on the wheel and burnt in 1762, having been found guilty of the murder of his twenty-nine-year-old son Marc-Antoine. The motive was supposed to be that Jean was determind to prevent his son becoming a Roman Catholic. The evidence was circumstantial although suicide was perhaps the most obvious conclusion to draw. The widow's case was taken up by Voltaire in his book *Sur la Tolérance*, with the result that the family, who had also suffered the penalities of intolerance, were declared innocent and given 30,000 livres by Louis XV.

Calendar. The Julian Calendar. *See* JULIAN.
The Gregorian Calendar. *See* GREGORIAN.
The Jewish Calendar. This dates from the Creation, fixed at 3761 BC and consists of 12 months of 29 and 30 days alternately, with an additional month of 30 days interposed in embolismic years to prevent any great divergence from the months of the Solar year. The 3rd, 6th, 11th, 14th, 17th, and 19th years of the Metonic cycle are embolismic years.

Calixtines. A Bohemian religious sect of the 15th century; so called from calix (the chalice), which they insisted should be given to the laity, i.e. communion of both kinds. They were also called ULTRAQUISTS.

Call. A summons, or invitation felt to be divine, as a 'call to the ministry'.
A call to the pastorate. An invitation to a clergyman by the members of a PRESBYTERIAN or NONCONFORMIST congregation to serve as their minister.
The call of Abraham. The invitation or command of God to Abraham, to leave his idolatrous country, under the promise of becoming father of a great nation (*Gen.* xii, 1–2).
The call of God. An invitation, exhortation, or warning by the dispensations of Providence (*Isa.* xxii, 12); divine influence on the mind to do or avoid something (*Heb.* iii, 1).

Callistus (or **Callixtus**), **St** (d. 222). Little is known of him except from the *Refutation of Heresies*, a work of invective attributed to St HIPPOLYTUS. Callistus had the distinction of being a slave who became a pope. He was said to have been involved in dubious financial transactions and sentenced to the treadmill.

Released from this, he was re-arrested for brawling and sent to work in the mines of Sardinia. He was again released, this time through the influence of Marcia, mistress of the Emperor Commodius, and was appointed to be manager of the cemetery named after him. He proved an able administrator and was ordained deacon. In 217 he was elected pope but was severely criticized for both his style of life and the doctrines he promulgated; these were strongly opposed by both Hippolytus and TERTULLIAN. Callistus was venerated as a martyr but there is no evidence of a persecution at the time and he was probably killed by a rioting mob. Another tradition was that he was thrown down a well. He was said to have instituted EMBER DAYS.

Caloyers. Monks in the Greek church, who follow the rule of St Basil. They are divided into *cenobites,* who recite the offices from midnight to sunrise; *anchorites,* who live in hermitages; and *recluses,* who shut themselves up in caverns and live on alms (Gr. *kalos* and *geron,* beautiful old man).

Calvary. The Latin translation of the Gr. GOLGOTHA which is a transliteration of the Hebrew word for a skull. It is the name given to the place of our Lord's crucifixion. Legend has it that the skull of ADAM was preserved here, but the name is probably due to a fancied resemblance of the configuration of the ground to the shape of a skull.
The actual site may be that occupied by the Church of the Holy Sepulchre, or possibly an eminence above the grotto of Jeremiah not far from the Damascus Gate.
A Calvary. A representation of the successive scenes of the PASSION of Christ in a series of pictures, etc., in a church; the shrine containing such representations. Wayside calvaries or crosses, representing the Crucifixion, are common in parts of Europe and some notable examples are to be found in Brittany.
A calvary cross. A Latin CROSS mounted on three steps (or grises).
Calvary clover. A common trefoil, *Medicago echinus,* said to have sprung up in the track made by PILATE when he went to the cross to see his 'title affixed' (Jesus of Nazareth, King of the Jews). Each of the three leaves has a little carmine spot in the centre; in the daytime they form a sort of cross; and in the flowering season the plant bears a little yellow flower, like a 'crown of thorns'. Julian tells us that each of the three leaves had in his time a white cross in the centre, and that the centre cross remains visible longer than the others.

Calvin, Jean Cauvin (1509–64). Born at Noyon in France, Calvin studied both law and theology, but after adopting reformed and evangelical principles he had to leave France and retire to Basel in Switzerland where he studied Hebrew and wrote his *Institutes of the Christian Religion*. A short stay at Geneva was followed by residence at Strasbourg where he translated the NEW TESTAMENT, then returning to Geneva where he established a strict PROTESTANT government, from whence his influence spread to the Netherlands, Scotland, England and New England.

Calvinism. The doctrines of the Reformer Jean Calvin (1509–1564), particularly as expressed in his *Institutio Religionis Christianae* (1536). Some chief points of his teaching are:

(1)   the transcendence of God;
(2)   the total depravity of natural man. He can achieve nothing without God;
(3)   predestination of particular election. Before the world began God chose some men for salvation through Christ;
(4)   the scriptures and the Holy Spirit are the sole authority;
(5)   the community must enforce the Church's public discipline.

Camaldolese Order. A ROMAN CATHOLIC order founded by St ROMUALD OF RAVENNA who established small communities of hermits, the chief being at Camaldoli in the Tuscan Apennines, in about the year 1012. His aim was to reintroduce to the West the early eremitical form of monasticism within the RULE of St BENEDICT. After his death the movement developed into a separate congregation which exists to this day, there being both eremitical and cenobitical Camaldolese; also several nunneries. The order wore a loose, flowing white garment with wide sleeves. Also called Camaldulians, Camoldeolites or Camaldulensians.

Cameronians. Also known as Reformed PRESBYTERIANS they were organized by the strict COVENANTER and field preacher, Richard Cameron, who was slain in battle at Aird's Moss in 1680. He objected to the alliance of Church and State under Charles II and seceded from the Kirk. His followers refused to take the Oath of Allegiance and thus deprived themselves of some of the privileges of citizenship. In 1876 the majority of Cameronians united with the Free Church.

Camillus of Lellis, St (1550–1614, f.d. 14 July). A soldier of fortune, noted for his height, hasty temper and addiction to gambling, he lost his all at play and became a hod-man in building a CAPUCHIN monastery. He was converted and applied to join the FRANCISCANS but was rejected on health grounds, having an incurable ulcer on his leg. He then studied and became a priest on the advice of St PHILIP NERI and founded an order of male nurses, the Ministers of the Sick, whose special work was serving in hospitals, homes, in prisons and among the galley-slaves. He also founded hospitals and sent units to serve on battlefields, the first of their kind. His treatments included innovations such as the importance of fresh air, isolation of infectious cases and suitable diet. His own ill-health forced him to resign the headship of the order but he continued his personal care until his death. He is the patron saint of nurses and the sick.

Camisards. In French history the PROTESTANT insurgents of the Cévennes, who resisted the violence of the DRAGONNADES occasioned by the Revocation of the Edict of NANTES in 1685 and carried on a fierce war of reprisals with Louis XIV's forces until finally suppressed in 1705. Their leader was Jean Cavalier (1681–1740), afterwards governor of Jersey and later of the Isle of Wight. So called from the *camise* or blouse worn by the peasantry.

Campanile. A bell tower or belfry, but especially one which is detached from the main building of a church. Italian in origin.

Campbellites. Followers of John McLeod Campbell (1800–1872), who taught the universality of the atonement, for which he was ejected from the CHURCH OF SCOTLAND in 1831.

In the USA the name is sometimes given to the *Disciples of Christ*, a body founded by Thomas and Alexander Campbell of Pennsylvania in 1809. They reject creeds and practise baptism by immersion and weekly communion, and uphold Christian union on the foundation of the Bible alone. They are also known simply as *Christians*.

Campion, St Edmund (1540–81, f.d. 25 October). Born in London, the son of a bookseller, he was educated at Christ's Hospital and St John's College Oxford. Showing particular scholarship and brilliance, he became a notable personality at Oxford and was chosen to welcome Queen Elizabeth when she visited the university. Campion was ordained deacon in the CHURCH OF ENGLAND but, going to Dublin University, he experienced doubts and decided to go to the ENGLISH COLLEGE at Douai and there turned to Catholicism. He went to ROME and became a JESUIT and was ordained sub-deacon, serving his novitiate in Moravia. He was chosen, with Robert Persons, to undertake a mission in England, travelling in disguise and working from north to south of the country, achieving considerable success not only with his outstanding scholarship but impressing people with his personality and courage. He was arrested and sent to the Tower where he was tortured and then tried on false charges, together with others, in Westminster Hall and was condemned to be hanged, drawn and quartered at Tyburn. He was canonized in 1970 among the FORTY MARTYRS OF ENGLAND AND WALES.

Candle. Candles in Christian churches are symbols rather than illumination, representing the Divine Light shining in the darkness of the world, also Christ as the Light of the World, and spiritual joy. They are an essential part of worship at the MASS, such candles being white, while at funerals and requiems they are orange-coloured. Votive candles are lighted before shrines, the HOST, images and relics. Candles on either side of the cross on the altar depict the dual nature of Christ, the human and the divine. See also PASCHAL CANDLE; TENEBRAE.

Bell, book, and candle. *See* BELL.

Candlemas Day. 2 February, formerly the Feast of the Purification of the Virgin Mary, now called the Presentation of Our Lord; one of the Quarter Days in Scotland. In ROMAN CATHOLIC churches all the candles which will be needed in the church throughout the year are consecrated on this day; they symbolize Jesus Christ, called 'the light of the world', and 'a light to lighten the Gentiles'. The ancient Romans had a custom of burning candles to scare away evil spirits.

If Candlemas Day be dry and fair,
The half o'winter's come and mair;
If Candlemas Day be wet and foul,
The half o'winter was gone at Youl.

Scotch Proverb

The badger peeps out of his hole on Candlemas Day, and, if he finds snow, walks abroad; but if he sees the sun shining he draws back into his hole.

German Proverb

Canice, St Kenneth or **Cainnech** (*c.* 525–600, f.d. 11 October). A pupil of St FINNIAN and friend of St COLUMBA, he was born in Ireland, the son of a bard, and became an Irish abbot. He founded monasteries in Ireland, went to Llancarfan in Wales and worked in the Western Isles of Scotland and on the mainland. Various churches were dedicated to him. He was a noted preacher and copier of manuscripts, particularly the *Four Gospel Legends* associated with him. They include the stories of his banishing mice which had chewed his slippers and remonstrating with birds for being vocal and interrupting services on Sundays.

Canon. The body of books in the BIBLE which are accepted by the Christian Church generally as genuine and inspired; the whole Bible from *Genesis* to *Revelation,* excluding the APOCRYPHA.

Called also the *sacred canon* and the *Canonical Books.*

The Church dignitary known as a *Canon* is a capitular member of a cathedral or COLLEGIATE CHURCH, usually living in the precincts, and observing the rule or *canon* of the body to which he is attached. The canons, with the DEAN or provost at their head, constitute the governing body, or CHAPTER, of the cathedral. These are the *canons-residentiary;* there are also *honorary canons* who have no share in the cathedral government, or emoluments. *Minor canons* are mainly concerned with the singing of the services and have no part in the decisions of the chapter.

The title once had a much wider application and was used to designate most of the diocesan clergy. When its use came to be limited to the secular clergy of a cathedral, they were called *secular canons* as distinct from the *canons regular* such as the Austin or AUGUSTINIAN CANONS (*see under* AUGUSTINE).

Canoness. The title was given to certain women living under rule, less strict than that of nuns, in the Frankish empire from the late 8th century. Like their male counterparts they came to be divided into canonesses *regular* and *secular.*

Book of Canons. A collection of 178 canons enacted by the councils of Nicaea, Ancyra, Neocaesarea, Laodicea, Gangra, Antioch, Constantinople, Ephesus, and Chalcedon. It was first published in 1610 and is probably of late 4th-or early 5th-century origin.

The CHURCH OF ENGLAND 'Book of Canons' was adopted in 1604 as the basis of ecclesiastical law. A *Book of Canons* for the Scottish Church was drawn up under Charles I's command and issued in 1636. It mainly helped to precipitate religious strife in Scotland.

Canons of the Mass. The fixed form of consecratory prayer used in the GREEK and ROMAN CATHOLIC churches—from the *Sanctus* to the PATERNOSTER.

Canonical. Canonical dress. The distinctive or appropriate costume worn by the clergy according to the direction of the canon; BISHOPS, DEANS and archdeacons, for instance, wear canonical hats. This distinctive dress is sometimes called simply 'canonicals'; Macaulay speaks of 'an ecclesiastic in full canonicals'.

Canonical Epistles. The seven CATHOLIC EPISTLES as distinct from those of Paul which were addressed to particular churches or individuals.

Canonical hours. The different parts of the Divine Office which follow, and are named after the hours of the day. They are seven—MATINS, PRIME, tierce, sext, NONES, VESPERS and COMPLINE. Prime, tierce, sext and nones are the first, third, sixth and ninth hours of the day, counting from six in the morning. (*See*

BREVIARY.) The reason why there are seven canonical hours is that David says, 'Seven times a day do I praise thee' (*Ps.* cxix, 164).

In England the phrase means more especially the time of the day within which persons can be legally married, i.e. from 8 in the morning to 6 p.m.

Canonical obedience. The obedience due by the inferior to the superior clergy. Thus bishops owe canonical obedience to the archbishop of the same province.

Canonization. The solemn act by which the Pope proclaims the sanctity of a person, subsequent to the lesser act of BEATIFICATION; whereupon he or she is worthy to be honoured as a SAINT and is put upon the *Canon* or Catalogue of Saints of the Church. Now a lengthy legal process is involved in which the Congregation of Sacred Rites considers the merits of the candidate and the *Promotor Fidei* acts as *Advocatus Diaboli,* or Devil's Advocate, and produces arguments against the proposed person. No one may be venerated as a saint in the ROMAN CATHOLIC CHURCH without the sanction of the Congregation. In the Eastern ORTHODOX CHURCH canonizations are carried out by the HOLY SYNOD acting within a particular AUTO-CEPHALOUS church. The first historical canonization was that of St ULRIC of Augsburg in 993.

Canopy. An awning carried over the Blessed Sacrament or high dignitaries of the church in procession.

Cantate Sunday. ROGATION Sunday, the fifth Sunday after EASTER. So called from the first word of the introit of the MASS: 'Sing to the Lord'. Similarly LAETARE SUNDAY, the fourth in LENT, is so called from the first word of the introit of the mass. *Cp.* QUASIMODO SUNDAY.

Canterbury. BEDE states that St AUGUSTINE, sent on a mission to England, converted a Roman basilica to the Cathedral Church of Christ, establishing a centre there from which to convert England to Christianity. It became the seat of the Archbishop of Canterbury, Primate of All England. At the REFORMATION the CHURCH OF ENGLAND maintained the office and the Archbishop as a principal officer of State. He takes precedence after princes of the royal blood and is responsible for crowning kings and queens; he sits in the House of Lords and is spiritual adviser to the Crown. St Augustine himself was the first Archbishop of Canterbury, appointed by Pope GREGORY THE GREAT in 598.

Canterbury cap. A soft flat cloth cap sometimes worn by dignitaries of the CHURCH OF ENGLAND.

Canticle. (Lat. *canticulum,* little song). A short non-metrical hymn, song or chant, usually taken from the BIBLE, included in CATHOLIC and ANGLICAN liturgies and services, e.g. Te Deum Magnificat, Jubilate. In the OLD TESTAMENT the song of Songs, the Song of Solomon are also called canticles.

Cantor. A leader of a church choir in liturgical music and processions; a precentor. Either a priest or a layman may act as a cantor and wears a surplice, or on solemn occasions a cope.

Cantoris. The place of the cantor on the north side of the choir in a cathedral or church; the antiphonal opposite the decanal.

Canute or **Cnut, St** (d. 1086, f.d. 10 July and 19 January). Illegitimate son of Sweyn Estrithson, nephew of Cnut, King of England, he succeeded his brother Harold to the throne of Denmark. Canute was a man of few morals and of tyrannical disposition, but he built churches and endowed them, taxing his nobility to maintain them. He was famous for his attempted raids on England. The *jarls,* or earls, whom he had suppressed, revolted against him and murdered him in the church of St ALBAN at Odersee. After his death miracles were reported at his tomb and a deputation sent to Pope Paschal II persuaded the pope to canonize him. He is Patron of Denmark.

Capitular Mass. The daily Mass in ROMAN CATHOLIC cathedrals and collegiate churches, sung or said in public and attended by the chapter.

Cappadocian Fathers. St BASIL THE GREAT and his brothers St GREGORY OF NYSSA and St GREGORY OF NAZIANZUS, from Cappadocia, then a Roman province. From noble and intellectual families, they combined early classical culture with Christianity; all were followers of ORIGEN and were noted for their trinitarian teaching and anti-Arianism.

Cappa Magna. A lined cloak having a long train and a hood, usually violet in colour, worn by cardinals and bishops of the ROMAN CATHOLIC CHURCH.

Capuchin. A friar of the strict group of FRANCISCANS that arose about 1520; so called from the *capuce* or pointed cowl. They became a separate order in 1619.

Caradoc or **Caradog** (d. 1124) venerated on 13 April). Born in Brecknock and attached to the court of Rhys, Prince of South Wales, he was a harpist. When he lost Rhys' hounds he fell out of favour and left the court for the service of the bishop. He later became a hermit, then was ordained priest and retired to an island off the

Pembrokeshire coast where he was taken prisoner by the Vikings, but later released. He was buried in the cathedral of St DAVID, where his shrine still exists and it was said that his body remained incorrupt. He was greatly venerated and the church of Lawrenny was dedicated to him but he was not formally canonized.

Cardinal (Lat. *cardo,* a hinge). The adjective *cardinalis* meant originally 'pertaining to a hinge' hence 'that on which something turns or depends', thus 'the principal or chief'. In Rome, a cardinal church was a parish church as distinct from an oratory attached to it and the word was next applied to the senior priest of such a church. From the mid-8th century it denoted urban as distinct from rural clergy, and subsequently the clergy of a diocesan town and its cathedral but it was later restricted to the cardinals of the Roman see. In 1567 Pius V formally reserved the title for members of the Pope's Council, the COLLEGE OF CARDINALS.

The Cardinal's red hat was made part of the official vestments by Innocent IV in 1245. This 30-tasselled hat (not worn) was abolished in 1969. *See also* BISHOP.

College of Cardinals, or **Sacred College.** Originally formed from the clergy of the see of ROME, it now contains members from many nations who take their titles, as has always been customary, from a Roman parish. It consists of Cardinal–Bishops, Cardinal–Priests, and Cardinal–Deacons (the latter possibly deriving from the seven deacons appointed by St PETER), but these terms are essentially of historical significance only, as all cardinals are now consecrated bishops. The number of cardinals was fixed at 70 by Sixtus V in 1586. John XXIII (1958–63) raised it to 87, and in 1969 it reached 136. The POPE is elected by and from the College of Cardinals.

Cardinal virtues. Justice, prudence, temperance, and fortitude, on which all other virtues hang or depend. A term of the SCHOOLMEN, to distinguish the 'natural' virtues from the 'theological' virtues (faith, hope and charity).

Care. Care Sunday. The fifth Sunday in LENT. 'Care' here means trouble, suffering; and Care Sunday means PASSION SUNDAY (as in OH Ger. *kar-fritag* is GOOD FRIDAY.

Care Sunday is also known as *Carle* or *Carling Sunday.* It was an old custom, especially in the north, to eat parched peas fried in butter on this day, and they were called *Carlings.*

Care-cloth. In the ROMAN CATHOLIC CHURCH, the fine silk or linen cloth formerly laid over the newly-married, or held over them as a canopy.

Carey, William (1761–1834). A PROTESTANT missionary born near Towcester, the son of a shoe-maker, he became a BAPTIST minister and was mainly responsible for the formation of the Baptist Missionary Society in 1792. He went to India, translated the NEW TESTAMENT into Indian dialects and was Oriental Professor at the New College at Fort William, Calcutta.

Carle Sunday; Carlings. *See* CARE SUNDAY.

Carlisle, Wilson (1847–1942). Founder of the CHURCH ARMY as an Anglican counterpart to the SALVATION ARMY. Born at Brixton, he was successful in business before being ordained in the CHURCH OF ENGLAND in 1880. He was made a prebendary of St Paul's in 1906. He directed the Church Army for sixty years.

Carmelites. A mendicant order of friars of 12th-century origin, taking its name from Mount Carmel in Syria and with a mythical history associating them with the prophet Elijah. Also called White Friars from their white mantle. *See* BAREFOOTED.

Carnival. The season immediately preceding LENT, ending on SHROVE TUESDAY and a period in many Roman Catholic countries devoted to amusement; hence revelry, riotous amusement. From the Lat. *caro, carnis,* flesh; *levare,* to remove; signifying the abstinence from meat during Lent. The earlier word *carnilevamen* was altered in Italian to *carnevale* as though connected with *vale,* farewell—farewell to flesh.

Carol (O.Fr. *carole,* probably from Lat. *choraula,* a flute-player). The earliest use of the word in English was for a round dance, then later a light and joyous hymn particularly associated with the Nativity. The following verse is a translation from Old English of our earliest extant Christmas carol:

Lordlings listen to our lay—
We have come from far away
To seek Christmas;
In this mansion we are told
He his yearly feast doth hold;
  'Tis today!
May joy come from God above,
To all those who Christmas love.

The first printed collection came from the press of Wynkyn de Worde in 1521; it included the *Boar's Head Carol,* which is still sung at Queen's College, Oxford.

Carthusians. An order of monks founded about 1084 by St Bruno of Cologne, who with six companions retired to the solitude of La Grande Chartreuse, thirteen miles north-east of Grenoble, and there built his famous monastery. It was here they made the famous liqueur called Chartreuse. In 1902 monks were evicted by order of the French government and they moved to the Certosa (Charterhouse) near Lucca.

The first English Charterhouse was founded by Sir Walter de Menny at London in 1371 and the Carthusians were among the staunchest opponents of Henry VIII at the time of the Dissolution of the Monasteries. In 1833 the Carthusians were re-established in the Charterhouse at Parkminster, Sussex.

Casimir, St (1458–84, f.d. 4 March). A prince of Poland, second son of King Casimir IV. An attempt to make him King of Hungary failed and he was banished to a castle near Cracow but later was established as viceroy during his father's absence. He was devout and virtuous and committed to a life of celibacy. He was buried at Vilna and miracles were reported at his tomb. In 1602 he was instated as patron saint of Poland.

Cassock. A long close-fitting robe worn by priests, choristers, sacristans, etc., while engaged in services in the church; it reaches to the heels and is usually black, but bishops wear purple cassocks, cardinals red and the pope white.

Catacomb. A subterranean gallery for the burial of the dead, especially those at ROME. The origin of the name is unknown but the cemetery of St SEBASTIAN on the Appian Way was called the *Catacumbas,* probably a place-name and in the course of time the name was applied to similar cemeteries. Their extensive development in Rome took place in the 3rd and 4th centuries and was due to the spread of Christianity. At times they were used by the Christians for their meetings. They suffered much destruction from the Goths and Lombards and eventually came to be forgotten until rediscovered in 1578 as the result of a landslip.

Catafalque. A draped platform on which a coffin is placed at a funeral or lying-in-state. At REQUIEM MASS in a ROMAN CATHOLIC CHURCH it can represent the corpse.

Catechism. A method of religious instruction, usually in the form of question and answer; it was employed by the early Church for the CATE-CHUMENS. Various books of catechism appeared at the REFORMATION for the PROTESTANT churches. The CATHOLIC CHURCH had that of Peter Canisius from 1555, but has recently published a new Catechism (1993), the first since the 16th century. It covers some 680 pages and gives detailed guidance to all Catholics. It is traditionalist in its teaching.

Catechumen. One taught by word of mouth (Gr. *katecheein,* to din into the ears). Those about to be baptized in the Early Church were first taught by word of mouth, and then *cate-chized* on their religious faith and duties.

Cathari. *See* ALBIGENSES.

Cathedral. Cathedrals of the Old Foundation. The ancient cathedrals that existed in England before Henry VIII founded and endowed new cathedrals out of some of the revenues from the Dissolution of the Monasteries. These latter are known as **Cathedrals of the New Foundation;** they are Chester, Gloucester, Peterborough, Bristol and Oxford.

Cathedral Schools. Schools established in association with cathedrals for the education of choir boys. In mediaeval times the education was free; the oldest such foundation is that of York.

Catherine. Catherine, St (d. *c.* 310, f.d. 25 November). Virgin and martyr of noble birth in Alexandria. She adroitly defended the Christian faith at a public disputation (*c.* 310) with certain heathen philosophers at the command of the Emperor Maximinus, for which she was put on a wheel like that of a chaff-cutter. Legend says that as soon as the wheel turned, her bonds were miraculously broken; so she was beheaded. Hence the name CATHER-INE WHEEL. She is the patron saint of wheelwrights.

Catherine of Bologna, St (1413–63, f.d. 9 March). Born in Bologna she was a maid of honour at the court of Nicholas III of d'Este at Ferrara. She joined the FRANCISCANS who later became the POOR CLARES. On going back to Bologna she was appointed prioress. Catherine was famous for her visions and when she died her body was shown in a glass case, incorrupt and richly clothed, at her convent.

Catherine of Genoa, St (1447–1510, f.d. 15 September). Of noble birth, she was married at sixteen to a nobleman of dissolute habits. She changed from a society life to one of devotion and self-mortification after a spiritual experience and influenced her husband, who joined her in living in modest circumstances. They devoted themselves to the care of the poor and the sick in the Pammatone Hospital where Catherine lived after the death of her husband. She intensified her life of austerity and good works and was noted as a visionary.

Catherine of Siena, St (1347–80). A patron saint of Italy, she was canonized in 1461 and in 1970 the second woman to be made a DOCTOR OF THE CHURCH. As well as serving the poor she was instrumental in bringing about the return of the POPE from AVIGNON to ROME.

Catherine of Sweden, St (1331–81, f.d. 24

March). The fourth daughter of St BRIDGET OF SWEDEN, she was married to Eggard Lydersson who was an invalid and whom she nursed devotedly. She accompanied her mother on pilgrimages and on a visit to ROME. On returning to Sweden she combined the care of her husband with her mother's religious works and after Eggard's death became the abbess of her convent at Vadstena, working for the BRIDGETTINES and obtaining papal approval for them; she also made great efforts to achieve the canonization of her mother.

Catherine Théot. A French prophetess like the English Joanna Southcott, calling herself 'The Mother of God' and changing her name to Theos (God). In the height of the Revolution she preached the worship of the Supreme Being and announced that Robespierre was the forerunner of The Word. She called him her well-beloved son and chief prophet. She died in prison in 1794.

Catherine wheel. A kind of firework, in the form of a wheel, which is driven round by the recoil from the explosion of the various squibs of which it is composed. *See* St CATHERINE.

Catherine-wheel window. A wheel window, sometimes called a *rose-window*, with radiating divisions.

The Order of St Catherine. (1) An extinct military order established in 1063 to guard the remains of St CATHERINE and to protect pilgrims. It followed the rule of St Basil.

(2) A Russian order founded by Peter the Great, confined to female members, and so named as a compliment to his second wife, who succeeded him as Catherine I in 1725.

To braid St Catherine's tresses. To live a virgin.

Catholic. The word (Gr. *katholikos*) means general, universal, comprehensive. It is used in this sense in the following extract:

> Creed and test
> Vanish before the unreserved embrace
> Of Catholic humanity.
>
> WORDSWORTH: *Ecclesiastical Sonnets*, III, xxxvi

Hence from the Church viewpoint it distinguishes (1) the whole body of Christians as apart from 'Jews, heretics and infidels', (2) a member of a church which claims the APOSTOLIC SUCCESSION and direct descent from the earliest body of Christians; (3) the ROMAN CATHOLIC CHURCH, i.e. the Western or Latin branch of the ancient Catholic or universal Church.

Alphonso I, King of the Asturias, 739–57, was surnamed the *Catholic* on account of his zeal in erecting and endowing monasteries and churches. *See* CATHOLIC KING.

Catholic Church. The whole body of Christians as distinct from the Churches and sects into which they are divided. The Latin Church called itself Catholic after the separation from the Eastern or ORTHODOX CHURCH. At the REFORMATION the Reformers called the Western Church under papal jurisdiction the ROMAN CATHOLIC CHURCH as opposed to their own Reformed or PROTESTANT Churches. Members of the CHURCH OF ENGLAND hold themselves to be Catholics but in popular usage Catholic usually means Roman Catholic.

> I believe in the Holy Ghost; The holy Catholic Church; etc.
>
> *Book of Common Prayer*: *Apostles' Creed*

Catholic and Apostolic Church. The name given to the followers of Edward Irving (1792–1824), and to the Church founded in 1835, after his death (also called IRVINGITES). He was a former member of the CHURCH OF SCOTLAND from which he was expelled for heresy in 1833.

Catholic Association (1823–29). Founded in Ireland by Daniel O'Connell and supported by the Roman Catholic clergy to promote the political emancipation of Roman Catholics. It became a powerful organization, aided by the monthly subscriptions of the peasantry called 'Catholic Rent', and achieved its objective with the passing of the Catholic Emancipation Act in 1829.

Catholic Epistles. Those Epistles in the NEW TESTAMENT not addressed to any particular church or individual; the epistles of James, Peter, and Jude and the first of John; II John is addressed to a 'lady', and III John to Gaius, but they are often included. *See* CANONICAL.

Catholic King, or **His Most Catholic Majesty.** A title given by Pope Innocent VIII to Ferdinand of Aragon and Isabella of Castile, and confirmed by Pope Alexander VI on account of their conquest and subsequent expulsion of the Moors in 1492. Those who remained and became nominal Christians were called Moriscos. The title was thereafter used as an appellation of the kings of Spain. *Cp.* RELIGIOUS.

Catholic League. (1) The party headed by the Guise faction in France (1584) in alliance with Philip II of Spain. Their object was to prevent the succession of Henry of Navarre to the French crown and place the Cardinal of Bourbon on the throne on the death of Henry III. (2) A Catholic confederacy formed in Germany in 1609 to counterbalance the Protestant Union of 1608. These rival groupings resulted in the Thirty Years' War (1618–48).

Catholic Roll. A document which Roman Catholics were obliged to sign on taking their seats as Members of Parliament. It was abolished when a single oath was prescribed to all members by an Act of 1866.

Old Catholics. In the Netherlands, the

Church of Utrecht which separated from ROME in 1724 after allegations of Jansenism. (*See* JANSENISTS). The term is more particularly associated with members of the German, Austrian and Swiss Churches who rejected the dogmas of papal INFALLIBILITY after the VATICAN COUNCIL of 1870 and were joined by others as a result of the Kulturkampf. Their episcopal succession is derived from the Church of Utrecht and they are in communion with the CHURCH OF ENGLAND. There are also others in the USA and small groups of Poles and Croats.

Catholicos. The head of the Assyrian NESTORI-ANS. Since called the Patriarch of Armenia.

Catholic Emancipation Act. In 1829 an Act was passed allowing Roman Catholics to sit in Parliament and be admitted to most public offices. Later, in 1926, the remaining restrictions were abolished except for the law which prohibits a Roman Catholic from sitting on the throne.

Catholic Truth Society. Founded in 1884 for the propagation of Roman Catholic faith. It publishes devotional and educational tracts and leaflets.

Cause. The Cause, or **The Good Old Cause** in the 17th century is the PURITAN cause, and was commonly used by the supporters of the Puritan Revolution in Cromwellian times and afterwards.

> The army, resolute as it still remained for the maintenance of 'the cause', was deceived by Monk's declarations of loyalty to it...
>
> J. R. GREEN: *A Short History of the English People,*
> ch. viii, sec. x

Cecilia, St. Patron SAINT of the blind and patroness of music and especially of Church music. Born in Rome, she is usually supposed to have been martyred in A.D. 230, but the date is uncertain. She was blind, and according to tradition, was inventor of the organ. An angel fell in love with her for her musical skill; her husband saw the heavenly visitant, who gave to both a crown of martyrdom which he brought from paradise. Her day is 22 November, on which the Worshipful Company of Musicians, a livery company of the City of London, meet and go in procession for divine service in St Paul's Cathedral.

Cedd, St (d. 664, f.d. 26 October, 3 January). Brother of St CHAD, educated at Lindisfarne, he went to Mercia as a missionary at the invitation of King Penda who had become a Christian. Cedd founded monasteries at Tilbury and Bradwell-on-Sea and was consecrated bishop by St FINAN OF LINDISFARNE. He attended the Synod of Whitby and supported the Roman usage in the dispute between the Celtic and Roman dates for EASTER. He founded the monastery of Lastingham, in Yorkshire, and died there of the plague.

Celestines. An order of reformed BENEDICTINES founded about 1260 by Pietro di Murrone, who became Pope Celestine V in 1294.

Celibacy. The unmarried state of a person who has taken vows to remain single, such as a monk or nun. Celibacy is obligatory for the clergy of the ROMAN CATHOLIC CHURCH. At first attempts to enforce the rule were spasmodic, but the Synod of Elvira in 305 forbade the marriage of the higher clergy while the DECRETAL of Pope Siricius in 385 enjoined strict celibacy for all clergy and insisted on the separation of those already married. Later, in 1917, the *Codex Iuris Canonici* prohibited the ordination of a married man. In the ANGLICAN CHURCH (*see* CHURCH OF ENGLAND) the celibacy of the clergy was abolished in 1549. In the Eastern ORTHO-DOX CHURCH celibacy of priests does not obtain but they may not marry twice.

Cell. A small, simple private room in a monastic house for either monks or nuns, or the isolated dwelling of a hermit. The term is also applied to a religious house dependent on a mother house. **Cellerar.** A monk responsible for the stores in a monastery, primarily of food and drink but also of general necessities. For this he was allowed freedom from many monastic rules and could attend markets and fairs.

Celsus, or **Cellach, St** (1079–1129, f.d. 1 April or 7 April). An Irishman of a saintly family of archbishops of Armagh by hereditary succession. He reformed the see which had lapsed into disorder and rebuilt Armagh cathedral. He was best known for his association with St MALACHY whom he appointed as his archdeacon and who succeeded him in the archbishopric.

Cemetery properly means a sleeping-place (Gr. *koimeterion,* a dormitory). The Persians call their cemeteries 'the Cities of the Silent'. The term appears to be used mainly for Christian burial grounds.

Cenydd, St. *See* KYNED.

Cenobites. *See* COENOBITES.

Censer. A sacred vessel in which incense is burnt during religious rites, it is usually suspended on chains and swung by an acolyte; it is also called a thurible. The rising smoke symbolizes ascending prayer. The censer is an attribute of the deacons LAURENCE and STEPHEN.

Ceolfrith, St (d. 716, f.d. 25 September). Of noble Northumbrian family, he became a monk and then was ordained priest at the monastery at Ripon, under the RULE of St BENEDICT, when only twenty-seven years of age. He was a friend and coadjutor of St BENEDICT BISCOP and became head of the community at Wearmouth and Jarrow during Biscop's absence in ROME, and abbot after the death of Biscop. Under his rule the community increased greatly. Towards the end of his life he set out for Rome but died at Langres, in Burgundy, where he was buried. His remains were soon translated to Wearmouth; from there they were removed to Glastonbury after the Viking invasions. He was renowned for his great learning.

Ceolwulf, St (d. *c.* 760, f.d. 15 January, 14 March). A weak Northumbrian king who was captured and shut up in a convent where he was tonsured by his enemies. He escaped, reigned for a few years, then abdicated and retired to the monastery of Lindisfarne where his generosity gave the community beer and wine in place of the former milk and water. BEDE praised his piety. Miracles were reported at his tomb.

Chad, St (*Ceadda*) (f.d. 2 March). A Northumbrian by birth and a pupil of St Aidan, he subsequently became BISHOP of Mercia with Lichfield as his SEE. He died in 672 and was the patron SAINT of springs. The New River which was once London's main water supply has its source in Chad's Well Springs between Hertford and Ware. There was also a spa at King's Cross opened early in the reign of George III called St Chad's Well. He was abbot of Lastingham and later made archbishop of York but was removed by St THEODORE OF CANTERBURY and retired to Lichfield, where he died. His relics are held in the cathedral at Birmingham, dedicated to him. In art he is depicted as a bishop holding a church, or with a vine.

Chair of St Peter. The office of the POPE of Rome, founded by St PETER, the apostle; but *St Peter's Chair* means the Catholic festival held in commemoration of the two episcopates founded by the apostle, one at Rome, and the other at Antioch (18 January; 22 February). The reputed chair itself in St Peter's at ROME is kept locked away and only exhibited once every century. It is of wood with ivory carvings, the wood being much decayed. It is probably 6th-century Byzantine work.

Chalcedon, Council of (451). Convened by the Emperor Marcian at Chalcedon, it was regarded as the fourth of the oecumenical councils. It met to settle the question of the heresy of Eutyches and to reinstate those condemned at the Council of Ephesus in 449. The creeds of the councils of NICAEA and CONSTANTINOPLE were ratified. The bishops attending were mainly from the Eastern Church but its decisions were accepted by the West.

Chamuel. *See* ARCHANGEL.

Chancel. That part of the church (usually at the eastern end) containing the altar and choir, which is often separated from the nave by a screen of wood or iron lattice-work and often with a raised floor level.

Chanel, St Peter (1803–41). The son of a peasant, he joined the missionary Society of Mary which had been established at Lyons in 1822 and was sent to Futuna in the New Hebrides with a group of lay brothers and an English layman. At first well received and successful, the jealousy of the chief was aroused when his son was converted. In the absence of his companions Fr Chanel was clubbed to death. He was the first martyr of the South Pacific.

Chant. In church music, a melody or song of a slow, solemn type with a long note on which words are recited, usually accompanying psalms and canticles. Ambrosian chants are named after St AMBROSE of the 4th century and Gregorian after St GREGORY THE GREAT.

Chantal, St Jane Frances de (1572–1641, f.d. 12 December). Born of a noble family in Burgundy, she married the Baron de Chantal but was widowed after nine years. She raised her family, then took a vow of chastity and worked under the direction of St FRANCIS DE SALES with whom she founded the Order of the Visitation. Its purpose was to allow women of delicate health to dedicate themselves to a life of religion and devotion. A convent was established at Annecy and the movement spread to Paris where Jane Frances met St VINCENT DE PAUL who said she was 'one of the holiest of souls' he had ever met. The order spread rapidly, and she made a point of visiting all its houses and working for the sick and the bereaved, especially during an outbreak of the plague.

Chantry. A religious and often charitable endowment usually connected with a chapel (often part of the parish church) and mainly to provide for the chanting of masses for the founder. Their spoliation was begun by Henry VIII in 1545 and completed under Edward VI in 1547. Little of the proceeds was used for charitable or educational purposes.

Chapel. Originally a chest containing relics or

the shrine thereof, so called from the *capella* (little cloak or cope) of St MARTIN, which was preserved by the Frankish kings as a sacred relic. The place in which it was kept when not in the field was called the *chapelle,* and the keeper thereof the *chapelain.* Hence the name came to be attached to a sanctuary, or a private place of worship other than a parish or cathedral church; and is also used for a place of worship belonging to the Free Churches, as a METHODIST Chapel, Baptist Chapel, etc., or a separately dedicated oratory within a church.

Chapel of ease. A place of worship for the use of parishioners residing at a distance from the parish church.

Lady chapel. A chapel dedicated to the Virgin within a larger church.

Chapelle Ardente (Fr.). The chapel or resting-place of kings or exalted personages when lying in state, so called from the many candles which were lit round the catafalque, a custom at least dating from the funeral rites of Dagobert, king of the Franks in 638. The term is now also applied to other mortuary chapels.

Chaplain. A clergyman who officiates at a private chapel, or who is commissioned to serve in the Forces, at a university, school, hospital or prison.

Chapter. From Lat. *caput,* a head. The chapter of a cathedral, composed of the canons (*see* CANON) and presided over by the DEAN or provost is so called from the ancient practice of the canons and monks reading at their meetings a *capitulum* or chapter of their Rule or of Scripture. *Ire ad capitulum* meant to go to the meeting for the reading of the chapter, hence to the meeting, hence to the body which made up the meeting.

Chardin, Marie-Joseph Pierre Teilhard de (1881–1955). Teilhard de Chardin was born in France, educated at a JESUIT school and entered the Order. His work was a combination of religious fervour, devotion and an over-riding interest in science and the theory of evolution. He was a noted palaeontologist and adopted a scientific, evolutionary interpretation of Christianity, maintaining that evolution was growing towards a peak point, which he named the Omega, the Christ. His scientific and neo-Marxist theories came into conflict with orthodox Catholicism, especially those theories put forward in his 'Hyper Physics' and 'Neo-Christianity' and he was dismissed from his professorship, exiled from Paris, and his works prohibited. They were, however, published posthumously, the best known being *The Phenomenon of Man, The Future of Man* and *The Milieu Divin.*

Chare Thursday. Another form of *Shear* or *Shere* Thursday; the same as MAUNDY THURSDAY.

Charismatic Movement. Having a certain affinity with the PENTECOSTALS, and sometimes referred to as neo-Pentecostalism, the movement maintains that the Gifts of Grace of the HOLY SPIRIT are as valid today as in the times of the NEW TESTAMENT and the early Church and that spiritual experience should be demonstrated in such gifts of the Spirit as speaking with tongues, prophecy and healing by faith and the laying on of hands. The convert is baptized in the Spirit, is able to testify to the Spirit, exercise spiritual gifts, and be in direct experience of God and Christ. Experience and spontaneity are more vital than liturgy and tradition. The movement involves both PROTESTANTS and CATHOLICS. Worship is characterized by spontaneity and is largely emotional; it stresses the importance of the Holy Spirit in life and worship.

Charlemagne (742–814). Charles the Great became sole king of the Franks in 771 and first Holy Roman emperor in 800. He ruled over most of western Europe and was noted as a lawgiver, administrator, protector of the Church and promoter of education. He was married nine times.

Charlemagne and his Paladins are the centre of a great series of chivalric romances. We are told that he was eight feet tall and of enormous strength and could bend three horseshoes at once in his hands. He was buried at Aix-la-Chapelle (Aachen), but according to legend he waits, crowned and armed, in Oldenburg, Hesse, for the day when ANTICHRIST shall appear; he will then go forth to battle and rescue Christendom. Another legend says that in years of plenty he crosses the Rhine on a bridge of gold, to bless the cornfields and vineyards.

Charles. St Charles Borromeo (1538–84, f.d. 4 November). One of the influential figures of the Counter REFORMATION, he was born of a noble family at Arona, Lake Maggiore, and was nephew of Cardinal de Medici, later Pope Pius IV. At the age of twelve he received the clerical tonsure and assumed control of the revenues of an abbey. At twenty-two he took his doctor's degree and held office under Pius IV who showered many honours upon him; he was appointed archbishop of Milan and made a cardinal. He carried out many reforms, among them the TRIDENTINE decrees; held councils and synods and did important work in overcoming ignorance both among the clergy and the people, one of his measures being the founding of SUNDAY SCHOOLS. Suffering from a speech impediment, he was unable to preach with ease but overcame this disability. He insisted on a simple style of living and on dignity in public worship; he had resigned all his family honours and estates. A group of Englishmen visited Borromeo in Milan, among them Ralph SHER-WIN and Edmund CAMPION. He died at Milan when only forty-six years old and his body was preserved in a crystal shrine in an underground chapel of his cathedral. In art his attributes are a crucifix and a skull.

Charles Lwanga, Joseph Mkosa and Companions, SS (d. 1886, f.d. 3 June). In Uganda, under the rule of Mwanga, there was a determined attempt to eradicate Christianity; PROTESTANT missionaries were murdered and the work of the Catholic WHITE FATHERS was attacked. Joseph Mkasa, a Christian in charge of the royal 'pages', reproached Mwanga for his unnatural vices and was beheaded. Learning that many of his pages were Christian, Mwanga challenged them to renounce their faith and when they refused they, with Charles Lwanga who had succeeded Joseph Mkosa, were put to death with the utmost cruelty. There were twenty-two so martyred, seventeen being young royal servants. They were beatified in 1920 and canonized in 1964.

Charterhouse. From Fr. *maison chartreuse,* a religious house of the CARTHUSIANS, the early monastery having wooden cells grouped round a wooden refectory but with a stone church.

Chasuble (Fr. from Med. Lat. *casabula,* a little cottage). The principal vestment worn by the priests in celebrating MASS. It is a roughly rectangular sleeveless garment, with a hole for the head in the middle, thus hanging down both back and front. It is usually richly decorated with embroidery, and mediaeval chasubles were finely ornamented with gold wire and gilded silver, this form of work being known throughout Europe as opus anglicanum. The City of London was the home of some of the best work of the 12th and 13th centuries. The chasuble is said to represent the seamless coat of Christ.

> And ye, lonely ladyes, with youre longe fyngres,
> That ye han silke and sendal to sowe, what tyme is,
> Chesibles for chapelleynes cherches to honoure.
> PIERS PLOWMAN

Cherub (*pl. cherubim*). A winged creature, and an order of ANGELS in attendance on God. In art a cherub is represented as a winged child's head.
Cherubicon. The 'cherubic hymn' sung by the Choir in the Eastern ORTHODOX CHURCH at the GREATER ENTRANCE; it is the mystical representation of the cherubim.

Child. Child of God. In the CHURCH OF ENGLAND

and the ROMAN CATHOLIC CHURCH, one who has been baptized; others consider the phrase to mean one converted by special grace and adopted into the holy family of God's Church.

> In my baptism; wherein I was made a member of Christ, the child of God, and an inheritor of the kingdom of heaven.
> *Catechism, Book of Common Prayer*

Childermas. The Old English name for the festival, of MASS of the HOLY INNOCENTS (28 December).

Chiliasts (Gr. *chilias,* a thousand). Also called MILLENARIANS (*see under* MILLENNIUM). Those who believe that Christ will return to this earth and reign a thousand years in the midst of his SAINTS. Originally a Judaistic theory, it became a heresy in the early Christian Church, and though it was condemned by St Damasus, who was POPE from 366 to 384, it was not extirpated. Article xli of the English Church further condemned Chiliasm in 1553; this Article was omitted in 1562.

China Inland Mission (CIM). Founded in 1865 by J. Hudson Taylor, it was an interdenominational missionary society of EVANGELICAL persuasion for the propagation of Christianity in the interior of China. The mission made no appeal for funds and its members 'lived by faith', having no fixed salary. It also ran schools and medical centres. With other missions it was expelled from China under the Communists and transferred much of its work to Africa.

Choir (Lat. *chorus*). The body of singers leading the choral services in church. It is also the part of a cathedral, church or abbey between the nave and the altar containing the seats of the clergy and the singers. Members of a choir usually wear a SURPLICE over a CASSOCK.

Chrism, Chrisom (Gr. *chrisma,* anointing, unction). The mixture of oil and balm consecrated for use in baptism, confirmation, etc. Originally *chrisom* was merely a variant of *chrism* resulting from a frequent form of pronunciation but later differentiated from the latter when it came to designate the white cloth or robe worn at baptism. This was used as a shroud if the child died within the ensuing month. In the Bills of Mortality as late as 1726, such infants were called *chrisoms.*

> 'A made a finer end, and went away, an it had been any chrisom child.
> SHAKESPEARE: *Henry V,* II, iii

Christen. To receive a person, usually an infant, into the Church by the rite of baptism, and to give a name.

Chrismation. The anointing at the post-baptismal rites of the Eastern ORTHODOX CHURCH when the bishop or priest anoints the baptized on the forehead, eyes, nose, ears and mouth with the consecrated CHRISM. The rite can be extended, in some cases, to other places; as many as thirty-six.

Christadelphians, or Brethren of Christ, sometimes called *Thomasites* after their founder Dr John Thomas (1805–1871), who migrated from London to Brooklyn and established the sect in 1848. They believe in 'conditional immortality' for the faithful and the full inspiration of the BIBLE, and look for the return of Christ to reign on this earth.

Christendom. All Christian countries generally; formerly it also meant the state or condition of being a Christian.

By my christendom,
So I were out of prison, and kept sheep,
I should be as merry as the day is long.
SHAKESPEARE: *King John*, IV, i

Christian. A follower of Christ. So called first at Antioch (*Acts* xi, 26). Also the hero of Bunyan's *Pilgrim's Progress* who fled from the CITY OF DESTRUCTION and journeyed to the celestal city. He started with a heavy burden on his back, which fell off when he stood at the foot of the cross.

Christian Brothers. A secret society formed in London in the early 16th century to distribute the NEW TESTAMENT in English. The name is now better known as that of the Roman Catholic teaching congregation of laymen, founded by the Abbé de la Salle in 1684. It still flourishes in France, Great Britain and elsewhere.

Christian Science. The religion founded at Boston by Mrs Mary Baker Eddy in 1879, 'the scientific system of divine healing'. Her views were put forward in her book *Science and Health, with key to the Scriptures*, first published in 1875. Christian Science is founded on the BIBLE, but distinguishes between what is taught in the NEW TESTAMENT and what is taught in the creeds and later dogma. It now has a considerable following and is not limited, as is popularly assumed, to the healing of those who are ill.

Most Christian Doctor. John Charlier de Gerson (1363–1429), French theologian.

Most Christian King. The style of the king of France since 1429, when it was conferred on Louis XI by POPE Paul II. Previously the title had been given in the 8th century to Pepin le Bref by Pope Stephen III (714–768), and again in the 9th century to Charles le Chauve. *See* RELIGIOUS.

Christiana. The wife of CHRISTIAN in Pt. II of Bunyan's *Pilgrim's Progress*, who journeyed with her children and Mercy from the city of destruction some time after her husband.

Christians of St Thomas. A sect of Christians from Malabar, India, who believe that the Apostle THOMAS reached that part of India, preached the GOSPEL and was martyred there. It is also called the Syrian Church of India and has NESTORIAN leanings. There is an archbishop and a metropolitan, and the clergy are nominally celibate.

Christmas. 25 December is Christmas Day although almost certainly not the day on which Christ was born, as is popularly supposed. The date was eventually fixed by the Church in AD 440, the day of the winter solstice, which had anciently been a time of festival among heathen peoples. In Anglo-Saxon England, the year began on 25 December, but from the late 12th century until the adoption of the Gregorian Calendar in 1752 the year began on LADY DAY, 25 March. See GREGORIAN YEAR. In the Eastern ORTHODOX CHURCH the Day of the Nativity and the Theophany, or Epiphany, are so closely linked as to form a single festival. The Coming of the Magi is celebrated at the Nativity and the baptism of Christ at Epiphany.

Christmas box. A gratuity given on Boxing Day (the day after Christmas Day), St Stephen's Day. Boxes placed in churches for casual offerings used to be opened on Christmas Day, and the contents, called the 'dole of the Christmas box', or the 'box money', were distributed next day by priests. Apprentices also used to carry a box around to their masters' customers for small gratuities.

Christology. The branch of theology which is concerned with the nature of Christ and particularly with the relationship between his divine and human natures.

Christopher, St (f.d. 25 July). Legend relates that St Christopher was a giant who one day carried a child over a brook, and said, 'Chylde, thou hast put me in gret peryll. I might bere no greater burden.' To which the child answered 'Marvel thou nothing, for thou hast borne all the world upon thee, and its sins likewise.' This is an allegory: Christopher means Christ-bearer; the child was Christ, and the river was the river of death. St Christopher was removed from the Church Calendar of Saints in 1969 as being of doubtful historicity.

Chrodegang, St (d. 766, f.d. 6 March). He was bishop of Metz and appointed secretary and chancellor of France by Charles Martel. He also acted as ambassador for Pepin to Stephen III. Chrodegang built and reformed monasteries and was famous for establishing the Rule for Canons and for founding a school of music at

Metz, noted for the GREGORIAN CHANT. He was a man of outstanding character and ability in both the political and ecclesiastical worlds.

Chrysanthus and Daria, SS (3rd cent. f.d., 25 October). A popular legendary pair of early martyrs. Chrysanthus was said to be a young Alexandrian in ROME whose father was anti-Christian and the young man suffered many extraordinary tortures unhurt. Daria had been a Vestal Virgin who, after her conversion and a virginal marriage to Chrysanthus, was thrown into a brothel where she was miraculously protected by a lion. The two were responsible for many conversions, especially among soldiers, who were also martyred. Finally, after many attempts which failed to kill them, the two were stoned and buried alive in a quarry on the Salarian Way. Christians praying at their tomb were also buried alive on the orders of the Emperor.

Church. This is the O.E. *circe*, or *cirice*, which comes through W.Ger. *kirika*, from Gr. *kuriakon*, a church, the neuter of the adjective *kuriakos*, meaning of or belonging to the Lord. It denotes the whole body of Christians; the place of worship; a particular sect or group of Christians; the CLERGY.
Anglican Church. The CHURCH OF ENGLAND.
Broad Church. *See* BROAD.
Catholic Church. *See* CATHOLIC.
Collegiate Churches. So called from having a college or chapter of CANONS or prebends since a DEAN. There were many such in mediaeval England but they were mainly suppressed during the reign of Edward VI (1547–53). St George's Chapel, Windsor and Westminster Abbey are surviving examples. Some of them eventually became cathedrals of new dioceses (e.g. at Manchester and Ripon).
Established Church. The church officially recognized and established by law and enjoying a privileged position. In England the established Church is Episcopalian, in Scotland it is PRESBYTERIAN. *See* EPISCOPACY.
Church of England. First severed its connexion with ROME under Henry VIII and subsequently under Elizabeth I (1559). Doctrinal changes were largely effected in the reign of Edward VI (1547–53) and embodied in the BOOK OF COMMON PRAYER of 1549 and the more definitely PROTESTANT version of 1552.
Church of Ireland. This became PROTESTANT in the same way as the Church of England and, although most of the Irish remained Roman CATHOLIC, it was not disestablished and largely disendowed until 1869.
Church of North America (Episcopalian), was established in November 1784, when Bishop Seabury, chosen by the churches of Connecticut, was consecrated in Scotland. The

first convention was held at Philadelphia in 1787.
Church of Scotland. It first became PRESBYTERIAN in 1560, but EPISCOPACY was cautiously restored by James VI and I from 1599, to be rejected finally in 1638. It is an ESTABLISHED CHURCH.
Church in Wales was separated from the province of Canterbury in 1920, after the long-standing agitation for disestablishment, which resulted in the Act of 1914 for this purpose.
Church Commissioners. *See* ECCLESIASTICAL COMMISSIONERS; QUEEN ANNE'S BOUNTY.
Church-ale. Also called *Easter-ale* and *Whitsun-ale* from their being sometimes held at EASTER and WHITSUNTIDE; a church festivity akin to the WAKES, when specially brewed ale was sold to the populace and money was collected in addition for church purposes. The word 'ale' is used in such composite words as *bride-ale, church-ale, clerk-ale, lamb-ale, Midsummer-ale, Scot-ale*, etc., for revel or feast, ale being the chief liquor provided. Church–ales were unsuccessfully forbidden in 1603 but mostly came to an end during the Interregnum.

which mault being made into very strong ale, or beer, is set to sale, either in the church, or in some other place... If all be true which they say, they bestow the money which is got thereby for the repair of their churches and chappels; they buy bookes for the service, etc. ...
PHILLIP STUBBS: *Anatomie of Abuses* (1595)

Church scot. A tribute, earlier known as *food-rent*, paid on St MARTIN'S Day (11 November) in corn and poultry, etc., to support the parish priests in Saxon times. It is named from the Early Saxon silver coin called a *sceat*.
High Church. *See* HIGH.
Low Church. *See* LOW.
Orthodox Church. *See* ORTHODOX.
The Church Army. A CHURCH OF ENGLAND evangelical body founded by the Rev. Wilson Carlile in 1882. It began its work among the poor of London on somewhat similar lines to those of the SALVATION ARMY.
The Church Invisible. Those who are known to God alone as His sons and daughters by adoption and grace. *See* CHURCH VISIBLE.

There is... a Church visible and a Church invisible; the latter consists of those spiritual persons who fulfil the notion of the Ideal Church—the former is the Church as it exists in any particular age, embracing within it all who profess Christianity.
F. W. ROBERTSON: *Sermons* (series IV, ii)

The Church Militant. The Church or whole body of believers who are said to be 'waging the war of faith' against 'the world, the flesh and the DEVIL'. It is therefore militant, or in warfare.
The Church Triumphant. Those who are dead and gone to their rest. Having fought the fight and triumphed, they belong to the Church

Triumphant in HEAVEN.

The Church Visible. All ostensible Christians; all who profess to be Christians; all who have been baptized and admitted into the communion of the Church. *Cp.* CHURCH INVISIBLE.

The Seven Churches of Asia. *See* SEVEN.

To go into the Church. To take HOLY ORDERS; to enter the ministry.

Uniat Churches. *See* UNIAT.

Churchwarden. A long clay pipe, such as churchwardens used to smoke a century or so ago when they met together in the parish tavern, after they had made up their accounts in the VESTRY, or been elected to office at the EASTER meeting. The warden is the senior lay official of the church congregation, having special supervisory duties and overseeing the observance of laws and regulations in church matters. Technically wardens are the bishop's representatives in the parish. The office, which is unpaid, is one of the oldest in English church customs.

Churchyard. The enclosed ground surrounding a church, often used as a burial ground. In the Middle Ages it was also used for public ceremonies and festivals.

Churches of Christ. A PROTESTANT sect in the USA which split from the DISCIPLES OF CHRIST after the Civil War and is still strong in the South. They advocate following the theology-pattern of the early Christians; they repudiate the organ as a church instrument and they abjure any missionary activity.

Church Fathers. *See* FATHERS OF THE CHURCH.

Church Missionary Society (CMS). Founded as the Society for Missions in Africa and the East in 1799, it was a CHURCH OF ENGLAND mission of EVANGELICAL persuasion. Starting with five missionaries, it spread worldwide in the 19th century.

Churching of Women. Derived from the Jewish rite of Purification (*Lev.* xii, 6), the service is one of thanksgiving for a safe childbirth. In the ROMAN CATHOLIC Church there is also a blessing and an ASPERSION. In the Eastern ORTHODOX CHURCH the ceremony is more elaborate; it usually takes place on the fortieth day after the birth and the priest meets the mother and child at the West Door and takes the child into the church with words of reception which are repeated in the middle of the church and before the royal doors of the Sanctuary. The child is given back to the mother with the blessing.

Ciborium. In CATHOLIC use, the vessel containing the consecrated HOST; the vessel has a lid. A ciborium is also a canopy over a shrine.

Circuit Rider. A METHODIST minister in America who rode on horseback round the outlying stations of his circuit to preach and perform other pastoral duties. Francis Asbury, a follower of John Wesley, began the practice in 1771.

Circumcellions. *See* AGONISTICS.

Circumcision. A religious rite among the Jews which became the issue between St PAUL's and St BARNABAS' missions to the GENTILES. The Conference at Jerusalem (*c.* 50) reached a compromise; Gentiles need not be circumcised but should abstain from practices offensive to the Jews. Christians had a 'true circumcision of the heart' (*Phil.* iii, 3). The rite remains in the ETHIOPIAN CHURCH.

Cistercians. A monastic order, founded at Cistercium or Cîteaux (near Dijon) in 1098, by Robert, abbot of Molesme, as strict BENEDICTINES. They are also known as Grey or White Monks from their habit and as *Bernadines* from St Bernard of Clairvaux, who with thirty companions joined the abbey of Citeaux in 1113. They were noted agriculturalists, and in the 13th-century England became a great producer of wool.

City. The City of David. Jerusalem. So called in compliment to King David (II *Sam.* v, 7, 9).

The City of Destruction. In Bunyan's *Pilgrim's Progress*, the world of the unconverted.

The City of God. The Church, or whole body of believers; the Kingdom of Christ, in contradistinction to the CITY OF DESTRUCTION. The phrase is from St Augustine's famous work, *De Civitate Dei*.

The City of St Michael. Dumfries, of which St MICHAEL is the patron SAINT.

The City of Saints. Montreal is so named because of its streets named after SAINTS. Salt Lake City, Utah, USA, is also so called, from its MORMON inhabitants.

The City of the Three Kings. Cologne; the reputed burial place of the MAGI.

Cities of Refuge. Six walled cities (*Joshua*, xxxv, 6), three on each side of the Jordan, set aside under MOSAIC LAW as a refuge for those who committed accidental homicide. Such refuges were necessitated by the primitive law which exacted blood vengeance by next of kin. All seeking asylum were tried, and if found guilty of murder right of asylum was withdrawn. The cities were Ramoth, Kedesh, Bezer, Shechem, Hebron, and Golam (*Joshua* xx, 7, 8). In *Numbers* xxxv, and other references, the choice of cities is attributed to Moses, but in *Joshua* xx, to Joshua.

The Cities of the Plain. Sodom and Gomorrah.

Abram dwelled in the land of Canaan, and Lot dwelled in the cities of the plain, and pitched his tent towards Sodom.

Gen. xiii, 12

Clapham Sect. The name bestowed by Sydney Smith upon the group of EVANGELICALS with common social and political interests most of whom lived in Clapham at the end of the 18th and in the early 19th centuries. William Wilberforce (1759–1833) was their leader. Henry Thornton the banker, Zachary Macaulay, John Venn and James Stephen were among his close associates. Their opponents derisively called them 'the Saints'.

Clare. Clare, St (1194–1253, f.d. 11 August, formerly 12 August). Born of a noble family at Assisi, there is nothing known of her early life but, at the age of eighteen, under the influence of St FRANCIS OF ASSISI, and against her parents' will, she first entered a BENEDICTINE nunnery, and then founded the Order of Poor Clares in association with the FRANCISCANS. She remained at the convent at Assisi but other convents were established in Italy, France and Germany. When Assisi was threatened by the Emperor Frederick II and the Saracens her convent was surrounded. Clare, though ill, was carried to the wall carrying a MONSTRANCE and the armies scattered. In art she is depicted with a PYX or monstrance, or a CROSIER as founder of an order.
Clare, Order of St. A religious order of women founded in 1212, the second that St Francis instituted. The name derives from their first abbess, Clare of Assisi. The nuns are also called Clarisses, Poor Clares, Minoresses, or Nuns of the Order of St Francis. *See* FRANCISCANS.
Clare of Montefalco, St (d. 1308, f.d. 17 April and 30 October). Became a FRANCISCAN hermit when very young. The order was re-established as Augustinian and she was appointed abbess. Clare was noted for her devotion to the Passion and said the marks would be engraved on her heart; she was also famed for her extreme austerities, visions and miracles. The miracles continued after her death, her body being incorrupt and her blood liquefying. Her cult still continues.

Claver, Peter, St (1580–1654, f.d. 9 September). Born at Verdu in Catalonia and educated at Barcelona University, he became a JESUIT and was sent to Cartagena, now in Colombia, and was ordained priest. Under the influence of an older Jesuit priest he devoted himself to work among the negro slaves, Cartegena being one of the main centres of the slave trade. He attempted to alleviate the appalling conditions suffered by the negroes, meeting the ships and following the slaves to the mines and plantations, working among them in conditions as fearful as their own and calling himself 'the slave of the negro for ever'. He did not confine his work to this cause alone but visited hospitals and prisons and carried out missions to seamen and traders, regardless of their religion or nationality. After an illness his last years were spent in physical suffering and neglect by his negro attendant, but he was honoured at his death with a civic funeral. Miracles and the gift of prophecy and reading minds were attributed to him. He was canonized in 1888 and named patron saint of missions among negroes.

Clean and unclean animals. Among the Jews of the OLD TESTAMENT (*see Lev.* xi) those animals which chew the cud and part the hoof were clean and might be eaten. Hares and rabbits could not be eaten because (although they chew the cud) they do not part the hoof. Pigs and camels were unclean, because (although they part the hoof) they do not chew the cud. Birds of prey were accounted unclean. Fish with fins and scales were accounted fit food for man.

Clement. Clement of Alexandria (c. 160–217, f.d. 4 December). One of the FATHERS OF THE CHURCH, he was born into a Greek pagan family, probably at Athens, but was resident for most of his life in Alexandria where he studied with Christian teachers after his conversion and where he also taught later, ORIGEN being one of his pupils. His writings are philosophical rather than theological and make reference to the mystery religions and gnosticism. He was the first Christian writer to mention the Buddha.
Clement, St (f.d. 23 November). Patron SAINT of tanners, being himself a tanner. His symbol is an anchor, because he is said to have been martyred by being thrown into the sea tied to an anchor where angels made him a tomb which was exposed yearly at low tide. He was bishop of ROME, said to have followed St PETER, and ranks as a Pope; he was the first of the APOSTOLIC FATHERS. Though little is known of his life he was believed to have had contact with the APOSTLES and was famous for the First Epistle of Clement to the Corinthians. Various legends are associated with him, one that he was banished to the Crimean quarries for hard labour; there, suffering from thirst, he, like Moses, miraculously obtained water by striking a rock. Many English churches are dedicated to him, including St Clement Danes in London. He is also patron of Trinity House, as being responsible for lighthouses and lightships. In art he may also be depicted with a lamb or wearing the papal TIARA.
Clement Slovensky, St (d. 916, f.d. 27 July). The most important of the SEVEN APOSTLES OF BULGARIA, he worked with St METHODIUS as a missionary in Moravia, from where he was driven by the German element, and went to evangelize the Bulgars. Clement was consecrated bishop at Velico and was the founder of this see,

and the first Slav to be appointed to a bishopric. He also founded a monastery at Okhrida. He is venerated in the Russian ORTHODOX CHURCH as well as in Bulgaria.

Clerestory, or **Clearstory.** A series of windows rising clear above the central nave of a church below the roof.

Clergy. Ultimately from Gr. *kleros*, a lot or inheritance, with reference to *Deut.* xviii, 21 and *Acts* i, 17; thus, the men of God's lot or inheritance. In St Peter's First Epistle (ch. v, 3) the Church is called 'God's heritage' or lot. In the OLD TESTAMENT the tribe of Levi is called the 'lot or heritage of the Lord'.

Clergy, Benefit of. *See* BENEFIT.

Clerical Titles. *Clerk.* In remote times the clergyman was usually one of the few who could read and write, so the word *clerical,* as used in 'clerical error', came to mean an orthographical error. As the respondent in church was able to read, he received the name of clerk, and the assistants in writing, etc., were so termed in business (Late Lat. *clericus,* a clergyman).

Curate. One who has the cure of souls in a parish. Properly a rector, vicar, or perpetual curate, but the word curate is now generally used to denote an 'assistant' curate or unbeneficed clergyman.

Parson. The same word as person. As Blackstone says, a parson is *'persona ecclesiae,* one that hath full rights of the parochial church'.

> Though we write 'parson' differently, yet 'tis but 'person'; that is the individual person set apart for the service of such a church, and 'tis in Latin *persona,* and *personatus* is a parsonage. Indeed with the canon lawyers, *personatus* is any dignity or preferment in the church.
>
> SELDEN: *Table-talk*

Rector. One who received the great TITHES. From Lat. *rector,* a ruler—the man who rules and guides the parish.

Vicar. Originally one who does the 'duty' of a parish for the owner or owners of the tithes (Lat. *vicarius,* a deputy). *Perpetual Curates* are now termed Vicars.

The French *curé* equals our vicar, and their *vicaire* our curate.

In the USA a vicar is the priest of a chapel, dependent on a church.

Clerical vestments. *White.* Emblem of purity, worn on all feasts, saints' days, and sacramental occasions.

Red. The colour of blood and of fire, worn on the days of martyrs, and on WHITSUNDAY, when the HOLY GHOST came down like tongues of fire. Now also used on GOOD FRIDAY.

Green. Worn on days which are neither feasts nor fasts.

Purple. The colour of mourning, worn on ADVENT Sundays, in LENT, and on EMBER DAYS. Now used on Good Friday in some churches.

Black. Formerly worn on Good Friday; worn when masses are said for the dead.

Clerks Regular. Bodies of ROMAN CATHOLIC clergy who live in a community under religious vows and are active in pastoral work, e.g. THEATINES, BARNABITES, JESUITS.

Clitherow, St Margaret (1556–86, f.d. 25 October). One of the FORTY MARTYRS OF ENGLAND AND WALES, she was canonized in 1970. She was born and lived in York, married to a prosperous PROTESTANT tradesman, but she became a CATHOLIC and was openly active in the cause. She was imprisoned for not attending the parish church and came under suspicion of hiding priests and attending MASS. She was arrested and interrogated but refused to plead, saying she had no offence to answer. Her family remained loyal but she was betrayed by a Flemish boy and was condemned to death by 'peine forte et dure' and was thus crushed to death. Margaret was an attractive and popular personality, a help to all and generally loved.

Cloister. He retired into a cloister, he entered a monastery. Most monasteries had a cloister or covered walk, which generally occupied three sides of a quadrangle. Hence *cloistered,* confined, withdrawn from the world in the manner of a recluse.

Cloud (or **Clodald**), **St** (6th cent., f.d. 7 September). Third son of Clodomir, second son of Clovis, his two elder brothers were murdered by their ambitious uncle but Cloud escaped and when he grew up he rejected any claim to the Frankish throne and became a priest and hermit. He built and endowed a monastery where the palace of St Cloud now stands. He was noted for his good works. In art he is represented with nails, being the patron saint of nailmakers.

Cluniacs. In 10th-century France discipline in the Benedictine abbeys had declined almost completely and wealth and luxury predominated. At Cluny, N.W. of Mâcon a reformed abbey was established in 910 and in due course many old abbeys adopted the rigid rule of the Cluniacs. By the end of the 12th century there were over 300 European monasteries linked with Cluny and some 30 or so Cluniac houses in England, including those of Bermondsey, Reading and Faversham. As with the BENEDICTINES wealth and laxity took over and the next major revival was that of the CISTERCIANS.

Cockle hat. A pilgrim's hat. Pilgrims used to

wear cockle (scallop) shells on their hats, the symbol of St JAMES of COMPOSTELA in Spain. This supposed shrine of James, the son of Zebedee, was especially favoured by English pilgrims. The polished side of the shell was scratched with some crude drawing of the Virgin, the Crucifixion, or some other object related to the pilgrimage. Being blessed by the priest, the shells were considered as amulets against spiritual foes, and might be used as drinking vessels.

> How should I your true love know
> From another one?
> By his cockle hat and staff,
> And by his sandal shoon
>
> SHAKESPEARE: *Hamlet,* IV, v

Codex. An ancient manuscript book with leaves, as distinct from a roll or scroll, especially of the BIBLE. There are five great biblical codices:

Codex Sinaiticus, in Greek, 4th cent., discovered in 1844 in the monastery of Mt Sinai and now in the British Museum.

Codex Vaticanus, also Greek, 4th cent., now in the Vatican Library.

Codex Alexandrinus, 5th cent., given by the Patriarch of Constantinople to Charles I of England, now in the British Museum.

Codex Bezae, 5th or 6th cent., Greek and Latin, given by Theodore Beza, a French Protestant scholar, to Cambridge University.

Codex Ephraemi, 5th cent., Greek, now in the Bibliothèque Nationale, Paris.

Coemgen, Comgan, Congen. *See* KEVIN.

Coenobites, or **Cenobites** (Gr. *koinos bios*). Monks who live in common, in contradistinction to hermits or anchorites.

Colette, St (1381–1447, f.d. 6 March). Born at Cologne, the daughter of a carpenter at Corbie Abbey, she took to the religious life at an early age and became a recluse and a Franciscan TERTIARY. She had visions and dreams in which she was exhorted to reform the POOR CLARES. She joined the order, was made superior-general, and reformed and established convents in France, Savoy and Flanders. Many miracles were attributed to her. She was said to have met St JOAN OF ARC, also to have recruited many noble devotees. Like St FRANCIS she was a noted lover of animals.

Colettines. *See* FRANCISCANS.

Collation. A light meal, permitted on fast days in addition to the one full meal. The term is also applied to the *Lives of the Fathers* put together for reading in monasteries.

Collect. A short prayer for the day, usually containing a petition, an invocation and a pleading; it is said before the EPISTLE at the EUCHARIST.

Collegiate Church. One which is not a cathedral or bishop's see but which has a college or chapter of clergy, called canons, and in the CHURCH OF ENGLAND a dean. An example is Westminster Abbey.

Collyridians. A sect of women of the 4th century who worshipped the VIRGIN MARY as Queen of Heaven and regarded her as actually divine. They were mentioned by bishop Epiphanius who held office at that time.

Colman. Colman of Kilmacduagh, St (d. *c.* 632, f.d. 29 October). Born at Corker in Kiltartan, he was consecrated bishop against his will and fled with one disciple to the forest of Connaught where he lived as a hermit, subsisting on a diet of vegetables and water. He founded the church of Kil-mac-duarch *c.* 620. He had three animal companions: a cock to wake him for the night office, a mouse to prevent him from going to sleep and a bluebottle kept his place in his book. The usual marvellous tales are told of him and his relics.

Colman of Lindisfarne, St (d. 676, f.d. 18 February and 8 August). Born in Ireland, he became bishop and abbot of Lindisfarne as successor to St AIDAN. At the synod of Whitby, where the date of EASTER and Celtic versus Roman usages were the subject of dispute, St WILFRID spoke for the Roman while Colman upheld the Celtic customs. When the king pronounced in favour of the Roman view, Colman, with a body of monks, bearing the bones of St Aidan, went to Iona but soon left for Ireland, establishing a monastery on the island of Inishbofin. Here, the English and Irish monks disagreed and to resolve the dispute Colman left the Irish at Inishbofin and founded a Saxon settlement on the mainland at Mayo, known as 'Mayo of the Saxons'. BEDE praised the learning, frugality and simplicity of the community and the bishop.

Colmcille. *See* COLUMBA.

Cologne. The Three Kings of Cologne. The three Wise Men of the East, the MAGI, whose bones, according to mediaeval legend, were deposited in Cologne Cathedral.

Colours in SYMBOLISM, ECCLESIASTICAL USE, etc.

Black:

> *In blazonry,* sable, signifying prudence, wisdom and constancy; it is engraved by perpendicular and horizontal lines crossing each other at right angles.

In art, signifying evil, falsehood, and error.

In Church decoration it was used for GOOD FRIDAY.

As a mortuary colour, signifying grief, despair, death. (In the Catholic Church violet may be substituted for black.)

In metals it is represented by lead.

In precious stones it is represented by the diamond.

In planets it stands for Saturn.

Blue:

Hope, love of divine works; (in dresses) divine contemplation, piety, sincerity.

In blazonry, azure, signifying chastity, loyalty, fidelity, it is engraved by horizontal lines.

In art (as an angel's robe) it signifies fidelity and faith; (as the robe of the Virgin Mary) modesty and (in the Catholic Church) humility and expiation.

In Church decoration, blue and green were used indifferently for ordinary Sundays in the pre-Reformation Church.

As a mortuary colour it signifies eternity (applied to Deity), immortality (applied to man).

In metals it is represented by tin.

In precious stones it is represented by sapphire.

In planets it stands for Jupiter.

Pale Blue:

Peace, Christian prudence, love of good works, a serene conscience.

Green:

Faith, gladness, immortality, the resurrection of the just; (in dresses) the gladness of the faithful.

In blazonry, vert, signifying love, joy, abundance; it is engraved by diagonal lines from left to right.

In art, signifying hope, joy, youth, spirit (among the Greeks and Moors it signifies victory).

In Church decoration it signifies God's bounty, mirth, gladness, the resurrection; used for weekdays and Sundays after TRINITY.

In metals it is represented by copper.

In precious stones it is represented by the emerald.

In planets it stands for Venus.

Pale Green:

BAPTISM.

Purple:

Justice, royalty.

In blazonry, purpure, signifying temperance; it is engraved by diagonal lines from right to left.

In art signifying royalty.

In Church decoration it is used for ASH WEDNESDAY and HOLY SATURDAY.

In metals it is represented by quicksilver.

In precious stones it is represented by amethyst.

In planets it stands for Mercury.

Red:

Martyrdom for faith, charity; (in dresses) divine love.

In blazonry, gules; blood-red is called sanguine. The former signifies magnanimity, and the latter fortitude; it is engraved by perpendicular lines.

In Church decoration it is used for martyrs and for WHITSUNDAY.

In metals it is represented by iron (the metal of war).

In precious stones it is represented by the ruby.

In planets it stands for Mars.

White:

In blazonry, argent; signifying purity, truth, innocence; in engravings argent is left blank.

In art, priests, MAGI, and Druids are arrayed in white. Jesus after the resurrection should be draped in white.

In Church decoration it is used for festivals of Our Lord, for MAUNDY THURSDAY, and for all Saints except Martyrs.

As a mortuary colour it indicates hope.

In metals it is represented by silver.

In precious stones it is represented by the pearl.

In planets it stands for Diana or the moon.

Yellow:

In blazonry, or; signifying faith, constancy, wisdom, glory; in engravings it is shown by dots.

In modern art, signifying jealousy, inconstancy, incontinence. In France the doors of traitors used to be daubed with yellow, and in some countries Jews were obliged to dress in yellow. In Spain the executioner is dressed in red and yellow.

In Christian art JUDAS is arrayed in yellow; but St PETER is also arrayed in golden yellow.

In metals it is represented by gold.

In precious stones it is represented by the topaz.

In planets it stands for Apollo or the sun.

Violet, Brown or Grey:

are used in Church decoration for ADVENT and LENT; and in other symbolism violet usually stands for penitence, and grey for tribulation.

Columba (or **Colmcille**), **St** (*c.* 521–97, f.d. 9 June). Reputedly descended from Irish kings, he was born at Gartan, Donegal, and was trained and ordained by St FINNIAN. He founded many monasteries in Ireland. With twelve companions he left Ireland for Iona where he founded the monastery which became so important a centre of Christianity in North Britain. He travelled extensively on the mainland, founding monasteries and converting the people. Much has been written of his impressive and attractive personality, of his scholarship, skill as a bard and scribe, of his visions, prophecies and miraculous deeds, one of these being the expulsion of a 'water monster' from the river Ness by making the sign of the cross. After Viking raids on Iona his relics were translated to Dunkeld in 849. His 'Cathach', the psalms in his own hand, still exists.

Columbanus, St (*c.* 543–618, f.d. 21 November, in Ireland 23 November). Born in Leinster, he became a monk but left Ireland on account of the temptations of the beauty of the Irish girls. He went to Gaul as a wandering preacher, making friends on his travels with the wolves and the bears. He attracted many followers and founded monasteries and a colony of ascetic monks. Columbanus fell foul of the licentious Queen Brunhild and the King by refusing to bless the illegitimate sons of Theuderic II and was banished to his own country, but the ship encountered a storm and was forced back; he then found refuge at the court of Clothair II, after which he moved from place to place carrying out missions and becoming one of the great Irish apostles to Europe. He was involved in ecclesiastical controversy with Pope Benedict IV. Settling finally at Bobbio, he founded a monastery and died there. In art he is depicted with a bear as his attribute.

Comgall, St (*c.* 517–603, f.d. 11 May, in Ireland 10 May). Born in Ulster and reputed to have been first a soldier, but later trained by St FINTAN and ordained priest, he lived as a hermit and then founded a monastery at Bangor, near Belfast, and was said to have established another in Britain. He trained St COLUMBANUS and visited St COLUMBA at Iona and was thought to have accompanied him on his mission to the Picts. Many strange miracles are told of him; his saliva had magical powers, spitting in a beggar's pocket turned it into a gold ring and spitting at a rock shattered it into fragments.

Comgan. *See* KEVIN.

Commandment. The Ten Commandments. *See* DECALOGUE.

Commendam. A living in commendam is one temporarily held by someone (often a BISHOP) until an incumbent is appointed, and the practice arose of commending several livings to the bishops of poorer sees. The custom was abolished in 1836.

Common Prayer. The Book of Common Prayer. *See under* BOOK.

Communion. *See* EUCHARIST.
  Communion Table. In the 'LOW' CHURCH in the CHURCH OF ENGLAND, in NONCONFORMIST or FREE CHURCHES, a table is placed instead of the ALTAR for the ceremony of the Lord's Supper.

Community of the Ressurection. *Osc. f.* 133.

Compline. The last of the CANONICAL HOURS, said about 8 or 9 p.m., and so called because it completes the series of the daily prayers or hours. From M.E. and O.Fr. *complie,* Lat. *completa* (*hora*).
  In ecclesiastical Lat. *vesperinus,* from *vesper,*

means evening service, and *completinus* appears to be formed on this model.

Complutensian Polyglot. *See* BIBLE, SOME SPECIALLY NAMED EDITIONS.

Compostela, or **Compostella.** Santiago de Compostela, the city in Spain where the relics of St JAMES the Great are supposed to be preserved; a corruption of *Giacomopostolo* (James the Apostle). *See* COCKLE HAT.

Conan (or **Conon**), **St** (d. 648, f.d. 26 January). Has been called the first bishop of Sodor but the evidence is doubtful. He worked in the Hebrides and the Isle of Man where several places are named after him. He was tutor to St FIACRE.

Conceptionists. *See* FRANCISCANS.

Conclave. Literally, a room or set of rooms, all of which can be opened by one key (Lat. *cum clavis*). The word is applied to small cells erected for the CARDINALS who meet, after the death of a POPE, to elect a successor; hence the assembly of cardinals for this purpose; hence any private assembly for discussion. The conclave of cardinals dates from 1274 and was limited to 120 cardinals in 1973. Those assembled in the VATICAN are secluded in the conclave apartments and votes are taken morning and evening until one candidate has secured a two-thirds majority of votes. He is then acclaimed Pope.

> And once more in my arms I bid him [Cardinal Campeius] welcome,
> And thank the holy conclave for their loves.
> SHAKESPEARE: Henry VIII, II, ii

To meet in solemn conclave is to meet together to decide matters of importance.

Confession, Seal of. The obligation which binds a priest not to divulge outside the confessional anything he may hear therein. He cannot be forced to reveal in the witness-box of a court of law any information he may have thus obtained. The sacrament of Confession is the acknowledgement of sin or fault, either made publicly or in private to a priest. It is practised in ROMAN CATHOLIC, ORTHODOX and most Eastern Churches and was revived in Anglican Churches by the Tractarians. The practice originated with the Jews and JOHN THE BAPTIST's converts made public confession; this continued in the early church. The term is also applied to the tomb of a martyr or CONFESSOR and a shrine containing the relics of a saint. It is also a declaration of a faith. *See also* CONFESSOR.
Confessor. A title used in the early church for one who affirmed his faith in spite of

persecution, torture or danger but did not suffer martyrdom; later it denoted a person of outstandingly dedicated Christian life, e.g. St JEROME. A confessor is also a priest who hears confessions and grants ABSOLUTION.

Confirmation. A rite in which the SACRAMENT of BAPTISM is confirmed, the grace of the HOLY SPIRIT is received, and the baptized are admitted to the full membership of the Church. The ceremony takes the form of the Laying on of Hands by a bishop. Vows made by the SPONSORS at the Christening are confirmed and the CATECHISM or the fundamentals of the Christian doctrines must have been learned.

Congen. *See* KEVIN.

Congregation. In the ROMAN CATHOLIC CHURCH the word is used as a congregation or committee of cardinals forming administrative departments; also the branches of a religious order following a general rule but forming separate groups with special constitutions and observances; also communities of RELIGIOUS under rule, composed of persons who have taken no sacred vows, e.g. OBLATES, LAZARISTS, ORATORIANS.

Congregationalists. Those PROTESTANT Dissenters maintaining that each congregation was independent with a right to govern its own affairs and choose its own minister. They derived from the BROWNISTS and BARROWISTS of Elizabeth I's reign. The Congregational Union was formed in 1832. *See* UNITED REFORMED CHURCH.

Congregation of Sacred Rites. *See* CANONIZATION.

Conon. *See* CONAN.

Consanguinity. A kinship or blood relationship within which Christian marriage is not permitted and in CANON LAW is null and void. The Table of Kindred and Affinity of 1563 defines the degrees of intermarriage prohibited in *Lev.* xviii.

Consistory (Lat. *consistorium,* a place of assembly). As an ecclesiastical court in the Church of ROME it is the assembly in council of the POPE and CARDINALS; in England it is a diocesan court presided over by the Chancellor of the diocese.

Constantine. Constantine the Great (*c.* 274–337). The first Christian Emperor of Rome, establishing Christianity as the religion of the state; said to have been converted on the eve of battle by a vision of a flaming CROSS with the words in Greek: 'In this sign conquer', which he adopted as his symbol, the LABARUM. At the Council of NICAEA he dealt with the DONATIST schism and the ARIAN heresy. After defeating the Eastern Emperor he moved his capital to Byzantium and called it Constantinople. In art he is depicted with a crown and sceptre, but more frequently with the Labarum.

Constantine, Donation of. *See* DECRETALS.

Constantine's Cross. *See* CROSS.

Constantinople, First Council of (381). When THEODOSIUS became Emperor in 379 he determined to eliminate ARIANISM and called a council for this purpose. It met at Constantinople and was dominated by the CAPPADOCIAN FATHERS, no Western bishops being present; in spite of this it was called OECUMENICAL and was regarded as the second of such councils. It condemned the heresies of Arianism, MACEDONIANISM and APOLLINARIANISM. It was thought that the NICENE CREED arose from this council.

Constantinople, Second Council of (553). The fifth Oecumenical Council. After the Council of CHALCEDON serious disputes arose between the Antiochene and Alexandrian Schools dividing the Eastern Church. JUSTINIAN called the Second Council at Constantinople, which endeavoured to reconcile the conflicting schools of thought as to the nature of Jesus Christ. Fifteen anathemas were issued against the teachings of ORIGEN and Evagrius and the Alexandrian viewpoint was ratified.

Constantinople, Third Council of (680–1). The sixth decumenical Council. It produced a 'Definition of Faith' that the CURIA had 'piously given its full assent to the Five Holy Oecumenical Synods'. It was concerned with, and condemned, the MONOTHELITES and anathematized Pope Honorius.

Constitution. Apostolic Constitutions. A comprehensive rule in eight books concerning church doctrines and customs. Of unknown authorship, they are probably of Syrian origin and probably date from the 4th century. They are certainly post-Apostolic.

Consubstantiation. Having the same substance of essence. The doctrine of Christ's presence in the EUCHARIST, his divine nature being consubstantial with the bread and wine. In the TRINITY the Three Persons are consubstantial. *Cp.* TRANSUBSTANTIATION.

Consummatum est (Lat.). It is finished; the last words of our Lord on the CROSS (*John* xix, 30).

Contakion. *See* KONTAKION.

Conval, St (d. *c.* 630, f.d. 28 September). Said to have been the son of an Irish chieftain and a disciple of St KENTIGERN, he sailed on a stone from Ireland to Scotland. The stone had magical properties and healed people and cattle who touched it.

Convent (Lat. *conventus,* an assembly). A religious community and the buildings in which the community lives; the term is more usually applied to a house of nuns.

Conventicle. The word was applied by the early Christians to their meeting places and inevitably acquired the derogatory sense of a clandestine meeting. With the advent of Protestantism in England it came to be applied to the meetings and meeting-places of DISSENTERS.
Conventicle Act. In 1593 such an Act was passed containing severe penalties against those attending religious conventicles. The better-known Act of 1664 forbade religious conventicles of more than five persons except in accordance with the BOOK OF COMMON PRAYER. It was repealed in 1812.

Conversion (Lat. *conversio,* a changing round). A change from one state to another; in religion a change from one belief to another. In Christianity to be changed from a state of sin to one of holiness. In EVANGELICAL and REVIVALISTIC meetings it is applied to the sudden realization and acceptance of Christ as Saviour, a conversion by the HOLY SPIRIT. *See also* BORN AGAIN CHRISTIANS.

Convocation. In the ANGLICAN CHURCH (*see* CHURCH OF ENGLAND) there are the provincial COUNCILS of CANTERBURY and York, divided into the Upper House, comprising the archbishop and bishops, and the Lower House of those elected and ex-officio representative of the clergy. Convocation assembles annually at the opening of Parliament.

Cope. A long, semicircular vestment worn by priests in procession over the SURPLICE or ALB; it has no sleeves and is fastened across the breast by a clasp. It is usually elaborately embroidered. It is also worn at solemn LAUDS and VESPERS.

Copts. Christian descendants of the Ancient Egyptians who became MONOPHYSITES and JACOBITES and who have retained the patriarchal chair of Alexandria since the Council of Chalcedon in 451, which still has nominal jurisdiction over the Ethiopian Church. Coptic ceased to be a living language in the 16th or early 17th century but is still used in their liturgy. The word is derived from the Gr. *Aigyptos* which became *Qibt* after the 7th-century Arab invasion. Coptic tradition says that the Church was founded by St MARK at Alexandria. The head of the Church is the Patriarch of Alexandria and the clergy consists of bishops, archpriests, priests and deacons. They may marry before ordination but may not marry a second time. Prayer should be undertaken seven times a day and fasts are frequent and severe. Images are not permitted in churches but sacred pictures are allowed. There is a monastic system of monks and nuns. CIRCUMCISION is practised and there is a considerable ancient Jewish influence evident.

Cordelier (*i.e.* cord-wearer). Franciscan Observantists or 'brethren of more strict observance' are called Cordeliers in France on account of their girdles of knotted cord (*see* FRANCISCANS). The story is that when these Minorites repulsed an army of infidels, St LOUIS of France (Louis IX, 1226–70) is reputed to have asked who those *gens de cordeliés* (corded people) were. From this they received their name.

Cornerstone. A large stone laid at the base of a building to strengthen the two walls forming a right-angle. In figurative use, Christ is called (*Eph.* ii, 20) the chief corner-stone because He united the Jews and Gentiles into one family; and daughters are called corner-stones (*Ps.* cxliv 12) because, as wives and mothers, they unite together two families.

Corporal. A white square of linen cloth used to cover the elements in the EUCHARIST.

Corpus Christi. A church festival kept on the Thursday after TRINITY SUNDAY, in honour of the Blessed Sacrament. It was instituted by Pope Urban IV in 1264. It was the regular time for the performance of religious dramas by the trade guilds and in England, many of the Corpus Christi plays of York, Coventry, and Chester are extant.

Cosmas and Damian, SS (date unknown, f.d. 27 September, 1 July, or 1 November in the East). Reputed to have been two surgeons and physicians, twin brothers, known as 'the holy moneyless ones', as they took no fees. They treated both people and animals. Little is known of them except for their martyrdom at Cyrrhus in Syria. They were said to have survived being cast into the sea, stoned and crucified, then were finally beheaded. Many legends and miracles have been associated with them; one said that they amputated a cancerous leg from a Moor and grafted on a white one, so that the man woke to find he had one black and one white leg, this was the subject of a painting by Fra Angelico. The brothers are patron saints of surgeons and barbers and were patrons of the Medici family, several of whom adopted the name of Cosmo. In art they are depicted holding a box of ointment, a lancet or other surgical instruments, sometimes a pestle and mortar.

Cotta. A shortened SURPLICE with a square neck, worn by choristers in place of the fuller surplice.

Cottolengo, St Joseph (1780–1842, f.d. 29 April). Born at Bra, Piedmont, and ordained priest in 1811, becoming a canon in 1818, he founded the Little House of Divine providence, caring for the sick and poor along the lines of St VINCENT DE PAUL. He opened hospitals and houses for the disabled and afflicted of every kind, catering for their spiritual as well as physical needs, running his work on faith that their financial needs would be provided. He died of typhoid fever at Chieri. He was canonized in 1934.

Councils. *See* OECUMENICAL.

Counter Reformation. *See* REFORMATION.

Countess of Huntingdon. *See* HUNTINGDONIANS.

Court of Arches. *See* ARCHES.

Covenanters. A term applied to those Scottish PRESBYTERIANS subscribing to various bonds or covenants for the security and advancement of their cause. The first was entered into by the Lords of the Congregation in 1557 and another by ordinance of King James VI in 1581. In 1638 the National Covenant was directed against the Laudian prayer-book imposed by Charles I. In 1643 a Solemn League and Covenant pledged the Scots and their English Parlimentarian allies to preserve Presbyterianism in Scotland and to establish it in England and Ireland.

The name Covenanter is particularly applied to those who adhered to the Covenants after they were declared unlawful in 1662. Between the Restoration and the Revolution of 1688 they were harried and proscribed but exhibited a brave and often fanatical resistance. *See* CAMERONIANS.

Coventry Mysteries. Miracle plays supposed to have been acted at CORPUS CHRISTI at Coventry until 1591. Called *Ludus Coventriae* by Sir Robert Bruce, Cotton's librarian in the time of James I, their special connexion with Coventry or Corpus Christi is doubtful, although there are two such plays extant, the play of the Shearman and Tailors, and the play of the Weavers. *See also* MYSTERY.

Cowl. The hood attached to a monk's habit, or, in an earlier meaning, a garment with a hood.

Cowley Fathers. An ANGLO-CATHOLIC order of The Society of Mission Priests of St John the Evangelist, founded in 1865 at Cowley, near Oxford, by R. M. Benson. It is the oldest such Anglican foundation for men.

Cradle Crown. In mediaeval England a fine paid by a priest (in lieu of penance) for fathering a child in his house and keeping a concubine. *Cp.* SIN RENT.

Cranmer, Thomas (1490–1556). Regarded as the founder of the REFORMATION in England. Appointed Archbishop of Canterbury by Henry VIII in 1532 when Henry broke with the Papacy, Cranmer instituted the CHURCH OF ENGLAND and the BOOK OF COMMON PRAYER. He continued in office through the reign of Edward VI, then was involved in the Lady Jane Grey plot and was condemned for treason. He was tried for heresy of which he was found guilty and excommunicated. He signed a recantation but later repudiated it under Mary and was burnt at the stake.

Cranmer's Bible. *See* BIBLE, THE ENGLISH.

Creationism. Originating in a FUNDAMENTALIST environment in the USA, creationism is based on the belief that the world was created at a relatively modern period, in six days of twenty-four hours, and was later subject to a universal flood as described in *Genesis* in the OLD TESTAMENT. Rejecting the Darwinian theory of evolution, fundamentalists, led by William Jennings Bryan, demanded a ban on the teaching of biological evolution in schools. This led to the famous Scopes ('Monkey') trial in 1925, which resulted in a serious setback for the Creationist Movement and its subsequent decline. Since then 'Creationist Science' has been propounded by fundamentalist and EVANGELICAL Christians who established a Creation Research Society in 1963 and endeavoured to make it compulsory for schools to teach Scientific Creationism wherever biological evolutionary theories were taught. Though American in origin, Creationism has adherents worldwide among fundamentalists and evangelicals.

Creatura Christi, or **Creature.** At one time newly-born children, in danger of dying before the arrival of a priest, were often baptized by a midwife. In the flurry of the moment mistakes could occur over the sex of the child, and to avoid the possibility of boys being baptized with girls' names, or the reverse, midwives often named them *Creature* or *Creatura Christi*—Christ's Creature being suitable in either case.

Credence Table. The table near the altar on which the bread and wine are placed before they are consecrated. In former times food was placed on a credence table to be tasted prior to being set before the guests, to assure them that the meat was not poisoned (Ital. *credenza,* a shelf or buffet).

Credo (Lat.). A statement of belief. Literally 'I believe'.

Credo quia impossibile (Lat.). I believe it because it is impossible. A paradox ascribed to St Augustine, but founded on a passage in Tertullian's *De Carne Christi, IV*:

Credibile est, quia ineptum est … certum est quia impossibile.

Crib. A barred wooden manger for animal fodder, in which, according to *Luke* ii, 7 the Christ Child was laid at birth. It is now a CHRISTMAS custom in the Western Church to have a model of the NATIVITY placed in the church on Christmas Eve. A stable scene is represented with the crib and the Child, the VIRGIN MARY and St JOSEPH surrounded by cattle, shepherds and ANGELS. The figures of the MAGI are added at EPIPHANY.

Crispin and Crispianus (f.d. 25 October). Shoemakers who became patron saints of their craft. It is said that the two brothers, born at Rome, went to Soissons in France to propagate the Christian religion, and they maintained themselves wholly by making and mending shoes. They were martyred in *c*. 286.

St Crispin's Day. 25 October, the day of the battle of Agincourt, Shakespeare makes Crispin Crispian one person, and not two brothers. Hence Henry V says to his soldiers:

And Crispin Crispian shall ne'er go by—
But we in it shall be remembered.
Henry V, IV, iii

St Crispin's holiday. Every Monday, with those who begin the working week on Tuesday, still a common practice with some butchers, fishmongers, etc.; a no-work day with shoemakers.

St Crispin's lance. A shoemaker's awl.

Crockford. The popular name for *Crockford's Clerical Directory*, published since 1838 and first compiled by John Crockford. It is a reference book of all the clergy of the CHURCH OF ENGLAND and of the other churches in communion with the see of Canterbury.

Cromwell's Bible. *See* BIBLE, THE ENGLISH.

Crosier, or **Crozier** (from L., Lat. *crocia*; connected with our *crook*; confused with Fr. *croisier* from *crois*, a cross). The pastoral staff of an abbot or BISHOP, and sometimes applied to an archbishop's staff, which terminates in a cross and not in a crook as does the bishop's crosier.

A bishop turns his staff outwards to denote his wider authority; an abbot turns it inwards to show that his authority is limited to his own convent. The abbot covers his staff with a veil when walking in the presence of a bishop, his superior.

Cross. The cross is not solely a Christian symbol originating with the crucifixion of the Redeemer. In Carthage it was used for ornamental purposes; runic crosses were set up by the Scandinavians as boundary marks, and were erected over the graves of kings and heroes. Cicero tells us (*De Divinatione*, ii, 27, and 80, 81) that the augur's staff with which they marked out the heaven was a cross; the Egyptians employed it as a sacred symbol, and two buns marked with a cross were discovered at Herculaneum. It was also a sacred symbol among the Aztecs; in Cozumel it was an object of worship; at Tabasco it symbolized the god of rain. It was one of the emblems of Quetzalcoatl, as lord of the four cardinal points, and the four winds that blow therefrom.

The cross of the crucifixion is said to have been made of palm, cedar, olive, and cypress, to signify the four quarters of the globe.

In his *Monasteries of the Levant* (1848) Curzon gives the legend that Solomon cut down a cedar and buried it on the spot where the pool of Bethesda stood later. A few days before the crucifixion the cedar floated to the surface of the pool, and was used as the upright of the Saviour's cross.

Constantine's Cross. It is said that Constantine on his march to ROME saw a luminous cross in the sky with the motto *In hoc vinces*, by this [sign] conquer. In the night before the battle of Saxa Rubra (312) he was commanded in a vision to inscribe the cross and motto on the shields of his soldiers. He obeyed the voice and prevailed. The LABARUM of Constantine was not really in the form of a cross but a monogram ☧ (XPI) formed of the first three letters of the word *Christ* in Greek. The legend of the Dannebrog is similar and there are others. The Scots are said to have adopted St ANDREW's cross because it appeared in the heavens the night before Achaius, King of the Scots, and Hungus, King of the Picts, defeated Athelstan.

The cross as a mystic emblem may be reduced to the four following:

1. **The Greek cross,** found on Assyrian tablets, Egyptian and Persian monuments, and on Etruscan pottery.
2. **The crux decussata,** generally called St ANDREW's cross, an x-shaped cross. Quite common in ancient sculpture.
3. **The Latin cross,** or **crux immissa**. This symbol is found on coins, monuments, and medals long before the Christian era.
4. **The tau cross** or **crux commissa**. Very ancient indeed. It is also the cross of St ANTHONY.

True Cross. *See* THE INVENTION OF THE CROSS.

Creeping to the Cross. The GOOD FRIDAY ceremony of the *Veneration of the Cross* was commonly so called in England, when priest and people kneel and kiss the cross on the sanctuary steps. The custom derives from the venera-

tion of the True Cross at Jerusalem. *See* THE INVENTION OF THE CROSS.

On Good Friday above all in holy Church men creep to the church and worship the cross.
Dives and Pauper (printed by Wynkyn de Worde in 1496)

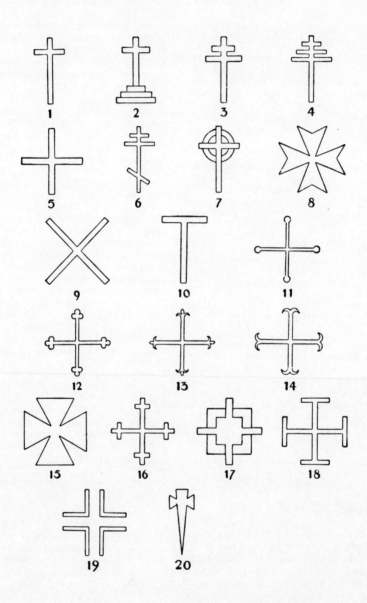

CROSSES.—1. Latin.   2. Calvary.   3. Patriarchal, Archiepiscopal, Lorraine.
4. Papal.   5. Greek.   6. Russian.   7. Celtic.   8. Maltese.   9. St. Andrew's.
10. Tau.   11. Pommé.   12. Botonné.   13. Fleury.   14. Moline.   15. Patté.
16. Crosslet.   17. Quadrate.   18. Potent.   19. Voided and couped.   20 Patté fiché.

The Invention of the Cross. Until its abolition by Pope John XXIII in 1960, a church festival held on 3 May, in commemoration of the finding (Lat. *invenire*, to find) of the 'true cross of Christ' by St HELENA. At her direction, after a long and difficult search in the neighbourhood of the HOLY SEPULCHRE (which had been over-built with heathen temples), the remains of the three buried crosses were found. These were applied to a sick woman, and that which affected her cure was declared the True Cross. The Empress had this enclosed in a silver shrine (after having taken a large piece to ROME) and placed in a church built on the spot for the purpose.

The Judgment of the Cross. An ordeal instituted in the reign of CHARLEMAGNE. The plaintiff and defendant were required to cross their arms upon their breast; and he who could hold out the longest gained the suit.

The Stations of the Cross. *See under* STATION.

To take the Cross. In mediaeval times to take the pledge to become a crusader. *See* CRUSADES.

Veneration of the Cross. *See* CREEPING TO THE CROSS.

Cross-roads, Burial at. All excluded from holy rites (criminals and suicides) were at one time buried at cross-roads. The ancient Teutonic peoples used such places for holding sacrifice and they thus by association came to be places of execution.

CROSSES.—1. Latin. 2. Calvary. 3. Patriarchal, Archiepiscopal, Lorraine. 4. Papal. 5. Greek. 6. Russian. 7. Celtic. 8. Maltese. 9. St Andrew's. 10. Tau. 11. Pommé. 12. Botonné. 13. Fleury. 14. Moline. 15. Patté. 16. Crosslet. 17. Quadrate. 18. Potent. 19. Voided and couped. 20. Patté fiché. 21. Fylfot, Swastika.

Crouchmas. An old name for the festival of the INVENTION OF THE CROSS (*see under* CROSS), also for ROGATION Sunday and Rogation week. 'Crouch', here from Lat. *crux,* means cross.

From bull-cow fast,
Till Crouchmas be past.

TUSSER: *May Remembrances*

Crown. The Crown of St Stephen. *See under* STEPHEN, St.

Crown of Thorns. The crown of Christ upon the Cross.

Crozier. *See* CROSIER.

Crucifix. An image of Christ on the CROSS, seen in all CATHOLIC churches, in some Lutheran churches, in wayside SHRINES in Catholic countries and carried about in processions and on the person.

Cruets. The small vessels for wine or water brought to the ALTAR at the EUCHARIST.

Crusades. Wars undertaken by Christians in the late Middle Ages to secure the right of Christian pilgrims to visit the Holy Sepulchre and to recover the HOLY LAND from its Muslim conquerors. The name is derived from the CROSS which the Crusaders wore on their dress. Ideas of chivalry as well as hopes of material gain were prominent. According to Matthew Paris, each nation had its special colour, which was *red* for France; *white* for England; *green* for Flanders; *blue* or *azure* for Italy; *gules* for Spain; for Scotland, a *St Andrew's cross*; for the Knights TEMPLAR, *red on white. See* TO TAKE THE CROSS *under* CROSS; PALMER. There were eight principal crusades:

1. Proclaimed by Urban II in 1095. The futile expeditions under PETER THE HERMIT and Walter the Penniless were destroyed by the Turks, but the main expedition (1096–99) under Raymond of Toulouse, Robert of Normandy, and Godfrey of Bouillon, ended with the capture of Jerusalem. The Latin Kingdom of Jerusalem was set up in 1100 under Baldwin I.

2. After the loss of Edessa an unsuccessful expedition (1147–49) was promoted by St BERNARD under the leadership of the Emperor Conrad III and Louis VII of France.

3. Inspired by the fall of Jerusalem in 1187, and led by Frederick Barbarossa, Philip Augustus of France and Richard I of England. Begun in 1188, it reached a stalemate in 1192.

4. Promoted by Innocent III in 1202 and led by Thibaut of Champagne and Baldwin of Flanders it was diverted, in spite of the Pope's prohibitions, into an attack on Constantinople. Baldwin became the first Latin Emperor of Constantinople in 1204.

5. Proclaimed by Innocent III for 1217 to recover Jerusalem. The main force was directed against Egypt. Damietta was taken but given up in 1221.

6. The Emperor Frederick II obtained Nazareth, Bethlehem and Jerusalem by negotiation (1222–29), although he was under excommunication at the time, but was absolved on his return.

7. Followed the loss of Jerusalem in 1244. It was organized and led by St LOUIS (Louis IX) of France in 1248. The main expedition against Egypt led to his capture in 1250. After release he made fruitless efforts to recover the Holy Land and returned home in 1254.

8. The Last Crusade. Undertaken by St Louis, Charles of Anjou, and Prince Edward of England. St Louis died in 1270 at Tunis and the project finally petered out in 1272.

The Children's Crusade of 1212 was due to misguided zeal. There were two main expeditions. Some 40,000 German children under one Nicholas, set off over the Alps for Italy. Only a few reached Genoa and ROME, where Innocent III ordered them home. Some hundreds possibly sailed from Brindisi to disappear from history. Another 30,000 French children, under Stephen of Cloyes, set out for Marseilles and about 5,000 were eventually offered passage by scoundrelly ship masters only to be wrecked or sold as slaves to the Muslims.

Crutched Friars. Crutched is the Lat. *cruciati,* crossed, from the cross at the top of their staves, later embroidered on their dress. They were a mendicant order established in Italy by 1169 and followed an Augustinian rule. They arrived in England in 1244 and the order was suppressed by the POPE in 1656.

Crux. A knotty point, an essential point, that on which a decision depends. It does not refer to the CROSS as an instrument of punishment, but to the crossing of two lines, called a *node* or knot; hence trouble or difficulty. *Quæ te mala crux agitat?* (Plautus); What evil cross distresses you?—i.e. what difficulty, what trouble are you under?

Crux ansata. *See* TAU CROSS *under* CROSS.

Crux decussata. *See* CROSS.

Crux pectoralis (Lat. *pectus,* breast). A cross suspended over the breast usually worn by BISHOPS, abbots and CARDINALS.

Crypt (Gr. *krypto,* I hide). An underground room beneath a Church, usually for the provision of a place of burial for SAINTS and MARTYRS.

Culdees. A religious order in Ireland and Scotland from about the 8th century to the 13th, although they continued in Ireland until the REFORMATION. So called from the Old Irish *céle dé* servants of God. They seem to have originated as independent communities of hermits or anchorites and latterly were essentially secular CANONS.

Cumberland Presbyterians. A separatist group formed in Cumberland, Kentucky, in 1810, following a dispute with the Kentucky Synod of the American PRESBYTERIAN Church over the formal requirements for the ministry. Those of the Cumberland presbytery unsuccessfully urged the need to dispense with the usual high educational standards in a frontier environment.

Cunegund, St (*c.* 978–1033, f.d. 3 March). Wife of Emperor Henry II of Germany and the HOLY ROMAN EMPIRE. It was claimed that their childless marriage was due to a vow of CELIBACY, but there is no authority for this belief. The Empress was accused of marital infidelity and was subjected to the trial of walking over redhot ploughshares, from which she emerged unharmed. In art she is depicted as dressed in royal robes, crowned, and either walking over the ploughshares or holding one in her hand.

Curate. *See* CLERICAL TITLES.

Curé de Meudon i.e. Rabelais (*c.* 1495–1553),

who was first a monk, then a physician, then a CANON of St Maur, and lastly (1550) nonresident curé of Meudon.

Curia Romana. The Papal Court at ROME, consisting of Cardinals and the Cardinal Secretary of State; the administrative and judicial institution governing the ROMAN CATHOLIC CHURCH and, by extension, the persons forming a part of it.

Curse. The curse of Cain. One who is always on the move and has no abiding place is said to be 'cursed with the curse of Cain'. The allusion is to God's judgment on Cain after he had slain his brother Abel.

> And now art thou cursed from the earth ... a fugitive and a vagabond shalt thou be in the earth.
> *Gen.* iv, 11–12

Curtal Friar. A curtal was a horse with its tail docked, whence its application to other things that were cut down or shortened. A curtal friar was one who wore a short cloak. In later use, especially by Scott, it acquired a vaguely derisory or belittling significance.

Cuthbert, St (634–87, f.d. 20 March). It is disputed whether Cuthbert, northern England's most popular saint, was Celtic or Anglo-Saxon by birth, but the name suggests that he was from northern England. Most accounts say he was a shepherd, but he was also said to have been of good Northumbrian family. After seeing a vision of St AIDAN conducted to heaven by an ANGEL on the night he had died, Cuthbert entered the monastery at Melrose. Following a period of missionary activity in the North and in the Lowlands of Scotland he became Abbot of Melrose. In 664 he left Melrose for Lindisfarne after the Synod of Whitby and became Prior, but later left to live as a hermit on the lonely isle of Farne. Here he was visited by many pilgrims, attracting people not only by his holiness but by his charm, character and great ability. He was also a great naturalist. Miracles were attributed to him and Bede referred to him as 'the Child of God'. At the request of King Egfrid Cuthbert accepted the bishopric of Hexham but soon left it for that of Lindisfarne. He died at his hermitage on Farne. His body, buried at Lindisfarne, was found to be incorrupt when translated in 1104 and after the Danish raids was removed to Durham Cathedral. The bearers of his relics were said always to have become monks.

St Cuthbert's Beads. Single joints of the articulated stems of encrinites (fossil crinoids), also called *stone lilies.* They are perforated in the centre and bear a fanciful resemblance to a CROSS; hence they were once used for rosaries. Legend relates that the 7th-century St Cuthbert sits at night on a rock in HOLY ISLAND and uses the opposite rock as an anvil while he forges the beads.

Cyrillic Alphabet

St Cuthbert's Duck. The eider duck, so called because it breeds in the Farne Islands.

Cuthburga, St (d. *c.* 725, f.d. 31 August). Daughter of Kenred, King of Wessex and sister to Ine King of Wessex and to Quenburga, she married Aldfrid, King of Northumberland, but they agreed to separate so that Cuthburga could become a nun at Barking. With her sister Quenburga she founded a monastery at Wimborne, in Dorset. She became abbess and ruled the nunnery with the utmost strictness, allowing no communication with the outside world and communicating herself only through a small grille.

Cuthman, St (8th cent., f.d. 8 February). Said to have been a shepherd in Devon or Cornwall, after his father's death he wandered to Steyning, in Sussex, taking with him his bedridden mother, for whom he made a special handcart. At Steyning he built a hut for his mother and himself and erected a church single-handed; there he preached to the people until his death. His memory was revived in 1939 when Christopher Fry wrote the play *The Boy with a Cart.*

Cybi (or **Cuby**), **St** (6th cent., f.d. 13 August in Cornwall, also 5, 6, 7 and 8 November in Wales). A native of Cornwall and grandson of Geraint, he travelled widely and lived in various parts as a hermit in Wales and is particularly associated with evangelistic work in Anglesey. He founded churches and was particularly noted for bringing forth springs and wells, one of which is still called St Cybi's Well; it was used for baptisms and had healing waters.

Cyprian, St (*c.* 200–58, f.d. 14 or 16 September). Thascius Cascilius Cyprianus was from an upper-class Carthaginian family and was converted to Christianity late in life. He had previously taught rhetoric at Carthage, but lost any chance of promotion on becoming a Christian. Soon after his conversion he became a priest, then bishop of Carthage, thus causing some jealousy. He proved an efficient organizer and distinguished himself during the plagues at Carthage. He was banished to Corubis by order of Valerian and suffered martyrdom in 258. He was buried at Carthage but later, in 806, his remains were taken to Arles in France. **Cyprian and Justina, SS** (*c.* 300, f.d. 26 September). Cyprian was reputed to be a magician who attempted to seduce the beautiful Christian Justina, sending devils to tempt her at night, but was himself converted by her; later he became a bishop and she an abbess. They were martyred by being put into boiling pitch but remained unharmed, and were then decapitated. The feast day of the two martyrs was suppressed by the HOLY SEE in 1969, in the reform of the CALENDAR, as one of doubtful authority.

Cyprus. Traditionally founded by St BARNABAS, the Eastern ORTHODOX CHURCH on the island is AUTOCEPHALOUS, independent since 431 and ruled by the Archbishop of Constantia.

Cyr, St *See* QUIRICUS.

Cyril. Cyril of Alexandria, St (376–444, f.d. formerly 9 June (East), 9 February (West), now 27 June). Alexandrian by birth, little is known of his early life. He was a noted theologian, a FATHER OF THE CHURCH and Patriarch of Alexandria in 412, in succession to his uncle Theophilus. Cyril was also famed for his opposition to the heresy of the NESTORIANS in general and to the Bishop of Constantinople in particular and for his persecution of the Jews and pagans which precipitated twelve years of civil war. He was also thought to be responsible for the murder by his monks of the Neo-Platonic woman philosopher Hypatia, when he became jealous of her influence and popularity. She was seized as she was returning home from a lecture. The monks took her to the church of the Caesareans, stripped her and hacked her to pieces with oyster-shells, then burnt the corpse. She is the heroine of Charles Kingsley's eponymous novel.

Cyril of Jerusalem, St (d. *c.* f.d. 18 March). One of the Greek FATHERS OF THE CHURCH, he was a bishop and theologian, but was accused of being a semi-ARIAN and was exiled, returning in 378. He was present at the Council of CONSTANTINOPLE in 381 and *c.* 386. He was patron saint of Jerusalem.

Cyril (827–69) **and Methodius** (815–85), **SS** (f.d. 14 February). Two brothers, known as the Apostles of the Slavs, were born in Thessalonika. Cyril, who had been baptized Constantine, assumed the name of Cyril on becoming a monk shortly before his death; he was librarian at Santa Sophia at CONSTANTINOPLE, while Methodius was governor of a province and later Archbishop of Sirmium. Both were learned men. They were sent as missionaries to Moravia where they translated the LITURGY and parts of the SCRIPTURES into Slavonic and invented the Glagolitic alphabet from which the CYRILLIC form of letters was derived, now in Russian, Bulgarian and Serbian usage. In 1981 Pope John Paul II declared them joint patrons of Europe with St BENEDICT.

Cyrillic Alphabet. The form of letters traditionally used by the Slavonic peoples, a form of the Greek alphabet invented by two brothers, the apostles of the Slavs, Constantine and Methodius of Thessalonika. Constantine was more popularly known by his religious name of CYRIL.

D

Dalmatic (Lat. *dalmatica* (*vestis*), (robe) of Dalmatian wool). A loose-sleeved liturgical vestment, originally made of Dalmation wool, worn by officiating deacons and by bishops. A similar robe is worn by the sovereign at coronation. The robe is sometimes partially slit at the sides and embroidered at the neck, cuffs and hem.

Damasus, St (*c.* 304–84, f.d. 11 December). Son of a priest of Spanish descent, he became a deacon and followed Liberius as Pope. There was great opposition to his election as bishop of ROME and Damasus was accused of violence, corruption and bribery. He was noted for his suppression of the heresies of the ARIANS, DONATISTS and MACEDONIANS and for his support for the work of St JEROME, at one time his secretary, and for the restoration of the CATACOMBS and the tombs of the Roman martyrs.

Damian, St. *See* COSMAS AND DAMIAN.
Damian, P. *See* PETER DAMIAN.

Damnation. Condemnation to eternal punishment in HELL (*Matt.* xxv, 46).

Dan. From Dan to Beersheba. From one end of the kingdom to the other; everywhere. The phrase is scriptural, Dan being the most northern and Beersheba the most southern cities of the HOLY LAND.

Dancing Sun. A phenomenon reported to have occurred in various places in Europe (notably the Ukraine), in Africa, South America, Georgia and Louisiana. The sun was seen to 'dance', this being variously described as spinning, pulsating, dropping or zig-zagging and was said to have a darker centre with light and prismatic colours streaming from the edges. It was possible to look directly into it for a considerable period without retinal damage, a million pilgrims having gazed at it for fifteen minutes. Miracles of healing, physical, mental and spiritual, were claimed and, though mainly CATHOLIC, the phenomena were seen by people of different religions and sects, by journalists and sightseers. In 1984, at a Croat enclave near Mostar, predominantly Eastern ORTHODOX, CATHOLIC and Muslim, the Dancing Sun was accompanied by visions of the VIRGIN MARY, said to have made exhortations to peace and given warnings of evil to come. The visions appeared mainly at Marian shrines; such apparitions have been reported in the Ukraine from the Middle Ages, often being associated with springs and healing waters.

Daniel the Stylite, St (409–93, f.d. 11 December). One of the first followers of St SIMEON STYLITES, he was born at Maratha in Mesopotamia and entered a monastery at a very early age. When later the monks wished to make him abbot he refused, then went to consult St Simeon and received instruction from him. Daniel then retired to a deserted temple, inhabited by devils, near CONSTANTINOPLE, making a hermitage there and fighting the devils; he remained there for nine years. At the death of St Simeon Daniel inherited his cloak and followed his lifestyle, taking up residence on a pillar by the Bosphorus. Later he lived on a structure of two pillars with a shelter on top. Here he was ordained priest by the patriarch Gennadius. From his pillars Daniel preached to the crowds who gathered, healing the sick and being consulted by the Emperor Leo I, by Zeno and by the patriarch of Constantinople. He was greatly venerated and when he died at the age of eighty-four he was buried in the chapel at the foot of his pillar.
Daniel, St. *See* DEINIOL.

David. The youngest son of Jesse and slayer of GOLIATH. He temporarily rose in favour through comforting Saul by his skill as a harpist. Saul's eventual jealousy led to David's flight, effected with the aid of his wife Michal and her brother Jonathan, both children of Saul. After many vicissitudes David eventually became King of Israel (I *Sam.* xvi–xxxi, II *Sam.*; I *Kings* i–ii). The Davidic authorship of the *Psalms* has largely been discounted.
St David, or **Dewi Sant.** Patron SAINT of Wales, whose day is 1 March. Historical information is scanty. He lived in the 6th century and died *c.* 600, and as the chief bishop of South Wales moved the ecclesiastical centre from Caerleon to Menevia (St David's). Legend is far more prolific and says that he was the son of Xantus, prince of Cereticu (Cardiganshire), and became an ascetic in the Isle of Wight; that he visited Jerusalem, confuted Pelagius, and

was preferred to the see of Caerleon. Geoffrey of Monmouth makes him the uncle of King Arthur.

David of Scotland, St (*c.* 108–1153, f.d. 24 May). Sixth and youngest son of Malcolm III of Scotland and St MARGARET OF SCOTLAND, he became Earl of Northampton and Huntingdon and Prince of Cumbria, then in 1124 King of Scotland, where he replaced the Celtic tribal system with feudalism. He founded bishoprics, numerous churches and monasteries, and set an example of pious life and giving of alms, these often given in person. He organized the Church in Scotland, keeping it in touch with ROME. He was buried at Dunfermline and his cult flourished until the REFORMATION.

David of Sweden, St (d. *c.* 1080, f.d. 15 July or 25 June). An English monk who went to Sweden to work with St SIGFRID, bishop of Vaxio and Apostle of Sweden. He is also called David of Munkthorp, having built a monastery there, and was also reputedly the first bishop of Vasteras. He was active in extensive missionary work and hoped to die as a martyr, but his death occurred peacefully and quietly of old age. Miracles were reported at his tomb.

Deacon. A member of the CLERGY, the lowest order in the Christian ministry dating from Apostolic times; literally a servant, one who ministered to the poor and who superintended church property and funds. Deacons were appointed by the APOSTLES to 'serve tables' and distribute charity; they could be laymen who assisted with secular affairs or they could be lay preachers. Later a deacon was ordained by the laying on of hands by a bishop and this became a preliminary step to full priesthood. In PRESBYTERIAN and FREE CHURCHES the deacon functions as a layman, assisting the minister.

Deaconess. A woman ordained to assist in the parish and engage in religious work, usually wearing a distinctive dress. In the early church deaconesses were chosen from widows and spinsters of at least forty years of age; they arranged the AGAPE, or love feast, cared for the sick and took part in adult baptisms of women for the sake of decorum. The office fell into disuse in the 6th century, but was reinstituted in the CHURCH OF ENGLAND in 1861 and was then the highest office for women. In 1994 women were admitted into the priesthood. There are deaconesses in the CHURCH OF SCOTLAND and FREE CHURCHES.

Dead Sea. The Palestinian Salt Sea or Sea of the Plain of the OLD TESTAMENT, in the ancient Vale of Siddim; called by the Romans *Mare Mortuum* and *Lacus Asphaltites*. It is about 46 miles long and 5 to 9 miles wide and is fed by the Jordan from the north, but has seemingly no outlet. The water is of bluish-green colour and its surface is about 1,300 ft. below the level of the Mediterranean. The northern end is some 1,300 ft. deep and its salt content is 25 per cent while that of sea-water is usually between 3 and 4 per cent. It supports no life other than microbes and a few very low organisms.

Dead Sea Scrolls. In 1947 a Bedouin goatherd, Muhammed the Wolf, made the first scroll discoveries in a cave at the N.W. end of the Dead Sea, since when some hundreds more have been found and more discoveries are probable. Most scholars accept them as originating from the monastery of the Jewish sect of the ESSENES at Qumran. There is still much controversy over their interpretation but it is expected that these manuscripts (from the period 150 BC to AD 70) will add very considerably to the understanding of Old Testament textual criticism and the background of the NEW TESTAMENT.

Dean (Lat. *decanus*, one set over ten). The ecclesiastical dignitary who presides over the CHAPTER of a cathedral or COLLEGIATE CHURCH, this having formerly consisted of ten canons. In the more recent foundations decanal functions are carried out by a provost. The Bishop of London is an *ex officio* Dean of the Province of Canterbury and Dean of the Chapels Royal. The Dean of the Chapel Royal of Scotland (Holyrood), is also Dean of the Order of the Thistle. The Dean of Christchurch, Oxford, is head of the college and also Dean of the cathedral. The Dean of King's College, London, controls the Theological Department.

Dean of the Arches. The judge presiding over the Court of ARCHES, formerly at Bow Church, once a PECULIAR.

Deans of Peculiars. Once numerous, and including those of Collegiate Churches such as Westminster and Windsor, surviving examples are those of Battle, Bocking, Jersey and Guernsey. *See* COLLEGIATE CHURCH; PECULIAR.

Dean of the Sacred College, is the senior cardinal-bishop who is given the title of Bishop of Ostia and Velletri. He ranks next to the POPE in the hierarchy. *See* CARDINAL.

Rural Dean. An incumbent who assists in administering part of an archdeaconry. An ancient office effectively revived from the mid-19th century.

Decade. The group of ten beads of the ROSARY with their corresponding prayers, the Hail Marys, an Our Father and Gloria.

Decalogue (Gr. *deka logos*, ten words or sentences). The name given by the Greek Fathers to the TEN COMMANDMENTS referred to in *Exodus* xxxiv, 28 and elsewhere. They have sometimes been divided into those which define our duty to God and those which state our duty to others. The 'classic' version occurs in *Exodus* xx, 2–17; another is found in *Deuteronomy* v, 6–21. The form adopted by the CHURCH OF ENGLAND and most Protestant churches is that which Josephus says was used by his Jewish contemporaries.

Decani. The part of the choir stalls in a cathedral or church where the DEAN sits. Its opposite side is the CANTORIS. The terms are used in antiphonal singing.

Declaration of Indulgence. *See* INDULGENCE.

Decretals. The name given to papal decrees or letters which embody decisions in ecclesiastical law.

The False, or **Forged Decretals** aimed at enhancing the position of BISHOPS and papacy and strengthening the Church against inroads by the temporal power. The collection contains many spurious letters and documents, ranging from the 1st to the 7th century, including the pretended DONATION OF CONSTANTINE, intermingled with, and thus supported by, genuine decretals. They appeared in the mid-9th century and were issued under the name of Isidore Mercator. They were first seriously challenged in the 15th century and finally discredited by the PROTESTANT minister David Blondel in 1620. They are also known as the ISIDORIAN DECRETALS.

The Isidorian Decretals. The False Decretals wrongly assigned to Isidore, Archbishop of Seville, a noted 7th-century scholar and codifier of canon law. They were probably compiled in France and accepted by Pope Nicholas I. Since their forgery became manifest they commonly came to be called the *Pseudo-Isidorian Decretals*.

Defender of the Faith (Lat. *fidei defensor*). A title given to Henry VIII by Pope Leo X (11 October 1521) for his treatise *Assertio Septem Sacramentorum* attacking Luther's teachings. The initials 'F.D.' continuously appeared on the British coinage from the reign of George I.

Defenders. An association of Irish Catholics (1784–98), formed in Northern Ireland in opposition to the Peep-of-the-day Boys. In 1795 a pitched battle was fought between the two and the Defenders suffered severe losses.

Degrees, Songs of. Another name for the GRADUAL PSALMS.

Dei Gratia (Lat.). By the grace of God. As early as *c*. 690 we find 'I, Ine, by God's grace King of the West Saxons', and in an ordinance of William I, '*Willelmus gratia Dei Rex Anglorum*'. It was first used on the Great Seal by William II and all Great Seals from the reign of Edward I.

It still appears on British coins, where it was originally introduced on the gold coins of Edward III in 1344.

The style was also sometimes used by the Archbishops of Canterbury and York, until as late as the 17th century, and is still so used by BISHOPS of the ROMAN CATHOLIC CHURCH.

Dei Judicium (Lat.). The judgement of God; so the judgement by ordeal was called, because it was taken as certain that God would deal rightly with appellants.

Deiniol (**Daniel**), **St** (6th cent., f.d. 11 September). Also known as Deniol Wyn, or the Blessed, and as 'of the Bangors' since he founded the monasteries of Bangor Fawr and Bangor Iscoed, he was reputedly the first bishop of Bangor. He was said to be a descendant of a Celtic chieftain of North Britain. He assisted St DAVID at the Synod of Brefi which was thought to be concerned with the heresy of Pelagianism. He was buried at Bardsey and the mediaeval cathedral of Bangor is dedicated to him.

Deist. *See* THEIST.

Deluge. The Biblical story of the flood (*Gen.* vi, vii, viii) has its counterpart in a variety of mythologies. In Babylonia it appears in the 11th tablet of the Gilgamesh Epic, but on a higher level of civilization, for Utnapishtim takes both craftsmen and treasure into his ark.

Demetrius (**or Dmitry**) **of Rostov, St** (1651–1709, f.d. 28 October). Of wealthy Cossack family, Demetrius, or Dmitry, was a priest and monk and became bishop of Rostov. He was a noted scholar, educationalist and preacher who left his mark on Russian religious literature, writing dramas and verse and a *Spiritual Alphabet* detailing the duties of the clergy towards their flocks. He accompanied Mazeppa, the Cossack military leader (the hero of Byron's poem of that name) to Moscow. He was canonized by the Russian ORTHODOX CHURCH in 1757.

Demiurge (Gr. *demiourgos*, artisan, handicraftsman, etc.). In the language of the Platonists, that mysterious agent which made the world and all that it contains. The Logos, or Word, spoken of by St JOHN in the first chapter of his gospel, is the *Demiurgus* of Platonizing Christians. Among the GNOSTICS, JEHOVAH (as an eon or emanation of the Supreme Being) is the Demiurge. *See* MARCIONITES.

Denarius Dei (Lat. God's penny). An earnest of a bargain, which was given to the Church or poor.

Denys or **Dionysius, St,** (d. *c.* 272, f.d. 9 October). The apostle to the Gauls and a traditional patron saint of France, said to have been beheaded at Paris. Legendarily, after martyrdom he carried his head in his hands for two miles and laid it on the spot where stands the cathedral bearing his name. The tale may have arisen from an ancient painting of his martyrdom in which the artist placed the head between the hands so that the martyr might be identified. One tradition said that he was born in Italy, another that he was an Athenian and bishop of Athens, sent by St CLEMENT on a mission to Paris where he carried out a successful evangelization but was persecuted, exposed to wild beasts, put in a fiery furnace, then crucified, from all of which he emerged unharmed, but was finally beheaded on the Martyrs' Mount (Montmartre) together with a priest and deacon, their bodies being thrown into the Seine. These legends were fabricated by Hilduin, abbot of St Denys, in about the year 800; he also confused him with DIONYSIUS THE AREOPAGITE. The bodies of the martyrs were retrieved from the river and a tomb was built; this became the site of the Abbey of St Denys, later the burial place of the French kings.

Deo gratias (Lat.). Thanks to God. *Cp.* DEI GRATIA.
Deo juvante, or adjuvante (Lat.). With God's help.
Deo volente (Lat.). God be willing; by God's will; usually contracted into D.V.

Depart. Literally, to part thoroughly; to separate effectually. The marriage service in the old prayer-books had 'till death us depart', which had been corrupted into 'till death us do part'.

'Depart' is sound English for 'part asunder', which was altered to 'do part' in 1661, at the pressing request of the Puritans, who knew as little of the history of their national language as they did of that of their national Church.

J. H. BLUNT: *Annotated Book of Common Prayer*

Derfel Gdarn (the Mighty), St (6th cent., f.d. 5 April). A great Celtic warrior who later in life became a hermit and then abbot of Bardsey. He was founder and patron of Llanderfel where there can still be seen the remains of the wooden statue of him mounted on a large horse and holding a staff. He was greatly venerated by the people who made pilgrimages to him, bearing gifts for which he would deliver them from hell.

Desert Fathers. *See under* FATHER.

Deus vult (Lat. God wills it). The war-cry of the First CRUSADE, enjoined by Pope Urban II because these words were spontaneously used by the crowd in response to his address at Clermont in 1095.

Devil, The. Represented with a cloven foot, because by the Rabbinical writers he is called *seirizzim* (a goat). As the goat is a type of uncleanness, the prince of unclean spirits is aptly represented under this emblem. As the Prince of Evil he is also called SATAN.
The Devil's Advocate. A carping or adverse critic, from *Advocatus Diaboli* (Devil's Advocate). In the ROMAN CATHOLIC CHURCH, the popular name given to the Promoter of the Faith whose duty it is to promote vigorously the arguments against a proposed BEATIFICATION or CANONIZATION. The supporter was (until 1983) called *Advocatus Dei* (God's Advocate).

Dewi Sant. *See* ST DAVID *under* DAVID.

Diaconicon. In the Eastern ORTHODOX CHURCH, an area south of the Sanctuary, in the charge of the deacon, for the storing and cleansing of sacred vessels and vestments; the counterpart of the sacristy in the WESTERN CHURCH.

Dial of Ahaz. The only time-measuring device mentioned in the BIBLE. It was probably a form of sun-clock and its introduction by Ahaz may have been due to his contacts with the Assyrians. It is referred to in II *Kings* xx, 9–11 and *Isa.* xxxviii, 8.

And he brought the shadow ten degrees backward, by which it had gone down in the dial of Ahaz.
II *Kings* xx, ii

Didache (Gr. teaching). An early Christian treatise, also known as *The Teaching of the Twelve Apostles*, probably belonging to the late 1st or early 2nd century. It was discovered in the Patriarchal Library at Constantinople in 1875 and falls into two parts. The first is concerned with moral teachings and is based on an earlier document, seemingly of Jewish origin, called *The Two Ways*, with additions from the Sermon on the Mount, etc. The second part is concerned with church ordinances.

Didymus. This Greek word for a twin was applied to St THOMAS, as the name Thomas in Aramaic means a twin.

Dies Irae (Lat. Day of Wrath). A famous mediaeval hymn on the Last JUDGEMENT, probably the composition of Thomas of Celano (in the Abruzzi), who died *c.* 1255. It is derived from the VULGATE version of *Zeph.* i, 15, and is used by Roman Catholics in the MASS for the Dead and on ALL SOULS' DAY. Scott has introduced the opening into his *Lay of the Last Minstrel* (Canto vi, xxx).

Dies irae, dies illa
Solvet saeclum in favilla.

Digamy. A second marriage, looked upon with disfavour by the early Church, but the Council of NICAEA, in 325, stated that people twice-married should not be excluded from the church. In the Eastern ORTHODOX CHURCH such marriages are forbidden to priests and are generally discouraged, there being a modified nuptial blessing in the service.

Diocese. A district under the authority of a bishop, originally based on the provinces of the Roman Empire.

Dionysius the Areopagite, St (date unknown, f.d. 3 or 9 October). The actual identity of Dionysius (or Denys) the Pseudo-Areopagite is unknown; he was said to be one of St PAUL's converts at Athens (*Acts* xvii, 34) and to have been the first bishop of Athens. The title 'Areopagite' implies that he was a member of the Council of the Areopagus. It is now generally accepted that he belonged to the Severian circles of Syria, and was a monk living about the year 500, associated with the moderate MONOPHYSITES. His mystical writings were inspired by the Neo-Platonic Proclus but he departs from Platonism when he says 'all essence is transcended by the Superessential Indefinite'—the transcendence of God. His work aims at building a bridge between Neo-Platonism and Christianity, the chief works attributed to him are: *Divine Names, Mystical Theology, Heavenly Hierarchy* and *Ecclesiastical Hierarchy*. He has been confused with St DENYS or Denis, patron saint of France, also called Dionysius.

Diophysite. One who holds that the two natures of Christ exist together, both divine and human.

Diptych. A tablet of wood, metal or ivory, of writings or paintings, hinged so as to fold in two wings, usually portraying a sacred subject; originally it was a depiction of those to be remembered at the celebration of the MASS. It could also be used as an altarpiece.

Discalced. *See* BAREFOOTED.

Discharge Bible, The. *See* BIBLE, SOME SPECIALLY NAMED EDITIONS.

Disciples (Lat. *discipulus*, a pupil). The twelve APOSTLES of Christ, or one of the seventy followers mentioned by St LUKE.
Disciples of Christ. *See* CAMPBELLITES.

Discipline, A. A scourge used for penitential purposes.

Before the cross and altar,... a lamp was still burning,... and on the floor lay a discipline, or penitential scourge of small cord and wire, the lashes of which were stained with recent blood.

SCOTT : *The Talisman*, ch. iv

This is a transferred sense of one of the ecclesiastical uses of the word—the mortification of the flesh by penance.
Discipline, Books of. The books which formed the basis of the constitution and procedure of the CHURCH OF SCOTLAND after the REFORMATION. The first was drawn up under John Knox in 1566, and the second, which amplified the first, between 1575 and 1578.

Dismas, St. *See* DYSMAS.

Dispensation (Lat. *dispensatio*, from *dis-* and *pendere*, to dispense, distribute, arrange). The system which God chooses to dispense or establish between himself and man. The dispensation of ADAM was between Adam and God; the dispensation of ABRAHAM, and that of MOSES, were those imparted to these holy men; the GOSPEL dispensation is that explained in the Gospels.
A Papal dispensation. Permission from the POPE to dispense with something enjoined; a licence to do what is forbidden, or to omit what is commanded by the law of the ROMAN CATHOLIC CHURCH.

A Papal dispensation enabled Catherine to wed the brother of her late husband, the younger sovereign himself.

J. R. GREEN: *History of the English People*, ch. vi

Dissenters. In England another name for the NONCONFORMISTS and commonly used from the Restoration until the 19th century, when it gradually fell into disuse.

Distaff. St Distaff's Day. 7 January. So called because the CHRISTMAS festival terminated on Twelfth Day, and on the day following the women returned to their distaffs or daily occupations.

Give St Distaff all the right,
Then give Christmas sport good night,
And next morrow every one
To his own vocation.

(1657)

It is also called Rock Day, 'rock' being an old name for the distaff.

What! shall a woman with a rock drive thee away?
Fye on thee, traitor!

Digby Mysteries

Dives. The name popularly given to the rich man (Lat. *dives*) in the parable of the Rich Man and

LAZARUS (*Luke* xvi, 19).

Lazar and Dives liveden diversely
And diverse guerdon haddon they ther-by.
CHAUCER: *Somnour's Tale*, 169

Divine Office. Daily office of prayer and praise undertaken by CATHOLIC priests, monks and nuns at the CANONICAL HOURS. *See also* OPUS DEI.

The Divine Right of Kings. A theory, of mediaeval origin, that kings reign by divine ordination, was first formulated in a rudimentary way during the struggle between the Papacy and the Empire. It was developed more fully to strengthen the European monarchies when they were later threatened by the activities of PROTESTANT and CATHOLIC extremists and others. Monarchy based on primogeniture was held to be divinely anointed and therefore unquestioning obedience could be demanded from subjects. Monarchs were responsible to God alone and their model was the patriarchal rule portrayed in the OLD TESTAMENT. The theory was expounded fully by James I in his *True Law of Free Monarchies* (1598) and in Sir Robert Filmer's *Patriarcha* (1642—published 1680). Divine Right was destroyed in Great Britain by the Glorious Revolution of 1688.

The Right Divine of Kings to govern wrong.
POPE: *Dunciad*, IV, 188

Divine Service. A service of public worship, usually liturgical in form, but often applied to MATTINS and EVENSONG only.

Divorcement. A Bill of Divorcement is a phrase from former days of divorce procedure. Before the Matrimonial Causes Act, 1857, 'divorce', or in effect judicial separation, could be granted only by the ecclesiastical courts, but remarriage was prohibited except when a special bill was promoted and passed in Parliament for either of the parties. Few could afford such an expensive process. Marriage being indissoluble according to CANON LAW, divorce is not permitted in the CATHOLIC CHURCH, but the Pope may annul marriages on certain grounds. In the CHURCH OF ENGLAND and the Eastern Church canon law allows divorce in special serious issues, such as adultery.

Dmitry. *See* DEMETRIUS.

Docetes. An early GNOSTIC sect, which maintained that Jesus Christ was divine only, and that his visible form, the crucifixion, resurrection, etc., were merely illusions. Christ had no real body on earth, but only a phantom body. The word is Greek and means phantomists.

Doctor. Doctors of the Church. Certain early Christian Fathers, and other saints whose doctrinal writings gained special acceptance and authority.

(a) *Eastern Church.* St Athanasius, who defended the divinity of Christ against the ARIANS; St Basil the Great; St Gregory of Nazianzus; St JOHN CHRYSOSTOM.

(b) *Western Church.* St Alphonsus Liguore; St AMBROSE; St Anselm of Canterbury; St AUGUSTINE of Hippo; St BERNARD of Clairvaux; St Bonaventura; St Francis de Sales; St GREGORY THE GREAT; St Hilary; St JEROME; St THOMAS AQUINAS.

Doctors of Learning, Piety, etc.

Admirable Doctor (*Doctor Admirabilis*) Roger Bacon (*c.* 1214–94).
Angelic Doctor: St Thomas Aquinas (*c.* 1225–74).
Divine Doctor } *Johannes van Ruysbroeck*
Ecstatic Doctor } (1293–1381)
Eloquent Doctor: Peter Aureolus (14th Century).
Evangelic Doctor: John Wyclif (*c.* 1320–84).
Illuminated Doctor: Raymond Lully (1235–1315); Johann Tauler (*c.* 1300–61).
Illustrious Doctor: Adam de Marisco (*d.* 1257).
Invincible Doctor: William of Occam (*c.* 1280–1349).
Irrefragable Doctor: Alexander of Hales (*c.* 1175–1245).
Mellifluous Doctor: St Bernard of Clairvaux (1090–1153).
Perspicuous Doctor: Walter Burley (1275–1345).
Profound Doctor: Thomas Bradwardine (*c.* 1290–1349).
Resolute Doctor: John Baconthorpe (*d.* 1346).
Seraphic Doctor: St Bonaventura (John of Fidanza) 1221–74).
Singular Doctor: William of Occam (*c.* 1280–1349).
Solid Doctor (i.e. sound); Richard Middleton (*fl.* 1280).
Subtle Doctor: Duns Scotus (*c.* 1265–1308).
Universal Doctor. Albert of Cologne or Albertus Magnus (*c.* 1206–80); Alain de Lille (*c.* 1128–1202).
Wonderful Doctor: Roger Bacon (*c.* 1214–94).
See SCHOLASTICISM; SCHOOLMEN.

Doctors' Commons. The association and buildings established on St Bennet's Hill, St Paul's Churchyard, for practitioners of canon and civil law, under the presidency of the DEAN OF THE ARCHES. This self-governing body was established in the 16th century and dissolved after the passing of the Court of Probate Act and the Matrimonial Causes Act of 1857. The buildings were demolished in 1867. The name arises from the fact that the doctors had to dine there four days in each term.

Doctrine. Formulated belief; a creed; that which is taught by the Church in Christianity, from the Lat. *doctrina*, teaching.

Dogma. A DOCTRINE authoritatively asserted; a principle of belief.
Dogmatics. The study and science of systematized Christian DOCTRINES and their theological and philosophical implications.

Dogs. In Christian art and symbolism the dog depicts fidelity and watchfulness and as a guardian of the flock represents the GOOD SHEPHERD, and by extension, a bishop or priest. Black and white dogs denote the order of the DOMINICANS and a dog carrying a torch is depicted with St DOMINIC. Among other saints the dog is an emblem of St BERNARD and is portrayed lying at his feet. St ROCH and his dog, who fed him and licked his wounds, are emblematic of inseparable companions. The dog is also associated with St Wendelin and with Tobias.

Dom (Lat. *dominus*). A title applied in the Middle Ages to the POPE, and later to other Church dignitaries. It is now largely restricted to monks of the BENEDICTINE and CARTHUSIAN Orders. The Sp. *don*, Port. *dom*, and M.E. *dan* are the same word.

Domine, quo vadis? (Lat. Master, whither goest thou?). According to tradition, when St PETER was fleeing from Nero's persecution in Rome, he met Christ on the Appian Way and greeted Our Lord with these words. The reply *'Veno Roman, iterum crucifigi'* (I am coming to Rome to be crucified again) so shamed the apostle that he returned to martyrdom in Rome. The meeting is commemorated by a church on the Appian Way. He is said to have requested to be crucified head downwards and to have given this account when nailed upon the cross. The story is found in the Gnostic *Acts* and other texts and is featured in an historical novel by H. Sienkiewicz, *Quo Vadis?* (1896).

Dominic St., (de Guzman) (1170–1221), the founder of the Dominican Order, or Preaching Friars, noted for his vehemence against the ALBIGENSES and called by the POPE 'Inquisitor-General'. He was canonized by Gregory IX. He is represented with a sparrow at his side and a dog carrying in its mouth a burning torch. It is said that the DEVIL appeared to him in the form of a sparrow, and the dog refers to his mother's dream, during her pregnancy, that she had given birth to a dog which lighted the world with a burning torch.
Dominicans. The order of preaching friars founded by St Dominic in 1215, their rule being based on that of St AUGUSTINE. Their first home in England was at Oxford (1221). They gained the name of BLACK FRIARS and in France they

were called JACOBINS. They were also called *Domini canes* or Hounds of the Lord. Albertus Magnus, St Thomas Aquinas and Savonarola were representatives of an order notable for its intellectual distinction.

Dominical Letters, or **Sunday Letters.** The first seven letters of the alphabet used in calendars, almanacs, etc., to mark the Sundays throughout the year (Lat. *Dominica Dies*, the Lord's Day, Sunday). If 1 January is a Sunday the Dominical Letter for the year will be A and if 2 January is a Sunday the Letter will be B, and so on. Dominical Letters are used for finding on what day of the week any day of the month falls in any particular year, also in determining EASTER. Tables and instructions are to be found in Prayer Books, Breviaries, etc.

Dominions. The sixth of the nine orders in the mediaeval hierarchy of angels, also known as *Dominations* and symbolized in art by an ensign. *See* ANGEL.

Domitian, St (d. 560, f.d. 7 May). Born in France, he was bishop of Maastricht. He was reputed to have rid the district of Huy on the Meuse of a huge serpent. He is patron of Huy, where his relics are venerated, and he is invoked against fever.

Domneva, St. *See* ERMENBURGA.

Donan, (Donnan or Dounan), St (d. 618, f.d. 17 April). An Irish monk who visited St COLUMBA on Iona and settled with companions on Eigg in the Inner Hebrides, where he founded a monastery with his companions. Pagan raiders landed on the island, herded the fifty-two monks into the building on Easter Sunday and set fire to it, beheading any who escaped. It was held by some that this was the work of a chieftainess who laid claim to the island, or of Viking pirates. There are several Scottish churches named after the saint.

Donation of Constantine. The presumed grant by the Emperor Constantine (306–37) to Pope Silvester and his successors in perpetuity, consequent upon his baptism of Constantine in 326, of the temporal jurisdiction over ROME and Italy, etc. The document is now accepted as an 8th-century forgery. *See* DECRETALS.
Donation of Pepin, or **Pippin.** When Pippin III (the Short) conquered Aistulf the Lombard king, the exarchate of Ravenna fell into his hands (756). Pippin gave it with the surrounding country and the Republic of Rome to Pope Stephen II, thus founding the Papal States and the temporal power of the papacy.

With the exception of the city of ROME, the Papal States were incorporated in the Kingdom of Italy in 1860 and when Rome was made the Italian capital in 1870 the Pope declared himself a 'prisoner' in the VATICAN. This seclusion was ended by the concordat with Mussolini's government in 1929.

Donatists. Schismatic followers of Donatus, a Numidian bishop of the 4th century who, on puritanical grounds, opposed the election of Caecilianus to the bishopric of Carthage (311).

Their chief dogma was that the Church was a society of holy people and that mortal sinners were to be excluded. St AUGUSTINE of Hippo vigorously combated their heresies.

Donatus (or Donat), St (d. 876, f.d. 22 October). An Irish monk who, returning from a pilgrimage to ROME, arrived at the cathedral of Fiesole at a time when a new bishop was being elected. As soon as Donatus entered the cathedral, bells rang and lamps and candles were kindled supernaturally and he was at once acclaimed bishop. He was reputed to be a scholar, poet and teacher of note. He founded a hospice dedicated to St Brigit for the use of Irish pilgrims. He played a part in the Roman Council of 861.

Door-keeper. One of the minor orders of the Western CHURCH.

Dorcas Society. A woman's circle making clothing for charitable purposes. So called from Dorcas in *Acts* ix, 39, who made 'coats and garments' for widows.

Dorothea, St (d. *c.* 300, f.d. 6 February). A martyr under Diocletian, she is represented with a rose-branch in her hand, a wreath of roses on her head, and roses with fruit by her side. The legend is that Theophilus, the judge's secretary, scoffingly said to her as she was going to execution, 'Send me some fruit and roses, Dorothea, when you get to Paradise.' Immediately after her execution, a young angel brought him a basket of apples and roses, saying 'From Dorothea in Paradise', and vanished. Theophilus was a convert from that moment. The story forms the basis of Massinger and Dekker's tragedy, *The Virgin Martir* (1622).

Dorsal. The cloth, usually embroidered, which is hung at the back of the ALTAR instead of the REREDOS.

Dorter. A dormitory in a monastery, often directly connected with the church for easy access for the night office.

Douai. Douai Bible. *See* BIBLE, THE ENGLISH.
Douai University. A university in Flanders which founded English colleges for the benefit of priests exiled under the anti-CATHOLIC laws of England in the time of Queen Elizabeth I. Many who trained there returned to England as missionary priests.

Dounan, St. *See* DONAN.

Dove. The name means 'the diver-bird'; perhaps from its habit of ducking its head. So also Lat. *columba* is the Gr. *kolumbis*, a diver.

In Christian art the dove symbolizes the HOLY GHOST, and the seven rays proceeding from it the seven gifts of the Holy Ghost. It also symbolizes the SOUL and as such is sometimes represented coming out of the mouth of saints at death. A dove bearing a ring is an attribute of St AGNES; St DAVID is shown with a dove on his shoulder; St DUNSTAN and St Gregory the Great with one at the ear; St Enurchus with one on his head; and St REMIGIUS with the dove bringing him holy chrism. The dove as the Holy Spirit is pictured with the VIRGIN MARY at the ANNUNCIATION. A dove on the staff of St JOSEPH depicts the husband of a pure virgin. A flock of doves represents the faithful. The dove with the olive branch is peace and deliverance and as the dove of Noah's Ark brought back the olive branch and found no resting place outside the Ark, so the Christian finds no safety outside the Church. Doves in a vine are the faithful seeking refuge in Christ. With a palm branch the dove is victory over death, while the white dove is victory over sin, the purified and saved soul as opposed to the black raven of sin. It also represents innocence and gentleness. The dove was the emblem of the Knights of the GRAIL.

Dowelling Money. Dwelling-house money. In mediaeval England the equivalent of a church rate i.e., a parochial levy in each household. *See* PENTECOSTAL; SMOKE-FARTHINGS.

Doxology (Gr. *Doxologia*). The word means a hymn of praise to God. The Greater Doxology is the hymn *Gloria in Excelsis Deo* at the EUCHARIST. The Lesser Doxology is the *Gloria Patri* (Glory be to the Father, etc.) sung or said at the end of each psalm in the liturgy. The hymn 'Praise God from whom all blessings flow' is also known as the Doxology.

Dragonnades. The name given to Louis XIV's persecutions of the HUGUENOTS from 1681, until after the Revocation of the Edict of NANTES in 1685. The name arises from the billeting of dragoons on those PROTESTANTS who refused to renounce their 'heresy'. The soldiery were given a free hand with the obvious results.

Dubtach, St. *See* DUTHAC.

Duchesne, St Philippine (1769–1852, f.d. 17

November). Born at Grenoble and educated at a convent there, she wished to join the community but was refused permission by her father in view of the political situation. During the French Revolution, in 1791, the nuns were expelled. Philippine engaged in good works and in 1802 she took over the convent buildings and tried, without success, to revive the religious life there. She then joined the Society of the Sacred Heart, founded by St Madeline Barat, and later left with a group of nuns on a mission to North America. She travelled up the Mississippi and Missouri and founded free schools. The conditions were pioneering and difficult among the Indians, and Philippine lived in extreme poverty. In spite of ill health she continued in the work until her death at the age of eighty-three. She was canonized in 1988.

Dulcinists. Heretical followers of Dulcinus (in northern Italy) who rejected papal authority and church rites and ceremonies. Dulcinus was burnt (1307) by order of Clement IV.

Dulia. *See* LATRIA.

Dumb Ox, The. St Thomas Aquinas (1224–74), known afterwards as 'the ANGELIC DOCTOR' or 'Angel of the Schools'. Albertus Magnus, his tutor, said of him: 'The dumb ox will one day fill the world with his lowing.' So called from his great bulk and taciturnity.

Dunkers. *See* TUNKERS.

Dunce. A dolt; a stupid person. The word is taken from Duns Scotus (*c.* 1265–1308), the famous SCHOOLMAN so called from his birthplace, Duns, in Scotland. His followers were called Dunsers or SCOTISTS. Tyndal says, when they saw that their hair-splitting divinity was giving way to modern theology, 'the old barking curs raged in every pulpit' against the Classics and new notions, so that the name indicated an opponent to progress, to learning, and hence a dunce.

Duns Scotus was buried at Cologne; his epitaph reads:

Scotia me genuit, Anglia me suscepit, Gallia me docuit, Colonia me tenet.

Duns Scotus. Blessed (1265–1308, f.d. 8 November). The mediaeval theologian and SCHOOLMAN John Duns Scotus was born at Duns, Berwickshire. Little is known of his early life beyond that he became a FRANCISCAN priest in Northampton in 1291. He studied and lectured at Oxford and later in Paris and Cologne, where he died and was buried. He was one of the most celebrated of Franciscan theologians and philosophers and was known as Doctor Subtilis on account of his fine distinctions. He

was the leader of the theologians pioneering the cult of the VIRGIN MARY and the belief that she was born without sin; this ultimately became the doctrine of the IMMACULATE CONCEPTION. He also maintained that will is superior to intellect and love superior to knowledge. His followers were called SCOTISTS, Dunsmen or Dunsers and the name is said to have given rise to the word 'dunce' as one who 'indulged in hair-splitting theology'. He was attacked by humanists such as ERASMUS and Tyndal. Duns Scotus has been immortalized in Raphael's frescoes in the VATICAN. Although Franciscans called him 'Blessed' he was not beatified until 20 March 1993. *See* DOCTORS OF LEARNING; DUNCE.

Dunstan, St (*c.* 925–88, f.d. 19 May, at Canterbury 21 October). Archbishop of Canterbury (961), and patron saint of goldsmiths, being himself a noted worker in gold. He is represented in pontifical robes, and carrying a pair of pincers in his right hand, the latter referring to the legend that on one occasion he seized the DEVIL by the nose with a pair of red-hot tongs and refused to release him till he promised never to tempt Dunstan again. Another legend is that the devil one day asked St Dunstan, who was noted for his skill as a farrier, to shoe his 'single hoof'. Dunstan, knowing who his customer was, tied him tightly to the wall, and proceeded with the job, but purposely put the devil to such pain that he roared for mercy. Dunstan at last agreed to release his captive on condition that he would never again enter a place where he saw a horseshoe displayed.

Little is known of his early life, but that he was educated at Glastonbury, ordained priest by the bishop of Winchester and returned to Glastonbury for a time as a hermit. He was of royal Wessex blood and was a trusted adviser to the kings of Wessex. He founded or restored many abbeys, carried out reformations in the Church, and at the same time was famous as a statesman and administrator. As a craftsman he was not only known as a goldsmith but also as an illuminator, embroiderer and musician. He was a visionary and prophet and many miracles were attributed to him. He is one of the great figures of the 10th century.

Dust. Dust and ashes. In Old Testament times, a person sprinkled earth, dust and ashes over the head as a sign of mourning. *Dust and ashes* was expressive of one's deep humiliation, insignificance and worthlessness. *Cp.* WEAR SACKCLOTH AND ASHES *under* SACK.

And Abraham answered and said, Behold now, I have taken upon me to speak unto the Lord, which am but dust and ashes.

Gen. xviii, 27

To shake the dust from one's feet. To show extreme dislike of a place, and to leave it with the intention of never returning. The allusion is to the Eastern custom.

> And whosoever shall not receive you, nor hear your words, when ye depart out of that house or city, shake off the dust of your feet.
>
> *Matt.* x, 14

> But the Jews… raised persecution against Paul and Barnabas, expelled them out of their coasts. But they shook off the dust of their feet against them, and came into Iconium…
>
> *Acts.* xiii, 50, 51

Duthac (Dubtach or Dothow), St (d. 1065, f.d. 8 March). A Scotsman, educated in Ireland, he returned to his native country and was appointed bishop of Ross, being greatly venerated. He was buried at Tayne, but his body was found to be incorrupt after seven years and was translated to an elaborate shrine which was visited by royalty. Several miraculous legends are recorded in the *Aberdeen Breviary*: he carried red-hot coals in his hands; mysterious lights guided his visitors at night and birds obeyed his commands, among them a kite who had stolen some pork and a gold ring. An inebriated guest at a party had sent the pork to St Duthac with a request to be cured of his headache and the ring had been left on a grave. The kite was ordered to return the ring but allowed to eat the pork.

Dymphna. The patron SAINT of the insane. She is said to have been the daughter of a 6th-century Irish chieftain, who fled to Gheel in Belgium to escape her father's incestuous attentions, and devoted herself to charitable works. She was eventually murdered by her father. In art she is shown dragging away a DEVIL. Gheel has long been a centre for the treatment of the mentally afflicted.

Dysmas. The traditional name of the Penitent Thief, who suffered with Christ at the Crucifixion. His relics are claimed by Bologna, and in some calendars he is commemorated on 25 March. In the apocryphal GOSPEL OF NICODEMUS he is called *Dimas* (and elsewhere *Titus*), and the Impenitent Thief *Gestas*.

E

Eadburga (or Edburga) of Thanet, St (d. 751, f.d. 12 December). Variously said to have been a princess of Wessex or of the royal house of Kent, she entered the nunnery of Minster-on-Thanet as a disciple of St MILDRED and succeeded her as abbess. She was famed for her correspondence with St BONIFACE, the *Letters of Boniface*, and as a scribe; also for her generosity. She built a church at Minster, consecrated by Cuthbert, archbishop of Canterbury, for the relics of Mildred; and also built a nunnery there. She was buried at Minster and cures were reported at her tomb.

Eadsin, St (d. 1050, f.d. 28 October). Little is known of his early life. He was chaplain to the Danish King Harold and was bishop of Winchester, later becoming archbishop of Canterbury. He crowned EDWARD THE CONFESSOR.

Eagle. In Christian symbolism the eagle represents the Spirit, spiritual endeavour, ascension, aspiration. Looking at the sun without blinking, it is Christ gazing on the glory of God; plunging into the sea to bring out fish, it is Christ rescuing souls from the sea of sin. It was believed that the eagle renewed its plumage by flying up to the sun then plunging into the sea, this symbolized new life in baptism and resurrection, renewal by grace. When depicted grasping the serpent in its talons, it is victory over sin and the DEVIL. At the LAST JUDGEMENT it throws the damned out of the nest. In Christian art, it is the symbol of St JOHN THE APOSTLE (hence its use on church lecterns), St PRISCA, St Medard and St Servatius. It is one of the Four Beasts of the APOCALYPSE.

Eanflaed, St. *See* ENFLEDA.

Ear. The Ears to Ear Bible. *See* BIBLE, SOME SPECIALLY NAMED EDITIONS.

East. In the Christian Church the custom of turning to the east when the creed is repeated is to express the belief that Christ is the Dayspring and sun of Righteousness. The altar is placed at the east end of the church to remind us of Christ, the Dayspring and Resurrection; and persons are buried with their feet to the East to signify they died in the hope of the Resurrection.

Easter. The name was adopted for the Christian Paschal festival from O.E. *eastre*, a heathen festival held at the vernal equinox in honour of the Teutonic goddess of dawn, called *Eostre* by Bede, which fell about the same time.

Easter Day is the first Sunday after the Paschal full moon, i.e. the full moon that occurs on the day of the vernal equinox (21 March) or on any of the next 28 days. Thus Easter Sunday cannot be earlier than 22 March, or later than 25 April, as laid down by the Council of NICAEA in 325. The Eastern Church still celebrates Easter independently and in 1963 the VATICAN Council declared itself in favour of fixing the date of Easter when agreement with other churches could be reached.

It was formerly a common belief that the sun danced on Easter Day.

> But oh, she dances such a way,
> No sun upon an Easter day
> Is half so fine a sight.
> SIR JOHN SUCKLING: *Ballad upon a Wedding*

Sir Thomas Browne combats the superstition:

> We shall not, I hope, disparage the Resurrection of our Redeemer, if we say the Sun doth not dance on Easter day. And though we would willingly assent unto any sympathetical exultation, yet cannot conceive therein any more than a Tropical expression.
> *Pseudodoxia Epidemica*, V, xxii

Easter Eggs, or Pasch Eggs. The egg as a symbol of fertility and renewal of life derives from the ancient world, as did the practice of colouring and eating eggs at the spring festival. The custom of eating eggs on Easter Sunday and of making gifts of Easter Eggs to children probably derives from the Easter payment of eggs by the villein to his overlord. The idea of the egg as a symbol of new life was adopted to symbolize the Resurrection. *Pasch Eggs* or *pace eggs*, hard-boiled and coloured, were rolled down slopes as one of the Easter games, a practice surviving in the yearly egg rolling held on the lawn of the White House in Washington.

Eata, St (d. 685, f.d. 26 October). Taken from Iona by St AIDAN, he was one of the twelve boys trained by him at Lindisfarne. He then entered the monastery at Melrose, later becoming its abbot; St CUTHBERT was among the monks under him. Eata was appointed bishop of Hexham and was involved in the controversy over the calculation of EASTER, at first adhering to the Celtic but later accepting the Roman date after the Synod of Whitby. When the archbishop of York endeavoured to remove Eata's relics to York, since there was no local shrine there, the dead saint appeared to him in a dream, beating him with his pastoral staff and so effectively preventing the translation.

Ebba (or Ebbe), St (d. 683, f.d. 25 August). Daughter of Ethelfrith, King of Northumbria, she became a nun at Coldingham, a monastery for monks and nuns, and later became its abbess. Ebba was famous for her wisdom and holiness, but in her old age the monastery obtained a bad name for laxity and the neglect of religious duties, the nuns thinking only of dressing themselves like brides, wearing fine clothes and attracting men. The monastery was burned, some said on account of the scandal. Ebba gave her name to St Abb's Head and Ebchester.

Ebenezer. A name often adopted by NONCONFORMIST chapels from the Heb. word meaning 'stone of help' (I *Sam.* vii, 12) and thus sometimes used as a symbol of Nonconformity.

Lest there should be any well-intentioned persons who do not perceive the difference ... between religion and the cant of religion ... let them understand that it is always the latter and never the former which is satirized here ... whether it establish its headquarters, for the time being, in Exeter Hall or Ebenezer Chapel, or both.

CHARLES DICKENS: *Posthumous Papers of the Pickwick Club (Preface)*

Ebionites (Heb. *ebion*, poor). In the early Church the name was given to the ultra-Jewish Christians, many of whom rejected the Virgin Birth and who kept the Jewish Sabbath as well as the Lord's Day. As a separate heretical sect from the 2nd century, they called themselves the Poor Men, and remained isolated from the Church, developing a mixture of creeds.

Ecce homo (Lat. Behold the man). The name given to many paintings of Our Lord crowned with thorns and bound with ropes, as He was shown to the people by PILATE, who said to them, 'Ecce homo!' (*John* xix, 5). Especially notable are those by Correggio, Titian, Guido Reni, Van Dyck, Rembrandt, Poussin, and Albrecht Dürer. In 1865 Sir John Seeley published a study of Christ under this title.

Ecclesiastes. This book of the OLD TESTAMENT was formerly ascribed to Solomon, because it says (i, I), 'The words of the Preacher, the son of David, King in Jerusalem.' It is now generally assigned to an unknown author of about the 3rd century BC.

Ecclesiastical. Ecclesiastical Commissioners, The, of the CHURCH OF ENGLAND were established in 1836 consisting of the archbishops, bishops and deans of Canterbury, St Paul's and Westminster with certain judges and ministers of State together with eleven eminent laymen. Essentially they administered surplus episcopal and cathedral endowments for relief of the poorer clergy and parochial ministries. In 1948 they merged with QUEEN ANNE'S BOUNTY as the Church Commissioners, basically to manage the ancient endowments of the Church for the support of the ministry.
The Father of Ecclesiastical History. Eusebius of Caesarea (*c.* 264–340).

Ecclesiasticus. The Latin name, probably meaning 'church book' (from its frequent use in the church), for the Book of Sirach, traditionally ascribed to Jesus the son of Sira. It is perhaps the most important book of the Old Testament APOCRYPHA and both the German hymn *Nun danket alle Gott* (Now thank we all our God) and the *Jubilee Rhythm* of St BERNARD of Clairvaux are taken from it. It has been much used by the Lutheran Church.

Eckhart, Johannes (*c.* 1260–1327). Known as Meister Eckhart, he was a German philosopher and mystic, his philosophy being influenced by Neo-Platonism. Born near Gotha, he became a DOMINICAN and taught in Paris, Strasburg and Cologne. He was accused of heresy but died before he could be brought to trial; many of his works were condemned by the Pope. Eckhart is regarded as one of the great mystics of all time.

Economy. The Christian Economy. The religious system based on the teachings of Jesus Christ as recorded in the NEW TESTAMENT.
The Mosaic Economy. The religious system revealed by God to Moses and set forth in the OLD TESTAMENT.

Ecstasy (Gr. *ek*, out; *stasis*, a standing). Literally, a condition in which one stands out of one's mind, or is 'beside oneself'. St PAUL refers to this when he says he was caught up to the third HEAVEN and heard unutterable words, 'whether in the body, or out of the body, I cannot tell' (II *Cor.* xii, 2–4). St JOHN also says he was 'in the spirit'—i.e. in an ecstasy—when he saw the apocalyptic vision (*Rev.* i, 10). The belief that the soul left the body at times was common in former ages, and there was a class of diviners among the ancient Greeks called **Ecstatici**, who used to lie in trances, and when they came to themselves gave strange accounts of what they had seen while they were 'out of the body'. **The Ecstatic Doctor.** Jan van RUYSBROECK (1293–1381), the Dutch mystic.

Ecumenical. *See* OECUMENICAL.

Edana, St. *See* MODWENNA.

Edburga, St. *See* EADBURGA.

Eddy, Mary Baker (1821–1910). American founder of CHRISTIAN SCIENCE, born in New Hampshire (née Baker). Brought up as a CON-GREGATIONALIST, she founded the Church of Christ, Scientist, after experiencing a rapid recovery from a serious accident which led her to study divine healing as given in the account of Christ's healing of the man of the palsy. She published her *Science of Health with Key to the Scriptures*, and founded the church in 1879. Her third husband, A. G. Eddy, whom she had married in 1877, was among her first disciples.

Eden. PARADISE, the country and garden in which ADAM was placed by God (*Gen*. ii, 15). The word means delight, pleasure.

Edgar, St (943–75, f.d. 8 July). Son of King Edmund of Wessex, he became King of All England at the age of sixteen years. He was educated by St DUNSTAN who was said to have reproved him severely for his loose living and association with nuns; St EDITH was his daughter by the nun Wulfrida or Wulfthryth. His reign was notable for instigating a close co-operation between Church and State and for the introduction of law-codes. Edgar founded a number of monasteries and encouraged learning. He was buried at Glastonbury and it was said that his body remained incorrupt and bled when his tomb was opened in 1052.

Edilbertus of Kent, St. *See* ETHELBERT.

Edith of Wilton, St (*c*. 961–84, f.d. 16 September). The natural daughter of King Edgar and the nun Wulfrida or Wulfthryth. The child was brought up and remained at Wilton Abbey where her mother had returned after the birth. Edith was educated by two chaplains. She refused all offices and advancement and became a nun. She founded the church of St DENYS, or Dionysius, at Wilton and was noted for her service to the sisters and to the poor, also for her sympathy and rapport with wild animals. She died at the age of twenty-three and miracles occurred at her tomb; it was also said that she appeared at the christening of a child, to stand sponsor, three years after her death; she vanished immediately after the ceremony.

Edmund. Edmund, St (841–69, f.d. 20 November). King of East Anglia; at an early age he led his troops against the invading Vikings and was defeated. Refusing to renounce his Christianity, he was bound to a tree, scourged, transfixed with so many arrows that his body was 'like a thistle', and then beheaded. He was first buried at a small chapel and later, his body being incorrupt, was translated to Boedricsworth (Bury St Edmunds). His cult became widespread in the Middle Ages.

Edmund of Abingdon, St (*c*. 1175–1240, f.d. 16 November, 30 May at Abingdon). Born at Abingdon, the eldest son of a wealthy merchant who became a monk, he was educated at Oxford and Paris universities. Returning to England he taught theology and scholasticism at Oxford. He was appointed treasurer of Salisbury and in 1233 was made archbishop of Canterbury. Becoming involved in disputes with King Henry III and the Black BENEDICTINE community at Canterbury, Edmund went to Rome, endeavouring to follow a middle course and reconcile the disputing parties, but with little success. He died at Soisy, in Burgundy, on his second journey to Rome, and was buried there; he was called St Edme in the local cult. In England his cult became widespread, particularly at Abingdon and in Northamptonshire, where his sisters were nuns. In Oxford St Edmund's Hall is named after him, and he was the first master at Oxford to be canonized. He was a man of devout character, an effective administrator and a notable scholar, teacher and preacher. He experienced heavenly visions.

Edmund Gennings, St. *See* GENNINGS.

Edward. Edward the Confessor. The last Anglo-Saxon king (1042–66) of the old royal house, so called for his piety and monk-like virtues although conspicuously deficient as a ruler. He was canonized in 1161 by Pope Alexander III.

Edward the Martyr, St (*c*. 962–79, f.d. 18 March). Although called a martyr, he was not martyred for his religion but was assassinated in a power-struggle for the throne. He was the son of King Edgar and his first wife Ethelfleda and came under the influence of St DUNSTAN. Edward was murdered at the instigation of his stepmother Elfrida or Aelfthryth, being killed by a henchman of hers while drinking a stirrup-cup at Corfe; she had 'allured him to her female blandishments' to have him slain so that she could attain power for herself and her son. Edward was buried at Wareham but his remains were translated to Shaftesbury by St Dunstan. Miracles were reported at his tomb and he became venerated as a saint.

Edwin, St (684–633, f.d. 12 October). The first Christian king of Northumbria; he was the son of Aella, King of Deira, but spent his early life in exile. In 616 he defeated Ethelfrith and became King of Northumbria; he was not then a Christian but was converted by St PAULINUS, who baptized him at York, of which the king made Paulinus archbishop. Edwin was killed at Hatfield Chase in a battle against Penda, King of Mercia. Edwin's cult was centred on York and Whitby and he was regarded as a hero and model king.

Efflam, St (6th cent., f.d. 6 November). A legendary Irish saint, son of an Irish king, said to have left his wife, Enora, on the marriage night and gone to Brittany as a recluse. Enora had herself sewn up in a cow-hide and thrown into the sea, and eventually was cast up on the shore by Efflam's cell. He was greatly displeased at her arrival and walled her up in a separate cell adjacent to his. He fed her through a window for the rest of her life. At King Arthur's request Efflam later emerged from his cell to slay a dragon and bring forth a fountain. He finally settled at Cornouailles, where he died.

Egbert, St (d. 729, f.d. 24 April). A nobleman of Northumbria who went to Ireland to study. After recovering from the plague he became a monk at Lindisfarne. A dream prevented him from going on an evangelizing mission on the Continent and instructed him to go to Iona. There he converted the monks from the Celtic to the Roman calculation of EASTER and died on the day it was used for the first time.
Egbert, St (d. 766, f.d. 19 November). Son of St EATA, he was appointed bishop of York, which see became an archbishopric through the influence of BEDE. Egbert founded the famous school at York where ALCUIN was a pupil; he also enlarged and decorated the cathedral. He died in a monastery and was buried in the cathedral.

Egwin, St (d. 717, f.d. 30 December, 11 January and 10 September). Of the royal blood of Mercia, he was made bishop of Worcester and was responsible for the foundation of Evesham Abbey, at which he was said to have seen a vision of the VIRGIN MARY. He incurred enmity and opposition by his vigorous denunciation of the immorality of the times, and was exiled. Setting out for ROME to vindicate himself, he went fettered and manacled and threw the keys into the Avon. One version of the story said that on his way to Rome a fish jumped on board the ship, or in another legend, that he bought a fish in the market, and that the keys were found inside it. Egwin was vindicated by the Pope and returned to Worcester. His cult, among others, was queried in the eleventh century but his relics were defended by ordeal by fire and by miracles on a journey to collect funds for a new church.

Einne, St. *See* ENDA.

Elder. The importance of elders as people of authority in ancient communities was a natural development. In the OLD TESTAMENT they appear as official authorities of a locality; and as the elders of the Synagogue they exercised religious discipline. The members of the Sanhedrin were called elders. The name was also applied to officers of the early Christian Church and is still used in this sense by the PRESBYTERIAN Church.

Election. The doctrine, held by Calvinists in particular, that there are certain numbers of people chosen by God as his elect; they inherit eternal salvation while all others are eternally damned. Robert Burns satirizes the doctrine in his 'Holy Willie's Prayer'.

Elevation of the Host. In the MASS, after the consecration, the raising of the Host and the Chalice by the celebrant for the adoration of the faithful.

Eleven. At the eleventh hour. Just in time; from the parable in *Matt.* xx, 1–16.
The Eleven Thousand Virgins. *See* URSULA.

Elfgiva, St. *See* ELGIVA.

Elfleda, (Ethelfleda, or **Elgiva), St** (656–716, f.d. 8 February). Daughter of Oswy, King of Northumbria, she was dedicated to the religious life at birth and was sent to Hartlepool, to the monastery of St HILDA, who later founded that at Whitby; Elfleda became its abbess in 681. As a friend of St CUTHBERT she at first opposed the innovations of St WILFRID, but eventually brought about a reconciliation between him and the conflicting northern bishops.
Elfleda, St (10th cent., f.d. 23 October). Of royal blood, niece to King Athelstan, when she was widowed she retired to Glastonbury, where she 'mothered' St DUNSTAN and where she died. She was famous for her little barrel of beer which was only large enough to supply Athelstan and his large retinue with one round of drinking horns when they visited her, but, on invoking the Blessed VIRGIN for 'abundance of ale' the barrel never ran dry.

Elgiva, St (d. 944, f.d. 18 May). Also called Elfgiva, she was probably the wife of King Edmund of Wessex, who succeeded Athelstan as King of England. She was the mother of kings Edwyn and Edgar. Elgiva was either the foundress or second after Alfred in the foundation of the monastery at Shaftesbury, where she died after a life of good works and famed for her generosity, wisdom, gift of prophecy and miracles.

Elian the Pilgrim, St (6th cent., f.d. 13 January, 22 February). A saint of Cornwall and Wales invoked against disease, he was also patron of a 'curing well' in Denbighshire. Here, on payment of a fee, a pebble inscribed with the name of the person to be cursed is dropped into the well, and the victim is stricken with ague, cramp or misfortune. The saint is also called St Allen or Elwyn and was founder of St Allen's church in Cornwall. He gave his name to Llanelian in Anglesey and Llanelian in Clwyd.

Eligius, St. *See* ELOI, St.

Elijah's Mantle. Metaphorically the assumption of powers previously enjoyed by another, as Elisha took up the mantle of Elijah (II *Kings* ii, 13).

Elijah's Melons. Certain stones on Mount Carmel are so called from the legend that the owner of the land refused to supply food for the prophet, and for punishment his melons were turned into stones.

Elim. The Elim Foursquare Gospel Movement, or Gospel Alliance, was founded by the Revivalist George Jeffreys at Belfast in 1915. The Movement preached the coming of the King, Jesus, the Saviour, Healer and Baptizer. Jeffreys later founded the Bible Pattern Fellowship with the same message.

Elizabeth. St Elizabeth of Hungary (1207–31, f.d. 19 November). Patron SAINT of the Third Order of St FRANCIS of which she was a member. She was noted for her good works and love of the poor. She is commemorated in Kingsley's poem *The Saint's Tragedy*. The story is told that her husband Louis at first forbade her abounding gifts to the poor. One day he saw her carrying away a bundle of bread and told her to open it asking what it contained. 'Only flowers, my lord,' said Elizabeth and, to save the lie, God converted the loaves into flowers and the king was confronted with a mass of red roses. This miracle converted him.

Elizabeth (or Isabel) of Portugal, St (1271–1346, f.d. 4 July). Daughter of King Peter III of Aragon and named after ELIZABETH OF HUNGARY, a relative, she married King Denis of Portugal at the age of twelve. He proved a difficult husband and father, although a good ruler. In spite of his infidelities and the revolt of their son Alfonso against him, Elizabeth remained a peacemaker, not only in the royal household, but in averting war between Portugal and Castile. After devotedly nursing her husband through his last illness she became a FRANCISCAN Tertiary, retiring to a small house at

Coimbra, near the convent she had founded for POOR CLARES. She was buried there and many miracles were reported at her tomb.

Elizabeth Seton, St (1774–1821, f.d. 4 January). The first native-born American to be canonized. Born Elizabeth Ann Bayley, she came from a well-known New York family and married a Professor Seton. After he died in 1803 Elizabeth became a CATHOLIC and in spite of opposition and social difficulties she organized a community in Emmitsburg which ultimately developed into the American Sisters of Charity, caring for children of the poor. She was canonized in 1975.

Elkesaites. A Jewish Christian sect founded in the first century which held that the *Book of Elkesai* had been revealed to them by an angel ninety-six miles high. They observed the MOSAIC LAW but condemned sacrifice. Christ's sufferings were apparent, not real. The rite of BAPTISM was of great importance in its power of redemption.

Elmo's Fire, St. *Elmo* through *Ermo*, is an Italian corruption of St *Erasmus*, a 4th-century Syrian bishop who came to be regarded as the patron SAINT of seamen, and St Elmo's Fire was attributed to him. Through some confusion the name St Elmo was also applied by Spanish sailors to the 13th century DOMINICAN, Blessed Peter Gonzalez, who revered him as their particular guardian for his labours among them.

Elohim. The plural form of the Heb. *eloah*, God. It expresses the general notion of Deity in the same way as the more widely used *El*, which is found in Babylonian, Aramaean, Phoenician, Hebrew, and Arabic. JEHOVAH (*Jahweh* or *Yahve*), however, is used with the special meaning of the God of Israel.

Elohistic and Yahwistic Sources. The Mosaic authorship of the PENTATEUCH is no longer held by Biblical scholars and the first six books of the BIBLE (the Hexateuch) are usually regarded as a literary entity compounded of a variety of sources. Among the evidence used to support this view, is the use of the names ELOHIM and YAHWEH. In some sections of the Hexateuch Elohim is used, in others Yahweh, and in some the names are used indifferently, the general conclusion being that the various sources, written at different periods, were subsequently blended. *See also* JEHOVAH.

Eloi (or Eligius), St (588–659). Patron SAINT of goldsmiths and metal-workers, and apostle of Flanders. Trained as a goldsmith, he was treasurer to Dagobert I (King of the Franks) and Bishop of Novon.

Eloquent Doctor, The. The SCHOOLMAN, Peter

Aureolus (Pierre d'Auriol, 14th century), Archbishop of Aix.

Elphege, St. *See* ALPHEGE.

Elstan, St (d. 981, f.d. 6 April). A monk of Abingdon, under St ETHELWOLD, founder of the house. Elstan was the cook but ultimately became abbot of Abingdon and was buried there. It was said that, at Ethelwold's command, he had plunged his hand into boiling water but it remained unharmed. He was promoted to the Wessex see of Ramsbury. There is little evidence of his cult except at Abingdon.

Eltut, St. *See* ILLTYD.

Elwyn, St. *See* ELIAN THE PILGRIM.

Elzear and Delphine, SS (f.d. 27 September). Elzear (*c.* 1285–1323) was a Provençal nobleman who married at an early age the fifteen-year-old Delphine of Signe. A devout couple, they were said to have lived as brother and sister and to have managed their estates with great wisdom and charity, practising asceticism from early years. Tradition says they were Franciscan TERTIARIES. Elzear was also tutor to the son of Robert, King of Naples, and took part in the political affairs of the day. He died at the age of thirty-eight; Delphine long survived him, dying in 1361 and being buried with him. Elzear was canonized by Pope Urban V who was his nephew and godson.

Ember Days. The Wednesday, Friday, and Saturday of the four EMBER WEEKS once observed as days of fasting and abstinence, the following Sundays being the days of Ordination. The name is the M.E. *ymber*, from O.E. *ymbren*, a period, course or circuit (as the rotation of the seasons).
Ember Weeks. The weeks next after the first Sunday in LENT, WHITSUNDAY, HOLY CROSS DAY (14 September), and St Lucia's Day (13 December). Uniformity of observance was fixed by the Council of Placentia in 1095, but they were introduced into Britain by AUGUSTINE.
Ember goose. The northern diver or loon; called in Norway *imbre*, because it appears on the coast about the time of Ember days in ADVENT. In Germany it is called *Adventsvogel*.

Emblem. A symbolic figure or representation; a pictorial design with an allusive meaning which is inserted or 'cast into' the visible device (Gr. *em*, in; *ballein*, to cast). Thus a *balance* is an emblem of justice, *white* of purity, a *sceptre* of sovereignty.
Some of the most common and simple emblems of the Christian Church are:
A chalice. The EUCHARIST.

The circle inscribed in an equilateral triangle, or *the triangle in a circle.* To denote the co-equality and co-eternity of the TRINITY.
A cross. The Christian's life and conflict; the death of Christ for man's redemption.
A crown. The reward of the perseverance of the SAINTS.
A dove. The HOLY GHOST.
A hand from the clouds. To denote God the Father.
A lamb, fish, pelican etc. The Lord Jesus Christ.
A phoenix. The RESURRECTION.

Emilian, St (d. 767, f.d. 16 November). A servant in the house of a nobleman at Vannes, Brittany, he was said to have made a practice of giving away his master's goods in charity. When caught with a basket of clothes he was asked what he was taking and replied 'chips of wood' and the clothes immediately changed into shavings. This type of legend is told of many saints, notably including St ELIZABETH OF HUNGARY whose concealed loaves turned into roses. Emilian, dismissed from the nobleman's service, became first a baker, then retired to a grotto in the Dordogne as a hermit.

Eminence. A title given to cardinals in the ROMAN CATHOLIC CHURCH, dating officially from 1630.

Emmanuel, or **Immanuel** (Heb. God with us). The name of the child whose birth was foretold by Isaiah, and who was to be a sign from God to Ahaz (*Is.* vii, 14). The name was later applied in the NEW TESTAMENT to the Messiah.

> Behold, a virgin shall be with child, and shall bring forth a son, and they shall call his name Emmanuel, which being interpreted is, God with us.
>
> *Matt.* i, 23

Encratites. In the early Church, and especially among the GNOSTICS, those ascetics who condemned marriage, forbade eating flesh or drinking wine, and rejected all the luxuries and comforts of life. The name is Greek, and signifies 'the self-disciplined' or 'continent'.

Encyclical. A solemn, circular letter from the Pope, written in Latin and addressed to archbishops and bishops of the ROMAN CATHOLIC CHURCH, dealing with some contemporary question of a moral, theological or social nature.

End of the World, The. According to rabbinical legend, the world was to last six thousand years. The reasons assigned are (1) because the name *Yahweh* contains six letters; (2) because the Hebrew letter *m* occurs six times in the book of *Genesis*; (3) because the patriarch Enoch, who was taken to heaven without dying, was the sixth generation from ADAM (Seth, Enos, Cainan, Mahalaleel, Jared, Enoch); (4) because God created the world in six days; (5) because six contains three binaries—the first 2,000 years were for the law of nature, the next 2,000 the written law, and the last 2,000 the law of grace. *See* LAST TRUMP *under* TRUMP.

Enda (Enna or **Einne), St** (d. *c*. 530, f.d. 21 March). Born in Ireland and regarded as the earliest founder of monasticism in Ireland, he was first a soldier, then a monk, training under St NINIAN at his monastery at Whithorn in Scotland. Enda returned to Ireland, founded monasteries and built churches, finally retiring to the rocky isle of Inishmore in the Aran Islands, where he was joined by a large number of his disciples, among them St Ciaran of Clonmacnoise. He was buried at Inishmore and the islands became the home of many saints.

Enfleda (or **Eanflaed), St** (d. *c*. 704, f.d. 24 November). Daughter of St EDWIN, King of Northumbria, and the Kentish princess St ETHELBURGA, she was baptized by St PAULINUS. When Edwin was killed at the battle of Hatfield Chase, mother and daughter, with St Paulinus, went to Kent. Enfleda married Oswiu of Bernicia in a move to unite the two factions in Northumbria, but in the dispute over the Celtic or Roman EASTER, calculation, Enfleda followed her Roman instructors while Oswiu adhered to the Celtic system. The dispute was settled at the Synod of Whitby. After the death of her husband Enfleda became a nun and abbess of Whitby.

English College, The. Founded in ROME in 1362 as a hospice for English pilgrims, it was converted in 1578 into a seminary for training English candidates for the ROMAN CATHOLIC priesthood. It was directed by the Jesuits until 1773, when it was taken over by Italian secular priests, but was closed during the French invasion. In 1818 Pope Pius VII restored the seminary under the direction of English secular clergy.

Enlightened Doctor, The. Raymond Lully of Palma (*c*. 1235–1315), a Spaniard, and one of the most distinguished of the 13th-century SCHOOLMEN.

Entrance. In the Eastern ORTHODOX CHURCH the *Greater Entrance* is the procession of priests and deacons which enters the SANCTUARY after the Cherubic hymn, in preparation for the ceremony in which the PATEN and Chalice are placed on the CORPORAL at the EUCHARIST.

Eparchy. In the Eastern ORTHODOX CHURCH an administrative division of an ecclesiastical province, ruled over by an eparch or metropolitan.

Ephor. In the Eastern ORTHODOX CHURCH the custodian of monastic property.

Ephraem Syrius (or **the Syrian), St** (*c*. 306–73, f.d. 1 February, 9 June). Also known as 'the Deacon', he was a Syrian-speaking FATHER OF THE CHURCH, born at Nisibis in Mesopotamia on the Persian border, the son of poor parents who had suffered under Diocletian. He became a monk and wrote learned treatises and poems, especially Mariological hymns which were influential in Catholic dogma. He was made a deacon at Edessa and opposed Arianism, he was thought to have been ordained by St BASIL. During a famine Ephraem severely reproached the rich, many of whom handed over their wealth for him to distribute among the poor and sick.

Ephrata. A communistic and celibate colony established by J. Conrad Beissel, in 1732, at Ephrata in Pennsylvania. It comprised unmarried men and women and married couples who remained celibate. Religious beliefs were mainly those of BAPTISTS, SEVENTH-DAY ADVENTISTS and MILLENARIANS (*see under* MILLENNIUM).

Epiclesis (Gr. invocation). The invocation of the HOLY GHOST which follows the words of institution of the office of the EUCHARIST in the Eastern ORTHODOX CHURCH. It is maintained that at this point the TRANSUBSTANTIATION occurs, while ROMAN CATHOLICS hold that it takes place during the recitation of the words of institution.

Epiphanius of Salamis, St (*c*. 315–403, f.d. 12 May). Born in Palestine and known as 'the Oracle of Palestine', Epiphanius was a disciple of St HILARION. He became Bishop of Salamis in Cyprus, and visited Egypt where he studied, then preached against, various heresies. He wrote against ORIGEN and Arianism in his *Panarion*, which earned him the approval of St JEROME, but he incurred the displeasure of St JOHN CHRYSOSTOM over his hasty and immoderate condemnation of persons as heretics and for interfering in places beyond his jurisdiction.

Epiphany (Gr. *epiphaneia*, an appearance, manifestation). The manifestation of Christ to the Gentiles, i.e. to the Wise Men from East. 6 January is the feast of the Epiphany in commemoration of this. The vigil of the Epiphany (5 January) was the time for choosing the bean-king. *See* TWELFTH NIGHT.

Episcopacy (Gr. *episkopos*, overseer, Late Lat. *episcopus*, bishop). Church government by

BISHOPS. Hence an *episcopalian church* is a church governed by bishops and its supporters are designated *episcopalians*. Episcopacy in the CHURCH OF ENGLAND was contested early on by Calvinists, who advocated a PRESBYTERIAN system, and was abolished by Parliament in 1643, but restored with the return of the Stuarts.

Episcopal Signatures. It is the custom of BISHOPS of the CHURCH OF ENGLAND to sign themselves with their Christian name and name of their SEE. In some of the older dioceses the Latin form is used, sometimes abbreviated:

Cantuar:	Canterbury	*Gloucestr:*	Gloucester
Ebor:	York	*Norvic:*	Norwich
Carliol:	Carlisle	*Oxon:*	Oxford
Cestr:	Chester	*Petriburg:*	Peterborough
Cicestr:	Chichester	*Roffen:*	Rochester
Dunebn:	Durham	*Sarum:*	Salisbury
Exon:	Exeter	*Winton:*	Winchester

Episcopalian. One who is a member of a church which is governed by bishops. The term is also applied to a member of the Episcopal Church in Scotland and in general to the ANGLICAN Communion; also to the PROTESTANT Episcopalian Church of the USA.

Epistle. This word, related in origin to APOSTLE, comes from a Greek verb meaning 'to send to'. The word is particularly applied to the NEW TESTAMENT letters, from which extracts are read at the Communion service. There are thirteen from St PAUL, one from St JAMES, two from St PETER, three from St JOHN, and one from St JUDE, and the *Epistle to the Hebrews*, of unknown authorship, written to the various churches with which they were concerned.
The epistle side of the altar. That side from which the Epistle has been customarily read at the Communion service according to the BOOK OF COMMON PRAYER. It is to the right of the celebrant as he faces the altar.

Epitaphion. In the Eastern ORTHODOX CHURCH a veil embroidered with the burial of Christ. It is used on GOOD FRIDAY and HOLY SATURDAY in procession and is then placed on the ALTAR during Eastertide.

Epitrachelion. The form of the STOLE which is worn by priests of the Eastern ORTHODOX CHURCH.

Era. The Christian Era begins theoretically from the birth of Christ, though the actual date of the Nativity is uncertain and was probably 6 or 7 BC. The epoch of the Christian Era was fixed by the calculations of Dionysius Exiguus in 527 and was inexact.

Erasmus (*c.* 1466–1536). Desiderius Erasmus

was the illegitimate son of a priest, Rogerius Gerardius (the subject of *The Cloister and the Hearth*, by Charles Reade). Erasmus somewhat reluctantly became a monk in an AUGUSTINIAN monastery near Gouda, but after becoming a priest he went to study in Paris, then travelled in Europe, visiting England where for a time he was Professor of Greek and Divinity at Cambridge. Later he went to Basel where he edited the *Christian Fathers*; he also wrote *Praise of Folly*, a satire against the loose living of the popes and priesthood and the intellectual abstruseness of the Scholastics. He was the outstanding scholar and Christian Humanist of his time and his writings laid the basis for the REFORMATION, although he disagreed with LUTHER in many respects.

Erastianism. A term derived from Thomas Erastus (1524–83), denoting the supremacy of the State in ecclesiastical affairs. *Erastus* (Gr. lovely, or beloved) was the name adopted by Thomas Lieber (Liebler, or Luber), professor of medicine at Heidelberg and at Basel, where he later held the chair of ethics. He was a follower of Zwingli, noted for his opposition to Calvinistic claims, and held that punishment for sin was the prerogative of the civil authority.
The term was popularized in England after its use in the WESTMINSTER ASSEMBLY, and the CHURCH OF ENGLAND is sometimes called Erastian because in certain matters it is subject to State control.

Erigena. Johannes Scotus, or John the Scot (*c.* 815–*c.* 877), philosopher and theologian. The name *Erigena* is taken to mean 'born in Erin' (Ireland) but nothing is known of his early life. According to tradition he was an Irishman (Scotus) and visited Greece and Italy before settling at the court of Charles the Bald as head of the school in Paris. His philosophy was a combination of Neo-Platonism and Christianity, he being one of the few, and last, of the scholars who knew Greek. He was reputed to have visited Oxford and to have taught, or been abbot, at Malmesbury and to have been stabbed to death by his pupils. He was involved in debates on PREDESTINATION and on TRANSUBSTANTIATION and was accused of pantheism, teaching that God and the world are closely linked in Nature. He was noted as a wit and when the Emperor asked him what separated Scot from sot, he replied: 'This table.'

Erik of Sweden, St (d. *c.* 1160, f.d. 18 May). King of Sweden from 1150 to 1160. Erik established Christianity in upper Sweden and the neighbouring Finland and built the first large church at Uppsala. He was famous as a law-giver, but was opposed by a faction of the nobles who joined with the Danes in marching against him.

He was killed at Uppsala, where his relics are preserved. His son Canute, or Cnut, established his father's veneration as the national saint.

Erkenwald (or Erconwold), St (d. 693, f.d. 30 April, 1 February, 13 May). Reputed to be of royal descent, he was appointed bishop of London by St THEODORE OF CANTERBURY. He founded Chertsey Abbey, which he ruled, and a convent at Barking, of which his sister St ETHELBURGA was abbess. Erkenwald was instrumental in resolving the dispute between St Theodore and St WILFRID. St Paul's Cathedral was enlarged during his time and his relics, several times translated, were enshrined there, becoming the centre of an important cult in the Middle Ages; miracles were reported there.

Ermenburga (or Domneva), St (d. *c.* 700, f.d. 19 November). Of royal Kentish blood, she married Merewold, son of Penda, King of Mercia and evangelized Mercia. After obtaining *wergild* or blood-money from Egbert, King of Kent, who had murdered her brothers, she founded a nunnery at Minster-in-Thanet and became its first abbess.

Ermenhilda (Ermengild or Hermynhilda), St (d. *c.* 700, f.d. 13 February, 17 October at Ely). Daughter of Erconbert, King of Kent, and of St SEXBURGA, she married Wulfhere, King of Mercia, and was mother of St WERBURGA. She worked to convert the Anglo-Saxons to Christianity and, after the death of her husband, became a nun at her mother's convent, succeeding her as abbess. At her death her daughter followed her in that office, thus giving Ely three royal abbesses in succession.

Eschatology (Gr. *eschatos*, last). The study of the last things in Christian theology, concerned with death, judgement, heaven and hell, the MILLENNIUM and the fate of both the individual and society. In both the OLD and NEW TESTAMENTS eschatology is associated with the coming of the MESSIAH; the last things, the end of the world and the last judgement are all based on the Second Coming of Christ.

Eskil, St (d. *c.* 1080, f.d. 12 June). He went with St SIGFRID, to whom he was related, to Sweden to reclaim the people, who had lapsed into paganism after the death of St ANSKAR. Eskil was appointed bishop of Strangnas but was stoned to death when a storm destroyed a pagan ALTAR.

Essenes. A Jewish fraternity originating about the 2nd century BC who lived a monastic kind of life and who rejected animal sacrifices. They were distinguished for their piety and virtue

and were strict observers of the SABBATH. They were given to acts of charity and maintained themselves by manual labour (chiefly agriculture), lived in fellowship, and held their goods in common. Their way of life was akin to that of Jesus and His disciples. *See* DEAD SEA SCROLLS.

Ethelbert, St (d. 794, f.d. 20 May). Successor to Ethelred as King of the East Angles, he was assassinated on the orders of Offa, King of Mercia, legend says through the machinations of Offa's queen. In contrition Offa built Hereford Cathedral, dedicating it to Ethelbert. There are also several churches in his name in Herefordshire, Gloucestershire and East Anglia. His cult flourished in the Middle Ages and Hereford was an important centre of pilgrimage, second only to CANTERBURY.

Ethelbert (or Edilbertus) of Kent, St (560–616, f.d. 24 February). King of Kent, he married Bertha, a Frankish princess who was a Christian; she converted Ethelbert who became the first Christian Anglo-Saxon king. He received the mission of St AUGUSTINE in 597, before he had been converted, later establishing Christianity in Kent and being instrumental in the conversion of Sebert, King of the East Saxons, and Redwold, King of the East Angles. Ethelbert built cathedrals at CANTERBURY, Rochester and St PAUL'S in London, and also some churches. He was famous for his Code of Laws. He was buried in his church of SS PETER and PAUL at Canterbury and it was said that a light was kept burning at his tomb for nearly a thousand years, until the time of Henry VIII. Miracles occurred there.

Ethelburga (or Aedilburgh), St (d. 675, f.d. 11 October, 7 March, 4 May). Of noble family and sister to St ERKENWALD, she refused marriage and took refuge in the monastery of Barking, founded by her brother; she was its first abbess. Legend tells of many marvels. When the abbey was being built a beam was found to be too short, but Ethelburga and her brother stretched it to the required length. Miracles occurred at the nunnery; Ethelburga was attended by angels and, after her death, she appeared to a dying nun.

Etheldreda (Aethelthryth, Ediltrudia or Audrey), St (d. 679, f.d. 23 June, 17 October). Daughter of Anna, King of the East Angles; at an early age she dedicated her virginity to God and maintained it through two marriages. Through the influence of St WILFRID she left her second husband Egfrith after twelve years when he wished to establish marital relationships. Etheldreda, or Audrey as she is better known, retired to Coldingham, becoming a nun under her aunt St EBBA. She later founded the dual monastery at Ely where she was consecrated abbess by Wilfrid in 673. A large number of monks and nuns gathered under her. She died there, it was said of a tumour of the neck, though more probably of the plague which was then prevalent, and the tumour was regarded as retribution for her youthful indulgence in quantities of jewellery. The word 'tawdry' is derived from the cheap necklaces, etc., which were sold at her fair, formerly held in the Isle of Ely and elsewhere on 17 October. When her body was translated it was said to be incorrupt and the linen shroud in pristine condition; the incision for the tumour had healed. Many miracles were reported and her shrine was greatly venerated and visited. She was regarded as the most popular of the women saints of the Anglo-Saxons.

Ethelhard, St (d. 805, f.d. 12 May). Abbot of Louth in Lincolnshire, he was appointed archbishop of Canterbury and was involved in the power struggle between the kingdoms of Kent and Mercia. He was noted for maintaining the importance and prestige of CANTERBURY against London as an archbishopric. He died at Canterbury and was buried in his cathedral there.

Ethelwold, St (c. 912–84, f.d. 1 August, 2 August (Abingdon), 10 September). Born of noble family at Winchester, he went to the court of King Athelstan but became a priest and received the TONSURE from St ALPHEGE The Bald together with his friend St DUNSTAN, with whom he went to Glastonbury. Ethelwold was made abbot of the ruined abbey of Abingdon, which he restored, and was consecrated by St Dunstan. He was a noted reformer and expelled the secular clerks from Winchester and other places when he became bishop of the diocese and rebuilt the cathedral. He was said to have been miraculously preserved from death when poison was administered by priests he had dispossessed in his reforms. He was highly skilled in musical, mathematical and mechanical arts, taking part himself in such practical work as building and cooking. He translated the RULE of St BENEDICT into Anglo-Saxon so that it could be read by nuns and those who had no Latin. He wrote a treatise on squaring the circle and established a school of vernacular writing at Winchester. He died at Winchester and was buried in the cathedral.

Ethiopian Church, The. This dates from the time of Frumentius, Bishop of Axium, in the 4th century, under the rule of the Patriarch of Alexandria. It is unique among Christian churches in its worship, rites and the language of its literature and LITURGY which is in Ge'ez, an ancient Semitic dialect. Its CANON of SCRIPTURES contains a number of apocryphal books.

VESTMENTS are of Coptic and Byzantine origin and certain Jewish customs are retained, such as CIRCUMCISION, the Sabbath and ritual purification. Churches are often built to resemble the ancient Jewish temple. The Church fiercely and successfully resisted Muslim invasions, but in the 1970s Marxism took over the government.

Eucharist (Gr. eucharistos, grateful). An ancient name for the *Lord's Supper, Holy Communion,* or MASS; also the consecrated *Elements* in the Communion. Literally, a thank-offering. Our Lord gave thanks before giving the bread and wine to His disciples at the LAST SUPPER. The Church offers the Eucharist as a service of praise and thanksgiving. See IMPANATION.

Eucharistic Vestments. In the Western Church the vestments used for the celebration of the Eucharist are six in number: the ALB, AMICE, CHASUBLE, GIRDLE, MANIPLE, and STOLE. In the Eastern Church they differ only in shape.

Euchites (Gr. euche, a prayer). A mid-4th-century mystical sect in Syria and Palestine called 'the praying people', since they relied entirely on prayer and ignored all ceremonies and forms as a means of salvation.

Eudes, St John (1601–80, f.d. 19 August). A JESUIT by education, at Caen, he joined the French ORATORIANS of St PHILIP NERI, preaching and caring for the sick, his preaching being of an inspired quality. He founded the order of the Congregation of Jesus and Mary, known as the EUDISTS. His missions particularly emphasized devotion to the SACRED HEART. He was canonized in 1925.

Eudists. Members of the order of Secular Catholic priests, the Congregation of Jesus and Mary, founded by St John Eudes in 1643, for the education of priests in seminaries; there were houses at Constances, Rouen and Lisieux. He also established houses for fallen women. The work of the society is now mainly in Canada.

Eudoxians. Followers of Eudoxius, a 4th-century patriarch of Constantinople, who maintained the heresies of the ARIANS.

Eulalia, St (d. c. 304, f.d. 10 December). Eulalon (i.e. the sweetly spoken) is one of the names of Apollo, and there are two 4th-century virgin martyrs called Eulalia both presumed to have been put to death under Diocletian in 304—St Eulalia of Barcelona and St Eulalia of Merida, whose ashes were scattered over a field upon which a pall of snow is said to have descended.

Eulogius, St (d. 606, f.d. 13 September). Eulogius of Alexandria was by birth a Syrian, entering the monastic life at an early age; he became the head of the monastery at Antioch and was elected Patriarch of Alexandria. He knew St GREGORY THE GREAT, with whom he maintained a long correspondence on the conversion of England. Eulogius also wrote many treatises against heresies.

Eulogius of Cordova, St (d. 859, f.d. 11 March). Born into a wealthy land-owning family in Spain, in a Muslim-controlled region, where Christians had to pay taxes to worship, it was forbidden on pain of death to convert people to Christianity. Eulogius became a priest and laboured in visiting monasteries and drawing up new rules; he also visited the sick in hospitals. He was elected archbishop of Toledo, but before he could be consecrated he was imprisoned and beheaded for having protected a girl converted from Islam. He was a person of great learning and courage; he wrote *The Memorial of the Saints*.

Euphemia, St (4th cent., f.d. 16 September). She was martyred at Chalcedon at the time of the Diocletian persecution, having refused to worship the pagan gods. Her history is one of the many tortures she suffered and miraculously survived, finally being thrown to the beasts and being hugged to death by a bear. Her parents buried her body and miraculous powers were attributed to it. Another tradition says she was burnt at the stake. Her 'Acts' are now regarded as fictitious and her cult, which was mainly confined to the Greek ORTHODOX CHURCH, has been relegated to local calendars since the revisions of 1969.

Euphrasia, St (d. c. 410, f.d. 13 March). Born in Constantinople, the daughter of the Governor of Lycia, and of imperial blood, she was betrothed at the age of five to the son of a wealthy senator, but her mother took her to Egypt and placed her in a convent where she remained at her own wish for the rest of her life. Her early life is recorded in the *Acta Sanctorum*.

Euphrasia Pelletier, St (1796–1868, f.d. 24 April). Born Rose Virginia Pelletier, on the island of Noirmontier, the family had taken refuge from the Vendée wars. She joined the Institute of Our Lady of Charity and Refuge at Tours, of which she became Mother Superior. She founded a new institute of the Good Shepherd at Angers, for which she obtained official approval, and became its director, carrying out missions among women in moral danger. She visited London in 1844. So successful was her mission among women that she established 110 convents in four continents. She died at Angers and was canonized in 1940.

Eusebius Pamphili (c. 260–340). Called the Father of Ecclesiastical History, Eusebius was born in Palestine and worked with Pamphilius at the library of ORIGEN in Caesarea, becoming bishop of Caesarea about 313. He played an important part in the Council of NICAEA in 325, at which he supported Arius, and was a favoured counsellor of CONSTANTINE THE GREAT, whom he had baptized. His *Ecclesiastical History* deals somewhat favourably with Christian history down to 324.

Eusebius, St (d. 371, f.d. 2 August, 16 December). A Sardinian who became bishop of Vercelli; he was said to have been the first bishop to live with his clergy, instituting a union of monastic and clerical life in the West. He played a leading part at the Council of Milan in 355 in the ARIAN controversy, vigorously defending St ATHANASIUS. For this he was exiled, imprisoned and cruelly maltreated. At the death of Constantius he was allowed to return and, at Alexandria with Athanasius and others, drew up a letter against the new heresy on the nature of the Incarnation. He died peacefully at Vercelli.

Eusebius of Samosata, St (4th cent., f.d. 21 or 22 June). Bishop of Samosata in Syria, he was exiled by the ARIAN Emperor Valens for assisting the orthodox bishops, but on the Emperor's death he was recalled. He was killed by an Arian woman who threw a tile at his head from the roof of her house. Eusebius was a close friend of SS BASIL and GREGORY OF NAZIANZUS.

Eustace (or Eustachius), St (date unknown, f.d. 2 November (East), 20 September (West)). A legendary Roman general under Trajan. He was one of the Fourteen Holy Helpers. He was said to have been converted to Christianity, when out hunting, by the vision of a white stag which confronted him with a CRUCIFIX between its antlers. (The same legend is told of St HUBERT.) Formerly called Placidas, he was baptized with all his household. When he refused to sacrifice to the gods the emperor had them all roasted to death in a brazen bull. Eustase is the patron saint of hunters. In art he appears either with the stag and crucifix or as carrying his children across a river. His story, omitting the martyrdom, appears in the *Gesta Romanorum*. His cult was suppressed by the HOLY SEE in 1969.

Eutychians. Followers of Eutyches (c. 380–c. 456), archimandrite of Constantinople, and author of the Eutychian controversy. He fiercely opposed the NESTORIANS and held that Christ, after the incarnation, had only one nature, the divine. He was excommunicated, reinstated, and later exiled. They were the forerunners of the MONOPHYSITES.

Eutychius, St (1st cent., f.d. 24 August). A Phrygian by birth, he was reputed to be a disciple of St JOHN the Apostle, recorded in the apocryphal *Acts of St John*. He has also been regarded as the young man raised from the dead (*Acts* xx) by St PAUL at Troas.

Evangelic Doctor, The. John Wyclif (*c.* 1320–84), 'the morning star of the Reformation'.

Evangelical. From the time of the REFORMATION, protestant Churches were often called Evangelical Churches from their insistence that their teachings were based on the *evangel*, or Gospel (i.e. the BIBLE). Those known as *Evangelicals* in the CHURCH OF ENGLAND emerged at the same time as the METHODISTS and they notably emphasized the importance of scriptural authority and salvation by faith in Christ, etc. *Cp*. CLAPHAM SECT; LOW CHURCH.
Evangelical Alliance. Founded in London in 1846 to form an international body committed to maintaining 'an enlightened PROTESTANTISM against the encroachments of Popery and PUSEYISM and to promote the interests of Scriptural Christianity'. In 1951 it was superseded by the World Evangelical Fellowship.

Evangelists. The four Evangelists, MATTHEW, MARK, LUKE and JOHN, are usually represented in art as follows:

Matthew. With pen in hand and scroll before him, looking over his left shoulder at an ANGEL.
Mark. Seated writing, and by his side a couchant winged lion.
Luke. With a pen, in deep thought, looking over a scroll, with a cow or ox nearby chewing the cud. Also shown painting a picture, from the tradition that he painted a portrait of the Virgin.
John. As a young man of great delicacy, with an EAGLE in the background to denote sublimity.

The more ancient symbols were: for Matthew, a man's face; for Mark, a lion; for Luke, an ox; and for John, a flying eagle, in allusion to the four living creatures before the throne of God, described by St John the Divine.

> And the first beast was like a lion, and the second beast was like a calf, and the third beast had a face as a man, and the fourth beast was like a flying eagle.
>
> *Rev*. iv, 7

Another explanation is that Matthew is symbolized by a man because he begins his gospel with the humanity of Jesus, as a descendant of David; Mark by a lion, because he begins with the scenes of JOHN THE BAPTIST and Jesus in the Wilderness; Luke by a calf, because he begins

with the priest sacrificing in the temple; and John by an eagle, because he soars high, and begins with the divinity of the Logos. The four symbols are those of Ezekiel's cherubim (*Ezek.* i, 10).

Irenaeus says: 'The lion signifies the royalty of Christ; the calf His sacerdotal office; the man's face His incarnation; and the eagle the grace of the Holy Ghost.'

The name evangelist was applied in the early Church to preachers of the Gospel and is often used today to denote a revivalist preacher.

Evans, St Philip (d. 1679, f.d. 25 October). Born at Monmouth and educated at St Omer, he became a JESUIT priest and worked in South Wales. He was arrested and imprisoned in Cardiff on suspicion of being involved in the 'Popish Plot' and was condemned to be executed. He was playing tennis when informed that the sentence would be carried out on the morrow, but continued his game. He was one of the FORTY MARTYRS OF ENGLAND AND WALES canonized in 1970.

Even-Christian. An old term for a fellow-Christian, a neighbour in the Gospel sense.

> He that hath desdayn of his neighebore, that is to seyn, of his evene Cristene.
>
> CHAUCER: *Parson's Tale (De Superbia)*

> The more pity that great folk should have countenance in this world to drown and hang themselves more than their even Christian.
>
> SHAKESPEARE: *Hamlet*, V, i

Evensong. The evening service, or Evening Prayer, in the ANGLICAN CHURCH (*see* CHURCH OF ENGLAND), corresponding to VESPERS in the ROMAN CATHOLIC CHURCH.

Evil. Evil communications corrupt good manners. The words used by St PAUL (I *Cor.* xv, 33); but he was evidently quoting Menander (*Thais*). A similar proverb is, 'he that toucheth pitch shall be defiled therewith' (*Ecclesiasticus*, xiii, 1).

The Evil One. The DEVIL, SATAN.

Ewald, SS. *See* HEWALD.

Ex cathedra. With authority. The POPE speaking *ex cathedra* (from the chair, or Papal throne) is said to speak with an infallible voice—as the successor and representative of St PETER. The phrase is applied to dicta uttered by authority and ironically to self-sufficient, dogmatic assertions.

Exaltation of the Cross. A feast held in the ROMAN CATHOLIC CHURCH on 14 September

(HOLY CROSS DAY), in commemoration of the restoration of the true cross to CALVARY in 629, after the victory of Heraclius over the Persians. The CROSS had been taken by Chosroes in 614.

Exarch. In the Eastern ORTHODOX CHURCH the exarch is the head of a self-governing church, a deputy of the PATRIARCH, ranking between a Patriarch and a METROPOLITAN; he visits and generally supervises the churches of a province.

Exclusive Brethren. A breakaway group from the PLYMOUTH BRETHREN; it excludes all contact or eating with non-members. Television and radio are prohibited and children may not join in school meals.

Excommunication. An ecclesiastical censure which excludes a person from the communion of the Church and sometimes accompanied by other deprivations. If clerics, they are forbidden to administer the sacraments. As a form of discipline, it no doubt derives from the Jewish practice at the time of Christ, which entailed exclusion from religious and social intercourse. It was a common punishment in mediaeval times and was on occasions applied to whole nations. Pope Adrian IV used it against ROME in 1155, and Pope Innocent III employed it against England in 1208. (*See* I *Cor.* v, 5.) The practice was also adopted by PROTESTANT Churches at the REFORMATION. The thirty-third of the *Articles of Religion* in the *Book of Common Prayer* is headed 'Of Excommunicate Persons, how they are to be avoided'. *Cp.* INTERDICT; BELL, BOOK AND CANDLE.

Exegesis. A literary commentary, especially the branch of THEOLOGY concerned with the interpretation of the SCRIPTURES.

Exhortation. This played an important part in the apostolic ministry. It is not mentioned in the GOSPELS but appears in *Acts* and in the EPISTLES. In apostasy it was admonitory, but in times of persecution it was encouragement and comfort. It is also used as a term for a persuasive sermon addressed to the will and the heart of the hearer.

Exorcism. The expelling of evil spirits by prayers and incantations. An ancient practice taken over by the Christian Church, after the example of Jesus Christ and the APOSTLES who healed those possessed of evil spirits. The use of this rite in the ROMAN CATHOLIC CHURCH is now carefully regulated.

> And when he had called unto him his twelve disciples, he gave them power against unclean spirits, to cast them out.
>
> *Matt.* x, 1

Exorcist. One of the minor orders of the Church. *See* EXORCISM.

Expectation Week. Between ASCENSION and WHIT-SUNDAY, when the APOSTLES continued praying 'in earnest expectation of the Comforter'.

Expiation. Atonement; making reparation for an offence or sin; the means by which amends are made.

Extreme Unction. The last sacramental unction, the anointing with oil when a person is *in extremis*, now usually called 'The Anointing of the Sick'. One of the seven SACRAMENTS of the ROMAN CATHOLIC CHURCH founded on *James* v, 14, 'Is there any sick among you? let him call for the elders of the church; and let them pray over him, anointing him with oil in the name of the Lord.'

Eye-service. Unwilling service, of the sort only done when one's master is looking.

> Servants, be obedient to them that are your masters, ... not with eye-service, as menpleasers; but as the servants of Christ.
>
> *Eph.* vi, 5, 6

Eystein (or **Augustine**) **Erlendsson, St** (d. 1188, f.d. 26 January). Second archbishop of Trondheim, then called Nidaros, he was noted for his political and episcopal activity in controlling the power of the nobles and enhancing the associations of the Norwegian Church with ROME. Pope Alexander III appointed him papal LEGATE. When involved in the power struggle between two kings Eystein was forced to flee to England where he took refuge in the abbey of St Edmondsbury. He wrote a chronicle of St OLAF, the manuscript being discovered in England. Returning to Norway, he died a few years later at Trondheim where his body was enshrined at the cathedral.

Eznik (5th cent.). An Armenian bishop of Bagrevand who was involved in translating the BIBLE into Armenian. He wrote a *Confutation of the Sects*.

F

Fabian, St (d. 250, f.d. 20 January). A layman who succeeded St Antheros as Pope; legend says he was elected because a DOVE fluttered down on him. According to St CYPRIAN he was 'an incomparable man, the glory of whose death corresponded with the holiness of his life. He was martyred under the persecution of the Emperor Decius. He was buried in the CATACOMB of St CALLISTUS and his body was rediscovered in 1915.

Faculty. A permission or licence or dispensation from a superior, such as are required in the Church for alterations to church properties. The Court of Faculties was established in 1534 when dispensations, licences and faculties were transferred from the Pope to the Archbishop of Canterbury.

Faith (Lat. *fidere*, to trust). The acceptance of truths, particularly those of divine revelation, those contained in the SCRIPTURES or taught by the Church, which cannot be proved by logical reasoning; a system of belief in religion.
Faith (or Foy), St (date unknown, f.d. 6 October, 14 January). Legendary rather than historical, her cult was widespread in the Middle Ages and many churches were dedicated to her. She was said to have been martyred at Agen in Gaul, her body being stretched on a brazen grate and roasted, then beheaded. A heavy fall of snow covered the body. She is confused with other saints of the same name and appears in France as Sainte Foy. In England chapels were dedicated to her in Westminster Abbey and the crypt of St Paul's Cathedral. Some of her relics were taken to Glastonbury. In art she is represented with a grate, a palm branch, a sword or a bundle of rods. She is invoked by pilgrims, soldiers and prisoners.
Faithful. The active supporters of any cult are called *the faithful* and in former times a PURITAN was sometimes *Brother Faithful*.
Father of the Faithful. ABRAHAM (*Rom*. iv, 16; *Gal*. iii, 6–9).
Faith and Order. The Faith and Order movement was responsible for inaugurating the first phase of the 20th-century OECUMENICAL MOVEMENT between the Edinburgh Conference of 1910 and the founding of the WORLD COUNCIL OF CHURCHES in 1948. It served as a means of theological dialogue and prepared the way for the world conferences of Faith and Order at Geneva in 1920, Lausanne in 1927 and the second Edinburgh Conference in 1937 at which there was an agreement to 'form a council of churches' in 1948. After the founding of the World Council of Churches, Faith and Order operated within the body, the members meeting every three or four years. It provides 'the most representative theological forum in the world', and offers study projects in both small and international groups which cover 'a broad spectrum of theological issues to assist the churches in overcoming their dividing and doctrinal differences'. Its work is supervised by a standing commission of thirty members at the Secretariat in Geneva.

Fall. The Fall of Man. The degeneracy of the human race in consequence of the disobedience of ADAM, when he and his wife Eve ate of the Tree of Forbidden Fruit in the Garden of EDEN. From this act the human race has inherited Original Sin, the knowledge of evil, and has lost immortality. Driven out of PARADISE, Adam and Eve were forced to toil for a living.

Familists. Members of the 'Family of Love', an extremist sect founded by Hendrik Niclaes at Emden, about 1540. He derived his mysticism from David George, or Jorizoon, an Anabaptist of Delft, whose followers are sometimes called Davidists or Davists. He implanted his ideas in England in the reign of Edward VI and the sect gained a hold in the eastern counties in spite of persecution. It revived under the Commonwealth, and lingered on until the 18th century. They maintained that all people were of one family and that religion consisted essentially of love.

Family of Love. *See* FAMILISTS.

Fara (or Burgundofara), St (d. 657, f.d. 7 December, 3 April). Sister of St FARO, she fled to a monastery to escape the marriage her father had arranged for her, and later founded the dual monastery of Faremontier-en-Brie. Several English nuns, including St ETHELBURGA, trained under her there and subsequently founded monasteries in England.

Faro, St (d. *c.* 672, f.d. 28 October). Of noble Burgundian family and brother to St FARA, he served as chancellor at the court of King Dagobert. He was married but separated from his wife by mutual consent and became a monk; he received holy orders and was appointed bishop of Meaux; he was noted for fostering monasticism. It was said that he entertained St ADRIAN OF CANTERBURY on his journey to ROME.

Fasting. Strictly a complete abstention from food and drink, but the word is more usually applied to an extreme or fairly strict limitation of diet, and is of proved value in treating certain complaints. It is ancient and widespread as a form of penance, or purification, and was so used by the Jews. It was practised by Christ and adopted by the early Church. As currently practised in the Church, it is marked by abstinence from flesh meat and observance of a light diet. Throughout the ROMAN CATHOLIC CHURCH fasting is obligatory on ASH WEDNESDAY and GOOD FRIDAY.

> Moreover when ye fast, be not, as the hypocrites, of a sad countenance; for they disfigure their faces, that they may appear unto men to fast.
>
> *Matt.* vi, 16

Father. In the HOLY TRINITY, God. The name is given as a title to Roman Catholic priests, and sometimes to CHURCH OF ENGLAND clergy of the HIGH CHURCH persuasion.
Father of Christian Monasticism. St Anthony (*c.* 250–350). *See* FATHERS OF THE DESERT.
Father of Ecclesiastical History. EUSEBIUS PAMPHILI (*c.* 260–*c.* 340).
Father of the Faithful. ABRAHAM.
Father of Lies. SATAN.
Fathers of the Church. All those church writers of the first twelve centuries whose works on Christian doctrine are considered of weight and worthy of respect. But the term is more strictly applied to those teachers of the first twelve, and especially of the first six, centuries who added notable holiness and complete orthodoxy to their learning. Representative among them are:

1st cent., Clement of Rome; 2nd cent., Ignatius of Antioch, Justin, Irenaeus, Polycarp; 3rd cent., Cyprian, Dionysius, Origen, Tertullian, Clement of Alexandria, Gregory Thaumaturgus; 4th cent., Hilary, Cyril of Jerusalem, Gregory Nyssen, John Chrysostom, Eusebius, Jerome, Epiphanius, Athanasius, Basil, Ambrose; 5th cent., Rufinus, Augustine, Pope Leo the Great, Cyril of Alexandria, Vincent of Lerins; 6th cent., Caesarius of Arles; 7th cent., Isidore, Pope Gregory the Great; 8th cent., John of Damascus, Venerable Bede; 11th cent., Peter Damian; 12th cent., Anselm, Bernard.

Cp. APOSTOLIC FATHERS.
Fathers of the Desert (or Desert Fathers). The monks and hermits of the Egyptian deserts in the 4th century from whom Christian monasticism derives. The most famous were St ANTHONY, who founded his first monastery in 305; St Pachomius, the hermit and founder of monasteries; and St Hilarion. There is a good description of their mode of life in Kingsley's *Hypatia.*
Pilgrim Fathers. *See* PILGRIM.

Fatima (Portugal). In 1917 three peasant children (Lucia dos Santos, 10; Francisco Marto, 8, and his sister Jacinta, 7), herding sheep, saw visions, a flash of light, an angel and a woman who said she was the VIRGIN MARY, 'Our Lady of the Rosary'. She told the children to come to the same place on the 13th of each month for six months. The Virgin confided a secret to Lucia. A chapel was built there in honour of the Virgin. Later visions were accompanied by the phenomenon of the DANCING SUN, witnessed by large crowds. After the apparitions the place became, and continues to be, a centre of pilgrimage. The apparitions were acknowledged by the ROMAN CATHOLIC CHURCH at the Second VATICAN COUNCIL.

Feast (or Festival). A day or days specially set apart for religious observances which is an ancient practice common to all religions. The number of Feasts in the ROMAN CATHOLIC and Greek CHURCHES is extensive; the CHURCH OF ENGLAND after the REFORMATION only retained a certain number. The Feasts in the Christian CALENDAR have been divided in various ways, one of which is to group them as **movable** or **immovable**. All SUNDAYS are Feast Days.
The **chief immovable feasts** are the four quarter-days—*viz.* the ANNUNCIATION, or LADY DAY (25 March); The Nativity of St JOHN THE BAPTIST (24 June); MICHAELMAS DAY (29 September); CHRISTMAS Day (25 December). Others are the Circumcision (1 January), EPIPHANY (6 January), ALL HALLOWS (1 November), the several Apostles' days and the anniversaries of martyrs and saints.
The **movable feasts** depend upon EASTER Day and also among them are the Sundays after the EPIPHANY, SEPTUAGESIMA SUNDAY, the Sundays of LENT, Rogation Sunday, ASCENSION DAY, PENTECOST or WHITSUNDAY, TRINITY SUNDAY, and the Sundays after Trinity.

February. The month of purification amongst the ancient Romans (Lat. *februo*, I purify by sacrifice).
2 February, CANDLEMAS DAY, is the feast of the Purification of the Blessed Virgin Mary. It is said that if the weather is fine and frosty at

the close of January and the beginning of February, there is more winter ahead than behind.

Si sol splendescat Maria Purificante,
Major erit glacies post festum quam fuit ante.

SIR T. BROWNE: *Vulgar Errors*

Fechin, St (d. 665, f.d. 20 January). An Irishman of the family of King Conn of the Hundred Battles. Fechin trained at Achonry then, having so many followers, founded a monastery, the first at Meath, which he ruled as its abbot. He also had a cult in Scotland, having connections with Arbroath and Ecclefechan.

Felicity of Rome, St (2nd cent., f.d. 23 November). Little is known of her history, but traditionally she was a Roman matron whose seven sons were Christians. All of them refused to worship pagan gods and were martyred one after the other in different ways in the presence of their mother, who encouraged them to remain steadfast, she herself being finally beheaded or thrown into boiling oil. Their cult became general in early times. Their story bears strong resemblance to that of the Seven Jewish Brothers and their mother in 2 *Maccabees* vii.

Felix of Dunwich, St (d. 647, f.d. 8 March). A Burgundian, sent to England by St HONORIUS to undertake a mission to the East Angles who were then ruled by the Christian king St SIGE-BERT. Felix was made bishop of Dunwich by the archbishop of Canterbury and founded the monastery of Soham; he also established a school for boys with teachers from CANTERBURY. He was buried at Soham, but his relics were translated to Ramsey Abbey. Several churches were dedicated to him and he gave his name to Felixstowe in Suffolk.

Felix of Nola, St (d. 260, f.d. 14 January). A CONFESSOR, son of a Syrian soldier; he lived at Nola, near Naples, where his church was famous for its OLD TESTAMENT murals and became a centre of pilgrimage. He was an active and outstanding priest and on this account was imprisoned and tortured under the Decian persecution of the 3rd century. Legend says he was miraculously released by an angel who sent him to the relief of his bishop, Maximus, who had gone into hiding in the hills and was perishing of cold and starvation. Felix eluded pursuit and carried Maximus to safety. He is patron of Nola and his relics are preserved there. In view of the large number of saints of the name of Felix it is likely that several Felixes have been combined in the legends.

Felix of Thibiuca, St (247–303, f.d. 24 October, 15 July). One of the early martyrs under Diocletian's persecution, he refused to obey the edict of 303 which ordered the destruction of the Christian SCRIPTURES and liturgical works. He was arrested and given time to change his attitude, but, saying it was better to obey God than man, he was beheaded at Carthage.

Fellowship. Fellowship of St Alban and St Sergius. Founded at St Albans, England, in 1928, at Anglo-Russian conferences organized by members of the British and Russian STU-DENT CHRISTIAN MOVEMENT, the fellowship is 'an independent society whose aim is to increase understanding and co-operation between Christians of the ORTHODOX and Western traditions'. Its name is derived from St ALBAN, the first martyr in Britain, and St SERGIUS, patron saint of the Russian theological academy in Paris. In 1943 the fellowship established a permanent base in London at St Basil House. There are branches in North America, Australia, Greece and Scandinavia. Although largely Orthodox and Anglican in membership, interest is also shown by some ROMAN CATHOLICS and FREE CHURCH members. There is a yearly pilgrimage to St Albans where the Orthodox LITURGY is celebrated.

Fellowship of Reconciliation. Founded in 1914 at Cambridge, England, by an English QUAKER and a German LUTHERAN pastor. After World War I an international Fellowship of Reconciliation was inaugurated in Holland and now operates in twenty-seven countries; both CATHOLICS and PROTESTANTS co-operate within the movement which is pacifist but committed to active work for world peace within Christian belief and ethics. Its headquarters are in Alkmaar.

Fénelon (1651–1715). French prelate and writer, son of the Comte de Fénelon, he was also tutor to the Duke of Burgundy, grandson of Louis XIV. Fénelon was spiritual director to a community of converts from the HUGUENOTS, and in 1685 was sent on a mission to preach to them. His *Explication des Maximes des Saints* was condemned as QUIETIST and he was banished to Cambrai where he had been appointed archbishop in 1695. The mystical tone of his work led to a quarrel with the JANSENISTS and his condemnation by the Pope.

Ferdinand III, St (1199–1252, f.d. 30 May). King of Castile and son of King Alfonso IX of Leon and Queen Berengaria, granddaughter of King Henry II of England, he united the kingdoms of Leon and Castile and conducted a rigorous crusade against the Moors in Spain, driving them back to Africa and establishing a Christian state. Legend says that St JAMES was seen leading the Christian army on a white horse. Ferdinand rebuilt the cathedral of Santiago de

Compostela, the bells having been removed by the Moors. He founded the university of Salamanca and probably also that of Valladolid. He proved a wise and tolerant ruler and had a widespread cult. He was buried in Seville cathedral, dressed in the habit of a FRANCISCAN. In art he is depicted with a greyhound.

Ferghil, St. *See* VIRGIL.

Feria. Days on which no special observance is decreed by church authorities; the opposite of *Feriae*, or holidays on which work ceased to allow for special church services.

Ferrara Bible, The. *See* BIBLE, SOME SPECIALLY NAMED EDITIONS.

Festivals. *See* FEASTS.

Feuillant. A reformed CISTERCIAN order instituted in 1577 by Jean de la Barrière, Abbot of the Cistercian monastery of Feuillants in Languedoc.

Fiacre, St. (f.d. 30 August). Legend has it that he was a 7th-century hermit of Irish origin. He settled in France and built a monastery at Breuil. He is the patron saint of gardeners. He had a reputation for caring for the sick, being associated particularly with those suffering from venereal disease and haemorrhoids; a stone on which he sat and left a curved impression was preserved and used by sufferers who were cured miraculously. As a skilled gardener and horticulturist he is often depicted with a trowel or shovel in his hand.

Fidei Defensor. *See* DEFENDER OF THE FAITH.

Fidelis of Sigmaringen, St (1577–1622, f.d. 24 April). Born at Sigmaringen, Hohenzollern, and named Mark Rey, he studied at Freiburg, taking degrees in philosophy and law. He became known as the 'advocate of the poor', but resigned his profession and was ordained priest, and then joined the CAPUCHINS. He was noted for his preaching and for his work among the sick during a pestilence. He was sent on a mission to heretics, converting CALVINISTS and working among ZWINGLIANS in Switzerland, where he was murdered in the church at Seewis by peasants infuriated at his success.

Fifth-Monarchy Men. Religious extremists of Cromwellian times who maintained that the time had come for the rule of Christ and His Saints—the Fifth Monarchy, succeeding those of Assyria, Persia, Macedonia, and Rome; as the four monarchies described in the *Book of Daniel* (ch. ii) give way to that set up by the 'God of Heaven'. Venner's Rising of 1661

marked the end of their attempts to establish the Fifth Monarchy.

Fig. Fig leaf. The leaf of the fig-tree was used by ADAM and Eve to cover their nakedness after the Fall (*Gen.* iii, 7). Hence its use in statuary and paintings in times when 'modesty' was in fashion, notably in the Victorian period.
Fig Sunday. An old provincial name for PALM SUNDAY. Figs were eaten on that day in commemoration of the blasting of the barren fig-tree by Our Lord (*Mark* xi). Many festivals still have their special dishes, as, the goose for MICHAELMAS, pancakes for SHROVE TUESDAY, hot cross buns for GOOD FRIDAY, etc.
Fig-tree. It is said that Judas hanged himself on a fig-tree.

Fighting Prelate, The. Henry Spenser, or Despenser, Bishop of Norwich (1370–1406), who put down the insurgents of Norfolk and Suffolk during the Peasants Revolt of 1381. At North Walsham he burnt down the church in which they took refuge. He later fought in Flanders and France for Pope Urban VI against the antipope's followers, and was denounced by Wyclif as a fighting bishop.

Filioque Controversy. An argument concerning the 'Procession of the Holy Spirit' that long disturbed the Eastern and Western Churches, and the difference of opinion concerning which still forms one of the principal barriers between them. The point was: Did the HOLY GHOST proceed from the Father *and the Son (Filio-que)*, or from the Father only? The argument basically is this: If the Son is one with the Father, whatever proceeds from the Father must proceed from the Son also. The *filioque* was first introduced by the Western Church at the Council of Toledo in 589 and was added to the NICENE CREED in the 11th century. For both sides it was a profoundly important matter which could not be settled by compromise. For the Eastern Church Peter of Antioch said that to deny the *filioque* was 'a wicked thing, and among wicked things the most wicked', this was what Christ had meant as to the blasphemy against the Holy Spirit. Photius urged: 'O Latin, cease and desist from saying that there are many principles and many causes, and acknowledge that the Father is the one cause'. For the Western Church PETER DAMIAN argued that: 'When the Holy Spirit is said to proceed from the Father, it is necessary that he proceed also from the Son, because Father and Son are undoubtedly of the same *ousia*.'

Fillan, St (8th cent., f.d. 9 January). Also known as Foellan, he was a monk of Irish family who went with his mother St KENTIGERNA and his kinsman St COMGAN (*see* KEVIN) on a mission to

Scotland. His cult became of sufficient importance for Robert the Bruce to take his relics to the battle of Bannockburn, which was won due to the saint's intervention. Fillan's bell and staff still survive and a pool at Strathfillan, in which the mentally sick were bathed, was used until comparatively recent times. The sick were tied to a corner of his chapel and left overnight; if they broke loose they were considered cured.

Finan the Leper, St (6th cent., f.d. 16 March). An Irishman, a disciple of St COLUMBA who was reputed to have made him abbot of Swords, near Dublin. Finan was said to have contracted leprosy from a child he had cured of the disease. He was buried at Clonmore, which he also possibly ruled.

Finan of Lindisfarne, St (d. 661, f.d. 17 February). An Irishman, a monk of Iona who followed St AIDAN as bishop of Lindisfarne, where he built a wooden cathedral. He baptized St SIGEBERT, King of the East Saxons and ordained St CEDD and others, sending them on missions to Mercia and East Anglia. In the controversy over the date of EASTER he adhered to the Celtic and opposed the Roman date.

Finbar (Barr or Barry), St (c. 560–610, f.d. 25 September). Born in Co. Cork, his father was illegitimate and his mother a slave girl. He was reputed to have gone with St DAVID to ROME, but this was probably as legendary as were his great wonders, such as crossing the Irish Sea on horseback and the appearance of Christ in person at his consecration. At his death the sun itself kept the wake and did not set. Finbar is patron of Cork which grew round the monastery he founded and of which he was the first bishop.

Finnian. Finnian of Clonard, St (d. 549, f.d. 12 December). A man of Leinster who founded monasteries in Ireland at Rossacurra, Drumfea and Kilmaglish before going to Wales with SS DAVID, CADOC and GILDAS. He studied traditional monasticism and founded churches. Returning to Ireland he founded more churches and the important monastery of Clonard, of which he was abbot and where he had numerous disciples and pupils including SS COLUMBA of Iona and BRANDAN the Voyager. Finnian became famous as the 'Master' and 'Teacher of Saints' and of the Twelve Apostles of Ireland; he was also renowned for his biblical studies, though some of his records contain anachronisms. He died of the yellow plague.

Finnian of Moville, St (d. 579, f.d. 10 September). Reputedly of royal blood of Ireland, he was educated at Dromore and then under St NINIAN at his monastery at Whithorn. He was said to have gone to ROME, and had been ordained priest and studied ecclesiastical and apostolic traditions before returning to Ireland, bringing with him a biblical manuscript. He then founded a monastery at Moville and another at Dromin. Finnian gained a reputation as a notable scholar and teacher and had St COLUMBA under him. Miracles were told of him but much of his history is doubtful, being confused with that of St Frigidian or Frediano of Lucca or of St FINNIAN OF CLONARD.

Fintan. Fintan of Clonenagh, St (d. 603., f.d. 17 February). Born in Leinster, he founded the famous monastery of Clonenagh, noted for the strictness of its rules and austerity in living. Fintan himself was said to have lived on barley bread and muddy water. The agricultural work of the monastery was carried out by the monks alone, without using animals. Fintan had a reputation as a man of great courtesy and forbearance; St COLUMBA of Iona spoke of him as a handsome, holy-looking man who had ruddy cheeks and shining eyes.

Fintan Munnu (or Mundus), St (d. 635, f.d. 21 October). Of the Neill family, he was trained under St COMGALL of Bangor at one of St COLUMBA's monasteries at Kilmore. He went to Iona to be with St Columba, but the saint had recently died and his successor Baithen would not permit Fintan to stay. He said that St Columba had left instructions before his death that when Fintan arrived he was to be sent back to Ireland to found a monastery at Taghmon and be its abbot. He was said to suffer from leprosy which he had contracted voluntarily to gain merit and that he never bathed or scratched himself except on MAUNDY THURSDAY when he did both. An angel visited him on Sundays and Thursdays.

Fintan of Reinau, St (d. 879, f.d. 15 November). Born in Leinster, he was carried off by Vikings and taken to the Orkneys as a slave. He escaped, wandered on the Continent, and made a pilgrimage to ROME. He later joined some hermits on an island in the Rhine, near Schaffhausen, remaining there for the rest of his life, his relics being enshrined there.

First. First cause. A cause that does not depend on any other. The Creator.

First-fruits. The first profitable results of labour. In husbandry, the first corn that is cut at harvest, which by the ancient Hebrews was offered to JEHOVAH. Such offerings became customary in the early Christian Church. ANNATES were also called First-fruits. The word is used figuratively as well in such expressions as 'the first fruits of sin', 'the first fruits of repentance'.

Fish. The fish was used as a symbol of Christ by the early Christians because the letters of its Greek name *ichthus* (*see* ICHTHYS) formed an acronym of the initial letters of the words Jesus

Christ, Son of God, Saviour. This applies in the Roman but not in the Eastern Orthodox Church. Three fishes with one head represent the three-in-one of the TRINITY and three intertwined fishes denote baptism under the Trinity. The fish is an emblem of SS ANTHONY OF PADUA, COMGALL, BEUNO, PETER the Fisherman, ULRIC and ZENO. Fish takes the place of meat on fast days.

He eats no fish. In the time of Elizabeth I, a way of saying he is an honest man and one to be trusted, because he is not a Papist. Roman Catholics were naturally suspect at this time, and PROTESTANTS refused to adopt their custom of eating fish on Fridays (*see* FISH DAY).

> I do profess to be no less than I seem; to serve him truly that will put me in trust ... to fight when I cannot choose, and to eat no fish.
> SHAKESPEARE: *King Lear*, I, iv

The government, however, sought to enforce the observance of fish days in order to help the fishing ports and the seafaring population; and to check the consumption of meat which encouraged the conversion of arable into pasture.

> It shall not be lawfull ... to eat any flesh upon any days now usually observed as fish dayes, or upon any Wednesday now newly limited to observed as fish day.
> *Act 5 Eliz. c.* 5, 1564

Fish day. In France known as *jour maigre* (a lean day), a day when Roman Catholics and others used to abstain from meat and customarily eat fish. In the ROMAN CATHOLIC CHURCH there was a general law of abstinence on all Fridays (unless FEASTS), but bishops now urge the faithful voluntarily to practise this or some other form of self-denial.

Fisherman's Ring. A seal-ring with which the POPE is invested at his election, bearing the device of St PETER fishing from a boat. It is used for sealing papal briefs, and is officially broken up at the Pope's death by the Chamberlain of the Roman Church.

Fisher, St John (1469–1535, f.d. 22 June, formerly 9 July). Born at Beverley and educated at Cambridge University, he was elected a fellow of Michaelhouse (Trinity College) when only fourteen years of age. Later he became Master of the College. He was ordained priest and was chaplain to Lady Margaret Beaufort, the King's mother; he advised her in using her fortune for the benefit of the University. Reforms were made and Greek and Hebrew were introduced into the curriculum, and a fine library was collected. ERASMUS was invited to lecture. Fisher also became chancellor of the University and bishop of Rochester. When Henry VIII came to the throne Fisher was chosen as confessor to

Queen Catherine of Aragon, but he fell foul of the King over the divorce and was imprisoned. He was also accused of sympathy with Elizabeth Barton, a nun who had visions and predicted punishment for the king if he did not renounce Anne Boleyn. After he had refused to take the Oath of Succession Fisher was imprisoned in the Tower and was deposed from his office. The Pope then made him a cardinal, but the King said that even if Fisher received a red hat he would have no head to put it on. He was tried and beheaded in spite of great physical weakness, showing remarkable fortitude at his execution. He was a friend of Thomas MORE and now shares the feast day of 22 June with him. He was canonized in 1935.

Five. The Five-Mile Act. An Act passed in 1665 (repealed in 1812), the last act of the Clarendon Code prohibiting NONCONFORMIST clergy from coming within five miles of any corporate town or within that distance of the place where they had formerly ministered.

The Five Points of Calvinism. *See* CALVINISM.

Flagellants. The Latin *flagellum* means a scourge, and this name is given to those extremists who scourged themselves in public processions in mediaeval times, and subsequently, as penance for the sins of the world. There was a particular outbreak in Italy in 1260 and again in 1348–9, at the time of the black death, when the movement spread over Europe. The Church has never encouraged such practices.

Flagellum Dei (Lat. the scourge of God).

Flannan, St (7th cent., f.d. 17 December). Born in Ireland and said to have been the first bishop of Lillaloe, he was a wandering preacher and had associations with the Isle of Man and with Scotland, where the Flannan Islands were named after him and on one of which are the remains of the chapel of Flannon. Many legends are told of him, among them that he was reputed to have sailed from Ireland to ROME on a stone. He replaced the eye of a boy after it had been pecked out and swallowed by a bird and, in common with various other Irish saints, his fingers shed light. It was said that in spite of his numerous activities he recited the entire psalter daily.

Flavian of Constantinople, St (d. 449, f.d. 18 February). Elected archbishop of Constantinople, he immediately came into conflict with the imperial chamberlain Chrysaphine whose godfather, the heresiarch Eutyches, was excommunicated for his teaching on the person of Christ. Eutyches appealed to Pope LEO THE GREAT who put forth the orthodox doctrine in his famous *Tome of Leo*. The Emperor

Theodosius II convened the OECUMENICAL COUNCIL of Ephesus together with Archbishop Dioscorus of Alexandria—a meeting called the 'Robber Council' on account of its disorderly conduct. Eutyches was reinstated while Flavian was deposed, exiled and imprisoned in Lydia where he was so ill–treated that he died soon after. He was vindicated later at the Council of Chalcedon in 451 and his remains were removed to Constantinople by St PULCHERIA.

Flood, The. *See* DELUGE.

Florence, Council of (1438–45). Called the Council of Florence although it was held in three different places, including ROME and Ferrara. Its chief aim was the reconciliation of the Eastern and Western branches of the Church, and it was the last of these attempts. It was here that the ORTHODOX CHURCH had to give way on the *filioque* argument, but the reconciliation was not lasting and the East and West still remain separate.

Flowers. Flowers and Trees, etc.
(1) Dedicated to saints:

Canterbury Bells	to	St AUGUSTINE of CANTERBURY
Crocus	"	St VALENTINE
Crown Imperial	"	EDWARD THE CONFESSOR
Daisy	"	St MARGARET
Herb Christopher	"	St CHRISTOPHER
Lady's-smock	"	the Virgin MARY
Rose	"	MARY MAGDALENE
St John's-wort	"	St JOHN
St Barnaby's Thistle	"	St BARNABAS

(2) In Christian Symbolism:

Box	a symbol of	the Resurrection
Cedars	"	the faithful
Corn-ears	"	the Holy Communion
Dates	"	the faithful
Grapes	"	this is my blood
Holly	"	the Resurrection
IVY	"	the Resurrection
Lily	"	purity
OLIVE	"	peace
Orange-blossom	"	virginity
PALM	"	victory
Rose	"	incorruption
Vine	"	Christ our Life
Yew	"	death

NB—The laurel, oak, olive, myrtle, rosemary, cypress, and amaranth are all funereal plants.

Flowers in Christian Tradition. Many plants and flowers play a part in Christian tradition. The aspen is said to tremble because the cross was made of its wood and there are other traditions connected with the elder-tree, FIG-TREE, passion flower, thistle, etc. *See also* FIG LEAF; GLASTONBURY.

The following are said to owe their stained blossoms to the blood which trickled from the CROSS: the red anemone; the arum; the purple orchis; the crimson-spotted leaves of the rood-selken (vervain, or the 'herb of the cross'); the spotted persicaria or snake-weed.

Foellan, St. *See* FILLAN.

Foillan (Faolan or **Feuillan), St** (d. *c.* 655, f.d. 31 October). An Irish monk, brother of SS Ultan and FURSEY. He accompanied the latter on a mission to East Anglia and established a monastery there of which Fursey was abbot. Fursey then left for Gaul and Foillan succeeded him. The monastery was destroyed by the ravages of King Penda of Mercia and Foillan went with Ultan to Brabant and founded a monastery at Fosses; there he carried out missionary work. He worked with St GERTRUDE, visiting her abbey and other establishments, and was murdered by robbers in the forest on one of these journeys. Ultan succeeded him as abbot of Fosses.

Font. A receptacle for water, occupying a permanent place in a church, and used for holy water in BAPTISM. The font is placed to the west of the NAVE, near the entrance to the church, symbolizing admission by baptism. A square font depicts the Holy City; as a pentagon it represents the five wounds of Christ; as an octagon, the most usual shape, the font takes on the significance of the number eight as regeneration and rebirth.

Fool. The Feast of Fools. A kind of clerical Saturnalia, popular in the Middle Ages and not successfully suppressed until the REFORMATION, and even later in France. The feast was usually centred on a cathedral and most commonly held on the Feasts of St STEPHEN (26 December), St JOHN (27 December), HOLY INNOCENTS (28 December). The mass was burlesqued and braying often took the place of the customary responses. Obscene jests and dances were common as well as the singing of indecent songs. The ass was a central feature and the **Feast of Asses** was sometimes a separate festival. *Cp.* BOY BISHOP.

Forbidden Fruit. Forbidden or unlawful pleasure of any kind, especially illicit love. The reference is to *Gen.* ii, 17, 'But of the tree of knowledge of good and evil, thou shalt not eat of it.' According to Muslim tradition the forbidden fruit partaken of by ADAM and Eve was the banyan or Indian fig.

Formal Sin. Deliberate transgression; an act known to be wrong in itself and known to be sinful by the perpetrator.

Forty. A number of frequent occurrence in the SCRIPTURES and hence formerly treated as, in a manner, sacrosanct. Moses was 'in the mount forty days and forty nights'; Elijah was fed by ravens for forty days; the rain of the FLOOD fell forty days; and another forty days expired before Noah opened the window of the ark; forty days was the period of emblaming; Nineveh had forty days to repent; Our Lord fasted forty days; He was seen forty days after His Resurrection, etc.

St SWITHIN betokens forty days' rain or dry weather; a quarantine extended to forty days; in Old English law forty days was the limit for the payment of the fine for manslaughter; a stranger, at the end of forty days, was compelled to be enrolled in the tithing; the privilege of SANCTUARY was for forty days; the widow was allowed to remain in her husband's house for forty days after his decease; a KNIGHT enjoined forty days' service of his tenant; a new-made burgess had to forfeit forty pence unless he built a house within forty days, etc., etc.

Forty stripes save one. The Jews were forbidden by MOSAIC LAW to inflict more than forty stripes on an offender, and for fear of breaking the law, they stopped short of the number. If the scourge contained three lashes, thirteen strokes would equal 'forty save one'.

The THIRTY-NINE ARTICLES of the CHURCH OF ENGLAND used sometimes to be called 'the forty stripes save one' by theological students.

Forty-two Line Bible, The. *See* BIBLE, SOME SPECIALLY NAMED EDITIONS.

Forty Martyrs of England and Wales, The (1535–1679, f.d. 25 October). In 1970 Pope Paul VI canonized forty ROMAN CATHOLICS, selected from among two hundred already beatified, as the Martyrs of England and Wales. All had suffered martyrdom under the persecution of Catholics which resulted from the changes made by King Henry VIII. Some had refused to take the Oath of Supremacy, others had become priests or had harboured priests. Among them were JESUITS, CARTHUSIANS, BENEDICTINES, FRANCISCANS, an AUGUSTINIAN FRIAR and a BRIDGETTINE, they were:

John Almond: Secular clergy.
Edmund Arrowsmith: Jesuit.
Ambrose Barlow: Benedictine.
John Boste: Secular clergy.
Alexander Briant: Secular clergy.
Edmund Campion: Jesuit.
Margaret Clitherow: Laywoman.
Philip Evans: Jesuit.
Thomas Garnet: Jesuit.
Edmund Gennings: Secular clergy.
Richard Gwyn: Layman.
John Houghton: Carthusian.
Philip Howard: Layman.
John Jones: Franciscan priest.
John Kemble: Secular clergy.

Luke Kirby: Secular clergy.
Robert Lawrence: Carthusian.
David Lewis: Jesuit.
Anne Line: Laywoman.
John Lloyd: Secular clergy.
Cuthbert Mayne: Secular clergy.
Henry Morse: Jesuit.
Nicholas Owen: Jesuit.
John Payne: Secular clergy.
Polydore Plasden: Secular clergy.
John Plessington: Secular clergy.
Richard Reynolds: Bridgettine.
John Rigby: Layman.
John Roberts: Benedictine.
Alban Roe: Benedictine.
Ralph Sherwin: Secular clergy.
Robert Southwell: Jesuit.
John Southworth: Secular clergy.
John Stone: Augustinian Friar.
John Wall: Franciscan.
Henry Walpole: Jesuit.
Margaret Ward: Laywoman.
Augustine Webster: Carthusian.
Swithun Wells: Layman.
Eustace White: Secular clergy.

Forty Martyrs of Sebasta (d. 320, f.d. 10 March). A group of soldiers of the 12th Thunder-struck Legion, of various nationalities, defied the order of the Emperor Licinius to renounce their Christian faith. They were stationed at Sebasta, in Armenia. Stripped naked, they were immersed in a frozen pond in full view of warm baths and a fire. All remained faithful but one, and his place was taken by another who had a dream of angels and became converted. Those who were not dead the next day were killed. It was said that the youngest, Melito, was supported throughout by his widowed mother. Their cult was widespread in the East, and there are variations in the story.

Four. In Christian symbolism four is the number of the body, associated with three as the number of the soul. There are four GOSPELS, EVANGELISTS, chief ARCHANGELS, chief DEVILS, FATHERS OF THE CHURCH, GREAT PROPHETS, rivers of PARADISE, CARDINAL VIRTUES, Horsemen of the Apocalypse, Letters.

Four Crowned Martyrs, The (4th cent., f.d. 8 November). Also known as the Four Crowned Brothers, or the Four Crowned Ones, there are two distinct legends as to their identity. One says they were four Roman soldiers, brothers, who were martyred under the Diocletian persecution in 304, their individual names being unknown. They refused to renounce their Christianity and worship Aesculapius, and so were scourged to death with leaden whips and then thrown into the drains. Pope Militades designated them martyrs and their bodies were reburied on the Via Lavicana. A church was dedicated to them in ROME. The alternative, and more popular, version is that four highly skilled Persian stonemasons named Claudius, Nicostratus, Simpronian and Casterius, from the quarries at Sirmium, refused to carve a statue of Aesculapius and worship the gods. They were placed alive in lead coffins and drowned. Their cult flourished in the Middle Ages and they were popular in England, having a chapel dedicated to them at Canterbury and being patrons of stonemasons. Accounts of them appear in the *Golden Legend*, and there is a Freemasons' *Quatuor Coronati* Lodge in London which publishes a journal entitled *Ars Quatuor Coronatorum.*

Four Horsemen of the Apocalypse. In *The Revelation of St John the Divine* (ch. vi), four agents of destruction, two being agents of war and two of famine and pestilence. The first appeared on a white horse, the second on a red horse, the third on a black horse, and the fourth on a pale horse.

Vicente Blasco Ibáñez (1867–1928), the Spanish writer, published a novel of this title in 1916 which appeared in English in 1918.

Four Letters, The. *See*, TETRAGRAMMATON.

Foursquare Gospel. A PROTESTANT Evangelical and FUNDAMENTALIST denomination founded by Pastor George Jeffreys in 1915, believing in adult BAPTISM by immersion, healing the sick by anointing, speaking with tongues, literal HEAVEN and Hell, the immanent coming of Christ and the MILLENNIUM. The organization is incorporated with the ELIM Foursquare Alliance.

Fourteen Holy Helpers. *See* EUSTACE.

Fox, George (1624–91). Founder of the Society of Friends or QUAKERS. Born at Fenny Drayton, in Lincolnshire, the son of a weaver, Fox was first a weaver, then apprenticed to a shoemaker. He said he was called by God to forsake all, after which he travelled widely as a preacher, but was imprisoned at Derby for blasphemy. He refused to bear arms or to take off his hat to anyone, but when he was examined by Cromwell, the Lord Protector, his beliefs and character were pronounced blameless. Fox travelled to Wales and Scotland and went on missionary journeys to the West Indies, North America, Germany and Holland. His *Journal*, appearing in 1694, became a religious classic.

Foy, St. *See* FAITH.

Frances (or **Francesca**) **of Rome, St** (1384–1440, f.d. 9 March). Of noble Roman family, she wished to become a nun. Instead, she was married, at the age of thirteen, to Lorenzo de Ponziani, but with other like-minded women she carried out charitable works, relieving the poor and tending those in hospital. She had several children, two of whom died young, and her husband was forced into exile by the sack of Rome in 1409, but Frances carried on her good works in difficult circumstances. She founded a society under BENEDICTINE rule but not under vows. This she first called the Oblates of Mary then, later, the Oblates of Tor de' Specci. Her husband was able to return from exile, but in poor health, and he died in 1436, after which Frances retired to her community as its head, remaining there until her death four years later. This community still remains active, now as the Casa degli Esercizi Pii, a centre of pilgrimage. Her relics are enshrined in the Church of Santa Francesca Romano. She was reported to have many visions, mystical experiences and visitations, particularly of her GUARDIAN ANGEL. Pope Paul V canonized her in 1605 and later Pope Pius named her as the patron saint of motorists. In art her work for plague victims is represented with her at prayer among the dead and dying, or as holding broken arrows to symbolize the conquest of disease. She wears a black habit and white veil; sometimes she carries a basket of food or is accompanied by her guardian angel.

Francis. Francis of Assisi, St (1182–1226, f.d. 4 October). The founder of the FRANCISCANS. The son of a wealthy merchant, he was rejected by his father for his generous gifts to the poor folk of Assisi and his little chapel, called the *Portiuncula,* was soon thronged with disciples. His love of nature was a characteristic as was his purity and gentleness of spirit and his preaching to the birds became a favourite subject for artists. His begging friars lived in extreme poverty and he was canonized two years after his death (in 1228). There are numerous representations of him in art: as holding up the LATERAN church; the mystic marriage of St Francis to the Lady Poverty; with the STIGMATA; with the CRIB he originated in a grotto at Greccio and numbers of animal and bird scenes, particularly with the wolf Gubbio. In 1979 Pope John Paul II named him the patron saint of ecologists.

Franciscans. The Friars Minor, founded by St FRANCIS OF ASSISI in 1209 and now divided into three distinct and independent branches, the Friars Minor, the Friars Minor Conventual and the Friars Minor CAPUCHIN. These constitute the First Order. The Franciscans first appeared in England in 1224 and were called *Grey Friars* from the indeterminate colour of their habit, which is now brown. They had 65 religious houses in England at the time of the REFORMATION. Especially notable for its preaching among the poor, the distinguishing feature of the order at the outset was insistence on poverty, which later produced dissension. Many of the stricter members called *Spirituals* or *Zealots*, the less strict FRATICELLI, and in 1517 the *Observants*, separated from the *Conventuals*, and in the 1520s the Capuchins became another Order. Later groups were the *Reformati*, the *Recollects*, and the *Discalced* (*see* BAREFOOTED). The whole Order was reorganized into its present branches by Pope Leo XIII in 1897. *See* CORDELIER; TERTIARIES. For the Second Order (or Nuns) *see* CLARE, ORDER OF ST.

Those nuns following a milder rule instituted by Urban IV in 1263 were called *Urbanists*, and a reformed order of *Colettines* founded by St Colette arose in the 15th century, other offshoots being the *Grey Sisters, Capuchin Nuns, Sisters of the Annunciation*, and *Conceptionists*.

St Francis's Distemper. Impecuniosity; being moneyless. Those of the Order of St Francis were not allowed to carry any money about them.

Francis, Society of. An ANGLICAN community of FRIARS at Cerne Abbas in Dorset, having a home farm and gardens and workshops where the destitute can find refuge and be trained for useful work.

Francis Borgia, St (1510–72, f.d. 10 October). Born at Gandia, in Spain, the son of the Duke of Gandia and descended from Pope Alexander VI, he married Eleanor de Castro and they had eight children. He was made governor of Catalonia and was active in suppressing corruption in administration and controlling the menace of brigands. After the death of his wife he renounced his titles, was ordained priest, and became a JESUIT; later he was appointed Father General of the Society. He founded many religious houses and colleges, improved the Roman College, and accompanied Pope PIUS V on missions to other countries. He was a notable preacher, known for his kindness and nobility of character, and he was acclaimed as a saint wherever he went. Kind and courteous to others, he was austere in his own life.

Francis of Paola, St (1416–1507, f.d. 2 April). Born of a poor family in Calabria, he joined a FRANCISCAN order when only thirteen years of age, but left to make a pilgrimage to Assisi and ROME, and then became a hermit in a cave by the sea near Paola. There he was later joined by others and together they formed the order of FRIARS known as MINIMS, the 'least', because of their humility and austerity. Francis gained a reputation as a healer, a worker of miracles and a mind-reader. He demonstrated immunity from burning and was said to have put his arm into boiling oil, carried burning charcoal in his hands and taken lime from a burning kiln. He was sent by the pope to attend the dying Louis XI of France, who was suffering from great fear of death. Thereafter Francis remained in France, founding orders, becoming tutor to the future King Charles VIII, and acting as a peace-maker. Many legends are attached to his name, and in art he is represented as spreading his cloak on the waters to calm a storm in the Straits of Messina to enable his companions to cross safely. This, and other miracles, made him the patron saint of seafarers in the appointment of 1943. He is depicted as an old, grey-bearded friar with *Caritas* (charity) written across his breast.

Francis de Sales, St (1567–1622, f.d. 24 January). Born at Thorens, in Savoy, in the Château de Sales, he studied at the University of Paris and then in Padua, where he became a Doctor of Law. He rejected a brilliant marriage and worldly advancement in favour of becoming a priest. He was sent on a difficult and dangerous mission to reinstate Catholicism in the Chablais district of Switzerland, which had been converted to CALVINISM. The success of his labours was due to his zeal, sincerity, noble character and teaching of love. A Calvinist minister said: 'If we honoured any man as a saint, I know of no one since the days of the APOSTLES more worthy than this man.' Francis was appointed coadjutor to the bishop of Geneva, after a rigorous examination in theology in ROME, and proved an excellent administrator. He succeeded to the bishopric in 1602. In conjunction with Jane Frances de CHANTAL he founded the Order of the VISITATION. He visited France, founding the Académie Florimantane at Annecy and died at Lyons; his body was later translated to Annecy. He was declared a DOCTOR OF THE CHURCH and was famed for his *Introduction to the Devout Life*. In 1923 the pope named him the patron saint of writers.

Francis Xavier, St (1506–51, f.d. 3 December). A Spaniard of noble birth, he was born at the Castle of Xavier, in Navarre. He went to the University of Paris where he met St IGNATIUS LOYOLA, and joined him and others as the first members of the SOCIETY OF JESUS. From the beginning the Society undertook foreign missions, and Francis set out for Goa on a mission to the East Indies, spending the rest of his life working in the East. In Goa he laboured against the evil-living of the Europeans and their exploitation of the people. He worked for seven years among the Paravas of S.E. India, Ceylon, the Malay Peninsula and the Molucca Islands. He left for Japan in 1549 where, after initial difficulties, he met with success as representative of the King of Portugal. He was given the use of a Buddhist monastery, and made many converts. After two years he returned to Goa and organized the mission of the priests who had arrived there, then set out for China, arriving at the island of Shangchwan where he fell ill and died. His body was taken to Goa and enshrined there. In 1927 the pope named him patron saint of Foreign Missions.

Frankalmoin (or frankalmoigne) tenure (free alms). A form of feudal tenure whereby the Church held land granted by pious benefactors in return for some form of praying service, usually praying for the soul of the donor. The Church also held some of its lands by knight service. *See* CHANTRY; MORTMAIN.

Frankincense. The literal meaning of this is pure or true incense. It is a fragrant gum exuded from several trees of the genus *Boswellia*, abundant on the Somali coast and in South Arabia. It was ceremonially used by the Egyptians, Persians, Babylonians, Hebrews, Greeks, and Romans and is an ingredient of the modern incense used in certain churches.

> They presented unto him gifts; gold, and frankincense, and myrrh.
>
> *Matt.* ii, 11

Fraticelli (Ital. Little Brethren). A name given to several groups of monks and friars in Italy in the 13th, 14th, and 15th centuries, many of whom were originally FRANCISCANS. They were mostly fanatical ascetics and came to be branded as HERETICS.

Free. Free Churches. The NONCONFORMIST churches, so called because they are free from any kind of official connexion with the State.
Free Church of Scotland (or Free Church). Formed by those who left the established CHURCH OF SCOTLAND after the disruption of 1843.
Wee Frees. A minority of the FREE CHURCH which refused to join the United Free Church in 1900. It had some 16,000 members in 1988.
Free Will Baptists. A PROTESTANT sect in the USA which adheres to Arminian free-will doctrines as opposed to the PREDESTINATION of CALVINISM. One of the oldest sects in the States.

French Prophets. The name bestowed upon a group of CAMISARDS who arrived in England in 1706 claiming prophetic and wonder-working gifts and the speedy arrival of the second ADVENT.

Friar (Lat. *frater*, a brother). A member of one of the mendicant orders, notably the AUGUSTINIANS, CARMELITES, DOMINICANS, and FRANCISCANS. *See also* CRUTCHED FRIARS.
Crutched Friars. *See* CRUTCHED.
Friars Major (*Fratres majores*). Sometimes applied to the DOMINICANS in contrast to the Friars Minor (*see* FRANSISCANS).
Friars of the Sack. *See under* SACK.

Friday. The sixth day of the week (until 1971 when it became the fifth (*see* SUNDAY). Friday was regarded by the Norsemen as the luckiest day of the week, the day of weddings, etc., but among Christians it has been regarded as the unluckiest, because it was the day of the Crucifixion. While no longer a day of compulsory abstinence for Roman Catholics, they are urged to set Friday apart for some voluntary act of self-denial.
Good Friday. *See under* GOOD.
Long Friday. GOOD FRIDAY was so called by the Saxons, probably because of the long fasts and offices associated with that day.

Frideswide, St (*c.* 680–727, f.d. 19 October, 12 February). Traditionally a princess who, to avoid marriage, or the unwanted attentions of a prince of Mercia, fled to the forest and remained there for three years. Her suitor was struck blind and abandoned his pursuit, but his sight was restored later at Frideswide's intercession. She established, and was abbess of, a monastery at Oxford and remained there for the rest of her life. The monastery was built on the site of Christ Church and was the beginning of the town of Oxford, of which she is patron. In the 15th century she was adopted as patron of the University. Miracles were attributed to her and her shrine at Christ Church is still visited by pilgrims.

Friend. A QUAKER, i.e. a member of the Society of Friends.
The Society of Friends. The QUAKERS.

Fringe. The fringe, or more correctly twisted cords or tassels worn on the four corners of the Jewish outer garment (*tzitzith*) in OLD TESTAMENT times and later, were anciently supposed to have a special virtue. Hence the desire of the woman who had the issue of blood to touch the fringe of Our Lord's garment (*Matt.* ix, 20–22). From the 13th century an undergarment with tassels attached, the *arba kanfoth* (four corners) worn at all times by orthodox Jews, replaced the *tzitzith*.

> Thou shalt make thee fringes upon the four quarters of thy vesture, wherewith thou coverest thyself.
>
> *Deut.* xxii, 12

Frithebert, St (d. *c.* 766, f.d. 23 December). Succeeded St ACCA as bishop of Hexham and was said to have been responsible for Lindisfarne while bishop Cynewulf was imprisoned. He served Hexham for thirty-four years.

Frontal. An ornamental panel, usually of embroidered cloth, hanging in front of the ALTAR and changed in colour according to the ecclesiastical season.

Frost Saints. *See* ICE SAINTS.

Fructuosus, St (d. 259, f.d. 21 January). Bishop

of Tarragona who, with his deacons Augurius and Eulogius, was martyred for refusing to obey the edict of Valerian and Gallienus to worship the gods. They were arrested and sentenced to be burnt alive. Much sympathy was shown them at their death and Fructuosus was offered drugged wine which he jokingly refused, saying it was a fast day. It was also said that when the flames had burnt through their hands they stretched out their arms to form a cross as they died. Fructuosus is patron of Tarragona.

Frumentius, St (d. *c*. 380, f.d. 27 October). A Tyrian who was wrecked off the coast of Ethiopia and stayed to carry out a mission there, becoming venerated as its first APOSTLE. He was given positions of trust at the court of the king and obtained permission to build chapels. He travelled to Alexandria to enlist the support of St ATHANASIUS, who appointed him bishop of Ethiopia to establish Christianity there. He achieved great success and it was said that his work was accompanied by 'apostolic signs'.

Fulgentius, St (d. 533, f.d. 1 or 3 January). A Carthaginian of a family of senatorial rank who was appointed procurator but abandoned office to become a monk; he became abbot of his monastery. He was elected bishop of Ruspa and was involved in the ARIAN controversy, being banished with other bishops to Sardinia and spending much of his episcopate in exile. He was a noted writer against ARIANISM. So respected and beloved by his flock was he that they prevented him from retiring to a monastery in his last years when he had returned to Africa.

Fundamentalism. The maintenance of traditional PROTESTANT Christian beliefs based upon a literal acceptance of the SCRIPTURES as fundamentals. Fundamentalism as a religious movement arose in the USA about 1919 among various denominations. What was new was not so much its ideas and attitudes, but its widespread extent and the zeal of its supporters. It opposed all theories of evolution and anthropology, holding that God transcends all laws of nature and that He manifests Himself by exceptional and extraordinary activities, belief in the literal meaning of the Scriptures being an essential tenet. In 1925, John T. Scopes, a science teacher of Rhea High School, Dayton, Tennessee, was convicted of violating the State laws by teaching evolution, an incident arousing interest and controversy far beyond the religious circles of the USA. Their leader was William Jennings Bryan (1860–1925), the politician and orator. *Cp*. MODERNISM.

Fursey, St (d. 650, f.d. 16 January). Said to be the son of an Irish prince, he became a monk and left Ireland with his brothers SS FOILLAN and Ultan for East Anglia where they were received by King SIGEBERT who gave them Burgh Castle, in Suffolk, as a monastery. After the death of Sigebert Fursey went to France and founded a monastery at Lagny-sur-Marne. While on a journey he died at Mezerolles and was buried at Péronne, his tomb becoming a place of pilgrimage, surviving the French Revolution. He was famed for his good works and as a visionary. According to BEDE he saw visions of spirits, of the future of the world and the after-life and had considerable influence on the thought of the Middle Ages, probably being the source of Dante's *Divina Commedia*.

G

Gabriel (i.e. man of God). One of the ARCHANGELS, sometimes regarded as the ANGEL of death, the prince of fire and thunder, but more frequently as one of God's chief messengers, and traditionally said to be the only angel that can speak Syriac and Chaldee. Muslims call him the chief of the four favoured angels and the spirit of truth. Milton makes him chief of the angelic guards placed over PARADISE (*Paradise Lost*, IV, 549).

In the Talmud Gabriel appears as the destroyer of the hosts of Sennacherib, as the man who showed Joseph the way, and as one of the angels who buried MOSES.

Gabriel Bell. In mediaeval England, another name for the ANGELUS or AVE Bell, in remembrance of the archangel's salutation of the Virgin Mary.

Gabriel's hounds, called also *Gabble Ratchet.* Wild geese. The noise of geese in flight is like that of a pack of hounds in full cry. The legend is that they are the souls of unbaptized children wandering through the air till the Day of JUDGEMENT.

Gabriel Lalemont, St (1610–49, f.d. 26 September). Born in Paris and died in Canada. He became a JESUIT and dedicated himself to foreign missionary work, but was unable to go abroad for some years, due to ill health. He ultimately went to Canada and undertook a mission to the Huron with Father Brébeuf. Both priests were captured, terribly tortured and killed. Father Lalemont was canonized in 1930.

Galgani, St Gemma (1878–1903, f.d. 14 May). Losing her devout parents at the age of eighteen, Gemma entered the household of Matteo Giannini, at Lucca, as a domestic servant. Her desire to become a nun of the PASSIONIST CONGREGATION was frustrated by ill health. She was a visionary, seeing on the one hand visions of CHRIST, the VIRGIN MARY and her GUARDIAN ANGEL, and on the other hand subject to a form of demonic possession and sacrilegious acts. She spoke in trance in a strange voice and her sayings were recorded. She manifested the STIGMATA and marks of the scourging. She was canonized in 1941; her cult spread and was responsible for the popularity of the name Gemma in Italy, Britain and America.

Galilee. A chapel or porch at the west end of some mediaeval churches where penitents waited before admission to the body of the church and where clergy received women who had business with them. Examples remain at Durham, Ely and Lincoln cathedrals. The name derives from *Matt.* iv, 15.

Galilean. An inhabitant of Galilee, and specifically Jesus Christ, who was called 'the Galilean'. The term was also applied to Christians as his followers. The dying words attributed to the Roman Emperor Julian the Apostate were '*Vicisti, Galilaee*'.

Gall. Bile; the very bitter fluid secreted by the liver; hence used figuratively as a symbol for anything of extreme bitterness.

Gall and wormwood. Extremely bitter and mortifying.

> And I said, My strength and my hope is perished from the Lord: Remembering mine affliction and my misery, the wormwood and the gall.
>
> *Lam.* iii, 18, 19

The gall of bitterness. The bitterest grief; extreme affliction. The ancients taught that grief and joy were subject to the gall as affection was to the heart, and knowledge to the kidneys. The 'gall of bitterness' means the bitter centre of bitterness, as the 'heart of hearts' means the innermost recesses of the heart or affections. In the *Acts* it is used to signify 'the sinfulness of sin', which leads to the bitterest grief.

> For I perceive that thou art in the gall of bitterness, and in the bond of iniquity.
>
> *Acts* viii, 23

Gall (Gilianus or Gallech), St (d. *c.* 630, f.d. 16 October, 20 February). Of noble Irish family, he trained as a monk at Bangor, in Ireland, under SS COLUMBANUS and COMGALL, going with the former to Switzerland where they founded monasteries. Gall refused office and settled near Bregenz as a hermit. Although he was not the founder of the monastery bearing his name he was one of the chief apostles of Christianity in Switzerland and was noted as an eloquent preacher. There were fanciful legends of his exorcising devils and driving out gnomes from the mountains, also of his friendship with bears. In art he is depicted with a bear at his feet.

Gallicanism. Influenced by William of OCCAM and the councils of the 14th and 15th centuries, the Gallicans maintained that the authority of the POPE was subject to the judgement of the General Council and was not infallible; their views were opposed by the Ultramontanists.

Gallwell, St. *See* GUDWAL.

Garden of Eden, The. *See* EDEN. Traditionally supposed to be sited in Mesopotamia.

Garnet, St Thomas (*c.* 1575–1608, f.d. 25 October). Born in Southwark and educated at Horsham Grammar School, he was a nephew of Henry Garnet, SJ, who was hanged on the suspicion of being involved in the Gunpowder Plot; his father had also been imprisoned for his beliefs. Thomas was a page to Lord William Howard and went to the JESUIT College at St Omer and then to the ENGLISH COLLEGE at Valladolid where he became a priest and later a Jesuit. He returned to England and was arrested and questioned in connexion with his uncle's alleged involvement, but was able to establish his innocence. In spite of this he, with other priests, was exiled. Returning to England against the law, he was again arrested and imprisoned, tried and condemned to be executed at Tyburn. He was canonized in 1970 as one of the FORTY MARTYRS OF ENGLAND AND WALES.

Gaudentius, St (d. *c.* 410, f.d. 25 October). A bishop of Brescia, northern Italy, chiefly known for his association with St JOHN CHRYSOSTOM, whom he defended, and his friendship with St AMBROSE. He was sent on a mission to the Emperor Arcadius at Constantinople, carrying letters from Pope Innocent I, but was intercepted by officials, who took the letters. Recognizing that the mission had failed, Gaudentius finally obtained permission to return home. The ship they were given was so unseaworthy that it had to be abandoned at Lampsacus. Finally he was imprisoned near Thrace and died soon after.

Gaudy, or **Gaudy-day** (Lat. *gaudium*, joy). A holiday, a feast-day; especially an annual celebration of some event, such as the foundation of a college.

Gaudy is also one of the beads in the ROSARY marking the five joys or JOYFUL MYSTERIES of the Virgin, and the name given to one of the tapers burnt at the commemoration of the same.

Gehenna (Heb.). The place of eternal torment. Strictly speaking, it means the 'Valley of Hinnom' (Ge-Hinnom), where sacrifices to Baal and Moloch were offered (*Jer.* xix, 6, etc.). It came to be regarded as a place of unquenchable fire, possibly from the fires of Moloch.

> And made his grove
> The pleasant valley of Hinnom, Tophet thence
> And black Gehenna called, the type of hell.
> MILTON: *Paradise Lost*, I, 403

Go to Gehenna. The same as saying 'Go to Hell'.

Gemma, St. *See* GALGANI.

General. The head of a religious order or CONGREGATION.

General Assembly. The highest court and governing body of the PRESBYTERIAN Church.

Genesius (or Gennys) of Arles, St (d. *c.* 303, f.d. 3 June). Martyred during the Maximian and Diocletian persecutions, he was a CATECHUMEN and held the office of a notary, responsible for summarizing judicial proceedings, at Arles. One day, having to record and read out an edict of persecution of Christians, he threw it down, declaring himself a Christian, and fled from the town. He sought a bishop to baptize him but was told that shedding his blood for Christ was an effective baptism. He was pursued, captured and beheaded. His cult became widespread. There is a church of St Gennys in Cornwall.

Genesius the Actor, St (4th cent., f.d. 25 August). In legend Genesius was a Roman actor who, while playing in a farce mimicking Christian baptism, in front of Diocletian, was suddenly converted and confessed his faith before the emperor. He was tortured and beheaded. The story is also told of Gelasius of Heliopolis and other actors, and has been used by dramatists such as Lope de Vega, Karl Lowe and Felix Weingartner. In art Genesius, or Genes, is depicted with a clown's cap and bells.

Geneva Academy. Founded in 1559 by CALVIN as a school for PROTESTANT theologians; it later became the University.

Geneva Bands. Two strips of white cloth, hanging from the collar, worn by some PROTESTANT clergy.

Geneva Bible. *See* BIBLE, THE ENGLISH.

Geneva Bull. A nickname given to Stephen Marshal (*c.* 1594–1655), a PRESBYTERIAN divine and one of the authors of 'Smectymnuus', because he was a disciple of John Calvin of Geneva, and when preaching 'roared like a bull of Bashan'. His influence on political and religious affairs was considerable.

Geneva doctrines. CALVINISM.

Geneva Gown. A loose-fitting black preaching-gown originally worn by CALVIN and adopted by Geneva reformers and by dissenting clergy in England. It is still worn by Calvinists and PRESBYTERIAN ministers.

Geneviève, St (422–512, f.d. 3 January). Patroness of Paris. She is represented in art with the keys of Paris at her girdle, a DEVIL blowing out her candle, and an ANGEL relighting it; or as restoring sight to her blind mother; or guarding her father's sheep. She was born at Nanterre and was influential in saving Paris from the Franks and the threatened attack of Attila the Hun. Her church has since become the Pantheon.

Gennings, St Edward (1567–91, f.d. 25 October). Born at Lichfield of a PROTESTANT family, he became a page to Richard Sherwood and was converted to CATHOLICISM. He left England for the ENGLISH COLLEGE at Reims and was ordained priest. Returning to England, he went to Lichfield for the purpose of converting his brother, but being unsuccessful, he went back to France. In 1591 he returned to London, becoming a friend of Polydore PLASDEN with whom he celebrated MASS in the house of Swithun WELLS. They were discovered by the pursuivant Topcliffe, arrested, tried and executed together at Gray's Inn Fields. Wells was subsequently tried and executed for harbouring priests. All three were canonized in 1970 as among the FORTY MARTYRS OF ENGLAND AND WALES.

Gennys of Arles, St. *See* GENESIUS.

Gentile. One who is not a Jew; especially applied to Christians. MORMONS use the term for a non-Mormon.

Genuflection. A brief bending of the knee as a formalized gesture of reverence in worship, used in the WESTERN CHURCH.

George. St George (f.d. 23 April, (Coptic) 18 April). The patron SAINT of England since his 'adoption' by Edward III. The popularity of St George in England stems from the time of the early CRUSADES, for he was said to have come to the assistance of the Crusaders at Antioch in 1098. Many of the Normans under Robert Curthose, son of William the Conqueror, took him as their patron.

Gibbon and others argued that George of Cappadocia, the Arian bishop of Alexandria, became the English patron saint but it is more generally accepted that he was a Roman officer martyred (*c.* 300) near Lydda during the Diocletian persecution. He is also the patron saint of Aragon and Portugal.

The legend of St George and the dragon is simply an allegorical expression of the triumph of the Christian hero over evil, which St JOHN the Divine beheld under the image of a dragon. Similarly, St MICHAEL, St MARGARET, St Sylvester, and St MARTHA are all depicted as slaying dragons; the Saviour and the Virgin as treading them under their feet; St John the Evangelist as

charming a winged dragon from a poisoned chalice given him to drink; and Bunyan avails himself of the same figure when he makes CHRISTIAN prevail upon Apollyon. The legend forms the subject of the ballad *St George for England* in Percy's Reliques.

In the reform of the Roman calendar in 1969 St George's status was reduced to that of a local cult, but he holds a highly important position in the calendar of the Orthodox Catholic Church. He is venerated as 'georgos', the husbandman, the patron of agriculture, of herds, flocks and shepherds; he is also 'the deliverer of prisoners and protector of the poor', giving help during his life and after his death. St George the Victorious, striking the dragon, is one of the most popular subjects in Orthodox ICON painting, particularly in the Novgorod school of the 15th century. He is also depicted with an ANGEL descending from heaven, holding the crown of victory and martyrdom over him.

George the Hagiorite, St (1009–65, f.d. 30 June, 24 May). Born in Tao-Klardzheti, in Georgia, of aristocratic parentage, he was educated in Constantinople. He returned home to become a monk, then travelled to the HOLY LAND where he became a follower of George the Recluse, at whose instigation he retired to Mount ATHOS to translate Greek religious works into Georgian. He lived in a Georgian monastery, was ordained priest, and then appointed as abbot. His literary work was of great importance in spreading orthodoxy, and after a time he abandoned his administrative labours to concentrate on the literary. He was involved in the controversy on Greek Orthodoxy and was active in opposing the MONOPHYSITE heresy. He returned to Georgia at the request of the king and the archbishop, but insisted that he should not be concerned with administration again. He laboured on the groundwork of the Council of Ruis-Urbnisi. After five years he left for the Holy Mountain at Athos, hoping to die there, but instead died on the way at Constantinople. His body was translated to the Holy Mountain.

George Haydock and Companions, BB. Dated from 1584 to 1679 this group consisted of eighty-five people who, for their faith, were martyred in England, Scotland and Wales. Among them were JESUITS, DOMINICAN and FRANCISCAN friars, SECULAR CLERGY and laymen. They were beatified by Pope John Paul II in 1987.

Gerald of Aurillac, St (855–909, f.d. 13 October). Succeeding to large estates in Auvergne, as Count of Aurillac, he administered them with proficiency, justice and kindness. He personally led a devout life of prayer and fasting, an exemplary layman's life. He built a church and founded a monastery at Aurillac which was later taken over by the CLUNIAC order.

Gerald of Mayo, St (d. 732, f.d. 13 March). A monk at Lindisfarne who was responsible for establishing the English part of a community when he went with St COLMAN to Inishbofin. Known as Mayo of the Saxons, the community developed into an important centre of studies which attracted the attention of ALCUIN, who corresponded with its members.

Gerard. Gerard Csanad (Sagredo) St (d. 1046, f.d. 24 September). Born in Venice, he became a monk at San Giorgio Maggiore and later its prior. He set out on a pilgrimage to the HOLY LAND, intending to remain there as a hermit, but was turned from his course and went to Hungary where he laboured to convert the people to Christianity. King STEPHEN founded the see of Csanad and established Gerard as its first bishop; he also appointed him tutor to his son. After Stephen's death there was a reaction against Christianity and Gerard was martyred, being stoned, transfixed to a lance and his body thrown from the Blocksburg cliff into the Danube. His relics were enshrined with those of Stephen, but some were translated to Venice where he was venerated as its first martyr and was known as St Gerard Sagredo.

Gerard Majella, St (d. 1755, f.d. 16 October). Born at Muro Lucano, in Italy, the son of a tailor, and trained as a tailor, he served in the household of the bishop of Lacedogna who treated him badly. Gerard had hoped to join the CAPUCHINS but was rejected on the grounds of ill-health. Instead he became a REDEMPTIONIST lay brother through the influence of the founder, St ALPHONSUS LIGUORI. Many marvels were attributed to Gerard, he was seen in two places at the same time, experienced ecstasies, had the gift of prophecy, of mind-reading and healing. He was also noted for his generosity, forbearance and caring for the poor. He died at an early age of consumption at the Redemptionist house at Caposele, where he had been the porter. He was beatified in 1889 and canonized in 1904. He was taken as patron of lay brothers and regarded as one of the most famous wonder-workers.

Germaine of Pibrac, St (d. 1601, f.d. 15 June). Born on a farm near Toulouse, she was a deformed and unhealthy child, ill-treated and ill-fed by her father and stepmother, sleeping in the stables or under the stairs. She was sent out daily to attend the sheep. She showed great religious devotion and patience under the mockery of the neighbours. Her stepmother accused her of stealing a loaf of bread, concealed in her apron to feed a beggar in winter, but when the apron was opened it was full of spring flowers. (A similar miracle is also told of SS ELIZABETH OF HUNGARY and ELIZABETH OF PORTUGAL.) Germaine died soon after at the age of twenty-two, alone, under the stairs. Miracles were reported at her grave, which became a place of pilgrimage.

Germanus. Germanus of Auxerre, St (d. 446, f.d. 31 July, 1 October). Born into a noble family of Romano-Gallican origin, he became an advocate in ROME, attained high position and married. At the death of the bishop of Auxerre he was appointed his successor, much against his will. He immediately changed his way of life, repudiating his marriage and devoting himself to his duties. He was sent to Britain to oppose the PELAGIAN HERESY and attended the conference at Verulamium, visiting the tomb of St ALBAN and exchanging relics. He accompanied the British army, defeating the combined forces of Picts and Scots, in the famous 'Alleluia Victory', it was said without bloodshed. He returned to France but was again in Britain where there was a revival of Pelagianism, which he successfully defeated. On his way home he interceded for the Armoricans with the emperor against the barbarian ruler. He died at Ravenna and his body was translated to Auxerre where his shrine became a centre of pilgrimage. Many accounts are given of his travels and miracles. In art he is depicted with an ass at his feet, having restored the animal to life. He is vested as a bishop and may carry a knife.

Germanus of Constantinople, St (d. c. 733, f.d. 12 May). He was raised from the see of Cyzicus to become Patriarch of Constantinople and was then involved in the dispute over iconography, opposing the edict of the Emperor Leo III and the ICONOCLASTS who forbade public veneration of ICONS, saying: 'When we show reverence to representations of Jesus Christ we do not worship paint laid on wood; we worship the invisible God in spirit and in truth.' Germanus was deposed and died at an advanced age. He was famous for his *Homilies on the Virgin Mary*, and as a composer of hymns.

Germanus of Man, St (c. 410–75, f.d. 3 July (Man), 31 July (Wales)). Born in Brittany, he went to stay with St PATRICK in Ireland, then left for Wales to live in the monastery of SS BRIOC and ILLTYD. Later he met St Patrick in Britain and took part in a magic contest with Gwrtheyrn. He was appointed bishop of Man. There are a number of churches dedicated to Germanus, but it is probable that there was some confusion with Germanus of Auxerre.

Germoe (Germoc or Germanus) MacGuill, St (date unknown, f.d. 30 July). Patron saint of Germoe, in Cornwall, where his chair was in the churchyard and a well outside. One legend says he was a king, and he is depicted with a crown and sceptre in St Brega's church. He was possibly an Irish monk, one of a party who went to Cornwall before going to Gaul.

Gerson, Jean Charlier de (1363–1429). A French mediaeval churchman and nominalist theologian, chancellor of the University of Paris, given the title 'the Most Christian Doctor'. He attended the Council of Constance and contributed to the condemnation of Hus. Gerson maintained that a Church Council should supersede the authority of the POPE. He opposed the FLAGELLANTS and is one of the writers to whom *The Imitation of Christ* has been attributed.

Gertrude. Gertrude the Great, St (d. 1302, f.d. 17 November, (Benedictine) now 16 November). All that is known of her early life is that she was placed in the nunnery of Helfta at the age of five. She remained there all her life, being well-educated. At the age of twenty-five she had a mystical experience, after which she abandoned all the secular studies in which she had been so well-grounded, and devoted her life to the SCRIPTURES, the LITURGY and the works of the FATHERS. St Mechtilde was both her preceptress and friend at Helfta and much of Gertrude's writing incorporated Mechtilde's notes and revelations. The *Revelations of St Gertrude and St Mechtilde* give an account of their spiritual and mystical experiences. Other works are: *The Herald of God's Loving-Kindness* and the *Book of Special Grace*. Gertrude became one of the most noted of mediaeval mystics, although there is some query about her confusion with Gertrude of Hackeborn, who was abbess of Helfta at the time when the child Gertrude was admitted. In art she is depicted as an abbess, holding a flaming heart; often a mouse, or mice, accompany her as with Gertrude of Nivelles.

Gertrude of Nivelles, St (d. *c.* 664, f.d. 17 March). The daughter of Pepin of Landen, aunt of Charles Martel's father, Pepin of Heristal. As abbess of Nivelles she was noted for her care of the poor and was reputed to have known most of the BIBLE by heart. In art she is usually represented as so rapt in contemplation that a mouse climbs her pastoral staff unnoticed.

Gervase and Protase, SS (no date). Two unknown martyrs, there being no historical evidence for their lives. Their remains were discovered at Milan, in 386, it was said as the result of revelations in dreams and visions. St AMBROSE ordered a search to be made, and he and St AUGUSTINE testified to miracles which followed the removal of the relics. Their cult became widespread and St Ambrose elected to be buried beside them. It has been suggested that there are affinities with the Dioscuri. In England a church was dedicated to them at Little Plumstead, in Essex.

Gestas. The traditional name of the impenitent thief. *See* DYSMAS.

Gethsemane. The word means 'oil-press' and the traditional site of the Garden of Gethsemane, the scene of Our Lord's agony, is on the Mount of Olives, east of the ravine of the Kidron. There was presumably an oil-press on this plot of ground.

The *Orchis maculata* is called 'gethsemane' from the legend that it was spotted by the blood of Christ.

Ghost. The Holy Ghost. *See under* HOLY.

Giants, i.e. persons well above normal height and size, are found as 'sports' or 'freaks of nature'; but the widespread belief in pre-existing races of giants among primitive peoples is due partly to the ingrained idea that mankind has degenerated—'There were giants in the earth in those days' (*Gen.* vi, 4)—
Giants of the Bible.

Anak. The eponymous progenitor of the Anakim (*see below*). The Hebrew spies said they were mere grasshoppers in comparison with these giants (*Josh.* xv, 14; *Judges* i, 20; and *Numb*, xiii, 33).

GOLIATH of Gath (I *Sam.* vii, etc.). His height is given as 6 cubits and a span: the cubit varied and might be anything from about 18 in. to 22 in., and a span was about 9 in.; this would give Goliath a height of between 9 ft. 9 in. and 11 ft. 3 in.

Og, King of Bashan (*Josh.* xii, 4; *Deut.* iii, 10, iv, 47, etc.). was 'of the remnant of the Rephaim'. According to tradition, he lived 3,000 years and walked beside the Ark during the Flood. One of his bones formed a bridge over a river. His bed (*Deut.* iii, II) was 9 cubits by 4 cubits.

The Anakim and Rephaim were tribes of reputed giants inhabiting the territory on both sides of the Jordan before the coming of the Israelites. The Nephilim, the offspring of the sons of God and the daughters of men (*Gen.* vi, 4), a mythological race of semi-divine heroes, were also giants.

Gichtelians. *See* ANGELIC BROTHERS.

Gideons. An international association of Christian business and professional men founded in 1899 and now functioning in over 65 countries. They seek to lead others to Christianity, particularly by the distribution of Bibles and New Testaments on a large scale. Bibles are provided in hotel bedrooms and hospitals and New Testaments are presented to pupils in schools. They are named after Gideon's men who overthrew the Midianites (*Judges* vii).

Gilbert of Caithness, St (d. 1245, f.d. 1 April). Son of William de Moravia, lord of Duffus and Strabrok, who owned large estates in Scotland,

Gilbert was appointed archdeacon of Moray by King Alexander II and, after the murder of Adam of Caithness, Gilbert was chosen bishop to succeed him. He ruled a difficult and turbulent district with wisdom and success, founding hospices for the poor and building the cathedral of Dornoch, whose patron saint he became. He firmly upheld the independence of Scotland against the archbishop of York. Gilbert's relics were used for swearing oaths until the REFORMATION.

Gilbert of Sempringham, St (*c.* 1083–1189, f.d. 4 February). Founder of the GILBERTINES, he was of Norman and Anglo-Saxon blood, his father being a knight, but Gilbert was physically deformed and so could not follow in his footsteps. Instead he was educated in France. He returned to Sempringham and founded a school for boys and girls; he became vicar of the parish and, on his father's death, lord of the manor. He was ordained priest but refused all advantageous preferment. He gathered a group of women in the parish and established an order for them under the Rule of St BENEDICT, then added lay sisters to the community, which became known as the GILBERTINES. He then founded an order of CISTERCIAN lay brothers to provide the necessary labour, and then an order of AUGUSTINIAN CANONS to supply the need for chaplains, Gilbert administering the whole in exemplary manner. Later in life he was in conflict with King Henry II, having assisted St THOMAS OF CANTERBURY to escape to the Continent and openly supporting his cause. Trouble was also caused by a revolt among Gilbert's lay brothers, who complained of their conditions and slandered him. The case was taken to ROME where the pope decided in Gilbert's favour, but the lives of the brothers were improved. Gilbert lived to be over 100 years old; he died and was buried at Sempringham, having founded thirteen monasteries and established orphanages and leper hospitals. The orders were suppressed by Henry VIII.

Gilbertines. The only mediaeval religious order of English origin, founded at Sempringham in Lincolnshire *c.* 1135 by GILBERT OF SEMPRINGHAM. The monks observed the rule of the AUGUSTINIANS and the nuns that of the BENEDICTINES. There were some 25 houses at the Dissolution.

Gildas the Wise, St (*c.* 500–70, f.d. 29 January). Also known as **Badonicus**, having been born in the year in which the Britons defeated the Saxons at Bath. Little is known of his life, but he was said to have been born in Clydeside, to have studied in South Wales under St ILLTYD, to have ended his days as a hermit in Brittany and to have founded a monastery there, in Rhuys, which became a centre of his cult. He was

highly educated and his fame rests on his importance in the development of monastic life in Wales and on his work *De excidio et conquestu Britanniae*, which gives a vivid history of Britain under the Romans and the corruption of the rulers and the clergy.

Giles, St. (f.d. 1 September) Patron SAINT of cripples and beggars. The tradition is that Childeric, king of France, accidentally wounded the hermit in the knee when hunting; and he remained a cripple for life, refusing to be cured that he might the better mortify the flesh.

His symbol is a hind, in allusion to the 'heaven-directed hind', which went daily to his cave near the mouth of the Rhône to give him milk. He is sometimes represented as an old man with an arrow in his hand and a hind by his side.

Churches dedicated to St Giles were usually situated in the outskirts of a city, and originally outside the walls, cripples and beggars not being permitted to pass the gates.

Gilianus, St. *See* GALL.

Girdle. A belt or sash worn round the waist with the ALB. It is one of the six EUCHARISTIC VESTMENTS.

Giuliani, St Veronica (1660–1717, f.d. 9 July). One of the outstanding, and one of the best documented, examples of physical phenomena, including the STIGMATA (which stopped bleeding on command); the imprint of the Crown of Thorns; levitations and mystical visions of Christ and the Passion. The phenomena were carefully examined and documented on the orders of the local bishop. Veronica was born into a wealthy family at Mercatello and became a CAPUCHIN nun, in spite of family opposition. She was appointed first mistress of novices and then abbess; during her rule she greatly improved both the spiritual and physical life of the community, enlarging and modernizing the buildings. She was an excellent administrator, both practical and level-headed.

Glastonbury. An ancient town in Somerset, almost twelve miles from Cadbury Castle, 'the many-towered Camelot'. It is fabled to be the place where Joseph of Arimathea brought the Christian faith to Britain, and the Holy GRAIL in the year 63. It was here Joseph's staff took root and budded—the famous Glastonbury Thorn, which flowers every Christmas in honour of Christ's birth. The name is now given to a variety of *Crataegus* or hawthorn, which flowers about old Christmas Day.

Glebe. Land belonging to an ecclesiastical

benefice or parish, intended for the support of the incumbent or to yield an income for the Church. The land is extra to that on which the house stands.

Gloria. Gloria in Excelsis. The opening words of the ANGELIC HYMN, also called the Greater DOXOLOGY. The Latin *Gloria in Excelsis Deo*, etc., is part of the ORDINARY OF THE MASS and the English translation 'Glory be to God on high' forms part of the CHURCH OF ENGLAND service for Holy Communion.

Gloria mundi, Sic transit (Lat.). So passes away the glory of the world. A quotation from *De Imitatione Christi* (Bk. I, ch. iii) by Thomas à Kempis (*c.* 1380–1471)—a classic statement on the transitory nature of human vanities. At the coronation ceremony of the POPE, a reed surmounted with flax is burnt, and as it flickers and dies the chaplain intones—*Pater sancte, sic transit gloria mundi.*

Gloria Patri. *See* DOXOLOGY.

Gloria Tibi. The brief DOXOLOGY, *Gloria tibi Domine*, Glory be to thee, O Lord. In the Roman Catholic Mass the Latin words are used after the announcement of the Gospel. In the CHURCH OF ENGLAND service for Holy Communion the English version is used similarly.

Glorious Mysteries. There are five Glorious Mysteries: the RESURRECTION, ASCENSION, the Descent of the HOLY SPIRIT, the ASSUMPTION of the Blessed Virgin Mary, the Coronation of the Blessed Virgin Mary.

Glossolalia. The gift of speaking with tongues. *See* TONGUE.

Gnostics. Various sects, mainly of Christian inspiration, which arose and flourished in the 2nd century with offshoots which survived into the 5th century. The name derives from the Gr. word *gnosis*, knowledge, but it was usually used by the Gnostics in the sense of 'revelation' which gave them certain mystic knowledge for salvation which others did not possess. It was essentially based on oriental dualism, the existence of two worlds, good and evil, the divine and the material. The body was regarded as the enemy of spiritual life. In most Gnostic systems there were seven world-creating powers, in a few their place was taken by one DEMIURGE. Christ was the final and perfect Aeon. The Gnostic movement caused the Christian Church to develop its organization and doctrinal discipline. In 1945 fifty-two Gnostic texts were found in Upper Egypt which underline its intellectual challenge to the early Church. *See also* MANICHAEANS; MARCIONITES.

Goat. From early times the goat has been associated with the idea of sin (*see* SCAPEGOAT) and associated with devil-lore. The legend that the DEVIL created the goat may well be due to its destructiveness, and the Devil was frequently depicted as a goat. It is also a type of lust and lechery.

Gobnet, St (5th cent., f.d. 11 February). An Irishwoman, born in County Clare, who went to the Isle of Aran and built a church there, but was told in a vision to seek another place where she would find nine white deer grazing. She went to Southern Ireland and built a church at Kilgobnet and founded a nunnery at Ballyvourney. A well there still exists and is named after her. Legend says that she prevented a robber from building a castle there by throwing a stone across the valley; the stone is still preserved as a relic. Gobnet was a notable bee-keeper and in art is depicted with bees.

Godparents. Godfathers and Godmothers who act as sponsors to a child at BAPTISM and accept responsibility for religious education up to CONFIRMATION.

Godric, St (*c.* 1069–1170, f.d. 21 May). Born in Walpole, Norfolk, of Anglo-Saxon parents, he was first a pedlar then went to sea and became a successful trader in Scotland, Flanders and Denmark. He also went on pilgrimages to St Andrews, COMPOSTELA, ROME and JERUSALEM. On one visit to Rome he was accompanied by his aged mother, both walking barefoot. Godric lived for a time as a hermit in various places in the HOLY LAND, in the desert of St JOHN THE BAPTIST. Returning to England, he took to learning in middle age and finally settled at Finchale in the diocese of Durham. He practised extreme austerities and lived in complete simplicity to atone for his earlier lax morals and dubious trading. He was noted for his affinity with, and care for, animals, bringing them into his hut out of the snow, giving them refuge from the hunt and even giving shelter to adders. He also had the gift of prophecy and of mind-reading, and poltergeist phenomena occurred towards the end of his life. He was famous as the author of the 'Hymn to the Blessed Virgin', and the earliest Middle English verse, set to music, is attributed to him. He maintained that he had no knowledge of music but received it in a vision of the Virgin and of his dead sister Burchwen, who had been a solitary.

Godwold, St. *See* GUDWAL.

Gog and Magog. In British legend, the sole survivors of a monstrous brood, the offspring of demons and the thirty-three infamous daughters of the Emperor Diocletian, who murdered their husbands. Gog and Magog were taken as prisoners to London after their fellow giants had been killed by Brute and his companions, where they were made to do duty as porters at the royal palace, on the site of the Guildhall, where their effigies have stood at least from the reign of Henry V. The old giants were destroyed in the Great Fire, and were replaced by figures 14 ft. high, carved in 1708 by Richard Saunders. These were subsequently demolished in an air raid in 1940 and new figures were set up in 1953. Formerly wickerwork models were carried in the Lord Mayor's Shows.

In the BIBLE Magog is spoken of as a son of Japhet (*Gen*. x, 2), in the *Revelation* Gog and Magog symbolize all future enemies of the Kingdom of God, and in *Ezekiel* Gog is prince of Magog, a ruler of hordes to the north of Israel.

Golden. The golden bowl is broken. Death. A Biblical allusion:

> Or ever the silver cord be loosed, or the golden bowl be broken, or the pitcher be broken at the fountain, or the wheel broken at the cistern; then shall the dust return to the earth as it was; and the spirit shall return unto God who gave it.
>
> *Eccles*. xii, 6, 7

The Golden Bull. In particular, an edict the Emperor Charles IV issued at the Diet of Nuremberg in 1356 for the purpose of regularizing the election to the throne of the Empire. It was sealed with a golden *bulla* or seal. *Cp*. PAPAL BULL *under* BULL.

Golden calf, To worship the. To bow down to money, to abandon one's principles for the sake of gain. The reference is to the golden calf made by Aaron when Moses was absent on Mount Sinai. For their sin in worshipping the calf the Israelites paid dearly (*Exod*. xxxii).

The Golden Legend (*Aurea Legenda*). A collection of so-called lives of the SAINTS made by the Dominican, Jacobus de Voragine, in the 13th century; valuable for the picture it gives of mediaeval manners, customs, and thought. It was translated from the Latin into most of the languages of western Europe and an English edition was published by Caxton in 1483.

Longfellow's *The Golden Legend* is based on a story by Hartmann von Aue, a German Minnesinger of the 12th century.

The Golden-mouthed. St JOHN CHRYSOSTOM (d. 407), a FATHER of the GREEK CHURCH, was so called for his great eloquence.

Golden Number. The number of the year in the Metonic Cycle which may therefore consist of any number from 1 to 19. In the ancient Roman and Alexandrian CALENDARS this number was marked in gold, hence the name. The rule for finding the golden number is:

> Add one to the Year of our Lord, and then divide by 19; the Remainder, if any, is the Golden Number; but if nothing remaineth, then 19 is the Golden Number.
>
> *Book of Common Prayer* (*Table to find Easter Day*)

It is used in determining the Epact and the date of EASTER.

Golden Rose. An ornament made of gold in imitation of a spray of roses, one rose, containing a receptacle into which is poured balsam and musk. The rose is solemnly blessed by the POPE on LAETARE SUNDAY, and is conferred from time to time on sovereigns and others, as well as churches and cities distinguished for their services to the ROMAN CATHOLIC CHURCH. The last to receive it was Princess Charlotte of Nassau, Grand Duchess of Luxembourg in 1956. That presented by Pius IX to the Empress Eugénie in 1856 is preserved in Farnborough Abbey.

The Golden Rule. 'Do as you would be done by.'

> Whatsoever ye would that men should do to you, do ye even so to them: for this is the law and the prophets.
>
> *Matt*. vii, 12

Golgotha. The place outside Jerusalem where Christ was crucified. The word is Aramaic and means a 'skull'. It may have been a place of execution where bodies were picked clean by animals or named from the round and skull-like contour of the site. There is no Biblical evidence for supposing that it was a hillock. The traditional site is that recovered by Constantine. *Calvaria* is the Greek and Latin equivalent of Golgotha. *See* CALVARY.

Golgotha, at the University church, Cambridge, was the gallery in which the 'heads of the houses' sat; so called because it was the place of skulls or heads. It has been more wittily than truly said that Golgotha was the place of empty skulls.

Goliath. The Philistine GIANT, slain by the stripling David with a small stone hurled from a sling (I *Sam*. xvii, 49–51). *See* GIANTS OF THE BIBLE.

Gonzaga, St Aloysius (1568–91, f.d. 21 June). Son of the Marquis of Castiglione whose wife was lady-in-waiting to the Queen of Spain. He showed great early piety and, to the annoyance of his family, became a JESUIT instead of following the intended military career. He became a novice and was professed in 1587. In opposition to the corrupt society of the time he advocated, and practised, rigid austerities, though he was forced to modify these as his health was poor and was further weakened by contracting the plague while nursing the sick in the plague hospital. He died young soon after, and was named patron of youth in 1729.

Good. Good Friday. The Friday preceding EASTER Day, held as the anniversary of the Crucifixion. 'Good' here means *holy*; CHRISTMAS, as well as SHROVE TUESDAY, used to be called 'the Good Tide'.
Born on Good Friday. According to old superstition, those born on CHRISTMAS Day or GOOD FRIDAY have the power of seeing and commanding spirits.
Good Samaritan. *See* SAMARITAN.
Good Shepherd, The. A title given to Christ, derived from *John* x, 11; it symbolizes his humanity and compassion, also the redemption of those gone astray. In art Christ is often depicted carrying a lamb over his shoulder, representing one that has been lost and found, or leading the flock.

Goose Bible, The. *See* BIBLE, SOME SPECIALLY NAMED EDITIONS.

Goretti, St Maria (1890–1902, f.d. 6 July). Of peasant family, near Ancona, she was a devout child. After the death of her father, when she was ten years old, her mother went out to work leaving Maria in charge of the house. In this situation she was approached by a young man who, when she resisted, first attempted to rape her then finally stabbed her to death. Her killer was imprisoned, repented, and lived to see Maria canonized in 1950 as representing martyrdom for chastity.

Gorkum, Martyrs of (d. 1572, f.d. 9 July). After Gorkum had been taken by an extremist group of Dutch CALVINISTS, nineteen priests from different orders were arrested and transported, half-naked and jeered by the crowd, to a ship where the admiral interrogated them, offering them freedom for a denial of their faith. On their refusal and in spite of orders by William of Orange and the Gorkum magistrates for their release, they were hanged in a deserted monastery and their bodies thrown into a ditch. They were translated to the FRANCISCAN church in Brussels in 1616, beatified in 1675 and canonized in 1867.

Gospel. From O.E. *godspel* (good tidings), a translation of the Med. Lat. *bonus nuntius*. It is used to describe collectively the lives of Christ as told by the EVANGELISTS in the NEW TESTAMENT; it signifies the message of redemption set forth in those books; it is used to denote the entire Christian message; and it is also applied to any doctrine or teaching set forth for some specific purpose.
The first four books of the New Testament, known as **The Gospels**, are ascribed to MATTHEW, MARK, LUKE and JOHN, although their exact authorship is uncertain. The first three of these are called the **Synoptic Gospels** as they follow the same lines and may be readily brought under one general view or *synopsis*. The fourth Gospel stands apart as the work of one mind. There are many **Apocryphal Gospels**, examples of which are given below. *See* APOCRYPHA.
The Gospel of Nicodemus, or 'The Acts of Pilate', is an apocryphal book of uncertain date between the 2nd and 5th centuries. It gives an elaborate and fanciful description of the trial, death, and resurrection of Our Lord; names the two thieves (DYSMAS and GESTAS); PILATE's wife (Procla); the centurion (Longinus), etc., and ends with an account of the *descensus ad inferos* of Jesus, by Charinus and Leucius, two men risen from the dead. The title first appears in the 13th century and the Gospel was much used by the writers of Miracle and MYSTERY plays.
The Gospel of Peter is an apocryphal book in fragmentary form, first mentioned by Serapion, bishop of Antioch in the last decade of the 2nd century, and part of which was found in 1892.
The Gospel of Thomas is a GNOSTIC work, probably of the 2nd century, containing much that is fanciful.
Gospel according to... The chief teaching of [so-and-so]. *The Gospel according to* Mammon is the amassing of wealth or money.
The Gospel side of the altar is to the left of the celebrant facing the altar.
The Gospel of wealth. Wealth is the great end and aim of man, the one thing needful, the Gospel according to Mammon.
Gospeller. The priest who reads the Gospel in the Communion Service; also a follower of Wyclif, called the 'Gospel Doctor'.
Hot Gospellers was an old nickname for PURITANS and is now frequently applied to the more energetic and colourful EVANGELISTS and revivalists.

Gossamer. According to legend, this delicate thread is the ravelling of the Virgin Mary's winding-sheet, which fell to earth on her ascension to HEAVEN. It is said to be *God's seam*, i.e. God's thread. Probably the name is from M.E. *gossomer*, goose-summer or St MARTIN's SUMMER (early November), when geese are plentiful. Other suggestions are *God's summer* and *gaze à Marie* (gauze of Mary).

Gothard, St (*c.* 960–1038, f.d. 4 May). Born in Bavaria, he became abbot of Nieder Altaich, a monastery which had recently come under the RULE of St BENEDICT. Gothard was also entrusted, by the Emperor Henry II, with the reform and discipline of other monasteries and, at the death of St Bernard, was appointed bishop of Hildesheim, where he continued his reforms. He was particularly concerned with the work of the cathedral school; he also founded a home for the poor. The hospice for travellers and the chapel dedicated to him gave the name to the St Gothard Pass.

Grace. A supernatural act of divine aid and good-will, unconditional, unearned and free, but given for salvation, showing God's care and mercy and enabling the human will to work in unison with the divine will.

Grace before, or **after meat.** A short prayer asking a blessing on, or giving thanks for, one's food; as the old college grace *Benedictus benedicat* before the meal followed by *Benedicto benedicatur* at the end. Here the word (which used to be plural) is a relic of the old phrase to *do graces* or to *give graces*, meaning to render thanks (Fr. *rendre grâces*; Lat. *gratias agere*), as in Chaucer's 'yeldinge graces and thankinges to hir lord Melibee' (*Tale of Melibeus*, 71).

Gradual. An antiphon sung between the Epistle and the GOSPEL as the deacon ascends the steps (Late Lat. *graduales*) of the altar or pulpit. Also the book containing the musical portions of the service at mass—the *graduals, introits, kyries,* GLORIA IN EXCELSIS, *credo,* etc.

The Gradual Psalms. Psalms cxx to cxxxiv inclusive; probably because they were sung when the priests made the ascent to the inner court of the temple at JERUSALEM. In the Authorized Version of the BIBLE they are called *Songs of Degrees,* and in the Revised Version *Songs of Ascents.*

Grail, The Holy. The cup or chalice traditionally used by Christ at the LAST SUPPER, the subject of a great amount of mediaeval legend, romance, and allegory.

According to one account, JOSEPH OF ARIMATHEA preserved the Grail and received into it some of the blood of the Saviour at the Crucifixion. He brought it to England, but it disappeared. According to others it was brought by angels from HEAVEN and entrusted to a body of knights who guarded it on top of a mountain. When approached by anyone not of perfect purity it vanished, and its quest became the source of most of the adventures of the knights of the Round Table.

There is a great mass of literature concerning the Grail Cycle, and it appears to be a fusion of Christian legend and pre-Christian ritual origins. Part of the subject matter appears in the Mabinogion in the story of *Peredur son of Efrawg.* The first Christian Grail romance was that of the French trouvère Robert de Borron who wrote his *Joseph d'Arimathie* at the end of the 12th century, and it next became attached to the Arthurian legend. In Robert de Borron's work the Grail took the form of a dish on which the Last Supper was served.

Malory's *Le Morte d'Arthur* (printed by Caxton in 1485) is an abridgement from French sources. The framework of Tennyson's *Holy Grail (Idylls of the King)* in which the poet expressed his 'strong feeling as to the Reality of the Unseen' is based upon Malory.

Grande Chartreuse, La. *See* CARTHUSIANS.

Grandmontines. An order of BENEDICTINE hermits, founded by St Stephen of Thiers in Auvergne about 1100, with its mother house at Grandmont. They came to England soon after the foundation and established a few small houses in remote places as that at Craswall, Herefordshire.

Great Bible, The. *See* BIBLE, THE ENGLISH.
Great Schism. *See* SCHISM.
Greater Entrance. *See* ENTRANCE.

Greek Church. A name often given to the Eastern or ORTHODOX Church of which the Greek Church proper is an autocephalous unit, recognized as independent by the Patriarch of Constantinople in 1850.
Greek Cross. *See* CROSS.

Gregorian. Gregorian Calendar. A modification of the JULIAN CALENDAR, introduced in 1582 by Pope Gregory XIII. This is called 'the New Style'. *See* GREGORIAN YEAR.

Gregorian chant. Plainsong; the traditional ritual melody of the Christian Church of the West, so called because it was reformed and elaborated by GREGORY THE GREAT at the end of the 6th century.

Gregorian Epoch. The epoch or day on which the Gregorian CALENDAR commenced in October 1582. *See* GREGORIAN YEAR.

Gregorian Year. The civil year according to the correction introduced by Pope Gregory XIII in 1582. The equinox which occurred on 25 March in the time of Julius Caesar fell on 11 March in the year 1582. This was because the Julian calculation of 365-days to a year was 11 min. 14 sec. too long. Gregory suppressed 10 days by altering 5 October to 15 October, thus making the equinox fall on 21 March 1583. Further simple arrangements prevented the recurrence of a similar error in the future. The change was soon adopted by most CATHOLIC countries, but the PROTESTANT countries did not accept it until much later. The *New Style* was not adopted by England and Scotland until 1752. At the same time the beginning of the civil or legal year was altered from LADY DAY (25 March) to 1 January, a change adopted in Scotland in 1600.

Gregory. A feast held on St Gregory's Day (12 March), especially in Ireland.

Gregory the Enlightener, St (*c.* 240, f.d. 1 October or 30 September). Apostle of Armenia. Grigor or Kritor, called 'Lusavorich', the Enlightener or Illuminator, or 'Partev', the Parthian, was, according to Armenian tradition, the son of the Parthian Anak who murdered King Khosrov I of Armenia; in dying he ordered the extermination of the Anak family. The child Gregory was smuggled out to Caesarea, in Cappodocia, was baptized and reared a Christian. Later, he married and had two sons, SS Aristakes and Vartanes. Gregory became an official at the court of King Tridates who at first persecuted Christians, but was subsequently converted and made Christianity the state religion. Armenia was thus nominally the first Christian country in history. Gregory visited Caesarea and was appointed bishop there by the metropolitan Leontius, establishing the see at Artishat. He organized the church, recruited clergy and taught Greek and Syrian, Armenian not then being a written language. He sent his son Aristakes to represent the Armenian Church at the Council of NICAEA, in 325, and shortly afterwards appointed Aristakes to succeed him. He then retired to a hermitage on Mount Manyea. A year later he was found dead by a shepherd and was buried at Thortan, and Greeks say he was later translated to Constantinople. There are unfounded legends of the troubles he encountered and the twelve torments he suffered. He is the patron saint of Armenia.

Gregory the Great, or **St Gregory** (540–604, f.d. 3 September), the first Pope of this name, and DOCTOR OF THE CHURCH. The outstanding figure of his age, notable for church and monastic reform, for dealing with heresies, for wise administration, and kindness to the poor. He also re-fashioned the liturgy of the Church and made a lasting contribution to Church music (*see* GREGORIAN CHANT).

Gregory was born into a patrician Roman family, the son of a senator, and he held office in ROME. He devoted his wealth to founding monasteries, six in Sicily and one in Rome which he entered the following year. He was called from this by the Pope and sent as papal ambassador to Byzantium. On his return he became abbot of his own monastery of St ANDREW's in Rome. It was then that the famed incident occurred in which, seeing some Anglo-Saxon slaves in a Roman market, he was told they were Angles. To this he replied, 'Not Angles but angels,' and he determined to set out on a mission to the Anglo-Saxons. In this he was frustrated by having been elected Pope, the first monk to attain that office, and in his place he sent St AUGUSTINE OF CANTERBURY and forty monks from his own monastery.

However, he maintained a keen personal interest in the mission throughout, and this resulted in England becoming closer than Gaul to the papacy. Gregory was famed not only for his noble qualities and brilliant diplomacy and administration, but also for his writings, which were of lasting importance and popularity. Among them were *Pastoral Care*, which King Alfred later translated into English, the *Dialogues, Lives of the Saints* and the *Moralia*, on the Book of *Job*. His influence also extended further than the WESTERN CHURCH when, in the ICONOCLASTIC disputes, he upheld the validity of ICONS.

Gregory II, St (d. 731, f.d. 11 or 13 February). A Roman, he was at first a subdeacon, then deacon, and accompanied Pope Constantine on a mission to Constantinople which arose from doctrinal and disciplinary difficulties. He became bishop of Rome at Constantine's death, rebuilding churches and establishing monasteries and hospitals. He maintained the independence of ROME against the Emperors, Saracens and Lombards; he also opposed the iconoclasm of LEO III. He continued GREGORY THE GREAT's interest in the Anglo-Saxons and King Ina of Wessex was received by him when he became a monk in Rome.

Gregory III, St (d. 741, f.d. 18 November, 10 December). A Syrian, he was elected pope to succeed GREGORY II. He was a man of great character, being wise, learned and a notable preacher, and he had great care for the poor, monks and nuns, widows and oprhans. He continued Gregory II's opposition to the Emperor Leo III's iconoclasm and excommunicated the iconoclasts. He supported St BONIFACE's missions and gave him the PALLIUM. Gregory founded new monasteries, enriched existing shrines, and built new ones for the housing relics. The images which surrounded his burial witnessed his esteem for ICONS in the WESTERN CHURCH.

Gregory VII, St (*c.* 1021–85, f.d. 25 May). Known also as Hildebrand, his family name, he was of humble origin, born in Tuscany and educated in France. He became a BENEDICTINE and held various offices at the papal court, serving five popes as archdeacon, then becoming a cardinal. He was elected Pope in 1073 and was noted for opposing simony, lay investiture and clerical concubinage; he asserted and increased the spiritual over the temporal power of the papacy and limited the imperial authority. This brought him into conflict with the devious Emperor Henry IV, who was excommunicated; but Gregory was exiled after the Normans (who had been called in to his support) so tyrannized the Romans that they rose against Gregory. He died in exile at Salerno.

Gregory IX (*c.* 1148–1241). Born Ugolino de Segni, he was papal legate to his uncle Innocent

III, and later Pope, noted for his quarrel with the Emperor Frederick II, whom he excommunicated twice. Gregory systematized the INQUISITION and entrusted it to the DOMINICANS; he sent monks to Constantinople to work for church unity but was unsuccessful. He was noted for his learning, blameless life and character. He was a friend of St FRANCIS OF ASSISI and responsible for his canonization.

Gregory X (1210–76). Born Theobald Visconti, he was a native of Piacenza, in Italy. While archdeacon of Liège, in Belgium, he undertook the preaching of the last CRUSADE and went with the crusaders to the HOLY LAND. He was elected pope while still there. He is chiefly noted for holding the Council of Lyons, at which there was a temporary, short-lived reconciliation between the Eastern and Western CHURCHES. He also introduced the CONCLAVE at the election of the pope by the Constitution of 1274. He was beatified in 1713.

Gregory XIII (1502–85). Pope from 1572 to 1585 he was noted for his support of the COUNTER REFORMATION and the founding of many JESUIT colleges and seminaries, also the ENGLISH COLLEGE at ROME. He was prominent in the Council of TRENT. Gregory tried unsuccessfully to depose Queen Elizabeth I of England. He was responsible for the GREGORIAN CALENDAR which superseded the JULIAN CALENDAR.

Gregory of Nazianzus, St (c. 330–98, f.d. 9 May, 2 January). Of Cappadocian noble family, he was one of the four great Cappadocian FATHERS of the Eastern CHURCH. His father was bishop of Nazianzus, and Gregory was educated at Athens where he met BASIL THE GREAT. He became a defender of orthodox Christianity against ARIANISM and was appointed bishop of Caesarea; he played a leading part in the Council of CONSTANTINOPLE where his famous discourses on the TRINITY earned him the title of 'theologus'. He was one of the Three Holy Hierarchs of the Eastern Church, together with SS BASIL THE GREAT and JOHN CHRYSOSTOM.

Gregory of Nyssa, St (c. 335–94, f.d. 9 March (West), 10 January (East)). Brother and disciple of BASIL THE GREAT and one of the Cappadocian FATHERS, he was an intellectual and rhetorician, a follower of ORIGEN and a noted opponent of ARIANISM. He wrote many theological works. Basil persuaded him to become bishop of Nyssa, but he was deposed in 376 and replaced by an Arian. He was reinstated on the death of the Arian emperor Valens, remaining as bishop for the rest of his life.

Gregory Palamas, St (c. 1296–1350, f.d. 14 November). A saint of the ORTHODOX CHURCH, he entered the monastery at Mount ATHOS and became the chief exponent of Hesychasm, the HESYCHASTS being also called Palamists after him. He was accused of heresy and excommunicated in 1344 but was reinstated, becoming

bishop, and then archbishop, of Thessalonika in 1347. He was canonized in 1368. He wrote *Triads in defence of the Holy Hesychasts* and his Hesychasm, though integrated with Orthodox theology, was not accepted by the WESTERN CHURCH, causing a further rift between the two branches of the CATHOLIC CHURCH. There has been a considerable renewal of interest in Hesychasm in recent times and its theory and practice is spreading widely in the West.

Gregory of Sinai, St (c. 1290–1346, f.d. 17 November). Born near Smyrna, Gregory was kidnapped by Turks but ransomed by a neighbour. He became a monk at Mount Sinai, but left and went to Crete, where he learned the practice of mental prayer. Later, he went to Mount ATHOS but, finding the monks knew little of meditation and contemplation, instructed them in the exercises of breath control and concentration. Leaving Mount Athos, he went to Sozopol and established a monastery on Mount Paroria, spending the rest of his life there. He was canonized by the ORTHODOX CHURCH and holds an important position in its history.

Gregory Thaumaturgus, St (c. 213–70, f.d. 17 November). Little is known of his life but he was said to have been born of noble pagan parents. He was converted to Christianity when he went to Caesarea and studied under ORIGEN, becoming his friend and the most famous of his pupils. Gregory was appointed bishop of Neocaesarea, converting great numbers of people, and he was indefatigable in serving them during the plague. He was one of the early Greek Fathers and is highly venerated in the Eastern Church. He was said to have worked many miracles which earned him the name of Thaumaturgus or Wonder-worker; he was reputed to have moved a mountain, drained a swamp and changed the course of a river. Also attributed to him is the first record of the appearance of the VIRGIN MARY who revealed herself to him with St JOHN THE APOSTLE, to elucidate the doctrine of the HOLY TRINITY.

Gregory of Tours, St (c. 538–94, f.d. 17 November). A French churchman and historian, and bishop of Tours, he was born at Clermont-Ferrand of an illustrious family. His *Historia Francorum*, a history of the world from its creation to the 6th century AD, provided a valuable source of information on early European history. He also played an important part in the politics of his day and was highly successful as a diplomat. He rebuilt Tours Cathedral, where he was ultimately buried, built and enriched churches, oratories and a baptistry and enshrined relics of the saints. He was a successor and devotee of St MARTIN OF TOURS. As well as his history of France, his numerous other writings included *De Gloria Martyrum, De Gloria Confessorium*, the Lives of the Desert Fathers, and a book on the Offices of the Church.

Gregory of Utrecht, St (*c*. 707–75, f.d. 25 August). Born at Maastricht, he became a follower of St BONIFACE of Crediton and later directed a religious house at Utrecht for the training of missionaries, several of whom were English. He has been called the bishop of Utrecht, but this title is in doubt. He was noted for pardoning the murderers of his two half-brothers, admonishing them instead of condemning them to death.

Grey Friars. *See* FRANCISCANS.
Grey Sisters. *See* FRANCISCANS.

Gridiron. The emblem of St LAWRENCE of Rome. One legend says that he was roasted on a grid-iron; another that he was bound to an iron chair and thus roasted alive. He was martyred in 258, under Valerian.

Grimbald, St (*c*. 825–901, f.d. 8 July). Born at Thérouanne, he became a monk at Saint-Bertin and was later ordained priest. King Alfred invited him to become a court-scholar in England to work with him in translations of Latin treatises into English, but Grimbald refused and was appointed dean at Winchester in the Church as distinct from the Cathedral. His work was of interest in providing the first account of the founding of Oxford University.

Guardian Angel. In CATHOLIC angelology, a guardian angel takes care of a particular human soul, to guard, bless and guide it in this world. In the oldest extant Roman sacramentary, reference is made to angels as individual guardians and ALCUIN, who died in 804, mentions them in his letters. It also became customary in the Middle Ages to have guardian angels of cities and districts in Spain, and in England the bishop of Norwich, Herbert Losinga (d. 1119), spoke of them, while the Invocation '*Angele Dei qui custos mei*' appeared in the writings of Reginald of Canterbury at about the same period.

Gudule (Gudula, or Gudila), St (d. 712, f.d. 8 January). Patron saint of Brussels, daughter of Count Witger. She is represented with a lantern, from a tradition that she was one day going to the church of St Morzelle with a lantern which went out, but the Holy Virgin lighted it again with her prayers.

Gudwal (Godwold, Gurval or Gallwell), St (6th cent., f.d. 6 June). Little is known of him, but he was said to have been an abbot who pioneered early Christianity in Brittany. He was patron of Finstall, Worcester, and the Gulval

church in Cornwall is dedicated to him. He was reputed to have been of noble family and to have resigned office to live in a monastery on a rock by the sea; he ordered the sea to remain at low tide and it never came near the monastery. Miracles are attributed to him, healing the sick and raising the dead.

Guerinists. An early 17th-century sect of French ILLUMINATI, founded by Peter Guérin.

Guthlac, St (d. 714, f.d. 11 April), of Crowland, Lincolnshire, is represented in Christian art as a hermit punishing demons with a scourge, or consoled by ANGELS while demons torment him. He was a Mercian prince who died as a hermit.

Guyon, Madame (1648–1717). Born Jeanne-Marie de la Motte, she married the wealthy Jacques Guyon but was left a widow after twelve years. She then travelled, with her spiritual director, in the south of France and northern Italy teaching QUIETISM. She was arrested and accused of heresy and of corresponding with the Spanish Quietist Molinos, but was released owing to the influence of powerful friends. She corresponded with Fénelon and greatly influenced his work. She was again arrested and imprisoned in the Bastille, but was allowed to retire to her son's estate where she devoted her life to good works and writing.

Gwinear, St (date unknown, f.d. 23 March). One of a band of missionaries, coming either from Wales or Ireland, to evangelize Cornwall. Some, including Gwinear, were killed by the pagan king of Cornwall. Many miracles were attributed to the saint; one is that, being in need of water while hunting, he was said to have struck the ground with his lance and three springs welled up, one for himself, another for his horse and one for his dog. He is patron of Gwinear in Cornwall.

Gwyn, St Richard (*c*. 1537–84, f.d. 25 October). Born at Llanidloes in Montgomeryshire, he was educated at St John's College, Cambridge, and then took up the profession of a schoolmaster in Wales. As a CATHOLIC, he refused to attend CHURCH OF ENGLAND services. He was twice arrested, imprisoned and fined and when he could no longer pay he was placed in the stocks. After his eighth assize in Wrexham he was falsely accused of treason and was condemned to death for refusing to accept Queen Elizabeth as head of the church. He was hanged, drawn and quartered. He was canonized in 1970 as one of the FORTY MARTYRS OF ENGLAND AND WALES.

H

Habit. The distinctive dress of religious orders worn by monks, nuns and friars.

Haddock. Traditionally it was in a haddock's mouth that St PETER found the piece of money, the *stater* or *shekel* (*Matt.* xvii, 27), and the two marks on the fish's neck are said to be impressions of the finger and thumb of the apostle. Haddocks, however, cannot live in the fresh water of the Lake of Gennesaret.

Hagiographa (Gr. *hagios*, holy, *graphos*, written; sacred writing). The books of the canonical OLD TESTAMENT other than the Law and the Prophets. **Hagiography.** Writings concerned with the lives of the SAINTS and their critical examination, or books consisting of such lives.

Hail Mary. *See* AVE MARIA.

Hall Sunday. The Sunday before SHROVE TUESDAY; the next day is called *Hall Monday* or *Hall Night. Hall* is a contraction of *hallow* meaning holy. *Hall Monday* is also known as *Collop Monday* from the custom of celebrating with a dish of collops.

Hallel. A Jewish hymn of praise recited at certain festivals, consisting of *Ps.* cxiii to cxviii inclusive, also called the *Egyptian* or *Common Hallel.* The name *Great Hallel* is given to *Ps.* cxxvi and sometimes to *Ps* cxx–cxxxvi, thus including the GRADUAL PSALMS.

Hallelujah is the Heb. *halelu-Jah*, 'Praise ye Jehovah'. *Alleluia* is one of the several variant spellings.
Hallelujah Lass. In the early days of the SALVATION ARMY, a name given to female members. Defined somewhat censoriously by Dr Brewer as: 'A young woman who wanders about with what is called "The Salvation Army".'

Halloween. 31 October, which in the old Celtic calendar was the last day of the year, its night being the time when all the witches and warlocks were abroad. On the introduction of Christianity it was taken over as the Eve of ALL HALLOWS or All Saints.

Hallvard, St (d. 1043, f.d. 15 May). Of noble Norwegian family, little is told of his life except that he was a Viking. When about to cross the Drammerfjord by boat he was appealed to by a woman who said she had been falsely accused of stealing and was being pursued. Hallvard, accepting her innocence, took her on board, but her pursuers arrived, demanded her surrender, and when this was refused, shot them both with arrows. They threw Hallvard's body into the sea, weighted with stones, but it floated. His body was enshrined at a church in Oslo and he was venerated as a protector of innocence. He is patron saint of the city.

Halo. In Christian art, the same as a NIMBUS. The luminous circle round the sun or moon caused by the refraction of light through a mist is called a halo. Figuratively it implies the ideal or saintly glory surrounding a person and is often used derisively, as 'you ought to be wearing a halo'. It is the Gr. *halo*, originally a circular threshing-floor, then the sun or moon's disc. *Cp.* AUREOLE.

Hampton Court Conference. Discussions held at Hampton Court in 1604 between James I, the BISHOPS, and four PURITAN clergy in the presence of the Council. The bishops would make no concessions of importance and their most valuable decision was to effect a new translation of the BIBLE, which became the Authorized Version of 1611.

Hand. In early art, the Deity was frequently represented by a hand extended from the clouds, with rays issuing from the fingers, but generally it was in the act of benediction, i.e. two fingers raised. In Christian art the hand appearing from a cloud depicts the presence and power of God the Father; it sometimes looses the DOVE of the HOLY SPIRIT. A hand raised with the palm outwards is blessing, divine grace and favour; with three fingers raised it represents the TRINITY; with the whole hand the thumb denotes the Father, the first finger the Holy Spirit, the second Christ and the third and fourth the two natures of Christ. A hand holding a bag of money represents JUDAS Iscariot.
Laying on of hands. In church usage, the imposition of hands is the laying on or touch of a BISHOP's hands in confirmation and ordination, and is the transmission of the Spirit, power and grace.

To wash one's hands of a thing. To have nothing to do with it after having been concerned in the matter; to abandon it entirely. The allusion is to PILATE's washing his hands at the trial of Jesus.

> When Pilate saw that he could prevail nothing, but that rather a tumult was made, he took water, and washed his hands before the multitude, saying, I am innocent of the blood of this just person: see ye to it.
>
> *Matt.* xxvii, 24

Harding, St Stephen (d. 1134, f.d. 17 April). Little is known of his parentage or early history beyond that he was educated at a BENEDICTINE monastery at Sherborne, Dorset. He travelled abroad and became a monk at Molesme, in Burgundy, but, dissatisfied with observances, he founded a new, reformed and stricter order at Cîteaux, together with Robert of Molesme and others. Stephen was elected prior, then abbot, establishing the CISTERCIAN Order and introducing lay brothers. His foundations on the Continent gave rise to such famous Cistercian abbeys as Tintern, Waverley, Rievaulx and Fountains in England.

Hard-shell Baptists. Extreme Calvinistic Baptists in the Southern USA who opposed all missionary activities and benevolent schemes. Also known as *Anti-Mission Baptists. Hard-shell* here is the colloquial American term meaning rigid, uncompromising, narrowly orthodox.

Harmonists. A sect founded in Württemberg by George and Frederick Rapp. They emigrated to western Pennsylvania in 1803 and moved to Indiana, founding New Harmony in 1815. This was sold to Robert Owen in 1824 and they returned to Pennsylvania. They looked forward to the second ADVENT, practised strict economy and self-denial, amassed wealth, and favoured celibacy.

Harris, Thomas Lake (1823–1906). Born in England, he emigrated to the USA where he became a UNIVERSALIST minister and a Spiritualist. He returned to England in 1850 and founded a society, which he took back to America, called the Brotherhood of the New Life. He directed this from New York state. He wrote works on the sexual make-up of angels.

Hart. In Christian art, the emblem of solitude and purity of life. It was the attribute of St HUBERT, St JULIAN, and St EUSTACE. It was also the type of piety and religious aspiration (*Ps.* xlii, 1). *Cp.* HIND.

Harvest Thanksgiving. On 1 October 1843, the Rev. R. S. Hawker, Vicar of Morwenstow in Cornwall, set aside that Sunday in order to thank God for the harvest. The popular CHURCH OF ENGLAND festival largely derives from this; the practice became widespread and nowadays churches are decorated with corn, fruit, vegetables and produce of all kinds, especially in country parishes. Hawker also reverted to the offering of the LAMMAS DAY bread at the EUCHARIST.

> Come, ye thankful people, come,
> Raise the song of harvest-home!
> All is safely gathered in,
> Ere the winter storms begin.
>
> H. ALFORD: *Harvest Hymn*

> The modern harvest-festival, as a parochial thanksgiving for the bounties of Providence, is an excellent institution, in addition to the old harvest-feast, but it should not be considered as a substitute for it.
>
> R. CHAMBERS: *The Book of Days*, Sept. 25

Hazazel. The scapegoat. *See* AZAZEL.

He Bible. *See* BIBLE, SOME SPECIALLY NAMED EDITIONS.

Heart. In Christian art the heart is an attribute of St TERESA of Avila.

The flaming heart is a symbol of charity, and an attribute of St AUGUSTINE, denoting the fervency of his devotion. The heart of the Saviour is sometimes so represented. A heart in the hand portrays love and piety; pierced by an arrow it is the contrite heart, repentance; the heart crowned with thorns is an emblem of St IGNATIUS LOYOLA; with a cross, an emblem of SS BERNARDINO OF SIENA, CATHERINE OF SIENA and TERESA.

The Immaculate Heart of Mary. In the ROMAN CATHOLIC CHURCH, devotion to the heart of Mary is a special form of devotion to Our Lady which developed from the 17th century. In 1947 Pius XII recognized 22 August as the Feast of the Immaculate Heart of Mary.

The Sacred Heart. In the ROMAN CATHOLIC CHURCH, devotion to the Sacred Heart of Jesus, essentially directed at the Saviour himself. It originated from a vision experienced by a French nun, Marguerite Marie Alacoque (1647–90). This devotion in France was approved by Clement XIII in 1758 and extended to the whole church in 1856 by Pius IX. The festival is celebrated on the Friday after the Octave of CORPUS CHRISTI. There are various Congregations of the Sacred Heart. *Cp.* IMMACUALTE HEART (*above*).

Heaven (O.E. *heofon*). The word properly denotes the abode of the Deity and His ANGELS—'heaven is my throne' (*Is.* lxvi, 1, and *Matt.* v, 34)—but it is also used in the BIBLE and elsewhere for the air, the upper heights, as 'the fowls of heaven', 'the dew of heaven', 'the clouds of heaven'; 'the cities are walled up to heaven' (*Deut.* i, 28); and a tower whose top should 'reach unto heaven' (*Gen.* xi, 4); the starry firmament, as 'Let there be lights in the firmament of the heaven' (*Gen.* i, 14).

In the Ptolemaic system, the heavens were the successive spheres surrounding the central earth. *See also* PARADISE.

Hedda. Hedda (or Haeddi) of Peterborough, St (d. 870, f.d. 10 April). An abbot of East Anglia who was killed, with his entire community, by the Danes who had previously murdered EDMUND of East Anglia. In mediaeval times the Hedda Stone stood over his grave and those of his companions. There were holes cut for candles at MASS and visitors and pilgrims placed their fingers in these holes.

Hedda of Winchester, St (d. 705, f.d. 7 July). A monk at Whitby, he was appointed bishop of the West Saxons and changed the seat from Dorchester (Oxon.) to Winchester. He assisted King Ina in drawing up laws, and BEDE remarked on Hedda's wisdom and prudence. He translated the relics of St BIRINUS to Winchester. His own relics are there and cures and miracles were reported at his tomb where dust mixed with water healed both men and animals.

Hedwig, St (*c.* 1174–1243, f.d. 16 October). Hedwig or Jadwiga was of noble family in Bavaria; she married, at the age of twelve, the Duke of Silesia, Henry I. Both were of a religious temperament and Henry encouraged his wife's activities in founding religious houses. After having seven children, both parents lived separate lives. Hedwig became a CISTERCIAN and her daughter Gertrude was abbess of Trebnitz where Hedwig lived and died. Miracles and prophecy were claimed for her and she was said to wear filthy and scanty clothes and go about barefoot. In art she is depicted as crowned, veiled and carrying her shoes in her hand.

Hegumenos (Gr. leader). The abbot or superior of a monastery of Basilian monks in the Eastern ORTHODOX CHURCH.

Helen (or Elia) of Skovde, St (d. *c.* 1160, f.d. 31 July). Of noble Swedish family in Vastergötland, she was married young and widowed; she then devoted her life and wealth to a life of religion and service to the poor. She went on a pilgrimage to the HOLY LAND but was murdered by her son-in-law's relatives, who held her responsible for her death. Helen was buried at Skovde in a church she had built and her cult was widespread in Scandinavia in the Middle Ages. She was patron of Vastergötland and is sometimes regarded as patron of Sweden.

Helena, St (*c.* 250–*c.* 330, f.d. 18 August). Mother of Constantine the Great. She is represented in royal robes, wearing an imperial crown as an empress, sometimes carrying a model of the HOLY SEPULCHRE, sometimes carrying a large cross (*see* INVENTION OF THE CROSS *under* CROSS). Sometimes she also bears the three nails by which the Saviour was affixed to the cross.

The island of St Helena in the South Atlantic was discovered by the Portuguese on 21 May 1502 (St Helena's Day as observed in the Eastern Church). It was the place of Napoleon's exile from 1815 until his death in 1821.

Helier, St (6th cent., f.d. 16 July). Son of a pagan nobleman of Belgium, he was educated by a priest whom his father murdered when he found his son had been converted to Christianity. Helier fled to Jersey where he lived as a hermit in a cave near the town which took his name. He was murdered by pirates and was venerated as a martyr; he was said to have been trying to convert the pirates.

Hell. The abode of the dead, then traditionally the place of torment or punishment after death (O.E. *hel*, hell, from root *hel-*, hide).

Henoticon. The formal statement of doctrine, or instrument of union, put forward by the Emperor Zeno, in 482, with the object of ending the MONOPHYSITE dispute. It was accepted by the ORTHODOX CHURCH but not by ROME.

Henry. Henry, St (d. 1127, f.d. 16 January). Of Danish birth, he left his homeland to avoid marriage and settled as a hermit on the island of Coquet, off Northumberland, where there was a community of monks where SS BEDE, CUTHBERT and ELFLEDA used to meet. He lived simply on his garden produce and practised austerities. He resisted the persuasions of a party of Danes to accompany them back to Denmark, and became the centre of a cult in England, people being drawn by his gifts of prophecy, mind-reading and telekinesis. His body was taken to the monastery of Tynemouth and buried in the sanctuary.

Henry II, St (973–1024, f.d. 13 or 15 July). Born in Bavaria, the son of Henry the Quarrelsome, he succeeded him as Duke of Bavaria and later, in 1002, was elected King of the Romans, and in 1014 Emperor of the Holy Roman Empire. Having used the Church for political ends, he restored much of its property and founded churches and the cathedral of Bamberg. The fact that his marriage was childless was one of deliberate celibacy is probably a later legend. There is also a legend that his wife CUNEGUND, accused of infidelity, proved her virtue by walking unharmed over red-hot ploughshares.

Henry of Finland, St (d. 1156, f.d. 19 January, 18 June). An Englishman, he was appointed bishop of Uppsala by Nicholas Breakspear, papal legate to Scandinavia. Henry joined St ERIK on a successful crusade to Finland to impose Christianity on the defeated Finns and remained among them as a missionary when Erik returned to Sweden. Henry built a church at Nousis where a few years later he was buried, having been murdered by either a soldier or peasant whom he had excommunicated. Miracles occurred at his tomb. His body was translated to Abo Cathedral and enshrined with elaborate sepulchral brass and paintings, said to be the best of mediaeval iconography.

Henry Morse, St. See MORSE.

Heptateuch. (Gr. *hepta*, seven; *teuchos*, a tool, book). A name given to the first seven books of the BIBLE, the PENTATEUCH plus *Joshua* and *Judges*.

Herbert of Derwentwater, St (d. 687, f.d. 20 March). Ordained priest, he lived as a hermit on the island in Derwentwater in the Lake District. He was a friend of St CUTHBERT whom he visited yearly at Lindisfarne. Meeting instead at Carlisle in 686, Cuthbert prophesied that they would both die soon at the same time, this was fulfilled when they both died on 20 March the next year. A sung MASS was celebrated each year on St Herbert's Island.

Heretic. From a Greek word meaning 'one who chooses'. A heretic is one who holds unorthodox opinions in matters of religion, i.e. he chooses his own creed.

The principal heretical sects of the first six centuries were:

FIRST CENTURY: The *Simonians* (from Simon Magus), *Cerinthians* (Cerinthus), EBIONITES (Ebion), and *Nicolaitans* (Nicholas, deacon of Antioch).

SECOND CENTURY: The *Basilidians* (Basilides), *Carpocratians* (Carpocrates), *Valentinians* (Valentinus), GNOSTICS (Knowing Ones), NAZARENES, MILLENARIANS, CAINITES (Cain), *Sethians* (Seth), *Quartodecimans* (who kept EASTER on the 14th day of *Nisan*, our April), *Cerdonians* (Cerdon), MARCIONITES (Marcion), MONTANISTS (Montanus), *Alogians* (who denied the 'Word'), *Angelics* (who worshipped angels), *Tatianists* (Tatian), QUINTILIANS.

THIRD CENTURY: The *Patri-passians, Arabici, Aquarians*, NOVATIANS, *Origenists* (followers of Origen), *Melchisedechians* (who believed Melchisedec was the Messiah), SABELLIANS (from Sabellius), and MANICHAEANS (followers of Mani).

FOURTH CENTURY: The ARIANS (from Arius), *Colluthians* (Colluthus), MACEDONIANS, AGNOETAE (they denied that God knew the past and the future), APOLLINARIANS (Apollinaris), *Collyridians* (who offered cakes to the Virgin Mary), *Seleucians* (Seleucus), *Priscillians* (Priscillian), *Anthropomorphites* (who ascribed to God a human form), *Jovinianists* (Jovinian), *Messalians*, and *Bonosians* (Bonosus).

FIFTH CENTURY: The PELAGIANS (Pelagius), NESTORIANS (Nestorius), EUTYCHIANS (Eutychus), MONOPHYSITES (who held that Christ had but a single, and that a Divine, nature), *Predestinarians*, *Timotheans* (Timothy, Monophysite Patriarch of Alexandria).

SIXTH CENTURY: *Theopaschites* (Monophysites who held that God was crucified in Christ's Passion), the new *Agnoetae* (Monophysite followers of Themistus). See also ALBIGENSES; BOGOMILS, WALDENSIANS.

Hermas. One of the APOSTOLIC FATHERS (2nd century), author of *The Shepherd* which consists of Visions, Commandments, and Similitudes or Parables.

Hermeneutics (Gr. *hermeneuein*, to interpret). The science of interpretation and explanation of texts, especially of the SCRIPTURES; exegesis.

Hermes (or **Erme**), **St** (3rd cent., f.d. 28 August). Probably of Greek origin, he was said to have been a convert who, with companions, was martyred under the Emperor Hadrian. Hermes was buried in the cemetery of Basilla on the old Salarian Way at ROME. After his body had been translated to Renaix, in Flanders, his tomb became a centre of pilgrimage, noted for its cure of lunacy. His cult was relegated to local calendars after the revision of 1969.

Hermit, or **Eremite** (Gr. *eremos*, solitary). One who has renounced the world with all its pleasures and the society of other people and lives in solitude, devoted to prayer and meditation. In early Christian times many retreated from the decadence, conflicts and persecutions of the Roman Empire to deserts in Africa and Asia. The first of the famous hermits was St ANTHONY. The hermits of the Egyptian deserts in the 4th century AD were known as the DESERT FATHERS. From these hermits monasticism was born.

Hermynhilda, St. See ERMENHILDA.

Herod. To out-herod Herod. To outdo in wickedness, violence, or rant, the worst of tyrants. Herod, who destroyed the babes of Bethlehem (*Matt.* ii, 16), was made (in the old mediaeval MYSTERIES) a ranting, roaring tyrant.

Hesperinos. The counterpart in the Eastern ORTHODOX CHURCH of VESPERS in the WESTERN CHURCH.

Hesychasts. In the Eastern Church, supporters of the ascetic mysticism propagated by the monks of Mount Athos in the 14th century. Also called *Palamists* after GREGORY PALAMAS who became the chief exponent of Hesychasm. The object of their exercises was to attain a vision of the 'Divine Light' which they held to be God's 'energy'. Hesychasm lasted until the 17th century; the name is from the Gr. *hesychos*, quiet.

Heterodoxy (Gr. another opinion). The opposite of orthodoxy; religious opinions which are not in accordance with established doctrines, principles or standards.

Hewald (or **Ewald**), **SS** (d. 695, f.d. 3 October). Two Northumbrians, traditionally brothers, who lived for some time in Ireland and were both called by the same name; they were distinguished by the colour of their hair as the 'Dark and the Fair' or the 'Black and the White'. They accompanied St WILLIBRORD to Frisia as missionaries to the Old Saxons on the Continent, but, suspicious of the new religion, the people murdered them and threw their bodies into the Rhine. Pepin had the bodies recovered and enshrined at Cologne. The Hewalds are patron saints of Westphalia.

Hexameron (Gr.). A period of six days, especially the six days of the Creation, and the commentaries thereon.

Hexateuch. *See* ELOHISTIC; *cp*. HEPTATEUCH, PENTATEUCH.

Hibbert, Robert (1770–1849). A West India merchant who left a fortune for the foundation of a trust for training students for the UNITARIAN ministry and for the endowment of the Hibbert Lectures and the *Hibbert Journal*. Both were to treat religion from a broad, interdenominational point of view.

Hickory Mormons. MORMONS of half-hearted persuasions.

Hicksites. QUAKERS in the USA who seceded from the main body in 1827 under the leadership of Elias Hicks.

Hierarchy (Gr. sacred government). A sacred system of graded government. In Christianity generally, an ecclesiastical establishment of bishops, priests and deacons.

Hieronymites. A monastic order named after St JEROME (Lat. *Hieronymus*) who, with St Paula, established a monastery for men and convents for women near the BASILICA of the Nativity at Bethlehem.

High. High Church. That section of the CHURCH OF ENGLAND distinguished by its 'high' conception of Church authority, upholding sacerdotal claims and asserting the efficacy of the SACRAMENTS. It also stresses the historical links with CATHOLIC Christianity. It has its origins in the reign of Elizabeth I, although the name is of the late 17th century. Archbishop Laud was of this persuasion and High Church opinions were again strengthened and re-established by the Oxford Movement. *Cp*. LOW CHURCH.

High Mass. *See* MASS.

High places. In the Authorized Version of the BIBLE this is a literal translation of the Heb. *bamah* and applied to the local places of sacrifice where JEHOVAH was worshipped. Such sites were often on a hilltop or mound, which may account for the origin of the name. Because of their association with forms of idolatry, and sometimes immoral rites, they were denounced by Hosea. Hezekiah removed the high places. (II *Kings* xviii, 4), so did Asa (II *Chron*. xiv, 3) and others. *Cp*. HILLS.

Higher Criticism. Critical inquiry into the literary composition and sources, especially of the BIBLE, also called *historical criticism*. The term is used in contradistinction to textual or verbal criticism which is to establish the correctness of the text.

Hilarion, St (*c*. 291–371, f.d. 21 October). Born into a pagan family at Gaza, he was educated at Alexandria and converted to Christianity, coming under the influence of St ANTHONY, on whose regime he based his life, living simply as a hermit and eating only figs, vegetables, bread and oil. However, he drew so many disciples of both sexes that he left to become a solitary. He went first to Egypt, then to Sicily and finally to Dalmatia. Again, his life and miracles attracted so much attention that he fled to Cyprus where he died at the age of eighty; his relics were then translated to Majuma. He had a reputation for great austerities, for victory over many temptations and being able to cast out demons. His cult was confined to local calendars in the revision of 1969.

Hilary. Hilary of Arles, St (d. 449, f.d. 5 May). Of noble parentage, he was related to St Honoratus of Arles and joined him as a monk at Lérins. He then succeeded to the bishopric of Arles. He presided at various councils but came into conflict with Pope LEO THE GREAT over the exceeding of his episcopal powers. He is remembered largely for his discourse on the life of St Honoratus.

Hilary of Poitiers, St (*c*. 315–68, f.d. 13 January). Born of wealthy and cultivated parents at Poitiers, he was converted to Christianity after he had married. Having studied seriously, he was elected bishop of Poitiers, becoming famous as an orator and theologian; St MARTIN OF TOURS was one of his disciples. Hilary was a noted opponent of ARIANISM and, following the Council of Milan, he was exiled for four years by the Emperor Constantinus II, but returned to Gaul in 360 when orthodoxy was re-established. In England the 'Hilary Term' of the Law Courts and some universities began on his feast day. Among his works are: *De Trinitate*, an anti-Arian treatise, and *De Synodis*, the history of the SYNODS. He also wrote some HYMNS and commentaries. He was named a DOCTOR OF THE CHURCH in 1851.

Hilda (or **Hild**), **St** (614–80, f.d. 17 November, 25 August). A princess of Deira and grandniece of King Edwin of Northumbria, she was baptized at York by St PAULINUS. The first half of her life was secular; she then took the veil at Hartlepool, where she became abbess at the instigation of St AIDAN. She then founded a double monastery at Whitby, ruling there until her death. Hilda was one of the great women of England, showing great wisdom and devotion and taking a serious interest in education, establishing libraries, encouraging the use of Latin and making the monastery famous for its learning. At least five bishops were trained there and the poet CAEDMON was among the great names associated with Whitby. At the Synod there, in the dispute between the Celtic and Roman ecclesiastical orders, Hilda upheld the Celtic against St WILFRID and the Roman usage, but later submitted to the adoption of the Roman. After Whitby had been sacked by the Danes in 800, Hilda's remains were translated to GLASTONBURY, though they were also claimed by Gloucester. She was a woman of 'wonderful godliness and grace'.

Hildebrand, St. *See* GREGORY VII.

Hildegard, St (1098–1179, f.d. 17 September, 25 August). Also known as the Sibyl, of the Rhine, Hildegard was one of the noted visionaries of the Middle Ages. Born in Western Germany, she was educated by a recluse, Jutta, at Diessenberg, and succeeded her as abbess in 1136. After the order grew too large she moved it to Rupertsberg, from where her prophecies and visions became widely known, and she corresponded with five popes, the Emperor Frederick Barbarossa and Henry II of England. She was a voluminous and versatile writer, recording her visions and revelations, reproving rulers, writing commentaries on the GOSPELS, the Rule of St BENEDICT, HYMNS, poetry

and plays, as well as works on natural history and science and medical treatises on both the human body and mind, showing considerable powers of observation. She was also a musician and artist. In later times her writings and illustrations were compared with those of Dante and William Blake.

Hills. Prayers were offered on the tops of high hills, and temples built on 'HIGH PLACES', from the notion that the gods could better hear prayer on such places, as they were nearer HEAVEN. It will be remembered that Balak (*Num*. xxiii, xxiv) took BALAAM to the top of Peor and other high places when Balaam wished to consult God. We often read of 'idols on every high hill' (*Ezek*. vi, 13).

Hind. Emblematic of St Giles. *See under* GILES. *Cp*. HART.
The milk-white hind, in Dryden's *Hind and the Panther*, means the ROMAN CATHOLIC CHURCH, milk-white because 'infallible'. The panther, full of the spots of error, is the CHURCH OF ENGLAND.

> Without unspotted, innocent within,
> She fear'd no danger, for she knew no sin.
> Part I, 3, 4

Hippolytus, St (d. 235, f.d. 13 August (Western), 30 January (Eastern)). A priest and theologian at ROME, of whom little is known. He accused the bishops St CALLISTUS and St ZEPHYRINUS of laxity in doctrinal and disciplinary matters, and when he opposed the heresy of Sabellius he was exiled to Sardinia by Maximus. There he set up a schismatic party, becoming the first anti-pope. He was said to have been martyred, and his body was brought to Rome and buried in the cemetery on the Via Tiburtina. He was an important theological writer. His works include the *Philosophoumena*, which refutes various heretical teachings in philosophical systems, and commentaries on *Daniel* and the *Canticle of Canticles*, also the *Apostolic Tradition*, formerly called *The Egyptian Church Order*. He has been confused with other saints of the same name and associated with the legendary martyr torn asunder by wild horses, echoing the myth of Hippolytus, son of Theseus. His cult was suppressed in the revision of 1969.

Hock-day, or **Hock Tuesday.** The second Tuesday after EASTER Day, long held as a festival in England and observed until the 16th century. According to custom, on Hock Monday, the women of the village seized and bound men, demanding a small payment for their release. On the Tuesday of Hocktide the men similarly waylaid the women. The takings were paid to the churchwardens for parish work. This was later modified, as shown over:

Hock Monday was for the men and Hock Tuesday for the women. On both days the men and women, alternately, with great merriment, intercepted the public roads with ropes, and pullsed passengers to them, from whom they exacted money, to be laid out in pious uses.

BRAND: *Antiquities*, vol. I

Hofbauer, St Clement-Mary (1751–1820, f.d. 15 March). Born at Tasswitz in Moravia, the son of a butcher and trained as a baker, he joined a monastery at Klosterbuch. He made pilgrimages to ROME and went to Vienna. He was then educated for the priesthood in Rome and joined the REDEMPTIONIST CONGREGATION in the lifetime of its founder, St ALPHONSUS LIGUORI. Hofbauer returned to Vienna, but was not able to found a house there. He then went to Warsaw, founding several houses in Poland and conducting a successful mission. After the Napoleonic invasion he returned to Vienna, becoming famous as a preacher and spiritual adviser and working devotedly for the sick and dying. He died in Vienna and his funeral was attended by a vast crowd. Soon after he died Redemptorist houses were established in Austria. In 1909 the pope canonized him and named him patron of Vienna.

Holidays, or **Holy days of Obligation.** Days on which Roman Catholics are bound to hear MASS and to abstain 'from servile work'. These *Feasts of Obligation* vary slightly in different countries. In England and Wales they are: all SUNDAYS, CHRISTMAS Day, the EPIPHANY (6 January), ASCENSION DAY (40th day after EASTER Sunday), CORPUS CHRISTI (Thursday after Trinity Sunday), SS PETER and PAUL (29 June), the ASSUMPTION of the Blessed Virgin Mary (15 August), ALL HALLOWS (1 November). St JOSEPH (19 March) and St PATRICK (17 March) are observed in Ireland and Scotland. The former and the feasts of the Octave Day of Christmas (1 January) and the IMMACULATE CONCEPTION (8 December) are not observed in England and Wales. Epiphany, Corpus Christi, SS Peter and Paul, and St Joseph are not kept in the USA.

Holiness Churches. PROTESTANT sects in the USA which teach the possibility of attaining to and maintaining a state of perfection and love through Divine Grace. They are also called Perfectionists and date from the time of the Civil War.

Holy. Holy Alliance. A treaty signed originally by the rulers of Austria, Prussia, and Russia in 1815 (after the fall of Napoleon) and joined by all the kings of Europe, except Great Britain and the President of the Swiss Republic. Sponsored by the Tsar Alexander, the rulers undertook to base their relations "upon the sublime truths which the Holy religion of Our Savious teaches". In effect it became a reactionary influence seeking to maintain autocratic rule.

Holy City. The city which the religious consider most especially connected with their faith. Thus:

Benares is the Holy City of the Hindus.
Cuzco of the ancient Incas.
Fez of the Western Arabs.
Jerusalem of the Jews and Christians.
Mecca and *Medina* as the places of the birth and burial of Muhammad.

Figuratively, the Holy City is HEAVEN.

Holy Club. The nickname given to the group of earnest Christians formed at Oxford in 1729 by Charles and John Wesley and joined by George Whitefield. They held meetings to study the Scriptures, fasted, and carried out pastoral work. *See* METHODISTS.

Holy Coat. Both the cathedral at Trèves (Trier) and the parish church of Argenteuil claim the ownership of Christ's seamless coat, which the soldiers would not rend and therefore cast lots for it (*John* xix, 23, 25). The traditions date from about the 12th century and the coat was supposed to have been found and preserved by the Empress HELENA in the 4th century. There are other places claiming this relic.

Holy Cross, or **Holy Rood Day.** 14 September, the day of the Feast of the EXALTATION OF THE CROSS, called by the Anglo-Saxons 'Roodmass-day'.

It was on this day that Jews in ROME used to be compelled to go to church and listen to a sermon—a custom abolished about 1840 by Pope Gregory XVI. It is the subject of Browning's *Holy-Cross Day* (1845).

Holy Door. The specially walled-up door of each of the four great basilicas at ROME (St Peter's, St John Lateran, St Paul's-Outside-the-Walls, St Mary's Major). That of St Peter's is ceremoniously opened by the Pope on Christmas Eve, to inaugurate the Holy Year; the others are opened by Cardinals-Legate. They are similarly closed the following Christmas Eve. Many Pilgrims pass through these doors during the year to perform their devotions and receive INDULGENCES.

Holy Family. Properly, the infant Jesus, MARY, and JOSEPH; in art, the infant Saviour and His attendants, usually Joseph, Mary, Elisabeth, Anne the mother of Mary, and JOHN THE BAPTIST.

Holy Father, The Most. A title given to the POPE.

Holy Ghost. The third person of the TRINITY, the Divine Spirit, also called the Holy Spirit; represented in art as a dove.

The seven gifts of the Holy Ghost are: (1) Counsel, (2) the fear of the Lord, (3) fortitude,

(4) piety, (5) understanding, (6) wisdom, and (7) knowledge.

The Procession of the Holy Ghost. *See* FILIOQUE CONTROVERSY.

The Sin against the Holy Ghost. Much has been written about this sin, the definition of which has been based upon several passages in the GOSPELS such as *Matt.* xii, 31, 32 and *Mark* iii, 29, and it has been interpreted as the wilful denouncing as evil that which is manifestly good, thus revealing a state of heart beyond the divine influence. Borrow in his *Lavengro* draws a graphic picture inspired by fear of this sin and its consequences, the danger of 'eternal damnation'.

The Order of the Holy Ghost. A French order of knighthood (*Ordre du Saint-Esprit*), instituted by Henry III in 1578 to replace the Order of St MICHAEL. It was limited to 100 Knights and was not revived after the revolution of 1830.

Holy Grail. *See* GRAIL.

Holy Innocents, or **Childermas.** This Feast is celebrated on 28 December, to commemorate Herod's MASSACRE OF THE INNOCENTS. It used to be the custom on *Childermas* to whip the children (and even adults) 'that the memory of Herod's murder of the Innocents might stick the closer'. This practice forms the plot of several tales in the *Decameron*.

Holy Island, or Lindisfarne. In the North Sea, some 9 miles south-east from Berwick-on-Tweed, it became the SEE of St AIDAN in 635 and a missionary centre. St CHAD, St Oswy, St EGBERT, and St WILFRID were among those educated there. It was the see of St CUTHBERT (685–7) and is now in the diocese of Newcastle. At low-water it can be reached across the sands by a causeway.

Ireland was called the Holy Island on account of its numerous saints.

Guernsey was so called in the 10th century in consequence of the great number of monks residing there.

The Holy Land Christians call Palestine the Holy Land, because it was the scene of Christ's birth, ministry, and death.

The Holy League. A combination formed by Pope Julius II in 1511 with Venice, Ferdinand of Aragon and the Emperor Maximilian of Germany to drive the French out of Italy. England joined subsequently.

Among other leagues of the same name, that formed by Henry II of France in 1576, with the support of Henry of Guise and the JESUITS is noteworthy. It was formed to defend the Holy Catholic Church against the encroachments of the reformers, i.e. to destroy the HUGUENOTS.

The Holy Maid of Kent. Elizabeth Barton (*c*. 1506–1534) who incited the Roman Catholics to resist the REFORMATION, and imagined that she acted under inspiration. Having announced the doom and speedy death of Henry VIII for his marriage with Anne Boleyn, she was hanged at Tyburn in 1534.

Holy of Holies. The innermost apartment of the Jewish temple, in which the Ark of the Covenant was kept, and into which only the High Priest was allowed to enter, and that but once a year on the Day of Atonement. Hence, a private apartment, a *sanctum sanctorum*.

The Holy Office. *See* INQUISITION.

Holy Orders. *See* ORDERS.

Holy Places. A name particularly applied to those places in Palestine and especially Jerusalem, associated with some of the chief events in the life of Christ, his death, and Resurrection. Jerusalem is also a HOLY CITY for Jews and Muslims and in the course of history this has produced bitter quarrels. Christian pilgrimages to the Holy Places were a familiar feature of mediaeval life and the CRUSADES began when Muslims interfered with pilgrims visiting the HOLY SEPULCHRE.

The Crimean War (1854–6) had its origins in a dispute between orthodox and Roman Catholic rights over the Holy Places, which included the churches of the Holy Sepulchre and the Virgin in Jerusalem, GOLGOTHA, and the church of the Nativity at Bethlehem.

Holy Rollers. A PROTESTANT EVANGELICAL sect in the USA, of the PENTECOSTALS who believe in the 'gift of tongues' and when the gift descended on them rolled about in ecstasy.

Holy Roman Empire. The mediaeval Western Empire, said to be neither Holy, nor Roman, nor an Empire.

Holy Rood Day. *See* HOLY CROSS DAY.

Holy Saturday. *See* HOLY WEEK.

Holy See. The SEE of Rome. Often used to denote the papacy and papal jurisdiction, authority, etc.

Holy Sepulchre. The cave in Jerusalem, where according to tradition Christ was entombed, said to have been found by St HELENA. Successive churches have been built on the site which includes that of CALVARY.

The Holy Spirit. *See* HOLY GHOST.

Holy Synod. The supreme Instrument of Government in the Russian ORTHODOX CHURCH, founded by Peter the Great in 1721 and lasting to the revolution in 1917. It is a committee of bishops and priests. It has now been reinstituted.

Holy Thursday. In England an old name for ASCENSION DAY, the Thursday next but one before WHITSUNDAY; by Roman Catholics and others MAUNDY THURSDAY, i.e. the Thursday before GOOD FRIDAY, is meant. *See also* IN COENA DOMINI.

Holy Trinity. *See* TRINITY.

Holy War. A war in which religious motivation plays, or is purported to play, a prominent part. The CRUSADES, the Thirty Years War, the wars against the ALBIGENSES, etc., were so called.

John Bunyan's *Holy War*, published in 1682, tells of the capture of Mansoul by SATAN and its recapture by the forces of Shaddai (EMMANUEL).

Holy Water. Water blessed by a priest for religious purposes. It is particularly used in the ROMAN CATHOLIC CHURCH at the *Asperges*, the sprinkling of the altar and congregation before High MASS, and generally in the Church at blessings, dedications, etc., and kept in Holy Water stoups near church doors for the use of those entering.

Holy Week. The last week in LENT. It begins on PALM SUNDAY; the fourth day is called SPY WEDNESDAY; the fifth is MAUNDY THURSDAY; the sixth is GOOD FRIDAY; and the last 'Holy Saturday', or the 'Great Sabbath'.

Holy Week has been called *Hebdomada Muta; Hebdomada Inofficiosa; Hebdomada Penitentialis; Hebdomada Indulgentiae; Hebdomada Luctuosa; Hebdomada Nigra*; and *Hebdomada Ultima*.

Holy Writ. The BIBLE.

Hombonus, St (d. 1197, f.d. 13 November). The son of a prosperous merchant of Cremona, he inherited his father's business and continued it with great diligence and probity. Having been christened 'Good Man', he fully justified his name. He lived a devout life and gave generously to the poor, being an excellent example of a lay saint. He died suddenly at MASS, falling on his face with outstretched arms in the form of a cross. Miracles were attributed to him and he was canonized. He is the patron saint of tailors and clothworkers.

Homily. An expository sermon in which spiritual matters are discussed; it is delivered by a bishop or presbyter for the instruction and edification of the congregation. The term can also apply to an over-moralizing and tedious address.

Honorius, St (d. 653, f.d. 30 September). He came to England as a missionary sent by St GREGORY THE GREAT and succeeded St Justin as archbishop of Canterbury. Nothing is known of his life and character, except that he was of Roman birth, but his episcopate was marked by the appointment of St ITHAMAR, the first English bishop, and the evangelization of East Anglia by St FELIX OF DUNWICH. Honorius was buried at Canterbury, the centre of his cult. In art his attribute is a baker's peel, sometimes there are loaves on it.

Hopkinsians. A sect of Independent Calvinists (*see* CALVINISM) who followed the teachings of Samuel Hopkins (1721–1803) a minister of Newport, Rhode Island. He was one of the first New England Congregational ministers to oppose slavery. His theological teachings are to be found in his *System of Doctrines contained in Divine Revelation* (1793).

Horn. The horn was a symbol of power and dominion and as such is found in classical writers and similarly in the OLD TESTAMENT. The original Hebrew *shofar* or trumpet was made of a ram's horn.

My horn hath He exalted (I *Sam.* ii, 10; *Ps.* lxxxix, 24, etc). He has given me the victory, increased my sway. Thus, *Lift not up your horn on high* (*Ps.* lxxv, 5) means, do not behave scornfully, maliciously, or arrogantly. In these passages 'horn' symbolizes power, and its exaltation signifies victory or deliverance. In DANIEL's vision (*Dan.* vii, 7) the 'fourth beast, dreadful and terrible, and strong exceedingly,' had ten horns, symbolic of its great might.

Horsemen. Four Horsemen of the Apocalypse. *See under* FOUR.

Hospital. Hospital Sunday. The SUNDAY nearest St LUKE's day (18 October), when churches have special collections for hospitals. The practice began in London in 1873.

Hospitallers. First applied to those whose duty it was to provide *hospitium* (lodging and entertainment) for pilgrims. The most noted institution of the kind was founded at Jerusalem (*c.* 1048), which gave its name to an order called the Knights Hospitallers or the Knights of St John of Jerusalem; later they were styled the Knights of Rhodes; and then the Knights of Malta; the islands of Rhodes (1310) and Malta (1529) being, in turn, their headquarters. The order became predominantly military in the 12th century but in late 18th century reverted to its earlier purposes of tending the sick and poor, moving to ROME in 1834.

The order came to an end in England after the REFORMATION but a branch was revived in 1831 which declared itself an independent order in 1858, now styled the Order of the Hospital of St John of Jerusalem. It founded the St John Ambulance Association in 1877.

Host (Lat. *hostia*, a sacrifice). The consecrated bread of the EUCHARIST regarded as the sacrifice of the Body of Christ.

The Elevation of the Host. At the EUCHARIST, the raising by the celebrant of the sacred elements immediately after consecration to symbolize the offering to God and to show them for adoration.

Host, as an army or multitude, is from the Lat. *hostis*, enemy. In Med. Lat. *hostem facere* came to mean 'to perform military service'. *Hostis* (military service) then came to mean the army that went against the foe, whence our word *host*.

The heavenly host. The ANGELS and ARCHANGELS.

The Lord God of Hosts, Lord of Hosts. JEHOVAH, the hosts being the ANGELS and celestial spheres.

Houghton, St John (1487–1535, f.d. 25 October). Born into a family of Essex landed gentry, he read Law at Christ's College, Cambridge, then became a secular priest before entering the CARTHUSIAN Order at Smithfield. He was elected prior of Beauvale, in Nottinghamshire, but was soon recalled to be prior of Charterhouse in London. This office he fulfilled admirably, gaining a reputation for sanctity and learning. After the passing of the Act of Succession of Henry VIII, Houghton, with two other priors, Robert LAWRENCE and Augustine WEBSTER, became involved in the conflict over the Oath of Supremacy which required recognition of Henry's marriage to Anne Boleyn and acceptance of the King as Supreme Head of the Church. Refusing to take the oath, all three were tried for treason, found guilty and condemned to be hanged, drawn and quartered at Tyburn, going to their deaths with great fortitude. They were canonized among the FORTY MARTYRS OF ENGLAND AND WALES by Pope Paul VI in 1970.

Hour. Book of Hours. A book of devotions for private use, especially during the CANONICAL HOURS (*see under* CANON). Such books in the later Middle Ages were often beautifully and lavishly illuminated and have a particular importance in the history of the book arts.

Canonical Hours. *See under* CANON.

At the eleventh hour. Just in time; only just in time to obtain some benefit. The allusion is to the parable of the labourers hired for the vineyard (*Matt.* xx).

House. A or **The House of God.** A church or place of worship; also any place sanctified by God's presence. Thus JACOB in the wilderness, where he saw the ladder leading from earth to HEAVEN, said, 'This is none other but the House of God, and this is the gate of heaven' (*Gen.* xxvii, 17).

Housel. To give the Sacrament (O.E. *husel*, sacrifice). *Cp.* UNANELED.

Unhouseled is without having had the EUCHARIST, especially at the hour of death.

Howard, St Philip (1557–95, f.d. 25 October). Earl of Arundel and son and heir to the Duke of Norfolk, Philip was reared as a PROTESTANT to conform with the CHURCH OF ENGLAND, his tutor being John Foxe, the martyrologist. Philip then went to Cambridge. Although the family was disgraced and the duke executed for high trea-

son when he proposed to marry Mary Queen of Scots, Philip remained in favour with Queen Elizabeth until he was reconciled with his wife, Anne Dacres, and he became a CATHOLIC. He was arrested at sea while trying to escape to the Continent, was imprisoned in the Tower and sentenced to death but was not executed, remaining a prisoner until he died at the age of thirty-eight. He was canonized in 1970 as one of the FORTY MARTYRS OF ENGLAND AND WALES.

Hubert, St (d. 727, f.d. 3 November). Patron saint of huntsmen, reputedly son of Bertrand, Duke of Guienne. He so neglected his religious duties for the chase that one day a stag bearing a crucifix menaced him with eternal perdition unless he reformed. Upon this he entered the cloister and duly became Bishop of Liège, and the apostle of Ardennes and Brabant. Those who were descended of his race were supposed to possess the power of curing the bite of a mad dog.

In art he is represented as a BISHOP with a miniature stag resting on the book in his hand, or as a huntsman kneeling to the miraculous crucifix borne by the stag.

Hugh. Hugh of Grenoble, St (1052–1132, f.d. 1 April). Born at Châteauneuf, he became a canon at the cathedral school of Valence, where he had been educated, although he was a layman and only twenty-five years of age. He was elected bishop of Grenoble and carried out vigorous reforms against the prevalent abuses of simony, usury and moral laxity among the clergy. He restored the cathedral, built hospitals, a bridge and a market-place and founded houses of CANONS Regular. He is famous as the co-founder of the CARTHUSIAN Order, in which his father died as a monk at 100 years of age. Hugh himself stayed frequently with the monks when the pope refused to allow him to resign his see. He supported Pope Innocent II, with St BERNARD, against the anti-pope Anacletus.

Hugh of Lincoln, St. There are two saints so designated.

(1) St Hugh (*c.* 1140–1200, f.d. 17 November), a Burgundian by birth, and founder of the first CARTHUSIAN house in England. He became bishop of Lincoln in 1186. He was noted for his charitable works and kindness to the Jews.

(2) St Hugh (13th century), the boy of about ten years of age allegedly tortured and crucified in mockery of Christ. The story goes that the affair arose from his having driven a ball through a Jew's window while at play with his friends. The boy was finally thrown into a well from which he spoke miraculously. Eighteen Jews were purported to have been hanged. The story is paralleled

at a number of other places in England and on the Continent (*cp.* WILLIAM OF NORWICH), and forms the subject of Chaucer's *The Prioress's Tale*. It is also found in Matthew Paris and elsewhere.

Huguenot. The French Calvinists (*see* CALVINISM) of the 16th and 17th centuries. The name is usually said to derive incorrectly from the Ger. *Eidgenossen*, confederates, but according to Henri Estienne (*Apologie pour Hérodote*, 1566), it is from *Hugo*, from the fact that the PROTESTANTS of Tours used to meet at night near the gate of King Hugo. *See also* BARTHOLOMEW, MASSACRE OF ST.

Hulsean Lectures. Since 1777, a course of lectures on Christian evidence, etc., delivered annually at Cambridge, instituted and endowed by the Rev. John Hulse (1708–90) of Cheshire.

Humanae Vitae. The ENCYCLICAL of Pope Paul VI, in 1968, which prohibited abortion and artificial birth-control.
Humani Generis. The ENCYCLICAL of Pope Pius XII, in 1950, which condemned Existentialism among other modern movements in the Church.

Humanitarians. A name given to certain ARIANS who held that Christ was only man. The name was also used of the UNITARIANS and of the followers of Saint-Simon (1760–1825), an early exponent of socialism. Nowadays the term is usually applied to philanthropists in general.

Humbert, St (d. 680, f.d. 25 March). Born at Maisières, Picardy, of noble family, he was ordained priest at the monastery of Laon, living as a recluse. He accompanied St AMANDUS to ROME, then entered the monastery of Marolles, Hainault, endowing it with all his worldly possessions and dying there. In art he bears the mark of a cross on his head and is accompanied by a bear, representing the legend that when his horse had been killed by a bear he placed the pack-saddle on the bear's back, and made it carry him for the rest of the journey to Rome.

Humeral. A priest's vestment in the Western CATHOLIC CHURCH; a silk scarf placed over the shoulders at the celebration of HIGH MASS and at processions of the Blessed SACRAMENT and at BENEDICTION.

Humiliati. An Italian lay fraternity of the 12th century, formed by a group of Lombards. Members of the order lived in their own homes in humility and piety, wearing simple clothes of one colour. The order spread rapidly and established two new branches, one for women and another for priests, and was recognized by Pope Innocent III. The rule of life forbade unnecessary oaths and the taking of God's name in vain; it allowed voluntary poverty and marriage and instituted pious exercises.

Huntingdonians. Members of 'the Countess of Huntingdon's Connexion', a sect of Calvinistic METHODISTS founded in 1748 by Selina, widow of the ninth Earl of Huntingdon, and George Whitefield , who had become her chaplain. The churches founded by the countess, numbering some 36, were mostly affiliated with the Congregational Union. *See* UNITED REFORMED CHURCH.

Hussites. Followers of John Hus, the Bohemian religious reformer (1369–1415), sometimes called WYCLIFFITES from the fact that many of the teachings of John Hus were derived from those of Wyclif.

Hutterite Brethren. A PROTESTANT group which left Germany on account of persecution, first settling in different parts of Europe but finally establishing themselves in South Dakota and Western Canada in 1873–5. They are farmers practising communal living and are pacifists.

Hwaetbert (or **Huaetberet**), **St** (716–*c.* 747, f.d. not recorded). Sent to the monastery of Wearmouth and Jarrow as a child and educated there in theology and monastic learning, he was ordained priest and later elected as abbot, being confirmed by St ACCA. Letters from Pope GREGORY II still survive, as do letters from St BONIFACE, requesting Hwaetbert to send the works of BEDE and a bell, accompanied by a present of a goat-hair bed-covering. Bede dedicated his *Commentary on the Apocalypse* and his *De Temporum ratione* to him. Hwaetbert was also known as 'Eusebius' on account of his holiness.

Hyacinth of Cracow, St (1185–1257, f.d. 17 August). Known as the 'Apostle of Poland', he was born of a noble Polish family and was educated at Cracow, Prague and Bologna. In ROME he met St DOMINIC, was converted by him, and entered the DOMINICAN Order. He founded houses of the order in Poland and was credited with remarkable missionary journeys to Scandinavia, Russia and eastwards to Great Tartary, and even as far as Tibet and China, but of this there is no reliable evidence. He died and was buried at Cracow in the Dominican church. His name was said to be 'Jacek' or Jacob, in Polish, changed to Jacinthus. He was credited with numerous miracles, one of which was to save from the Tartar invaders a MONSTRANCE and a heavy statue of the VIRGIN and carry them to safety, walking across the waters of the Dnieper river. His cult is now confined to local calendars since the revision of 1969.

Hyacinthus, St. *See* PROTUS.

Hymn (Gr. *hymnos*, a song composed in honour of the gods). A sacred song or ode of praise or of supplication to God, it is set to music and sung at religious services. Singing has been an essential part of religious activity from all time, according to anthropologists, probably preceding speech, and expressing emotions both in the individual and in unison. Christian hymnology had its origins in Hebrew sources. In the NEW TESTAMENT Christ and the DISCIPLES sang a hymn at the LAST SUPPER before going to the MOUNT OF OLIVES (see OLIVET) (*Mark* xiv, 26). St JAMES recommended psalm-singing (the distinction between hymns and psalms being modern and arbitrary); SS PAUL and SILAS sang hymns in prison at Philippi and St Paul speaks of 'psalms and hymns and spiritual songs'. At the AGAPE members of the congregation sang hymns of their own composition or taken from the SCRIPTURES. St AUGUSTINE defined a hymn as 'praise to God with song' and said that 'in singing we are doubling our prayers'. The first prolific hymn-writer was Ephraem Syrius (4th century) and the first great Latin hymn-writer was St HILARY OF POITIERS (d. 367), but the main instigator of hymn-singing at services in the Western Church was St AMBROSE (d. 397). The Middle Ages saw a number of important hymn-writers, largely monastic; many of their hymns are included in the Roman BREVIARY. English hymnology dates from Anglo-Saxon times, but the first hymn book proper was George Withen's *Hymns and Songs of the Church* (1623), while the first collection of original hymns, rather than translations from the Latin and psalms, was John and Charles WESLEY's *Collection of Psalms and Hymns* (1737).

Hyperdulia. A CATHOLIC term for the homage paid to the VIRGIN MARY, differing from LATRIA and DULIA.

Hypostatic Union. The union of three Persons in the TRINITY; also the union of the Divine and Human in Christ, in which the two elements, although inseparably united, each retain their distinctness. The *hypostasis* (Gr. *hypo*, under; *stasis*, standing; hence foundation, essence) is the personal existence as distinguished from both *nature* and *substance*.

Hyssop. David says (*Ps.* li, 7): 'Purge me with hyssop, and I shall be clean.' The reference is to the custom of ceremonially sprinkling the unclean with a bunch of hyssop (marjoram or the thorny caper) dipped in water in which had been mixed the ashes of a red heifer. This was done as they left the Court of the Gentiles to enter the Court of the Women (*Numb.* xix, 17, 18).

I

I.H.S. The Greek I H Σ, meaning IHΣους (Jesus), the long η(H) being mistaken for capital *H*, the abbreviation 'ihs' was often expanded as 'Ihsesus'. St Bernadine of Siena in 1424 applied them to *Jesus Hominum Salvator* (Jesus, the Saviour of men). Other explanations were *In Hac Salus* (safety in this, i.e. the Cross) and *In Hoc Signo* [*vinces*] (in this sign [ye shall conquer]). *See* CONSTANTINE'S CROSS *under* CROSS.

I.N.R.I. The initial letters of the inscription affixed to the CROSS of Christ by order of Pontius Pilate—*Iesus Nazarenus, Rex Iudaeorum,* Jesus of Nazareth, King of the Jews (*John* xix, 19). It was written in Greek, Latin, and Hebrew (*Luke* xxiii, 38).

Ice Saints, or **Frost Saints.** Those saints whose days fall in what is called 'the blackthorn winter'—that is, the second week in May (between 11 and 14). Some give only three days, but whether 11, 12, 13, or 12, 13, 14, it is not agreed. 11 May is the day of St Mamertus, 12 May of St PANCRAS, 13 May of St Servatius, and 14 May of St BONIFACE.

Ichthys (Gr. *ichthus,* fish). From the 2nd century the fish was used as a symbol of Christ and the word is also an acronym formed from the initial letters of *Jesous CHristos, THeou Uios, Soter* (Jesus Christ, Son of God, Saviour). It is found on many seals, rings, urns and tombstones of the early Christian period and was believed to be a charm of mystical efficacy.

Icon, or **Ikon** (Gr. *eikon,* an image or likeness). A representation in the form of painting, low-relief sculpture or mosaic of Our Lord, The Blessed Virgin, or a SAINT, and held as objects of veneration in the Eastern Church. Excepting the face and hands, the whole is often covered with an embossed metal plaque representing the figure and drapery. Saints are usually represented full-face since profile breaks the communion and is generally only used for those who have not attained sanctity, e.g. the Wise Men and shepherds. The oldest surviving icons date from the Justinian period and were produced mainly by the monastery of St CATHERINE on Mount Sinai. Discovered in the 1880s, they were taken to the Museum of the Theological Academy in Kiev. The first reference to Russian painters occurred in the 11th century, with SS Alimpiy (or Alipy) and Grigoriy, monks who had trained under Greek masters. An icon is never signed, as the iconographer does not work for his own glory, nor is an icon an object of aesthetic admiration and study, but a transmission of spiritual quality. Icons are 'theology and spirituality in colour', as Archbishop Pitirim said, and 'held to be embodiments of the eternal and hence to radiate the spiritual'. They symbolize the microcosm and are sacramental in that they are the outward and visible sign of an inward and spiritual grace. The colours must be unmixed and the gold background represents the Light of God. A natural development was the idea of powers working within the images which could afford protection, supply help and work miracles. We are told that St EUPHRASIA committed a child to the image of Christ for safe keeping, and, later, images were reputed to speak. Principal Festivals, in the sequence of the Church Year, are depicted in icons as:

Birth of the Holy Virgin.
Raising of the Cross.
Protection of the Mother of God.
Presentation of the Holy Virgin in the Temple.
Nativity of Christ.
Baptism or Ephipany.
Presentation of Christ in the Temple.
Annunciation.
Raising of Lazarus.
Entry into Jerusalem.
Crucifixion. The Cross.
Descent into Hell.
Spice-bearers at the Sepulchre.
Mid-Pentecost (Wednesday of 4th week after Easter).
Ascension.
Pentecost.
Holy Trinity.
Descent of the Holy Ghost on the Apostles.
Transfiguration of Our Lord.
The Dormition of the Mother of God (Assumption).

The Resurrection, or Easter, does not enter into the twelve principal feast days of the Church as it is 'the Feast of Feasts and the Celebration of Celebrations and excels all other festivals' (St Gregory the Theologian).

Iconoclasts (Gr. image-breakers). In the 8th

century reformers, essentially in the Eastern Church, opposed to the use of sacred pictures, statues, emblems, etc. The movement against the use of images was begun by the Emperor Leo III, the Isaurian, who was strongly opposed by the monks and also by Pope Gregory II and Pope Gregory III. The controversy continued under successive *Iconoclast Emperors*, notably Constantine V, called insultingly 'Copronymus' by his opponents (he is said to have fouled the font at baptism). It was finally ended by the Empress Theodora in 843 in favour of the image-lovers, and Iconclasm was proscribed.

Iconostasis. One of the most important features of an ORTHODOX Catholic CHURCH; it is a screen composed of five or more rows of ICONS; there is a door in the middle, flanked by figures of Christ and the VIRGIN MARY. The screen separates the SANCTUARY, where the EUCHARIST is celebrated, from the NAVE, the central part where the congregation stands. It existed from early times and is mentioned by early CHURCH FATHERS (*see* FATHERS OF THE CHURCH) such as St Gregory the Theologian and St JOHN CHRYSOSTOM, and historians such as EUSEBIUS. The central door leading to the Sanctuary is the Holy or Royal Door; it is only entered by clergy at the times the church services require.

Idelphonsus of Toledo, St (*c.* 607–77, f.d. 23 January). Of noble Spanish family, he was ordained priest and became abbot of a monastery near Toledo and later archbishop of that city. He was a writer and musician and his fame rests on his treatises on BAPTISM and on the VIRGIN MARY, the latter being an enthusiastic and emotional work. The Virgin was said to have appeared to him, when he was seated on his episcopal throne, presenting him with a CHASUBLE. In art this scene has been painted by Velázquez and El Greco.

Idle Bible, The. *See* BIBLE, SOME SPECIALLY NAMED EDITIONS.

Ignatius, St. According to tradition St Ignatius was the little child whom our Saviour set in the midst of his disciples for their example. He was a convert of St JOHN THE APOSTLE. was consecrated Bishop of Antioch by St PETER, and is said to have been thrown to the beasts in the amphitheatre by Trajan about 107. His day is 17 October and he is represented in art with lions, or chained and exposed to them.

Ignatius Loyola, St. *See* LOYOLA.

Father Ignatius. The Rev. Joseph Leycester Lyne (1837–1908), a deacon of the CHURCH OF ENGLAND, who founded a pseudo-BENEDICTINE monastery at Capel-y-ffin, near Llanthony, Monmouthshire, in 1870. He was an eloquent preacher, but his ritualistic practices brought him into conflict with his ecclesiastical superiors

who would not admit him to priest's orders. In 1898 he was ordained by Joseph Villatte, a wandering BISHOP who had been consecrated by a schismatic 'JACOBITE' prelate in Ceylon.

The Rev. and Hon. Geo. Spencer (1799–1864), a clergyman of the Church of England, who joined the ROMAN CATHOLIC CHURCH and became Superior of the English province of the Congregation of Passionists, was also known as 'Father Ignatius'.

Ignatius of Laconi, St (1701–81, f.d. 11 May). Born at Laconi, in Sardinia, he became a CAPUCHIN LAY BROTHER; he was said to have taken to the religious life after the shock of his horse bolting but leaving him unharmed. He was given the position of QUESTOR for the FRIARS, and in execution of his duties went on foot in all weathers, meeting every section of the public, treating all with love and care. Legend relates that he refused to ask alms of a notorious moneylender, who complained of being ignored. Ignatius was ordered to remedy this, calling on him and being given a sack of food which, when opened, dripped blood. Ignatius had power as a healer and miracles were attributed to him.

Ignorantines. A name given to the Brothers of the Christian Schools, A Roman Catholic religious fraternity founded at Reims by the Abbé de la Salle in 1680 for giving free education to the children of the poor. They now carry out teaching work in many countries. A clause in their constitution prohibited the admission of priests with theological training, hence the name, which was also given to a body of Augustinian mendicants, the Brothers of Charity, or Brethren of Saint Jean-de-Dieu, founded in Portugal in 1495.

Illtyd (Illtud or **Eltut), St** (6th cent., f.d. 6 November). Founder and abbot of a large monastic school at Llantwit, in Glamorgan, he was a notable figure in the religious history of Wales, reputed to be 'the most learned of Britons on both Testaments and in all kinds of knowledge'. Many Welsh churches are dedicated to him. He was said to have sailed to Brittany to relieve a famine and churches and villages there bear his name. The numerous legends associated with him have no historical foundation.

Illuminated Doctor. *See* DOCTORS OF LEARNING.

Illuminati. The baptized were at one time so called, because a lighted candle was given them to hold as a symbol that they were illuminated by the HOLY GHOST.

The name has been given to, or adopted by, several sects and secret societies professing to have superior enlightenment, especially to a republican society of deists founded by Adam Weishaupt (1748–1830), at Ingolstadt in Bavaria in 1776, to establish a religion consistent with 'sound reasons'. They were also called *Perfectibilists*.

Among others to whom the name has been applied are the HESYCHASTS; the Alombrados of 16th-century Spain; the French GUERINISTS; the ROSICRUCIANS; the French and Russian MARTINISTS; and in the USA to the Jeffersonians, etc.

The Illuminator. The surname given to St Gregory of Armenia (*c*. 240–322), the apostle of Christianity among the Armenians.

Image-breakers, The. ICONOCLASTS.

Immaculate Conception. This dogma, that the Blessed Virgin Mary was 'preserved immaculate from all stain of original sin' from 'the first moment of her conception' was not declared by the ROMAN CATHOLIC CHURCH to be an article of faith until 1854 when Pius IX issued the Bull *Ineffabilis Deus*. It has a long history as a belief and was debated by the SCHOOLMEN. It was denied by St Thomas AQUINAS (*see* THOMISTS), but upheld by Duns Scotus.

The Feast of the Immaculate Conception is on 8 December; it is a HOLIDAY of obligation in some countries.

Immersion. BAPTISM by Immersion is a form of baptism in which the whole body is submerged in the waters; it is practised by BAPTISTS and the Disciples of Christ. It can also take place in the Eastern Church and is permitted amongst ROMAN CATHOLICS.

Impanation. The dogma that the body and blood of Christ are locally present in the consecrated bread and wine of the EUCHARIST, just as God was present in the body and soul of Christ. The word means 'putting into the bread' and is found as early as the 11th century. *Cp*. TRANSUBSTANTIATION.

Imposition. Imposition of hands. *See* LAYING ON OF HANDS *under* HAND.

Imprimatur (Lat., let it be printed). An official licence to print a book. Such a licence or *royal imprimatur* was required under the Licensing Act of 1662 to secure ecclesiastical conformity. The act, initially for two years, was not renewed after 1695, and was in abeyance from 1679 to 1685.

In the ROMAN CATHOLIC CHURCH, if a priest writes on theological and moral subjects the book has to receive an *imprimatur* and NIHIL OBSTAT. The former is granted by the BISHOP or his delegate. *Cp*. INDEX.

Impropriation (Lat. *impropriare*, to take as one's own). Profits of an ecclesiastical BENEFICE in the hands of a layman, who is called the *impropriator*. When the benefice is in the hands of a spiritual corporation it is called *appropriation*. At the REFORMATION, many appropriated monastic benefices passed into the hands of lay rectors, who usually paid only a small part of the TITHE to incumbents, hence the need for QUEEN ANNE'S BOUNTY.

In. In Coena Domini (Lat., on the Lord's Supper). A papal BULL issued from the 13th century until its suspension in 1773 owing to the opposition of the civil authorities. It contained excommunications and censures against heresies, schism, sacrilege, and the infringement of papal and eccclesiastical privileges by temporal powers, etc. Its publication came to be restricted to MAUNDY THURSDAY and many of its ecclesiastical censures were incorporated in Pius IX's bull *Apostolicae Sedis* (1869).

In commendam (Lat., in trust). The holding of church preferment for a time, during a vacancy; and later restricted to livings held by a BISHOP in conjunction with his SEE. There were many abuses, and the practice was ended in England in 1836.

In petto (Ital.). Held in reserve, kept back, something done privately and not announced to the general public. (Lat. *in pectore*, in the breast.)

Cardinals in petto. CARDINALS chosen by the POPE, but not yet proclaimed publicly. Their names are *in pectore* [of the Pope].

Incarnation. The Christian doctrine that the Son of God took human flesh and that Jesus Christ is truly God and truly man (L. Lat. *incarnari*, to be made flesh).

Incense. Gums and spices which when burnt emit a sweet scent, used in religious ceremonies, especially in ROMAN and ORTHODOX Catholic CHURCHES. It symbolizes prayer rising to heaven, the perfume of virtue and the pure life; it can also be regarded as symbolizing a substitute for the 'burnt offering'. Incense is also apotropaic as it puts demons to flight and is used in the exorcising of evil spirits.

Incombustibility. Immunity from injury when exposed to fire or excessive heat. Numerous incidents of this phenomenon are recorded in the lives of the saints, giving them the title of 'human salamanders' from one Marie Somet, who was nicknamed 'Marie la Salamandre'. She would be suspended over a fiery brazier, wrapped in a sheet, and neither she nor the sheet sustained any damage. The earliest recorded example was St POLYCARP of Smyrna, (*c*. 155) who was condemned to be burnt at the stake but 'fiercely burning fire encircled the saint and left him unharmed'. A notable case was that of St Francis of Paula, who was also said to be able to transmit the immunity. There are frequent accounts of saints carrying live coals in their hand or in the habit or apron. Other such saints are: St CATHERINE OF SIENA, St Austreberta, the Blessed Angeline di Marsciano and Emma, mother of St EDWARD THE CONFESSOR.

Incumbent. The holder of an ecclesiastical benefice in the CHURCH OF ENGLAND, responsible for the duties of the sacred office.

Independent. Independent Methodists. A PROTESTANT NONCONFORMIST CHURCH in Britain, dating from 1806. Its ministry is unpaid, is EVANGELICAL, and has CONGREGATIONAL affinities in its organization.

Independents. A collective name for the various PROTESTANT separatist sects, especially prominent in 17th-century England, who rejected both Presbyterianism and EPISCOPACY, holding that each congregation should be autonomous or independent. The earliest were the BARROWISTS and BROWNISTS of Elizabeth I's reign, and the BAPTISTS and CONGREGATIONALISTS became the two main groups, but there were others more eccentric such as the FIFTH-MONARCHY MEN. They were notably strong in the Cromwellian army.

Index, The (Index Librorum Prohibitorum). The 'List of Prohibited Books' of the ROMAN CATHOLIC CHURCH which members were forbidden to read except in special circumstances. The first Index was made by the INQUISITION in 1557, although Pope Gelasius issued a list of prohibited writings in 494 and there had been earlier condemnations and prohibitions. In 1571 Pius V set up a *Congregation of the Index* to supervise the list, and in 1917 its duties were transferred to the Holy Office. The Index was abolished 14 June 1966. In addition to the Index there was the *Codex Expurgatorius* of writings from which offensive doctrinal or moral passages were removed. Since 1897 diocesan bishops were given greater responsibility in the control of literature and the Index became less prominent.

All books likely to be contrary to faith and morals, including translations of the BIBLE not authorized by the Church, were formerly placed on the Index. Among authors wholly or partly prohibited were Chaucer, Bacon, Milton, Addison, Goldsmith, Locke, Gibbon; Montaigne, Descartes, Voltaire, Hugo, Renan; Savonarola, Croce, D'Annunzio; and for a long time Galen, Copernicus, and Dante. *Cp.* IMPRIMATUR.

Indract, St (d. *c.* 700, f.d. 5 February or 8 May).

Said to be an Irish chieftain or of Royal descent, he settled near GLASTONBURY with nine companions. All were murdered by brigands who supposed them to be carrying treasure. Another legend says that Indract and his sister St Drusa, or Dominica, were murdered by Saxon pagans on their way home from a pilgrimage to ROME. King Ina of Wessex had their relics translated to Glastonbury beside the high altar of the old church.

Induction (Lat., the act of leading in). When a clergyman is inducted to a living he is led to the church door, and his hand is laid on the key by the archdeacon. The new incumbent then tolls the bell.

Indulgence. In the ROMAN CATHOLIC CHURCH, the remission before God of the earthly punishment due for sins of which the guilt has been forgiven in the sacrament of Penance. Such indulgences are granted out of the TREASURY OF THE CHURCH; they are either plenary or partial. In the later Middle Ages the sale of indulgences by PARDONERS became a grave abuse and it was the hawking of indulgences by Tetzel and the DOMINICANS in Germany that roused Luther and precipitated the REFORMATION.

Declarations of Indulgence. Declarations issued by Charles II (1662 and 1672) and James II (1687 and 1688) suspending the penal laws against DISSENTERS and Roman Catholics. Except for that of 1662, they were issued under royal prerogative; that of 1688 led to the trial of the SEVEN BISHOPS.

Industrial Christian Fellowship. A PROTESTANT group organized by the Rev. P. T. R. Kirk; it met at the MALVERN CONFERENCE in 1941 and published *Social Justice and Economic Reconstruction*, which laid down Christian principles for the industrial, economic and social systems of the world.

Infallibility. In the ROMAN CATHOLIC CHURCH, the POPE, when speaking EX CATHEDRA on a question of faith and morals is held to be free from error. This dogma was adopted by the VATICAN COUNCIL of 1870 (many members dissenting or abstaining from voting) and was publicly announced by Pius IX at St Peter's. The term is also used by PROTESTANT FUNDAMENTALISTS when applied to the BIBLE.

Inferno. We have Dante's notion of the infernal regions in his *Inferno*: Homer's in the *Odyssey*, Bk. XI; Virgil's in the *Aeneid*, Bk. VI; Spenser's in *The Faerie Queene*, Bk. II, canto vii; Aristo's in *Orlando Furioso*, Bk. XVII; Tasso's in *Jerusalem Delivered*, Bk. IV; Milton's in *Paradise Lost*; Fénelon's in *Télémaque*, Bk.

XVIII; and Beckford's in his romance of *Vather*. *See* HELL.

Infralapsarian. The same as SUBLAPSARIAN.

Infusion (Lat. *fundere*, to pour). BAPTISM by pouring water over the candidate, as in the ROMAN CATHOLIC CHURCH.

Innocents. Feast of the Holy Innocents. *See under* HOLY.
The massacre of the Innocents. *See* MASSACRE.

Inquisition, The (Lat. *inquisitio*, an enquiry). The name given to the ecclesiastical jurisdiction in the CATHOLIC Church dealing with the prosecution of heresy. In the earlier days of the Church excommunication was the normal punishment, but in the later 12th and early 13th centuries, disturbed by the growth of the Cathari (*see* ALBIGENSES), the Church began to favour seeking the aid of the State. The Inquisition as such was instituted by Pope Gregory IX in 1231, influenced by the activities of the Emperor Frederick II against HERETICS. Inquisitors were appointed, chiefly from the DOMINICAN and FRANCISCAN Orders to uphold the authority of the Church in these matters. They held court in the local monastery of their order. Proceedings were in secret, and torture, as a means of breaking the will of the accused, was authorized by Pope Innocent IV in 1252. Obstinate heretics were handed over to the secular authorities for punishment which usually meant death at the stake (*see* AUTO DA FÉ). In 1542 the *Congregation of the Inquisition* was set up as the final court of appeal in trials of heresy, and its title was changed to *The Congregation of the Holy Office* in 1908 and it was renamed *The Sacred Congregation for the Doctrine of the Faith* in 1965, concerned with the maintenance of ecclesiastical discipline.

The famous Spanish Inquisition was established in 1479, closely bound up with the State, and at first directed against 'converts' from Judaism and Islam. Its famous first Grand Inquisitor was Torquemada (1420–98), and during his term of office some 2,000 heretics were burned. The Spanish Inquisition was abolished by Joseph Bonaparte in 1808, reintroduced in 1814 and finally terminated in 1834.

Installation. The correct term for the induction of a CANON or prebendary to his *stall* in a cathedral or collegiate church. Members of certain orders of chivalry are also *installed*.

Institution. The investing, by a bishop, of a cleric with the spiritual care of a parish.

Insufflation. The act of breathing upon a person, or on water, at BAPTISM, symbolizing the inspiration of the HOLY SPIRIT and the expulsion of evil spirits.

Interdict. In the ROMAN CATHOLIC CHURCH, an ecclesiastical punishment placed upon individuals, particular places, or a district, restrictions being placed upon participation in, or performance of, certain SACRAMENTS, solemn services and public worship. *Cp.* EXCOMMUNICATION. Notable instances are:

1081. Poland was put under an interdict by Pope Gregory VII because Boleslaw II, the Bold, slew Stanislaus, Bishop of Cracow, on the altar steps of his church.

1180. Scotland was similarly treated by Pope Alexander III for the expulsion of the Bishop of St Andrews.

1200. France was interdicted by Pope Innocent III because Philip Augustus had his marriage with Ingelburge annulled.

1208. England was put under an interdict lasting until 1213 by Innocent III for King John's refusal to admit Stephen Langton as archbishop of Canterbury.

International. International Association of Mission Studies. A meeting in Oslo in 1970 was followed by a formal organization in 1971, in Holland, 'to promote the scholarly study of theological, historical, social and practical questions relating to missions, to promote fellowship, co-operation and mutual assistance in the study, and to relate studies in mission to studies in theological and other fields'. Originally western PROTESTANT, the movement now includes ROMAN CATHOLICS.

International Association for Religious Freedom. Founded in 1900, in the USA, for UNITARIAN and other 'Liberal Religious Thinkers and Workers', it has fifty-four member groups in twenty-one countries and holds a triennial congress. The movement is concerned with social aid and relief work and includes other faith groups as well as Christians.

International Christian Youth Exchange. Initiated in 1949 as an offshoot of the Church of the Brethren, in the USA, its object is to provide opportunities for oecumenical exchange for young people of 16–18 years of age. The movement spread to Asia, Latin America and Africa, in co-operation with the WORLD COUNCIL OF CHURCHES Youth Movement. Following disputes, the organization was dissolved and reformed on liberal lines, allowing members to develop programmes according to their own convictions.

Introit. In the WESTERN CHURCH, the PSALM or HYMN which opens the act of worship at the EUCHARIST.

Invention of the Cross. *See under* CROSS.

Investiture (Med. Lat. *investitura*, investing; from *vestire*, to clothe). The ceremonial clothing or investing of an official, dignitary, etc., with the special robes or insignia of his office. **Investiture Controversy.** The name given to disputes between the Church and the Emperor and other princes over the right to invest abbots and BISHOPS with the ring and staff and to receive homage. The political and religious issues were strongly contested in the 11th and 12th centuries, especially between HILDEBRAND and the Emperor Henry IV. A compromise was reached in 1122, when the Emperor gave up his claim to invest with the ring and the staff but continued to grant the temporalities. In England the controversy between Anselm and Henry I over lay investiture was settled in a similar fashion in 1107.

Invincible Doctor. William of Occam (*c*. 1280–1349) or Ockham (a village in Surrey), FRANCISCAN friar and scholastic philosopher. He was also called *Doctor Singularis*, and *Princeps Nominalium*, for he was the reviver of Nominalism.

Invocation of Saints. The practice of involving the souls of SAINTS to intercede with God on behalf of the believer.

Irenaeus of Lyons, St (*c*. 130–200, f.d. 28 June). A Greek-speaking presbyter of Smyrna who was a disciple of St POLYCARP. He taught against the MONTANISTS, GNOSTICS and other heretics, and took part in the Eastern–Western controversy regarding EASTER. He went to Gaul, became bishop of Lyons in 178 and was said to have been crucified, but of this there is no proof. The beginning of the veneration of Mary as the Blessed VIRGIN MARY in the CATHOLIC CHURCH may be found in Iranaeus's conception of Mary as the Universal Mother, the Eve of the new creation. He is also noted as one of the first great ecclesiastical writers of the WESTERN CHURCH, stressing the importance of the OLD and NEW TESTAMENTS and the GOSPELS. **Irenaeus of Sirmium, St** (d. 304, f.d. 6 April (East), 25 March (West)). Bishop at Pannonia, in Hungary, who, at a comparatively young age, was martyred at Sirmium under the Diocletian and Maximian persecutions for refusing to sacrifice to the gods. All the pleas and weeping of his relatives and friends, and of his servants, failed to break his resolution, he was imprisoned and tortured, then beheaded, his body being thrown into the river Sava.

Iron. The iron entered his soul. This expression, used of one experiencing the pangs of anguish and embitterment, is found in the Prayer Book Version of *Ps.* cv (verse 18). It is a mistranslation of the Hebrew which appeared in the VULGATE. It was corrected in the Authorized Version of the BIBLE which says 'whose feet they hurt with fetters: he was laid in iron', i.e. he was put in irons or fetters. Coverdale, following the Vulgate, says—'They hurte his feet in the stocks, the yron pearsed his herte.'

Irvingites. Members of the CATHOLIC AND APOSTOLIC CHURCH. Edward Irving, a friend of the Carlyles, claimed to revive the college of the APOSTLES, and established a complex hierarchy, with such symbolical titles as 'ANGEL', 'Prophet', etc. In their early days they claimed to have manifested the gift of tongues.

Isaac the Great, St (d. 438, f.d. 9 September). Son of St NARSES I and, like his father, an important figure in the history of the Church in Armenia, being its virtual founder and being responsible for the rise of Armenian literature in the translating of the BIBLE; he also founded monasteries. In 427 he was driven out by the Persians for his opposition to the NESTORIANS.

Isaac Jogues, St (1607–46, f.d. 19 October). Born at Orleans, he joined the Society of Jesus in 1624 and in 1636 went to Canada as a missionary to the Indians, travelling one thousand miles inland, and being the first European to penetrate so far into the interior. He was taken prisoner, but managed to escape; three years later he was again captured and was believed to be a sorcerer responsible for a famine and an outbreak of sickness which, in fact, he had gone to help to cure. He and his friend St John Brebeuf were tortured, then tomahawked to death by the Mohawks. Both priests were canonized in 1930.

Isidore. Isidore the Farmer, St (*c*. 1080–1130, f.d. 15 May). An interesting example of sanctity in a devout layman of humble parentage and life. He was employed as a farm labourer, serving the same master all his life on a farm near Madrid and marrying a woman who was equally devout and saintly, St Maria de la Cabeza. Though little is known of his history, many legends are attached to his name. For example, when he was late for work a team of white oxen, led by angels, was seen ploughing in his place. In mid–winter he gave half his sack of corn to some starving birds he saw perched on a branch; the other half of the grain yielded a double crop. He was said to have guided King Alphonsus of Castile to a victory over the Moors and his relics and intercession cured King Philip III of a mortal fever. Miracles occurred after his death and his body remained incorrupt. He became patron saint of Madrid.

In art he is represented with a sickle.

Isidore of Seville, St (*c.* 560–636, f.d. 4 April). Son of a governor of Cartagena and grandson of King Theodoric. His brothers Leander and Florentina were also canonized. Isidore was made bishop of Seville in 601; he presided at various councils and reorganized the Church in Spain. He was a noted theologian, writer, historian, astronomer and grammarian and was named a DOCTOR OF THE CHURCH by Benedict XIV. His body lies in his church at Leon. In art he is represented holding a pen, as one of the great scholars, and with a hive of bees, as a swarm of bees was said to have settled about him in his infancy.

Isidorian Decretals. *See* DECRETALS.

Ita, St (*c.* 480–570, f.d. 15 January). Originally called Deirdre, there are various spellings of her name as Ita, Ide, Mida, Ytha; and in Devon she is known as St Ide or St Syth. Next to St BRIDGET she is probably the most famous of Ireland's women saints. Of royal descent, she took the veil at an early age and gathered round her a community of nuns at Killeedy, in County Limerick. It is also probable that she had a school for young boys and, among them, was reputed to have brought up St BRANDAN. Ita has been called the 'fostermother of the saints of Ireland'. Her legends stress the austerity of her life and numerous extravagant miracles have been attributed to her. She was one of the Irish saints invoked on the Continent in ancient litanies.

Ithamar, St (d. *c.* 660, f.d. 10 June). Little is known of his life other than that according to BEDE he was 'a man of Kent' and a man of great learning. His chief interest is that he was the first Anglo-Saxon to become an English bishop. He was consecrated to the see of Rochester by St HONORIUS to succeed St PAULINUS. In 655 Ithamar consecrated Deusdedit, or Frithona, as Archbishop of Canterbury. Buried at Rochester, Ithamar's tomb had a reputation for miracles.

Ives (Ivo, Ia or **Hya), St** (6th cent., f.d. 3 February, 27 October). An Irish virgin of noble birth who settled with others in Cornwall, having crossed the Irish Sea on a leaf which grew in size to support her. She was joined by St Barrices, and they built churches in Cornwall. She is the patron saint of St Ives in that county.

Ivo (Ives or **Yves), St** (date unknown, f.d. 24 April). In 1001 four bodies were discovered at Slepe, near Ramsey Abbey, one bearing a bishop's insignia. It was revealed, in a peasant's dream, that this was the Persian bishop Ives, or Ivo, who had lived as a hermit in Britain. The bodies were translated to Ramsey Abbey; miracles followed, and a spring appeared by the relics which had curative powers. Later the relics were translated back to Slepe after the miraculous appearance of a light at night which stretched there from Ramsey. Ives is the patron saint of St Ives in Huntingdon.

Ivo (Yvo or **Helory) of Brittany, St** (*c.* 1235–1303, f.d. 19 May). Born at Kermartin, in Brittany where his father was lord of the manor, he studied canon law and theology at Paris and Orleans but lived a monastic life, practising austerities and fasting. When he returned to Brittany he was appointed judge of the church courts at Rennes and later at Tréquier. He had a reputation for complete impartiality and incorruptibility, but gave special care to poor litigants. In 1284 he was ordained priest, abandoned his legal career, and devoted himself to his parish of Tredrez and later to Lovanec, building a hospital, attending the sick and poor, giving away his own clothes and housing beggars. He was also a noted preacher. He is the patron saint of lawyers.

Ivy (O.E. *ifig*). In Christian symbolism ivy typifies the everlasting life, from its remaining continually green. It also represents death and immortality and fidelity.

Iwi (or Ywi), St (7th cent., f.d. 8 October). Ordained deacon, he was a monk and disciple of St CUTHBERT at Lindisfarne. With the object of becoming 'an exile for Christ' he boarded a ship with some sailors for an unknown destination, landing in Brittany where he became a hermit noted for miracles of healing. Over 200 years later, Breton clerics brought his relics to England, to Wilton Abbey, where they were received in solemn procession and placed on the altar of St EDITH. When the time came for departure and return to Brittany the relics were found to be immovable, in spite of all efforts and the despair of the Bretons. The abbess, Wulftrudis, gave them a large sum of money in consolation and the relics remained at Wilton.

J

Jacob. Jacob's ladder. The ladder seen by Jacob leading up to HEAVEN (*Gen.* xxviii, 12); hence its application to steep ladders and steps, especially the rope ladder with wooden rungs slung from a ship's boom to the water. There is also a garden plant of this name so called from the ladder-like arrangement of its leaflets.

Jacob's staff. A pilgrim's staff; from the Apostle JAMES (Lat. *Jacobus*), who is usually represented with a staff and scallop shell.

> As he had traveild many a sommers day
> Through boyling sands of Arabie and Ynde;
> And in his hand a Jacobs staffe, to stay
> His wearie limbes upon.
> SPENSER: *The Faerie Queene*, I, vi, 35

Jacob's stone. The Coronation stone of Scone, in Scotland, is sometimes called, from the legend that Jacob's head had rested on this stone when he had the vision of the ANGELS ascending and descending the ladder (*Gen.* xxviii, 11).

Jacobins. The DOMINICANS were so called in France from the 'Rue St Jacques', the location of their first house in Paris.

Jacobites. A sect of Syrian MONOPHYSITES, so called from Jacobus Baradaeus, BISHOP of Edessa in the 6th century. The present head of their church is called the PATRIARCH of Antioch. The term is also applied to the Monophysite Christians in Egypt.

Jadwiga, St. *See* HEDWIG.

Jahveh, or **Jahweh.** *See* JEHOVAH.

Jambert (or **Jaenbeorht**), **St** (d. 792, f.d. 12 August). A man of Kent, he became a monk of St Augustine's Canterbury and was later elected abbot. Under King Offa of Mercia, Lichfield became the metropolitan see, thus reducing Kent to a sub-kingdom, but Offa's successor restored the status of Canterbury which retained it thereafter. Jambert was chosen archbishop and was buried there at St Augustine's.

James. James, St (f.d. 25 July). The APOSTLE **St James the Great** is the patron saint of Spain. One legend states that after his death in

Palestine his body was placed in a boat with sails set, and that next day it reached the Spanish coast. At Padron, near COMPOSTELA, they used to show a huge stone as the veritable boat. Another legend says that it was the relics of St James that were miraculously conveyed from Jerusalem, where he was BISHOP, to Spain, in a marble ship. A knight saw the ship entering port and his horse took fright and plunged into the sea but the knight saved himself by boarding the vessel and found his clothes entirely covered with scallop shells.

The saint's body was discovered in 840 by Bishop Theudemirus of Iria through divine revelation, and a church was built at Compostela for its shrine.

St James is represented in art sometimes with the sword by which he was beheaded, and sometimes attired as a pilgrim, with his cloak covered with shells.

St James the Less, or **James the Little.** He has been identified both with the APOSTLE James, the son of Alphaeus, and with James the brother of the Lord. He is commemorated with St PHILIP on 1 May (3 May by Roman Catholics).

James of the Marches, St (1394–1476, f.d. 28 November). Born at the Marches of Ancona, of humble parentage, he joined the FRANCISCANS, studied law at Perugia, and was ordained priest, living a life of great austerity. He was involved in controversies between branches of the order, and later between Franciscans and DOMINICANS. He was a notable preacher and refused the see of Milan in order to maintain his itinerant life. He helped the poor, setting up pawn shops to help them over financial difficulties. He preached against the BOGOMIL and HUSSITE heresies; took part in the Council of Basle in 1431 and FLORENCE (1438), and promoted reunion with the Greeks. He followed JOHN OF CAPISTRANO as Papal LEGATE in Hungary, after which he went to Naples, where he died and was buried. There is a portrait of him by Crivelli in the Louvre.

Jane Frances de Chantal. *See* CHANTAL.

Jansenists. A sect of Christians, who held the doctrines of Cornelius Jansen (1585–1638), Bishop of Ypres. Jansen professed to have formulated the teaching of AUGUSTINE, which resembled CALVINISM in many respects. He taught the doctrines of 'irresistible grace', 'original sin' (*see under* SIN), and 'the utter helplessness of the natural man to turn to God'. Louis XIV took part against them and they were put down by Pope Clement XI, in 1713, in the famous Bull UNIGENITUS.

Januarius, St (d. 304, f.d. 19 September). The patron saint of Naples, a bishop of Benevento who was martyred during the Diocletian persecution. His head and two vials of his blood are preserved in the cathedral at Naples. This congealed blood is said to liquefy several times a year.

Japan, The Martyrs of (d. 1597, f.d. 6 February). The successful mission of St FRANCIS XAVIER to Japan, in 1549, left a considerable number of converts who increased under FRANCISCAN, JESUIT and DOMINICAN missions. In 1597 the boasting of a Spanish captain so incensed the shogun Hideyoshi that he set out to exterminate Christianity in his country. The persecution killed 26 people among the Franciscans, 36 Jesuits, 21 Dominicans and 107 lay people, including three young boys. Their deaths were extremely cruel, first having their ears cut off, they were displayed in various towns and finally bound to crosses on the ground then raised and stabbed to death. A second persecution took place in 1614 and following years. They were beatified at different dates and canonized in 1862, their feast being chiefly local, but included in the revised Roman Calendar in 1970 as the first martyrs of the Far East.

Jarlath, St (d. *c.* 550, f.d. 6 June). Of noble family in Galway, he was reputed to have been a disciple of St Edna, to have founded a monastery at Cluain Fois, and to have been the first bishop of Tuam. His monastery was noted as a centre of learning and St Brendan of Clonard and St Colman of Cloyne were educated there.

Jassy, Synod of. A synod of the Eastern ORTHODOX CHURCH which met at Jassy in 1642 to condemn the CALVINIST heresy of Cyril Lucar and to ratify the text of Mogila's *Orthodox Confession*.

Javan. In the BIBLE, the collective name of the Greeks (*Is.* lxvi, 19, and elsewhere), who were supposed to be descended from *Javan,* the son of Japheth (*Gen.* x, 2).

Jehovah. The name *Jehovah* is an instance of the extreme sanctity with which the name of God was invested, for this is a disguised form of JHVH, the TETRAGRAMMATON which was too sacred to use, so the scribes added the vowels of Adonai, thereby indicating that the reader was to say Adonai instead of JHVH. At the time of the Renaissance these vowels and consonants were taken for the sacred name itself and hence *Jehovah* or *Yahweh*.

Jehovah's Witnesses. A religious movement founded in 1872 by Charles Taze Russel in Philadelphia, and known as International Bible Students until 1931. It does not ascribe divinity to Jesus Christ, regarding him as the perfect man and agent of God. Recognition of Jehovah as their sole authority involves the Witnesses in refusal to salute a national flag or to do military service. *The Watch Tower* is their official organ.

Jehovistic. *See* ELOHISTIC.

Jerome, St (*c.* 340–420, f.d. 30 September). A father of the Western Church, and compiler of the VULGATE. He died at Bethlehem and is usually represented as an aged man in a cardinal's dress, writing or studying, with a lion seated beside him. Born Eusebius Hieronymus Sophronius at Aquileia, in Dalmatia, he was highly educated both by his father and by Donatus, the grammarian at ROME, and became noted as the most learned of the Latin FATHERS and a master of rhetoric. He went to Syria as a hermit, learning Hebrew and studying the SCRIPTURES, and was later ordained priest at Antioch, but did not use his orders. He left for Constantinople where he studied under St GREGORY NAZIANZUS, writing and translating. Returning to Rome he acted as interpreter to PAULINUS and as secretary to POPE St DAMASUS. At Damasus's death he went to Bethlehem, where he was followed by some disciples, among them a group of ladies he had instructed in Rome, SS PAULA, Eustochium and Marcella. They led a semi-monastic life and established a hospice for travellers, and free schools where Jerome taught Greek and Latin. Being of an irascible nature and a master of invective, Jerome was frequently involved in controversy and made many enemies. He wrote treatises against various heresies, particularly PELAGIANISM, and on celibacy and the teachings of ORIGEN.

Jerome Emiliani, St (1481–1537, f.d. 8 February, 20 July). Born in Venice of illustrious family, he was an officer in the army and led a dissolute life until he was captured and imprisoned. Legend says that he repented, prayed to the VIRGIN MARY and vowed to serve God, whereupon an angel appeared and released him, opening doors and leading him to freedom. He founded hospitals, orphanages and penitentiaries for prostitutes. He also founded a Congregation of Clerks Regular, the *Somaschi,* who carried out his charitable works. He died of fever, caught while serving the sick. He was named patron saint of orphans and homeless children by Pope Piux XI, in 1928, and was placed on the revised Roman Calendar of 1969.

Jerusalem. JULIAN THE APOSTATE, the Roman Emperor (d. 363), to please the Jews and humble the Christians, said that he would rebuild the temple and city, but was mortally wounded before the foundations were laid, and his work set at nought by 'an earthquake, a whirlwind, and a fiery eruption' (*see* Gibbon's *Decline and Fall,* ch. dxiii).

Much has been made of this by early Christian writers, who dwell on the prohibition and curse pronounced against those who should attempt to rebuild the city. The fate of Julian is cited as an example of Divine wrath.

The New Jerusalem. The paradise of Christians, in allusion to *Rev.* xxi.

Jerusalem Chamber. This chamber adjoins the south tower of the west front of Westminster Abbey and probably owes its name to the tapestries hung on its walls depicting scenes of Jerusalem. Henry IV died there, 20 March 1413.

> It hath been prophesied to me many years,
> I should not die but in Jerusalem.
> SHAKESPEARE: *Henry IV, Pt. II,* IV, iv

The WESTMINSTER ASSEMBLY (1643–9) which drew up the Calvinistic WESTMINSTER CONFESSION met in the Jerusalem Chamber, as did the compilers of the Revised Version of the BIBLE. It is now the chapter-room.

Jerusalem Cross. A CROSS potent.

Jerusalem Delivered. An Italian epic poem in twenty books by Torquato Tasso (1544–95). Published in 1581, it was translated into English by Edward Fairfax in 1600. It tells the story of the First CRUSADE and the capture of Jerusalem by Godfrey of Bouillon in 1099.

Jesse, or **Jesse Tree.** A genealogical tree, usually represented as a large vine or as a large brass candlestick with many branches, tracing the ancestry of Christ, called a 'rod out of the stem of Jesse' (*Is.* xi, 1). Jesse is himself sometimes represented in a recumbent position with the vine rising out of his loins; hence a stained glass window representing him thus with a tree shooting from him containing the pedigree of Jesus is called a *Jesse window.*

Jesuit. The name given to members of the Society of Jesus, begun by Ignatius LOYOLA in 1534, and formally approved by Pope Paul III in 1540. It was founded to combat the REFORMATION and to propagate the faith among the heathen. Through its discipline, organization, and methods of secrecy it accquired such power that it came into conflict with both the civil and religious authorities. It was driven from France in 1594, from Portugal in 1759, and from Spain in 1767, was suppressed by Pope Clement XIV in 1773, but formally reconstituted by Pius VII in 1814.

Owing to the casuistical principles maintained by many of its leaders, the name Jesuit acquired an opprobrious signification and a *Jesuit* or *Jesuitical person* means (secondarily) a deceiver, a prevaricator, etc. Such associations have often obscured the extent of their achievements.

Jesus. The Greek form of the Hebrew Joshua; the name given to the Christ, son of MARY, and founder of the Christian religion.

Jesus People. Also called the Jesus Movement, or Jesus Revolution. An EVANGELICAL revivalist movement of the 1960s in California; it combined a 'hippie' lifestyle with Christian FUNDAMENTALISM and a millenarian outlook.

Jesus Prayer. A prayer widely used in the ORTHODOX Catholic CHURCH and dating from the 6th century: 'Lord Jesus Christ, Son of God, have mercy upon me.'

Jezreelites. A small sect founded in 1875 by James White (1849–85), a one-time army private, who took the name James Jershom Jezreel. They were also called the 'New and Latter House of Israel' and believed that Christ redeemed only souls, and that the body is saved by belief in the Law. Their object was to be numbered among the 144,000 (*see Rev.* vii, 4) who, at the Last JUDGEMENT, will be endowed with immortal bodies. Their headquarters were at Gillingham, Kent, where their Tower of Jezreel was formerly a familiar landmark.

Joachim. Joachim, St. The father of the Virgin Mary. Generally represented as an old man carrying in a basket two turtledoves, an allusion to the offering made for the purification of his daughter. His wife was St Anne.

Joachim of Fiore (de Floris), Bl. (*c.* 1130–1202). Born at Celica in Calabria, he was converted to the monastic life while on a pilgrimage to the HOLY LAND. Joachim became a monk in the CISTERCIAN Order at Sambucina. Later he founded a new Cistercian congregation at Fiore in South Italy. He wrote commentaries and his particular conception was that of history being divided into the Three Ages. In the first age the Father directed the Age of Law, the OLD TESTAMENT teaching; the second was the Age of the Son, the GOSPEL and the NEW TESTAMENT; this ended about 1260 when the Third Age of the Spirit would begin, the age of contemplation and spiritual understanding, directed by the Holy Spirit after the age of corruption and the Anti-Christ. But when the fatal 1260 came and went, the Joachimists faded into the general body of the Cistercians. Joachim was one of the great mystics of the Middle Ages and Dante called him 'the Calabrian abbot Joachim, endowed with prophetic spirit' (*Paradiso* XII).

Joan of Arc, St (1412–31, f.d. 30 May) the Maid of Orleans (*La Pucelle d'Orléans*). Born at Domrémy in Lorraine, the daughter of a peasant, she was directed by heavenly voices to undertake her mission to deliver France, then undergoing the ravages of the Hundred Years War. She convinced the Dauphin of her sincerity, donned male dress, and inspired the French army in the relief of Orléans (1429) and then the advance to Rheims. She was captured by the Burgundians at Compiègne (May 1430) and sold to the English by the Count of Luxembourg for 10,000 livres. She was condemned to death by the Bishop of Beauvais for witchcraft and heresy and burned at the stake at Rouen (30 May 1431). Her last words were the name of Jesus repeated thrice. She was canonized in 1920 as the second patron of France but as such is not recognized by the State. There has been no official patron saint of France since the separation of Church and State in 1905.

Pope Joan. *See under* POPE.

Joan of Lestonnac, St (1556–1640, f.d. 2 February). Born at Bordeaux, niece of Montaigne, the essayist, and married to Gaston de Montferrant, she was widowed in 1597 and devoted the rest of her life to the education of girls, for which she founded the Sisters of Notre Dame of Bordeaux, taking the office of Superior. She was deposed for a time as the result of a conspiracy, but was reinstated, bearing her troubles with great patience. She was canonized in 1949.

Joan Thounet, St (1765–1826, f.d. 24 August). Born near Besançon, the daughter of a tanner, she joined the Sisters of Charity of St VINCENT DE PAUL in Paris. The community was dissolved at the Revolution and Joan returned to her native village to run the school. She then opened a school at Besançon which developed into the Congregation of the Sisters of Charity under St Vincent's protection. The movement spread to Switzerland, Savoy, Italy and in France. There her work was hindered by the archbishop of Besançon, but she continued steadfastly to the end of a long life. She was canonized in 1934.

Joan of Valois, St (1464–1505, f.d. 4 February). Daughter of Louis XI, she was deformed and pock-marked and disliked by her father, who married her off at the age of twelve to Louis, Duke of Orléans. To her joy, the marriage was dissolved and, being of a devout nature, she devoted her life to good works at Bourges, founding the Order of the Annunciation, the 'Annonciades', to work and pray for concord among the people. She was venerated at Bourges at her death and canonized in 1775.

Joanna Southcott. *See* SOUTHCOTTIANS.

Jogues. *See* ISAAC JOGUES.

John. The English form of Lat. and Gr. *Johannes,* from Heb. *Jochanan,* meaning 'God is gracious'. The feminine form, *Johanna* or *Joanna,* is nearer the original. The French equivalent of 'John' is *Jean* (formerly Jehan), the Italian *Giovanni,* Russian *Ivan,* Gaelic *Ian,* Irish *Sean* or *Shaun,* Welsh *Evan,* German *Johann* or *Johannes,* which is contracted to *Jan, Jahn,* and *Hans.* For many centuries John has been one of the most popular of masculine names in England—probably because it is that of St JOHN THE APOSTLE, St JOHN THE BAPTIST and many other saints.

The name *John* has been used by Popes more than any other, its last holder being John XXIII. Among the SAINTS of this name are:

John the Almoner (or **Almsgiver**), **St** (*c.* 616, f.d. 23 January (West), 11 November (East)). Of noble and wealthy Cypriot family, he became a widower and lost all his children; he then devoted all his great wealth to the poor. On becoming Patriarch of Alexandria, though still a layman, he issued orders protecting the poor from taxes and exploitation and forbade his officers to accept any presents. He lived in great poverty himself and was said to have only one blanket, and that a poor one. There are many stories of his generosity and compassion and of giving gold to hospitals and making a list of some 7,500 poor needing help.

John the Apostle or **Evangelist,** or **the Divine, St** (f.d. 27 December). The 'beloved disciple'. Tradition says that he took the Virgin Mary to Ephesus after the Crucifixion and that in the persecution of Domitian (AD 93–6) he was plunged into a cauldron of boiling oil but was delivered unharmed, and afterwards banished to the Isle of Patmos where he wrote the *Book of Revelation*. He died at Ephesus. He is usually represented bearing a chalice from which a serpent issues, in allusion to his driving the poison from a cup presented to him to drink.

Called 'the Divine', John was a fisherman of Galilee, a son of Zebedee and brother of St PETER and St JAMES. Christ called the brothers 'Boanerges', 'sons of thunder' as an allusion to their impetuous and impassioned temperaments. John was traditionally the author of the Fourth GOSPEL. In pictures of the LAST SUPPER he is depicted leaning on Christ's breast.

John of Avila, St (1500–69, f.d. 10 May). Born at Almodovar-del-Campo, of wealthy Jewish family, he studied law at Salamanca but abandoned it to live a religious life. He then read theology and philosophy at Alcalá and was ordained priest. He hoped to go on a mission to Mexico but was persuaded to remain in Spain to convert the Moors. He was counsellor to such famous people as St TERESA of Avila, St FRANCIS BORGIA and St JOHN OF GOD, and was noted as a mystic and writer; he is called 'the Apostle of Andalusia'. His most outstanding work is *Audi Filia*. Beatified in 1894, he was canonized in 1970.

John the Baptist, St (f.d. 24 June). The forerunner of Jesus, who was sent 'to prepare the way of the Lord'. He is represented in a coat of sheepskin (in allusion to his life in the desert), either holding a rude wooden CROSS with a pennon bearing the words, *Ecce Agnus Dei*; or with a book on which a lamb is seated; or holding in his right hand a lamb surrounded by a HALO, and bearing a cross on the right foot.

John of Beverley, St (c. 640–721, f.d. 7 May). Bishop of Hexham and subsequently Archbishop of York. The Venerable BEDE was one of his pupils. His healing gifts are recorded by his biographers and his shrine at Beverley Minster (which he founded) became a favourite resort of pilgrims.

John Bosco, St. *See* BOSCO.

John of Bridlington, St (d. 1379, f.d. 21 October). Born at Thwing, near Bridlington, he was educated at Oxford University, then became an AUGUSTINIAN CANON. He led an exemplary life and was an excellent superior, also acting as precentor and cellarer. Miracles were reported at his tomb and the legend of the transformation of bread which was being carried to the poor was told of him, as of other saints.

John de Britto, St (1667–93, f.d. 4 February). Born in Lisbon, he became a JESUIT, going to India as a missionary at Malabar, Taniore and Madua. He tried to convert the Brahmin class, but he condemned polygamy and so provoked a persecution against the Christians during which he was executed for subversion of the religion of the country.

John of Capistrano, St (1386–1456, f.d. 23 October). Born at Capistrano, he studied law at Perugia where he later became governor. He had married, but at the age of thirty the marriage was dissolved and he entered the FRANCISCAN Order. He was ordained in 1420 and was a noted preacher, attracting large crowds; he also worked assiduously in trying to reconcile the factions among the Franciscans. The Pope appointed him papal legate in various states and sent him as inquisitor against the HUSSITE heretics in Austria, which office he fulfilled with great ferocity. At the fall of Constantinople in 1453 he was sent on a mission to the Turks, accompanying the Hungarian general Hunyady's army and being present at the victory of Belgrade in 1456, but dying of battle-field plague. Many miracles were reportedly worked by him.

John Cassian, St (c. 360–432, f.d. 23 July (West), 29 February (East)). A monk at Bethlehem, he left for Egypt to study monasticism. Later he went to Constantinople, was ordained deacon and was a disciple of St JOHN CHRYSOSTOM, following him to Italy when he was dismissed at the Synod of the Oak. Cassian was ordained priest and founded two monasteries, one for monks, the other for nuns. His works, the *Institute* and the *Conferences,* were guides to life in the community and the life of the hermit. His writings against the teaching of St AUGUSTINE on predestination were said to be the beginning of SEMI-PELAGIANISM.

John Chrysostom, St (c. 347–407, f.d. 13 September, formerly 27 January). (Gr. Golden tongued). Bishop of Constantinople and DOCTOR OF THE CHURCH, he did much to purify the life of his SEE. He was banished by his enemies in 403 and died in exile. He was noted for his holiness and liturgical reforms. He was one of the Three Holy Hierarchs of the Eastern Church, a great orator, and his sermons give valuable information on contemporary customs and worship. He was an iconodule, saying that images encourage piety. Born at Antioch, he was a hermit in the desert before being unwillingly appointed Bishop of Constantinople.

John of the Cross, St (1542–91, f.d. 14 December). Founder of the Discalced CARMELITES under the influence of St TERESA. He is noted for his mystical writings, *The Ascent of Mount Carmel, The Dark Night, The Spiritual Canticle,* etc. He was canonized in 1726.

John Damascene, St (c. 675–c. 749, f.d. 4 December, formerly 27 March). DOCTOR OF THE CHURCH and a defender of images during the Iconoclastic controversy. (*See* ICONOCLAST.) He was born at Damascus, son of a wealthy Christian who lived as an official under Muslim rule. He was well educated in theology and science by a Greek Sicilian monk. After succeeding his father for some time, John, also called Mansur, became a monk and was ordained priest. He was a noted writer of hymns, poetry and theological works which included *The Fount of Wisdom,* of which the last part, *De Fide Orthodoxa,* was an important exposition of the doctrines of the Greek Fathers. Legend says his head was cut off by Saracens, but was restored on praying to the Virgin.

John Fisher, St. *See* FISHER.

John of God, St (1495–1550, f.d. 8 March). Patron of hospitals, nurses and the sick, and a native of Portugal. In Ireland he is also held popularly to be the patron of alcoholics, through association with the Dublin clinic devoted to their cure and bearing his name. He founded the Order of Charity for the Service of the Sick, or Brothers Hospitallers.

John Houghton, St. *See* HOUGHTON.

John of Kanti, St (1390–1473, f.d. 23 December, formerly 20 October). Born at Kanti, in Poland, and educated at the University of Cracow, he was ordained priest and appointed a lecturer. He became famous as both a teacher and preacher, for his abstemious life and his generosity to the poor. He imbued his students with the need of meeting all controversy with courtesy and forbearance, and was held in great esteem by all.

John of Nepomuk, St (*c.* 1340–93, f.d. 16 May). Patron saint of Bohemia, he was drowned by order of the dissolute King Wenceslaus IV, allegedly because he refused to reveal to the king the confessions of the queen.

John Ogilvie, St. *See* OGILVIE.

John and Paul, SS (4th cent., f.d. 26 June). Early Roman martyrs, said to be brothers, whose remains were reputed to be in the church of SS John and Paul in ROME. Little is known of them except that they were martyred under JULIAN THE APOSTATE as soldiers of the Emperor Constantine; they had refused to obey a summons to court. Their Acts are generally held to be legendary and in the 1969 revision of the Calendar their cult was confined to their church.

John I, Pope, St (d. 526, f.d. 18 May). A Tuscan who succeeded Hormisdas as Pope after having held office as archdeacon. His episcopate was short, owing to his advanced age and ill health, and his main work was to remonstrate with the Eastern Emperor to obtain toleration for the ARIANS, a mission he undertook unwillingly on the orders of Theodoric, King of the Goths. On his return he was imprisoned by Theodoric who was dissatisfied with the partial success of his efforts, although he had been well received by the Greeks. He died in prison in hard conditions and in want.

John of Rila, St (d. 946). Founder of the great monastery of Rila and one of the earliest of the Bulgarian monks. He spent his life in the Rhodope mountains at his monastery which continued to modern times until it was converted into a meteorological station by the Communists in 1947.

John Roberts, St. *See* ROBERTS.

John-Baptist de la Salle, St (1651–19, f.d. 7 April). Born at Rheims, in comfortable circumstances, he gave these up to devote himself to educating the poor. He was ordained priest and appointed a canon at Rheims but resigned to found schools run by lay brothers, rather than priests; he also inaugurated SUNDAY SCHOOLS. King James II of England, in exile, asked him to undertake the education of the sons of his retinue. La Salle suffered considerable opposition from the established teaching profession in his innovations. He is regarded as the founder of Teacher Training Colleges as such, and his work *The Conduct of Christian Schools*, which advocated teaching in the native language rather than in Latin, became a classic and was translated into English in 1935.

John the Silent, St (454–558, f.d. 13 May). A native of Nicopolis in Armenia, he became a monk and had founded a monastery before he was twenty years of age, becoming a bishop at twenty-eight. He relinquished office to lead the life of a hermit in Palestine. When it was discovered that he was a bishop he again left and lived in a hut in the desert, spending the rest of his life in the LAURA of St SABAS near Jerusalem. It was said that he was guarded by a lion during the Saracen invasions.

John Southworth, St. *See* SOUTHWORTH.

John Stone, St. *See* STONE.

John-Baptist Vianney, St. *See* VIANNEY.

John Dory. A golden yellow fish, the *Zeus faber*, common in the Mediterranean and round the south-western coasts of England. Its name was dory (Fr. *doré*, golden) long before the John was added.

There is a tradition that it was from this fish that St PETER took the stater or shekel, and it has an oval black spot on each side, said to be his finger-marks when he held the fish to extract the coin. It is called in France *le poisson de St Pierre*, and in Gascon the *golden* or *sacred cock*, meaning St Peter's cock. *Cp.* HADDOCK.

Jones, St John Buckley (1559–98, f.d. 25 October). Born at Clynog Fawr, in Caernarvonshire, he entered the FRANCISCAN Order at Pontoise in France. After being professed in ROME he returned to England and worked with the JESUIT Henry GARNET. He was arrested and accused of returning to minister in England after having been ordained abroad. He admitted the charge and was executed in London. He was canonized in 1970 by Pope Paul VI as one of the FORTY MARTYRS OF ENGLAND AND WALES.

Jophiel. *See* ARCHANGEL.

Jordan passed. Death over. The Jordan separated the wilderness of the world from the PROMISED LAND, and thus came to be regarded as the Christian Styx.

Josaphat of Polotsk, St (1580–1623, f.d. 12 November, formerly 14 November). From a wealthy merchant family at Vladmir, he was first involved in merchandise in Vilna, then became a Byzantine monk. He was ordained priest, later becoming abbot of Vilna, then archbishop of Polotsk in Lithuania. He was noted as a preacher and for his unremitting work for his see. However, he was embroiled in much controversy in his efforts to unite the province of Kiev with ROME and yet maintain the integrity of the Byzantine clergy; he suffered from prejudice and nationalism on both sides. He was murdered by a mob in an outbreak of anti-Rome violence at Vitebsk. In 1867 he was the first Uniate to be canonized by Rome.

Joseph, St (f.d. 19 March). Husband of the Virgin Mary and the lawful father of Jesus. He is patron saint of carpenters, because he was of that craft.

In art Joseph is represented as an aged man with a budding staff in his hand. In 1955 Pope Pius XII instituted the feast of St Joseph the Workman on 1 May.

Joseph of Arimathea, St (f.d. 17 March). The rich Jew, probably a member of the Sanhedrin, who believed in Christ, but feared to confess it, and, after the Crucifixion, begged the body of the Saviour and deposited it in his own tomb (*see Matt.* xxvii, 57–60; *Mark* xv, 43–46).

Legend relates that he was imprisoned for 12 years and was kept alive miraculously by the holy GRAIL, and that on his release by Vespasian, about the year 63, he brought the Grail and the spear with which Longinus wounded the crucified Saviour to Britain, and founded the abbey of GLASTONBURY whence he commenced the conversion of Britain.

The origin of these legends is to be found in a group of APOCRYPHAL writings of which the *Evangelium Nicodemi* is the chief; these were worked upon at Glastonbury and further established by Robert de Borron in the 13th century, the latter version (by way of Walter Map) being woven by Malory into his *Morte d'Arthur.*

Joseph of Calasanz, St (*c.* 1557–1648, f.d. 25 August). Born at Peralta de la Sal, he studied law and divinity at Spanish universities and was ordained priest. He went to ROME and joined the Confraternity of Christian Doctrine, a system of education founded to combat the ignorance of ordinary people and the poor, and which worked with free schools in slum districts. The movement spread rapidly, and St Joseph organized it into a religious order which became known as the Piarists or *Le Scuole Pie*, Clerks Regular of the Religious Schools. His schools were organized on a primary and secondary basis, foreshadowing the work of St JOHN-BAPTIST DE LA SALLE; they spread in Spain and to Poland and Bohemia. He was a man of great character and forbearance, suffering troubles from the ambitions of subordinates in his later years and from the persecutions of others in the same work. He was unjustly accused, removed from his order, but later reinstated.

Joseph of Copertino, St (1602–63, f.d. 18 September). Joseph Desa was born at Copertino into a poor family. His father having been forced to sell the house, the birth took place in a shed and the child was sickly, ungainly and slow-witted. He was nicknamed 'the Gaper', and was disliked by his mother, who was widowed early in his life. He tried unsuccessfully several times to join a community, being rejected on account of his clumsiness and inefficiency. Finally, with difficulty, he joined the MINORITES at Grotella as a stableboy. He rose steadily in efficiency and in the religious life and was admitted as a novice, and

ordained priest. He moved about the country preaching, and collected great crowds for his ecstasies and miraculous healing, and for psychic phenomena, particularly that of levitation, which was well attested and which gave him the title of 'the Flying Friar'. He was seen to have flown above altars, and on one occasion to have raised into place a huge cross, some thirty-six feet high, when it had defeated the efforts of ten workmen, treating it 'as if it were straw'. These marvels were such that they drew large crowds. As a result of the disturbances caused, Joseph was confined to a solitary life, being moved from one place to another when his presence was discovered by the people. He bore all with resignation and humility and lived a life of great austerity. He was noted for a close kinship with animals and birds.

Joseph Benedict Cottolengo, St (1786–1842, f.d. 30 April). Born at Brà, in Piedmont, he was a canon of the collegiate church in Turin, in which town he founded a hospital, transferring it to Valdocco after an outbreak of cholera. This was the inception of a movement which gave rise to 'The Little House of Divine Providence', and a succession of establishments to care for the distressed and afflicted of every kind, asylums, almshouses, schools, workshops and hospitals, served by men and women he had organized into religious societies and run on faith, there being no systematized funds or accounts. The Little House at Turin continues as a testimony to this foundation and its relief of suffering. St JOHN BOSCO was associated with this work. Joseph was canonized in 1934.

Josepha Rossello, St (1811–80, f.d. 3 October). Born at Albisola Marina into the large family of a potter, she showed early signs of organizing ability. With the permission of the bishop of Savona she instituted work among young women, opening schools, hospitals and rescue-homes which developed into the Congregation of Daughters of Our Lady of Mercy. The movement spread to the Americas and, against strong opposition, the bishop authorized her to set up a house for the encouragement of men with a vocation for the priesthood. She died at Savona and was canonized in 1949.

Joy. The five Joyful Mysteries. The first chaplet of the ROSARY, made up of the ANNUNCIATION, the Visitation, the Nativity of Christ, the Presentation of Christ in the Temple, and the finding of the Child Jesus in the Temple.

The seven joys of the Virgin. *See* MARY.

Jubilate (Lat., Cry aloud) is the name given to two psalms which begin with this word in the VULGATE (lxv and xcix). In the English psalter they are *Psalms* lxvi and c.

Jubilate Sunday is the third Sunday after

EASTER, when the introit at the MASS begins with two verses of the first of the Jubilate Psalms.

Judas. Judas Iscariot, who betrayed Christ, his Master; hence a traitor.
   Judas Kiss. A deceitful act of courtesy or simulated affection. Judas betrayed his Master with a kiss (*Matt.* xxvi, 49).

> So Judas kiss'd his Master,
> And cried, all hail! when as he meant all harm.
> SHAKESPEARE: *Henry VI, Pt. III*, V, vii

Jude, St (f.d. 28 October). One of the twelve apostles, brother of James (i.e. the Lord's brother), also identified as brother of JAMES THE LESS. He is represented in art with a club or staff, and a carpenter's square in allusion to his trade. His day coincides with that of St SIMON, with whom he suffered martyrdom in Persia. He is the author of the *Epistle of Jude* and nowadays is regarded as the patron of hopeless cases.

Judgement, The Last, or **General Judgement,** is God's final sentence on mankind on the LAST DAY. The **Particular Judgement** is the judgement on each individual soul after death.

Judica Sunday. The fifth Sunday in LENT (formerly also known as Passion Sunday) is so called from the first word of the Introit at the MASS, *Judica me, Deus*, Give sentence with me, O God (*Ps.* xliii).

Judicium Crucis. Trial of the CROSS. A form of ordeal which consisted in stretching out the arms before a cross, till one party could hold out no longer, and lost his cause.

Judoc (or **Josse**), **St** (d. *c.* 668, f.d. 13 December). Son of Juthael or Hoel, King of Brittany, he renounced his worldly status and was ordained priest. After a pilgrimage to ROME he became a hermit at Ponthieu, later named Salin-Josse-sur-Mer, where he died. Later, in 902, refugees took his relics to England where the New Minster was being built at Winchester, and the relics were enshrined in the church. It was said that his body remained incorrupt and that his beard and hair were kept trimmed. His cult became popular and spread in France and to Flanders, Germany, Alsace, Switzerland and Austria. In Chaucer's *Canterbury Tales* the Wife of Bath swears 'by God and by Seint Joce'. In art he is depicted with a pilgrim's staff and with a crown at his feet, symbolizing his early renunciation of royalty.

Julian. Julian the Apostate (332, 361–63). Flavius Claudius Julianus, Roman emperor, and nephew of Constantine the Great. So called from his attempts to restore paganism, having abandoned Christianity at about the age of 20. He set an example by the austerity of his life and zeal for the public welfare and was notable for his literary and philosophical interests. Christians were not actively persecuted but there was discrimination against them. See GALILEAN.
Julian Calendar. The calendar instituted by Julius Caesar in 46 BC, which was in general use in Western Europe until the introduction of the GREGORIAN CALENDAR in 1582, and still used in England until 1752 and until 1918 in Russia. To allow for the odd quarter of a day, Caesar ordained that every fourth year should contain 366 days, the additional day being introduced after the 6th before the Calends of March, i.e. 24 February. Caesar also divided the months into the number of days they at present contain. It is now called 'the Old Style'.
Julian, St (f.d. 12 February). A patron SAINT of travellers and of hospitality, looked upon in the Middle Ages as the epicure of saints. Thus Chaucer says that the Franklin was 'Epicurus owne sone', and:

> An house holdere, and that a greet was he;
> Seint Julian in his contree.
> *Canterbury Tales: Prologue*, 339

He seems to be essentially a mythical saint. He is supposed to have unwittingly slain his parents and devoted his life to helping strangers by way of atonement.
Julian Sabas, St (d. *c.* 378, f.d. 18 October). A hermit of Mesopotamia who ate only a little bread weekly. He attracted disciples, and they rose at midnight to sing psalms till sunrise. He visited Sinai and Antioch. Miracles were attributed to him and his prayers were said to have brought about the death of JULIAN THE APOSTATE and the ARIAN bishops. St JOHN CHRYSOSTOM named him as the perfect example of a Christian.
Julian of Toledo, St (d. 690, f.d. 8 March). Appointed bishop of Toledo, he consolidated the diocese and made it a centre of Christendom under Moorish rule. He was an important writer of the history of the Spanish Church and was responsible for establishing the MOZARABIC rites of worship. Said to have been of Jewish blood, he nevertheless took part in a council which promulgated severe laws against Jews.

Juliana (or **Mother Julian**) **of Norwich** (*c.* 1342–*c.* 1413). A religious recluse and mystic who recorded her visions in *XVI Revelations of Divine Love.*
Juliana Falconieri, St (1270–1341, f.d. 19 June). Born into a wealthy family of Florence, she entered the SERVITE Order as a TERTIARY at the age of fifteen. Her uncle St Alexis Falconieri was one of the SEVEN SERVITE founders and her parents had built the Annunziata church in Florence. At the death of her mother, Juliana moved to

another convent, called the 'Mantellate', organized and ruled the community of tertiary sisters, and from it founded the Servite nuns who were dedicated to prayer and good works. It was claimed that she worked miracles.

Julitta. *See* QUIRICUS.

Julius the Veteran, St (d. 304, f.d. 17 May). A Roman soldier with a reputation for great bravery and devotion, who had re-enlisted as a veteran. He was interrogated by the prefect Maximus who realized his worth and did all he could to persuade him to accept the worship of the gods, offering him every excuse and expedient to save him, but Julius steadfastly refused any such equivocation and was sentenced and beheaded.

Jumpers. A nickname applied to the SHAKERS, and also to Welsh METHODISTS who were supposed to 'jump for joy' during divine service.

Justin Martyr, St (*c.* 100–65, f.d. 1 June). An APOLOGIST and FATHER OF THE CHURCH. Born in Samaria of Greek descent and often called the Philosopher, he was a Stoic and Platonist before conversion to Christianity at about thirty years of age; he then became one of the great Apologists against pagan attack. He founded a school for the teaching of Christianity in ROME and wrote numerous works in defence of the Faith, for which he was martyred. He is regarded as the first of the Fathers of the Church. His two *Apologies* and the *Dialogue with the Jew Trypho* survive and are important documents of the 2nd century.

Justinia of Padua, St (*c.* 300, f.d. 7 October). Little is known of her life but that she was one of the martyrs of the Diocletian persecution. The church dedicated to her at Padua became famous, and in the 10th century a monastery was attached to it under her patronage and was liberally endowed. Later it was reformed under the Rule of St BENEDICT. It was said to have had some relics of St LUKE the Evangelist. In art she is depicted with both breasts pierced with a sword; she also has the attributes of a martyr, the sword, crown and palm.

Justinian, St (6th cent., f.d. 5 December). A native of Brittany, of noble birth, he settled on the Isle of Ramsey off Pembrokeshire as a hermit. He was a friend of St DAVID. Many conventional legends are attached to his name, such as his capture by devils masquerading as sailors; he defeated them but a subsequent attack resulted in Justinian being murdered. His head was cut off, but his body rose and carried it across to the mainland where he wished to be buried by St David. A church was built there and

became a place of many miracles. A healing spring issued from the spot where the head had fallen. The devils were punished by being inflicted with leprosy and were condemned to live on a barren rock, the Lepers' Rock.

Justus (or **Just**), **St** (d. 627, f.d. 10 November). One of the missionaries sent to England by St GREGORY THE GREAT. He was the first bishop of Rochester, but at the outbreak of a pagan uprising he fled to Gaul when St AUGUSTINE died. He returned later and succeeded St MELLITUS as archbishop of Canterbury, He was sent the PALLIUM by Pope Boniface V. In art he is depicted as an archbishop with the Primatial Cross.

Justus of Beauvais, St (3rd cent., f.d. 18 October). A legendary boy–martyr, said to have died at the age of nine years under the Diocletian persecution for declaring himself a Christian and for hiding other Christians. He was beheaded near Beauvais by soldiers, but the severed head continued to speak. His cult spread in France, Belgium and Switzerland, and in England some of his relics were claimed by Winchester Cathedral.

Juthwara, St (date unknown, f.d. variously 28 November, 13 July, 6 January). Said to have been the sister of SS Paul Aurelian and Sidewell of Exeter, she was naturally pious, practising prayer and fasting, but suffered under a jealous stepmother, who had a son Bana. They accused Juthwara of infidelities and of being pregnant, and Bana struck off her head, which she then carried back to the church. A spring welled up where the head had fallen. Her body was translated to Sherborne Abbey at the time of Aelfwold II. Bana repented and became a monk, founding the abbey of Gerbar. Juthwara is depicted in art with a sword or with her head in her hand.

Jutta, St (d. 1260, f.d. 5 May). In a legend similar to that of St ELIZABETH OF HUNGARY, Jutta was happily married and had a family of children, but when her husband died on a pilgrimage to the HOLY LAND she renounced the world; she first provided for her children, then gave away all her possessions and spent the rest of her life in seclusion and caring for the poor. She died at her hermitage near Kulmsee and became the centre of a cult in Prussia, of which she is the patron saint.

Juventinus and Maximus, SS (date unknown, f.d. 25 January). Legendary officers of the bodyguard of JULIAN THE APOSTATE. They were said to have been put to death with horrible torture at Antioch for protesting at the mixing of the food of Christians with that which had been offered to the gods, and for refusing to sacrifice to the gods.

K

Kamelavchion. The black, cylindrical hat worn by monks and clergy of the Eastern ORTHODOX CHURCH.

Kathisma or **Cathesma.** A section of the PSALTER in the Eastern ORTHODOX CHURCH. It is divided into twenty sections.

Kea (Ke or **Quay), St** (6th cent., f.d. 5 November). A monk of Cornwall and Devon, said to have been of noble family, and who probably came from GLASTONBURY. He was associated with St GILDAS and was identified with Saint-Quay in Brittany. He is represented with stags and is invoked for curing toothache.

Keble, John (1792–1866). ANGLICAN churchman and poet who was regarded as the leader of the Tractarians. He was ordained in 1816 and was tutor at Oriel College, Oxford, but resigned this post to work with his father who was vicar of Coln St Aldwyn. In 1827 he published *The Christian Year*, a book of poems. His sermon at St Mary's, Oxford, on 'National Apostasy' was taken as the commencement of the Oxford Movement. He wrote eight of the *Tracts for the Times*.

Kells, The Book of. Kells is an ancient Irish town in County Meath, and was the SEE of a BISHOP until the 13th century. Among its antiquities, but now preserved in Trinity College, Dublin, is the 8th-century *Book of Kells*, one of the finest extant illuminated manuscripts of the Gospels in Latin.

Kemble, St John (1599–1679, f.d. 25 October). Born at St Weonards of a noted Wiltshire family, he was educated at the ENGLISH COLLEGE, DOUAI, and was ordained priest. He returned to England to his brother's house, Pembridge Castle, making it a centre of a lifelong mission which lasted unmolested through the reign of Charles I and the Commonwealth, but he was arrested, at the age of eighty, with other priests, following the POPISH PLOT. He was condemned to be hanged, drawn and quartered at Hereford. Before his execution he requested time to pray, smoke a last pipe and have a last drink. In this the under-sheriff joined him and the term 'Kemble pipe' came to denote the last of a sitting. So respected was he that the hangman ensured that he was dead before the final two executions. His room is still preserved at Pembridge Castle and he was canonized in 1970 as one of the FORTY MARTYRS OF ENGLAND AND WALES.

Kempis, Thomas à (*c.* 1379–1471). Thomas Hammerken was born at Kempen, near Cologne, hence his name of Kempis. He entered the AUGUSTINIAN monastery at Zwolle, in Holland, after attending school at Deventer under the Brethren of the Common Life, followers of Gehard Groote. His *Imitation of Christ* is one of the most famous of devotional works.

Kenelm, St (early 9th cent., f.d. 17 July). An English SAINT, son of Kenwulf, King of Mercia. He was only seven years old when he succeeded to the throne of his father. By his sister's order he was murdered at Clent, Worcestershire. The murder, says Roger of Wendover, was miraculously notified at ROME by a white dove, which alighted on the altar at St Peter's, bearing in its beak a scroll with

> In Clent cow pasture, under a thorn,
> Of head bereft, lies Kenelm, King-born.

Kenneth, St. *See* CANICE.

Kenosis. A theological term from the Greek, an emptying, taken from *Philippians* ii, 7, maintaining that Christ, in becoming a man, laid aside his divinity in an act of self-emptying and revealed God simply through the human experience.

Kensit, John (1853–1902). An English PROTESTANT of extreme views who founded the Protestant Truth Society in 1890, and devoted his life to anti-CATHOLIC propaganda and disruption of ANGLO-CATHOLIC services. He opened a Protestant bookshop in London. He was fatally injured in a religious riot in Liverpool; his followers were known as **Kensitites**.

Kentigern, St (*c.* 510–*c.* 600, f.d. 13 January). The patron SAINT of Glasgow; apostle of north-west England and south-east Scotland, and traditional founder of Glasgow Cathedral. He is represented with his episcopal cross in one hand, and in the other a salmon and a ring in allusion to the popular legend:

> Queen Langoureth had been false to her husband, King Roderich, and had given her lover a ring. The king, aware of the fact, stole upon the knight in sleep, abstracted the ring, threw it into the Clyde, and then asked the queen for it. The queen, in alarm, applied to St Kentigern, who after praying, went to the Clyde, caught a salmon with the ring in its mouth, handed it to the queen and was thus the means of restoring peace to the royal couple.

The Glasgow arms include the salmon with the ring in its mouth, an oak-tree with a bell hanging on one of the branches, and a bird at the top of the tree:

> The tree that never grew,
> The bird that never flew,
> The fish that never swam,
> The bell that never rang.

The oak and the bell are in allusion to the story that St Kentigern hung a bell upon an oak to summon the wild natives to worship.

St Kentigern is also known as 'St Mungo', for *Mungho* (dearest) was the name by which St Servan, his first preceptor, called him.

Kentigerna (or Quentigerna), St (d. *c.* 733, f.d. 7 January). Daughter of a prince of Leinster, she married an Irish chief and was the mother of St Coellan. After her husband's death she went to Scotland and lived as a recluse on Inch Cailleach, Loch Lomond, where a church was dedicated to her. Legend says that her son Fillan, or Faeltan, was saved from drowning by St Ibar who rescued him from playing with kelpies at the bottom of a loch.

Kessog (or Mackessog), St (6th cent., f.d. 10 March). Born at Cashel, he was an Irish prince who went to Scotland and became a monk, traditionally on Monks' Island on Loch Lomond; he later became bishop of that area. He was killed by assassins at Banbry. Several churches were dedicated to him in Scotland and a sanctuary was granted by Robert Bruce. Kessog was reputed to have worked miracles from an early age.

Kevin, St. An Irish saint of the 6th century, of whom legend relates that he retired to a cave on the steep shore of a lake where he vowed no woman should ever land. A girl named Kathleen followed him, but the saint flogged her with a bunch of nettles or, according to the more romantic story, hurled her from a rock and her ghost never left the place where he lived. A cave at Glendalough, Wicklow, is shown as the bed of St Kevin. Moore has a poem on this tradition (*Irish Melodies*, IV).

Traditionally he was born into a noble family of Leinster which was dispossessed. Kevin was educated by monks, was ordained, then became a hermit at Glendalough. As disciples were drawn to him, a monastery was built, of which he was the abbot. Among other legends it was said that the community was fed by an otter who brought them salmon; also that when a blackbird laid eggs on the hand of the saint, outstretched in prayer, he remained in that position until the birds were hatched. His cult spread and his monastery became an important centre of pilgrimage and famed in Irish history. He was said to have lived to a hundred and twenty. Kevin is one of the patron saints of Dublin. In art he is represented with a blackbird.

Key. St Peter's Keys. The cross-keys, the insignia of the Papacy borne, saltire-wise, one of gold and the other of silver, symbolizing the POWER OF THE KEYS.

The Cross Keys. The emblem of St PETER and also St Servatius, St HIPPOLYTUS, St GENEVIÈVE, St PETRONILLA, St OSYTH, St MARTHA, and St Germanus of Paris. They also form the arms of the Archbishop of York. The Bishop of Winchester bears two keys and a sword in saltire and the bishops of St Asaph, Gloucester, Exeter, and Peterborough bear two keys in saltire.

The Power of the Keys. The supreme ecclesiastical authority claimed by the POPE as the successor of St PETER. The phrase is derived from *Matt.* xvi, 19:

> And I will give unto thee the keys of the kingdom of heaven: and whatsoever thou shalt bind on earth shall be bound in heaven; and whatsoever thou shalt loose on earth shall be loosed in heaven.

The key shall be on his shoulder. He shall have the dominion, shall be in authority, have the keeping of something. It is said of Eliakim that God would lay upon his shoulder the key of the house of David (*Is.* xxii, 22). The cumbersome wooden or iron keys of Biblical times were often carried across the shoulder.

Keyne, St (5th cent., f.d. 8 October). A Celtic saint, daughter of Brychan, King of Brecknock. St Keyne's Well, near Liskeard, Cornwall, is reputed to give the upper hand to the first of the marriage partners to drink from it.

Kierkegaard, Søren Aaby (1813–55). Danish philosopher and theologian, born in Copenhagen of a wealthy family, and graduate of the university. He wrote many works in which the fundamentals of Christianity were reinterpreted, and he attacked the arid PROTESTANTISM of his time; he also wrote of the struggle for freedom and the loneliness and dread it entailed. He urged abandonment to the Absolute and God's will through divine grace and forgiveness. His most noted works are *Enter-Eller* (Either/Or) and *Concept of Dread*. His writings are generally regarded as the basis of Existentialism.

Kildare's Holy Fane. Famous for the 'Fire of St Bridget' which the nuns never allowed to go out. Every twentieth night St Bridget was fabled to return to tend the fire. St Bridget founded a nunnery at Kildare in the 5th century. Part of the chapel still remains and is called 'The Firehouse'.

Kilian, St. (d. *c.* 689, f.d. 8 July). An Irishman and apostle to Franconia, who set out with eleven others, eventually arriving at Würzburg, where he was successful in converting the pagan rulers to Christianity. He founded the see there, of which he became bishop. He journeyed to ROME and tradition says that on his return he discovered that King Gozbert had unlawfully married the widow of his brother; he denounced the marriage and was murdered at the instigation of the queen. Kilian became the patron of Würzburg, his image appearing on seals and coins. His cult spread and there was an annual Kilianfest with a mystery play of his life.

King. King James's Bible. *See* BIBLE, THE ENGLISH.
King of Kings. The Deity. The title has also been assumed by various Eastern rulers, especially the sovereigns of Ethiopia.
The Three Kings of Cologne. The MAGI.

Kirby, St Luke (*c.* 1548–82, f.d. 25 October). Born at Richmond in Yorkshire, he first received an education in England before leaving for the ENGLISH COLLEGE, DOUAI. He became a CATHOLIC, was ordained, then continued his studies in ROME. When he returned to England in 1580, accompanied by Edmund CAMPION, he was arrested as he landed at Dover and was imprisoned and tortured in London at the Tower. He was tried, with others, on a false accusation of plotting against the Queen and was hanged, drawn and quartered. His relics are at Stonyhurst. He was canonized in 1970 as one of the FORTY MARTYRS OF ENGLAND AND WALES.

Kirk (Gr. *kyriakon*, church). A term used in Scotland for the CHURCH OF SCOTLAND, the PRESBYTERIAN as distinguished from the Episcopal CHURCH. A kirk session is a petty ecclesiastical court, comprising the minister, lay elders and deacons of a parish.

Kiss (O.E. *cyssan*). An ancient and widespread mode of salutation frequently mentioned in the BIBLE as an expression of reverence and adoration, and as a greeting or farewell among friends. Esau embraced Jacob, 'fell on his neck, and kissed him' (*Gen.* xxxiii, 4), the repentant woman kissed the feet of Christ (*Luke*, vii, 45), and the disciples of Ephesus 'fell on Paul's neck, and kissed him' (*Acts* xx, 37). In the NEW TESTAMENT the kiss becomes a token of Christian brotherhood, 'Salute one another with an holy kiss' (*Rom.* xvi, 16). Kissing between the sexes occurs in *Prov.* vii, 13, 'So she caught him, and kissed him, and with an impudent face said unto him...'

The old custom of 'kissing the bride' comes from the Salisbury rubric concerning the PAX.
Kissing the Pope's toe. Matthew of Westminster (15th century) says it was customary formerly to kiss the hand of his Holiness; but that a certain woman in the 8th century not only kissed the POPE's hand but 'squeezed it'. Seeing the danger to which he was exposed, the Pope cut off his hand, and was compelled in future to offer his foot. In reality the Pope's foot (i.e. the cross embroidered on his right shoe) may be kissed by the visitor; BISHOPS kiss the knee as well. This is an old sign of respect and does not imply servility. It is customary to bend the knee and kiss the ring of a CARDINAL, bishop, or abbot.
To kiss the book. To kiss the BIBLE, or the NEW TESTAMENT, after taking an oath; the kiss of confirmation or promise to act in accordance with the words of the oath and a public acknowledgment of its sanctity.

In the English courts, the Houses of Parliament, etc., non-Christians are permitted to affirm without kissing the book, as a result of the struggle waged by the atheist Charles Bradlaugh to take his seat in the House of Commons. First elected in 1880 he was finally admitted to the House in 1886. Previously, in 1858, Baron Lionel de Rothschild, the first Jew to be admitted to Parliament, as a Jew, had been allowed to swear on the OLD TESTAMENT. He had been elected as Whig MP for the City of London in 1847. The position was legalized by the Oaths Act of 1888.

In Roman Catholic churches it is customary for the priest to kiss the Bible after reading the Gospel.
The kiss of Judas symbolizes betrayal.
Kiss of Peace. The general greeting of the congregation at the EUCHARIST. Originally a kiss, later a mutual greeting, now more usually a shaking of hands in the WESTERN CHURCH.

Kneeling. The usual posture adopted by Christians at prayer, but some churches, notably the REFORMED and LUTHERAN on the Continent, and the CHURCH OF SCOTLAND and FREE CHURCHES in Britain may sit or stand for prayers. In the ROMAN CATHOLIC CHURCH and the CHURCH OF ENGLAND worshippers kneel for prayer and in receiving the Sacrament.

Kneeling, bowing and standing were all adopted by early Christians; only sitting appears to have been excluded. Kneeling symbolizes homage to a superior, supplication and submission.

Knight. Knights Hospitallers. *See* HOSPI-TALLERS.

Knights of Columbus. A Roman Catholic fraternal and philanthropic society in the USA, founded in 1882 with the aim of uniting laymen of that Church in corporate religious and civic usefulness.

Knights Templar. *See* TEMPLARS.

Knipperdollings. Anabaptist followers of Bernard Knipperdolling (*c.* 1490–1536), who was one of the leaders of the Munster theocracy (1532–5). After the city was taken by the BISHOP and his supporters, Knipperdolling was tortured to death with red-hot pincers.

Knox, John (*c.* 1505–72). Scottish PROTESTANT reformer, born near Edinburgh, probably at Haddington. He trained as a CATHOLIC priest but was converted to Protestantism. He took part in the revolt by the Reformers, in 1547, at St Andrew's Castle, where the group was captured by the French and sent to the galleys, from which Knox was rescued in 1549. During the reign of Edward VI of England, he assisted in the compilation of the Prayer BOOK and emphasized its Protestant element. At Mary's accession, Knox went to live, first at Frankfurt, then in Geneva, where he was associated with CALVIN. Returning to Scotland in 1559, he played an important part in framing the 'Confession of Faith' and is generally held responsible for the establishment of the CHURCH OF SCOTLAND. He died at Edinburgh and was buried beside St Giles's Cathedral.

Kolbe, St Maximilian (1894–1941, f.d. 14 August). Born at Zdunska Wola, Poland, of a devout family which was reduced to poverty under Russian rule, the parents became FRANCISCAN TERTIARIES and Maximilian entered the Franciscan Order; he studied at ROME and was ordained. He was found to be suffering from tuberculosis and returned to Poland where he taught Church History at a seminary and edited a magazine for Christians in Cracow. He founded Franciscan communities near Warsaw and at Nagasaki in Japan, later becoming superior of his Polish monastery. At the German invasion of 1939 he was interned but released, returning to his monastery and making it a refugee camp for Poles and Jews. He also continued his independent publications, which resulted in his arrest by the Gestapo and his being sent to Auschwitz, with four companions. There they were subjected to all the horrors of the death-camp. Maximilian continued his priestly vocation in every way possible and comforted the sufferers. When, in revenge for an escape from the camp, men were selected for death by starvation, he announced that he was a Catholic priest and offered to take the place of a younger man, a sergeant, who had a wife and children. After two weeks in the death-cell Kolbe was still alive and was injected with phenol. He died at the age of forty-seven. He was beatified by Pope Paul VI in 1971 and canonized by John Paul II in 1982. The sergeant whose life he had saved was present at the ceremony.

Kontakion, or **Contakion.** A hymn or canticle in liturgical use in the Eastern ORTHODOX CHURCH.

Korea, Martyrs of, SS (1839, f.d. 20 September). In 1784 the first Korean Christian was baptized in Peking, Christianity having reached Korea through China in spite of being forbidden. By 1794 there were some 4,000 converts under a Chinese priest, but when he was killed they were without a priest for thirty years. In 1837 Pope Pius VII sent Laurence Imbert, a bishop, with two priests from the Paris Missionary Society; they arrived in disguise and worked in secrecy. When the growth in the number of converts became conspicuous a violent persecution took place and the three priests sacrificed themselves to avert a wholesale massacre. They were beheaded and seventy-eight Koreans were martyred at the same time, among them Agatha Kim and John Ri. A few years later the first Korean priest to be martyred was Andrew Kim. The martyrs were beatified in 1925 and canonized in 1984.

Kostka, St Stanislaus (1550–68, f.d. 13 November). Born at Rostovo Castle, in Poland, of a noble and wealthy family, he was educated first at home then at the JESUIT College in Vienna. He was brow-beaten by his elder brother and tutor and housed in unsuitable lodgings in Vienna, and became ill. On recovering, he wanted to become a Jesuit, and when the Austrian Provincial had not the courage to receive him he walked the 350 miles to ROME where, at the age of seventeen, he was admitted to the order by St FRANCIS BORGIA. He lived only nine months, during which time he led an exemplary religious life and experienced visions and ecstasies. His brother later also became a Jesuit.

Kralitz Bible. *See* BIBLE, SOME SPECIALLY NAMED EDITIONS.

Kyneburga, Kyneswitha and Tibba, SS (7th cent., f.d. 6 March). The first two were daughters of Penda, King of Mercia, a fierce opponent of Christianity, and the third a kinswoman. They assisted in the foundation of the abbey at Medehampstede (Peterborough) and Kyneburga founded, and was abbess of, Dormancaster (Castor) in Northamptonshire where she was succeeded by her sister. Their relics were enshrined at Peterborough.

Kyned (Cenydd or **Keneth), St** (6th cent., f.d. 27 June). Traditionally the son of St GILDAS, he married and had children, then became a monk under St ILLTYD and founded Llangenydd, in Gower, later going to Brittany. One legend says he was born a cripple and was put into a cradle made of osier and dropped into a river which carried him to the Island of Heniswergn. Miracles and angelic aid ensured his survival and he became a hermit. He was cured of his infirmity by St DAVID, but resented this and, at his request, it was restored.

Kyrie Eleison (Gr., 'Lord have mercy'). The short petition used in the liturgies of the Eastern and Western Churches, as a response at the beginning of the MASS and in the Anglican Communion Service. Also, the musical setting for this.

L

La Salette. In the Dauphiné, in 1864, two peasant children herding cattle (a girl of fifteen and a boy of eleven) saw a lady weeping and surrounded by a dazzling light; she was dressed in white and gold. She revealed herself as the VIRGIN MARY, and urged the people to repent and promised Divine Mercy. The place became a centre of pilgrimage.

Labadists. A Christian sect of communistic-type PROTESTANTS, founded by Jean de Labadin (1610–74) who left the JESUITS and joined the Reformed Church. He, with some fifty followers, settled in Holland, but after his death about one hundred went to North America and formed a community in Maryland. The Labadists believed in the 'inner light' and ignored outward forms; they were strictly celibate. The community prospered during the lifetime of its leader, Peter Sluyter, but died soon after his death.

Labarum. The standard of the later Roman emperors. It consisted of a gilded spear with an eagle on the top, while from a cross-staff hung a splendid purple streamer, with a gold fringe, adorned with precious stones. *See also* CONSTANTINE'S CROSS *under* CROSS.

Labouré, St Catherine (1806–76, f.d. 28 November). Born at Fain-les-Moutiers, near Dijon, into a large farming family. After caring for her widowed father she joined the SISTERS OF CHARITY at Châtillon-sur-Seine, then went to Paris as a nurse in the community at Reuilly. There she acted as porteress, poultry-keeper and attendant at the rest home. Her life was unremarkable until shortly before her death, when her visions as a young nun were disclosed; these were of St VINCENT DE PAUL, founder of the order, and of the VIRGIN MARY, with whom she held dialogues, receiving prophecies of future disasters. One of her visions of Mary was recorded in the form of a medal, authorized by the archbishop and struck in 1832; it was known as the 'miraculous medal' and was widely dispersed. Catherine's body remained incorrupt at the chapel of the convent in Paris and miracles have been reported there. She was canonized in 1947.

Labre, St Benedict Joseph (1748–83, f.d. 16 April). Born at Amette, near Boulogne, the oldest of fifteen children of a shopkeeper, he unsuccessfully tried to join first the CISTERCIANS and then the CARTHUSIANS. He was rejected on the grounds of his eccentricity. He then adopted the life of a pilgrim, going to ROME and visiting numerous shrines in Europe, subsisting on casual charity and living in extreme poverty. Later he settled in Rome, sleeping in the Colosseum and spending the days in prayer. He ended his life in a hostel for the poor, still selflessly serving others and giving away even his meagre portion of food. He was canonized in 1881 and nominated the patron saint of tramps and the homeless.

Lactean, St (3rd cent., f.d. 19 March). A legendary Irishman who was reputed to have founded the monastery of Clonfert early in the seventh century. In association with the name, many marvels were attributed to him in connection with milk. He turned water into milk and when his cow, who was white with a red face, died he revived her and she continued to nourish him on her milk.

Ladislas I (or **Laszlo**), **St** (1040–95, f.d. 27 June). King of Hungary and son of Bela of Hungary, he was elected to succeed his brother. He consolidated the kingdom and added Croatia and Dalmatia. He was a notable warrior and a just and enlightened ruler. When he died in 1095 he had been nominated leader of the CRUSADE and as such had a considerable cult in Bavaria.

Lady. Our Lady. A title frequently used by CATHOLICS for the VIRGIN MARY.
Lady Chapel. *See under* CHAPEL.
Lady Day. 25 March, to commemorate the ANNUNCIATION of Our Lady, the Virgin Mary; formerly called 'St Mary's Day in Lent', to distinguish it from other festivals in honour of the Virgin which were also, properly speaking, 'Lady Days'. Until 1752, Lady Day was the legal beginning of the year and dates between 1 January and that day are shown with the two years, e.g. 29 January 1648/9, on present reckoning 29 January 1649. *See* GREGORIAN YEAR.
Our Lady of Mercy. A Spanish order of knighthood instituted in 1218 by James I of

Aragon, for the deliverance of Christian captives among the Moors.

Laetare Sunday (Lat., rejoice). The fourth Sunday in LENT, so called from the first word of the Introit, which is from *Is.* lxvi, 10: 'Rejoice ye with Jerusalem, and be glad with her, all ye that love her.' It is also known as MOTHERING SUNDAY.

Lamb. An important symbol in Christianity, representing Christ as both suffering and triumphant. As the Good Shepherd Christ is depicted carrying the lamb, having rescued the lost lamb which went astray (the sinner), or he is leading his flock. The lamb with the cross depicts the crucifixion, the sacrificial lamb; with the pennant or flag it is the resurrection. The Apocalyptic lamb, with the book and seven seals is Christ as Judge at the Second Coming; with seven horns and seven eyes the lamb represents the Seven Gifts of the Spirit. Depicted with a hill and four streams it signifies the Church and the four Rivers of Paradise, also the Four Gospels. With a row of sheep the lamb is Christ and the sheep the disciples. In Christian art, the emblem of the Redeemer, in allusion to *John* i, 29, 'Behold the Lamb of God, which taketh away the sins of the world.'

It is also the attribute of St AGNES, St CATHERINE, St GENEVIÈVE, and St Regina. JOHN THE BAPTIST either carries a lamb or is accompanied by one.

Paschal Lamb. *See under* PASCH.

Lamb-ale. The 'ale' or merry-making given by the farmer when his lambing was over. *Cp.* CHURCH-ALE.

Lambert's Day, St. 17 September. St Lambert, a native of Maastricht, lived in the 7th century. He supported the missionary work of St Willibrord and was energetic in suppressing vice.

> Be ready, as your lives shall answer it,
> At Coventry, upon St Lambert's day.
>
> SHAKESPEARE: *Richard II*, I, i

Lambeth Conference. A convocation of bishops of the ANGLICAN COMMUNION worldwide, held every ten years at the Palace of the Archbishop of CANTERBURY at Lambeth, London; first held in 1867.

Lambeth Cross. A decoration awarded by the Archbishop of CANTERBURY. First given to Archbishop Germanos in 1942 as representative of the Oecumenical Patriarch of the Eastern ORTHODOX CHURCH.

Lambeth Degrees in divinity, arts, law, medicine, music, etc., are conferred by the Archbishop of Canterbury, who was empowered to do so by a statute of 1533.

Lambeth Palace. The London residence of the archbishops of Canterbury since the 12th century. The oldest part is the chapel built by Archbishop Boniface in 1245 and the buildings have been steadily added to and modified through the centuries. Originally called Lambeth House, it came to be called Lambeth Palace about 1658 owing to the decay of the palace at Canterbury. It is the archbishop's principal residence, but he now has another palace at Canterbury. The library and chapel were badly damaged in an air raid in 1940.

Lammas Day. 1 August, one of the regular QUARTER DAYS in Scotland and a half-quarter or cross-quarter-day in England, the day on which, in Anglo-Saxon times, the FIRST-FRUITS were offered. Formerly, bread for the Lammas Day EUCHARIST was made from the new corn of the harvest. So called from O.E. *hlaf-maesse*, the loaf-mass. It is also the feast of St PETER ad Vincula. *See* HARVEST THANKSGIVING.

Lance. An attribute in Christian art of St MATTHEW and St THOMAS, the apostles; also of St Longinus, St GEORGE, St ADALBERT, St BARBARA, St MICHAEL, and others. The lance and cup are also associated with the HOLY GRAIL as the cup which caught the blood of Christ when he was wounded by the lance. It is also an emblem of the Passion. In the Eastern ORTHODOX CHURCH the lance is a small knife used to cut the bread at the EUCHARISTIC rites at the PROSKOMIDE or Preparation.

Laodicea. A Graeco-Roman city in N.W. Syria which had an early Christian community, referred to in *Colossians* iv, 16.

Lapsi. 'The fallen', those who under persecution denied their Christian faith.

Laserian (or Molaisse), St (d. 639, f.d. 18 April). Said to have been the son of an Irish nobleman of Ulster and to have gone to ROME to be ordained and consecrated bishop, also to have been abbot of a monastery at Leighton, Leinster and the founder of Irishmurray, Co. Sligo. He led the movement which ended in the adoption of the Roman use of Easter. Legend says he had taken on a voluntary illness of thirty diseases at the same time to expiate his sins and avoid PURGATORY.

Last. Last Day. The final day of the present dispensation when Christ is to return to earth for the last judgement; the day of judgement.

The Last Judgement. *See* JUDGEMENT.

The Last Supper. The last meal Christ partook with his disciples on the night before the Crucifixion and the institution of the EUCHARIST.

Leonardo da Vinci's famous picture of this was painted on a wall of the refectory of the Convent of Santa Maria delle Grazie, Milan, in

1494–7. Although the refectory was reduced to ruins by Allied bombs in August 1943, the wall on which the Last Supper is painted was practically undamaged and the picture left quite intact. It has worn badly with time and is now protected against further deterioration.

The Last Trump. *See* TRUMP.

The Last of the Fathers. St BERNARD (1090–1153), Abbot of Clairvaux.

Laszlo, St. *See* LADISLAS I.

Lateran. The ancient palace of the Laterani family which was appropriated by Nero (AD 66) and later given to Pope (St) Sylvester by the Emperor Constantine. It remained the official residence of the Popes until the departure to Avignon in 1309. The present palace is now a museum. Fable derives the name from *lateo*, to hide, and *rana*, a frog, and accounts for it by saying that Nero once vomited a frog covered with blood, which he believed to be his own progeny, and had it hidden in a vault. The palace built on its site was called the 'Lateran', or the palace of the hidden frog.

Lateran Council. The name given to each of five OECUMENICAL COUNCILS held in the Lateran church at ROME. They are (1) 1123, held under Calixtus II; it confirmed the Concordat of Worms which ended the INVESTITURE CONTROVERSY; (2) 1139, when Innocent II condemned Anacletus II and Arnold of Brescia; (3) 1179, convoked by Alexander III to regularize papal elections; (4) 1215, when Innocent III condemned the ALBIGENSES and further defined CATHOLIC doctrine; and (5) 1512–17, under Julius II and Leo X, to invalidate the work of the antipapal Council of Pisa.

Lateran Treaty. A treaty concluded between the Holy SEE and the Kingdom of Italy in 1929, establishing the VATICAN CITY as a sovereign state, thus ending the 'Roman Question' begun in 1870 when the temporal power of the papacy was finally abrogated and ROME became the capital of the Italian Kingdom. *See* PRISONER OF THE VATICAN *under* VATICAN.

St John Lateran is called the *Mother and Head of all Churches* and is the cathedral church of ROME. It occupies part of the site of the old Lateran palace.

Latin. Latin American Council of Churches. An oecumenical body which includes Latin America and the Hispanic Caribbean; its headquarters is in Quito. It is a PROTESTANT missionary movement and includes METHODISTS, PRESBYTERIANS, LUTHERANS, Reformed ANGLICANS, WALDENSIANS, PENTECOSTALS, BAPTISTS, MORAVIANS, INDEPENDENT and ORTHODOX CHURCHES. Its object is to promote the 'unity of the people of God in Latin America as a local expression of the universal church of Christ and as a testimony and contribution to the unity of the Latin American people'. It consists of 140 churches and oecumenical bodies.

The Latin Church. The Western Church, in contradistinction to the Greek or Eastern Church.

The Latin Cross. *See under* CROSS.

Latitudinarians. In the CHURCH OF ENGLAND a name applied, at first opprobriously, from the mid-17th century to those clergy attaching little importance to dogma and practice in religion, which in the 18th century encouraged laxity and indifference. The Cambridge Platonists were prominent among them. Latitudinarianism was checked by the advent of the EVANGELICALS and the Oxford Movement. The term is widely applied to those attaching little importance to dogma and orthodoxy.

Latria and **Dulia.** Greek words adopted by the Roman Catholics; the former to express that supreme reverence and adoration which is offered to God alone; and the latter, that secondary reverence which is offered to saints. *Latria* is from the Greek suffix-*latreia*, worship, as in ido*latry*; *dulia* is the reverence of a *doulos* or slave. **Hyperdulia** is the special reverence paid to the Virgin Mary.

Latrocinium Council. The 'Robber Council' held at Ephesus in 449. It was convened by Theodosius II and was predominantly MONOPHYSITE, acquitting and reinstating Eutyches, but this was annulled at Chalcedon in 451.

Latter-day Saints. *See* MORMONS.

Laud, William (1573–1645). Archbishop of Canterbury 1633–45. He opposed the PROTESTANTS and maintained the CATHOLIC heritage of the Church. He was religious adviser to King Charles I and his attempts to impose episcopacy on the Scots led to the English Revolution. Laud was impeached by the Long Parliament for endeavouring to overthrow the Protestant religion, was imprisoned and beheaded on Tower Hill.

Lauds. In the Western Church, the traditional morning prayer, so called from the repeated occurrence of the word *laudate* (praise ye) in *Pss.* cxlvii–cl which form part of the office. It is said in the early morning by religious orders who rise for the Night Office, otherwise it is nowadays coupled with MATTINS and said overnight. It forms part of the BREVIARY of the ROMAN CATHOLIC CHURCH, and the service of Morning Prayer, in the BOOK OF COMMON PRAYER, is essentially composed of parts of Lauds and Matins.

Laura (Gr. *laura*, an alley). In early monachism, a collection of separate cells under a superior, their occupants meeting in chapel and for a common meal in the refectory. Monastic life proper was a much more communal affair. The community can include monks and nuns.

Laurence, St. *See* LAWRENCE.

Lausanne Conference. *See* WORLD COUNCIL OF CHURCHES.

Lavabo. The ritual washing of the celebrant's hands at the offering of the oblations in the EUCHARIST; also the towel and basin used. The term is derived from the first word of *Psalm* xxvi, 6: 'I will wash.'

Law. Canon Law. *See* CANON.
The Law of Moses, or **Mosaic Law.** *See under* MOSES.
The law of the Medes and Persians. That which is unalterable.

> Now O King, establish the decree, and sign the writing, that it be not changed, according to the law of the Medes and Persians, which altereth not.
>
> *Dan.* vi, 8

Lawn. Fine, thin cambric, used for the rochets of Anglican BISHOPS. So called from *Laon* (O.Fr. *Lan*), a town in the Aisne department of France, once noted for its linen manufacture.
Man of lawn. A BISHOP.

Lawrence. Lawrence, St (of Rome) (f.d. 10 August). The patron saint of curriers, who was roasted on a GRIDIRON. He was archdeacon to Pope (St) Sixtus II and was charged with the care of the poor, the orphans, and the widows. When summoned by the praetor to deliver up the treasures of the church, he produced the poor, etc., under his charge, and said, 'These are the church's treasures.' Fragments of his relics were taken to the Escorial.

The phrase **Lazy as Laurence** is said to originate from the story that when being roasted over a slow fire he asked to be turned. 'For', said he, 'that side is quite done.' This expression of Christian fortitude was interpreted by his torturers as evidence of the height of laziness, the martyr being too indolent to wriggle.

His feast day is associated with weather-prophecy. 'If the day of St Laurence be sunny and fine, expect a good autumn and much good wine.' In art he is depicted as a young man, wearing the deacon's DALMATIC. He stands on, or holds, the gridiron and can also be represented with a book in his hand and a cross on his shoulder, or he may carry a purse, a CENSER, or martyr's PALM.

Lawrence of Brindisi, St (1559–1619, f.d. 21 July). Born at Brindisi, in southern Italy, the son of a wealthy Venetian, he joined the CAPUCHINS at the early age of sixteen and studied at the University of Padua, showing an exceptional gift for languages and acquiring a great knowledge of the BIBLE. Clement VIII appointed him a missioner to the Jews and LUTHERANS in Europe and he established reformed Capuchin houses in Germany, Prague, Vienna and Gorizia. He was also entrusted with diplomatic and political missions and became NUNCIO at Munich. In the war against the Turks in Hungary he held the office of chaplain-general and led the troops into battle, holding only a crucifix. After a period of retired contemplative devotion he was sent to Spain and Portugal on a diplomatic mission to Philip III and died at Lisbon. He was noted for his theological works, sermons and writings against the Lutherans. He was canonized in 1881 and made a DOCTOR OF THE CHURCH in 1959.

Lawrence of Canterbury, St (d. 619, f.d. 3 February, 13 September). Sent to England by Pope St GREGORY THE GREAT with St AUGUSTINE whom he succeeded as Archbishop of Canterbury. On the accession to the throne of Kent by Edbald, Christianity suffered a reversion in the pagan reaction and it was said that Laurence considered deserting his see, but he had a vision of St PETER who beat him so severely that he was black and blue. Laurence showed his scars to the king, thus converting him from paganism and enabling the church to expand. The saint was buried at the church of SS PETER and PAUL, which later became St Augustine's, Canterbury.

Lawrence Giustiniani, St (1381–1455, f.d. 5 September). Born in Venice, of noble family, he renounced fame and fortune and became a canon of the AUGUSTINIAN monastery of San Giorgio, on the island of Alga, which later became a CONGREGATION of CANONS REGULAR. He was ordained priest, then elected prior. In 1433 he was appointed bishop of Castello and moved to Venice as its first bishop. His personal life was one of great austerity and care for the poor. He adopted a policy of delegating the financial side of his work to his steward with himself toiling among the poor and attending to their spiritual needs. He died on a bed of straw, attended by those he had served and greatly venerated by his contemporaries.

Lawrence Loricatus, St (*c.* 1190–1243, f.d. 16 August). Born at Facciolo, Apulia, trained as a soldier in his youth, he accidentally killed a man and in atonement went on a pilgrimage to COMPOSTELA. He then became a hermit at Subiaco, in St BERNARD's cave, where he attracted disciples and formed a small community. He lived in extreme poverty, giving away all donations from pilgrims. His name was derived from the coat of chain-mail he wore next to his skin instead of a hair-shirt. Among those who visited him was Cardinal Ugolino, later Pope GREGORY IX, who induced him to discard his breastplate. Laurence lived as a hermit for thirty-four years and his life and miracles gave rise to a popular cult. He wrote a book of prayers which, with his breastplate, is kept at St Bernard's cave.

Lawrence, St Robert (d. 1535, f.d. 25 October). A CARTHUSIAN monk of CHARTER-HOUSE, London, he became prior of Beauvale in Nottinghamshire. With other Carthusians, John HOUGHTON and Augustine WEBSTER, he was unable to accept the Act of Supremacy which made King Henry VIII Supreme Head of the Church, and after they had visited Thomas Cromwell all were condemned to be martyred at Tyburn. They were canonized by Pope Paul VI in 1970 as among the FORTY MARTYRS OF ENG-LAND AND WALES.

Lawrence O'Toole, St (1128–80, f.d. 14 November). Born Loecan Ua Tuathail, son of a chieftain, Laurence was taken hostage by the King of Leinster, then at twelve years of age became an AUGUSTINIAN CANON at Glendalough and was appointed abbot at the age of twenty-five. In 1162 he was made archbishop of Dublin. When 'Strongbow' led the English forces in Ireland and took Dublin, Laurence negotiated with King Henry II and worked for the relief of the Irish people. He attended the third LATERAN COUNCIL in ROME and became Papal LEGATE throughout Ireland. He was noted for the sanctity and simplicity of his life, for his work in reforming the clergy and his relief of the poor.

Lay. Pertaining to the people of laity (Lat. *laicus*) as distinguished from the clergy. Thus, a **lay brother** is one who, though not in HOLY ORDERS (*see under* ORDERS), is received into a monastery and is bound by its vows and usually engaged in manual work or the business side of the community life. There are also **lay sisters** in convents.

A layman is, properly speaking, anyone not in HOLY ORDERS; (*see under* ORDERS); it is also used by professional men, especially doctors and lawyers, to denote one not of their particular calling or specialized learning.

Lay Baptism. Baptism by a person not in holy orders when the person baptized is dying with no priest at hand.

Lay investiture. *See* INVESTITURE CONTROVERSY.

Lay Reader. A LAYMAN may be invited by the incumbent of a parish to read the lessons in church. In the ROMAN CATHOLIC CHURCH lay readers have been one of the minor orders since the 3rd century. In the CHURCH OF ENG-LAND the order fell into disuse and the appoint-ment of lay readers was not revived until 1866. Today, with the decline in the numbers of the clergy, lay readers are more in demand.

Laying on of Hands. The sign universally used in the early church for ordination, with the exception in the case of the ordination of a bishop. It is mentioned in *Acts* vi in the election of the Seven and in *Acts* xiii, 3; *I Timothy* iv, 14 and v, 22; and *II Timothy* i, 6. In the 3rd century, attested by CYPRIAN, penitents and those who had been in schism or heresy were received by the laying on of hands. It is used in CONFIRMA-TION and in the healing of the sick as a transmission of the power of the HOLY SPIRIT.

Lazarus. Any poor beggar; so called from the Lazarus of the parable, who was laid daily at the rich man's gate. *See* DIVES.

Lazar house, or **Lazaretto.** A house for lazars or poor persons affected with contagious diseases; so called from LAZARUS.

Lazarists. The popular name for the 'Congregation of the Priests of the Mission' founded by St VINCENT DE PAUL in 1625 and re-established at St Lazare's College in Paris in 1832. They were also known as Vincentians and were secular priests, taking simple vows and working in missions in all parts of the world.

Lazarus, St (1st cent., f.d. 17 December (West), 4 May (East)). Tradition says that Lazarus, raised from the dead by Jesus (*John* xi, 1–44) was present, with his sisters Martha and Mary, when the APOSTLES received the GIFT OF TONGUES (*Acts* ii, 3/4) which they also received. Later the Jews expelled them, placing them in a leaky boat which drifted to Cyprus where Lazarus became its first bishop. Another legend of the 11th century said that the boat, rudderless and without oars, miraculously took them to the South of France where they landed at Marseilles. Lazarus became its first bishop, but was martyred under Domitian. Associated with this legend is that of the THREE MARYS. The Order of Knights HOSPITALLERS has Lazarus as its patron; he was also claimed by mediaeval lepers and leper-hospitals, but this is probably a confusion with the parable of Dives and Lazarus.

Leander, St (c. 550–600, f.d. 27 February). Son of the Duke of Cartagena and brother of St ISIDORE, he became a monk and later bishop of Seville. He went on a mission to Constantinople where he met St GREGORY THE GREAT, with whom he formed a friendship; when Gregory became Pope he rewarded Leander with the PALLIUM. He attended the Third Council of Toledo in 589, worked successfully for the conversion of the Visigoths from Arianism, combated the heresy in Spain and made the establishing of orthodoxy his life work. He wrote a Rule for Nuns for his sister and was responsible for introducing the custom of singing the NICENE CREED in worship. He founded the episcopal school at Seville and is venerated as a Liturgical Doctor in Spain. In art he is represented with a flaming heart.

Lebuin (or **Liafwine**), **St** (d. *c.* 775, f.d. 12 November). An Anglo-Saxon who became a monk at Ripon. He went with others as a missionary to Germany and Frisia and the eastern Netherlands, the centre of his work being Deventer where he preached and built a church. He was venerated mainly in Holland.

Lectern (Lat. *legere*, to read). A raised reading desk or movable stand in a church on which the BIBLE is placed and from which SCRIPTURE lessons are read. It is usually in the form of an eagle with outspread wings, as symbolizing St JOHN THE APOSTLE and the inspiration of the GOSPELS. A lectern may also support the music for the CHOIR.
Lector. In the WESTERN CHURCH, a member of the third-ranking minor order whose function is to read the SCRIPTURE lessons in church.

Leda Bible, The. *See* BIBLE, SOME SPECIALLY NAMED EDITIONS.

Legate (Lat. *legare*, to send). An ecclesiastic appointed by the POPE to represent his temporal authority. The highest class of legates are *legati a latere*, 'legates sent from the side', who are usually cardinals. When the legate represents the Pope in a permanent capacity he is styled a *nuncio*.

Leger (or **Leodegarius**), **St** (*c.* 616–78, f.d. 2 October). Of a Merovingian family, he was educated by his uncle the bishop of Poitiers at the court of Clotaire II. He was first a deacon at the age of twenty, then an archdeacon and later bishop of Autun. He then reformed church discipline and organized monasteries to conform to the Rule of St BENEDICT. He played a prominent part in political affairs and was involved in a struggle against Ebroin, the mayor of the palace and a tyrant. He pursued Leger, captured him, and had him cast into prison where his eyes were put out, his tongue and lips slashed, and he was finally beheaded. In art he is depicted with gimlets in his eyes, or with pincers holding his eyeballs or with other instruments of his tortures.

Lent (O.E. *lencten*, the spring). The Saxons called March *lencten monath* because in this month the days noticeably lengthen. As the chief part of the great fast, from ASH WEDNESDAY to EASTER, falls in March, it received the name *Lencten-faesten* or Lent.

The fast of 36 days was introduced in the 4th century, but it did not become fixed at 40 days until the early 7th century, thus corresponding with Our Lord's fast in the wilderness.
Lenten curtain, or **Lenten veil.** In the mediaeval Western Church, a white curtain hung down in parish churches between the altar and the nave, and parted on feast days kept during Lent. It was taken down in the last three days of HOLY WEEK and said to betoken 'the prophecy of Christ's Passion, which was hidden and unknown till these days' (*Liber Festivalis*). Similarly, all crucifixes and images were covered, a practice still followed in some Anglican churches.

Leo the Great, St (d. 461, f.d. 10 November (West), 18 February (East)). Nothing is known of his early life, but tradition says he was of Tuscan origin. He was famous for his powerful personality and his political skills; he was able to persuade Attila the Hun to refrain from attacking ROME and later, when the Vandals succeeded in the capture of Rome, he checked their killings and destruction. He campaigned indefatigably against heresies, expelling the MANICHAEANS and condemning the PELAGIANS and PRISCILLIANS. He wrote his *Tomos* to refute EUTYCHIANISM, the last of the ancient heresies. Leo died in 461 and was buried at St PETER's, but his remains were translated to the Vatican church in 1715. He was named a FATHER OF THE CHURCH in 1754 and was POPE from 440 to 461.
Leo III, St (d. 816, f.d. 12 June). A Roman priest who first became a cardinal and then pope. He was involved in much controversy, supporting CHARLEMAGNE and crowning him in St PETER's, ROME, in 800, thus instituting the Christian Empire in the West, similar to the Eastern Empire at Constantinople. He was also concerned with the FILIOQUE dispute, refusing to impose the clause in the NICENE CREED. Leo was involved in English affairs during the rivalry between Lichfield and Canterbury as the metropolitan see during Offa's reign, restoring Canterbury when Offa died.
Leo IX, St (1002–54, f.d. 19 April). Born in Alsace of noble family, and named Bruno, he was educated at Toul, of which he was later elected bishop. He carried out various reforms in the church and in monasteries. He was made POPE by the Emperor Henry III and held reforming synods, working against simony, nepotism and the power of the nobles. He was criticized by St PETER DAMIAN for himself leading troops against the Normans who were invading papal territory in Southern Italy; he was taken captive but released. Accusations of heresy were made against him from Constantinople by the Patriarch, which ultimately led to the Eastern Schism. Cures and miracles were reported from his tomb in St Peter's.

Leonard, St (6th cent., f.d. 6 November). A Frank at the court of Clovis, founder of the monastery of Noblac and patron SAINT of prisoners, Clovis having given him permission to release all whom he visited. He is usually represented as a deacon holding chains or broken fetters in his hand. He wears the DALMATIC of a deacon which may be adorned with fleurs-de-lys and is sometimes accompanied by the other deacons, St LAURENCE and St STEPHEN. Legend says that Clovis was hunting in the forest, together with his pregnant wife, when she gave birth and was saved by Leonard's help and prayers. He is thus the patron saint of pregnant women. In gratitude, Clovis gave him as much land as he could ride round on a donkey, this being the foundation of Noblac, where he died and was buried. His cult spread widely in Europe and in England. One hundred and seventy-seven churches were dedicated to him and in 1512 a college was founded in his name at St Andrew's in Scotland.

Leonard of Port Maurice, St (1676–1751, f.d. 26 November). Born at Porto Maurizio in Italy, the son of a master mariner, he was educated by JESUITS in ROME, then became a FRANCISCAN FRIAR and was later ordained priest. He was appointed Guardian of St Bonaventura's in Rome and undertook a mission all over the country, to soldiers, sailors, prisoners, galley-slaves and in parishes, achieving a reputation as the greatest missioner of his age. He was also a writer, leaving a large volume of letters and sermons. He was responsible for spreading devotion to the SACRED HEART and IMMACULATE CONCEPTION and founding the STATIONS OF THE CROSS (*see* CROSS) at the Colosseum in Rome, which gave rise to the service of that name.

Leonardi, St John (*c.* 1542–1609, f.d. 9 October). Born at Lucca, he first trained as an apothecary, then became a priest, founding the Clerks Regular of the Mother of God for the dissemination of Christian Doctrine. This was a congregation of diocesan priests who lived under vows at a time when clerical life was greatly in need of reform. Pope Clement VIII appointed him to reform various monasteries and he also shared in the founding of the Roman College called 'Propaganda'. He died of the plague while nursing the sick. He was canonized in 1938.

Leonore, St (6th cent., f.d. 1 July). Among Bretons he is known as St Lunaire. He was a Celt, ordained at Caerleon by St Dubricius, who went to Brittany and founded the diocese of Léon. It was said that the cornfields there originated from a grain of wheat brought to the saint by a robin when he had no bread. Many other legends are attached to his name: stags drew his plough and angels helped him to make clearings in the forest. Two white pigeons brought his altar up from the depth of the sea.

Leopard. So called because it was thought in mediaeval times to be a cross between the lion (*leo*) and the *pard*, which was the name given to a panther that had no white specks on it.

In Christian art, the leopard represents that beast spoken of in *Revelation* xiii, 1–8, with seven heads and ten horns; six of the heads bear a NIMBUS, but the seventh, being 'wounded to death', lost its power, and consequently is bare.

> And the beast which I saw was like unto a leopard, and his feet were as the feet of a bear, and his mouth as the mouth of a lion.
>
> *Rev.* xiii, 2

Leopold of Austria, St (1073–1136, f.d. 15 November). Born at Melk in Austria, he was the fourth Margrave of Austria but rejected a nomination for the imperial crown. He married and had eighteen children, one of whom was Otto of Friesing, the chronicler. Leopold founded three religious houses; the BENEDICTINE Abbey of Mariazell, the CISTERCIAN Abbey of Heiligenkreuz and the Augustinian CANONS of Klosterneuburg. He was noted for his generosity and good rule.

Leopolita Bible. *See* BIBLE, SOME SPECIALLY NAMED EDITIONS.

Lesser Entrance. *See* ENTRANCE.

Lestonnae, St Jeanne de (1556–1640, f.d. 2 February). Founder of the Congregation, The Company of Mary, nuns dedicated to the education of girls. She was born at Bordeaux, and her parents were of opposing beliefs, her mother a CALVINIST who endeavoured unsuccessfully to convert her daughter. Jeanne (a niece of Montaigne) married Gaston de Montferrand and, at his death, became a CISTERCIAN nun, but she was not physically able to maintain the regime. She returned to Bordeaux and, under the influence of a JESUIT priest, founded schools for girls. The movement spread to seventeen countries. When Jeanne died miracles were reported at her tomb, but she was not beatified until 1900, and canonized in 1949.

Letters of Orders. A certificate issued to one who has been ordained; it bears the seal of the officiating bishop.

Leviathan. The Hebrew name for a monster of the waters. In *Job* xli, 1, and *Ps.* lxxiv, 14, it appears to refer to the crocodile; in *Ps.* civ, 26, it is probably the whale; and in *Is.* xxvii, 1, it is a sea-serpent.

This great and wide sea, wherein are things creeping innumerable, both small and great beasts. There go the ships: there is that leviathan, whom thou hast made to play therein.

Ps. civ, 26

Hence the name is applied to any huge sea-animal or ship of great size.

Levitation is a term applied to the phenomenon of heavy bodies rising and floating in the air. It is frequently mentioned in Hindu and other writings, and is a not uncommon attribute of Roman Catholic saints. Joseph of Cupertino (1603–63) was the subject of such frequent levitation that he was forbidden by his superiors to attend choir, and performed his devotions privately where he would not distract others. Other saints, mentioned in the text, who levitated are:

Catherine of Siena.
Dunstan.
Edmund of Canterbury.
Francis of Assisi.
Gerard Majella.
Ignatius Loyola.
John of the Cross.
Peter de Alcantara.
Philip Neri.
Teresa.
Thomas Aquinas.

Lewis, David (or **Charles Baker**), **St** (1616–79, f.d. 25 October). Born in Monmouthshire, his father was a PROTESTANT and his mother a CATHOLIC. He was educated at Abergavenny and the Middle Temple, then took the position of tutor to the family of the Comte Savage. Lewis converted to Catholicism and entered the ENGLISH COLLEGE in ROME, being ordained priest and becoming a JESUIT. After being Spiritual Director to the College he returned to England and carried out a mission from a farmhouse at Llanrothal. He was arrested after the POPISH PLOT, his farmhouse was wrecked and his library given to Hereford Cathedral. He was condemned to death and finally hanged by a blacksmith as the hangman and others had refused to carry out the sentence. His tomb at Usk is still a centre for pilgrimage. He was canonized in 1970 as one of the FORTY MARTYRS OF ENGLAND AND WALES.

Liafwine, St. *See* LEBUIN.

Liberalism, or **Liberal Theology.** A movement within Christianity, developed largely since the 18th century, rejecting restraints on intellectual freedom and assuming the right to query and examine the basis and credentials of accepted beliefs. At first a PROTESTANT movement, it spread to CATHOLICISM and maintains that

blind faith, e.g. the fundamentalist view of the Creation and the age of the earth, should be replaced by careful analysis, judgement and intellectual freedom. Friedrich E. D. Schliermacher (1768–1834) is generally accepted as the founder of the school. He was a German Protestant professor of theology and pastor at Berlin and wrote *Discourses on Religion* and *Christian Dogmatics*, while his *Religion: Speeches to its Cultured Despisers*, is regarded as the introduction to Liberal Theology. For him dogma was an incrustation, while religion is feeling, an attitude of reverence towards God. 'Piety cannot be an instinct craving for a mess of metaphysical and ethical crumbs.' The BIBLE should be read as a record of experience rather than as a divine revelation. The reaction against Liberalism came with Karl Barth in his *Die kirchliche Dogmatik* (1932).

Liberation Theology. A modern movement in Latin America which criticizes the Church for being largely concerned with spiritual and moral teaching and ignoring the acute problems of poverty and social injustice. Originating in the climate of extreme poverty, it also opposes the oppression of the laity by a rigid sacramental system and the exploitation of the people by oppressive regimes, maintaining that the GOSPEL of Christ is first and foremost concerned with the poor and oppressed. The movement is Marxist in tone.

Libertine. A free-thinker in religion and morals, hence (more commonly) a debauchee, a profligate; one who puts no restraint on his personal indulgence. The application of the word to 16th-century Anabaptist sects in the Low Countries and certain of Calvin's opponents at Geneva had derogatory implications. In the NEW TESTAMENT (*Acts* vi, 9) it is probably used to mean a freedman (Lat. *libertinus*):

Then there arose certain of the synagogue, which is called the synagogue of the Libertines,... disputing with Stephen.

Lich. A body (O.E. *lik*).
Lich-gate. The covered entrance to churchyards intended to afford shelter to the coffin and mourners while awaiting the clergyman who is to conduct the cortège into church.
Lich-wake, or **Lyke-wake.** The funeral feast or the *waking* of a corpse, i.e. watching it all night.

In a pastoral written by Aelfric in 998 for Wilfsige, Bishop of Sherborne, the attendance of the clergy at lyke-wakes is forbidden.
Lich-way. The path by which a funeral is conveyed to church, which not infrequently deviates from the ordinary road. It was long supposed that wherever a dead body passed

became a public thoroughfare.

Life and Work. Organized at a meeting in Stockholm in 1925 under Archbishop Soderblom, the movement stated that: 'doctrine divides and service unites' and called on the churches to collaborate in 'applied Christianity' through world alliance and in promoting international friendship. The movement is now merged with the WORLD COUNCIL OF CHURCHES.

Light (O.E. *leoht*). The O.E. is the same for both senses of this word, i.e. illumination and smallness of weight, but in the former sense it is the O.H. Ger. *lioht* and in the latter O.H. Ger. *liht*. Light is a manifestation of divinity, of cosmic creation. The ancient Feast of Lights was adopted and adapted in Christianity as the PURIFICATION of the blessed VIRGIN MARY or CANDLEMAS, she being the 'Light-bearer' in her Son.

The Light of the World (Lat. *Lux Mundi*). Jesus Christ; allegorically portrayed by Holman Hunt in his famous picture (1854) showing Christ carrying a lantern knocking at the door of the soul. Sir Arthur Sullivan has an oratorio of this title (1873); and Sir Edwin Arnold a poem (1891) in which Christ is the central figure as the founder of Christianity.

> Then spake Jesus unto them, saying, I am the light of the world: he that followeth me shall not walk in darkness, but shall have the light of life.
>
> *John* viii, 12

The light of thy countenance. God's smile of approbation and love.

> Lift thou up the light of thy countenance upon us.
>
> *Ps.* iv, 6

Inner Light. Inward or spiritual light: knowledge divinely imparted; as used by QUAKERS, the light of Christ in the soul.

Liguori, St Alfonso Maria de. *See* ALPHONSUS.

Lily, The. There is a tradition that the lily sprang from the repentant tears of Eve as she went forth from PARADISE.

In Christian art the lily is an emblem of chastity, innocence, and purity. In pictures of the ANNUNCIATION, GABRIEL is sometimes represented as carrying a lily-branch, while a vase containing a lily stands before the Virgin who is kneeling in prayer. St JOSEPH holds a lily-branch in his hand, indicating that his wife Mary was a virgin.

The lily in the field in *Matt.* vi, 29, 'that even Solomon in all his glory was not arrayed like one of these', is the wild lily, probably a species of iris. Our 'lily of the valley', with which this is sometimes confused, is a different plant, one of the genus *Convallaria*.

Limbo (Lat. *limbus*, border, fringe, edge). The borders of HELL; that portion assigned by the SCHOOLMEN to those departed spirits to whom the benefits of redemption did not apply through no fault of their own.

The Limbo of Children (Lat. *limbus infantium*). The limbo for children who die before baptism or before they are responsible for their actions.

Limbo of the Fathers (Lat. *limbus patrum*). The half-way house between earth and HEAVEN, where the PATRIARCHS and prophets who died before Christ's crucifixion await the last day, when they will be received into Heaven. Some hold that this is the 'HELL' into which Christ descended after He gave up the ghost on the cross.

Shakespeare (*Henry VIII*, V, iv) uses *limbo patrum* for 'quod', jail, confinement.

> I have some of 'em in Limbo Patrum, and there they are like to dance these three days.

The Limbus of Fools, or **Limbus Fatuorum,** or **Paradise of Fools.** As fools or idiots are not responsible for their works, the SCHOOLMEN held that they were not punished in PURGATORY and could not be received into HEAVEN, so they were destined to go to a special 'Paradise of Fools'.

> Then might you see
> Cowls, hoods, habits, with their wearers tossed
> And fluttered into rags; then relics, beads,
> Indulgences, dispenses, pardons, bulls,
> The sport of winds. All these, upwhirled aloft,
> Fly o'er the backside of the world far-off,
> Into a Limbo large and broad, since called
> The Paradise of Fools.
>
> MILTON: *Paradise Lost*, III, 498

Lincoln. The devil looking over Lincoln. *See under* DEVIL.

Lincoln Imp. A grotesque carving having weird and prominent ears and nursing the right leg crossed over the left, in the ANGEL choir of Lincoln Cathedral. He is said to have been turned to stone by the angels for misbehaving in the Angel Choir. The Imp is now the county emblem.

Line, St Anne (c. 1565–1601, f.d. 25 October). Born at Dunmow, Essex, into a strongly CALVINISTIC family, she and her brother both became CATHOLICS and were rejected and disinherited. Anne also married a convert, Roger Line, who was arrested and imprisoned for attending MASS and was exiled. After his death Anne, being in straitened circumstances, became housekeeper to a JESUIT father, John Gerard, who harboured priests. She also taught children and did embroidery for a living. She was arrested with others at a Mass held in her house and was tried for harbouring a priest and having an altar. She was found guilty, sentenced to death and executed. She was canonized in 1970 among the FORTY MARTYRS OF ENGLAND AND WALES

Lioba, St (d. 786, f.d. 28 September). Of Anglo-Saxon family, born in Wessex and related to St BONIFACE. She was educated in convents at Minster-in-Thanet and Wimborne under the abbess Tetta who was requested by Boniface to send nuns to assist in the evangelization of Germany. Lioba went, as leader, with some thirty nuns, and was established in Franconia. It was said that she was beautiful, intelligent, of charming character and highly esteemed and consulted by the authorities of both the Church and State, including Queen Hildegard at the court of CHARLEMAGNE. She founded convents under the BENEDICTINE RULE, the nuns being taught Latin, trained as scribes, also undertaking manual work in the house and garden. She finally retired to the nunnery at Schönersheim where she died and was buried near St Boniface's tomb at Fulda.

Lion. In Christian symbolism the lion is ambivalent as both the kingly nature of Christ, his power and might, but also his power to deliver the Christian from the lion's mouth, the Devil, the 'roaring lion'. The lion was believed to sleep with its eyes open, hence it represented spiritual watchfulness and vigilance. As a solitary animal it depicted the hermit.

St MARK the EVANGELIST is symbolized by a lion because he begins his gospel with the scenes of St JOHN THE BAPTIST and Christ in the wilderness.

A lion is the emblem of the tribe of Judah; Christ is called 'the Lion of the tribe of Judah'.

Judah is a lion's whelp:... he couched as a lion, and as an old lion; who shall rouse him up?

Gen. xlix, 9

The story of Androcles and the lion has many parallels, the most famous of which are those related of St JEROME and St Gerasimus:

While St Jerome was lecturing one day, a lion entered the schoolroom, and lifted up one of its paws. All his disciples fled; but Jerome, seeing that the paw was wounded, drew a thorn out of it and dressed the wound. The lion, out of gratitude, showed a wish to stay with its benefactor, hence the SAINT is represented as accompanied by a lion.

St Gerasimus, says the story, saw on the banks of the Jordan a lion coming to him limping on three feet. When it reached the saint it held up to him the right paw, from which St Gerasimus extracted a large thorn. The grateful beast attached itself to the saint, and followed him about as a dog.

The Lion as an emblem of the

Resurrection. According to tradition, the lion's whelp is born dead, and remains so for three days, when the father breathes on it and it receives life.

A lion at the feet of crusaders, or martyrs, in effigy, signifies that they died for their cause.

The Lion of St Mark, or of Venice. A winged lion *sejant*, holding an open book with the inscription *Pax tibi, Marce, Evangelista Meus*. A sword-point rises above the book on the dexter side, and the whole is encircled by an AUREOLE.

Lip homage, or service. Verbal devotion; insincere regard; honouring with the lips while the heart takes no part or lot in the matter See *Matt*. xv, 8; *Is*. xxix, 13.

To shoot out the lip. To show scorn.

All they that see me laugh me to scorn: they shoot out the lip, they shake the head.

Ps. xxii, 7

Litany (Gr. supplication). An appointed form of public prayer recited by the clergy with responses from the congregation, having the same formula for several clauses in succession. Often used in processions, this being the original usage. The ANGLICAN and ROMAN CATHOLIC litanies closely resemble the ancient forms with the exception of the invocation to the VIRGIN MARY among Catholics. The processional litany is still maintained in the Eastern ORTHODOX CHURCH.

Liturgy. The established rites for public worship in a Christian Church, originally employed for the celebration of the MASS. The term is now used for the set framework of worship in Eastern ORTHODOX, ROMAN CATHOLIC and ANGLICAN CHURCHES (*see* CHURCH OF ENGLAND) it is the focal point of worship in the Russian ORTHODOX CHURCH where ritual has been said to take precedence over doctrine.

Lloyd, St John (1630–79, f.d. 25 October). Born at Brecon, he left Wales for the English seminary at Valladolid and was ordained priest. He returned to Wales and carried out a twenty-year mission until the time of the panic caused by the Titus Oates POPISH PLOT. Lloyd was arrested, imprisoned in Cardiff Castle and tried together with Philip EVANS; both were sentenced as priests and were hanged, drawn and quartered. They were canonized in 1970 among the FORTY MARTYRS OF ENGLAND AND WALES.

Loaf. In sacred art, a loaf held in the hand is an attribute of St PHILIP the Apostle, St OSYTH, St Joanna, St NICHOLAS, St Godfrey, and other saints noted for their charity to the poor.

Locus poenitentiae (Lat., a place or opportunity

of repentance). The interval when it is possible to withdraw from a bargain or course before being committed to it. In the interview between Esau and his father Isaac, St PAUL says that the former 'found no place of repentance, though he sought it carefully with tears' (*Heb*. xii, 17)—i.e. no means whereby Isaac could break his bargain with Jacob.

Logia (Gr. words). A collection of the supposed sayings of Christ, they are largely embodied in the Gospel According to St *Matthew* and to a lesser extent in the Gospel According to St *Luke*; they were disseminated in the early church. The term is also applied to the 'Sayings of Jesus' found in Egypt in 1897 at Oxyrhynchus on a 2nd or 3rd century papyrus.

Logos (Gr. reason or word). In Christian theology the Logos is identified with the Christ, the second person of the TRINITY. The main use of the term occurs in the Johannine writings in the NEW TESTAMENT, which show the Hellenistic influence of Philo.

Lollards. A name given to the followers of John Wyclif, and earlier to a sect in the Netherlands. It is probably from the Mid. Dut. *Lollaerd*, one who mumbles prayers or hymns. The word is recorded as having been used by William Courtenay, Archbishop of Canterbury, when he condemned their teachings in 1382.

The Lollards condemned TRANSUBSTANTIATION, INDULGENCES, clerical celibacy, the ecclesiastical hierarchy, and the temporal possessions of the church.

London Missionary Society. An interdenominational PROTESTANT mission 'to promote Christianity among the heathen'. Founded in 1795, it was mainly CONGREGATIONAL, WESLEYAN, PRESBYTERIAN and ANGLICAN in origin but it became increasingly Congregationalist, and in 1966 it was named the 'Congregational Council for World Missions'.

Longinus, or **Longius** (f.d. 15 March (West), 16 October (East)). The traditional name of the Roman soldier who smote Our Lord with his spear at the Crucifixion. The only authority for this is the apocryphal *Acts of Pilate*, dating from the 6th century. According to Arthurian Legend, this spear was brought by JOSEPH OF ARIMATHEA to Listenise, when he visited King Pellam, 'who was nigh of Joseph's kin'. Sir Balim the Savage seized this spear, with which he wounded King Pellam and destroyed three whole countries with that one stroke. William of Malmesbury says the spear was used by CHARLEMAGNE against the Saracens.

Many legends are associated with him, such as having kept Christ's blood which healed him

of increasing blindness. Tradition says that he then became a monk at Caesarea (there were no Christian monasteries at that date) and was arrested and tried for refusing to worship idols. He smashed an image which released devils; these possessed the Roman Governor, sending him mad. Longinius said that after his death the Governor would be healed; he died soon after and the Governor recovered and spent the rest of his life in good works. In art Longinus is depicted at the Crucifixion, holding a lance, or sometimes a pyx containing the blood; he symbolized the converted gentile. The pyx was said to have been taken to Mantua, of which Longinus is the patron saint. He was regarded as a martyr and venerated as such.

Lord. In the year of our Lord. *See* ANNO-DOMINI.
Lord of Creation. Man.

> Replenish the earth, and subdue it: and have dominion over the fish of the sea, and over the fowl of the air, and over every living things that moveth upon the earth... Behold, I have given you every herb bearing seed.... and every tree.
>
> *Gen*. i, 28, 29

Lord of Hosts. In the Old Testament, a frequently used title for JEHOVAH, no doubt arising from the belief that He led their armies in battle.
The Lord's Day. SUNDAY.
The Lord's Prayer. The words in which Jesus taught his disciples to pray (*Matt*. vi, 9–13). *See* PATERNOSTER.
The Lord's Supper. A name given to the Holy Communion which commemorates the LAST SUPPER of Jesus with his disciples.
Lords Spiritual. The bishops who have seats in the House of Lords.
When our Lord falls in our Lady's lap. When EASTER Sunday falls on the same date as LADY DAY (25 March). This is said to bode ill for England. In the 19th century this occurred in 1883 and 1894; in the 20th, its sole occurrence has been in 1951.

Loreto. The house of Loreto. The Santa Casa or Holy House, the reputed house of the Virgin Mary at Nazareth. It was said to have been miraculously moved to Dalmatia in 1291, thence to Recanati in Italy in 1294, and finally to a site near Ancona in 1295. It was reputed to have been transported by ANGELS to prevent its destruction by the Turks. The name is from the Lat. *lauretum*, a grove of laurels, in which it stood in Recanati. The Holy House itself is a small stone building, now surrounded by a marble screen.

Lost Tribes. The term applied to the ten tribes of Israel who were carried away from North Palestine (721 BC) into Assyria, about 140 years before the Babylonian captivity (586 BC) exiled the tribes of Judah. Their disappearance has caused much speculation, especially among those who look forward to a restoration of the Hebrews as foretold in the OLD TESTAMENT. In 1649, John Sadler suggested that the English were of Israelitish origin. This theory was expanded by Richard Brothers, the half-crazy enthusiast who declared himself Prince of the Hebrews and Ruler of the World (1792), and has since been developed by others. The British Israelite theory is still held by some without any serious supporting evidence.

Lost Sunday. Another name for SEPTUAGESIMA SUNDAY, from its having no special name.

Louis. Louis, St (1214, 1226–70, f.d. 25 August). Louis IX of France is usually represented as holding the Saviour's crown of thorns and the cross; sometimes he is pictured with a pilgrim's staff and sometimes with the standard of the cross, the allusion in all cases being to the CRUSADES. He was canonized in 1297. He is considered a saint offering special protection to France.

Louis Bertrand, St (1526–81, f.d. 9 October). Born at Valencia in Spain, he showed great piety as a child. After some difficulty, due to ill-health, he succeeded in joining the DOMINICANS. In 1562 he went as a missionary to South America, but had little success among the Indians, accounts of the conversions being greatly exaggerated. He did help to moderate the greed and barbarities of the Conquistadors. He returned to Spain in 1569 and became prior at Valencia. He was adviser to St TERESA and was noted as a preacher. His life was ascetic; he had visions and was said to have had the gift of tongues and supernatural powers.

Louis Grignion, St (1673–1716, f.d. 28 April). Born at Montfort, Brittany, of poor parents and educated by charity, he carried out missionary work among the poor and founded free schools. He adopted a controversial style in his missions, which alienated the authorities but appealed to the populace, so that his work encountered some opposition. He founded the Daughters of Wisdom, at Poitiers, who nursed the sick and taught the poor; later he instituted the Company of Mary, a society of priests involved in his work. He wrote the book *True Devotion to the Blessed Virgin*, which was widely translated.

Louis of Toulouse, St (1274–97, f.d. 19 August). The second son of Charles II, King of Naples, he was great-nephew of St LOUIS and related to St ELIZABETH OF HUNGARY. While held hostage for his father, by the King of Aragon, he studied under the FRANCISCANS, was ordained, and on his release joined the order in ROME. He was appointed bishop of Toulouse at an early age but lived a life of poverty and rejected all pomp and ceremony, wearing an old patched habit and renouncing all claim to the throne. He found the episcopate burdensome and wished to resign, but he died soon after at the age of twenty-three.

Louise de Marillac, St (1591–1660, f.d. 15 March). Born in Auvergne, she wished to become a nun but was married to Anthony le Gras, a court official. After his death she engaged in charitable work and met St VINCENT DE PAUL, who became her spiritual director and with whom she worked among the poor and sick. She later founded the SISTERS OF CHARITY, largely taken from the artisan and peasant classes, more able to deal with the horrifying conditions than were the aristocratic ladies. Louise employed the latter in fund-raising and organization. She worked from her own home, drew up a rule of life, and her sisters laboured in hospitals, orphanages and schools as well as in the houses of the poor in the plague-stricken areas. The work spread widely and there were forty houses of the Sisters at the time of Louise's death. She was canonized in 1934.

Lourdes. A famous centre of pilgrimage situated in the south-west of France. In 1858 Bernadette Soubirous, a simple peasant girl, claimed that the Virgin Mary had appeared to her on eighteen occasions. Investigations failed to shake her narrative, and a spring with miraculous healing properties that appeared at the same time began to draw invalids from all over the world. The pilgrimage received ecclesiastical recognition in 1862 and Bernadette was canonized in 1933.

Love. The Family of Love. *See* FAMILISTS.
Love Feast. *See* AGAPE.
A labour of love. Work undertaken for the love of the thing without regard to payment.

Remembering without ceasing your work of faith, and labour of love, and patience of hope in our Lord Jesus Christ, in the sight of God and our Father.
I *Thess.* i, 3

Low. Low Church. The essentially PROTESTANT section of the CHURCH OF ENGLAND which gives a relatively low place to the claims of the priesthood, episcopate, etc., and has more in common with NONCONFORMIST than CATHOLIC teaching. It is used in contrast to HIGH CHURCH.
Low Mass. In the Western Church, MASS said by the celebrant without the assistance of other clergy. No part of the service is sung.
Low Sunday. The Sunday next after EASTER. So called probably because of the contrast to the 'high' feast of EASTER Sunday. *Cp.* QUASIMODO-SUNDAY.
Lower Criticism. The section of Biblical Criticism concerned with the text and the

recovery of the original text of the BIBLE. *cp* HIGHER CRITICISM.

Loyola, St Ignatius (1491–1556). Founder of the Society of Jesus, is depicted in art with the sacred monogram. I.H.S. on his breast, or as contemplating it, surrounded by glory in the skies, in allusion to his claim that he had a miraculous knowledge of the mystery of the TRINITY vouchsafed to him. He was the son of the Spanish ducal house of Loyola and, after being severely wounded at the siege of Pamplona (1521), left the army and dedicated himself to the service of the Virgin. *See* JESUIT.

Lucar, Cyril (1572–1638). Patriarch of Constantinople who turned from ROMAN CATHOLICISM to sympathize with CALVINISM and the CHURCH OF ENGLAND, presenting the *Codex Alexandrinus* to Charles I in 1628. He attempted to reconcile the ORTHODOX faith with Calvinism, and his teaching was condemned by later synods.

Lucian of Antioch, St (4th cent., f.d. 7 January (West), 15 October (East)). Born at Samosata in Syria, he was a priest at Antioch where he founded a theological school which was attended by Arius. The followers of the Arian heresy were thus sometimes known as Lucianists, and tried to make him responsible for their unorthodoxy. Lucian was said to have been imprisoned for nine years under the Diocletian persecution, frequently refusing to renounce his faith and finally being put to death. According to another tradition he was starved to death and his body was cast into the sea but was brought ashore by a dolphin. In art he is sometimes represented with a dolphin.

Lucy, St. Patron SAINT for those afflicted in the eyes. She is supposed to have lived in Syracuse and to have suffered martyrdom there about 304. One legend relates that a nobleman wanted to marry her for the beauty of her eyes; so she tore them out and gave them to him, saying, 'Now let me live to God.' Hence she is represented in art carrying a palm branch and a platter with two eyes on it. Another legend says that she was persecuted under Diocletian and that her eyes had been torn out but miraculously restored. She was condemned to be sent to a brothel but became immovable, a whole team of oxen failing to move her, after which she was sentenced to be burned, but this was also unsuccessful. Finally she was stabbed in the throat. Her cult spread widely beyond Sicily and in Sweden, as St Lucia, her festival on December 13, the darkest day, is essentially a festival of light, her name signifying 'light'. She is also depicted with a lighted lamp in art. An ox at her feet symbolizes her martyrdom.

Ludger (or Liudger), St (*c.* 744–809, f.d. 26 March). A Frieslander, brought up at the monastery of Utrecht under St GREGORY. He went to England, to York, where he studied under ALCUIN and became a deacon. He returned to Utrecht and rebuilt the church at Deventer which had been destroyed by pagans. He carried out a mission to Friesland, wrecking many pagan shrines and building churches. He was raised to the priesthood in 778 and visited ROME and St BENEDICT's monastery at MONTE CASSINO, with a view to establishing a monastery of his own under the RULE of St BENEDICT. This he achieved on his return to Westphalia, founding a monastery at Werden. He was ordained bishop of Münster and founded a monastery for CANONS. Ludger was a man of gentle persuasion and a great missioner, making many converts. He was buried at his monastery at Werden.

Ludmilla, St (d. *c.* 925, f.d. 16 September). The daughter of a Slavonic prince and married to the Duke of Bohemia, she was converted to Christianity with her husband by St METHODIUS. She was noted for her piety, charity and gentleness. Ludmilla was responsible for the education of her grandson St WENCESLAS, who grew up under her influence. She was beloved by all except her daughter-in-law, mother of Wenceslas, who was jealous of her and had her murdered by hired assassins.

Luke, St (f.d. 18 October). Patron SAINT of artists and physicians. Tradition says he painted a portrait of the Virgin Mary and *Col.* iv, 14, states that he was a physician. *See also* SYMBOLS OF SAINTS.

Lull, St (*c.* 710–86, f.d. 16 October). Born in Wessex and educated at Malmesbury, where he became a monk, he went to Germany with his cousin St BONIFACE on a mission, later succeeding him as bishop of Mainz. He was involved in a protracted dispute with St STURM over the jurisdiction of the monastery of Felda. Lull was noted for his organization and learning, having a great appreciation of books and forming a notable library. He was a careful observer of the canons and fasts. In 781 he was appointed archbishop and received the PALLIUM. He founded monasteries at Bleidenstadt in Nassau and at Hersfeld in Hesse, where he died and was buried.

Luminary of the English Church, The. Bishop Bartholomew of Exeter, a Breton (1161–84), was so called by Pope Alexander III. He was one of the five bishops sent to Sens with Henry II's appeal to the Pope, after Archbishop Becket's flight to France in 1164. He conscientiously used his learning and abilities for the good of the Church.

Lupus of Troyes, St (d. 478, f.d. 29 July). Born at Toul, he married a sister of St HILARY but after seven years both partners agreed to separate and Lupus became a monk at Lérins. He was shortly afterwards appointed bishop of Troyes. In 429 he accompanied St GERMANUS to Britain to oppose the PELAGIAN heresy. Legend says that Lupus saved Troyes from being sacked by Attila, the Hun, by persuasion, but was himself taken hostage for some years before being able to return to his diocese, where he died.

Lustral. Properly, pertaining to the Lustrum; hence purificatory, as *lustral water*, the water used in Christian as well as many pagan rites for aspersing worshippers. In ROME the priest used a small OLIVE or Laurel branch for sprinkling infants and the people.

Lutgard, St (1182–1246, f.d. 16 June). Born at Tongres, she was educated at the nunnery of Saint-Trond in Belgium and became a nun there after a vision of Christ calling her. Later, to avoid being made abbess, she moved to a stricter order of the CISTERCIAN nuns at Aywieres. She had many visions and mystical experiences and was one of the noted mystics of the Middle Ages. She became totally blind during the last eleven years of her life.

Luther, Martin (1483–1546). German reformer, usually regarded as the founder of PROTESTANTISM. Born at Eisleben, the son of a miner, he was educated at the University of Erfurt and then entered an AUGUSTINIAN monastery, showing brilliant theological ability. He was ordained priest and became a professor at the new university of Wittenberg. After going on a mission to ROME, he became involved in the controversy over the sale of INDULGENCES and, in 1517, nailed a thesis on the church door of Wittenberg, attacking the system. He criticized many of the Church's doctrines and urged the authority of the SCRIPTURES. Leo X launched a papal BULL against him which Luther burnt in public. He was then summoned to appear before the Diet of Princes at Worms where he made the famous Declaration, taken as the birth of Protestantism.

Lutheranism. The PROTESTANT body originating from the life and works of Martin Luther, and the chief form of Protestant Christianity in Germany, Denmark, Norway, Sweden and Iceland. It spread into the Baltic States and neighbouring countries and later into the New World and other continents following German and Scandinavian immigration. Statistically, Lutheranism is the largest Protestant body, having some 70 million members. Arising between 1517 and 1530, it was defined by the AUGSBURG CONFESSION of 1530, with Luther's two *Catechisms* and *Book of Concord* setting forth the principle articles of faith. The doctrine of 'justification by faith' is the basis of its theology. There is no uniform liturgy and services are conducted in the native language, varying according to the country; there is only one order of clergy.

Lych Gate. *See* LICH.

Lyons, Martyrs of (d. 177, f.d. 2 June). The names of forty-eight martyrs were recorded at Lyons and Vienne under the persecution of Marcus Aurelius. They included St Pothinus, a bishop; St Blandina, a slave girl; Sanctus, a deacon; Maturus, newly baptized; Attalus, a man of repute; and Ponticus, a 15-year-old boy. They were denounced and charged during an outburst of anti-Christian zeal; some were tortured and died in prison, others were beheaded or killed in the arena by wild beasts. An account is preserved in a letter sent by the churches in Asia and Phrygia and in the pages of EUSEBIUS.

Lwanga, Charles and Companions, SS. *See* CHARLES.

M

Macanisius, St (d. *c.* 514, f.d. 3 September). Oengus Mac Nisse was one of the earliest recorded saints of Ireland, said to have been a disciple of St PATRICK. He was a hermit at Kells and later a bishop and founder of a monastery, probably at Kells. Little is known of his life, but his fame rests on the legend that his reverence for the SCRIPTURES was such that he was not content to carry them in a leather bag, as was the custom, but bore them elevated on his shoulders or on all fours.

Macarius the Great of Egypt, St (*c.* 300–90, f.d. 15 January). Born in Upper Egypt, he became a monk in the desert of Sketis where he lived in great austerity, following the example of St ANTHONY. He was constantly at prayer, but also tended sheep and plaited baskets. He was ordained priest and was one of the FATHERS of Egypt, founding a monastery and being noted for his wisdom. He was said to have been exiled for a time when he opposed the ARIAN heresy. Many writings and homilies were attributed to him, but their origin is doubtful. There has been considerable confusion between him and the contemporary St Macarius of Alexandria, also a monk in the Egyptian desert.

Macartan (or Aedh Mac Cairthinn), St (d. *c.* 505, f.d. 24 March). One of the earliest of the Irish saints, said to have been a disciple of St PATRICK and to have been consecrated bishop of Clogher by him. Little is known of Macartan's early life but his liturgical office is the only one to survive from an Irish source.

Maccabees, The. The family of Jewish heroes descended from Mattathias the Hasmonaean and his five sons, John, Simon, Judas, Eleazar, and Jonathan, which delivered its race from the persecutions of the Syrian King, Antiochus Epiphanes (175–164 BC). It established a line of priest-kings which lasted till supplanted by Herod in 37 BC. Their exploits are told in the four *Books of The Maccabees*, of which two are in the APOCRYPHA.

Although pre-Christian, there was a widespread cult of these OLD TESTAMENT characters as symbolizing Christian martyrs. The Jews had been persecuted for their refusal to worship other gods or eat swineflesh, showing an affinity with the later Christians who were mar-tyred for rejecting paganism, such as the SEVEN BROTHERS. The feast day was on August 1 but was withdrawn from the CALENDAR in the revision of 1969 and confined to a local calendar.

Macedonians. A religious sect named after Macedonius (d. *c.* 362), Bishop of Constantinople, an upholder of semi-Arianism. He was deposed by the ARIAN Council of Constantinople in 360.

Machalus (Machella or Magor), St (d. 498, f.d. 27 April). A legendary character, said to have become Bishop of the Isle of Man and to have been an Irish pirate who, for his misdeeds, was ordered by St PATRICK, as a penance, to set out to sea in a coracle without oars. He drifted to the Isle of Man and later was described as 'a rod of gold, a vast ingot, the great bishop MacCaille'. Another tradition said he came from the Orkneys.

Machan, St (6th cent., f.d. 28 September). A Scotsman who studied in Ireland and returned to Scotland. He was said to have been consecrated bishop at ROME. An ALTAR was erected to him at Glasgow Cathedral. Legend says that robbers who stole his oxen were turned to stone.

Machar (Mochar or Mochumma), St (6th cent., f.d. 12 November). Son of an Irish prince, he was baptized by St COLMAN and went to Iona as a missionary with St COLUMBA, to convert the Picts; from there he was sent to Mull and became a bishop of the Picts. He was associated with Aberdeen and was fabled to have visited ROME. His well at Aberdeen was used as baptismal water.

Mackessog, St. *See* KESSOG.

Macmillanites. A religious sect in Scotland which seceded from the CAMERONIANS in 1743 because they wished for stricter adherence to the principles of the REFORMATION in Scotland; so named from John Macmillan (1670–1753), their leader. They called themselves the 'Reformed Presbytery'.

Macrina the Elder, St (d. 340, f.d. 14 January). A disciple of St GREGORY THAUMATURGUS and grandmother of SS BASIL, GREGORY OF NYSSA and

MACRINA THE YOUNGER. She went into exile in Pontus with her husband during the persecution under Diocletian, suffering loss of property and much hardship. She died at Neo-Caesarea.

Macrina the Younger, St (*c.* 327–79, f.d. 19 July). Born of a distinguished family, the eldest of ten children, she was a daughter of Basil the Elder and sister to SS BASIL and GREGORY OF NYSSA. At the age of ten she was betrothed to a young lawyer, but he died early and although remarkably beautiful, highly educated and talented, Macrina elected to remain single. She devoted herself to the education of the younger members of the family, herself living a strict monastic life together with her widowed mother St Emmelia. Later both retired to Annesi, in Pontus, by the river Iris, where they established a religious community of women and nuns. Macrina's discussions with Gregory were embodied in *De Anima et Resurrectione* ('On the Soul and the Resurrection').

Madeleine Sophie Barat, St (1779–1865, f.d. 25 May). Born at Joigny, in Burgundy, the daughter of a cooper and vintner, her brother Louis, eleven years older, was her godfather and later, as a priest, undertook her education along religious lines. After the first turmoil of the French Revolution had abated, the Abbé Barat and Father Varin proposed that she should go to Amiens to teach in an institute of consecrated women for training girls. Thus were laid the foundations of the Society of the Sacred Heart, of which Madeleine became head and which she directed for sixty-three years, having been only twenty-three when first appointed. The order spread to twelve countries in Europe and in North America, becoming, in spite of difficulties raised by the ambitious chaplain of Amiens, one of the most famous and efficient of religious educational orders.

Madonna (Ital., my lady). A title especially applied to the Virgin MARY.

Madron (or **Madern**), **St** (5th cent., f.d. 17 May). Patron of the town of Madron in Cornwall where his chapel and well were a centre of pilgrimage and miraculous cures. It was reported that in 1641 the bishop of Exeter attested the cure of a cripple who had walked on his hands for sixteen years and was able to walk naturally after sleeping in the saint's bed. Nothing is known of Madron's life, and he is variously identified with Medron, Matronus and Piran. Services are still held at his chapel by ANGLICANS and METHODISTS.

Maedoc of Ferns, St (d. 626, f.d. 31 January). Born in Connacht, he was educated in Ireland at Leinster and in Wales at St David's School, Pembrokeshire. Returning to Ireland, he founded a monastery at Ferns, and others at Drumlane and Rossinver. His relics, bequeathed to his monasteries, still survive in Dublin and Armagh. He was reputed to practise extreme austerities and to have lived on barley bread and water for seven years, reciting 500 psalms each day. Legend recounts that some bogus beggars, having hidden their good clothes, applied to him for aid; seeing through their trickery, he took their clothes and gave them to the poor, sending them away naked and without alms. Maedoc is also identified with St AIDAN.

Maelruain, St (d. 792, f.d. 7 July). An Irish abbot and reformer, he founded the monastery of Tallaght, Co. Wicklow, and instigated the CULDEES reform movement. This sought to combat contemporary laxity and revive traditional asceticism, such as flagellation and vigils held in cold water; it also laid emphasis on manual labour as well as study. Women were of the devil, and all alcohol was prohibited. Little is known of his life, but he was noted for his writings, *The Teachings of Mael-ruain*, *The Rule of Celi-de* (Culdees), *The Monastery of Tallaght* and his *Stowe Missal*. In later times his feast day was celebrated by house-to-house processions, the dancing of jigs and drinking all night. This was suppressed by the DOMINICANS in 1856.

Maelrubba (or **Malrubius**), **St** (*c.* 642–722, f.d. 21 April, 27 August). Born in Ireland, a descendant of Irish kings, he was known as the Apostle of the Picts, going to Scotland where he founded a monastery at Applecross, Ross and Cromarty. He carried out a mission to Skye, and on the mainland he went to Loch Broom, and built a church also on an island in Loch Maree, where his spring was famous for its healing properties. One tradition said he was murdered by Norse pirates.

Mafalda of Portugal, St (1184–1257, f.d. 2 or 13 May). Daughter of King Sancho I of Portugal, she was married at the age of twelve to her cousin King Henry I of Castile, but the marriage was annulled on the grounds of consanguinity. Returning to Portugal, she entered a nunnery at Arouca which she converted to the CISTERCIAN Order. She led a life of extreme austerity in sackcloth and ashes. Her fortune was spent on founding a hospice for pilgrims, a refuge for widows, building a bridge over the river Talmeda and restoring Oporto Cathedral. Her body was exhumed in 1617 and was found to be incorrupt and flexible.

Magdeburg Centuries. The first great PROTESTANT history of the Christian Church, compiled in Magdeburg under the direction of Matthias Flacius Hyricus (1520–75). It was written in Latin and first published at Basle (1559–74) as the *Historia Ecclesiae Christi*, and takes the story to 1400.

Magdalene, St Mary (1st cent., f.d. 22 July (West), 4 May (East)). A follower of Christ, who 'cast seven devils' (*Luke* viii, 2) out of her. She is also referred to in the NEW TESTAMENT as standing by the cross (*Mark* xv, 40); going to anoint the body in the tomb (*Mark* xvi, 1); being one to whom he first appeared (*Mark* xvi, 9) and seeing the Risen Lord (*Matt.* xxviii, 9). She had also been identified with the sinner of *Luke* vii, 37, as anointing his feet, and with MARY sister of Martha (*John* xii, 3), who also anointed his feet, but these associations are problema-tical.

Magi (Lat., pl. of *magus*). Literally 'wise men'; specifically, the Three Wise Men of the East who brought gifts to the infant Saviour. Tradition calls them Melchior, Gaspar, and Balthazar, three kings of the East. The first offered gold, the emblem of royalty; the second, FRANKINCENSE in token of divinity; and the third, myrrh, in prophetic allusion to the persecution unto death which awaited the 'Man of Sorrows'.

Melchior means 'king of light'.
Gaspar or Caspar means 'the white one'.
Balthazar means 'the lord of treasures'.

Mediaeval legend calls them the *Three Kings of Cologne*, and the cathedral there claimed their relics. They are commemorated on 2, 3, and 4 January, and particularly at the Feast of the EPIPHANY.

Magisterium. The historic teaching of the ROMAN CATHOLIC CHURCH.

Maglorius (or Maelor), St (d. *c.* 575, f.d. 24 October). Educated under St ILLTYD, he joined St SAMSON in Brittany and founded monasteries, becoming abbot of one at Dol and succeeding St Samson as bishop. It was claimed that he became a hermit in Jersey in his old age.

Magnificat. The hymn of the Virgin (*Luke* i, 46–55) beginning 'My soul doth magnify the Lord' (*Magnificat anima mea Dominum*), used as part of the daily service of the Church since the beginning of the 6th century, and at Evening Prayer in England for over 800 years.
To correct the Magnificat before one has learnt Te Deum. To try to do that for which one has no qualifications; to criticize presumptuously.
To sing the Magnificat at matins. To do things at the wrong time, or out of place. The

Magnificat belongs to VESPERS, not to MATTINS.

Magnus, St (*c.* 1075–1116, f.d. 16 April). An earl and sea-king of Orkney, son of the Viking Erling, co-ruler of the islands; he was converted to Christianity after leading an adventurous life, but was captured by King Magnus Barefoot of Norway and forced to take part in the invasion of the west coast of Britain. At Anglesey he refused to fight, instead remaining on his ship at his devotions. He escaped to Scotland to the court of Malcolm III and was said to have lived in the house of a bishop. He was killed by his cousin Haakon in a political dispute concerning the succession, but was venerated as a martyr. He was ultimately buried in Kirkwall Cathedral, his relics being discovered there in 1919. Miracles were reported, and Magnus became the chief saint of Orkney and North Scotland. It was he who was said to have appeared to Robert Bruce before the battle of Bannockburn, in 1314, to promise him victory. In art he is depicted as in armour or richly robed and carrying an axe or club.

Magog. *See* GOG.

Magor. *See* MACHALUS.

Maid of Kent. *See* HOLY MAID OF KENT *under* HOLY.
Maid of Orleans. JOAN OF ARC.

Maieul, St (906–94, f.d. 11 May). Born at Avignon, he was heir to large estates in Provence, at that time under Saracen domination. He refused the see of Besançon and entered the monastery of Cluny, becoming librarian and bursar, and finally being appointed abbot. With his administrative abilities and notable character he greatly expanded Cluny and reformed other monasteries. He was offered, but refused, the papacy, named St ODILO his successor as abbot and retired to the contemplative life. Hugh Capet requested him to reform the Abbey of St Denis, near Paris, but Maieul died at Souvigny on the way.

Majella, St Gerard. *See under* GERARD.

Major Orders. As distinct from the MINOR ORDERS, the higher, or Major Orders of the Christian Church, are BISHOPS, PRIESTS and DEACONS.

Malabar Christians. A body of Christians in South West India who claim that they were founded by St THOMAS, and are also called 'Thomas Christians', but there is no evidence of their existence before the 6th century.

Malachy O'More, St (1094–1148, f.d. 3

November). Of noble Irish family, he was educated at Armagh where he became first a deacon, then a priest. He did much to reform the church in Ireland, pioneering the GREGORIAN reform, restoring the canon law, the rites of marriage, confirmation and confession, introducing Roman ceremonies in the liturgy and establishing the Order of Augustinian CANONS. He was appointed bishop of Connor and Down and rebuilt the neglected abbey of Bangor, Co. Down. He was nominated archbishop of Armagh, but encountered much opposition from the local chieftains. After restoring peace he resigned Armagh to the rule of the abbot of Derry, and in 1139 left for ROME to apply for the Pallia for Armagh and Cashel. He met St BERNARD at Clairvaux on his outward journey and again on his return, dying there in his arms. St Bernard said of him: 'His first and greatest miracle was himself. His inward beauty, strength and purity are proved in his life.' Malachy was buried at Clairvaux and was the object of a considerable cult there. The *Prophecies of St Malachy*, concerning the papacy from 1143 to the end of the world, are a forgery, published in 1595.

Malchus, St (d. *c*. 390, f.d. 21 October (West), 20, 26 March, 16 April (East)). The son of a wealthy family of Nisibis in Mesopotamia, he refused to marry and became a hermit in the desert. He decided to return home at his father's death to console his mother, but was captured by Bedouins, together with a young woman. The captors insisted that the two should marry, since a single man was considered incomplete, but Malchus had made monastic vows and the girl was already married, so they consented to live together in appearance only. After a time they planned to escape, he to his religious life, she to her husband. They took food and goat-skins, using the skins to cross the Euphrates, and hid in a cave. They were pursued by two Bedouins who were killed by a lioness, leaving their camels which were used by Malchus and the girl to escape to Edessa. Malchus returned to his desert hermitage but the girl did not find her husband, and so settled nearby. Malchus met St JEROME, who wrote the account of his life.

Malo, Maclouor, Machutus, St (6th–7th cent., f.d. 15 November, 11 July). Said to have been the son of a Welsh prince, he was one of the apostles of Brittany, founding a church at Aleth where now stands Saint-Malo. His work roused the hostility of the chieftains, and he was driven out, but later recalled. Many miracles are told of him. Once, being caught by the tide, the sands rose and formed an island for him, and when a wolf had eaten an ass belonging to a poor woman he made the wolf carry faggots for her.

Malta.
   Knights of Malta, or **Hospitallers of St John of Jerusalem.** *See* HOSPITALLERS.
   Maltese Cross. Made thus: ✠. Originally the badge of the Knights of Malta, formed of four barbed arrow-heads with their points meeting in the centre. In various forms it is the badge of many well-known Orders, etc., as the British Victoria Cross and Order of Merit, and the German Iron Cross. *See* CROSS.

Malvern Conference. Organized by the ANGLICAN Industrial Christian Fellowship, the conference met in 1941 to lay down the basic requirements in industrial life from the viewpoint of modern Christianity. Its conclusions were published in *Social Justice and Economic Reconstruction*.

Mammas, St (d. *c*. 274, f.d. 17 August). A shepherd of Cappadocia in the reign of Aurelian. Little is known of his life but he was greatly venerated in the East as a martyr who was stoned to death at an early age after wild beasts had refused to touch him in the arena.

Mammon. The god of this world. The word in Syriac means riches, and it occurs in the BIBLE (*Matt*. vi, 24; *Luke* xvi, 13): 'Ye cannot serve God and mammon.' Spenser (*Faerie Queene*, II, vii), and Milton, who identifies him with Vulcan or Mulciber (*Paradise Lost*, I, 738–51), both make Mammon the personification of the evils of wealth and miserliness.

> Mammon led them on—
> Mammon the least erected spirit that fell
> From Heaven; for even in Heaven his looks and
>   thoughts
> Were always donward bent; admiring more
> The riches of Heaven's pavement, trodden gold,
> Than aught divine or holy.
>
> MILTON: *Paradise Lost*, I, 678

The Mammon of Unrighteousness. Money; *see Luke* xvi. 9.

Mandaeans. A GNOSTIC sect, also called *Nasoreans* and *Christians of St John* which arose in the 1st or 2nd century and still found near Baghdad. Their teachings were akin to those of the MANICHAEANS, and St JOHN THE BAPTIST featured prominently in their writings. They favoured frequent baptism.

Mandorla. *See* VESICA PISCIS.

Mani, Manes, or **Manichaeus.** The founder of MANICHAEISM, born in Persia (*c*. 215) and prominent in the reign of Shapur or Sapor I (*c*. 241–272). Mani began his teaching *c*. 240 and was put to death in 275.

Manichaeans, or **Manichees.** Followers of

Mani, who taught that the universe is controlled by two antagonistic powers, light or goodness (identified with God), and darkness, chaos, or evil. The system was based on the old Babylonian religion modified by Christian and Persian influences. St AUGUSTINE was for nine years a Manichaean and Manichaeism influenced many Christian heretical sects and was itself denounced as a heresy. One of Mani's claims was that, though Christ had been sent into the world to restore it to light and banish darkness, his APOSTLES had perverted his doctrine, and he, Mani, was sent as the PARACLETE to restore it. Manichaeism survived in Turkestan until the 13th century.

Maniple. A eucharistic vestment, a strip of material about three feet long and three inches wide, worn over the left arm of the priest; it is of the same colour as the stole and is buttoned to the sleeve of the ALB. It is derived from the handkerchief used in earlier times when handling sacred vessels.

Manna. The miraculous food provided for the children of Israel on their journey from Egypt to the HOLY LAND.

> And when the children of Israel saw it, they said to one another, It is manna: for they wist not what it was. And Moses said unto them, This is the bread which the Lord hath given you to eat.
>
> *Exod.* xvi. 15

The word is popularly said to be a corrupt form of *man-hu* (What is this?) but is probably Heb. *man*, a gift, and ultimately the Arab. *mann*, an exudation of the tamarisk.

> And the house of Israel called the name thereof Manna: and it was like coriander seed, white; and the taste of it was like wafers made with honey.
>
> *Exod.* xvi, 31

Manse. The dwelling place of a MINISTER in Scotland, particularly that of a PRESBYTERIAN.

Maranatha (Syriac, the Lord will come—i.e. to execute judgement). A word which, with ANATHEMA, occurs in I *Cor.* xvi, 22, and has been erroneously taken as a form of anathematizing among the Jews; hence used for a terrible curse.

Marcellian and Mark, SS (date unknown, f.d. 18 June). Legendary Roman martyrs, reputedly twins, born into a noble family. Both were deacons who suffered under Maximian Herculeus; they rejected all appeals to recant and so save their lives. They were beheaded and buried at Balbina, their remains being discovered there in 1902. Their cult was confined to local calendars in the revision of 1969.

Marcellinus and Peter, SS (d. 304, f.d. 2 June). Romans martyred under the Diocletian persecution, one being a priest and the other an exorcist. Their cult was considerable, but their history doubtful. Legend says that they were imprisoned, but converted their gaoler and family. They were executed at the Black Wood, which afterwards became the White Wood, and were buried in the catacomb on the Via Lavicina. Constantine built a basilica over the tomb. Miracles were recorded there.

Marcellus the Centurian, St (d. 298, f.d. 30 October). A Roman centurion of the first class who, during the celebrations of the birthdays of the Emperors Maximian and Diocletian, threw off his military belt in front of the legion's standards, saying he served only Jesus Christ and despised the gods of wood and stone who were only deaf and dumb images. He was arrested and imprisoned and, when questioned over his actions, said it was not fitting for a Christian to fight for the armies of the world. He was sentenced to death and beheaded.

Marcellus the Righteous, St (c. 485, f.d. 29 December). Born at Apamea in Syria, he joined the monks of the Eirenion, near Constantinople, becoming abbot. The community was known as the 'Sleepless ones' since they followed the regime of maintaining a rote of ceaseless praise and prayer throughout the whole day and night. Marcellus also instituted a balance of worship with manual work, and strict adherence to the vows of poverty. He attended the Council of CHALCEDON in 451.

Marcionites. An heretical sect founded by Marcion of Sinope in the 2nd century, and largely absorbed by the MANICHAEANS in the late 3rd century. They rejected the God of DEMIURGE of the OLD TESTAMENT as a God of Law, and worshipped only Jesus Christ as the God of Love, whose mission was to overthrow the Demiurge. Much of the NEW TESTAMENT was regarded by them as uncanonical and they had a certain kinship with Gnosticism (*see under* GNOSTICS).

Marcoul (or Marculf), St (d. c. 558, f.d. 1 May, 2 May at Malmesbury). Born into a wealthy family at Bayeux, he was a priest at Coutances where he preached the GOSPEL; he then became a hermit on an island and later founded a monastery at Nazteuil, on the model of the Egyptian hermit monks. St HELIER was one of his disciples. His relics were venerated at Corbeny by the kings of France, at the coronation at Rheims. The saint was invoked against diseases of the skin.

Mardi Gras (Fr., 'fat Tuesday'). SHROVE TUESDAY, the last day of the LENT Carnival in France. At

Paris, a fat ox, crowned with a fillet, used to be paraded through the streets. It was accompanied by mock priests and a band of tin instruments in imitation of a Roman sacrificial procession.

Margaret. St Margaret of Antioch (3rd cent., f.d. 20 July). Virgin martyr, known as St Marina among the Greeks. It is said that Olybrius, governor of Antioch, captivated by her beauty, sought her in marriage but, being rejected, threw her into a dungeon, where the DEVIL came to her in the form of a dragon. She held up the cross and the dragon fled. Sometimes she is delineated as coming from the dragon's mouth, for one legend says that the monster swallowed her, but on her making the sign of the cross he suffered her to quit his maw.

She is the chosen type of female innocence and meekness, represented as a young woman of great beauty, bearing the martyr's palm and crown, or with the dragon as an attribute, sometimes standing upon it. She is the patron saint of the ancient borough of King's Lynn. Her cult was suppressed in the revision of the calendar in 1969.

Margaret of Cortona, St (c. 1247–97, f.d. 22 February). Born at Lavinio in Tuscany of a farming family, she lost her mother at an early age and was ill-treated by her step-mother. She became the mistress of a knight, who had seduced her, and bore him a son. At the death of the knight Margaret became a penitent and attempted to return home but her step-mother rejected her. Two ladies gave her a home where she led a life of extreme mortification in which she also involved her child who was later sent to school at Arezzo, and then entered the FRANCISCAN TERTIARIES. Margaret then devoted herself to good works and founded a community at Cortona. Here, following a revelation, she carried out a mission of attacking vice and calling sinners to repentance, her own life still being one of great austerity and self-inflicted suffering. She had a reputation for miraculous cures. Her body is in the church at Cortona and remains incorrupt. In art she is depicted looking at a corpse, or skull, with a dog at her side.

Margaret of England, St (d. 1192, f.d. 3 February). Invoked as 'Margaret the English-woman', she had an English mother and probably a Hungarian father. She and her mother went on a pilgrimage to the HOLY LAND, where her mother died. Margaret made further pilgrimages to Montserrat and Puy, and then entered the CISTERCIAN nunnery at Sauve Benite, where she died. Miracles were reported at her tomb.

Margaret of Hungary, St (1242–70, f.d. 26 January). Daughter of King Bela IV of Hungary, she was placed in the DOMINICAN convent at Visprem at the age of three. Later she was professed at the nunnery built by her

father on an island in the Danube, having rejected marriage with Ottokar, King of Bohemia. She indulged in extreme penances, mortification and fasting, reducing herself to squalor to identify with the poorest of the poor, and she spent long hours in prayer, during which she saw visions. Her excessive austerities wore her out and she died at the age of twenty-eight. She was canonized in 1943.

Margaret of Scotland, St (c. 1045–93, f.d. 16 November). She was a granddaughter of Edmund Ironside, King of England, daughter of Edward the Atheling and a Hungarian princess, and was a great-niece of St STEPHEN OF HUNGARY. Margaret was brought up mainly in Hungary, in exile from the Danish rule in England. She married King Malcolm III of Scotland and had eight children, four of whom became kings and queens. She devoted herself to the care of the poor, orphans and prisoners of war and was generous in almsgiving. She was also noted for her services to the Church in Scotland and for her learning, piety and religious benefactions. She was canonized in 1250, and was named the patron saint of Scotland in 1673, being the only Scottish saint to have a universal cult in the ROMAN CALENDAR. Her name is also associated with the pilgrims' passage across the Firth of Forth. She died in Edinburgh, soon after Malcolm's death in battle, and was buried beside him at Dunfermline at the abbey she had founded. When Scotland became PROTESTANT their remains were translated to Madrid.

Maria Goretti. See GORETTI.

Marian Cult. There is no evidence of the cult for the first 300 years, the first mention of an invocation of the VIRGIN MARY being that of St GREGORY NAZIANZUS in a sermon preached in Constantinople in 379, in which he tells the story of the Christian virgin, Justinia, and prays to the Virgin Mary to help her maintain her virginity. The cult was approved by the Church at the Council of Ephesus in 431; it was popular rather than ecclesiastical and it was then that Mary became 'The Mother of God'. The first Marian miracles were reported to have occurred in Constantinople during the 440s. The idea of the ASSUMPTION does not appear earlier than the 5th century.

Marian appearances have been reported in the last century and in recent times:

1830. To a nun, Catherine Labouré, at a convent in Paris.
1846. Two children (boy and girl) at La Salette.
1858. Bernadette Soubirous at Lourdes.
1871. At Portmain.
1917. At Fatima in Portugal.
1932. At Beauraing in Belgium.
1933. At Banneux in Belgium.

Marian appearances have been reported in the Ukraine since the Middle Ages, often in association with shrines or springs of healing waters. In more recent times there have been Marian appearances in connexion with the phenomenon of the Dancing Sun. In 1981, at Medjugorje, near Mostar, in the predominantly ORTHODOX CATHOLIC and Muslim enclave, a vision was reported of a young woman who announced herself to be the Virgin Mary, the vision being repeated on successive days in the presence of large crowds who were given exhortations to peace and apocalyptic warnings of evil.

In 1987 visions, lights and warnings were repeated at Hriushiw in the Ukraine.

At some appearances the sun danced, at others the Virgin appeared, or both; miracles were also reported. The places became the centres of pilgrimage. *Cp* DANCING SUN.

Marian Year. The method of reckoning 25 March, the Feast of the ANNUNCIATION, as the first day of the year. This was used until the reform of the CALENDAR in 1752. The beginning of the financial year follows this reckoning; the eleven days added in 1752 make it 5 April.

Marianus and James, SS (d. 259, f.d. 30 April (West), 6 May (East)). A deacon and lector who were martyred at Cirta, later Constantina, in Numidia, during the Valerian persecution. Refusing to recant, they were tortured and imprisoned, during which time they experienced visions. They prophesied disasters, earthquakes, famine and disease carried by flies. They and numerous others were beheaded, arranged in rows by the river Rummel, into which their bodies were thrown. Their 'Acts' are authentic.

Marillac, St Louise de. *See* LOUISE.

Marina, St. *See* MARGARET OF ANTIOCH.

Marinus of Caesarea, St (d. *c.* 260, f.d. 3 March). A wealthy noble who should have become a centurion in the Roman army at Caesarea but was denounced as a Christian by a jealous rival. He was interrogated by a magistrate and given three hours to recant. Theoctenus, bishop of Caesarea, encouraged him to stand fast, telling him to choose between a BIBLE and a sword. Marinus chose the Bible and was executed.

Marists. A ROMAN CATHOLIC order of priests and lay members, devoted to missionary and educational work and nursing the sick, especially in the West Pacific and New Zealand. Founded in France in 1816 by the Abbé Colin as the Society of Mary.

Mark, St (f.d. 25 April). The GOSPEL writer who died in prison *c.* 68 is represented in art as in the prime of life, sometimes habited as a BISHOP, and with a lion at his feet and scroll on which is written, 'Peace be to thee, O Mark, My Evangelist.' He is also represented with a pen in his right hand and in his left the Gospel. His body was translated to Venice in the 9th century and the cathedral dedicated to him. He is patron saint of the city.

St Mark's Eve. An old custom in North-country villages was for people to sit in the church porch on this day (24 April) from 11 p.m. till 1 a.m. for three years running, in order to see on the third year the ghosts of those who were to die that year, pass into the church. In other parts this custom was observed on Midsummer-Eve.

Poor Robin's Almanack for 1770 refers to another superstition:

> On St Mark's Eve, at twelve o'clock,
> The fair maid will watch her smock,
> To find her husband in the dark,
> By praying unto good St Mark.

Keats has an unfinished poem on the subject, and he also refers to it in *Cap and Bells* (lvi).

Mark and Marcellian, SS (d. *c.* 290, f.d. 18 June). Roman martyrs whose remains were found at the catacomb of St Balbina. They were reputed to be twins of high rank and noble birth martyred under the Diocletian persecution. They were said to be Christians who rejected the entreaties of their wives, children and parents to recant and so were beheaded. The sole authenticity for their story comes from the doubtful *Acts of St Sebastian* and their cult was confined to the local calendar in 1969.

Marnock (or Marnan), St (d. *c* 625, f.d. 1 March, 25 October). An Irish monk, a friend of St COLUMBA at Iona, and a Scottish bishop who gave his name to Kilmarnock. His head was kept at Kilmarnock and cures were effected by washing the head every Sunday and giving the water to be drunk by the sick.

Maro, St (d. 433, f.d. 14 February). A Syrian hermit living near Antioch; his reputation for virtue and powers attracted disciples. He was buried near Apamea and Emesa and a monastery was founded at his tomb. He was a friend of St JOHN CHRYSOSTOM and revered by Theodoret. The MARONITES of Lebanon were reputed to have taken their name from him.

Maronites. A UNIAT body, mainly in the Lebanon, in communion with ROME and having their own liturgy. Although probably of 7th-century origin, according to tradition, they arose in the early 5th century as followers of St MARO. They became MONOTHELITES, but recognized Rome's authority in the 12th century.

Marprelate Controversy. The name given to the vituperative pamphlet war between the PURITAN writer 'Martin Marprelate' and the supporters of the established Church. The Marprelate Tracts (1587–9) were scurrilous attacks on the BISHOPS, secretly printed and distributed. They threatened to establish a 'young Martin' in every parish 'to mar a prelate'. The Church commissioned John Lyly, Thomas Nashe and Robert Greene to launch a counter-attack. The tracts led to a Conventicle Act and another against seditious writings and the presumed chief author, John Penry, was caught and hanged in 1593.

Marriage. The sacramental rite which sanctions the union of man and woman as husband and wife. The ROMAN CATHOLIC CHURCH does not permit divorce, although nullity may be granted in certain cases. The ORTHODOX CHURCH has permitted divorce since Byzantine times.

Close seasons for marriage. These were of old, from ADVENT to St Hilary's Day (13 January); SEPTUAGESIMA to LOW SUNDAY; ROGATION SUNDAY to TRINITY SUNDAY. They continued to be upheld in the English Church after the REFORMATION, but lapsed during the Commonwealth.

> Advent marriage doth thee deny,
> But Hilary gives thee liberty.
> Septuagesima says thee nay,
> Eight days from Easter says you may.
> Rogation bids thee to contain,
> But Trinity sets thee free again.

The ROMAN CATHOLIC CHURCH does not allow nuptial MASS during what is left of the 'close season' i.e. between the first Sunday of Advent and the Octave of the EPIPHANY, and from ASH WEDNESDAY to Low Sunday.

Marrow Controversy. A controversy in the CHURCH OF SCOTLAND arising from the General Assembly's condemnation in 1720 of *The Marrow of Modern Divinity*, a book by 'E.F.' which first appeared in 1645 and which was considered to uphold ANTINOMIAN doctrines and too free in its offer of salvation. Who 'E.F.' was is not known.

Marrow-men. The twelve ministers in the MARROW CONTROVERSY who protested against the General Assembly condemnation of the 'Marrow'. Thomas Boston, Ralph and Ebenezer Erskine were prominent among them.

Martha, St. Sister of St LAZARUS and St MARY MAGDALENE; patron saint of good housewives. She is represented in art in homely costume, bearing at her girdle a bunch of keys, and holding a ladle or pot of water in her hand. Like St MARGARET she is accompanied by a dragon bound, for she is said to have destroyed one that ravaged the neighbourhood of Marseilles. She is commemorated on 29 July and is patron of Tarascon.

Martin. Martin I, St (d. 655, f.d. 13 April, formerly 12 November and 10 November at York). Born at Todi in Umbria, he became a deacon, went to Constantinople as NUNCIO, and in 649 was elected pope. He held a LATERAN COUNCIL which condemned the MONOTHELITES and in consequence of which he was deposed by the Emperor Constans II, was confined at Naxos in 653 and the following year sent to Constantinople. He suffered from dysentery, was imprisoned without water to wash and deprived of food, finally being exiled to the Tauric Chersonese where he again suffered neglect, insults and flogging, from which he died. He was the last pope to be venerated as a martyr. In art he is depicted as a pope and holds money.

Martin of Braga, St (*c.* 515–80, f.d. 20 March). Little is known of his early life, and his fame rests on his having introduced communal monasticism in North West Spain, founding the abbey of Dumium. He was first a bishop, then archbishop of Braga; he played an active part in missionary work among the ARIAN Suevians, converting their king. Martin was noted for his writings and for giving accounts of rural superstitions.

St Martin of Bullions. The St SWITHIN of Scotland. His day is 4 July, and the saying is that if it rains then, rain may be expected for forty days.

Martin de Porres, St (1579–1639, f.d. 3 November). Born at Lima in Peru, he was a mulatto, the illegitimate son of a Spanish grandee by an Indian woman. He became a DOMINICAN lay brother, acting as a general factotum, devoting himself to the poor and beggars at the gate of the friary and caring for stray animals. He was also a skilled negotiator in family and other difficulties and was consulted by people of standing. Supernatural powers were attributed to him and he had a reputation for great sanctity, but his canonization was delayed and did not take place until 1962.

Martin of Tours, St (d. *c.* 400, f.d. 11 November). The patron SAINT of innkeepers and reformed drunkards, usually shown in art as a young mounted soldier dividing his cloak with a beggar; in allusion to the legend that in midwinter, while a military tribune at Amiens, he divided his cloak with a naked beggar who sought alms and that at night Christ appeared to him arrayed in this very garment. This effected his conversion.

He was born of heathen parents in Pannonia but was converted at ROME and became Bishop of Tours in 371, dying at Candes. His feast day is also the day of the Feast of Bacchus; hence his purely accidental patronage and also the phrase Martin Drunk.

St Martin's beads, jewellery, lace, rings, etc. Cheap counterfeit articles. When the old collegiate CHURCH of St Martin's-le-Grand was demolished at the dissolution of the monasteries, hucksters established themselves on the site and carried on a considerable trade in artificial jewellery, and cheap ware generally. Hence the use of the saint's name in this connexion.

> Certain lyght braynes... wyll rather weare a Marten chayne, the pryee of viiid, then they woulde be unchayned.
>
> THOMAS BECON: *Jewel of Joy* (*c.* 1548)

St Martin's bird. The hen-harrier, called *l'oiseau de Saint Martin* in France, because it makes its passage through the country about 11 November (St Martin's day).

St Martin's goose. St Martin's day (11 November) was at one time the great goose feast in France. The legend is that St MARTIN was annoyed by a goose which he ordered to be killed and served up for dinner. Hence, the goose was 'sacrificed' to him on each anniversary. *Cp.* GOOSE FAIR; MICHAELMAS DAY.

St Martin's running footman. The DEVIL, traditionally assigned to St Martin for such duties on a certain occasion.

> How do we know whether St Martin's running footman is not brewing another storm?
>
> RABELAIS: *The Fourth Book: Pantagruel*, ch. xxiii

St Martin's summer. A late spell of fine weather. St Martin's day is 11 November.

Martinmas. The feast of St MARTIN, 11 November. November was the great slaughtering time of the Anglo-Saxons when fodder was exhausted and oxen, sheep and hogs were killed and salted.

Martyr (Gr.) simply means a witness, one who bears testimony; hence one who bears witness to his faith with his blood. In Christianity many of the members of the early church were martyred for refusing to renounce their faith or worship pagan gods; many of the saints were also martyrs.

Martyrology. A history or list of Christian martyrs; originally a calendar naming the martyr, the place of martyrdom and the date of the saint's festival.

Martyrs of Scillian (d. 180, f.d. 17 July). A group of twelve early Christian martyrs of North Africa. They were interrogated by the pro-consul at Carthage. Separatus acted as spokesman for the Christians, who all affirmed their faith. Given thirty days to alter their decisions, they were again examined but refused to recant and were condemned to be beheaded. A BASILICA was built at their tomb, and St AUGUSTINE

preached sermons in their honour.

Mary, the Mother of Christ, is represented in art as follows:

As *the Virgin*, with flowing hair, emblematical of her virginity.

As *Mater Dolorosa*. Somewhat elderly, clad in mourning, head draped, and weeping over the dead body of Christ.

As *Our Lady of Dolours*. Seated, her breast being pierced with seven swords, emblematic of her seven sorrows.

As *Our Lady of Mercy*. With arms extended, spreading out her mantle and gathering sinners beneath it.

As *The glorified Madonna*. Bearing a crown and sceptre, or an orb and CROSS, in rich robes and surrounded by angels.

Her seven joys. The ANNUNCIATION, VISITATION, NATIVITY, EPIPHANY, Finding in the Temple, Resurrection, Ascension.

Her seven sorrows. Simeon's Prophecy, the Flight into Egypt, the loss of the Holy Child, on meeting Our Lord on the way to CALVARY, the Crucifixion, the Taking Down from the CROSS, and the Entombment. Her festival is 8 September.

Mary of Egypt, St (?5th cent., f.d. 2 April, also 9 and 10 April). A courtesan of Alexandria who was converted to Christianity when she decided to join a pilgrimage to the Holy Sepulchre at Jerusalem. She saw a vision of an ICON of the VIRGIN MARY and was told to cross the Jordan. Taking with her three loaves, she went into the desert as a hermit, living on dates and herbs for the rest of her life. Her clothes wore out and she was then covered by her long hair. It was said that St Zosimus, an abbot of Palestine, met her when he was spending LENT in the desert and gave her a cloak; he arranged to meet her the next year to give her communion, but when he came he found her dead. As he had no spade, a lion came and dug a hole where they buried her. In art she is represented as naked, covered by her long hair, and carrying three loaves.

Mary Magdalene, St (f.d. 22 July). Patron SAINT of penitents, being herself the model penitent of GOSPEL story. (*See* MAGDALENE.) In art she is represented either as young and beautiful, with a profusion of hair, and holding a box of ointment, or as a penitent, in a sequestered place, reading before a CROSS or skull.

Mary di Rosa, St (1813–55, f.d. 15 December). Born at Brescia in North Italy, into a wealthy family, she was physically delicate but mentally strong and showed natural piety and care for the poor. From the age of seventeen she undertook work among the girls in factories and hospitals and among the deaf and dumb. She founded 'The Handmaids of Charity of Brescia' to work for the sick and suffering and engaged in nursing during a cholera epidemic. Her society was approved by Pope Pius IX in 1851. She was canonized in 1954.

Marys, The Three. (1st cent., f.d. 25 May). Legend says that MARY MAGDALENE, Mary wife of Cleophas (*John* xix, 25) and Mary Mother of James (*Mark* xv, 40), together with LAZARUS and MARTHA, were exiled from Palestine, placed in a boat without rudder or oars, and set adrift. They arrived at Marseilles and evangelized Provence. Another version adds an Egyptian servant girl, Sara, to the legend, while yet another tradition makes her Sara the Kali, chief of a tribe near the Rhône, who had a vision telling her of the arrival of the Marys. She went to meet them at the shore, but the sea was too rough for a landing, so Sara threw her mantle on the waters; it floated and brought the Marys safely to the shore. This legend is the basis of the festival of Les-Saintes-Maries-de-la-Mer, held by the gypsies, and to which they come from all over Europe, and which combines Christian and gypsy elements. Sara is represented as a dark-skinned person of similar origins to their own. *See also* LAZARUS.

Mass (Lat. *missa*, a dismissal). The EUCHARIST. In the early Church the unbaptized were dismissed before the Eucharist proper began and the remaining congregation were solemnly dismissed at the end. By the 8th century the name *missa* had become transferred to the service as a whole, and the original meaning of the word faded out. The name *Mass* is used by the ROMAN CATHOLIC CHURCH and by Anglo-Catholics in the CHURCH OF ENGLAND.

High Mass, or *Missa solemnis*, in which the celebrant is assisted by a deacon and subdeacon, requires the presence of choir and acolytes. Sung Mass, or *Missa Cantata*, is a simplification in which the celebrant and congregation sing the musical parts of the service, but without the deacon and subdeacon. The plain form of Mass is called Low Mass. A Pontifical High Mass is one celebrated by a BISHOP or higher prelate with very full ritual. A Nuptial Mass follows the marriage service and Requiem Mass is one offered for the dead. There are also other special forms of Mass.

Massacre of the Innocents. The slaughter of the male children of Bethlehem 'from two years old and under' when Jesus was born (*Matt.* ii, 16). This was done at the command of Herod the Great in order to destroy 'the babe' who was destined to become 'King of the Jews'.

Material Sin. An offence which, although wrong in itself or contravening God's law, is not blameworthy if committed in ignorance or under compulsion.

Mathew, Father. Theobald Mathew (1796–1856),

an Irish priest called *The Apostle of Temperance*. His work on behalf of total abstinence was truly remarkable. When the centenary of his death was celebrated in Cork (1956), 60,000 people gathered to honour his memory.

Matilda (or Maud), St (*c*. 895–968, f.d. 14 March). Born at Engern in Westphalia, she married King Henry I, the Fowler, King of Germany and Emperor of the Holy Roman Empire, and was the mother of the Emperor Otto I and St Bruno of Cologne. She was ill-treated by her sons Otto and Henry, who complained of her expenditure on the Church and the poor and she was exiled for a time. Later she returned to a monastery at Nordhausen and was greatly venerated for her character and good works.

Matins. *See* MATTINS.

Matthew. Matthew, St (f.d. 21 September). Is represented in art as (1) an EVANGELIST, old and with a long beard, with an ANGEL generally standing near by dictating his GOSPEL; (2) an APOSTLE, bearing a purse in reference to his being a publican; sometimes carrying a spear, sometimes a carpenter's rule or square. His symbol is an angel or a man's face.

One legend says that St Matthew preached for 15 years in Judaea after the Ascension, and that he carried the Gospel to Ethiopia, where he was murdered.

Matthew Parker's Bible; Matthew's Bible. *See* BIBLE, THE ENGLISH.

Matthias, St. The APOSTLE chosen by lot to take the place left by the traitor Judas Iscariot (*Acts* i, 21–26). The name is a shortened form of *Mattathias*. His day is 14 May (formerly 24 February).

Mattins, or Matins. The BREVIARY office for the night called *Vigiliae* until the 11th century, and originally held at midnight, but in the BENEDICTINE rule at 2 a.m. It is now anticipated and said the previous afternoon or evening. The name was retained in the BOOK OF COMMON PRAYER (1549) for the service of Morning Prayer which was derived from the ancient office. The name was discarded in the book of 1552.

Maughold (Maccaldus or Macul), St (6th cent., f.d. 27 April). An Irish brigand of dissolute life who was said to have been converted by St PATRICK and sent to the Isle of Man as a missionary where he subsequently became bishop. He was reputed to have divided the island into seventeen parishes.

Maul of Monks, The. Thomas Cromwell (1485–1540), VICAR-GENERAL (1535) who arranged for the visitation of the English monasteries and their subsequent dissolution.

Maundy Thursday. The day before GOOD FRIDAY is so called from the first words of the antiphon for that day being *Mandatum novum do vobis*, a new commandment I give unto you (*St John* xiii, 34), with which the ceremony of the washing of the feet begins. This is still carried out in Roman Catholic cathedrals and monasteries. It became the custom of popes, Catholic sovereigns, prelates, and priests to wash the feet of poor people. In England the sovereign did the same as late as the reign of James II. The word has been incorrectly derived from *maund* (a basket), because on the day before the great fast it was an ancient church custom to bring out food in maunds to distribute to the poor.
The Royal Maunds, or **Maundy Money.** Gifts in money given by the sovereign on MAUNDY THURSDAY to the number of aged poor men and women that corresponds with her (his) age. Broadcloth, fish, bread and wine were given in the reign of Elizabeth I, later clothing and provisions. The clothing was replaced by money in 1725 and the provisions in 1837. In due course the ceremony was transferred from the chapel at Whitehall to Westminster Abbey. Personal distribution of the doles ceased in 1688 until George V restarted it in 1932, as did Edward VIII in 1936. Queen Elizabeth II has made a personal distribution in most years since 1953 and the ceremony is no longer held at Westminster every year. Thus the 1979 service attended by the Queen and Prince Philip was held in Winchester Cathedral. The money is specially struck in silver pennies, twopennies, threepences, and fourpences and is unaffected by decimalization.

Maurice and Companions, SS (d. *c.* 287, f.d. 22 September). A popular legend in the West is that of a Theban legion in the army of the Emperor Maximian in Gaul, consisting of Christians recruited in Egypt, being put to death for refusing to sacrifice to the gods for success in battle. Tradition says that at Martigny, in Switzerland, the entire legion, with Maurice as their leader, was massacred, the numbers being given as some 6,600 or 6,666. Their cult became popular in the West. In art Maurice is depicted as a negro soldier; he is patron of soldiers, weavers and dyers. Eight churches were dedicated to him in England. The cult was confined to local calendars in the revision of 1969.

Maurists. A community of French BENEDICTINE monks, founded in 1621 at St Maur-sur-Loire, which later had its chief house in Paris where the Maurist Fathers produced scholarly editions of the CHRISTIAN FATHERS and Benedictine Chronicles. The congregation was suppressed at the Revolution and the Superior and forty monks died on the guillotine.

Mawes (or Maudez), St (5th cent., f.d. 18 November). Associated with St BUDOC, he went from Wales to Cornwall, settling near the mouth of the Fal and giving his name to the fishing village there, founding a monastery and miraculously producing a fountain. He went over to Brittany, the chief centre of his cult, and founded a monastery. Many marvels are told of him; he carried coals in his lap and the Black Rocks by Pendennis Point were hurled by him at a seal. He was noted as a teacher and is invoked against headaches, snake-bites and worms.

Maximillian, St (d. 295, f.d. 12 March). Son of a Roman veteran, he refused to join the army at a time when men were being recruited for the third Augustan Legion; as the son of a veteran he could not refuse to serve, but he rejected the new clothes and military badge issued, saying he was a soldier of Christ and already wore his saving sign. When told he would die, he said: 'I shall not perish, my soul shall live with Christ my Lord.' He was beheaded and his body was taken to Carthage and buried there by a devout Christian woman called Pompeiana.

Maximus the Confessor, St (*c.* 580–662, f.d. 13 August). Born into a noble family of Constantinople, he became a noted theologian and philosopher and was appointed secretary to the Emperor Heraclitus. In 649 he played a leading part in the LATERAN COUNCIL which condemned MONOTHELITISM (which taught that Christ had only one nature or will, the divine). In this he was supported by Pope MARTIN I and was opposed by the Emperor Constans who had Martin exiled and Maximus imprisoned. It was said that Maximus was scourged and had his tongue and right hand cut off, and that he died soon after. He is regarded as the most important of the ORTHODOX theologians and is known as the Father of Byzantine Theology. His notable and mystical writings still survive, the chief being the *Mystagogy*. Tradition says that a supernatural light appeared at his tomb at night.
Maximus of Turin, St (*c.* 350–415, f.d. 25 June). The first bishop of Turin; little is known of his life but that he held a council of Gaulish bishops at Turin in 398. He was a noted evangelist, propagating Christianity against the prevalent paganism, and was famous for his sermons, many of which still survive.

Mayeul (or Maiolus), St (*c.* 906–94, f.d. 11 May). Born at Avignon, he was made archdeacon of Mâcon at an early age but, when there was a probability that he would be appointed to a bishopric, he retired to the monastery at Cluny. The abbot chose him as his assistant and later Mayeul became abbot, greatly extending the Cluniac influence. Although of a commanding presence he was humble and retiring and when the Emperors Otto I and II wished him to become Pope he refused. He died on his way to the abbey of St DENYS in Paris where he was travelling at the request of King Hugh Capet.

Mayne, St Cuthbert (c. 1543–77, f.d. 25 October). Born at Youlston, North Devon, and educated at Barnstaple Grammar School and Oxford, he was given a living at the age of seventeen, through the influence of an uncle, and was ordained into the CHURCH OF ENGLAND. At Oxford he came under the influence of Edmund CAMPION, was converted to CATHOLICISM and went to the ENGLISH COLLEGE at DOUAI in 1573. He was ordained priest and became a Bachelor of Theology. He returned to England and joined the Catholic household of Francis Tregian, but in 1577 was arrested with others, accused of being a priest and refusing to acknowledge the Queen as supreme head of the Church. In spite of division among the judges, he was condemned and executed as an example to papists. He was the first seminary priest of the period of Elizabethan persecution to die for his faith. He was canonized in 1970 as one of the FORTY MARTYRS OF ENGLAND AND WALES.

Mazarin Bible. See BIBLE, SOME SPECIALLY NAMED EDITIONS.

Mazzarello, St Maria-Domenica (1837–81, f.d. 14 May). Born into a large farming family at Mornese, Piedmont, she was engaged in farm labour until she contracted typhoid when nursing relatives. This left her physically weak, and she turned to dressmaking and joined a local religious confraternity. She met St JOHN BOSCO who, having founded the SALESIAN Order, was attempting to found a boys' school at Mornese. He proposed that Maria should found a similar school for girls; and this was the beginning of the SALESIAN sisters of which Maria became superior-general. Although limited in education herself, she was efficient in organization. Later she sent nuns to South America to found a house in Argentina. Her work spread widely into fifty-four countries. Her body was enshrined in Turin beside that of Bosco. She was canonized in 1951.

Mecitarists. A congregation of BENEDICTINE monks named after their founder Abbot Peter Melchitar (1676–1749) who established them in Armenia but eventually moved to the island of St Lazzaro at Venice. They are also known as the UNIATES.

Medana, St. See MODWENNA.

Médard, St (6th cent., f.d. 8 June). The French St SWITHIN.

> Quand il pleut à la Saint-Médard
> Il pleut quarante jours plus tard.

He was bishop of Noyon and Tournai, and founded the Festival of the Rose at Salency, in which the most virtuous girl in the parish receives a crown of roses and a purse of money. Legend says that a sudden shower once fell which soaked everyone except St Médard who remained dry as toast, for an EAGLE had spread its wings over him, and ever after he was termed *maître de la pluie*. He was invoked against toothache.

Meditation. In Christianity a spiritual exercise of prayer or reflection on religious subjects or themes to attain spiritual insight.

Meen (Maine or Mewan), St (6th cent., f.d. 21 June). Born in South Wales, he followed St SAMSON to Brittany, through Cornwall, where he is patron of St Mewan. He was accompanied by St AUSTELL in Brittany, and together they founded churches and a monastery in the forest of Broceliande and another called Saint-Méen where there was a shrine which drew pilgrims from all over France. The saint lived to a great age.

Meinrad, St. Born in Swabia, he became a monk and priest at the BENEDICTINE abbey of Reichenau in Switzerland, later going to Einsiedeln as a hermit, living an austere life. He was bludgeoned to death by robbers who, although he had received them courteously, thought he had a hidden treasure. His body was enshrined at Reichenau and his cell was occupied by a succession of hermits. In the 10th century a Benedictine monastery was established at Einsiedeln, where it still stands.

Melaine (Melanius or Mellion), St (d. c. 535, f.d. 6 November, 6 January). Patron saint of Mullion and St Mellyan in Cornwall, he was a Breton by birth and followed St AMAND as bishop of Rennes. He was adviser to Clovis and carried out a campaign against paganism. Melaine had a considerable cult in Brittany, and the abby of St Melaine was built over his tomb. A letter of his, still extant, rebukes Breton priests and exhorts them to cease 'wandering from cabin to cabin, celebrating MASS on portable altars, accompanied by women who administer the chalice to the faithful'.

Melanchthon is the Greek name by which Philipp Schwarzerd (black earth), the German reformer (1497–1560), was called. Similarly

Oecolampadius is the Greek version of the German name *Hauschein*, and *Desiderius Erasmus* is one Latin and one Greek rendering of the name *Gheraerd Gheraerd*.

Melania the Younger, St (*c*. 383–439, f.d. 31 December). Daughter of a wealthy Roman patrician, she was married against her will to Valerius Pinianus. Her devotional and austere life were at first unacceptable to the family but they were finally reconciled and agreed to the sale of property to benefit the Church and the poor, and to the emancipation of slaves. She and her husband fled to Thagaste, in Africa, during the Visigoth invasion, she having estates there. Later they went to Palestine and Melania remained there after the death of her husband, founding a women's community on OLIVET. She led a life of prayer and good works and copying books. She was known to and respected by SS JEROME, AUGUSTINE and PAULINUS OF NOLA. She was the paternal granddaughter of St Melania the Elder, a widow who left ROME for Palestine where she also worked with St Jerome.

Melchites, or **Melkites.** Members of the Eastern ORTHODOX CHURCH in Syria and Egypt who accepted the decrees against MONOPHYSITE and NESTORIAN doctrines laid down by the Council of CHALCEDON in 415. They included the patriarchates of Alexandria, Jerusalem and Antioch. Their name derives from the charge that the Council was dominated by the Emperor Marcian. The name also applies to those following the Byzantine rite, both Orthodox and UNIAT, using mainly Arabic in the liturgy.

Mellifluous Doctor. St BERNARD of Clairvaux (1091–1153), the *Oracle of the Church*, whose writings were called a 'river of Paradise'. *See* DOCTORS OF LEARNING.

Mellitus, St (d. 624, f.d. 24 April). A member of the second group of missionaries sent to England in 601 by GREGORY THE GREAT to assist St AUGUSTINE. Mellitus became the first bishop of London and founded St Paul's on the site of an ancient temple of Diana, following Gregory's famous letter of instructions telling the Christians not to destroy pagan temples and rites but to adapt them to Christian usage. A pagan revolt and his refusing holy communion to the apostate sons of King Sigebert, forced Mellitus and JUSTUS to flee to Gaul, but they returned later and Mellitus became archbishop of Canterbury.

Melor (Mylor or **Melorius), St** (date unknown, f.d. 1 October). Said to have been the son of a king of Cornwall and to have been murdered as a child by his uncle Rivold who, at first deterred from actual murder, cut off the child's right hand and left foot. The child was then sent to a remote monastery; the hand and foot were replaced by a silver hand and brazen foot, and both artificial limbs grew to work as if natural. Rivold then ordered his guardian to kill Melor, who was beheaded, but Rivold touched the head and died three days later. The child's body and relics were preserved at Amesbury, and churches in Brittany, Dorset, Devon and Cornwall were dedicated to him. Many legends were attached to his name and he was reputed to have elicited fountains.

Menas (or **Mennas**), **St** (d. *c*. 300, f.d. 11 November). Regarded as one of the most famous of Egyptian saints, he was born in Egypt and martyred there for his faith under Diocletian. Menas was said to be an Egyptian soldier in the Roman army. His body was brought back to Egypt and enshrined near Alexandria and became an important centre of pilgrimage. Terracotta phials or ampullae of water from his well were taken away by the pilgrims. In modern times excavations have unearthed a complex of buildings, including a church, monastery and baths, at the site and in World War II the victory of El Alamein, in 1945, and the saving of Egypt was attributed by Christians to his intercession. In art he is represented as accompanied by a pair of camels; he is patron saint of merchants and caravans in the desert. In the revision of the calendar in 1969 his cult was confined to local festivals.

Mendicant Orders, or **Begging Friars.** The orders of the FRANCISCANS (Grey Friars), DOMINICANS (Black Friars), AUGUSTINIANS (Austin Friars), CARMELITES (White Friars), SERVITES, and other lesser orders.

Mennonites. Followers of Simon Menno (1492–1561), a parish priest of Friesland, who joined the Anabaptists in 1536. They still exist in Holland, Germany, and America and some other places. They reject church organization, infant baptism, and usually military service and the holding of public office.

Menology, or **Menologion.** An annotated calendar of the Eastern ORTHODOX CHURCH, containing notes on the lives of the saints and martyrs, arranged in the order of commemoration dates in the ecclesiastical year.

Mercedarian Order (The Order of Our Lady of Ransom). Also called Nolascans after St PETER NOLASCO, who in 1234 founded the order for the purpose of rescuing and ransoming slaves from the Moors, offering themselves as hostages. The confraternity followed the Rule of St

AUGUSTINE and was approved by Pope GREGORY IX in 1235. They also tended the sick.

Mercurius, St (d. *c.* 250, f.d. 25 November). Said to have been a Scythian soldier in the Roman army whose valour won the favour of the Emperor Decius. However, when he refused, as a Christian, to sacrifice to Artemis, he was tortured then sent to his home in Cappadocia and executed at Caesarea where he was venerated as a martyr. During torture he received angelic visions. He is numbered among the 'warrior' saints.

Mercurius and Companions, SS (d. *c.* 300, f.d. 10 December). A group of soldiers deputed to take Christian prisoners to the place of execution at Leontium, in Sicily. The behaviour of the Christians so impressed the soldiers that they were converted and were then beheaded with the prisoners.

Mercy. The seven corporal works of mercy are: (1) To tend the sick; (2) To feed the hungry; (3) To give drink to the thirsty; (4) To clothe the naked; (5) To harbour the stranger; (6) To minister to prisoners; (7) To bury the dead (*see Matt.* xxv, 35–45).
The seven spiritual works of mercy are: (1) To convert the sinner; (2) To instruct the ignorant; (3) To counsel those in doubt; (4) To comfort those in sorrow; (5) To bear wrongs patiently; (6) To forgive injuries; (7) To pray for the living and the dead.

Merewenna (or **Merwinna**), **St** (10th cent., f.d. 29 October, 10 February). The first abbess of the convent at Romsey, refounded by King Edgar; it prospered under Merewenna's rule. St Ethelfleda was one of her disciples and princesses joined the nunnery. SS Merewenna and Ethelfleda were buried near each other in the abbey church.

Meriadoc (or **Meriasek**), **St** (6th cent., f.d. 3, 7, or 9 June). Although nothing is known of his history, he is of literary interest as the hero of the mediaeval miracle play, written in the vernacular, *Buenaus Meriasek*. Possibly of Welsh birth, he was said to have founded a church in Cornwall before going to Brittany where he became a bishop at Vannes. His feast is kept in Breton dioceses on 7 June; elsewhere it is given as 3 or 9 June.

Merryn, St (date unknown, f.d. 4 April, 7 July in Cornwall). Probably confused with the legendary St Marina, both were said to be women, living in disguise as monks and even supposed to have been accused falsely of fathering a child. Patron saint of St Merryn in Cornwall.

Mesrob (or **Mesrop**), **St** (*c.* 354–439, f.d. 19 February, 25 November). One of the most noted of the churchmen of the Eastern Church, he was known as 'the Teacher'. He laboured as a missionary in Armenia and, with St ISAAC THE GREAT, was responsible for the expansion of the Armenian Church and the development of an Armenian alphabet, liturgy and a version of the NEW TESTAMENT and a Book of Proverbs. He organized schools and encouraged learning. He was a native of the Armenian province of Taron; he became a bishop and later succeeded the Patriarch Sahak.

Messiah (Heb. *mashiach*, one anointed). It is the title of the expected leader of the Jews who shall deliver the nation from its enemies and reign in permanent triumph and peace. Equivalent to the Greek word Christ, it is applied by Christians to Jesus.

Methodists. A name given (1729) to the members of Charles Wesley's HOLY CLUB at Oxford, from the methodical way in which they observed their principles. They were originally members of the CHURCH OF ENGLAND and the separatist Methodist Church was not established until after John Wesley's death (1791). The movement was itself soon faced with secessions, the first being the Methodist New Connexion (1797), followed by the Independent Methodists (1805), Primitive Methodists (1810), the Bible Christians (1815), the Wesleyan Methodist Association (1835), and the Wesleyan Reformers (1849). Reunion began in 1857 with the formation of the United Methodist Free Church and was completed with the formation of the Methodist Church of Great Britain in 1932. Methodism was introduced into the USA in the 1760s and grew steadily in importance.

The name was at one time applied to the JESUITS, because they were the first to give systematic representations of the method of polemics.

Since 1965 the Church of England and the Methodist Church have been seeking reconciliation.

Methodius, St. *See* CYRIL AND METHODIUS.
Methodius of Constantinople, St (d. 847, f.d. 14 June). Also known as the Confessor, he was a Syracusian holding an important place in the history of the second ICONOCLASTIC persecution under Michael the Stammerer. Methodius was imprisoned for nine years and was scourged and tortured. He was released on the accession of the Empress Theodora and was appointed Patriarch of Constantinople. He reinstituted the veneration of ICONS. He also inaugurated the festival of Orthodoxy which still takes place in Byzantine churches on the first Sunday of LENT. He founded a monastery on the island of Chios.

Methodius was noted as a writer, particularly of hymns, though none survives.

Methodius of Olympus, St (4th cent., f.d. 18 September). Little is known of his life except that he was a bishop in Asia Minor, nor is 'Olympus' known as a see. His fame rests on his writings, the chief of which is *The Symposium or Banquet of the Ten Virgins*, written in the style of Plato's *Symposium* and extolling the values of virginity. It has survived and was translated into English in 1958.

Methuselah. Old as Methuselah. Very old indeed, almost incredibly old. He is the oldest man mentioned in the BIBLE, where we are told (*Gen.* v, 27) that he died at the age of 969.

Metropolitan. A BISHOP who controls a province and its SUFFRAGANS. The two metropolitans of England are the archbishops of Canterbury and York, and in Ireland the archbishops of Armagh and Dublin. The Archbishop of Canterbury is *metropolitanus et primus totius Angliae*, and the Archbishop of York *primus et metropolitanus Angliae*. In the early Church the bishop of the civil metropolis (mother city) was usually given rights over the other bishops (suffragans) of the province. In the GREEK CHURCH a metropolitan ranks next below a PATRIARCH and next above an archbishop.

Mewan, St. *See* MEEN.

Michael, St. The ARCHANGEL. The great prince of all the ANGELS and leader of the celestial armies.

Go, Michael, of celestial armies prince,
And thou, in military prowess next,
Gabriel; lead forth to battle these my sons
Invincible; lead forth my armed saints
By thousands and by millions ranged for fight.
MILTON: *Paradise Lost*, VI, 44

His day (St Michael and All Angels) is 29 September (*see* MICHAELMAS DAY). He appears in the BIBLE in *Dan.* x, 13, and xii, 1; *Jude*, verse 9; and *Rev.* xii, 7–9, where he and his angels fight the dragon. His cult was popular in the Middle Ages and he was also looked on as the presiding spirit of the planet Mercury, and bringer to man of the gift of prudence.

In art St Michael is depicted as a beautiful young man with severe countenance, winged, and clad in either white or armour, bearing a lance and shield, with which he combats a dragon. In the final judgment he is represented with scales, in which he weighs the souls of the risen dead.

Michaelmas Day, 29 September, the Festival of St MICHAEL and all Angels, one of the QUARTER DAYS when rents are due and the day when magistrates are chosen.

The custom of eating goose at Michaelmas (*see also* St MARTIN'S GOOSE) is very old and is probably due to geese being plentiful and in good condition at this season. We are told that tenants formerly presented their landlords with one to keep in their good graces. The popular story is that Queen Elizabeth I, on her way to Tilbury Fort on 29 September 1588, dined with Sir Neville Umfreyville, and partook of geese, afterwards calling for a bumper of Burgundy, and giving as a toast 'Death to the Spanish Armada!' Scarcely had she spoken when a messenger announced the destruction of the fleet by a storm. The Queen demanded a second bumper, and said, 'Henceforth shall a goose commemorate this great victory.' The tale is marred by the fact that the Armada was dispersed by winds in July and the thanksgiving sermon for victory was preached at St Paul's on 20 August.

George Gascoigne, the poet, who died in 1577, refers to the custom of goose-eating at Michaelmas:

At Christmas a capon, at Michaelmas, a goose.
And somewhat else at New Yere's tide for feare the lease flies loose.

Mid-Lent Sunday. The fourth Sunday in LENT. It is called *dominica refectionis* (Refreshment Sunday) because the first lesson is the banquet given by Joseph to his brethren, and the GOSPEL of the day is the miraculous feeding of the five thousand. It is the day on which SIMNEL CAKES are eaten and it is also called MOTHERING SUNDAY.

Miki, St. *See* JAPAN, MARTYRS OF.

Milburga (or Milburgh), St (d. 715, f.d. 23 February, 25 June). Daughter of Merewold, King of Mercia, and of St ERMENBURGA of Kent, and sister of SS MILDRED and MILDGYTH, she founded a monastery for virgins at Wenlock and later was consecrated abbess. She led an exemplary life, was of an attractive character, and was credited with many miracles, among them restoring a child to life after it had been seen to have died, healing lepers and the blind and having power over birds and animals. Miracles were also reported at her tomb.

Mildgyth (or Mildgytha), St (7th cent., f.d. 17 January). Younger sister to SS MILBURGA and MILDRED, the Holy Virgins of Thanet, daughters of the King of Mercia and St ERMENBURGA, princess of Kent. Little is known of her, one tradition saying that she was a nun in Northumbria, another that she died a nun and abbess of the monastery of Eastry, in Thanet.

Mildred of Thanet, St (d. *c*. 700, f.d. 13 July). Daughter of Merewold, King of Mercia and St ERMENBURGA, princess of Kent, and sister of SS

MILBURGA and MILDGYTH, she was educated at a nunnery at Chelles, near Paris. Refusing to marry, she returned to England and entered a convent at Minster-in-Thanet where she succeeded her mother as abbess. She was of tranquil temperament, kind and generous to the poor, particularly widows and children, and was one of the most popular saints of mediaeval England. A pilgrimage is made to her shrine where her relics are venerated at Minster, and her nunnery is one of the oldest inhabited buildings in the country. In art Matilda is represented in BENEDICTINE habit, accompanied by a white hart.

Millenary Petition. An appeal to James I in 1603 from some, 1000 PURITAN clergy asking for certain changes in liturgy and worship, and for the prevention of pluralities and non-residence of clergy, etc. Their requests included the discontinuance of the sign of the CROSS in baptism, of the RING in marriage, and of Confirmation; also optional use of the cap and surplice, more scope for preaching, simplification of music, etc. As a result James summoned the HAMPTON COURT CONFERENCE.

Millennium. A thousand years (Lat. *mille, annus*). In *Rev.* xx, 2, it is said that an angel bound SATAN a thousand years, and in verse 4 we are told of certain martyrs who will come to life again who 'lived and reigned with Christ a thousand years'. 'This', says St JOHN, 'is the first resurrection'; and this is what is meant by the millennium—the period of a thousand years during which Christ will return to earth and live with His saints, and finally take them to heaven.
Millenarians, or **Chiliasts** (Lat. *mille,* Gr. *chilioi,* a thousand) is the name applied to early Christian sects who believed in a future MILLENNIUM. Such views were held by some post-REFORMATION sects and by some of the 17th-century Independents in England, and more recently by MORMONS, IRVINGITES, and ADVENTISTS.
Millennial Church. *See* SHAKERS.

Millerites. Followers of William Miller of Massachusetts (1782–1849). *See* SEVENTH-DAY ADVENTISTS.

Miltiades, St (d. 314, f.d. 10 December). Although little is known about the man, his papacy was notable for the Emperor Constantine's decree of religious tolerance and the end of the times of persecution, particularly of the Christians. Miltiades was pope from 311 to 314 and died a natural death in Rome, but he was canonized as a martyr on account of having suffered under Maximian persecution. He was said by St AUGUSTINE to be a man of peace and moderation.

His cult was limited to local calendars in the reform of 1969.

Minims (Lat. *Fratres Minimi,* least of the brethren). A term of self-abasement assumed by a mendicant order founded by St Francis of Paula in 1453. They went barefooted, and wore a coarse black woollen stuff, which they never took off, day or night. The FRANCISCANS had already adopted the title of *Fratres Minores* (inferior brothers). The superior of the minims is called *corrector.*

Minister. Literally, an inferior person, in opposition to *magister,* a superior. One is connected with the Lat. *minus,* and the other with *magis.* Our Lord says, 'Whosoever will be great among you, let him be your minister', where the antithesis is well preserved. Gibbon has:

a multitude of cooks, and inferior ministers, employed in the service of the kitchen.
Decline and Fall, ch. xxi

The minister of a church is one who serves the parish or congregation; and a minister of the crown is the sovereign's or state's servant.
Florimond de Remond, speaking of Albert Babinot, one of the disciples of Calvin, says, 'He was student of the *Institutes,* read at the hall of the Equity school in Poitiers, and was called *la Ministerie.*' Calvin, in allusion thereto, used to call him 'Mr Minister', whence not only Babinot but all the other clergy of the Calvinistic Church were called *ministers.*

Minor Orders. In the Western Church, below MAJOR ORDERS, come ACOLYTES, DOOR-KEEPERS, EXORCISTS and LECTORS; now called 'ministeria'. Door-keepers and exorcists are no longer included.

Minoresses. *See* CLARE, ORDER OF ST.

Minorites, or **Minors.** *See* FRANCISCANS.

Minster. A large church or CATHEDRAL to which a monastery or fraternity was attached, such as Westminster. However this is not invariable, as York Minster had no monastic origin. The term is a shortened form of 'monastery'.

Minver (or Menefreda), St (date uncertain, probably 6th cent., f.d. 23 or 24 November). Said to be a relation of St BRYCHAN, she probably came from Minwear in South Wales and became a nun at Tredresick in Cornwall. A church and well are named after her near Lundy Hole, and it was here that, while combing her hair by the well, the Devil came to tempt her. He fled when she threw her comb at him. She is the patron saint of Tredresick.

Miracle (Lat. *miraculum*, a marvel). This is traditionally defined as an effect in the physical world which contravenes or transcends any known human agency or natural law, and is therefore attributed to supernatural powers. Before Christianity there were always the unseen forces of the gods; in Christianity miracles are accepted as unique acts of intervention by God in the normal world, or as a means of divine revelation. In the CATHOLIC CHURCH miracles are also ascribed to the VIRGIN MARY and the saints, though the power of the relics of saints to work miracles precedes Christianity in the miraculous account of the dead man being revived by the bones of Elisha (*II Kings* xx–xxi). The miracle of the multiplication of food is seen in the account of Elijah and the widow (*I Kings* vii, 14ff) and (*II Kings* iv, 1ff), and repeated in that of Christ and the Feeding of the Five Thousand. It recurs throughout the history of the saints up to modern times with the curé d'Ars (d. 1859). In hagiography miracles are introduced to enhance the reputation of saints. Many of the events are based on folklore or myths, such as the Irish folklore incorporated in the life of St BRIDGET, and the myths of the Dioscuri in the twin-brother martyrs, miracles often being transferred from one saint to another.

Miracle plays. *See* MYSTERIES.

Mirfield. *See* COMMUNITY OF THE RESURRECTION.

Mirin (Merinus or **Meadhran), St** (7th cent., f.d. 15 September). Said to be a disciple of St COMGALL, he was a monk at Bangor, Co Down, who went to Scotland, founding a monastery at Paisley, where he died and was buried, his shrine becoming a place of pilgrimage. Inch Murryn, the largest island on Loch Lomond, has the ruins of his chapel.

Miserere. The fifty-first psalm is so called because its opening words are *Miserere mei, Deus* (Have mercy upon me, O God. *See* NECK VERSE). One of the evening services of LENT is called *miserere*, because this penitential psalm is sung, after which a sermon is given. The under side of a folding seat in choirstalls is called a *miserere*, or more properly, a **misericord**; when turned up it forms a ledge-seat sufficient to rest the aged in a standing position. A shorter dagger used by knights to end the agony of a wounded man was also known as a *misericord* (Lat. *misereri*, to have pity; *cor cordis* heart).

Missal (Lat. *liber missalis*, book of the mass). The book containing the liturgy of the MASS with ceremonial instructions as used in the ROMAN CATHOLIC CHURCH. *See* BREVIARY.

Missionary Movements. The term 'missionary' is applied to a person sent to a foreign country to spread a religion. Christianity has been one of the proselytizing religions from the days of the APOSTLES who followed Christ's charge: 'Go ye therefore, and make disciples of all nations, baptizing them into the name of the Father and of the Son and of the Holy Ghost' (*Matt.* xxviii, 19). At PENTECOST they were promised the power to become witnesses. The earliest activities, over the first five centuries, following the Apostles and PAUL, took Christianity to Britain and the borders of the Roman Empire, to Armenia, Syria, Antioch, Crete, Cyprus, Ethiopia and parts of Africa and the East. The Middle Ages saw the journeys of St FRANCIS OF ASSISI into Islam; the notable Celtic activity; the spread of missions in Europe, the Low Countries, Germany, Scandinavia, Greenland and Iceland; while the Eastern Church expanded into the Slavonic world and to the Balkans, which were evangelized from Constantinople. The travels of Marco Polo, accompanied by two DOMINICANS, took Christianity to the Far East, continuing the work of the earlier NESTORIANS.

Missionaries also followed the trade routes and voyages of discovery, such as the passage to India, the rounding of the Cape of Good Hope and the discovery of the American Continent, with Spanish and Portuguese settlements spreading the Church's influence. The founding of the SOCIETY OF JESUS, in 1543 gave rise to missionary work by a body of dedicated propagandists, such as Robert de Nobili in India, Matteo Ricci in China and the great pioneer missions of St FRANCIS XAVIER, reaching South India, Ceylon, the East Indies, China and Japan. They not only preached the GOSPEL, but fought against the scandalous exploitation of the native people by the traders.

The PROTESTANT movement in Britain began seriously in the 18th century with the SOCIETY FOR PROMOTING CHRISTIAN KNOWLEDGE in 1701, the English BAPTISTS in 1792, the LONDON MISSIONARY SOCIETY (predominantly CONGREGATIONALIST) in 1795, the CHURCH MISSIONARY SOCIETY (CHURCH OF ENGLAND) in 1799, the WESLEYAN METHODIST MISSION in 1813 and the CHINA INLAND Mission (interdenominational) in 1853, and various other societies. On the Continent, King Frederick IV of Denmark founded a mission to India in 1705 and the MORAVIANS began a widespread missionary movement. The final years of the century were marked by the foundation of several other societies, as well as the enterprises of individuals such as Dr David Livingstone. The 19th century flowering of missions worldwide was followed by Communist repression and consequent withdrawal, but at the same time, in the 20th century there was the birth of the OECUMENICAL (Gr. *oikumena*, worldwide) MOVEMENT. In 1910 the World Missionary conference met in Edinburgh to study the missionary situation in the world and 'to win the world for Christ in this generation' and in 1921 the International Missionary Conference met at Geneva; these conferences marked the beginning of the ecumenical approach of the WORLD COUNCIL OF CHURCHES.

Mitre (Gr. and Lat. *mitra*, a headband, turban). The episcopal mitre is supposed to symbolize the cloven tongues of fire which descended on the apostles on the day of PENTECOST (*Acts* ii, 1–12).

Mochta (Mochuta or **Mochteus), St** (5th cent., f.d. 19 August). Probably of British origin, he was said to have been a disciple of St PATRICK and to have gone to Rome, where he was made a bishop. He returned to Ireland and founded a monastery at Louth, becoming the first bishop of the diocese. Legends associated with him are that St Patrick had an understanding with him that each would be responsible for the other's community after the founder's death; also that, because he had doubted the accounts of the ages of the OLD TESTAMENT prophets, Mochta had to live for 300 years. He is the subject of numerous fabulous miracle stories.

Mock of the Church. When BANNS OF MARRIAGE are called and none takes place. Formerly the churchwardens often fined the offenders.

Modalism, or **Sabellianism.** A 3rd-century heresy maintaining that the three persons of the TRINITY are merely different manifestations of the one Godhead.

Moderator. The president of an assembly, synod or kirk session, especially in the PRESBYTERIAN and CONGREGATIONAL CHURCHES.

Modernism. A movement in the ROMAN CATHOLIC CHURCH which sought to interpret the ancient teachings of the Church with due regard to the current teachings of science, modern philosophy, and history. It arose in the late 19th century and was formally condemned by Pope Pius X in 1907 in the encyclical *Pascendi*, which stigmatized it as the 'synthesis of all heresies'.

The term **Modernist** is also applied to liberal and Radical critics of traditional theology in other churches. The Modern Churchmen's Union was founded in 1898 and was strongly critical of Anglo-Catholic and Roman Catholic ideals. Dean Inge (1860–1954) and Bishop Barnes (1874–1953) were prominent among its members.

Modomnoc, St (6th cent., f.d. 13 February). An Irishman of the princely O'Neill family, he was a pupil of St DAVID in Wales. Legend says he introduced bees into Ireland; when he left Wales a swarm settled on his boat and landed with him in Ireland, thus bringing 'the gifted race of Ireland's bees'. He was also said to have become bishop of Ossory.

Modwenna, St (7th cent., f.d. 5 July, 9 November). Born in Ireland, reputedly of a princely house, she was said to have lived as an anchoress in England, near Burton-on-Trent, where her shrine became famous for miracles. She was also supposed to have gone to Scotland and died there; her body was translated to Burton although it was wanted in both Scotland and Ireland. Modwenna has also been identified with other saints in those countries as Medana, Merryn, Monyna and Edana.

Molaisse, St. *See* LASERIAN.

Moling (or Mulligus), St (d. 697, f.d. 17 June). An Irishman who became a monk and founded the monastery of St Mullins, or Teghmoling, Co Carlow, and established a ferry-service over the river Barrow. He was said to have followed St AIDAN as bishop of Ferns and is famed for the *Book of Mulling*, which is extant in a shrine in the library of Trinity College, Dublin.

Molinism. The system of grace and election taught by the Spanish JESUIT, Louis Molina (1535–1600). His doctrine was that grace is a free gift to all, but consent of the will must be present before that grace can be effective. *Cp.* JANSENISTS.

Moluag (Molloch or **Moloc), St** (c. 530–92, f.d. 25 June). A monk of northern Ireland who crossed the sea to Scotland on a stone and then founded a monastery on the island of Lismore, and churches in East Scotland, Skye and the Outer Hebrides. On Lewis his name was invoked against madness. A relic of his, which still survives, is a staff of blackthorn in gilded copper. Moluag died at Rossmarkie, but his shrine was kept at Mortlach.

Monarchianism. Monarchians, Christians of the 2nd and 3rd centuries, maintained the unity (*monarchia*), the monarchy or sole rule, of the Divine Nature. Strictly monotheistic, they argued that the Father *is* the Son, *is* the Holy Ghost. Out of this grew 'Dynamistic Monarchianism', which said that Christ was only a man, becoming the Son of God by being filled with the Divine Essence to an exceptional degree. Moralistic Monarchians asserted that Christ contained the whole Godhead and that Father and Son were two terms for the same Being. This doctrine became the Patripassian Heresy.

Monastery. A house, or group of buildings, for the housing of a religious community.

Monasticism (Gr. *monachos*, alone, solitary). A pattern of religious life of withdrawal from the world into communities of monks or nuns dedicated to the service of God, devotional exercises, contemplation, meditation and ascetic practices, normally under vows of poverty, chastity and obedience. As an institution monasticism is ancient and widespread.

The earliest form of Christian withdrawal from the world was that of the hermits, eremites or anchorites, living in solitary cells in deserts and waste places, its foundation being ascribed to St ANTHONY, in the 3rd century, in Egypt. The first Christian monastic order was founded by St BASIL and still remains in the Eastern ORTHODOX CHURCH; St ATHANASIUS introduced it into the West in 340.

In the 6th century, St BENEDICT established his RULE of both spiritual and manual work in community life, under which monasteries became centres of learning in addition to serving the needs of the people as hostels and hospitals. The movement spread rapidly. In 910 the Cluny foundation introduced a system in which each monastery was subordinate to a 'mother' house.

Many orders were established in the Middle Ages: CISTERCIANS, CARTHUSIANS, AUGUSTINIANS, DOMINICANS, FRANCISCANS and CARMELITES, while the FRIARS combined the corporate life with active work among the populace. There were also CELESTINES and OLIVETANS, and the MENDICANT ORDERS. The CRUSADES gave rise to the military Orders of KNIGHTS HOSPITALLERS, KNIGHTS TEMPLARS and the TEUTONIC KNIGHTS. Later reformed orders were the CAPUCHINS, BAREFOOTED CARMELITES and TRAPPISTS.

The REFORMATION caused a decline in monasticism, but a revival took place in 1540 with the COUNTER REFORMATION and the founding of the JESUITS, the SOCIETY OF JESUS, in which the vows of a monk are taken but the members are sent into the world to preach, teach and do religious works.

Monasticism under the Eastern ORTHODOX CHURCH includes the first monastery founded at Mount ATHOS in the early 11th century and the Monastery of the Caves, at Kiev. Such communities had their own stringent rules, but there were no special orders governing the works and spiritual development of the members. Under the Mongol-Tartar yoke of the 13th–15th centuries monasticism was repressed, but it revived at the end of the 15th century when the divided and humiliated Rus was replaced by the independent Russia. Numerous great monasteries were founded under the HESYCHAST movement.

Monenna (Darerca or **Bline), St** (d. *c.* 518, f.d. 6 July). An Irishwoman associated with St PATRICK and St BRIDGET, she founded a nunnery with eight virgins and a widow whose son, Luger, later became a bishop. The community lived under extreme austerity. One member went to Whithorn in South West Scotland. Monenna was credited with miraculous powers.

Monica, St (332–87, f.d. 27 August). Born of Christian parents in North Africa, she was married to Patricus, a pagan, whom she later converted. Her fame rests on being the mother of St AUGUSTINE OF HIPPO. She tried to rear him as a Christian but, under his father's influence, he grew up a Manichee and lived a dissolute life until he went to Milan, where St Monica followed him. There she met St AMBROSE and became his disciple; the two together succeeded in converting Augustine and he prepared for, and received, baptism. Mother and son set out for Africa, but she died on the way, at Ostia. There appears to have been no early cult of St Monica and her life is known through the writings of St Augustine.

Monk (O.E. *munuc*; Med. Lat. *monachus*, a solitary). In the Western Church, properly a member of those religious orders living a community life under vows of poverty, chastity, and obedience. *See* BENEDICTINES; CARTHUSIANS; CISTERCIANS. *Cp.* FRIARS; MENDICANT ORDERS.

Monophysites (Gr. *monos*, one; *phusis*, nature). A religious sect in the Levant which maintained that Jesus Christ had only one nature, and that divine and human were combined in much the same way as body and soul were combined in man. It arose upon the condemnation of the EUTYCHIAN heresy at the Council of Chalcedon, 451, and is still represented by the Coptic (*see* COPTS), Armenian, Abyssinian, Syrian, and Malabar JACOBITE Churches.

Monotheism. The doctrine that maintains there is one God only.

Monothelites (Gr. *monos*, one; *thelein*, to will). A 7th-century heretical sect holding that Christ had only one will, the divine. Monothelitism was akin to the teaching of the MONOPHYSITES, and was an attempt to reconcile the latter to their fellow-Christians of the eastern Empire against Persian and Mohammedan invaders. It was condemned finally by the Council of Constantinople (680).

Monsignor (pl. *Monsignori*). A title pertaining to all prelatexs in the ROMAN CATHOLIC CHURCH, which includes all prelates of the Roman court, active or honorary. Used with the surname, as 'Monsignor Newman', it does away with the solecism of speaking of Bishop so-and-so.

Monstrance. A vessel of gold or silver, usually elaborately decorated, used in CATHOLIC churches to contain the HOST when exposed to the congregation for veneration. It dates from the 13th century.

Montanists. A short-lived 2nd-century heretical sect; so called from Montanus, a Phrygian, who asserted that he had received from the HOLY GHOST special knowledge that had not been vouchsafed to the APOSTLES. They were extreme ascetics and believed in the speedy coming of the Second ADVENT. *See* QUINTILIANS.

Montanus and Lucius, SS (d. 259, f.d. 24 February, 23 May (Carthage)). A group of early martyrs, disciples of St CYPRIAN at Carthage, who died under the Valerian persecution; there were priests among them. They were imprisoned and suffered hunger and thirst and, after several months, were executed. Montanus experienced visions, and at his execution was loud in his denunciations of the pagans, exhorting them to repentance. The *Acta* of the martyrs are accepted as authentic.

Monte Cassino. A monastery of South Latium in Italy, the principal house of the BENEDICTINE Order, founded by St BENEDICT of Nursia *c.* 529. It became a great centre of learning. Almost destroyed in World War II, it has been rebuilt.

Montfort, Louis Grignion de (1673–1716, f.d. 28 April). Born at Montfort in Brittany, he was educated at Rennes by JESUITS. He entered the seminary of Saint-Sulpice and was ordained. Horrified at the conditions of the poor in Paris, he embarked on a mission of popular preaching in emotional style and, though he met opposition, received papal authority as a 'missionary apostolic'. He was successful in converting CALVINISTS at La Rochelle. He founded the Company of Mary and the Daughters of Wisdom, which spread to other countries. Montfort was canonized in 1947.

Month. A month's mind. Properly the Requiem MASS said for the deceased on the 30th day after death or burial. The term often occurs in old wills in connexion with charities to be disbursed on that day.

Montserrat (Lat. *mons serratus*, the mountain jagged like a saw). The Catalonians aver that this mountain was riven and shattered at the Crucifixion. Every rift is filled with evergreens. The monastery of Montserrat is famous for its printing-press, its Black Virgin and the boy's choir.

Monuments and effigies in churches. The following points usually apply:

Founders of chapels, etc., lie with their monument built into the wall.

Figures with their hands on their breasts, and chalices, represent *priests*.

Figures with armour represent *knights*.

Figures with legs crossed represent either *crusaders* or *married men*, but those with a SCALLOP SHELL are certainly *crusaders*.

Female figures with a mantle and large ring represent *nuns*.

In the age of chivalry the woman was placed on the man's right hand; but when chivalry declined she was placed on his left hand.

It may usually be taken that ancient inscriptions in Latin, cut in capitals, are of the first twelve centuries; those in Lombardic capitals and French, of the 13th; those in Old English text, of the 14th; while those in the English language and roman characters are subsequent to the 14th century.

Tablets against the wall came in with the REFORMATION; and brasses are mostly post-13th century.

Monyna, St. *See* MODWENNA.

Moody and Sankey. Dwight Lyman Moody (1836–99) was the son of a Massachusetts bricklayer who began his evangelical work in 1860. He was joined by Ira David Sankey (1840–1908) in 1870, who backed up Moody's preaching with singing and organ music. The famous 'Sankey and Moody hymn book', first published in 1873, properly called *Sacred Songs and Solos*, was 'compiled and sung' by Sankey. Their type of 'Gospel Hymn' was partly popularized in Great Britain during their visits to this country and particularly by the SALVATION ARMY.

Moon. In Christianity the moon is represented in five different phases: (1) new; (2) full; (3) crescent or decrescent; (4) half; and (5) gibbous, or more than half. In pictures of the ASSUMPTION it is shown as a crescent under Our Lady's feet; in the Crucifixion it is eclipsed, and placed on one side of the CROSS, the sun being on the other; in the Creation and Last JUDGEMENT it is also depicted.

Moonies. A religious sect, properly called the *Unification Church*, founded by Sun Myung Moon in South Korea in 1954. It spread to the USA in the 1960s and subsequently to Great Britain, Australia, etc. Moon claims to be the Second MESSIAH and his devotees will save mankind from SATAN. Funds built up by his followers by selling artificial flowers and other items were used by Moon to create a large property and business organization in America where he has dwelt since 1972. Tax avoidance led to his prosecution and imprisonment (1984–5).

Moor-slayer, or **Mata-moros.** A name given to St JAMES, the patron saint of Spain, because, as the legends say, in encounters with the Moors he came on his white horse to the aid of the Christians.

Moral. Father of Moral Philosophy. St THOMAS AQUINAS (*c*. 1225–74).

Moral Re-armament (MRA). A movement founded in 1938 by Frank Buchman, who had earlier founded the Oxford Group. Its purpose is to counter the Materialism of present-day society by persuading people to live according to the highest standards of morality and love, to obey God, and to unite in a worldwide association according to these principles.

Morality Play. An allegorical dramatic form in vogue from the 15th to the 16th centuries in which the vices (*see* SEVEN DEADLY SINS) and VIRTUES were personified and the victory of the latter clearly established. It was a development from the earlier MYSTERY Plays. *Everyman*, a 15th-century play translated from the Dutch *Elkerlijk*, is the best-known. *Cp.* PASSION PLAY.

Moravians. A PROTESTANT Church which is a direct continuation of the BOHEMIAN BRETHREN. Theirs is a simple and unwordly form of religion and John Wesley was influenced by them. They are now to be found in Denmark, Holland, Germany, Switzerland, Great Britain, and America. The church was founded in Bohemia in 1457 by the followers of John Huss. At the Synod of Lhota, in 1467, the Brethren established their own organization with three orders: Bishop, Presbyter and Deacon. The church spread also into Moravia and Poland, but had to go underground after the PROTESTANT defeat at the Battle of the White Mountain in 1620; in 1722 it was revived in Saxony under the patronage of Count Zinzendorf. It was then spread by Moravian missionaries into India, Africa, the Caribbean, North America and Greenland. In Britain it greatly influenced John WESLEY in establishing METHODISM. The church now has eighteen self-governing provinces, and every seven years holds an International Unity Synod. It is a member of the WORLD COUNCIL OF CHURCHES.

More, St Thomas (1478–1535, f.d. 22 June, formerly 9 July). Son of the judge Sir John More, of London, Thomas entered the house of John Morton, Archbishop of Canterbury, who sent him to Canterbury College. In 1496 he entered Lincoln's Inn, in 1501 was called to the Bar and in 1504 became a Member of Parliament. He had considered joining the FRIARS Minor but instead he married and continued his legal career. He became friendly with ERASMUS and other leaders of the New Learning and was also a friend of King Henry VIII who used to visit the More household informally and who appointed More to a number of high offices. More was famous for his cultured household, painted by Hans Holbein, and for his writings, particularly *Utopia*. In spite of his worldly success More maintained an ascetic private life, always wearing a hair shirt, using the discipline and daily saying the Little Office. He initiated a programme for the reform of the clergy. When the king married Anne Boleyn More was unable to accept the validity of the mar.iage or the Act of Succession and, with John FISHER, his friend and adviser, was committed to the Tower and remained imprisoned for fifteen months until he was tried in Westminster Hall and, still refusing to recant, was condemned to death and beheaded on Tower Hill. He was buried in the church of St Peter and Vincula and, with Fisher, was beatified in 1886 and canonized in 1935. They are among the few English saints to have a universal cult in the Roman CHURCH.

Mormons. Properly the *Church of Jesus Christ of Latter-Day Saints* regarding itself as a restoration of the one and only Gospel of Christ.

Joseph Smith (1805–44), a farmer's son of Western New York, claimed in 1820 that God the Father and his Son Jesus Christ had appeared to him and in 1823 that an account of the early inhabitants of America and of the everlasting Gospel inscribed on gold plates had been revealed to him and subsequently, in 1827, these plates were delivered to him. The result was the *Book of Mormon* produced at Palmyra, New York, in 1830, the book taking its name from the prophet Mormon, who had condensed earlier plates. In the same year Smith and his associates founded the Church. Smith was later murdered by a mob when imprisoned by his enemies in Carthage, Illinois, and his place was taken by Brigham Young (1801–77), a carpenter. He led the persecuted 'Saints' to the valley of the Salt Lake, 1,500 miles distant, generally called Utah, but by the Mormons, *Deseret* (Bee-country) the New Jerusalem where they have been settled since 1847, despite many disputes with the US Government.

The Mormons accept the BIBLE as well as the *Book of Mormon* as authoritative, they hold doctrines of repentance and faith, that Zion will be built on the American continent, and believe in baptism, the EUCHARIST, the physical resurrection of the dead, and in the Second ADVENT when Christ will have the seat of His power in Utah. Marriage may be for 'time and eternity'. Popularly associated with polygamy the Mormons practised it until 1890 when the US Supreme Court finally declared against it and this was accepted by the Church. Hence the expression **a regular Mormon** for a promiscuous or flighty person who cannot keep to one wife or sweetheart.

After Smith's death those who refused to recognize Brigham Young's presidency subsequently established the *Reorganized Church of Jesus Christ of Latter-Day Saints* at Wisconsin in 1852. Notably it rejected polygamy, claiming that it is the true successor of the original Church. Its headquarters are now at Independence, Missouri.

Mormon missionaries first arrived in Britain in 1837 and there are now some 350 congregations in the United Kingdom following a strict code of behaviour and self-sufficiency.

Morse, St Henry (1595–1645, f.d. 25 October). Born at Brome in Suffolk and reared as a PROTESTANT, he became a CATHOLIC while reading law in London, and was ordained in Rome. On returning to England he was arrested as a priest and imprisoned in York and later released and banished. He went to Flanders, but in 1633 came back under the name of Cuthbert Claxton and ministered in London, doing admirable work among those suffering from the plague. After the proclamation of 1641, banishing all priests, he left for Ghent but again returned to the north of England, was arrested in Cumberland, imprisoned at Durham, then taken to London where he was sentenced to death and hanged at Tyburn. The French, Spanish and Portuguese ambassadors and their suites were present to honour him. He was canonized in 1970 as one of the FORTY MARTYRS OF ENGLAND AND WALES.

Mortal. A mortal sin. A 'deadly' sin, one which deserves everlasting punishment; opposed to VENIAL. An act committed with full knowledge of wrong.

> Earth trembled from her entrails... some sad drops
> Wept at completing of the mortal Sin
> Original; while Adam took no thought.
> MILTON: *Paradise Lost*, IX, 1003

Mortification. The act of humiliating or deadening the mortal body for the purpose of controlling its lusts and passions by means of ascetic practices.

Mortmain. The holding of land by an ecclesiastical corporation, such as a monastery; such land cannot be transferred to new ownership.

Moscati, St Giuseppe (1860–1927, f.d. 16 November). Born into a noble Italian family, he became a student at Naples University, joining the medical faculty, showing outstanding ability and being recognized as a forerunner of modern biochemistry. Of a deeply religious nature,

he took a vow of chastity and devoted himself to the sick and incurables; he was also involved in the cholera epidemic of 1911 after the eruption of Vesuvius. Throughout his charitable work he maintained his scientific research. He was beatified in 1975 and canonized in 1987.

Moses. Moses the Black, St (*c.* 330–405, f.d. 28 August). An Ethiopian robber of disreputable character and of great physical strength who had been dismissed from service in an Egyptian household on account of his thefts. He experienced conversion and became a monk in the desert of Sketis, reforming himself to the extent of being accepted for ordination into the priesthood. He was murdered by Berber invaders, having refused to defend himself. He was buried at Dair al-Baramus at a monastery which still exists.

The horns of Moses' face. Moses is conventionally represented with horns, owing to a blunder in translation. In *Exod.* xxxiv, 29, 30, where we are told that when Moses came down from Mount Sinai 'the skin of his face shone', the Hebrew for this *shining* may be translated either as '*sent forth beams*' or 'sent forth *horns*'; and the VULGATE took the latter as correct, rendering the passage: *quod cornuta esset facies sua. Cp. Hab.* iii, 4, 'His brightness was as the light; he had horns [rays of light] coming out of his hand.'

Michelangelo followed the earlier painters in depicting Moses with horns.

Mother Church. The church considered as the central fact, the head, the last court of appeal in all matters pertaining to conscience or religion. St John LATERAN, at ROME, is known as the *Mother and Head of all churches,* Also, the principal or oldest church in a country or district; the cathedral of a diocese.

Mothering Sunday. MID-LENT SUNDAY, LAETARE SUNDAY when the POPE blesses the GOLDEN ROSE, children feast on mothering cakes and SIMNEL CAKES. A bunch of violets is emblematic of this day, and it is customary for children to give small presents to their mothers. It is said that it is derived from the pre-Reformation custom of visiting the MOTHER CHURCH on that day. Children away from home, especially daughters in service, normally returned to their family.

Also known as Refreshment Sunday in view of the relaxation of the mid-Lenten discipline.

Mother's Union. A CHURCH OF ENGLAND women's society to safeguard and strengthen Christian family life, to uphold the lifelong vows of marriage, and generally to play a proper part in the life of the Church. It was incorporated by Royal Charter in 1926 and generally operates as a parish institution.

Movable Feast. A religious festival which

changes its date from year to year, varying according to certain rules, e.g. EASTER following on the first Sunday after the full moon of the spring equinox, falling between 21 March and 18 April.

Mozarab. The term applied to those of non-Arabic race who became absorbed into Arabic culture but were allowed to follow their own Christian religion. Mozarab was a mediaeval Christian in Spain, owing allegiance to the Moorish king but permitted to remain a Christian. The word Mozarabic was applied to Christian communities which existed in large cities in Spain, such as Cordova, Seville and Toledo; they had their own Mozarabic Rite which was replaced when the Christians reconquered Spain.

Mozetta. A short, buttoned cape, reaching to the elbows, with an ornamental hood of silk or wool, worn over a ROCHET by CATHOLIC prelates. It is red, black or violet in colour.

Muggletonian. A follower of Lodovic Muggleton (1609–98), a journeyman tailor, who, about 1651, set up for a prophet. He was sentenced for blasphemous writings to stand in the pillory, and was fined £500. The members of the sect, which maintained some existence until *c.* 1865, believed that their two founders, Muggleton and John Reeve, were the 'two witnesses' spoken of in *Rev.* xi, 3.

Mulligus, St. *See* MOLING.

Mungo, St. An alternative name for St KENTIGERN.

Muratorian Fragment. A fragment of a late 2nd-century document found embodied in an 8th-century codex. Written in Latin, it reveals the NEW TESTAMENT canon of the period as consisting of the four Gospels, thirteen Epistles of Paul, two Epistles of John, the Epistle of Jude, the Apocalypse of John, and the Apocalypse of Peter. It was discovered by L. A. Muratori, librarian of the Ambrosian Library at Milan.

Murderer's Bible, The. *See* BIBLE, SOME SPECIALLY NAMED EDITIONS.

Murialdo, St Leonard (1828–1900, f.d. 30 March). Born and educated at Turin, he became a priest, dedicating his life to the education of boys of the working class, following the labours of St JOHN BOSCO. Murialdo visited Saint-Sulpice, then returned to Turin to take over the direction of a Christian College of Further Education. He founded the Catholic Workers' Movement, working through the press and improving its standards through a nationwide federation. He was buried at the church of Santa Barbara in Turin, and was canonized in 1970.

Muscular Christianity. Hearty or strong-minded Christianity, which braces a man to fight the battle of life bravely and manfully. The term was applied to the teachings of Charles Kingsley (1819–75)—somewhat to his annoyance.

> It is a school of which Mr Kingsley is the ablest doctor; and its doctrine has been described fairly and cleverly as 'muscular Christianity.'
>
> *Edinburgh Review*, Jan. 1858

Myrrophores (Gr., myrrh-bearers). The Marys who went to see the sepulchre, bearing spices, are represented in Christian art as carrying vases of myrrh (*see Mark* xvi, i).

Mysterium. The letters of this word, which, until the time of the REFORMATION, was engraved on the Pope's tiara, are said to make up the number 666. *See* NUMBER OF THE BEAST.

> And upon her forehead was a name written, MYSTERY, BABYLON THE GREAT, THE MOTHER OF HARLOTS AND ABOMINATIONS OF THE EARTH.
>
> *Rev.* xvii, 5

Mystery. In English two distinct words are represented: *mystery*, the archaic term for a handicraft, as in *the art and mystery of printing*, is the same as the Fr. *métier* (trade, craft, profession), and is the M.E. *mistere*, from Med. Lat. *misterium, ministerium*, ministry, *Mystery*, meaning something hidden, inexplicable, or beyond human comprehension, is from Lat. *mysterium* (through French) and Gr. *mustes*, from *muein*, to close the eyes or lips.

It is from this latter sense that the old miracle plays, mediaeval dramas in which the characters and story were drawn from sacred history, came to be called **Mysteries**, though they were frequently presented by members of a guild or *mystery*. *Miracle plays* (as they were called at the time) developed from liturgical pageantry, especially in the CORPUS CHRISTI processions, and were taken over by the laity. They were performed in the streets on a wheeled stage or on stages erected along a processional route, and non-Biblical subjects were also introduced. They flourished in England from the 13th to the 15th century but MORALITY PLAYS continued into the 16th century. *Cp.* PASSION PLAY.

Mysteries of the Rosary. The fifteen subjects of meditation from the life of Christ and the Blessed Virgin Mary, connected with the decades of the ROSARY.

The three greater mysteries. The TRINITY, ORIGINAL SIN, and the INCARNATION.

Mysticism. A belief in, an experience of, communion with the Divine or the Absolute, transcending thought and reason; absorption in the Divine. Mysticism appears in all the higher religions, giving remarkable similar expressions. In Christianity mysticism is traced back to DENYS THE AREOPAGITE (5th cent.) and the great mystics include, among others, DUNS SCOTUS, ERIGENA, BERNARD of Clairvaux, the VICTORINES, BONAVENTURE, JOACHIM OF FIORE, THOMAS À KEMPIS, St TERESA, St JOHN OF THE CROSS, St FRANCIS OF SALES, and, among the QUIETISTS, Mme. GUYON and Molinos. Numbered among outstanding German mystics are Meister ECKHART, SUSO, TAULER, BÖHME and RUYSBROECK.

Eastern ORTHODOX mysticism was greatly influenced by Neo-Platonism, but also by the HESYCHAST movement instigated by St SIMEON, the New Theologian (d. 1022), who instituted a distinctive ascetic mysticism using psychological methods, meditation, breath-control and the repetition of the 'Jesus Prayer' ('Lord Jesus Christ, Son of God, have mercy on me a sinner').

Mystical sects are represented by the FRATI-CELLI, the BEGHARDS and BÉGUINES, the Brothers of the Common Life and the BRETHREN OF THE FREE SPIRIT.

Among PROTESTANTS the Anabaptists, SEEKERS and QUAKERS are mystical in essence. The 17th century saw the movement of the Cambridge Platonists and Henry More. The writings of SWEDENBORG are based on mysticism and, in the 18th century, came William Law and William BLAKE.

There has been a revival of interest in mysticism in the works of Evelyn Underhill, W. R. Inge and Aldous Huxley among others, while there is a new scientific and psychological approach evident in such works as William James' *Varieties of Religious Experience*.

Mystic Rose (Lat. *Rose mystica*). A name given to the VIRGIN MARY as suggested by *Ecclesiasticus* xxiv, 18 and xxxix, 17.

Mystics of St Victor. A school of mystical philosophy at the Abbey of St Victor, near Paris, founded by William of Champeaux in 1108. Among its members were Hugh St Victor, Peter Lombard and Richard Victor, a Scotsman.

N

N or M. The answer given to the first question in the CHURCH OF ENGLAND Catechism; and it means that here the person being catechized gives his or her *name* or *names*. Lat. *nomen vel nomina*. The abbreviation for the plural *nomina* was—as usual—the doubled initial (*cp.* 'LL.D.' for Doctor of Laws); and this when printed (as it was in old Prayer Books) in black-letter and close together, N.N. came to be taken for M.

In the same way the M. and N. in the marriage-service ('I M. take thee N. to my wedded wife') merely indicate that the name is to be spoken in each case; but the M. and N. in the publication of banns ('I publish the BANNS OF MARRIAGE between M. of—and N. of—') stand for *maritus*, bridegroom, and *nupta*, bride.

Naboth's Vineyard. The possession of another coveted by one who will use any means, however unscrupulous, to acquire it. (I *Kings* xxi.)

Nag's Head Consecration. An early 17th-century story designed to deride the validity of the APOSTOLIC SUCCESSION in the CHURCH OF ENGLAND and in particular the validity of Archbishop Parker's consecration. The story is that on the passing of the Act of Uniformity of 1559 in Queen Elizabeth's reign, 14 bishops vacated their sees, and all the other sees were vacant except that of Llandaff, whose bishop refused to officiate at Parker's consecration. He was therefore irregularly consecrated at the 'Nag's Head' tavern, in Cheapside, by John Scory who had been deprived of the SEE of Chichester under Mary. In fact the consecration took place at LAMBETH PALACE on 17 December 1559 by four bishops who had held sees under Edward VI (Barlow, Scory, Coverdale, and Hodgkin). Those who took part in the consecration apparently dined at the 'Nag's Head' afterwards. The story was first put about in 1604 by C. Holywood, a JESUIT.

Nail. The nails with which Our Lord was fastened to the Cross were, in the Middle Ages, objects of great reverence. Sir John Mandeville says, 'He had two in his hondes, and two in his feet; and of on of theise the emperour of Constantynoble made a brydille to his hors, to bere him in batayle; and throghe vertue thereof he overcam his enemyes' (*c.* viii). Fifteen are shown as relics.

Nantes, Edict of. An edict signed by Henry IV of France in 1598 granting freedom of worship to PROTESTANTS and ending the French wars of religion. It was revoked by Louis XIV, which caused many HUGUENOTS to leave France.

Narses I, St (*c.* 326–73, f.d. 19 November). Son of St ISAAC THE GREAT and descended from St GREGORY THE ENLIGHTENER, he was married, but after his wife's death was ordained priest and later appointed the chief bishop of the Armenian Church. He was reputedly deposed by King Arshak III for condemning Arshak's misdeeds, but was reinstated by King Pap who proved little better and was said to have poisoned Narses.

Nathalan, St (d. *c.* 678, f.d. 8 January). A Scotsman, said to have been a nobleman born in Tullicht and to have built churches, also to have worked on the land and produced crops to feed the people in times of famine. The legend of the lost key is associated with him; in his case he had locked his hand and leg together and thrown away the key, which was recovered from the inside of a fish in ROME.

National Church League. A CHURCH OF ENGLAND evangelical society for promoting the Church's scriptural heritage and recognition of the REFORMATION Settlement.

National Society. The shortened form of the name of the association formed in 1811 as the 'National Society for the Education of the Poor in the Principles of the Established Church'. It played a great part in the development of English education, especially before direct state participation and control. Principally known for the establishment of Church schools, or 'National Schools', and teacher training colleges, it still continues its work.

Nativity, The. CHRISTMAS Day, the day set apart in honour of the Nativity or Birth of Christ.

The Cave of the Nativity. The 'Cave of the Nativity' at Bethlehem, discovered, according to Eusebius, by the empress HELENA, is under the chancel of the BASILICA of the 'Church of the Nativity'. It is a hollow scraped out of rock, and there is a stone slab above the ground with a star cut in it to mark the supposed spot where Jesus was laid. There are no grounds for connecting the Nativity with a cave.

Natural Theology. The teaching that the knowledge of God is attained through reason rather than revelation; associated especially with the work of St THOMAS AQUINAS, who made a strict distinction between natural and Revealed Theology.

Nave (Lat. *navis*, a ship). The central part of a church, cathedral, etc., extending from the main entrance to the CHOIR or CHANCEL, so called on account of its resemblance to the shape of an inverted ship.

Nazarene. A native of Nazareth; Our Lord is so called (*John* xviii, 5, 7). He was brought up in Nazareth, but was born in Bethlehem (*see Matt.* ii, 23). Hence the early Christians were called *Nazarenes* (*Acts* xxiv, 5); also an early sect of Jewish Christians, who believed Christ to be the MESSIAH, but who nevertheless conformed to much of the Jewish law.
Can any good thing come out of Nazareth? (*John* i, 46). A general insinuation against any family or place of ill repute. Can any great man come from such an insignificant village as Nazareth?
Nazarites (Heb. *'nazar,* to separate). A body of Israelites set apart to the Lord under vows. They refrained from strong drink, and allowed their hair to grow. (*See Numb.* vi, 1–21.)

Nazarius and Celsus, SS (date unknown, f.d. 28 July). Nothing is known of their history, but the names were given by St AMBROSE to two bodies of early martyrs found after a dream or vision. One was said to have been an African and the other his disciple. Their Acts are said to be unreliable and their cult was restricted to local calendars in 1969.

Neck verse. The first verse of *Ps.* li. *See* MISERERE. 'Have mercy upon me, O God, according to thy loving kindness: according unto the multitude of thy tender mercies blot out my transgressions.'

> He [a treacherous Italian interpreter] by a fine cunny-catching corrupt translation, made us plainly to confess, and cry *Miserere,* ere we had need of our necke-verse.
> NASH: *The Unfortunate Traveller* (1594)

This verse was so called because it was the trial-verse of those who claimed BENEFIT OF CLERGY, and if they could read it, the ORDINARY of the prison said, '*Legit ut clericus*' (he reads like a clerk) and the prisoner saved his neck, but by an Act of Henry VII convicted clerks were branded on the hand before release.

Nectan (or **Nighton**), **St** (6th cent., f.d. 14

February, 17 June, 4 December). Said to have been the eldest and most noted of the family of St BRYCHAN, a legendary Welsh chieftain who had twenty-four children. Nectan became a hermit and settled at Hartland Point in North Devon. Legend says he was killed as a result of kindness; having helped a swineherd to find his lost pigs, he received a gift of two cows in gratitude from the swineherd's master. Thieves stole the cows and when Nectan found them and admonished the robbers and tried to convert them to Christianity they beheaded him. He was reputed to have carried his head half a mile to his spring at his hermitage. He had a considerable cult in Devon and Cornwall where five churches were dedicated to him and his shrine was a centre of pilgrimage. He is patron saint of Hartland.

Nectarius Kephalas (1846–1920, f.d. 9 November). A bishop of the ORTHODOX CHURCH, canonized in 1961 for his work on the island of Aegina, where he restored a nunnery and was rector of the Ecclesiastical College at Rhizarion. He was noted as a writer, greatly venerated in his lifetime, and his tomb is a place of pilgrimage. He is the most recently canonized saint of the Greek Orthodox Church.

Neophytes (Gr., newly-planted). Converts to the early Christian church who had recently been baptized. New entrants to religious orders.

Neot, St (d. *c.* 877, f.d. 31 July). Said to have been of royal blood, possibly related to King Alfred who visited him and sought his advice. The story of Alfred and the cakes is taken from one of the three accounts of St Neot's life. He was a monk at Glastonbury, then a hermit in Cornwall, at Neotstoke, where he founded a monastery. He gave his name to St Neot's in Cornwall and in Cambridgeshire. Several traditional legends are told of him: stags drew his plough when his oxen had been stolen and fish eaten were miraculously replenished.

Nepomuk. *See* St JOHN OF NEPOMUK *under* JOHN.

Nepotism (Ital. *nepote,* nephew). The practice of favouring relatives in matters of employment, promotion, etc. The usage derives from the days when Popes and high ecclesiastics gave preferment and advancement to their nehews as their illegitimate sons were euphemistically labelled.

Nereus and Achilleus, SS (date unknown, f.d. 12 May). Early Christian martyrs of whom there are conflicting accounts. Pope St DAMASUS said they were Roman soldiers, converted to Christianity, who abandoned their military life, threw away their weapons, confessed their new faith and were martyred and buried in the cemetery of Domitilla. Another account, taken from their legendary Acts says they were eunuchs in the household of the Lady Flavia Domitilla and shared her exile during Trajan's reign. All were martyred for refusing to sacrifice to the gods. Domitilla was burnt to death and Nereus and Achilleus were beheaded.

Neri, St Philip (1515–95, f.d. 26 May). Son of a Florentine official, he was educated at the DOMINICAN convent of St Marco. He started on a business career but abandoned it after a conversion experience and went to ROME to live in extreme poverty, studying theology and philosophy, then turning to a mission among young business men. He also founded a brotherhood for pilgrims to Rome and later the Congregation of the Oratory, the ORATORIANS, whose priests were not bound by vows. Neri was widely known for his attractive personality, wisdom and spiritual counsel and was consulted by great numbers, ranging from the poorest to cardinals and kings; he was also instrumental in averting conflict between the PROTESTANT Henry IV of Navarre and the Pope. Not only was his austerity famous but he was often in ecstasy and was said to be surrounded by light or radiance. He was seen to levitate at the Mass and other times and to have the power of bilocation. He also experienced so great a heat of ardour that it burned his throat 'as if suffering a raging fever or inward fire'; this fire entered his throat, dilated his heart and left a swelling on his left breast which displaced two ribs. The actual physical facts were established by examination after his death. That he was also said to have moved after death has been verified. He was buried at the church of St Maria in Vallicella. In England Cardinal NEWMAN became an Oratorian and founded the London and Birmingham Oratories. The musical form 'oratorio' is derived from the services of the Oratorians.

Nestorians. Followers of Nestorius, Patriarch of Constantinople, 428–31 (d. c. 451). He is traditionally supposed to have asserted that Christ had two distinct natures and that Mary was the mother of his human nature. His teaching was condemned by Pope Celestine I in 430. A separate Nestorian Church was established which spread to Asia where most of their churches were destroyed by Timur (Tamburlaine) about 1400. A small group called Assyrian Christians survived in parts of Asia Minor and Persia.

Neumann, St John (1811–60, f.d. 5 January). Born in Bohemia, of German–Czech parentage, he was educated at Budweis seminary and Prague University. He spoke eight languages.

When the Austrian government delayed his ordination he left for North America to work for German-speaking immigrants. He was ordained and later joined the REDEMPTIONIST CONGREGATION, was sent on a mission to the east coast and became parish priest at Baltimore. In 1852 he was appointed bishop of Philadelphia and was responsible for establishing 100 churches and 80 schools. He was a small man of great energy and influence. He was canonized in 1977.

Neume. A prolonged series of notes sung on one syllable, an early form of PLAINSONG.

New Church. *See* SWEDENBORG.

New English Bible. *See* BIBLE.

New Jerusalem. The city of HEAVEN foretold in *Rev.* xxi, 2, 'coming down from God out of heaven, prepared as a bride adorned for her husband'. Hence, figuratively, the perfect society.

The New Jerusalem Church. The name chosen (*c.* 1784) by Richard Hindmarsh for the sect founded by him on the doctrines of Emanuel Swedenborg. *See* SWEDENBORG.

New Testament, The. The name given to the second group of sacred writings in the BIBLE comprising 27 books in all (the four Gospels, The Acts of the Apostles, 21 Epistles and the Revelation of St John the Divine), but which more correctly could be called 'The New Covenant' or 'The New Dispensation'.

The religion of Israel was regarded as a covenant between Jehovah and his chosen people and in due time a new covenant was promised by the prophets:

> Behold, the days come, saith the Lord, that I will make a new covenant with the house of Israel, and the house of Judah.
>
> *Jeremiah* xxi, 31

This new covenant, for the Christians, was established by the life and death of Christ, and towards the end of the 2nd century a generally accepted collection of new scriptures, worthy of complementing the OLD TESTAMENT, was evolving. The present canon is that established by the Council of Carthage in 397. The name *Testament* is from the Lat. *testamentum* which is an inaccurate rendering of the Gr. *diathēkē*, 'disposition' or 'covenant'. Thus we have in the *Authorized Version* (*Luke* xxii, 20): 'This cup is the new testament in my blood, which is shed for you.' This in the *Revised Version* reads 'This cup is the new covenant in my blood, even that which is poured out for you.' *See* APOCRYPHA.

Newman, John Henry (1801–90). The son of a London banker of EVANGELICAL convictions, Newman was ordained into the CHURCH OF ENGLAND and became vicar of St Mary's, Oxford. Here he came under the influence of KEBLE and

Froude and their High Church emphasis on the CATHOLIC heritage of the Church of England. Keble's sermon on National Apostasy is generally regarded as the birth of the Oxford Movement, and a series of tracts published by the members of the movement, *Tracts for the Times*, led to their being called the Tractarians. Newman wrote *Tract Ninety* which caused considerable adverse reaction, and in which he maintained that the THIRTY-NINE ARTICLES were comparable with the ROMAN CATHOLIC creed. At St Mary's he preached a series of sermons emphasizing the Catholic heritage and character of the Church of England. In 1843 he resigned his living, retreated to Littlemore, and later went to ROME and was ordained priest. In 1870 he was made a cardinal by Pope Leo XIII. Newman's most famous works are his *Apologia pro Vita Sua*, his *Grammar of Ascent* and his poem *The Dream of Gerontius*.

Nicaea. The Council of Nicaea. The first OECUMENICAL COUNCIL of the Christian Church held under Constantine the Great in 325 at Nicaea in Bithynia, Asia Minor, primarily to deal with the ARIAN heresy, which it condemned. The second Council of Nicaea (787), the seventh General Council of the Church, was summoned by The Empress Irene to end the Iconoclastic Controversy (*see* ICONOCLASTS).

Nicene Creed. The creed properly so called was a comparatively short statement of beliefs issued in 325 by the Council of NICAEA to combat the ARIAN heresy. The 'Nicene Creed' commonly referred to is that properly called the *Niceno-Constantinopolitan Creed*, referred to in Article VIII of the THIRTY-NINE ARTICLES given in the BOOK OF COMMON PRAYER, which ultimately derives from the Baptismal Creed of JERUSALEM. It is used in the EUCHARIST of the ROMAN CATHOLIC CHURCH, the CHURCH OF ENGLAND, and the Eastern CHURCH, where it still forms part of the service of Baptism. It was first used at Antioch in the late 5th century and gradually gained acceptance in both East and West. *See also* FILIOQUE CONTROVERSY. *Cp*. APOSTLES' CREED; ATHANASIAN CREED (under ATHANASIUS).

Nicephorus, St (d. 828, f.d. 2 June, 13 March). Although a layman, he was appointed Patriarch of Constantinople and became a noted opponent of the ICONOCLASTS. He was secretary to the Emperor Constantine, but later was persecuted by Michael the Stammerer and deposed and excommunicated by the Iconoclastic bishops. He was exiled to a monastery he had founded on the Bosphorus, where he died fifteen years later.

Nicetas of Remesiana, St (d. *c*. 414, f.d. 22 June, 7 January). Little is known of his life except that he became bishop of Remesiana, in Serbia, where he carried out an active mission south of the Danube. His fame rests on his writings, among them an exegesis on the APOSTLES' CREED and another treatise on psalm-singing. He exhorted people to sing understandingly, 'thinking of what you are singing ... tunes should be in keeping with the sacredness of religion ... not savouring of the theatre ... and do not show off'; the object of worship is to do all 'in God's sight, not to please men'. It has been suggested that he was the author of the TE DEUM. St PAULINUS OF NOLA held him in high esteem as a poet and missionary 'among the rude inhabitants of a frozen land'.

Nicholas. Nicholas, St (early 4th cent., f.d. 6 December). One of the most popular saints in Christendom, especially in the East. He is the patron SAINT of Russia, of Aberdeen, of parish clerks, of scholars (who used to be called clerks), of pawn-brokers (because of the three bags of gold—transformed to the three gold balls—that he gave to the daughters of a poor man to save them from earning their dowers in a disreputable way), of little boys (because he once restored to life three little boys who had been cut up and pickled in a salting-tub to serve for bacon), and is invoked by sailors (because he allayed a storm during a voyage to the HOLY LAND) and against fire. Finally he is the original of SANTA CLAUS.

Little is known of his life but he is said to have been Bishop of Myra (Lycia) in the early 4th century, and one story relates that he was present at the Council of NICAEA (325) and buffeted Arius on the jaw. He is represented in episcopal robes with either three purses of gold, three gold balls, or three small boys, in allusion to one or other of the above legends. His cult was confined to local calendars in the revision of 1969.

St Nicholas's Bishop. *See* BOY BISHOP.

Nicholas the First, St (d. 867, f.d. 13 November). While still only a deacon in ROME he was elected Pope, somewhat against his will, at a time which involved him in many disputes, notably with St PHOTIUS, Patriarch of Constantinople; Archbishop John of Ravenna; Hincmar of Rheims and Lothair II of Lorraine, whom he excommunicated. Having a generous and reasonable temperament and being a skilled negotiator, he succeeded where a less able intermediary would have failed. His missionaries worked for the conversion of Bulgaria. Nicholas became one of the three popes entitled 'the Great'.

Nicholas of Flue, St (1417–87, f.d. 21 March, 25 September (Switzerland)). Born into a farming family at Flueli, Switzerland, and working on the farm, he joined the lay association of the Friends of God at an early age and lived a life of strict devotion, based on the *Imitation of Christ*. He was also involved in public affairs, being both a magistrate and judge and taking part in two wars. He married a farmer's daughter and they had ten children, but, at the age of fifty, he resigned his offices and, with his wife's consent, retired to a hermitage at Ranft, not far from his home, where he lived a life of prayer and contemplation for twenty years. It was said that during that time he took neither food nor drink. Many people visited him, seeking his advice in both spiritual and secular matters. In this way he played an important part in Swiss history at a time of turmoil and strife, resolving difficulties and averting civil war. It was thought that his diplomacy was responsible for the Edict of Stans, although it was known that he could neither read nor write. He was beatified as a patron and saint and was canonized in 1947. As patron saint of Switzerland he is venerated as 'Bruder Klaus'.

Nicholas of Tolentino, St (1245–1305, f.d. 10 September). Born at Sant' Angelo in the March of Ancona, he joined the AUGUSTINIAN FRIARS at the age of eighteen, living in various friaries until he settled at Tolentino. He was ordained and resolved to preach every day, becoming a famous preacher and confessor and gaining a reputation as a worker of miracles. His labours were mainly pastoral and in art he is represented as distributing rolls of bread to the sick and to women in labour. Many of the miracles attached to him were told also of St Nicholas of Myra, after whom he had been named. One of the more remarkable miracles of the effusion of blood was said to have occurred in 1345. Forty years after his death his remains were still incorrupt; a lay brother attempted to steal the arms as relics to take to Germany, but this caused a great flow of blood which exposed the outrage and led to the arrest of the thief. The arms were recovered and enshrined at Tolentino where it was said that they continued to emit blood at intervals during more than 300 years, the effusion usually portending some catastrophe. His cult remains widespread in Europe and America but was confined to local calendars after the revision of 1969. He was invoked against plague. He can be depicted with a star on his breast as an emblem of the comet seen at his birth; two pigeons accompanying him represent the legend that he restored the birds to life when they were brought to him, roasted, when he was sick.

Nicodemus, Gospel of. *See under* GOSPEL.

Nicodemus of Athos, St (*c.* 1748–1809, f.d. 14 July). Canonized by the ORTHODOX CHURCH in 1955, Nicodemus of the Holy Mountain is one of the most noted Greek writers of the Eastern Church, his most famous work being the *Philokalia*, a compilation of excerpts from the writings of the Greek Fathers; it had a deep and lasting influence, not only among Eastern Orthodox Christians, but also passing into English in 1951. He also wrote a volume of meditations based on the *Spiritual Exercises* of IGNATIUS LOYOLA and was a liturgist, canonist and hagiographer. Nicodemus was a monk at Dionysion on Mount ATHOS.

Night Office. Another name for MATTINS.

Nihil. Nihil obstat. The words by which a Roman Catholic censor of books (*Censor Librorum*) declares that he has found nothing contrary to faith or good morals in the book in question. The full Latin phrase is *nihil obstat quominus imprimatur*, nothing hinders it from being printed. The imprimatur is granted by the BISHOP or his delegate.

Nilus the Ascetic of Ancyra, St (d. *c.* 430, f.d. 12 November). Traditionally he was a courtier of Byzantium, but it is now known that he was actually bishop of Ancyra and a disciple and friend of St JOHN CHRYSOSTOM. Nilus was said to have retired to live a life of asceticism with his son on Mount Sinai. The son was captured by brigands but eventually was able to rejoin his father. Nilus was opposed to animal representations in the church and said the faithful would be confused by them; 'on the other hand it is fitting that a strong and manly spirit should set up a single cross in the sanctuary ... and fill the sacred temple on both sides with pictures from the Old and New Testaments'.

Nilus (or Neilos) of Rossano, St (*c.* 910–1005, f.d. 26 September). Born into a Greek family in Calabria, he was first an official of the treasury then entered a monastery, living as a cenobite. Later he became abbot of St Adrian's by San Dometrio Corone and was noted for his holiness and austerity. He lived at a time of constant threat from the Saracens and had to flee with his community to MONTE CASSINO where they were housed until they moved into the empty monastery of Vallelucio. They went finally to Serperi, where they were visited by the Emperor Otto III; he was amazed at the austerity of the life in the monastery and offered to rebuild it, but the offer was rejected in favour of a gift of money. When he visited Grottaferrata, near ROME, Nilus had a vision of a permanent home for his community there, although he died before the monastery was built. The abbey, which follows the Byzantine rite, has lasted as a centre of religious life and learning. Nilus was a scholar of both Greek and Latin literature, and composed hymns.

Nilus (or Nil) of Sora, St (*c.* 1433–1508, f.d. 7 April). Little is known of his youth, but he became a scribe and copyist and a monk at Belozersk, near Lake Beloe. From Russia he went to Mount ATHOS in Greece where he gathered a coterie of monks who engaged in the study and translation of mystical and ascetic works. Nilus also wrote a monastic rule which has been translated into English. Although of humble family he was a man of great learning, a noted preacher and educator and an authority on Greek manuscripts. A man of great piety and strict asceticism, he maintained that wealth and spiritual perfection were incompatible. He opposed 'possessions', saying that monks should live simply and work for their needs; also that churches should be unadorned in order to concentrate on the beauty of God. In this he was opposed by St Joseph of Volokolamsk, who, at the Council of Moscow in 1503, argued for possessions, saying that they should hold monastic property.

Nimbus (Lat., a cloud). In Christian art a HALO of light placed round the head of an eminent personage. There are three forms: (1) *Vesica piscis*, or fish form (*cp.* ICHTHYS), used in representations of Christ and occasionally of the Virgin Mary, extending round the whole figure; (2) a circular halo; (3) radiated like a star or sun. The enrichments are: (1) for our Lord, a CROSS; (2) for the Virgin, a circlet of stars; (3) for ANGELS, a circlet of small rays, and an outer circle of quatrefoils; (4) the same for SAINTS and martyrs, but with the name often inscribed round the circumference; (5) for the Deity the rays diverge in a triangular direction. Nimbi of a square form signify that the persons so represented were living when they were painted.

The nimbus was used by heathen nations long before painters introduced it into sacred pictures of saints, the TRINITY, and the Virgin Mary. Proserpine was represented with a nimbus; the Roman emperors were also decorated in the same manner because they were *divi*. *Cp.* AUREOLE.

Nine. Nine, Five, Three are mystical numbers—the *diapason*, *diapente*, and *diatrion* of the Greeks. Nine consists of a trinity of trinities. According to the Pythagoreans man is a full chord, or eight notes, and deity comes next. Three, being the TRINITY, represents a perfect *unity*; twice three is the perfect *dual*; and thrice three is the perfect *plural*. This explains why nine is a mystical number. There are triple triads of choirs of angels and there are nine spheres and rings round hell.
The Nine First Fridays. In the ROMAN CATHOLIC CHURCH the special observance of the first FRIDAY in each of nine consecutive months, marked by receiving the EUCHARIST. The practice derives from St Mary Alacoque (*see* SACRED HEART *under* HEART), who held that Christ told her that special grace would be granted to those fulfilling this observance.

Ninian, St (*c.* 360–432, f.d. 26 August). Son of a Cumbrian noble, he was said to have travelled to ROME and been consecrated as a bishop. On returning home he became an apostle to the Southern Picts in Galloway and built a church at Whithorn, dedicating it to his friend St MARTIN OF TOURS. His cult was popular among the Lowland Scots and there are many churches dedicated to him. In art he is depicted with heavy chains.

Nino, St (*c.* 320, f.d. 15 December). According to RUFINUS, who said he had the story from a Georgian prince, Bakur, Nino was a Christian girl sold as a slave in Georgia. People were so impressed by her virtue and devoutness that she gained great influence, particularly with the queen, by her powers of healing in the name of Christ. The king was also converted when, having become lost when hunting, he found his way by calling on Christ. Nino instructed him in Christianity and supervised the building of a church, showing such miraculous powers that great numbers of people were converted. The king requested the Emperor Constantine to send clergy to teach the people and in this way Christianity was brought to Iberia (Georgia), of which Nino is venerated as the apostle.

Noel Chabanel, St (1613–49, f.d. 26 September). He became a JESUIT novice at Toulouse and was sent to Canada on a mission to the Huron Indians, where he worked with St Charles Garnier who was killed by the Iroquois. Father Chabanel was away at that time but did not return when expected; later a Huron was said to have confessed to his death. He was canonized in 1930.

Nolo episcopari (Lat., I am unwilling to be made a BISHOP). The formal reply supposed to be returned to the royal offer of bishopric. Chamberlayne says (*Present State of England*, 1669) that in former times the person about to be elected modestly refused the office twice, and if he did so a third time his refusal was accepted.

Non (Nonna or **Nonnita), St** (5th cent., f.d. 3 March, 25 June, 3 July). Daughter of a Welsh prince and mother of St DAVID by a neighbouring prince who seduced her. One tradition says she was a nun early in life, another that she became a nun when widowed. She founded churches in Devon and Cornwall and went to Brittany, where she died and where her tomb survives at Dirimon. Her sacred wells gave healing waters, especially for curing blindness.

Nonconformists. In England, members of PROTESTANT bodies who do not conform to the doctrines of the CHURCH OF ENGLAND. They had their origins in the BROWNISTS and BAPTISTS of Elizabeth I's reign and among the 17th-century PURITANS and sectaries. After the Restoration and the subsequent Act of Uniformity of 1662, which enforced strict observance of the BOOK OF COMMON PRAYER, some 2,000 clergy were ejected and a lasting division resulted. The DISSENTERS or Nonconformists were subjected to the Clarendon Code until relief came with the Toleration Act of 1689 and later measures. Nonconformity received further recruits particularly with the advent of the METHODISTS.

Nones. In the ancient Roman CALENDAR, the *ninth* (Lat. *nonus*) day before Ides; in the ROMAN CATHOLIC CHURCH, the office for the *ninth* hour after sunrise i.e. between noon and 3 p.m.

Non-jurors. Those HIGH CHURCH clergy who refused to take the oath of allegiance to William and Mary after the Revolution of 1688 and who were deprived of their livings in 1690. Their numbers included Archbishop Sancroft and five other bishops. They maintained their own episcopal succession until the death of their last bishop in 1805. *Cp.* SEVEN BISHOPS.

Non-resistance. In the CHURCH OF ENGLAND passive obedience to royal commands was a natural corollary of the DIVINE RIGHT OF KINGS but it acquired a particular importance after the restoration, when Tory-minded clergy advocated non-resistance to combat NONCONFORMIST doctrines and Whig policies. When James II tried to promote Roman Catholicism, many advocates of non-resistance abandoned their support of the monarchy and others became NON-JURORS after the accession of William of Orange.

Norbert, St (1080–1134, f.d. 6 June). Founder of the PREMONSTRATENSIAN CANONS under the Order of St AUGUSTINE. He came from a noble Rhineland family, related to the emperor, and led a worldly life, although a minor canon, at Xanten where he was born. It was said that his conversion took place after he was thrown from his horse in a violent storm, narrowly escaping death by lightning and lying as one dead for an hour. He retired to Xanten, sold his estates and gave his possessions to the poor. He travelled to Languedoc where he saw the Pope Gelasius II who authorized him to preach wherever he chose. Failing to reform the canons of Xanten and rejected by the canons of St Martin, Norbert founded an order at Prémontré, under austere Augustinian rules, which received formal approval in 1126. He joined St BERNARD and St HUGH OF GRENOBLE in an effort to heal the schism caused by the death of Honorius II. Norbert was appointed bishop of Magdeburg, where he died. In art he may hold a MONSTRANCE or a chalice with a spider in it. Legend says he was about to take the SACRAMENT when he saw a poisonous spider in the chalice, but rather than spill the sacred blood he drank it and remained unharmed.

Notburga, St (*c.* 1265–1313, f.d. 13 September). A peasant's daughter, born in the Tyrol and employed as a servant at the local castle, she was dismissed for giving food to the poor when it should have been fed to the pigs. She then worked for a farmer, continuing to give food away and depriving herself. After a time she went back to the castle and remained there. In art she is portrayed with a sickle to illustrate the legend that a sickle hung in the air out of reach over her head when she refused to reap on a Sunday. She is patron saint of hired hands in the Tyrol and Bavaria.

Notes of the Church. The four characteristic marks of the Church, i.e. *one, holy, catholic,* and *apostolic*, as set forth in the NICENE CREED. These 'notes' were used by Roman Catholic theologians and others, and by the Tractarians to demonstrate their claims.

Nothelm, St (d. 739, f.d. 17 October). A priest in London who succeeded St TATWIN as Archbishop of Canterbury, having received the PALLIUM from Pope GREGORY III in 736. The Venerable BEDE was assisted by Nothelm in his compilation of the *Ecclesiastical History*, and Nothelm also corresponded with St BONIFACE. He was buried in the church of St AUGUSTINE, Canterbury, and his body was translated later to be grouped with other archbishops round Augustine's body.

Notre Dame (Fr. Our Lady). The name given to churches in France dedicated to the VIRGIN MARY, the most famous among them being the Cathedral of Notre Dame in Paris, on the Ile de la Cité.

Novatians. Followers of Novatian, a presbyter of ROME in the 3rd century. They were doctrinally orthodox, but objected to the readmission into the Church of those who had dallied with paganism. They were excommunicated, but Novatianist churches persisted until after the 5th century.

Novena (Lat. *novenus*, nine each). In Roman Catholic devotions, a prayer for some special object or occasion extended over a period of nine days.

Novice (Lat. *novitius*, new). A probationer

received into a religious order; during the noviate no vows are taken, and at the end of the period the novice may choose to return to the world or take the vows committing him/her to the religious life. The term can also apply to a new convert.

Numbers. In old ecclesiastical symbolism the numbers from 1 to 13 were held to denote the following:

1 The Unity of God.
2 The hypostatic union of Christ, both God and man.
3 The TRINITY.
4 The number of the EVANGELISTS.
5 The wounds of the Redeemer; two in the hands, two in the feet, one in the side.
6 The creative week.
7 The gifts of the HOLY GHOST and the seven times Christ spoke on the CROSS.
8 The number of BEATITUDES (*Matt.* v, 3–11).
9 The nine orders of ANGELS.
10 The number of the Commandments.
11 The number of the APOSTLES who remained faithful.
12 The original college.
13 The final number after the conversion of Paul.

Apocalyptic number, 666. *See* NUMBER OF THE BEAST, *below.*

The Number of the Beast. 666; a mystical number of unknown meaning but referring to some man mentioned by St JOHN.

> Let him that hath understanding count the number of the beast: for it is the number of a man: and his number is Six hundred threescore and six.
>
> *Rev.* xiii, 18

One of the most plausible suggestions is that it refers to Neron Caesar, which in Hebrew characters with numerical value gives 666, whereas Nero, without the final 'n', as in Latin, gives 616 (n = 50), the number given in many early MSS., according to Irenaeus.

One suggestion is that St John chose the number 666 because it just fell short of the holy number 7 in every particular; it was straining at every point to get there, but never could. *See also* MYSTERIUM.

Nun. A woman who has joined a religious order and taken its vows, usually of poverty, chastity and obedience, and living in a convent or community. Among the most notable orders are: POOR CLARES, CARMELITES, URSULINES, BENEDICTINES and AUGUSTINIAN CANONESSES.

Nunawading Messiah. James Cowley Morgan Fisher (*c.* 1832–1915) of Nunawading, Victoria, Australia, was so called. The son of Gloucestershire immigrants, he ran away to sea at the age of 14 and settled at Nunawading in the mid-1850s. In the 1860s he succeeded his mother-in-law as head of the New Church of the Firstborn. In a law suit of 1871 he was accused of claiming to be the Messiah or the Christ and of practising polygamy, with three sisters as his wives. His following was small, estimated at about 100 in 1871, but was probably less. *Cp.* SOUTHCOTTIANS.

Nunc dimittis. The Song of Simeon (*Luke* ii, 29), 'Lord, now lettest thou thy servant depart in peace', so called from the opening words of the Latin version, *Nunc dimittis servum tuum, Domine.*

Hence, *to receive one's Nunc dimittis*, to be given permission to go; *to sing one's Nunc dimittis*, to show satisfaction at departing.

The Canticle is sung at Evening Prayer in the CHURCH OF ENGLAND, and has been anciently used at COMPLINE or VESPERS throughout the Church.

> But, above all, believe it, the sweetest canticle is, 'Nunc dimittis' when a man hath obtained worthy ends and expectations.
>
> BACON: *Essays (Of Death)*

Nuncio. A representative or ambassador of the Pope residing at a foreign court; an ambassador of the highest rank.

O

O. The fifteen O's, or **The O's of St Bridget.**
Fifteen meditations on the PASSION composed
by St Bridget. Each begins with *O Jesu*, or a
similar invocation.

The Seven O's, or **The Great O's of Advent.**
The seven antiphons to the MAGNIFICAT sung
during the week preceding CHRISTMAS. They
commence respectively with *O Sapientia, O
Adonai, O Radix Jesse, O Clavis David, O Oriens
Splendor, O Rex gentium,* and *O Emmanuel.*
They are sometimes called *The Christmas O's.*

Oates, Titus (1649–1705). An ANGLICAN clergyman,
officiating at several parishes. He went to the
JESUIT College at Valladolid and St Omer as a spy
but was expelled from both. Returning to
England, Oates forged a plot, maintaining he had
discovered a 'Popish Plot' to murder Charles II
and re-establish CATHOLICISM; as a result many
innocent Catholics were executed on his evidence, but Oates was later flogged, pilloried and
imprisoned for perjury. After the revolution of
1688 he was pardoned and given a pension.

Oath. A solemn attestation of truth or the binding
of a statement or promise, often to God or to
some sacred person or object. Various PROTES-
TANT bodies forbid the taking of oaths, e.g.
QUAKERS (FRIENDS) and BAPTISTS, following the
prohibition in *Matthew* v, 33–7.

Obadiah. An old slang name for a QUAKER.

Obedience. One of the vows taken by a RELIGIOUS
on entering an order or congregation.

Oberammergau. *See* PASSION PLAY.

Obit. A CATHOLIC service on behalf of the soul of
the deceased, often on the anniversary of the
death.

Oblates (Lat. *oblatus*, offered). Lay people
attached to a monastery, or engaged in religious work, often making their possessions
over to the monastery. Also, children committed to a monastery or nunnery by their parents
or guardians, as opposed to *conversi*, who
entered voluntarily in maturity. The term has
been adopted by members of certain CATHOLIC
religious orders.

Observantins. *See* FRANCISCANS.

Occam's Razor. *Entia non sunt multiplicanda
praeter necessitatem* (entities ought not to be
multiplied except from necessity), which
means that all unnecessary facts or con-
stituents in the subject being analysed are to be
eliminated. These exact words do not appear in
Occam's works but the principle expressed
occurs in several other forms. Occam's razor
cuts away superfluities.
   William of Occam, the *Doctor Singularis et
Invincibilis* (d. 1349), the great FRANCISCAN
scholastic philosopher, was probably born at
Ockham, Surrey, *Occam* being the latinized
form of the name. *See also* SCHOLASTICISM. He
revived SEMI-PELAGIANISM, which had been condemned at the Council of Orange in 529.

Occurrence. When two festivals occur on the
same day in the ecclesiastical calendar, the
more important feast is celebrated: e.g.
Christmas falling on a Sunday.

Octateuch. The first eight books of the OLD TES-
TAMENT.

Octave. In liturgical usage the eighth day, including the festival itself, after a festival. It falls on
the same day of the week as the feast.

Octoechos. The liturgical book of the Eastern
ORTHODOX CHURCH containing the variable parts
of the service from the first Sunday after WHIT-
SUNDAY to the tenth Sunday before EASTER.

Oda (or **Odo**), **St** (d. 958, f.d. 2 June
(Canterbury), 29 May, 4 July). Born of Danish
pagan parents in East Anglia, he left them while
young and became a Christian. He was
ordained priest, later being appointed bishop of
Ramsbury in Wiltshire. He was a counsellor at
the court of King Athelstan and in 942 was
made archbishop of Canterbury. He was present at the battle of Brunanburh when
Athelstan's victory defeated the combined
forces of Northumbrians, Scots and Vikings.
Oda was a friend of St DUNSTAN, promoting the
reformation of morals in the Church and the
monastic revival in England, restoring churches and being known as 'Oda the Good'.
Miracles were attributed to him, such as the

repair of King Athelstan's sword in battle; also at a MASS the HOST dripped with blood.

Odila (or Ottilia), St (*c.* 720, f.d. 13 December). She was said to be the daughter of a Frankish nobleman, and to have founded a nunnery at Hoenburg in the Vosges mountains, of which she was the abbess. She was reputedly born blind and rejected by her father. She was adopted by a convent and her sight was restored when she was reconciled with her family. Her shrine at Odilienberg was a noted place of pilgrimage for the blind and those with diseases of the eyes. She is patron of Alsace.

Odilo, St (*c.* 962–1049, f.d. 1 January, 29 April). Born into an aristocratic family, he renounced the world and became a CLUNIAC monk and later, in 991, abbot of Cluny, following the rule of St MAIEUL, and remaining there some fifty-four years. He exerted great influence on other houses, reforming many and bringing them into line with the BENEDICTINE Black Monk tradition. His was a character of nobility, gentleness yet firmness, combined with diplomatic skills. He was described by Fulbert of Chartres as 'the archangel of monks'. He was consulted by both ecclesiastical and political leaders and as a peacemaker he succeeded in limiting fighting from Fridays to Mondays during LENT and ADVENT. He showed great generosity, giving bountiful help during famines. The spread of the observance of ALL SOULS' DAY was due to his institution of prayers for the dead monks, this being later extended to all the dead.

Odo of Cluny, St (879–942, f.d. 18 or 19 November). Born at Tours, he was the son of a knight, and was brought up in the household of William of Aquitaine, who founded Cluny. Odo became a monk at Baume after resigning the canonry of Tours and then, in 927, succeeded Berno as abbot of Cluny, increasing both its numbers and influence and instituting reforms. His influence and reforms spread widely to other monasteries, including MONTE CASSINO, Subiaco and St Paul's-outside-the-Walls in ROME. He also exerted great influence in political matters and was instrumental in obtaining monastic freedom and immunity from secular government and interference. He was noted for his care of the poor and prisoners. His rule was said to combine strict discipline with a sense of fun.

Odour. The odour of sanctity. In the Middle Ages it was held that a sweet and delightful odour was given off by the bodies of saintly persons at their death, and also when their bodies, if 'translated', were disinterred. Hence the phrase, *he died in the odour of sanctity*, i.e. he died a saint. The SWEDENBORGIANS say that when the celestial ANGELS are present at a deathbed, what is then cadaverous excites a sensation of what is aromatic.

Odran (or Otteran) of Iona, St (d. *c.* 563, f.d. 27 October). Traditionally one of the first companions of St COLUMBA on Iona and of note in that the cemetery at Iona was named after him. He died not long after his arrival on the island and St Columba saw angels and devils fighting for his soul before it ascended into heaven. He is patron of Wexford.

Odulf, St (d. 855, f.d. 12 June). Born in North Brabant, he was ordained priest and was sent on a mission to Frisia by St Frederick of Utrecht. He was a man of great piety and intellect and founded churches and monasteries, finally retiring to Utrecht. His relics were bought by Aelfward, bishop of London, for a large sum and were given to Evesham Abbey. Legend says that Queen Edith tried to take some of the relics but was smitten by blindness. Later an abbot of Evesham wanted to remove them to Winchcombe but the shrine became too heavy to carry until they turned back to Evesham, when it became as light as a feather. Odulf had a considerable cult in Holland and Belgium where churches were dedicated to him.

Oecumenical Councils (Gr. *oikoumenikos*, the whole inhabited world—*ge*, earth, being understood). Ecclesiastical councils whose findings are—or were—recognized as binding on all Christians.

Those commonly recognized in the East and West, which dealt with the heresies indicated, are:

Nicaea, 325 (Arianism); Constantinople, 381 (Apollinarianism); Ephesus, 431 (Nestorianism); Chalcedon, 451 (Eutychianism); Constantinople, 533 and 680–1 (Monothelitism); Nicaea, 787 (Iconoclasm).

The ROMAN CATHOLIC CHURCH also recognizes:

Constantinople, 869–870; Lateran, 1123, 1139, 1179, 1215; Lyons, 1245, 1274; Vienne, 1311–12; Constance 1414–18; Ferrara-Florence, 1438–9; Trent, 1545–63; (Protestantism and Reform); Vatican 1869–70 (Papal Infallibility); Vatican, 1962–5.

The Second VATICAN COUNCIL was attended by observers from the CHURCH OF ENGLAND and 26 other denominations.

Oecumenical Movement. The movement towards re-unity among the various Christian Churches, which has gathered strength in recent years, especially since the Second Vatican Council and the establishment of the

World Council of Churches inaugurated at Amsterdam in 1948 which comprises most of the prominent Christian bodies. *See* WORLD COUNCIL OF CHURCHES.

Oecumenical Patriarch. A title given to archbishops or patriarchs of Constantinople since the 6th century.

Oengus the Culdee, St (d. *c*. 824, f.d. 11 March). Born into a royal Ulster family and educated at Clonenagh, he became a hermit, practising austerities, fasting, and saying the psalter while immersed in cold water. He later entered a monastery near Dublin where his origins and scholarship were unknown; he was set to menial tasks until he was discovered coaching an unsuccessful student. He was recognized and honoured by the abbot Maelruain, with whom he compiled the *Tallacht Martyrology*. He was also author of the earliest Irish martyrology, the *Felire*.

Offa of Essex, St (d. *c*. 709, f.d. 15 December). A king of the East Saxons and son of King Sighere and St OSYTH. He abdicated and went to ROME, where he was tonsured and became a monk; he died soon afterwards.

Offertory. The part of the EUCHARIST at which the bread and wine are offered to God; it is also the anthem sung by the choir during the ritual of offering. The collection of money taken at a church service.

Office, The Divine. The obligatory prayers, etc., of the Church said by priests and the religious. The Divine Office (*horae canonicae*) of the ROMAN CATHOLIC CHURCH is contained in the BREVIARY.

Office, The Holy. *See* INQUISITION.

Ogilvie, St John (1579–1615, f.d. 10 March). Of a noble Scottish family of mixed CATHOLIC and PROTESTANT allegiance, he was brought up as a CALVINIST but was sent to the Continent to be educated; there he turned to Catholicism and became a JESUIT. Priests being forbidden entry to Britain, he took the name of John Watson and returned to Scotland to conduct a mission there, but was ultimately betrayed, questioned and tortured, accused of high treason and hanged. He was canonized in 1976, the first Scottish saint in five hundred years.

Olaf (Olave or **Tola), St** (995–1030, f.d. 29 July, 3 August). King of Norway, the son of a chief Harold Grenske, he became a Christian after having pursued a life of war and rapine; he continued to propagate Christianity through the sword. He helped Ethelred II of England against the Danes, then returned to Norway, seized power and established himself as king.

He was of cruel but just nature and, in spite of his intemperance and ferocity, ruled impartially and brought peace for a time until his cruelties provoked a rising against him, and he was exiled in 1029. He was killed in the following year at the battle of Stiklestad in an attempt to regain his throne. He is noted for establishing Christianity in Norway. Miracles were reported at a spring flowing from his grave and his body was said to have remained incorrupt. His cult spread to the Viking areas of England and many churches were dedicated to him. He is patron saint of Norway.

Old. Old Believers. Those members of the Russian ORTHODOX CHURCH who rejected the liturgical reforms of the patriarch Nikon and were excommunicated in 1667. They were subjected to violent persecution and eventually resolved into two groups, the *Popovtsy*, and the *Bespopovtsy*, the latter rejecting the priesthood altogether. The former attained state recognition in 1881.

Old Catholics. *See under* CATHOLIC.

Old Chapel, The. *See under* CHAPEL.

Old Cracow Bible. *See* BIBLE, SOME SPECIALLY NAMED EDITIONS.

Old Latin Bible. *See* BIBLE.

Old Testament, The. The collective name (*see* NEW TESTAMENT) of the first 39 books in the BIBLE inherited as sacred scripture from the Jewish church, and referred to by Christ and his disciples as 'the Scriptures'. *Matt.* xxi, 42 has:

> Jesus saith unto them, Did ye never read in the scriptures...

The Hebrew canon, which is that of the Reformed churches and comprises the 39 books printed in most bibles, is substantially that adopted by a Jewish council at Jamnia (*c*. 90 AD). The Roman Catholic canon includes the APOCRYPHA.

Olga, St (d. 968, f.d. 11 July). One of the most revered of the saints of the Eastern ORTHODOX CHURCH, she was the wife of the pagan Duke of Kiev and was converted to Christianity, taking the baptismal name of Helena and devoting her life to the conversion of the people. Olga was the first Russian woman to receive baptism and canonization. Her grandson St VLADIMIR carried out her work in Christianizing Russia.

Olive. In Christianity the olive symbolizes the fruit of the Church; peace and the faith of the just, making God's peace with mankind. The olive branch is sometimes carried by the Archangel GABRIEL in ANNUNCIATION scenes; it also appears occasionally as carried by the people in Christ's entry to Jerusalem. It is an emblem of St AGNES. The DOVE with an olive branch is a widespread symbol of peace, and in Christianity it also depicts the souls of the faithful at peace.

In the OLD TESTAMENT, the subsiding of the FLOOD was demonstrated to Noah by the return of a dove bearing an olive leaf in her beak (*Gen.* viii, 11).

Olivet, or the Mount of Olives. The range of hills to the east of Jerusalem, closely connected with ancient Jewish ceremonies and intimately associated with the events of the NEW TESTAMENT. Here Jesus retired for prayer and meditation and to talk to his disciples and here he came on the night of his betrayal.

> And in the daytime he was teaching in the temple, and at night he went out, and abode in the mount that is called the Mount of Olives.
>
> *Luke* xxi, 37

Olivetan. Pierre Robert (*c.* 1506–38), a cousin of CALVIN, PROTESTANT reformer and translator of the OLD TESTAMENT; called 'Olivetanus' in allusion to his 'burning the midnight oil'.

Olivetans. Brethren of Our Lady of Mount Olivet, an offshoot of the BENEDICTINES. The order was founded in 1319 by St Bernard Ptolemei. For a time they were total abstainers.

Ombrellino. In the Western CATHOLIC CHURCH, a small canopy covering the Blessed SACRAMENT when it is moved on informal occasions.

Omega. *See* ALPHA.

Omer (or Audomarus), St (d. *c.* 699, f.d. 9 September). Little is known of his life. Born near Coutances, he was a monk at Luxeuil and became bishop of Thérouanne. King Dagobert appointed him as a missionary in northern France where the people had lapsed into paganism. He carried out the mission with great diligence and was an eloquent preacher. He founded the abbey of Sithiu, near the present city of Saint-Omer. He became blind in his old age.

Omophorion. In the Eastern ORTHODOX CHURCH, a long scarf worn round the shoulders of a bishop during the LITURGY.

Oneida Community, The. *See* PERFECTIONISTS.

Ophir. An unidentified territory, famed in the OLD TESTAMENT for its fine gold, possibly in S.E. Arabia. (*See* I *Kings* ix, 26–28.)

Opus (Lat., a work).

Opus operantis, opus operatum; ex opere operato (Lat.). Theological terms long used in relation to the effectiveness of acts relating to the sacraments. *Opus operantis* means the 'act of doer'; *opus operatum*, the 'act done' irrespective of the qualities or disposition of the recipient. Thus baptism is held to convey regeneration to an infant. To hold that a SACRAMENT gives grace *ex opere operato* (from the act of being done) means that the sacrament, properly performed, itself conveys grace, irrespective of the merits of the performer or recipient.

Opus Dei (Lat. God's work). Used in BENEDICTINE monasticism as specifying the recitation of the DIVINE OFFICE, i.e. prescribed prayers at the set times of the CANONICAL HOURS.

It is also the name of an international ROMAN CATHOLIC secular organization, comprising priests and laity, men and women, which was founded in Spain in 1928 by Josemaria Escriva de Balaguer, to promote Christian ideals of perfection, particularly among intellectuals and in government circles. Pope Pius XII gave the organization approval, and in 1946 the headquarters of Opus Dei were removed to ROME.

Oracle of the Church, The. St BERNARD of Clairvaux (1091–115). *Cp.* MELLIFLUOUS DOCTOR.

Orange Lodges. *See* ORANGEMEN.

Orangemen, Orange Order. A society founded in 1795 in Ulster to maintain 'the PROTESTANT Constitution, and to defend the King and his heirs as long as they maintain the Protestant ascendancy'. It was formed after an armed clash between Roman Catholics and Protestants in Armagh, known as the Battle of the Diamond. The name commemorated William of Orange (William III), who defeated James II and his Catholic supporters at the Battle of the Boyne in 1690. Orange Lodges or clubs of militant Protestants spread throughout the province, their members being known as *Orangemen*, an earlier association of this name having been formed in the reign of William III. Gladstone's championship of Home Rule after 1886 led to a revival of the movement. The Orange Order still flourishes, imposing ethical obligations on its members.

Oratorians. (Med. Lat. *oratorium*, a place of prayer). A congregation founded at ROME by St Philip Neri (1515–95), but with origins in the late 1550s. Now called the Institute of the Oratory of St Philip Neri, membership consists of secular priests and lay brothers, who take no vows but live communally, and are free to leave if, and when, they wish. Each oratory is autonomous and its members work under the ORDINARY of their diocese. Dr J. H. Newman was so impressed with the Oratory at Rome that he obtained papal permission to found the Birmingham Oratory in 1847 and in 1849 sent F. W. Faber to found the London Oratory, which moved to Brompton in 1854. *See* ORATORIO.

Oratorio is sacred story or drama set to music, in which solo voices, chorus, and instrumental music are employed. St Philip Neri introduced the acting and singing of sacred dramas in his Oratory at ROME in the late 16th century, and it is from this that the term comes.

Oratory. A chapel in a church, or a private room, used for private worship. The term is now used for places of worship other than the parish church. *See* also ORATORIANS.

Orders. Holy Orders. A clergyman is said to be in *holy orders* because he belongs to one of the *orders* or ranks of the Church. In the CHURCH OF ENGLAND these are three, *viz.*, Deacon, Priest, and BISHOP; in the ROMAN CATHOLIC CHURCH there is a fourth, that of Sub-deacon.

In ecclesiastical use the term also denotes a fraternity of monks or friars (as the *Franciscan Order*), and also the Rule by which the fraternity is governed.

To take orders. To enter HOLY ORDERS by ordination.

Ordinary. In the CHURCH OF ENGLAND, an ecclesiastic who has *ordinary* or regular jurisdiction in his own right and not by depute, usually the BISHOP of a diocese and the archbishops. The Chaplain of Newgate Gaol was called the Ordinary thereof. In the ROMAN CATHOLIC CHURCH, the POPE, diocesan bishops, abbots, apostolic vicars, etc., are classed as ordinaries. In Scotland certain judges of the Court of Sessions are called *Lords Ordinary* and those legal experts appointed to aid the House of Lords in the determination of appeals are called *Lords of Appeal in Ordinary.*

A meal prepared at an eating-house at a fixed rate for all comers was called 'an ordinary'; hence, the place providing such meals.

'Tis almost dinner; I know they stay for you at the ordinary.

BEAUMONT and FLETCHER: *The Scornful Lady*, IV, i

In heraldry the 'ordinary' is a simple charge, such as the chief, pale, fesse, bend, bar, chevron, cross or saltire.

The Ordinary of the Mass. That part of the MASS which varies in accordance with the Church Calendar as opposed to the CANON of the MASS which does not change.

Ordination. The rite of ordaining to, or conferring, HOLY ORDERS of the Christian Church. Baptism and CONFIRMATION are prerequisites to ordination.

Origen (*c.* 185–254). A native of Alexandria, son of the Christian martyr Leonidas, Origen became one of the most influential and brilliant of the FATHERS OF THE CHURCH. Greatly influenced by Philo and Plato, he propounded the interpretation of the SCRIPTURES as allegorical and mythological and, as a result, many of his writings were condemned as heretical. He was said to have written some 6,000 works, of which few have survived; among these are the *De Principiis, Contra Celsum* and *Practical Works.* Origen was arrested and tortured under Decius and died at Tyre.

Origenists. Followers of Origen whose orthodoxy has constantly been called in question. There was a strong anti-Origenist movement in the 4th century, and in the 6th century he was finally condemned as a heretic. In 543 Justinian issued an edict against Origenists and issued fifteen anathemas against the teachings of Origen and Evagarius, a disciple.

Original Sin. *See under* SIN.

Orthodox. The Orthodox Church. The Eastern Church, properly, The Holy Orthodox Catholic Apostolic Eastern Church. Its separation from the Western Church was partly due to the historic division of the Empire by Constantine; but also to the differences arising between 'Greek' and 'Latin' Christianity which culminated in complete separation in 1054 over the FILIOQUE CONTROVERSY. The Eastern Church now consists of seven patriarchates and is oligarchical in structure, and autocephalous; there is no Pope. Churches conduct their worship in their own languages and the Church abstains from proselytism among other Christians. The largest churches are the Russian, Greek, Romanian, Serbian and Bulgarian; other communities are found in Georgia, Albania, Finland, Poland, Czechoslovakia, Cyprus and Mount Sinai. Emigration has led to Eastern Orthodox Churches being established in many other parts of the world. The leading Orthodox patriarchates are represented on the WORLD COUNCIL OF CHURCHES. *See also* CATHOLIC CHURCH; GREEK CHURCH.

Orthodox Sunday, or **Feast of Orthodoxy,** in the Eastern Church, is the First Sunday in LENT, to commemorate the restoration of the icons in 842. *See* ICONOCLASTS.

Orthodoxy. The adhering to and holding of the accepted beliefs, creeds and practices of a religious system, as opposed to heresy (*see* HERETIC).

Orthros. In the Eastern ORTHODOX CHURCH, the early morning office.

Osmanna (no date, f.d. 9 September). A legendary Irish princess of pagan family who fled to France rather than marry the man her parents chose. She lived in a wood near the Loire with her maid, but her hiding place was discovered during a wild boar hunt when the animal sought refuge with her. The bishop persuaded her to become a Christian, and she was dedicated as a virgin. A peasant was employed to make a garden to supply her needs, but he was tempted by the devil to seduce her; she resisted and the man was struck by blindness. Osmanna cured him by prayer. She also cured the queen and the daughter of the King of Spain when they were in the district.

Osmund, St (d. 1099, f.d. 4 December, 16 July). Of noble family in Normandy, he came to England in the train of William the Conqueror, and was his chancellor. He was also appointed bishop of Salisbury, where he was responsible for the completion and consecration of the cathedral. He was credited with drawing up the SARUM RITE and was involved in the preparation of the *Domesday Book*, attending the Council of Rockingham in 1095. He collected a library for the Church and was noted for his love of books, his learning, purity and strictness of discipline, tempered with moderation. He died at Salisbury and was buried in the cathedral at Old Sarum. Miracles were reported at his tomb and he is invoked against madness, toothache, rupture and paralysis.

Ostrog Bible, The. *See* BIBLE, SOME SPECIALLY NAMED EDITIONS.

Oswald. Oswald of Northumbria, St (*c.* 604–42, f.d. 5 August). He fled from King Edwin to Iona where he became a Christian. Later he succeeded Edwin as King of Northumbria and assisted St AIDAN in evangelizing his country, but he did not reign long and was killed in the battle of Maserfield by the pagan Penda of Mercia. His body was mutilated, and different parts were said to be possessed by various churches, his head being in St CUTHBERT's coffin in Durham. Miracles were recounted of his relics and Oswald became one of England's national heroes. In art he is depicted in various guises, either holding a bowl, trampling his murderers, carrying his head or a sword, or blowing a horn. His emblem is a raven with a ring in its beak.
Oswald of Worcester, St (992, f.d. 28 February). Born into a Danish military family, settled in England, he was educated under the direction of his uncle St ODA of Canterbury, who sent him to the CLUNIAC house at Fleury-sur-Loire. He was also related to Archbishop Oskytel of York. Oswald was ordained priest and returned to England, being appointed bishop of Worcester. He was closely associated with the monastic reforms of St DUNSTAN and St ETHELWOLD and founded monasteries, the most famous being at Ramsey. In 972 he was made archbishop of York, but also retained the diocese of Worcester. He was greatly favoured by King Edgar, who gave his monasteries considerable lands. Oswald also built churches. He died at Worcester while carrying out his habitual Lenten practice of serving twelve poor men at table and washing their feet. His remains were translated to York in 1086. He was said to be a man of sanctity, gentleness and kindness, combined with humour.

Oswin (or Oswini), St (d. 65, f.d. 20 August). The last King of Deira, son of King Osric, he was a friend of St AIDAN, whom he helped in spreading Christianity in Northumbria. He was slain by treachery in the battle of Oswy, or Oswin, and buried at Tynemouth where Eanfleda, wife of the murderer, built a monastery in expiation of the crime. Oswin was said to be a man of handsome appearance and great stature, with a courteous and kindly manner to all. He was regarded as a martyr as having died 'at least for the justice of Christ'.

Osyth, St (*c.* 700, f.d. 7 October). An East Anglian princess, married to Sighere, King of the East Saxons; their son Offa became king in 683. There are conflicting legends of her life. One tradition said that she fled from the bridal feast and took the veil; another that the king, an ardent hunter, was distracted by a magnificent white stag appearing each time he attempted to embrace his bride, and left her to go in pursuit of the stag. Osyth left the king, took the veil, and founded a monastery (*c.* 673). She was said to have been beheaded by invading Danes and to have walked three miles to the church with her head in her hands. Later AUSTINIAN CANONS established a priory near the present village of St Osyth in Essex. Her cult spread to Aylesbury, London and Hereford and she was recorded as a virgin and martyr, although the mother of Offa. In art she is depicted carrying her head or with a stag.

O'Toole. *See* LAURENCE, St.

Otteran, St. *See* ODRAN.

Ottilia, St. *See* ODILA.

Otto of Bamberg, St (1062–1139, f.d. 30 September). Born in Swabia, he was ordained priest and became chancellor to Emperor Henry IV, and was appointed bishop of Bamberg. He was invited by Duke Boleslav III of Poland to undertake a mission to Pomerania where, at great danger to himself, he made perilous journeys into the wilds of that country, to Bohemia and North Germany. He made many converts and destroyed a number of pagan temples, building churches in their place. He also played an important part in the political and ecclesiastical affairs of his time and was noted for his sense of justice and his care for the poor. He died at Bamberg, where his relics remain in the cathedral.

Ouen (Audoenus or **Dada), St** (*c*. 600–84, f.d. 24 August). Born near Soissons and brought up at the court of Clotaire II, where he was a friend of SS ELIGIUS or ELOI and Wandrille, he became chancellor to Dagobert and Clovis II, was ordained late in life and founded a monastery at Rebais. He was appointed bishop of Rouen where there is a church dedicated to him. Some of his relics were claimed by Canterbury, where they were responsible for miraculous cures.

Overy, or **Overie.** The priory church of St Mary Overy, renamed St Saviour's in 1540, and which became Southwark Cathedral in 1905, was legendarily founded by a ferryman's daughter called Mary (or Mary Overs). Her miserly father Awdrey feigned death in the hope that sorrow would restrain his household's consumption of victuals. Instead they rejoiced and made merry, whereupon Awdrey rose up in anger, only to be slain as a ghost. Mary, now possessed of his fortune, sent for her lover, but he was thrown from his horse and was killed. In sorrow she founded the nunnery which she entered. *Overy* is probably a corruption of 'over the river'.

Owen, St Nicholas (*c*. 1550–1606, f.d. 25 October). Born into a Catholic family in Oxfordshire, he was a carpenter and builder, in which capacity he built a number of 'priest's holes' and hiding places in country houses, many of which may be seen today; he thus saved many lives of priests and recusants. He was arrested and imprisoned three times following the arrest of those he had helped to save. He was tortured and twice put to the rack, still refusing to betray his companions. He died under extreme torture. He was canonized in 1970 as one of the FORTY MARTYRS OF ENGLAND AND WALES.

Owin (or **Owen), St** (d. *c*. 670, f.d. 4 March). Mentioned by the Venerable BEDE as a devout monk serving in the household of St CHAD's monastery at Lastingham, he was born in East Anglia and accompanied St ETHELDREDA to Northumbria on the occasion of her marriage. When St Chad was appointed bishop of Mercia and Linsey, Owin went with him. He experienced a vision foretelling Chad's death and himself died soon after.

P

Pachomius, St (d. 346, f.d. 15 May (East), 9 May (Coptic)). Regarded as the founder of Christian monasticism, he was born near Esmeh, in Egypt, into a pagan family. He became a Christian and at first lived as a hermit, organizing other hermits into groups living a communal life under written rules and being self-supporting by crafts and agriculture. He established the first monastery at Tabennisi, this being the precursor of nine monasteries for men and two nunneries for women. His Rule influenced the later monasticism of St BASIL and St BENEDICT.

Padre (Lat. *pater*, father). The popular term used for a priest in the armed forces. A title of address for a priest in Italy, Spain, Portugal and Latin America.

Padre Pio (Pio Forgione) (d. 1968). A priest who in 1918 developed the STIGMATA, which remained for the rest of his life. Miraculous cures were reported, sight restored, bilocation, fragrance, bodily heat, thought-reading, and clairvoyance. He was of peasant family and was practical and conscientious.

Pagan (Lat. *paganus*, a rustic). Its present meaning of a heathen or non-Christian has usually been held to be derived from the fact that heathen practices lingered in the villages long after the Christian Church was established in the towns. The word was also a Roman contemptuous name for a civilian and it is likely that when the early Christians called themselves *milites Christi* (soldiers of Christ) they adopted the military usage, *paganus*, for those who were not 'soldiers of Christ'. (See the penultimate note to ch. xxi of Gibbon's *Decline and Fall of the Roman Empire*.)

Paine, St John (1550–82, f.d. 25 October). Born at Peterborough and a member of the CHURCH OF ENGLAND, he was converted to ROMAN CATHOLICISM and entered the ENGLISH COLLEGE at DOUAI where he served as bursar and was ordained priest. Returning to England, he worked among recusants under the guise of the steward of Inglestone Hall in Essex. He was betrayed, arrested, imprisoned and charged with conspiracy against the Queen. He was tortured in the Tower and finally sentenced to be hanged, drawn and quartered at Chelmsford. His popularity was such that the people compelled the hangman to be sure he was dead before the rest of the sentence was carried out. He was canonized in 1970 as one of the FORTY MARTYRS OF ENGLAND AND WALES.

Palimpsest (Gr. *palin* , again; *psestos*, scraped). A parchment or other writing surface on which the original writing has been effaced and something else has been written, anciently common practice owing to the shortage of material. As the writing was not always entirely effaced, many works, otherwise lost, have been recovered. Thus Cicero's *De Republica* was restored, though partially erased to make way for a commentary of St AUGUSTINE on the PSALMS.

Pall. The small linen cloth stiffened by cardboard which covers the chalice at the EUCHARIST; also the covering thrown over a coffin. It is the Lat. *pallium*, a robe or mantle; also the long sweeping robe or pall worn by sovereigns at their coronation, by the POPE and archbishops. *See* PALLIUM.

> Sometimes let gorgeous Tragedy
> In sceptered pall come sweeping by.
>
> MILTON: *Il Penseroso*, line 97

Pall-bearers. The custom of appointing men of marks for pall-bearers came to us from the Romans. Julius Caesar had magistrates for his pall-bearers; Augustus Caesar had senators; Germanicus had tribunes and centurions; L. Aemilius Paulus had the chief men of Macedonia who happened to be at ROME at that time; but the poor were carried on a plain bier by ordinary citizens.

Palladius, St (5th cent., f.d. 7 July). Sent by Pope Celestine to Ireland in 431 to be the first bishop of the country. He probably accompanied St Germanus for the purpose of eradicating the PELAGIAN heresy. It was claimed that he founded three churches in Ireland and that his mission prepared the way for St PATRICK. Tradition says that he met with hostility and left for Scotland where he died at Fordunn. His cult flourished at Aberdeen.

Pallium. The Roman name for a square woollen cloak worn by men in ancient Greece, especially by philosophers and courtesans, corresponding to the Roman toga. Hence the Greeks called themselves *gens palliata*, and the Romans were *gens togata*.

At the present time, the scarf-like vestment of white wool with red crosses, worn by the POPE and archbishops, is called the *pallium*. Pallia are made by the OBLATES of St FRANCIS in ROME from wool taken from two lambs blessed in the church of St AGNES on her feast day. Until he has received his pallium no Roman Catholic archbishop can exercise his functions. Its use in the Church of England (*see under* CHURCH) ended with the REFORMATION, although it is still displayed heraldically in the arms of the Archbishop of Canterbury in the shape of a letter Y. It is also called a PALL.

Pallotti, St Vincent. *See* VINCENT PALLOTTI.
Pallottini Fathers. The SOCIETY OF THE CATHOLIC APOSTOLATE, founded by St Vincent Pallotti in 1835 as a society of ROMAN CATHOLIC priests and laity committed to conversion, missions and education, and to the promotion of reunion of the Roman and Eastern ORTHODOX CATHOLICS. In 1843 he also founded the Pallotti Sisters. The missions of both spread widely.

Palm. In Christianity the palm symbolizes divine blessing and righteousness, the righteous who 'shall flourish like the palm tree'. It can also represent immortality and, as such, is sometimes depicted with the PHOENIX. The palm is also an emblem of Christ's triumphal entry into Jerusalem and of the martyr's triumph over death. Palm branches signify triumph, glory, resurrection and victory over death and sin. Among early Roman Christians it was a funerary emblem. *See also* PALMER.
Palm Sunday. The Sunday next before EASTER. So called in memory of Christ's triumphant entry into JERUSALEM, when the multitude strewed the way (*John* xii, 12–19). In mediaeval England 'palms' were often made from willow, box, and yew.
Palmer (Lat. *palmifer*, palm-bearer). A pilgrim to the HOLY LAND who was given a consecrated palm-branch to carry back which was usually laid on the altar of his parish church on his return.

His sandals were with travel tore
Staff, budget, bottle, scrip he wore;
The faded palm-branch in his hand
Showed pilgrim from the Holy Land.
SCOTT: *Marmion*, i, 27

Pammachius, St (*c.* 340–410, f.d. 30 August). A Roman senator who married a daughter of St PAULA. He was a learned layman and a friend of St JEROME, writing to him to reprove him for his temper and for his quarrel with RUFINUS over the teachings of ORIGEN. After the death of his wife Pammachius devoted his time and fortune to good works in association with St Fabiola, founding a hospice and hospital for travellers.

Pamphilus, St (*c.* 240, f.d. 16 February, 1 June). Born in Berytus (Beirut), he studied at Alexandria, taught in the school and collected a noteworthy library for the church at Caesarea in Palestine, where he settled for life. He was a follower of ORIGEN, writing in his defence while imprisoned for his faith. Pamphilus was martyred together with St Elias and others, being flayed and roasted alive.

Pancras, St (d. 304, f.d. 12 May). One of the patron saints of children (*cp.* NICHOLAS), martyred in the Diocletian persecution at ROME at the age of 14. He is usually represented as a boy with a sword in one hand and a palm-branch in the other. The first church to be consecrated in England by St AUGUSTINE, at Canterbury, was dedicated to St Pancras.
Pancras of Taormina, St (1st cent., f.d. 3 April, 8 July). Said to have been sent by St PETER on a mission to Sicily; he preached and worked miracles but was stoned to death by brigands. His cult spread over all Sicily and even as far as Georgia. English churches are also dedicated to him.

Pannychis. In the Eastern ORTHODOX CHURCH a night-long vigil; a liturgical preparation for a festival.

Pantaleon, St (d. *c.* 305, f.d. 27 July). The name means the 'All compassionate' and Pantaleon was reputedly a physician who treated the Emperor Galerius. Legend says he was the son of a pagan father and Christian mother, reared in Christianity, but he lapsed into paganism and self-indulgence. Later he returned to the Church through the influence of a friend and became a wonder-worker. He suffered persecution under Diocletian, being tortured and finally beheaded after six different methods had been tried to put him to death. Milk was said to flow from his neck at the execution. Numerous churches claim his body and relics, and a phial of his blood at Ravello, in Italy, is said to liquefy on his festival. He was revered in the West as one of the FOURTEEN HOLY HELPERS and is patron of physicians.

Pantheism. The doctrine that God is everything and everything is God; a monistic theory elaborated by Spinoza, who by his doctrine of the Infinite Substance sought to overcome the opposition between mind and matter, body and soul. It also denotes pagan worship of all the gods.

Papa (Lat. Father). A title given to the Pope as

the 'Holy Father' at ROME. Clergy in the Eastern ORTHODOX CHURCH are styled 'Papa'.

Papacy. *See* POPE.

Paphnutius, St (*c.* 350, f.d. 11 September). At first a solitary in Egypt and a friend and disciple of St ANTHONY THE GREAT, he was called to be a bishop in Upper Thebaid. He suffered persecution, torture and mutilation under Maximinus, having an eye plucked out and a leg hamstrung. After being ordained bishop, he attended the first Council of NICAEA in 325, opposing the motion that married clergy should separate from their wives, but supporting the celibacy of the clergy after ordination. He also attended the Council of Tyre in 335 and was a supporter of St ATHANASIUS.

Papias (*c.* 70—160). Bishop of Hieropolis, in Phrygia, and said to have been a disciple of St JOHN and a friend of POLYCARP. His writings survive only as quoted by IRENAEUS and EUSEBIUS. He wrote on the origins of the GOSPELS of MATTHEW and MARK.

Parable (Gr. *parabole*, a comparison). A story used to illustrate a moral lesson or religious principle; an allegorical narrative. A method of teaching frequently employed by Christ in the GOSPELS.

Paraclete. The advocate; one called to aid or support another; from Gr. *parakalein*, to call to. The word is used as a title of the HOLY GHOST, the Comforter.

Paradise. The Greeks borrowed this word from the Persians, among whom it denoted the enclosed and extensive parks and pleasure grounds of the Persian kings. The SEPTUAGINT translators adopted it for the garden of EDEN, and in the NEW TESTAMENT and by early Christian writers it was applied to HEAVEN, the abode of the blessed dead.

Paragraph Bible. *See* BIBLE.

Paraguay, Martyrs of (d. 1628, f.d. 17 November). Three JESUITS, Roque Gonzales, Alonso Rodriguez and Juan de Castillo, were founders of the 'Reductions' of Paraguay, settlements for Indians converted to Christianity, which would preserve their ancient traditions. They opposed the Spanish colonists and the INQUISITION, and were suppressed in the 18th-century. Ultimately they were confronted by a powerful Medicine Man who incited the local Indians to kill them. Evidence came to light 200 years later and was collected in 1934. The three priests were canonized in 1988.

Paraskeva, St (no date, f.d. 28 October). A native of Iconia in Asia Minor, martyred in the Diocletian persecution. He was specially venerated among the Slavs from earliest times as the patron of the work of women. He was famed for his bold preaching of Christianity. He was tortured and was canonized in the Eastern Church as a martyr-confessor. In art he is depicted with the red cloak of martyrdom.

Pardon Bell. The ANGELUS bell. So called because of the INDULGENCE once given for reciting certain prayers forming the Angelus.
Pardoner. A mediaeval cleric licensed to preach and collect money for a definite object such as a CRUSADE or the building of a church, for contributing to which letters of INDULGENCE were exchanged. By many they were regarded as licences to sin and were denounced by Chaucer, Langland, and Wycliff.

Parish. An ecclesiastical administrative district or territorial division under the control of a priest.
Parish Clerk. A layman who assists a priest in the care of the parish.
Parochial Church Council. In the CHURCH OF ENGLAND a body of laity set up in each parish to assist in its administration.

Parousia (Gr., presence or coming). The expected return of Christ to the world in glory to rule the world. See MILLENNIUM.

Parson. *See* CLERICAL TITLES.
Grey-coat parson. An impropriator; a layman who owned the TITHES.

Particular Baptists. *See* BAPTISTS.

Parvis. An enclosed court in front of a cathedral or church, later used for the church porch.

Pascal, Blaise (1623–62). Born at Clermont-Ferrand, scientist, mathematician and apologist, he showed early signs of genius, especially in mathematics. He wrote scientific treatises of great importance. He came under JANSENIST influence and joined them at Port-Royal, where his sister was a nun. He argued the Jansenist doctrine against the JESUITS in his *Lettres Provinciales* (1656), a brilliant satirical work. After a mystical experience he turned to asceticism. The *Pensées*, his most famous work, were written on scraps of paper and were not published until after his early death. They were intended as the basis of an *Apology for the Christian Religion*, and their main object was to defend Christianity against freethinkers and to explore the limits of reason.

Pasch. EASTER, from the Greek form of the

Hebrew *Pesach*, PASSOVER.

Pasch eggs, or **Pace eggs.** EASTER eggs, given as an emblem of the Resurrection.

Paschal Candle. A tall candle burning for forty days from EASTER to ASCENSION, it is blessed on HOLY SATURDAY and represents Christ's presence with the Disciples for the 40 days after the RESURRECTION. Extinguished on Ascension Day it depicts Christ leaving the earth. It also symbolizes the light of the risen Christ; also representing the pillar of fire which led the Israelites for 40 years.

Paschal Lamb. The lamb sacrificed and eaten at the Jewish PASSOVER. For Christians, Jesus Christ is called the *Paschal Lamb* because He was called the 'Lamb of God' by *John* (i, 29) and in allusion to I *Cor.* v, 7—'For even Christ our passover is sacrificed for us.'

Pasque eggs. *See* PASCH EGGS.

Passes, St Bernard. Two Alpine passes into Italy, the Great St Bernard from Switzerland, the little St Bernard from France. On the former is the famous hospice founded by St Bernard of Menthon (923–1008, canonized 1681), served by the AUGUSTINIAN CANONS. From early days they have succoured pilgrims and others crossing the pass, for this purpose breeding the large and handsome **St Bernard dog,** trained to track and aid travellers lost in the snow.

Passion, The. The sufferings of Jesus Christ which had their culmination in His death on the CROSS.

Passion Play. A development of the mediaeval MYSTERY play with especial reference to the story of our Lord's passion and death. The best-known survival of such plays, which were common in 14th-century France, is the Oberammergau Passion Play, which takes place every ten years. In 1633 the black death swept over the village of Oberammergau; when it abated the inhabitants vowed to enact the passion every ten years and this has been done with one or two exceptions. It is now a highly commercial undertaking although the cast is still taken from the villagers.

Passion Sunday. *See* JUDICA.

Passionists. Members of the Congregation of Discalced Clerks of the Most Holy Cross and Passion of Our Lord Jesus Christ, founded by St Paul of the Cross in 1720. The first house, at Monte Argentario, an island off the coast of Tuscany, was opened in 1737. Their chief work is in the holding of retreats and missions. The fathers wear on the breast of their black habit a white heart with the inscription *Jesu Xpi Passio*, surmounted by a CROSS.

Passover. A Jewish festival to commemorate the deliverance of the Israelites, when the ANGEL of death (that slew the firstborn of the Egyptians) passed over their houses, and spared all who did as MOSES commanded them. The festival began on 14th of Nisan (i.e. about 12 April) when the PASCHAL LAMB was eaten, and the Festival of Unleavened Bread lasted seven days. Traditionally the time of the Last Supper and the institution of the EUCHARIST.

Pastophorion. In the Eastern ORTHODOX CHURCH the sacristy used for the Reserved Sacrament; it adjoins the APSE.

Pastoral Letters. Letters from a bishop directed to the whole diocese, as differing from ENCYCLICAL letters for the clergy only.

Paten. (Lat. *patina*, a dish). A small plate used to cover the chalice and on which the bread or wafers are placed at the EUCHARIST.

Paternoster (Lat., Our Father). The Lord's Prayer; from the first two words in the Latin version. Every eleventh bead of a ROSARY is so called, because at that bead the Lord's Prayer is repeated; the name is also given to a certain kind of fishing tackle, in which hooks and weights to suit them are fixed alternately on the line somewhat in rosary fashion.

A Paternoster-while. Quite a short time; the time it takes to say a paternoster.

Paternoster Row (London) was probably so named from the ROSARY or paternoster makers. There is mention as early as 1374 of a Richard Russell, a 'paternosterer', who dwelt there, and we read of 'one Robert Nikke, a paternoster maker and citizen', in the reign of Henry IV. Another suggestion is that it was so called because funeral processions on their way to St Paul's began their *Pater noster* at the beginning of the Row. For three centuries Paternoster Row was the home of publishers and booksellers. It was totally destroyed in an air raid in December 1940.

Patriarch (Gr. *patria*, family; *archein*, to rule). The head of a tribe or family who rules by paternal right; applied specially (after *Acts* vii, 8) to the twelve sons of Jacob, and to ABRAHAM, Isaac, and Jacob and their forefathers. In one passage (*Acts* ii, 29) David is spoken of as a patriarch.

In the early Church, 'Patriarch', first mentioned in the Council of Chalcedon, but virtually existing from about the time of the Council of Nicaea, was the title of the highest Church officers. A Patriarch ordained METROPOLITANS, convened councils, received appeals, and was the chief BISHOP over several countries or provinces, as an archbishop is over several dioceses. It was also the title given by the POPES to

Patrick, St

the archbishops of Lisbon and Venice, in order to make the patriarchal dignity appear lower and distinct from the papal. It is also the title of the chief bishop of various Eastern churches, as the JACOBITES, Armenians and MARONITES.

In the ORTHODOX Eastern Church the bishops of Constantinople, Alexandria, Antioch, and JERUSALEM are patriarchs, the Patriarch of Constantinople bearing the style of Oecumenical Patriarch. Within a religious order the title is given to the founder, as St BENEDICT. St FRANCIS, and St DOMINIC.

Patrick, St (*c.* 389–*c.* 461, f.d. 17 March). The apostle and patron SAINT of Ireland was not an Irishman but was born at Bannavem. Its location is unknown but it may have been in Glamorgan and his father, Calpurnius, was a Roman official and deacon. As a boy he was captured in a Pictish raid and sold as a slave in Ireland. He escaped to Gaul where he probably studied in the monastery of Lérins before returning to Britain. After receiving a supernatural call to preach to the heathen of Ireland, he returned to Gaul and was ordained deacon. He landed in Wicklow (432) and going north converted the people of Ulster and later those of other parts of Ireland. He established many communities and churches including the cathedral church of Armagh. He is said to have died in 461 and to have been buried at Down in Ulster.

St Patrick left his name to many places and numerous legends are told of his miraculous powers. Perhaps the best known tradition is that he cleared Ireland of its vermin. The story goes that one old serpent resisted him, so he made a box and invited the serpent to enter it. The serpent objected, saying it was too small; but St Patrick insisted it was quite large enough to be comfortable. Eventually the serpent got in to prove it was too small, whereupon St Patrick slammed down the lid and cast the box into the sea.

In commemoration of this he is usually represented banishing the serpents, and with a shamrock leaf.

St Patrick's Cross. The same shape as St Andrew's CROSS (×), only different in colour, viz. red on a white ground.

The Order of St Patrick. A British order of knighthood instituted by George III in 1783, originally consisting of the Sovereign, the Lord Lieutenant, and 15 knights (enlarged to 22 in 1833). Its motto is *Quis Separabit?* In 1968 the Order consisted of the Sovereign and 2 knights. There have been no elections since 1924. The Order ceased with the death of the Duke of Gloucester in 1974.

Patripassians (Lat. *Pater passus,* suffering father). An early Christian school of the 2nd century founded by Praxeas who, according to TERTULLIAN, taught that 'the Father Himself descended into the Virgin, was Himself born of her, Himself suffered; in fact Himself was Jesus Christ'.

Patripassian Heresy. *See* MONARCHIANISM.

Patristics, Patrology (Lat. *pater,* father). Study relating to the FATHERS OF THE CHURCH and their writings, given more particular prominence in CATHOLIC traditions. The most widely known texts are those collected by the French Father Migne; the Greek and Latin *Patrologia Graeca* and *Patrologia Latina,* and the ORTHODOX *Philokalia.* In England the founders of the Oxford Movement edited translations of the chief patristic texts, bringing about a revival of interest in the subject.

Patron Saints. *See* SAINTS.

Paul. Paul, St (d. *c.* 66, f.d. 25 January). Patron saint of preachers and tent-makers (see *Acts* xviii, 3). Originally called Saul, his name, according to tradition, was changed in honour of Sergius Paulus, whom he converted (*Acts* xiii, 6–12).

His symbols are a sword and open book, the former the instrument of his martyrdom and the latter indicative of the new law propagated by him as the apostle of the Gentiles. He is represented as of short stature, with bald head and grey, bushy beard; and legend relates that when he was beheaded at ROME after having converted one of Nero's favourite concubines, milk instead of blood flowed from his veins.

Paul Aurelian, St (6th cent., f.d. 12 March, later 10 October). Son of a Romano–British chieftain, he became a monk and priest and was educated under St ILLTYD, together with St DAVID. He left with companions for Brittany, where they founded churches. Paul became bishop of Saint Pol-de-Léon named after him. He died at the age of 104, and his body was translated to Fleuty; later his relics were taken to the cathedral of Saint Pol-de-Léon. He is patron of Paul in Cornwall.

Paul of the Cross, St (1694–1775, f.d. 19 October, formerly 28 April). Born at Ovada in Piedmont of a devout, noble, but impoverished family, he rejected his inheritance, and the opportunity of an advantageous marriage, and joined the Venetian army as a volunteer to fight the Turks. After a year he left the army to engage in a life of seclusion and prayer. Following a vision, he founded the PASSIONIST CONGREGATION in 1720; it combined the contemplative life and an active ministry among the sick and dying. He experienced many mystical states but at the same time was an active and noted preacher and had the gifts of healing, prophecy and reading minds. He worked actively for the reconciliation of England with the PAPACY. In 1771 he founded the Passionist nuns at an enclosed convent at Cornento. He was canonized in 1867.

Paul's Cross. A pulpit in the open air situated on the north side of Old St Paul's Cathedral, in which, from 1259 to 1643, eminent divines preached in the presence of the Lord Mayor and Aldermen every Sunday. The cross was demolished in 1643 by order of Parliament. A new pulpit and CROSS were erected on the site in 1910.

St Paul the Hermit (d. 341, f.d. 15 January). The first of the Egyptian hermits. When 113 years old, he was visited by St ANTHONY, himself over 90, and when he died St Anthony wrapped his body in the cloak given to him by St Athanasius, and his grave was dug by two lions. He lived in a cave, and he is represented as an old man, clothed with palm-leaves, and seated under a palm-tree, near which are a river and loaf of bread. Traditionally, he had gone to the desert to escape the persecution under Decius and was a man of good family and education. His attributes are a raven and two lions, but he is somewhat rarely depicted in art.

Paula, St (d. 404, f.d. 26 January). A Roman matron connected with the patrician families of the Scipios and Gracchi, she married the senator Toxotius. At his death and that of her eldest daughter, she left the world and followed an austere regime, giving generously to the poor. Under the influence of St JEROME she, with her daughter St Eustochium, journeyed to Egypt, visiting the hermits and going on to the HOLY LAND where she settled near Bethlehem and became the leader of a group of women under St Jerome's direction. She built a monastery for men and a convent for women, also a hospice for pilgrims. Her scholarship and knowledge of Greek helped St Jerome, as did her practical efficiency and tactfulness, although she incurred financial difficulties through her over-generosity. She died in Bethlehem and was buried under the Church of the Nativity. St Jerome wrote his noted *Letter 108* as her epitaph.

Paulicians. A heretical sect of the 7th century in Armenia, founded by Constantine of Mananalis, who was executed by order of the Emperor in 687. The Paulicians were dualists, rejecting the OLD TESTAMENT and the EPISTLES of PETER in the NEW TESTAMENT, they also rejected BAPTISM and the EUCHARIST and had no priesthood. They condemned Mariolatry since, matter being of the Devil, the HOLY SPIRIT could not enter into it. Many of the sect were transported to Bulgaria in 752 where they may have been connected with the BOGOMILS who held similar views.

Paulinus. Paulinus of Aquileia, St (*c.* 726–802, f.d. 11 January). Born near Cividale in northern Italy, he was well educated and went to the court of Charlemagne in 776, where he became a friend of ALCUIN of York. He was appointed bishop of Aquileia and proved a good administrator. He attended various Church councils, was involved in sending missions to the Avars and other pagans, working with Pepin in Italy. He denounced the baptism of uninstructed converts and wrote against the heresy of ADOPTIONISM. He also wrote hymns and poems.

Paulinus of Nola, St (d. 431, f.d. 22 June). Pontius Meropius Anicius Paulinus was born into a wealthy Roman patrician family at Bordeaux. He was educated by the poet Ausonius, then practised as a lawyer, travelled widely, and married a Spanish woman, Therasia. They became Christians, sold most of their French estates and gave generously to the poor. By popular demand Paulinus was ordained priest, although not then a deacon. He and Therasia settled at Nola, in Italy, where they lived frugally in the upper floor of a house, while the lower floor was devoted to the care of pilgrims and the needy. Paulinus was a noted poet and was considered comparable to Prudentius; he was also a keen student of the lives of the saints. He was appointed bishop of Nola in 409 and was greatly esteemed, both for his attractive personality and his scholarship.

Paulinus of York, St (d. 644, f.d. 10 October). A Roman monk and one of the second band of missionaries sent to England by GREGORY THE GREAT. He was the first apostle to Northumbria, accompanying St ETHELBURGA there on her marriage to the King St Edwin, whom he had converted. He also converted many people there and founded the see of York. He travelled southwards to Nottinghamshire and founded a church at Lincoln. After the death of Edwin, Paulinus had to fly and took refuge in Kent with Ethelburga and her children, becoming bishop of Rochester there. BEDE describes him as a 'tall, dark man ... his presence being venerable and awe-inspiring'.

Paulists. Members of the ROMAN CATHOLIC MISSIONARY SOCIETY of St PAUL the Apostle, founded in 1858 for missionary work in the USA. They were not bound by religious vows, being largely engaged in work and propaganda among non-Catholics.

Pax (Lat., peace). The 'kiss of peace', which is given at MASS. It is omitted on MAUNDY THURSDAY.

Also a sacred utensil used when mass is celebrated by a high dignitary. It is sometimes a crucifix, sometimes a tablet, and sometimes a reliquary, and is handed round to be kissed as a symbolic substitute for the 'kiss of peace'.

The old custom of 'kissing the bride', which took place immediately before the Communion of the newly married couple and still obtains in some churches, is derived from the Salisbury rubric concerning the Pax in the Missa Sponsalium:

Tunc amoto pallio, surgant ambo sponsus et sponsa; et accipiat sponsus pacem a sacerdote, et ferat sponsae osculans eam et neminem alium, nec ipse, nec ipsa; sed statim diaconus vel clericus a presbytero pacem accipiens, ferat aliis sicut solitum est.

Pax Romana. Founded in Switzerland in 1921 and having its headquarters in Geneva, Pax Romana is an international group of ROMAN CATHOLIC students, later incorporating a section for graduates and professionals, working for 'Christian presence and evangelization of culture', promoting intellectual dialogue and 'the search for more humane means of scientific development'. It has groups in every continent and some 80 countries.

Pax vobis(cum) (Peace be unto you). The formula used by a BISHOP instead of 'The Lord be with you', wherever this versicle occurs in Divine service. They are the words used by Christ to His apostles on the first EASTER morning.

Pazzi, St Mary Magdelene de (1566–1606, f.d. 29 May). Born into a wealthy family in Florence, with connections with the Medici, she became a CARMELITE nun against the wishes of her parents. She was famous as a mystic and for the visions which came to her when she became bedridden and in great pain; she was heard to hold conversations with Christ and the Saints, which were recorded. She had the gifts of prophecy and mind-reading. Her incorrupt body at St Maria degl'Angeli is the centre of a cult.

Pectoral Cross. *See* CRUX PECTORALIS.

Peculiar. A parish or group of parishes exempt from the jurisdiction of the ORDINARY of the diocese. There were many such in mediaeval England, e.g. monastic peculiars, royal peculiars, archiepiscopal, and diocesan, peculiars, peculiars belonging to Orders, and cathedral peculiars. In 1832 there were still over 300 peculiars which were abolished between 1838 and 1850, the exceptions being cathedral peculiars, Westminster Abbey and those of the royal residences including the Chapel Royal of the Savoy. *See also* DEAN OF THE ARCHES; DEANS OF PECULIARS.

Court of Peculiars. In particular, a branch of the Court of ARCHES which had jurisdiction over the peculiars of the Archbishop of Canterbury.

The Peculiar People. Properly, the Jews, the 'Chosen people'. The title was also assumed by a London sect, the 'Plumstead Peculiars', founded in 1838. They refuse medical, but not surgical aid and rely on the efficacy of prayer and on anointing with oil by the elders. The name is based on *Titus* ii, 14—'Purify unto himself a peculiar people'.

Pedestal. To set on a pedestal. To idolize or to idealize. From the custom of showing reverence to figures of SAINTS and others set on pedestals.

Pedilavium. The rite of foot-washing on MAUNDY THURSDAY. It commemorates Christ's action at the LAST SUPPER.

Pega, St (d. *c.* 719, f.d. 8 January). Sister of St GUTHLAC, a hermit at Croyland, they were of royal blood of a Mercian tribe. Pega lived as an anchoress not far from her brother. When he knew he was dying Guthlac invited her to his funeral, and she inherited his psalter and scourge. On the way to the funeral Pega healed a blind man. She later went on a pilgrimage to ROME, where she died.

Pelagia the Penitent, St (no date, f.d. 8 October). A legendary character, popular in both the East and West; the story, however, may be based on an account given by St JOHN CHRYSOSTOM of the conversion of an actress of Antioch. The legend says that she was a beautiful but licentious actress who, passing by some bishops attending a sermon by Nonnus, attracted their attention and disapproval, except for Nonnus who remarked on the attention and devotion she gave to her appearance and profession in contrast to the tepid attention given by the bishops to their calling. Later Pelagia, hearing Nonnus preach, was converted and baptized, giving away all her possessions and retiring to a solitary cave on OLIVET. She dressed as a man and was known as the beardless hermit 'Pelagius'. Her sex and identity were not known until after her death.

Pelagia of Antioch, St (d. *c.* 311, f.d. 9 June (West), 8 October (East)). Sometimes confused with the legendary Pelagia the Penitent, the historical Pelagia who appears in the Ambrosian Canon was a girl of fifteen, a Christian at Antioch, who, at a time of persecution, was arrested by soldiers. To avoid dishonour she pretended to go upstairs to change her clothes, but threw herself off the top of the house into the river below. She was venerated among the maiden martyrs.

Pelagians. Heretical followers of the British monk Pelagius (a Latinized form of his Welsh name *Morgan*, the sea). They denied the doctrine of ORIGINAL SIN (*see under* SIN) or the taint of ADAM, and maintained that we have power of ourselves to receive or reject the GOSPEL. They were opposed by St AUGUSTINE and condemned by Pope Innocent I in 417 and again by Pope Zosimus in 418.

Pelican. In Christian art, a symbol of charity; also an emblem of Jesus Christ, by 'whose blood we are healed'. St JEROME gives the story of the pelican restoring its young ones destroyed by serpents, and his own salvation by the blood of Christ. The popular fallacy that pelicans feed their young with their blood arose from the fact that the parent bird transfers macerated food from the large bag under its bill to its young. The correct term for the heraldic representation of the bird in this act is **a pelican in her piety,** *piety* having the classical meaning of filial devotion.

The mediaeval Bestiary tells us that the pelican is very fond of its brood, but, when they grow, they often rebel against the male bird and provoke his anger, so that he kills them; the mother returns to the nest in three days, sits on the dead birds, pours her blood over them, revives them, and they feed on her blood.

> Then sayd the Pellycane,
> When my byrdis be slayne
> With my bloude I them reuyue [revive].
> Scripture doth record
> The same dyd our Lord,
> And rose from death to lyue.
>
> SKELTON: *Armoury of Birdis*

Penance. Penalty or suffering undertaken voluntarily to atone for sin or wrongdoing. Penance is a SACRAMENT in the ROMAN and Eastern ORTHODOX CHURCHES; there are three stages: contrition and confession to a priest; priestly absolution; and the performance of some act of atonement as required by the priest. In the Roman Catholic Church Penance can now also be called the Rite of Reconciliation. Penance imposed is now more often set in good works rather than in the recitation of prayers or formulae. The fourth LATERAN COUNCIL of 1215 imposed confession and penance at least once a year.

Penitential Psalms. The seven psalms expressive of contrition (vi, xxxii, xxxviii, li, cii, cxxx, cxliii). From time immemorial they have all been used at the ASH WEDNESDAY services; the first three at MATINS, the 51st at the Commination, and the last three at Evensong.

Penitents. In the ROMAN and Eastern ORTHODOX CATHOLIC CHURCHES a penitent is one who receives the SACRAMENT of PENANCE. In earlier times penitents wore a special robe and occupied a separate part of the Church. 'Penitents'

was also the name given to fraternities which existed in France, Spain and Italy in the Middle Ages; they wore sombre clothing, practised flagellation as they went through the streets and devoted themselves to works of mercy, burying the dead and visiting the sick and prisoners. There are orders of women penitents who are dedicated to reclaiming prostitutes.

Penny fish. A name given to the JOHN DORY because of the round spots on each side left by St PETER'S FINGERS.

Pentateuch. The first five books of the OLD TESTAMENT, anciently attributed to MOSES (Gr. *penta*, five; *teuchos*, a tool, book).
The Samaritan Pentateuch. The Hebrew text of the Pentateuch as preserved by the Samaritans; said to date from the 4th century BC.

Pentecost (Gr. *pentecoste*, fiftieth). The festival held by the Jews on the fiftieth day after the second day of the PASSOVER; our WHITSUNDAY. The term came into use among the Greek-speaking Jews. TERTULLIAN was the first Christian writer to use the name as a Christian festival. Held on the seventh Sunday after EASTER, Pentecost commemorates the descent of the HOLY SPIRIT and the bestowal of the GIFT OF TONGUES on the Disciples (*Acts* ii). The ORTHODOX CHURCH holds a memorial service for the dead believers; the worshippers bring food to the service; this has affinities with the Roman Catholic ALL SOULS traditions.
Pentecostal Churches. PROTESTANT sects associated with manifestations of the gift of tongues such as had occurred at Pentecost (*see Acts* ii, 1–4), and evangelical and healing campaigns.
Pentecostals. In mediaeval England, offerings made to the parish priest at WHITSUNTIDE were called *Pentecostals*, or *Whitsun-farthings*. The term is also used of offerings paid by the parish church to the cathedral of the diocese. *Cp.* DOWELLING MONEY; PETER'S PENCE; SMOKE-FARTHINGS.
Pentecostarion. In the Eastern ORTHODOX CHURCH, the liturgical period between EASTER and the Sunday after Pentecost; also the book containing the prayers and lections then used.

Perfectionists. Certain Christians who believe it possible, through Divine Grace, to attain moral and religious perfection in this world. The belief occurred among early Christians and certain CATHOLIC theologians, but it is most notable in the USA, where a number of sects have flourished, such as the Oneida Community and the PENTECOSTALS.

Perpetua and Felicitas, SS (d. 203, f.d. 7

March). Perpetua was a young married woman of good family, with a baby son; Felicitas, or Felicity, was a heavily pregnant slave at Carthage. With four male companions, Saturnus, Revocatus, Secundulus and Saturninus, they were imprisoned under the persecution of Septimius Severus and condemned to be thrown to the beasts in the arena. Felicitas gave birth to a girl who was immediately adopted by a fellow Christian, and Perpetua's boy was taken by her family. During her imprisonment Perpetua experienced visions. At the Games the men were exposed to leopards, bears and boars, the women to a mad cow. After an AGAPE all the martyrs went cheerfully to the arena 'as though on their way to heaven'. Perpetua, who refused to wear the dress of Ceres, fell into ecstasy and was unaware of having been tossed by the cow, but got up and helped Felicitas to her feet. Finally they were despatched by a sword thrust into the throat. The first clumsy attempt greatly hurt Perpetua but failed to kill her, so she guided the sword to her throat. The martyrs were buried in the Basilica Majorum at Carthage, where, in 1907, an inscription was discovered in their honour. The account of their martyrdom was authentic and they were greatly revered in the early church.

Person. Confounding the Persons. The heresy of Sabellius (*see* SABELLIANISM), who declared that Father, Son, and Holy Ghost were but three names, aspects, or manifestations of one God, the orthodox doctrine being that of the ATHANASIAN CREED (*see under* ATHANASIUS):

> We worship one God in Trinity, and Trinity in Unity; Neither confounding the Persons, nor dividing the Substance (*Neque confundentes personas, neque substantiam separantes*).

Perth. The Five Articles of Perth (1618) were imposed on the CHURCH OF SCOTLAND by James VI and I, enjoining kneeling at communion; the observance of CHRISTMAS, GOOD FRIDAY, EASTER, and PENTECOST; confirmation; communion for the dying; and early baptism of infants. They were ratified by the Scottish Parliament, 4 August 1621, called Black Saturday, and condemned by the General Assembly at Glasgow in 1638.

Peter. St Peter (d. AD 65, f.d. 29 June). The patron saint of fishermen, being himself a fisherman; the 'Prince of the APOSTLES'. He is usually represented as an old man, bald, but with a flowing beard, dressed in a white mantle and blue tunic, and holding in his hand a book or scroll. His peculiar symbols are the keys, and a sword (*Matt.* xvi, 19, and *John* xviii, 10).

Tradition tells that he confuted SIMON MAGUS, who was at Nero's court as a magician, and that in AD 65 he was crucified with his head downwards at his own request, as he said he was not worthy to suffer the same death as Our Lord. The location of his bones under the high altar of St Peter's, ROME, was announced in 1950 and the POPE confirmed their authenticity in 1968.

St Peter's Fingers. The fingers of a thief. The allusion is to the fish caught by St Peter with a piece of money in its mouth. It is said that a thief has a fish-hook on every finger.

St Peter's Fish. The JOHN DORY; also the HADDOCK.

Peter's Pence. An annual tribute of one penny, paid at the feast of St Peter to the see of ROME, collected at first from every family, but afterwards restricted to those 'who had the value of thirty pence in quick or livestock'. This tax was collected in England from the late 8th century until its abolition by Henry VIII in 1534. It was also called *Rome-Scot, Rome fardynges*, or *Peter's farthings*. Much of it never got as far as Rome. *Cp.* PENTECOSTALS.

Peter's Pence now consists of voluntary offerings made to the HOLY SEE by Roman Catholics.

Peter of Alcantara, St (1499–1562, f.d. 19 October). Peter Gravito was the son of a lawyer of Alcantara, and studied law at Salamanca. At the age of sixteen, he became a FRANCISCAN Observant, leading an extremely austere life. He was sent as superior to a new foundation at Badajoz and, in 1524, was ordained priest. He became noted for his preaching and his visions and raptures, described by St TERESA of Avila, whom he encouraged and advised, sharing experiences of the mystical life. She recorded that for forty years he slept only one-and-a-half hours in twenty four, usually only ate once in three days, sometimes eating nothing for eight days. In 1538 he was elected head of the strict Estremadura province of his order and, when he failed in introducing further reforms, founded a new branch of the Franciscan Order called the Alcantrines, at Pedrosa. Here the friars lived in small groups in great poverty and austerity, devoting much time to prayer and contemplation. In 1862 Peter was made patron saint of Brazil and in 1962 of Estremadura. He is one of the great Spanish mystics.

Peter of Alexandria, St (d. 311, f.d. 26 November). An Alexandrian, tortured under the Diocletian persecution, he survived and was appointed patriarch of Alexandria in 300. He was forced into hiding under the persecution which continued under Maximinus, and was later martyred. He had opposed extreme ORIGENISM and been involved in controversy with bishop Melitus of Lycopolis on the question of church usage, leading to a rift in the Egyptian church, and had excommunicated Arius. His cult was relegated to local calendars in 1969.

Peter of Canterbury (d. 607, f.d. 6 January, 30

December (Canterbury)). A BENEDICTINE monk, one of the group of missionaries sent to England by St GREGORY THE GREAT. He became the first abbot of the monastery of SS PETER and PAUL, later called St AUGUSTINE's at Canterbury. He was sent on a mission to Gaul and was drowned near Boulogne. BEDE records that the body was buried 'in an unworthy place', but a mysterious light appeared over his grave at night, and so his relics were translated to Boulogne and duly honoured. His cult was confirmed in 1915.

Peter Celestine (Celestine V), St. Pierre de Moron, the eleventh child in a peasant family, was a hermit on Monte Morone and was ordained priest. Reluctantly he was appointed abbot of a monastery of hermits where he lived a devout life and founded the CELESTINES under the RULE of St BENEDICT. In order to resolve the apparently insoluble differences between Church and State, and on account of his holy life, Peter was chosen POPE, to become Celestine V, but his naive openness, unworldliness and ignorance of the prevailing political climate, made his rule a disaster and he became virtually a prisoner of Charles, King of Naples. Celestine resigned the PAPACY, making history as the only pope to do so voluntarily. He retired to a monastery and BONIFACE VIII was elected in his place. To counteract intrigue in favour of Celestine and against himself, Boniface captured and imprisoned him at Fumome where Celestine died, contented with his 'CELL'.

Peter Chanel, St. *See* CHANEL.

Peter Chrysologus, St (d. *c.* 450, f.d. 30 July, formerly 4 December). Little is known of his life. Born at Imola, near Ravenna, he was a deacon at the time he was elected archbishop of Ravenna. He supported the teaching of LEO THE GREAT on the INCARNATION and exhorted the MONOPHYSITE Eutyches to conform to the teaching of the Roman Church. His chief concern was with the persistence of paganism and increasing abuses in the Church. He was noted as a preacher, hence his name 'golden speech'; some of his sermons still survive. He was a guest of St GERMANUS OF AUXERRE and later presided over his funeral. Peter Chrysologus died at Imola and was made a DOCTOR OF THE CHURCH in 1729.

Peter Claver, St. *See* CLAVER.

Peter Damian, St (100–72, f.d. 21 February). Born at Ravenna, of a large family, he was orphaned while young; he was ill-treated by one brother, then adopted by another brother of naturally austere temperament. Peter joined the BENEDICTINES and taught at their monasteries, becoming head of his community of hermits at Fonte Avellana. He was a noted theologian and reformer, writing theological and canonical works and preaching against simony and laxity among the clergy, even reproving bishops for playing chess. He was appointed Cardinal Bishop of Ostia in 1057 and played a prominent part in ecclesiastical affairs, especially in the Gregorian Reform and the LATERAN SYNOD. Wishing to be relieved of his episcopal duties and to return to the life of a hermit, he finally went back to Fonte Avellana and practised austerities, but combined these with craftsmanship, making wooden spoons and other objects. Pope Leo XII enrolled him among the DOCTORS OF THE CHURCH in 1828.

Peter Fourier, St (1565–1640, f.d. 9 December). Born at Mirecourt in Lorraine, he was for thirty years parish priest of Mattaincourt in the Vosges where his main work was to arrest the spread of CALVINISM. He joined the AUGUSTINIAN CANONS. In advance of his time he saw the need for free education for children and, against opposition but with the aid of Mother Alix Le Clercq, he founded the Congregation of Augustinian Canonesses of Our Lady, thus establishing the idea of teaching nuns.

Peter the Hermit (*c.* 1050–1115). Preacher of the first CRUSADE. He took part in the siege of Antioch (1098) and entered JERUSALEM with the victorious crusaders. He afterwards became Prior of Huy, where he had founded the monastery of Neufmoutier and where he died. His feast day is 8 July but he was never officially beatified.

Peter of Luxemburg, Bl. (1369–87, f.d. 4 July). Born at Ligny in Lorraine of noble family, he showed religious zeal at an early age and was appointed to ecclesiastical benefices when only fourteen, being made bishop of Metz and elected a cardinal by the Pope. He ruled with great wisdom and mature judgement, dying at the age of eighteen. He was beatified in 1527.

Peter the Martyr (or **of Verona**), **St** (1205–52, f.d. 29 April). Born of Cathar parentage, he became a CATHOLIC and was educated at Bologna University. He joined the Order of St DOMINIC, became prior of various monasteries and was noted as a preacher. He worked zealously against heretics, mainly Cathars, and was appointed an inquisitor, arousing much antagonism. Whilst on his way between Como and Milan he was waylaid and his head was split with a hatchet. In art he is depicted with a hatchet embedded in his skull. His tomb became a centre of pilgrimage and he was famed as a wonder-worker.

Peter Nolasco, St (*c.* 1182–1258, f.d. 28 January). There is little of certainty and much legend concerned with his life, but he was said to be from Languedoc and to have worked against the ALBIGENSES. He was also reputed to be the founder of the MERCEDARIAN order (The Order of Our Lady of Ransom) in 1234, a confraternity which rescued and ransomed slaves from the Moors. The order followed the rule of

St AUGUSTINE. Peter was given the name of Nonnatus, 'not born', as he was reputed to have been taken from his mother's womb after she had died in labour. He became patron saint of midwives. Miracles were reported at his tomb. His cult was confined to local calendars in the revision of 1969.

Peter of Tarantaise, St (1102–74, f.d. 2 May). Born into a devout family at Saint-Maurice near Vienne, he became a CISTERCIAN monk at the age of twelve, and in 1132 was chosen abbot of Tamié. He was responsible for rebuilding the hospice at the Little St Bernard Pass and for instituting the free distribution of soup and bread at harvest time. He was elected archbishop of Tarantaise and undertook reforms to counteract the corruption of his predecessor. He was reputed to work miracles of healing and of the multiplication of food but, disturbed at the publicity of his wonder-working, he disappeared until he was found a year later in a monastery in Switzerland, living as a lay brother. He was later involved in the dispute between Pope Alexander III and the anti-pope Victor, upholding the cause of Alexander and attending several councils. He was also instrumental in making peace between Henry II of England and Louis VII of France. He was described as a man of modesty, joyfulness and sanctity.

Petroc (or Pedrog), St (6th cent., f.d. 4 June, 1 October, 14 September). Accounts of his life are mainly unreliable and derived from folklore, but traditionally he was the son of a South Wales chieftain. He became one of the most important saints of Cornwall. Padstow or Petrockstowe, where he founded a monastery of which he was the abbot, was the chief centre of his mission, and he established other monasteries. Later he retired to Bodmin Moor to live as a hermit, but a monastery was built nearby to house his disciples. When he died he was buried at Padstow, but his shrine and relics were later translated to Bodmin. This became the centre of a cult which spread to Devon and South Wales, also to Brittany where he was revered as St Perreux. In 1177 a disaffected AUGUSTINIAN CANON stole the relics, taking them to Brittany to Saint-Méen. King Henry II was appealed to and had them returned to Bodmin, leaving only a rib at Saint-Méen. In art Petroc is depicted as a bishop and, like several other saints with a reputation for sympathy with animals, he is represented with a stag which he was said to have saved from huntsmen. His feast day varies in several calendars.

Petronilla, St (date unknown, f.d. 31 May). An early legendary virgin martyr, said in one tradition to be of the Roman family of Domitilla, but in another to be the daughter of St PETER the

Apostle. When she rejected marriage to Count Flaccus he threatened to kill her, but she fasted three days and then died. A catacomb, a church at ROME, and an altar in the VATICAN are dedicated to her and she appears frequently in mediaeval stained glass windows, depicted as either holding St Peter's keys or being cured by him. Her cult was confined to local calendars in the revision of 1969.

Pew (Gr. *podion*, footstool). Pews date from about the 15th century. Formerly the body of the church was open space, but benches were placed along the walls for the use of those too weak to stand, hence the phrase 'the weakest go to the wall'. Originally pews were little more than benches; they were for the use of particular people or families, such as the squire's pew. After the REFORMATION larger pews were added and the 'box pew' was an enclosed structure, now seldom seen. There are no pews in Eastern ORTHODOX CHURCHES.

Pfister's Bible. *See* BIBLE, SOME SPECIALLY NAMED EDITIONS.

Pharisees (Heb. *perusim*; from *perash*, to separate) means 'those who have been set apart'. The Jewish party of this name first appeared in Judea in the reign of John Hyrcanus I (135–104 BC) and strove to ensure that the state was governed in strict accordance with the Torah. Their influence in the development of orthodox Judaism was profound. The condemnations of Jesus were essentially against the more extremist followers of the Pharisee Shammai, who were open to charges of narrow literalism and hypocrisy. The Talmud mentions the following groups:

(1) The 'Dashers' or 'Bandy-legged' (*Nikfi*), who scarcely lifted their feet from the ground in walking, but 'dashed them against the stones', that people might think them absorbed in holy thought (*Matt.* xxi, 44).

(2) The 'Mortars', who wore a 'mortier' or cap, which would not allow them to see the passers-by, that their meditations might not be disturbed. 'Having eyes they saw not' (*Mark* viii, 18).

(3) The 'Bleeders', who inserted thorns in the borders of their gaberdines to prick their legs in walking.

(4) The 'Cryers', or 'Inquiriers', who went about crying out, 'Let me know my duty, and I will do it' (*Matt.* xix, 16–22).

(5) The 'Almsgivers', who had a trumpet sounded before them to summon the poor together (*Matt.* vi, 2).

(6) The 'Stumblers', or 'Bloody-browed' (*Kizai*), who shut their eyes when they went abroad that they might see no women, being 'blind leaders of the blind' (*Matt.* xv, 14). Our Lord

calls them 'blind Pharisees', 'fools and blind'.

(7) The 'Immovables', who stood like statues for hours together, 'Praying in the market places' (*Matt.* vi, 5).

(8) The 'Pestle Pharisees' (*Medinkia*), who kept themselves bent double like the handle of a pestle.

(9) The 'Strong-shouldered' (*Shikmi*), who walked with their back bent as if carrying on their shoulders the whole burden of the law.

(10) The 'Dyed Pharisees', called by Our Lord 'Whited Sepulchres', whose externals of devotion cloaked hypocrisy and moral uncleanliness. (*Talmud of Jerusalem, Berakoth*, ix; *Sota*, v, 7; *Talmud of Babylon, Sota*, 22b.)

Philadelphists. *See* BEHMENISTS.

Phileas, St (d. 306, f.d. 4 February, 26 November). A wealthy Egyptian nobleman of great learning and eloquence who was converted to Christianity and became bishop of Thmuis. He was martyred with others under the Diocletian persecution in 304 for refusing to sacrifice to the gods. In his long imprisonment he wrote a vivid account of the sufferings and tortures of Christians in his see. His history was related by EUSEBIUS.

Philemon and Apphia, SS (1st cent., f.d. 22 November (West), 14 February or 6 July (East)). An early martyr, the Philemon of St PAUL'S EPISTLE, sent from ROME to Colossae. Philemon was said to have a runaway slave who met St Paul who sent him back to his master with a letter asking for forgiveness. This was granted and the slave was freed, but Philemon and his wife were martyred later at Colossae.

Philibert, St (*c.* 608–85, f.d. 20 August). Born in Gascony, he attended the court of King Dagobert I and was educated under St OUEN, entering his monastery and later becoming abbot at Rébais. He proved too inexperienced and unable to control the monks, and so resigned and visited other monasteries. He then founded his own monastery on land near Rouen given to him by Clovis II. He denounced and antagonized Ebroin, the West Frankish mayor, who had him imprisoned and then banished. Philibert went to the island of Heriou and there founded the monastery of Noirmoutier; he also later established a monastery and nunnery and was referred to by ALCUIN as a celebrated founder of religious houses.

Philip, St is usually represented bearing a large CROSS, or a basket containing loaves in allusion to *John* vi, 5–7. He is commemorated with St JAMES THE LESS on 1 May (since 1985, 11 May by Roman Catholics). He was one of the twelve APOSTLES and traditionally said to have been the Apostle of Upper Asia, preaching the GOSPEL in Phrygia and dying at Hierapolis. There are various accounts of his death, some saying that he was crucified, others that he was hanged on a pillar. Hierapolis was said to have the tomb of one of Philip's daughters. It is thought that in some cases Philip the Apostle has been confused with PHILIP THE DEACON.

Philip Benizi (or **Beniti**), **St** (1233–85, f.d. 23 August). Born at Florence of a noble family and educated at Paris and Padua universities, where he studied medicine and philosophy, he entered the SERVITE Order at Monte Senario, working in the garden as a lay brother. He was ordained priest and appointed novice master at Siena, then secretary to the Prior General, following him to that office in 1267. He attended the Council of Lyons and obtained confirmation of the Order, and was the practical founder of the Servite nuns. He was a noted preacher, also a peacemaker, working to end the strife between the cities of North Italy. It was said that he had been proposed as a candidate for the papacy, but avoided it by going into hiding in the hills. He was reputed to have performed miracles of healing. In Florentine art he is depicted as wearing the black Servite habit and healing a woman possessed, or giving his shirt to a leper. He appears in Andrea del Sarto frescoes.

Philip the Deacon, St (1st cent., f.d. 6 June (West), 27 April (East)). Said to be one of the SEVEN DEACONS (*Acts* vi, 5 and viii, 27). The eunuch he converted traditionally went to Arabia and Ceylon as a missionary and was martyred. Philip's four daughters (*Acts* xxi, 9) are also venerated as saints. Philip's cult is of greater importance in the Eastern ORTHODOX CHURCH.

Philip of Heraclea, St (d. 304, f.d. 22 October). Bishop of Heraclea, near Constantinople, during the Diocletian persecution, his church was closed and he was ordered to deliver up all treasures. He allowed the ritual vessels to be taken but refused to relinquish the SCRIPTURES. He and his deacons were brutally beaten and imprisoned and later taken to Adrianople where they were interrogated, again severely scourged and sentenced to be burned. Too weak to stand, Philip was dragged to the stake and the deacon Hermes cheerfully accompanied him.

Philip Howard, St. *See* HOWARD.

Philip of Moscow, St (1507–69, f.d. 9 January (Russian Orthodox)). Born Theodore Kolyshov, of a noble Russian family, little is known of his youth other than that he received a good education and training in arms. However, hearing a sermon on the impossibility of serving two masters, he became a monk at the remote monastery of Solovetsk, received the tonsure and took the name of Philip. He was ordained priest and was elected abbot in

1547, distinguishing himself not only as a religious leader but developing agricultural engineering systems on the monastery lands and producing and selling salt. He took an active part in the Councils of 1550/1 at Moscow. He was appointed metropolitan of Moscow and primate of the Russian ORTHODOX CHURCH at a time of political and religious massacres under Ivan the Terrible. Rebuked by St Philip, the Czar had him imprisoned, dragged from place to place in chains, and finally smothered. Later, under Czar Theodore, his body, found to be incorrupt, was translated to Solovetsk where he had wished to be buried. Miracles, visions and cures occurred there. He was canonized by the Russian Orthodox Church in 1636.

Philip Neri, St. *See* NERI.

Philomena, St. The cult of the entirely legendary Philomena rose from the discovery in 1802 of an ancient inscription, together with the bones of a young girl and a phial of blood, in a catacomb in ROME. These were assumed to be the relics of an early virgin martyr and were given to the church at Mungnano and enshrined. Miracles and answers to intercessions were reputed to have taken place and a nun claimed revelation and visions of Philomena. The cult spread and legends were added, but the chief influence was that of St J.-B. VIANNEY, the Curé d'Ars, who made Philomena the focal point of his devotions and attributed his own cures to her intervention. There was also the instance of a remarkable recovery from near-death at the shrine, which increasingly became a centre of pilgrimage. The cult was recognized by Pope Gregory XVI in 1835 and by Pius IX in 1855 but was suppressed by the HOLY SEE in 1961, and although her feast day was celebrated on 10 August, her name was not included in the Roman MARTYROLOGY.

Phocas, St (date unknown, f.d. 23 July or 22 September). An important saint in early martyrologies, he was a hermit and a professional gardener, supporting himself, the poor and pilgrims at Sinope on the Black Sea. He was condemned as a Christian under Diocletian and three soldiers were sent to kill him. Calling at his hermitage, they enquired if he knew where Phocas lived; he replied that he did and would give them directions on the morrow, and he invited them to stay as his guests for the night. This they did, and during the night Phocas dug his grave in his garden. He revealed his identity next morning, and assured the reluctant soldiers that he was willing to die. He was killed and buried in his garden grave. His relics were claimed by both Vienne and Antioch and he became the patron saint of sailors in the Black Sea, the Aegean and the Adriatic. Sea-shanties were sung in his honour.

Phoenix. In Christianity the phoenix is a symbol of the RESURRECTION; Christ consumed in the fires of the PASSION and rising again on the third day, triumphant over death.

Photius, St (*c*. 810–91, f.d. 6 February (Orthodox)). Born at Constantinople into a patrician Byzantine family, he filled various offices at the imperial court, including secretary of state. In 858 the Emperor Michael III banished the patriarch Ignatius, appointing Photius in his place. This caused endless difficulties with Popes Nicholas I and Adrian II and in the Church and Byzantine politics. Finally, at the death of Ignatius, Pope John VIII recognized the authority of Photius and the dispute between the two branches of the Church was resolved. Although the Western Church blamed Photius as a schismatic, the Eastern Church regarded him as a defender of its rights. He wrote extensively and was a man of great scholarship, talent and personal virtue.

Phrygians. An early Christian sect of the late 2nd century, so called from Phrygia, where they abounded; also called MONTANISTS.

Physician (Gr. *phusis*, nature). **The Beloved Physician.** St LUKE, so called by St PAUL in *Col.* iv, 14.

Piarists. Fathers of the Pious Schools, founded in ROME at the end of the 16th century, by Joseph Calasanctius. They were largely concerned with education in Europe.

Picards. An extremist early 15th-century sect prevalent in Bohemia and the Vaudois, said to be so called from Picard of Flanders, their founder, who called himself the New ADAM and tried to introduce the custom of living in the nude, like Adam in PARADISE. They were suppressed by Ziska in 1421. *Cp.* ADAMITES.

Picture Bible. A name given to the BIBLIA PAUPERUM.

Pietà. A representation of the Virgin embracing the dead body of her Son. Filial or parental love was called *pietas* by the Romans.

Pietism. A 17th-century Lutheran movement seeking to revive the life of the Lutheran Church in Germany. It was started by P. J. Spener (1635–1705) and the name was applied derisively by the orthodox in the same way as the term METHODIST was used in England. Spener was born in Alsace and was pastor at Frankfurt and later court chaplain at Dresden and finally at Berlin; his teaching stressed the practical and living aspect of Pietist Christianity as against the tendency elsewhere to increasing dogmatism and theological argument. It has been a potent force in EVANGELICAL PROTESTANTISM.

Pike. The Germans have a tradition that when Christ was crucified all fishes dived under the water in terror, except the pike, which, out of curiosity, lifted up its head and beheld the whole scene; hence the fancy that in a pike's head all the parts of the Crucifixion are represented, the CROSS, three nails, and a sword being clearly delineated.

Pilate. One tradition has it that Pontius Pilate's later life was so full of misfortune that in Caligula's time he committed suicide at ROME. His body was thrown into the Tiber, but evil spirits so disturbed the water that it was retrieved and taken to Vienne, where it was cast into the Rhône, eventually coming to rest in the recesses of a lake on Mount Pilatus. Another legend is that he committed suicide to avoid the sentence of death passed on him by Tiberius because of his having ordered the crucifixion of Christ. His wife is given as Claudia Procula, or Procla, and by some she has been identified with Claudia of II *Tim.* iv, 21: there is a story that they both became penitent and died peaceably in the faith.

In the Coptic Church he is regarded as a martyr, and his feast day is 25 June. Procla has been canonized in the GREEK CHURCH.

The Acts of Pilate. An apocryphal work, probably of the 4th-century, recounting the trial, death, and resurrection of Christ. In combination with another treatise on the *Descent of Christ into Hades*, the two are known as the *Gospel of Nicodemus*.

Pilate voice. A loud ranting voice. In the old mysteries all tyrants were made to speak in a rough ranting manner. Similarly Shakespeare has 'out-herods HEROD' (*Hamlet*, III, ii), and 'This is Ercles' vein, a tyrant's vein' (*Midsummer Night's Dream*, I, ii).

> The Miller, that for-drunken was al pale…
> in Pilates vois he gan to crye,
> And swoor by armes and by blood and bones,
> 'I can a noble tale for the nones
> With which I wol now quyte the Knightes tale.'
> CHAUCER: *Miller's Prologue*, 12–19

Pilgrim Fathers. The term (first used in 1799) applied to the emigrants who founded the colony of Plymouth, New England, in 1620. In 1608 a PURITAN congregation from Scrooby (Notts.) settled at Leiden and eventually decided to migrate to America. They finally left Plymouth in the Mayflower. Of the 102 settlers, 24 were women, and only 35 of the party were Puritans. Their tradition is part of American folklore.

The Pilgrim's Progress. The allegorical masterpiece of John Bunyan, the first part of which appeared in 1678 and the second in 1684. It tells of Christian's pilgrimage, beset with trials and temptations, but with incidental encouragement, until he reached the Celestial City where he was later joined by his wife and children. The rustic simplicity and directness of its story gave it lasting appeal and many expressions have become part of the language. 'The Slough of Despond', 'Vanity Fair', 'Mr Worldly Wiseman' and 'Mr Facing-both-ways' are notable examples.

Pilgrimage. A journey to a sacred place undertaken as an act of religious devotion, either as an act of veneration or penance, or to ask for the fulfilment of some prayer. In the Middle Ages the chief venues in the West were Walsingham and Canterbury (England), Fourvière, Le Puy, and St Denis (France); ROME, Loreto, and Assisi (Italy); COMPOSTELA, Guadalupe, and Montserrat (Spain); Mariazell (Austria); Cologne, Trier (Germany); Einsiedeln (Switzerland). The pre-eminent pilgrimage was of course to the HOLY LAND. LOURDES became a noted place of pilgrimage for Roman Catholics after 1858.

Miraculous cures were sometimes effected upon those who worshipped at these shrines and spiritual and bodily welfare was the main concern of most pilgrims; for others a pilgrimage was an occasion for a holiday and an opportunity to visit distant parts or foreign lands.

Pionius, St (d. *c.* 250, f.d. 1 February (West), 12 March (East)). A priest at Smyrna who was arrested with other Christians for celebrating the feast of St POLYCARP and refusing to sacrifice at the temple of Nemesis at the time of the Decian persecution. Pionus was an eloquent speaker and answered his accusers with wit and allusions to Homer and to biblical texts, which impressed his listeners. He was imprisoned, repeatedly interrogated and tortured, and finally burnt alive together with the MARCIONITE priest Metrodorus.

Piran, St (5th or 6th century, f.d. 5 March). The patron saint of Cornish miners, said to have been sent to Cornwall by St PATRICK. According to another legend he was cast into the sea by his fellow Irishmen bound to a millstone and landed at Perranzabuloe (St Piran in the Sands) near Perranporth. He set up a hermitage and discovered tin when he saw it streaming from the stone of his fireplace. Two churches of St Piran were buried in the sand dunes and the remains of one have been uncovered, hence legends of bells ringing in the sand.

Piscina. In old churches a stone basin with a drain, situated at the south side of the ALTAR; vessels were cleansed there after the EUCHARIST.

Pius V, St (1504–72, f.d. 30 April, formerly 5 May). Born at Bosco into a humble family, Michael Ghislieri entered the DOMINICAN Order at the age of fourteen. He was ordained in 1540 and lectured in philosophy and theology, became a master of novices and prior, then bishop of Nepi and Sutri. In 1557 he was appointed a cardinal and Inquisitor General. On the death of Pius IV, whose notorious nepotism he had denounced, Ghislieri was elected to succeed him as Pope Pius V. He proved an active reformer and enforced the decrees of the Council of TRENT; he also reformed the city of ROME, carrying out vigorous measures against the evils of prostitution, brigandage and bullfighting. In his personal life he followed the rules of a devout friar and, instead of pomp and banquets, gave money to hospitals and the poor, aided in this work by the support of St CHARLES BORROMEO. Pius V used the powers of the INQUISITION implacably against the PROTESTANT REFORMATION and issued a BULL excommunicating Elizabeth of England in 1570. He was successful in opposing the power of the Turks, who were defeated by Don John of Austria at the battle of Lepanto, also in ratifying the league against the Turks. Pius V encouraged learning and produced a new edition of the works of St THOMAS AQUINAS, declaring him a DOCTOR OF THE CHURCH in 1567.

Pius X, St (1835–1914, f.d. 21 August, formerly 3 September). Giuseppe Sarto was born into a poor family at Riese, so poor that the boy walked the four miles to school barefoot to save shoe-leather. He was the second of ten children. He was not ordained priest until 1858; he was curate to the parish priest of Tombolo for nine years, then in 1867 became parish priest at Salzano. In 1884 he was appointed bishop of Mantua and in 1893 patriarch of Venice, then a cardinal. In 1903 he succeeded Leo XIII as pope. He was responsible for the reform of Common Law, the reorganization of the Roman Congregation and of church music. He worked against liberal and modernistic movements and condemned both the SILLON and the Action Française. His aim was 'to restore all things to Christ' and he lived a simple life. The separation of Church and State in France occurred during his pontificate, and he sacrificed ecclesiastical property for the sake of the Church's independence from state control. He worked hard, but unsuccessfully, to avert World War I, dying on 20 August 1914. His life was throughout one of simplicity and deliberate poverty and miracles were associated with him. He was canonized in 1954.

Place. Place-makers' Bible. *See* BIBLE, SOME SPECIALLY NAMED EDITIONS.

Placebo (Lat., I shall please, or be acceptable). VESPERS for the dead; because the first antiphon at Vespers of the office of the Dead began with the words *Placebo Domino in regione vivorum*, 'I will walk before the Lord in the land of the living' (*Ps.* cxvi, 9).

Placid, St (6th cent., f.d. 5 October). Entrusted to the care of St BENEDICT, he was trained to become a monk. Legend says he fell into a lake and was saved miraculously by St Maurus. He was said to be one of a company of martyrs whose remains were found at Messina in Sicily. His cult spread and BENEDICTINE monasteries held him as the patron of novices, who celebrated his day on October 5 when they took part in offices usually confined to the professed. Later a combined feast day was authorized on that day for SS Placid and Maurus. The Abingdon Calendar designated him as 'abbot and martyr'.

Plainsong. *See* GREGORIAN CHANT.

Plasden, St Polydore (or **Oliver Palmer**) (1563–91, f.d. 25 October). Born in London, he was the son of a craftsman and went to France for his education at the ENGLISH COLLEGE of DOUAI, and was ordained priest at ROME. He returned to England and officiated in Sussex. He was arrested with St Edmund GENNINGS in London and condemned as a priest ordained abroad, being executed at Tyburn. Sir Walter Raleigh, who supervised the hanging, ensured that Plasden was dead before being cut down. Plasden and Gennings were canonized in 1970 as among the FORTY MARTYRS OF ENGLAND AND WALES.

Plechelm (Pleghelm or **Pechthelm), St** (8th cent., f.d. 16 July). One of the Northumbrian priests who went on a mission to the Low Countries. He built a church and monastery at Roermond with the assistance of Pepin of Herstal and worked closely with St Wiro. On a pilgrimage to ROME Plechelm was made a bishop. He died at Odilienberg and was buried there, but his relics were later translated to Roermond.

Plessington, St (John or **William Scarisbrick)** (*c*. 1637–79, f.d. 25 October). Born at Dimples in Lancashire, he was educated by JESUITS at Scarisbrick Hall and at Saint-Omer, going on to the English College at Valladolid in Spain. After having been ordained priest he returned to England and carried out a mission in Flintshire. Then, under the guise of a tutor to the Massey children, he went to Puddington Hall in the Wirral and acted as a missionary priest. He was arrested and accused at the time of the POPISH PLOT of Titus OATES, and was condemned to be hanged, drawn and quartered. His body was sent to Puddington Hall and placed in the four corners, but the Masseys buried the body in Burton churchyard. Plessington was canonized in 1970 as one of the FORTY MARTYRS OF ENGLAND AND WALES.

Plunket, St Oliver (1629–81, f.d. 1 July). Born at Loughcrew in Co. Meath, of an aristocratic family, he went to ROME at the age of sixteen to be educated for the priesthood. He was a brilliant scholar and later was appointed procurator for the Irish bishops to the HOLY SEE. In 1669, when the archbishop of Armagh and Primate of All Ireland died, Pope Clement IX appointed Oliver Plunket to succeed him; he was consecrated at Ghent. Returning to Ireland, he was involved in a dispute among CATHOLICS of various orders, but he maintained friendly relationships with the PROTESTANTS of Ulster who, for his sake, did not oppress Catholics. When the policies of Charles II of England brought about fresh persecution, Plunket had to go into hiding. After the POPISH PLOT of Titus OATES, Plunket, with others, fell under suspicion and he was tried in Ireland for conspiring against the state, and was transferred to Newgate in London. His first trial was inconclusive, but a second, biased trial condemned him to execution. He was hanged, drawn and quartered at Tyburn. He was the last Catholic to die there. Plunket was beatified in 1920 and canonized in 1975.

Pluralism. The holding of more than one ecclesiastical benefice by the same person. The Pluralistics Act of 1838 abolished pluralism in the CHURCH OF ENGLAND except for small livings in close proximity. A series of Acts followed which were nullified by the Pastoral Reorganization Measure in 1949.

Plymouth Brethren. A sect of Evangelical Christians founded in Ireland about 1828 by J. N. Darby, one-time Anglican priest (hence they are sometimes called Darbyites), and deriving their name from Plymouth, the first centre set up in England (1830). In 1849 they split up into 'Open Brethren' and 'Exclusive Brethren'. They have no organized ministry and lay emphasis on the Breaking of Bread each SUNDAY.

Polycarp, St (c. 69–155, f.d. 26 January). One of the most noted martyrs of the 2nd century whose life was linked with the Apostolic age. He was probably converted to Christianity by St JOHN THE APOSTLE and was Bishop of Smyrna for over 40 years where he became a staunch and vigorous leader. Persecution of Christians arose in Smyrna in 155 and the mob soon demanded Polycarp, 'the father of the Christians' as their next victim. The proconsul, Statius Quadratus, had him arrested and he was burnt alive after refusing to deny his faith. His faithfulness to the Apostolic tradition is recorded by Irenaeus, his disciple. Polycarp's only surviving writing is his *Epistle to the Philippians*.

Polyglot Bible. *See* BIBLE.

Pontiff. The term formerly applied to any BISHOP but now only to the POPE—the Supreme Pontiff. It means literally one who has charge of the bridges (Lat. *pons, pontis*, a bridge), and these were under the care of the principal college of priests in ancient Rome, the head of which was the *Pontifex Maximus*, a title which originally applied to the pagan chief priest in ROME and was taken over by Christianity.

Pontificals. Vestments and regalia worn by prelates at the celebration of Pontifical MASS; they are the CROSIER, DALMATIC, gloves. MITRE, PECTORAL CROSS, RING and sandals.

Poor. Poor as a church mouse. In a church there is no cupboard or pantry where a mouse may take his pickings and he thus has a lean time.
Poor as Job. The allusion is to Job being deprived by SATAN of everything he possessed.
Poor as Lazarus. This is the beggar LAZARUS, full of sores, who was laid at the rich man's gate and desired to be fed with crumbs that fell from Dives' table. (*Luke* xvi, 19–31).
Poor Clares. *See* CLARE.
Poor Preachers. Followers of John Wycliffe, disseminators of his theology, criticizing the papacy and teaching and preaching a biblical, evangelical theology.

Pope. The word represents the O.E. *papa*, from ecclesiastical Latin, and Gr. *pappas*, the infants' word for father.
In the early Church the title was given to many bishops; Leo I, the Great (440–61) was the first to use it officially, and in the time of Gregory VII (1073–85) it was, by decree, specially reserved to the Bishop of Rome. *Cp.* PONTIFF.
According to Platina, Sergius II (844–7) was the first pope who changed his name on assuming office. Some accounts have it that his name was Hogsmouth, others that it was 'Peter de Porca' and he changed it out of deference to St PETER, thinking it arrogant to style himself Peter II. However, the first clear case of changed name was when Peter, Bishop of Pavia, on election (983) changed his name for that of John XIV.
Gregory the Great (590–604) was the first pope to adopt the title *Servus Servorum Dei* (the Servant of the Servants of God). It is founded on *Mark* x, 44.

217

The title *Vicar of Christ*, or *Vicar of God*, was adopted by Innocent III, 1198.

Including John Paul II, there are commonly 263 popes enumerated, and the nationality of two of them is unknown. Of the remainder, 209 were Italians, 15 Frenchmen, 12 Greeks, 6 Germans, 6 Syrians, 3 Africans, 3 Spaniards, 2 Dalmatians, and 1 each Dutch, English, Polish, Portuguese, and Jew (St Peter).

The Black Pope. The General of the JESUITS.

The Pope of Geneva. A name given to Calvin (1509–64).

The Red Pope. The Prefect of the PROPA-GANDA.

The Pope's slave. So Cardinal Cajetan (d. 1534) called the Church.

Pope Joan. A mythical female POPE first recorded in the 13th century by the Dominican Stephen de Bourbon (d. *c.* 1261) who is said to have derived the story from Jean de Mailly. It was widely and long accepted. She was said to have been born in Germany of English parents and eventually went to ROME after living with a monk at Athens. Passing under the name of Johannes Anglicus, her wide learning gained her election to the papacy in 855 as John VIII. She was supposed to have died in childbirth during a solemn procession. The Calvinist scholar David Blondel exploded the myth in 1647 and it was finally demolished by Döllinger in 1863. Emmanuel Royidis published his novel *Papissa Joanna* on the subject in 1886.

Popish Plot (1678). A fictitious JESUIT plot to murder Charles II and others, enthrone the Duke of York, fire the City of London, after which, with the aid of French and Irish troops, a PROTESTANT massacre was to ensue. The plot was invented by the scoundrelly Titus OATES and before the anti-Catholic panic abated in 1681 some 35 Catholics were judicially murdered, including the Roman Catholic Primate of Ireland. Oates was eventually pilloried, whipped, and imprisoned when James II became King.

Porphyry of Gaza, St (*c.* 352), f.d. 26 February). Born at Salonika, of wealthy parents, he disposed of his inheritance and gave the money to the poor while he lived as a monk in the Egyptian desert. He then went to Jerusalem and worked as a shoemaker. At Calvary he was miraculously cured of lameness. Against his wishes he was appointed bishop of Gaza, a pagan district, and set to work to destroy temples and images, thus rousing much resentment, but he ultimately succeeded in converting the people. The life of Porphyry was recorded by his deacon Mark and is a valuable historical document.

Porres, Martin de, St (1579–1639, f.d. 5 November). The illegitimate son of a Spanish knight and a negress of Peru, he started life as a barber-surgeon and then became a DOMINICAN lay-helper, but his devotion and dedication were such that he was encouraged to become a lay brother. He worked assiduously for the poor and plague-stricken, dying himself of a fever, but his cures of others were miraculous and his rapport with animals marvellous. Miraculous cures were also reported at his tomb. While the people called him the 'Father of Charity', he called himself 'mulatto dog'. He was canonized in 1962 and named as the patron saint of race relations, because of his mixed birth and total service to people of any race or colour.

Port-Royal. A convent of CISTERCIAN nuns about 8 miles S.W. of Versailles, which in the 17th century became a centre of the JANSENIST influence. In 1626 the community had moved to Paris and Port-Royal des Champs was occupied mostly by laymen living a semi-monastic existence, among them many distinguished scholars. In 1648 some of the nuns returned and the hermits moved elsewhere in the neighbourhood.

From 1653 it came under papal condemnation for its adherence to Jansenism, and Louis XIV began active persecution from 1661. By 1669 the conformist nuns were all at the Paris house and the supporters of Jansen remained at Port-Royal des Champs until forcibly removed in 1709. The buildings were duly destroyed but Port-Royal-de-Paris remained in being till the French Revolution.

Possenti, St Gabriel (1838–62, f.d. 27 February). A son of the governor of Assisi, he was educated at the JESUIT College at Spoleto. His reputation for frivolity earned him the name of 'Il Damerino', the ladies' man. After two serious illnesses he resolved to enter the religious life, but did not carry out his intentions until during a procession of the ICON of Spoleto; his life changed and he entered the PASSIONIST CONGREGATION at Morrovalle. He died young before he could become a priest. His life as a religious was so outstanding that his shrine became a centre of pilgrimage. He was canonized in 1920 and named patron of youth and of the Abruzzi region.

Potamiaena and Basilides, SS (d. *c.* 208, f.d. 28 June). Little is known of these early martyrs except that EUSEBIUS says that they were disciples of ORIGEN. Potamiaena was a virgin who resisted attempts on her chastity. She was condemned as a Christian and killed by having boiling pitch poured over her. When she was reviled by a crowd of soldiers, Basilides protected her and showed compassion, for which she thanked him and promised to pray to the Lord in Heaven for him. Basilides became a

Christian, was arrested and imprisoned and beheaded. In prison he had a vision of Potamiaena placing a crown on his head.

Potter's Field. A name applied to a burial ground formerly reserved for strangers and the friendless poor. It is an allusion to the field bought by the chief priests with the thirty pieces of silver returned to them by the repentant JUDAS (*Matt.* xxvii, 7).

> And they took counsel, and bought with them the potter's field, to bury strangers in.

Powers. *See* THRONES.

Praemonstratensian. *See* PREMONSTRATENSIAN.

Praemunire. The title of numerous statutes passed from 1353, and especially that of 1393 designed to assert the rights of the Crown against encroachments from the Papacy, particularly rights of patronage, the removal of cases from the King's courts, and EXCOMMUNI-CATION. The name also denotes the offence, the writs, and the punishment under these statutes. The writ begins with the words *praemunire facias*, 'that you cause to be forewarned'. The most famous case of praemunire was when Henry VIII invoked the statute against Cardinal Wolsey in 1529 on account of his activities as Papal legate. A peer so charged cannot be tried by his peers, but must accept a jury. The last statute involving praemunire was the Royal Marriage Act of 1772.

Pragmatic Sanction (Gr. *pragmatikos*, businesslike, official). A term originating in the Byzantine empire to denote a public decree and later used by European sovereigns for important declarations defining their powers, settling the succession, etc. Prominent among such was the *Pragmatic Sanction* of St Louis, 1269, and that of Charles VII in 1438, asserting the rights of the Gallican Church against the Papacy; that which settled the Empire of Germany in the House of Austria in 1439; the instrument by which Charles VI of Austria settled the succession of his daughter, Maria Theresa, in 1713; and that of Naples, 1759, whereby Charles III of Spain ceded the succession to the Kingdom of Naples to his third son and his heirs in perpetuity.

Prayer. A devout supplication to God, gods, or objects of religious worship. In Christianity prayer offers entreaties to God for some benefit or favour, either spiritual or material; it may also include praise, adoration, confession and thanksgiving. The mystic's communication with the Divine is in the nature of prayer. In CATHOLICISM prayer is also addressed to the VIRGIN MARY and the SAINTS, but EVANGELICAL

Christianity holds that prayer should be offered to God only, or in the name of Christ. *See* LATRIA, HYPERDULIA, DULIA.

Prebend. Originally a certain portion of food given to each monk at the communal meal, now a stipend paid from a cathedral revenue to a **Prebendary**, a member of the CHAPTER, who renders certain clerical services.

Precentor. A member of a cathedral staff responsible for all musical organization at the cathedral; he ranks next to the dean.

Preceptor. Among the Knights Templar a *preceptory* was a subordinate house or community (the larger being a *commandery*) under a *Preceptor* or *Knight Preceptor*. The *Grand Preceptor* was the head of all the preceptories in a province, those of Jerusalem, Tripolis, and Antioch being the highest ranking.

Predella. A platform or step on which the ALTAR is raised. The term also applies to a carving or painting on the vertical face.

Predestination. The doctrine that all is determined by God and must inevitably come to pass; it is especially connected with the idea of divine omnipotence and the fate of the soul. It is distinctive especially of CALVINISM, but also occurs among Catholic theologians following St THOMAS AQUINAS.

Prelate. A church dignitary of high rank who exercises jurisdiction in his own right, a patriarch, metropolitan, archbishop or bishop; formerly also an abbot or prior. **Prelacy** is government by prelates and is synonymous with episcopalianism.

Premillenarians. *See* SECOND ADVENTISTS.

Premonstratensian or *Norbertine Order*. An order founded by St Norbert in 1120 in the diocese of Laon, France, which adopted the rule of St AUGUSTINE. A spot was pointed out to him in a vision, hence the name *Pré montré* or *Pratum Monstratum* (the meadow pointed out). In England the order possessed 35 houses before the dissolution and its members were called 'White Canons'.

Presbyter (Gre. *presbuteros*, senior or elder). An elder of the early church responsible for guiding and governing the believers, baptizing converts, preaching sound doctrine and leading the congregation in prayer and praise. Also an elder of the PRESBYTERIAN church, or a member of a PRESBYTERY.
Presbyterians. Members of a church governed by elders or presbyters and minister in a hierarchy of representative courts. Their doc-

trine is fundamentally Calvinistic. The CHURCH OF SCOTLAND (*see under* CHURCH) became presbyterian after the REFORMATION but the growth of Presbyterianism in 17th-century England was checked by the rise of the INDEPENDENTS and the Act of Uniformity of 1662. The Presbyterian Church of Wales is of 18th-century origin. In 1900 the Presbyterians joined the FREE CHURCH OF SCOTLAND and formed the United Free Church of Scotland, except for a small section which broke away to become the FREE CHURCHES.

Presbytery. Variously, the eastern part of a church beyond the choir stalls; the residence of a ROMAN CATHOLIC priest, and in PRESBYTERIANISM, the district court's area of jurisdiction and the body of ELDERS ruling it.

Pride. The first of the SEVEN DEADLY SINS.
Pride goes before a fall. An adaptation of *Proverbs* xvi, 18—'Pride goeth before destruction, and an haughty spirit before a fall.'

Prie-Dieu (Fr., pray God). A small, narrow prayer desk or a high-backed chair with a ledge for kneeling when engaged in PRAYER.

Priest (Lat., *presbyter*, an elder). An official minister of religion; one trained or ordained and authorized by a bishop in CATHOLIC and Episcopal CHURCHES, to administer the SACRAMENTS and conduct the rites of the Church. He or she is also responsible for the care of sacred buildings and treasures. The order is between that of a DEACON and BISHOP.

Primate. The title of the BISHOP of the 'first' or chief see of a state (Lat. *prima sedes*); originally the METROPOLITAN of a province. The Archbishop of York is called *Primate of England* and the Archbishop of Canterbury *Primate of All England*.

Prime (Lat. *primus*, first). In the Western Church, the office appointed for the first hour (6 a.m.), the first of the CANONICAL HOURS.

Primitive Methodists. The term 'primitive' was adopted to indicate a close association with the teachings of John WESLEY, and the name was used after the expulsion of the movement from the METHODISTS in 1810. This followed the holding of 'camp meetings' and open-air services instituted by Hugh Borne and William Clowes. They had allowed women preachers and admitted a large number of laymen to their conferences. The movement also became known as 'Ranters' from the extreme emotionalism of their meetings. Their chief following was among the industrial populations of North England and the Midlands. In 1932 the sect rejoined the Methodists.

Primus (Lat., first). The presiding BISHOP of the Episcopal Church of Scotland. He is elected by the other six bishops, and presides in Convocation, and at meetings relative to Church matters.

Primus and Felician, SS (d. *c.* 297, f.d. 9 June). Tradition says they were two aged brothers in a patrician Roman family who were martyred at Nomentum, near ROME, under the Diocletian persecution. They were tortured and beheaded, and are noted as the first Christian martyrs to have had their relics translated to a church inside Rome. Their cult was confined to local calendars in 1969.

Prince. Prince of the Church. A CARDINAL.
Prince of Darkness. The DEVIL; SATAN.
Prince of Peace. The MESSIAH; Jesus Christ.

> For unto us a child is born, unto us a son is given ... and his name shall be called Wonderful, Counsellor, The mighty God, The everlasting Father. The Prince of Peace.
>
> *Isaiah* ix, 6

Principalities. Members of one of the nine orders of angels in mediaeval angelology. *See* ANGEL.

> In the assembly next upstood
> Nisroch, of Principalities the prime.
>
> MILTON: *Paradise Lost*, VI, 447

Printer. The Printer's Bible. *See* BIBLE, SOME SPECIALLY NAMED EDITIONS.

Prior. The Superior in a PRIORY, but second in command to an ABBOT in a monastery.
Priory. A religious house governed by a Prior or Prioress, smaller and lower in status than an abbey, or dependent on it.

Prisca, St. A Roman Christian maiden tortured and beheaded (*c.* 270) under the Emperor Claudius II. There is a church of St Prisca at ROME. She is represented between two lions who, it is said, refused to attack her. Her feast day is 18 January, but her cult has been confined to her basilica in Rome since 1969.
St Priscilla, a Christian convert of the 1st century, and mentioned several times in the NEW TESTAMENT (*Acts* xviii, *Rom.* xvi, I *Cor.* xvi, 2 *Tim.* iv), is also known as St Prisca.

Priscillians. A sect of the 4th and 5th centuries, named after Priscillian, a Spanish bishop who was executed on the orders of the Emperor Maximus on a charge of heresy, this being the first instance of a sentence of death for heresy. Priscillian was accused of GNOSTIC and MANICHAEAN leanings; his followers practised extreme asceticism, remained celibate and ate no meat. The sect died out about 430.

Prisoner of the Vatican. *See under* VATICAN; LAT-ERAN TREATY.

Privileged Presses. The Oxford and Cambridge University Presses share the Royal Privilege of printing the AUTHORIZED VERSION (*see under* BIBLE, THE ENGLISH) of the BIBLE in England.

Pro Oriente. Founded in 1964 in Vienna, the movement was inaugurated by Cardinal Franz König to promote understanding between the ROMAN and ORTHODOX CATHOLIC CHURCHES, aiming 'to advance towards the re-establishment of full communion between the Catholic and Orthodox sister churches'. It holds theological conferences and symposia and publishes literature on oecumenical, historical and theological themes.

Probabilism. In ROMAN CATHOLIC theology, the principle that where there is reasonable doubt arising from a matter of conscience on the binding force of some law, it is permissible to act as one believes to be best, providing this is 'probable', that is to say that it has some support by an authority or by a theologian of repute. The authority on such reasoning is LIGUORI, a Roman Catholic saint, theologian and noted casuist.

Processional. A service book containing hymns, litanies and prayers used in processions.

Processus and Martinian, SS (date unknown, f.d. 2 July). Legend says that these early martyrs were warders of SS PETER and PAUL in the Mamertine prison, and were converted by St Peter. One tradition says that they were buried in the private cemetery of a woman called Lucina, another that the cemetery of Damascus was their burial place, or, again, that their tomb was the basilica on the Aurelian Way. They were greatly venerated in ROME, but their cult was confined to local calendars in the revision of 1969.

Procopius, St (d. 303, f.d. 8 July). Born at Jerusalem and a lector of the church at Scythopolis, he was also an exorcist and interpreter of Syriac. He was greatly esteemed for his virtuous life and humility. Ordered by Flavian to sacrifice to the gods, he refused and became the first Christian martyr under the Diocletian persecution. The bare facts of his life were recorded by EUSEBIUS, but fantastic legends were added, such as endless arguments with Flavius, appalling tortures with miraculous healing of wounds, the conversion of his mother Theodosia and other aristocratic women, with their subsequent martyrdom;

then the successful repulsion of thousands of bandits. There were shrines in his honour at Caesarea and Scythopolis.

Prolocutor. The president or spokesman of the Lower Houses of the convocation of the CHURCH OF ENGLAND at Canterbury and York.

Promised Land, or **Land of Promise.** Canaan; so called because God promised ABRAHAM, Isaac, and Jacob that their offspring should possess it. Figuratively, HEAVEN or any place of expected happiness or fulfilment.

Promotor Fidei. *See* CANONIZATION.

Proof Bible, The. *See* BIBLE, SOME SPECIALLY NAMED EDITIONS.

Propaganda. The CONGREGATION or College of the Propaganda (*Congregatio de propaganda fide*) is a committee of CARDINALS established at ROME by Gregory XV in 1622 for propagating the FAITH throughout the WORLD. Hence the term is applied to any scheme, association, publication, etc., for making PROSELYTES or influencing public opinion in political, social, and religious matters, etc.

Prophet. An inspired teacher; one who reveals the will of God or his judgements. In the OLD TESTAMENT there are two groups.
The Great, or **Major Prophets.** Isaiah, Jeremiah, Ezekiel, and DANIEL; so called because their writings are more extensive than the prophecies of the other twelve.
The Minor, or **Lesser Prophets.** Hosea, Joel, Amos, Obadiah, Micah, Jonah, Nahum, Habakkuk, Zephaniah, Haggai, Zechariah, and Malachi, whose writings are less extensive than those of the four GREAT PROPHETS.

They appear in the NEW TESTAMENT in association with the fulfilment of prophecies.

Proselytes. From Gr. *proselutos*, one who has come to a place; hence, a convert, especially (in its original application) to Judaism. Among the Jews proselytes were of two kinds—*viz.* 'The proselyte of righteousness' and the 'stranger that is within thy gates' (Hellenes). The former submitted to circumcision and conformed to the laws of MOSES; the latter went no farther than to refrain from offering sacrifice to heathen gods, and from working on the SABBATH. To **proselytize** is to engage in converting people to one's religious beliefs.

Prosfora. The sacrificial bread of the Russian ORTHODOX CHURCH; made from pure wheat in two parts, representing the two natures of Christ. It is imprinted with the Greek cross, which has four arms of equal length. The liturgy of the church employs five prosforae, the first, having the seal of the Lamb of God, is cut out and consecrated during the liturgy, the other four sacramental breads are dedicated to the VIRGIN MARY, to all souls, to the living and to the dead. The GREEK CHURCH now only uses one large loaf.

Proskomide. In the Eastern ORTHODOX CHURCH the ceremony of preparation of the bread and wine for the EUCHARIST.

Prosper of Aquitaine, St (*c.* 390–455, f.d. 7 July). Little is known of his life other than that he was a layman of learning and a noted controversialist and was later in the service of LEO THE GREAT in the papal chancery. He played an important part in writing against PELAGIAN heresies and in promoting the teachings of St AUGUSTINE in his work *Defence of St Augustine.* He also wrote a *History of the World* and his *De vocatione omnium gentium* was published in English in 1950.

Protestant. A member of a Christian Church upholding the principles of the REFORMATION or (loosely) of any Church not in communion with ROME. In the time of Luther his followers called themselves 'evangelicals'. The name arose from the Lutheran *protest* against the recess of the Diet of Spires (1529) which declared that the religious status quo must be maintained.
The Protestant Pope. Clement XIV (1769–75), who ordered the suppression of the JESUITS in 1773. He was a patron of art and a liberal-minded statesman but was under pressure from the Bourbon kings.

Protevangelium. The first (Gr. *protos*) GOSPEL; a term applied to an apocryphal gospel which has been attributed to St JAMES THE LESS. It was supposed by some critics that all the gospels were based upon this, but it appears to be the compilation of a Jewish Christian from a variety of sources and dates from the 2nd century. The name is also given to the curse upon the serpent in *Gen.* iii, 15, which has been regarded as the earliest utterance of the gospel:

> And I will put enmity between thee and the woman, and between thy seed and her seed; it shall bruise thy head, and thou shalt bruise his heel.

See APOCRYPHA.

Prothesis. In the Eastern ORTHODOX CHURCH, the table on which the EUCHARISTIC gifts are prepared at the PROSKOMIDE; it is also the chamber in the church, situated on the left of the APSE where the table stands.

Proto-martyr. The first martyr (Gr. *protos*, first). STEPHEN the deacon is so called (*Acts* vi, vii), and St ALBAN is known as the proto-martyr of Britain.

Protus and Hyacinth, SS (date unknown, f.d. 11 September). Traditionally two Roman eunuchs, in the religious romance of St Eugenia. They were thought to be legendary until in 1845 the tomb of St Hyacinth was found in the cemetery of Basilla, with his epitaph and date of burial; it contained charred bones. An empty tomb nearby bore the name of Protus, the relics having been translated to ROME by Leo IV. According to St DAMASUS, Protus and Hyacinth were brothers, while St JEROME's martyrology says they were 'teachers of the Christian law'. They also appeared in the O.E. Martyrology, the Martyrology of St BEDE and in the Sarum Calendar. Their cult was widespread in the Middle Ages, reaching as far as a church at Blisland in Cornwall.

Provincial. The Provincial of an Order. In a religious order, one who has authority over all the houses of that order in a province or given area. He is usually elected by the provincial CHAPTER.

Provost. The head of a CHAPTER of a religious community, or the head of a cathedral chapter where the cathedral is also a parish church.

Psalms. Of the 150 songs in the *Book of Psalms*, 73 are inscribed with David's name, 12 with that of Asaph the singer, 11 are attributed to the sons of Korah, a family of singers, and one (*Psalm* xc) to Moses. The whole compilation is divided into five books: Bk. 1, from i to xli; Bk. 2, from xlii to lxxii; Bk. 3, from lxxiii to lxxxix; Bk. 4, from xc to cvi; Bk. 5, from cvii to cl.

Much of the *Book of Psalms* was for centuries attributed to David (hence called the sweet psalmist of Israel) but it is doubtful whether he wrote any of them. The tradition comes from the author of *Chronicles*, and II *Sam.* xxii is a psalm attributed to David that is identical with *Ps.* xviii. Also, the last verse of *Ps.* lxxii ('The prayers of David the son of Jesse are ended') seems to suggest that he was the author up to that point.

In explanation of the confusion between the ROMAN CATHOLIC and PROTESTANT psalters, it should be noted that *Psalms* ix and x in the BOOK OF COMMON PRAYER version (also in the BIBLE, AUTHORIZED and REVISED VERSIONS (*see under* BIBLE, THE ENGLISH)) are combined in the Roman Catholic Psalter to form *Psalm* ix, and *Psalms* cxiv and cxv in the *Book of Common Prayer* are combined in the Roman Catholic Psalter to form *Psalm* cxiii. Again, *Psalm* cxvi in the *Book of Common Prayer* is split to form *Psalms* cxiv and cxv in the Roman Catholic Psalter, and *Psalm* cxlvii in the *Book of Common Prayer* is split to form *Psalms* cxlvi and cxlvii in the Roman Catholic Psalter. Thus only the first eight and the last three *Psalms* coincide numerically in both psalters. *See also* GRADUAL PSALMS; PENITENTIAL PSALMS.

Psalter. A version or copy of the PSALMS for liturgical use, as in the BOOK OF COMMON PRAYER, or a separate book with tunes for congregational singing.

Pseudepigrapha (Gr., falsely inscribed or ascribed). In Biblical scholarship, a term applied to certain pseudonymous Jewish writings such as the 'Book of Enoch', the 'Assumption of MOSES', the 'Psalms of Solomon', the 'Fourth Book of the MACCABEES' (*see under* MACCABEES), etc., which were excluded from the CANON of the OLD TESTAMENT and the APOCRYPHA.

Pucci, St Anthony Mary (1819–92, f.d. 12 January). Of peasant family in Tuscany, he was educated at Monte Senario, ordained priest and served the parish of Viareggio for the whole of his life. Though not of a prepossessing appearance or temperament, he was an excellent organizer. He had become a SERVITE FRIAR and worked for the Association for the Propagation of the Faith and was appointed provincial of the province of Tuscany. His care for the sick was unremitting, particularly during two epidemics of the plague, and he was responsible for the innovation of seaside nursing homes for children. He was greatly revered and miracles were reported at his tomb. He was canonized in 1962.

Pudens. A soldier in the Roman army, mentioned in II *Tim*. iv, 21, in connexion with Linus and Claudia. According to tradition, Claudia, the wife of Pudens, was a British lady; Linus, otherwise Cyllen, was her brother; and Lucius 'the British king', the grandson of Linus. Tradition further adds that Lucius wrote to Eleutherus, Bishop of ROME, to send missionaries to Britain to convert the people.

Pulcheria, St (399–453, f.d. 10 September). Daughter of the Emperor Arcadius, she acted as regent for her younger brother Theodosius II who, even after his marriage and accession, continued under her influence. When Theodosius died in 450, Pulcheria succeeded as Augusta or Empress. She married a general, Marcian, who ruled with her. The marriage was nominal, Pulcheria having earlier taken a vow of celibacy. She summoned councils for the suppression of such heresies as MONOPHYSITISM and NESTORIANISM. In atonement for the ill-treatment of St JOHN CHRYSOSTOM by her parents, she had his remains translated from Comana to the Church of the Apostles at Constantinople. She led a devout life and was a pillar of the Church.

Pulpit (Lat. *pulpitum*, platform). In a church, the raised or enclosed structure of wood or stone, usually approached by a short flight of steps, from which the preacher delivers the sermon. It is normally placed on the north side of the NAVE, against the CHANCEL arch. Pulpits also occur in monastery refectories.

Purgatory. The doctrine of Purgatory, according to which the souls of the departed suffer for a time till they are purged of their sin, is of ancient standing, and in certain phases of Jewish belief GEHENNA seems to have been regarded partly as a place of purgatory.

The early Church Fathers developed the concept of purgatory and support for the doctrine was adduced from *2 Macc*. xii, 39–45; *Matt*. xii, 32; 1 *Cor*. iii, 11–13; etc. The first decree on the subject was promulgated by the Council of Florence in 1439. It was rejected by the CHURCH OF ENGLAND in 1562 by the XXIInd of the *Articles of Religion*.

St Patrick's Purgatory. *See under* PATRICK.

Purification, Feast of. *See* CANDLEMAS DAY.

Puritans. The more extreme PROTESTANTS inside and outside the CHURCH OF ENGLAND who found the Elizabethan religious settlement unacceptable and wished a further 'purification' of religion. They looked more and more to the BIBLE as the sole authority, rejecting all tradition in matters of public worship, and were mainly CALVINIST in outlook and theology. They feature in the 16th and 17th century as BROWNISTS, BARROWISTS, PRESBYTERIANS, BAPTISTS, SEPARATISTS, and Independents, and were sometimes called *Precisionists* from their punctiliousness over religious rules and observances. After the Restoration and the Act of Uniformity (1662), they became collectively known as DISSENTERS or NONCONFORMISTS.

Puseyite. A HIGH CHURCH follower of E. B. Pusey (1800–82), Professor of Hebrew at Oxford, one of the leaders of the Oxford Movement, and a contributor to *Tracts for the Times*. Hence **Puseyism** as an unfriendly name for Tractarianism.

Pyx (Gr. *pyxis*, a boxwood vessel). A small metal receptacle or box in which the reserved HOST is taken to sick people. It is also the vessel in which the Host is reserved in the Tabernacle in Roman Catholic (and some Anglican) churches.

Q

'Q'. In Biblical criticism, the symbol used for the theoretical document used by MATTHEW or LUKE or both. In the SYNOPTIC GOSPELS there is much material common to both Matthew and Luke, which is designated 'Q' (usually held to be the German *Quelle*, source). These passages mainly consist of the sayings of Jesus.

Quadragesima. The forty days of LENT.
Quadragesima Sunday. The first Sunday in LENT; so called because it is, in round numbers, the fortieth day before EASTER.

Quadragesimals. The farthings or payments formerly made in commutation of a personal visit to the Mother-church on Mid-Lent Sunday. *Cp.* PENTECOSTALS. *See also* MOTHERING SUNDAY.

Quadrilateral. Lambeth Quadrilateral. The four points suggested by the LAMBETH Conference of 1888 as a basis for Christian reunion; the BIBLE, the APOSTOLES' and NICENE CREEDS, two Sacraments (BAPTISM and the EUCHARIST), and the historic Episcopate.

Quaker. A familiar name for a member of the Society of Friends, a religious body having no definite creed and no regular ministry, founded by George Fox, who began his preaching in 1647. His followers created an organized society during the 1650s and 1660s. It appears from the founder's *Journal* that they first obtained the appellation (1650) from the following circumstances: 'Justice Bennet, of Derby,' says Fox, 'was the first to call us Quakers, because I bid them Tremble at the Word of the Lord.'

> Quakers (that, like to lanterns, bear
> Their light within them) will not swear.
> BUTLER: *Hudibras*, II, ii

The name was previously applied to a sect whose adherents shook and trembled with religious emotion and was generally applied in the Commonwealth period as an abusive term to religious and political radicals. *Cp.* SHAKERS.
Quaker City. Philadelphia, which was founded by a group of Quakers led by William Penn and intended as a haven of religious freedom.
Quaker guns. Dummy guns made of wood, for drill purposes or camouflage; an allusion to the Quaker reprobation of the use of force.
The Quaker Poet. Bernard Barton (1784–1849); also John Greenleaf Whittier (1807–92).

Quare impedit (Lat., wherefore he hinders). A form of legal action by which the right of presentation to a Church of England BENEFICE is tried (from the opening words of the writ). When a BISHOP has failed to institute a clergyman presented by the patron of the benefice, the latter may apply for a writ of *Quare impedit* against the bishop. It is now only used where the bishop's objections relate to matters of doctrine and ritual.

Quarter Days. (1) New Style LADY DAY (25 March), Midsummer Day (24 June), MICHAELMAS DAY (29 September), and CHRISTMAS Day (25 December).
   (2) Old Style—Lady Day (6 April), Old Midsummer Day (6 July), Old Michaelmas Day (11 October), and Old Christmas Day (6 January).
Quarter Days in Scotland. CANDLEMAS DAY, (2 February), WHITSUNDAY (15 May), LAMMAS DAY (1 August), and MARTINMAS Day (11 November).

Quasimodo Sunday. The first Sunday after EASTER or LOW SUNDAY; so called from the Introit at MASS on this day which begins *Quasi modo geniti infantes*, as newborn babes (I *Pet.* ii, 2). *Cp.* CANTATE SUNDAY.

Quattro Coronati. *See* The FOUR CROWNED MARTYRS.

Quay, St. *See* KEA.

Queen Anne's Bounty. A fund established by Queen Anne in 1704 for the relief of the poorer clergy of the CHURCH OF ENGLAND. It was created out of the firstfruits (*see* ANNATES) and tenths, formerly given to the papacy, which were annexed to the Crown by Henry VIII. In 1809 there were 860 incumbents still getting less than £50 per annum and the fund was increased by Parliamentary grants (1809–20). Queen Anne's Bounty was merged with the Ecclesiastical Commission in 1948 to form the Church Commissioners.

Quenburga (or Coenburga), St (d. *c.* 735, f.d. 31 August or 3 September). A daughter of Conred, a Wessex chieftain, and sister of St CUTHBURGA. The sisters founded Wimborne, a double monastery, after Cuthburga had left her husband, Aldfrith, King of Northumbria, to become a nun at Barking. There were said to be about fifty nuns, and their seclusion was such that not even bishops were allowed within. Later there were three houses, one for monks and two for nuns, with Quenburga and Cuthburga as abbesses.

Quentigerna, St. *See* KENTIGERNA.

Quentin (or Quintin), St (date unknown, f.d. 31 October). Said to have been a Roman soldier who went with St Lucian of Beauvais on a mission to convert the pagans at Amiens. He was martyred under the Maximian and Diocletian persecutions with every kind of torture. An angel released him from prison, but he was again arrested and tortured; legend says that the men who scourged him were struck by paralysis. Finally he was beheaded. His relics were translated to Saint-Quentin on the Somme. In art he can be depicted as either a Roman soldier or a bishop, and holds spits.

Questor, or **Quaestor.** Originally a Roman judge or prosecutor; later a treasurer or tax-gatherer. In the CATHOLIC CHURCH, one who is appointed to beg for alms.

Quicunque Vult. The alternative name for the ATHANASIAN CREED (*see under* ATHANASIUS).

Quietism. A form of religious mysticism based on the doctrine that the essence of religion consists in the withdrawal of the SOUL from external objects, and in fixing it upon the contemplation of God; especially that taught by Miguel Molinos (1640–1696), who taught the direct relationship between the soul and God. His followers were called Molinists or *Quietists*. Outward acts of mortification were held superfluous and when a person has attained the mystic state by mental prayer, even if he transgresses in the accepted sense, he does not sin, since his will has been extinguished. *See* MOLINISM.

Quinguagesima Sunday (Lat., fiftieth). Shrove Sunday, or the first day of the week which contains ASH WEDNESDAY. It is so called because in round numbers it is the fiftieth day before EASTER.

Quintilians. Members of a 2nd-century heretical sect of MONTANISTS, said to have been founded by one Quintilia, a prophetess. They made the EUCHARIST of bread and cheese, and allowed women to become priests and BISHOPS. *See* HERETIC.

Quintin, St. *See* QUENTIN.

Quiricus (Cyricus or Cyr) and Julitta (d. *c.* 304, f.d. 16 June (West), 15 July (East)). Legendary martyrs; Quiricus being the three-year-old son of a widow who fled to Tarsus from Iconium to escape the Diocletian persecution. She was recognized, and she and her child were tortured. One legend says that the child attacked the torturers, another that the torments rebounded on the persecutors. As a child-martyr the cult of Quiricus became popular and he was frequently represented in art. Churches were named after him, such as the cathedral dedicated to St Cyr and the church of Newton St Cyres in Devon. He was the patron saint of children.

Quirinus, St (d. *c.* 130, f.d. 30 March). Said to have been the jailer of Pope Alexander I, he was converted by the pope and was then persecuted as a Christian under Hadrian. His tongue was cut out and thrown to a falcon but the bird rejected it; the same occurred when his hands and feet were cut off and given to the dogs. He was then beheaded. His relics were said to be held at several places including Troyes, Cologne and ROME.

Quis separabit? (Lat., Who shall separate us?) The motto adopted by the Most Illustrious ORDER OF ST PATRICK (*see under* PATRICK) when it was founded.

R

Raikes, Robert (1735–1811). Born at Gloucester, he became a printer and publisher. Being distressed by the miserable conditions and ignorance of poor children, he started a Sunday School in 1780 where they were taught to read and to repeat the CHURCH OF ENGLAND catechism. This was the foundation of the Sunday School movement in England.

Radegonde (or Radegund), St (f.d. 13 August). Wife of Clotaire, King of the Franks (558–61). Disgusted with the crimes of the royal family, she founded the monastery of St Croix at Poitiers.
St Radegonde's lifted stone. A stone 60 ft in circumference, placed on five supporting stones, said by the historians of Poitou to have been so arranged in 1478, to commemorate a great fair held on the spot in October of that year. The country people insist that Queen Radegonde brought the impost stone on her head, and the five uprights in her apron, and arranged them all as they appear to this day.

Raganer (or Ragenerius), St (d. c. 870, f.d. 21 November). Traditionally a soldier and martyr of Northampton. It was said that Bruning, a wealthy but devout priest of St Peter's at Northampton, had a simple-minded servant of Viking extraction who wanted to go on a pilgrimage to St Peter's, ROME, but was turned back by a vision which revealed that the body of a saint was buried under the floor of the Northampton church. Excavations were carried out and a tomb was found, but not identified. Miracles occurred and a miraculous light appeared. Alfgiva of Abingdon, a cripple, was cured and able to walk. Bruning opened the tomb after he had fasted for three days and a scroll, in with the bones, identified the relics as those of Ragener, a nephew of King EDMUND, with whom he had been martyred. A shrine was erected; miracles followed and Alfgiva became a nun.

Rainier (or Ranieri) of Pisa, St (1117–61, f.d. 17 June). Born into a wealthy merchant family of Pisa, he was well educated and learned Latin. He became a monk and set out on a pilgrimage to the HOLY LAND, staying there as a hermit for some twelve years before returning to Pisa and living in the monastery of St Andrew and then at San Vito. He lived a life of austerity and became known as a preacher and, with his knowledge of Latin, was able to use the BIBLE in his work. He was also known as a healer. In the 13th century he was named as the patron saint of Pisa.

Ranters. A sect which was founded in England at the time of the Civil War; its members said they were filled with the Spirit; they could not sin but were in the same state as was ADAM in PARADISE. Their slogan was 'Christ in men' and they were known as 'Ranters' from the extreme ranting and gesticulating adopted in preaching and praying. The name was also given to early PRIMITIVE METHODISTS nearly 200 years later, for the same reason.

Raphael. One of the principal ANGELS of Jewish angelology. In the book of TOBIT we are told how he travelled with Tobias into Media and back again, instructing him on the way how to marry Sara and to drive away the wicked spirit. Milton calls him the 'sociable spirit' and the 'affable archangel' (*Paradise Lost*, VII, 40) and it was he who was sent by God to warn ADAM of his danger.

> Raphael, the sociable spirit that deigned
> To travel with Tobias, and secured
> His marriage with the seven-times-wedded maid.
> *Paradise Lost*, V, 221

Raphael is usually distinguished in art by a pilgrim's staff or carrying a fish, in allusion to his aiding Tobias to capture the fish which performed the miraculous cure of his father's eyesight.

Raven. In Christian art, the raven is an emblem of God's Providence, in allusion to the ravens which fed Elijah. St Oswald holds in his hand a raven with a ring in its mouth; St Benedict has a raven at his feet; St PAUL THE HERMIT is drawn with a raven bringing him a loaf of bread.

On the other hand, the raven can be a symbol of the Devil, feeding on corruption or pecking out eyes to blind sinners. The raven also represents sin as opposed to the innocence of the white dove. The raven sent out from the Ark by Noah depicts wandering, unrest and the unclean. In the symbolism of the FALL the raven can appear in the TREE OF KNOWLEDGE from which Eve gathers the fruit.

Raymund Nonnatus, St (1204–40, f.d. 31 August). Called non-natus ('not born') as he was taken from his mother's womb after she had died in labour. His history is obscure, but he was known to have joined the MERCEDARIAN Order and was sent to Algeria on a mission to convert Muslims to Christianity. It was said that he redeemed slaves and offered himself as a ransom for their liberation. When freed from prison, he returned to Spain and was nominated cardinal by Pope GREGORY IX; he died at Cardona on his way to ROME. Many miracles were attributed to him, and the peculiarity of his birth made him patron saint of midwives. His cult was confined to local calendars in 1969.
Raymund of Pennafort, St (c. 1180–1275, f.d. 7 January, formerly 23 January). Born into a Catalonian family of aristocratic connections, he was educated at Barcelona and Bologna, taking doctorates in civil and canon law. He became archdeacon of Barcelona and in 1222 entered the DOMINICAN Order and worked to convert Moors and Jews, and also against WALDENSIAN and ALBIGENSIAN heresies. GREGORY IX called him to ROME where he compiled the Decretals of canon law; he also wrote the *Summa casuum* on penitential discipline. In 1238 he became Master-General of his order and revised the Dominican Constitutions. He returned to Spain where he encouraged St THOMAS AQUINAS to write his *Summa contra Gentiles*. There is little support for the claim that he assisted St PETER NOLASCO to found the MERCEDARIAN ORDER. He was a man of great learning and a lover of solitude; he had refused the archbishopric of Tarragona. He died at the age of nearly 100 in Barcelona.

Read. To read oneself in. Said of an Anglican clergyman on entering upon a new incumbency, because one of his first duties is to give a public reading of the THIRTY-NINE ARTICLES in the church to which he has been appointed, and to make the Declaration of Assent.
Lay Reader. In the CHURCH OF ENGLAND, a layman licensed by the BISHOP to conduct church services; namely, Morning and Evening Prayer (except the absolution and the blessing) and the Litany. A Lay Reader may also publish BANNS OF MARRIAGE, preach, catechize children, etc. The modern office dates from 1866.

Real Presence. The doctrine that Christ Himself is present in the bread and wine of the EUCHARIST after consecration, as contrasted with doctrines that maintain the Body and Blood are only symbolically present.

Realism. In mediaeval scholastic philosophy the opposite of Nominalism; the belief that abstract concepts or universals are real things existing independently of our conceptions and their expression. It was a development from Plato's metaphysic and was held in varying forms by ERIGENA, REMIGIUS, St ANSELM, ABELARD, ALBERT THE GREAT, THOMAS AQUINAS, DUNS SCOTUS, and others. *See* SCHOLASTICISM.

Reatus (Lat., a charge of sin). That which has to be purged by confession and absolution and by an act of atonement or reparation.

Rechabites. Members of a teetotal benefit society (the Independent Order of Rechabites), founded in 1835, and so named from Rechab, who enjoined his family to abstain from wine and to dwell in tents (*Jer.* xxxv, 6, 7).

Recluse. One who lives alone, avoiding the world on religious grounds and for self-discipline and meditation.

Recollects. The name given (1) to a reformed branch of the FRANCISCAN Observants first formed in France; and (2) a reformed group of AUGUSTINIAN Hermits founded in Spain. Both orders were first formed in the late 16th century.

Rector. *See* CLERICAL TITLES.

Recusants. The name given from the reign of Elizabeth I to those who refused to attend the services of the CHURCH OF ENGLAND (Lat. *recusare*, to refuse). The term commonly denoted 'popish recusants' although properly it included PROTESTANT dissenters. Fines were first exacted under statute in 1552 and 1559 at the rate of 1s. per Sunday but raised to the exorbitant sum of £20 per month in 1587. Fortunately they were intermittently imposed, and the last fines for recusancy were those in 1782 on two Yorkshire labourers and their wives. The CATHOLIC recusants were largely drawn from land-owning families; they were barred from political positions and the professions from the time of Queen Elizabeth I to Victorian times, when they were emancipated in 1829.

Red. The Red Hat. The flat broad-brimmed hat formerly bestowed upon cardinals, hence the office of CARDINAL.
Red-letter day. A lucky day; a day to be recalled with delight. In almanacs, and more commonly in ecclesiastical calendars, important FEAST days and saints' days were printed in red, other days in black.

Redemptionists. Members of a religious order whose object was to redeem Christian captives and slaves from Muslims. They are also known as TRINITARIANS.

Redemptorists. Members of the Congregation of the Most Holy Redeemer, a religious order founded at Scala, Italy, in 1732 by St ALPHONSUS Maria di Liguori. They are largely concerned with mission work among the poor and foreign missions.

Reed. A broken, or **bruised reed.** Something not to be trusted for support; a weak adherent. Egypt is called a broken reed, in which Hezekiah could not trust if the Assyrians made war on Jerusalem: 'which broken reed if a man leans on, it will go into his hand and pierce it.' *See* II *Kings* xviii, 21; *Is.* xxxvi, 6.
A reed shaken by the wind. A person blown about by every wind of doctrine. John the Baptist (said Christ) was not a 'reed shaken by the wind', but from the very first had a firm belief in the Messiahship of the Son of MARY, and this conviction was not shaken by fear or favour. *See Matt.* xi, 7.

Reformation, The. Specifically, the religious revolution of the 16th century which destroyed the religious unity of Western Europe and resulted in the establishment of 'Reformed' or PROTESTANT churches. It aimed at reforming the abuses in the Roman Church and ended in schism, its chief leaders being LUTHER, ZWINGLI, and CALVIN (*see* CALVINISM, ROMAN CATHOLIC CHURCH).
The Counter-Reformation. A name given by historians to the movement for reform within the Roman Church (much stimulated by the REFORMATION) and the measures taken to combat the spread of Protestantism and to regain lost ground. It is usually reckoned to extend from the mid-16th century, when the Council of Trent (1545–63) strengthened and reawakened the life and discipline of the Church, until the time of the Thirty Years War (1618–48). The JESUITS played a major role, whilst the INQUISITION and the INDEX strengthened Papal influence.

Reformed Church. A group of PROTESTANT churches which follow the doctrines of ZWINGLI and CALVIN, founded in Switzerland at the same time as the LUTHERAN branch was established in Germany. Zwingli, influenced by ERASMUS, instituted the church at Zürich in 1519, breaking away from the ROMAN CATHOLIC CHURCH. The movement spread to Germany, Holland, France, Hungary, England and Scotland and reached the USA in the 17th century.
Reformed Episcopal Church. A PROTESTANT EVANGELICAL offshoot from the CHURCH OF ENGLAND, inaugurated in the USA in 1873, having branches in Canada and India.

Refreshment Sunday. *See* MID-LENT SUNDAY; MOTHERING SUNDAY.

Regium donum (Lat., royal gift). An annual grant paid by the Crown from 1670 until 1871 to help PRESBYTERIAN ministers in Ulster. It was, however, withdrawn by James II and again in 1714. An English *regium donum* was introduced by Walpole in 1723 for the benefit of the widows of Dissenting ministers. NONCONFORMIST unease led to its discontinuance in 1851.

> The English 'Regium Donum' had all the demoralizing effects of a bribe. For more than a century and a quarter it continued to be a source of weakness, strife, discontent, and reproach.
> SKEATS and MIALL: *History of the Free Churches of England,* ch. V

Regular. One subject to religious vows and discipline and living in a community, as distinct from secular priests living in the world.
Regular Clergy. A term applied to CATHOLIC monks and friars who are members of an Order or Congregation, having taken vows and living under monastic conditions; as opposed to SECULAR CLERGY who live in the world as parish priests.

Regularis Concordia. In 972 the Synod of Winchester, attended by bishops, abbots and abbesses, drew up a code regulating monastic observance for all religious houses, male or female, in England.

Relic, Christian. The corpse of a saint, or any part thereof; any part of his clothing; or anything ultimately connected with him. The veneration of Christian relics goes back to the 2nd century and led to many spurious relics being brought back from the HOLY LAND. Miracle-working relics brought wealth to many monasteries and churches and the remains of saints were often dismembered and trickery and violence were used to obtain them. Relics such as the tip of Lucifer's tail, the blood of Christ, the candle which the ANGEL of the Lord lit in Christ's tomb, were among the many accepted by the credulous.

Relief Church. A secession from the CHURCH OF SCOTLAND led in 1752 by Thomas Gillespie (1708–74). He offered passive obedience respecting the settlement of ministers. The 'Presbytery of Relief' was constituted in 1761; in 1847 the sect was embodied in the United Presbyterian Church of Scotland.

Religious. His Most Religious Majesty. The title by which the kings of England were formerly addressed by the POPE. It still survives in the BOOK OF COMMON PRAYER in the Prayer 'for the High Court of Parliament under our most religious and gracious Queen at this time assembled' (which was written, probably by hand, in 1625), and in James I's *Act for Thanksgiving on the Fifth of November* occurs the expression 'most great, learned, and religious King'.

Similarly the Pope addressed the King of France as 'Most Christian', the Emperor of Austria as 'Most Apostolic', the king of Portugal as 'Most Faithful', etc.

The term is also used in CATHOLICISM to denote a man or woman, clerical or lay, who has taken vows and is a member of an institute such as an Order or Congregation.

Religious Tract Society. An EVANGELICAL organization, founded in 1799 by Churchmen and Nonconformists, for the purpose of the propagation of Evangelical literature and its distribution at home and abroad among missionary societies.

Reliquary. A receptacle of various kinds for RELICS. The smaller relics were preserved in monstrances, pyxes, pectoral reliquaries (usually in the form of a CROSS), shapes of arms and legs, etc. The entire remains of a saint were kept in shrines.

Remigius (or Remy), St (438–533, f.d. 1 October), BISHOP and confessor, and apostle of the Franks. He is represented as carrying a vessel of holy oil, or in the act of anointing therewith Clovis, who kneels before him. He is said to have given Clovis the power of touching for the king's evil.

Repenter Curls. The long ringlets of a lady's hair. *Repentir* is the French for penitence, and *les repenties* are the girls doing penance for their misdemeanours. MARY MAGDALENE had such long hair that she wiped off her tears from the feet of Jesus therewith. Hence the association of long curls and reformed (*repenties*) prostitutes.

Requiem. The first word of the prayer *Requiem aeternam dona eis, domine, et lux perpetua luceat eis* (Eternal rest give them, O Lord, and let everlasting light shine upon them) used as the introit of a MASS for the Dead; hence a Requiem Mass.

Requiescat (Lat. *requiescat in pace*, rest in peace). Abbreviated to R.I.P., it is a term used by CATHOLICS as a prayer for the dead. The abbreviation appears frequently on tombstones.

Reredos (Lat., rear, back). The screen behind the ALTAR, usually ornamental, adorned with paintings, embroidery, sculpture or figures; sometimes covering the entire east wall.

Reservation. The practice of reserving a portion of the consecrated HOST in the AMBRY or PYX, to be taken to the sick at need, or to be the focus of adoration. The term also applies to withholding the right of absolution in appropriate cases.

Resurrection. The belief contained in the APOSTLES' CREED of the rising of Christ from the dead on the third day, and the rising from the dead of the faithful at the Last Judgement.

Resurrection, Community of the. A body of CHURCH OF ENGLAND clergy who founded a community at Oxford in 1892 and lived under a rule of celibacy and a common purse. After 1898 this became the House of the Resurrection at Mirfield, Yorkshire. It trains clergy and undertakes mission work in South Africa.

Retable. A shelf or ledge at the back of the ALTAR on which ornaments may be placed, or a framework enclosing decorated panels.

Retreat. A period of withdrawal from the world for spiritual recollection and devotional exercises, usually held at some monastery or religious establishment under the direction of an experienced leader.

Reverend. An archbishop is *the Most Reverend* (Father in God); a BISHOP, *the Right Reverend*; a DEAN, *the Very Reverend*; an archdeacon, *the Venerable*; all the other CLERGY, *the Reverend*. A person in orders should always be referred to as 'the Reverend Mr Jones', or 'the Reverend John Jones'; never 'Reverend', or 'the Reverend Jones'.

Revised Version, The. *See* BIBLE, THE ENGLISH.

Revivalism. A re-awakening of religious fervour, particularly associated with Evangelism and evangelistic meetings and preachers or prayer meetings.

Reynolds, St Richard (*c.* 1492–1535, f.d. 25 October). Of a Devon family, he was educated at Cambridge, taking a doctorate in Divinity and becoming a Fellow of Corpus Christi. He joined the BRIDGETTINE community at Syon and was noted for his learning in Greek, Latin and Hebrew, as well as for the holiness of his life. He was commended by ERASMUS, MORE and FISHER, and many consulted him on theological matters.

At the time of the divorce of Henry VIII he was arrested and imprisoned in the Tower after having refused to take the Oath of Supremacy. He was tried at Westminster, rejecting all persuasions to conform, and was hanged at Tyburn with three CARTHUSIAN priors. He was canonized in 1970 as one of the FORTY MARTYRS OF ENGLAND AND WALES.

Rheims-Douai Version, The. *See* The DOUAI BIBLE, *under* BIBLE, THE ENGLISH.

Rhipsime and Gaiana, SS (d. *c.* 290, f.d. 29 September). Two of the somewhat legendary virgin martyrs venerated as the first martyrs of the Armenian Church. A band of Christian women in ROME was led by Gaiana, and all left together when one, Rhipsime, attracted the attention of Diocletian. They journeyed to Armenia, but there they suffered the same trouble with King Tiridates who, being rejected, ordered the execution of the whole group. Another version of the legend says that there was one survivor, St NINO, who is venerated in Georgia, but she was said to be a slave girl. The existence of the group is accepted, but their Acts are doubtful.

Ricci, St Catherine dei (1522–90, f.d. 13 February). Born in Florence into a wealthy family, she was an admirer of SAVONAROLA and became a nun in the Dominican convent which he had founded at Prato, ultimately becoming its prioress. She won great esteem for her wisdom and administrative abilities. She corresponded with St PHILIP NERI, and it was said that they talked together in ROME. Catherine was noted for her ecstasies and for her enactment of the Passion while she was unconscious; she also received the stigmata. She was canonized in spite of her continuing veneration for Savonarola.

Richard. Richard of Chichester, St (1197–1253, f.d. 3 April). Richard de Wyche was the son of a yeoman farmer, but was orphaned at an early age and had to work hard to keep the land in order. He then studied at Oxford, Paris and Bologna and was appointed chancellor of Oxford University by St Edmund Rich, his former tutor and Archbishop of Canterbury. Richard was ordained priest and joined the DOMINICANS at Orleans. Returning to England he was made Bishop of Chichester in spite of opposition from King Henry III, and went to ROME for consecration. He was regarded as a model prelate, opposing corruption, strict in discipline, but generous in giving and simple in his personal life. He was buried in his cathedral and canonized only nine years after his death. Miracles occurred at his shrine. In art he is depicted as a bishop with a chalice lying on its side at his feet.

Richard Gwyn, St. *See* GWYN.

Richarius, St. *See* RIQUIER.

Rigby, St John (d. 1600, f.d. 25 October). Born at Harrock in Lancashire, he was the son of a poor recusant but took service with a PROTESTANT family. Later, going to the Huddlestones, he came in contact with JESUITS and was reconciled to his CATHOLIC faith. Attending the Middlesex Sessions on behalf of his master's daughter, he was questioned on his religion and admitted his Catholicism. When he refused to renounce his loyalty to the Church he was sentenced to death and was executed at Southwark. He was canonized in 1970 as one of the FORTY MARTYRS OF ENGLAND AND WALES.

Rigorist. A term for a CATHOLIC theologian who, when a case of conscience is in doubt, adheres to the stricter course. *See* PROBABILISM.

Ring. The noun (meaning a circlet) is the O.E. *hring*; the verb (to sound a bell, or as a bell) is from O.E. *hringan*, to clash, ring, connected with Lat. *clangere*, to clang.

The wearing of a wedding-ring by married women is now universal in Christian countries, but the custom varies greatly in detail. It appears to have originated in the betrothal rings given as secular pledges by the Romans. Until the end of the 16th century it was the custom in England to wear the wedding-ring on the third finger of the right hand.

As the forefinger was held to be symbolical of the HOLY GHOST, priests used to wear their ring on this in token of their spiritual office. Episcopal rings, worn by CARDINALS, BISHOPS and abbots, are of gold with a stone—cardinals a sapphire, bishops and abbots an amethyst—and are worn upon the third finger of the right hand. The POPE wears a similar ring, usually with a cameo, emerald, or ruby. A plain gold ring is put upon the third finger of the right hand of a nun on her profession.

Ring of the Fisherman. *See* FISHERMAN'S RING *under* FISH.

Riquier (or Richarius), St (d. *c.* 645, f.d. 9 October or 26 April). Born at Celles, near Amiens, of pagan family, he defended some Irish missionaries who were threatened by the local people, and was converted to Christianity. Becoming a priest, he went to England for a time, then returned to France, founding a monastery at Celles. He became a noted preacher and rebuked King Dagobert. Later he became a hermit. His relics were translated to the town named after him, Saint-Riquier, and a monastery was built there.

Rita of Cascia, St (1377–1447, f.d. 22 May). Although she wanted to become a nun, she submitted to the wishes of her parents and married a man who proved violent and dissolute and under whom she suffered for twenty years until he was murdered. Rita then entered the AUGUSTINIAN convent at Cascia, living an austere life of prayer and meditation. Concentrating on the Passion of Christ, the wounds of the crown of thorns appeared on her forehead and did not heal. She was noted for her holiness and for her work with sick nuns, and she became famous as a mystic and miracle-worker. Her cult became widespread in many countries. Her body was translated to an elaborate shrine; it remained incorrupt and is a centre of pilgrimage to this day, a basilica, school and orphanage being built there in 1946. With St JUDE, she is a patron of hopeless cases, particularly in matrimony. There is an English centre at the Augustinian church at Honiton in Devon. She was beatified in 1624 and canonized in 1900.

Ritual. An established or prescribed procedure in religious use and liturgical practice; it plays an important part in CATHOLIC worship in the exposition of doctrine, and in the Russian ORTHODOX CHURCH has been said to take precedence over doctrine. Bishop Serafim, of the Orthodox Church, said: 'Ritual is symbolic form, reflecting the deepest spiritual content of religion ... it invokes both the external, inevitably finite, aspect of Christian faith and its enduring, innermost significance.' The Orthodox LITURGY is considerably longer than the ROMAN CATHOLIC MASS.

Rituale Romanum. The official service book of the ROMAN CATHOLIC CHURCH, setting out the rites for the administration of the SACRAMENTS by a priest other than the MASS and Divine Office.

Robert of Bellarmine, St (1542–1621, f.d. 17 September). Born at Montepulciano, he entered the JESUIT ORDER and became a famous theologian and controversialist at a time of conflict between the CATHOLIC CHURCH and PROTESTANTS. He taught at the Roman College, of which he became rector in 1592, and was appointed archbishop of Capua and cardinal. He was involved in the debate with King James I of England and with Bishop Lancelot Andrews on the question of the authority of kings. He was a friend and helper of Galileo. Bellarmine was an outstanding theologian, encouraging the study of Greek, Hebrew and the VULGATE and writing extensively; among his works are commentaries on the PSALMS, volumes of *Disputations* and two CATECHISMS. Several of his works were translated into English and one into Welsh. He was not canonized until 1930, since when he has been named a DOCTOR OF THE CHURCH.

Robert of Knaresborough (1160–1218, f.d. 24 September). Son of a burgher of York, he became a sub-deacon at the CISTERCIAN abbey of Newminster. After a few months he retired to a cave in Knaresborough as a hermit, moving to other places before settling at Rudfarlington,

where he kept four servants and livestock. He came into conflict with the constable of Knaresborough Castle, who accused him of harbouring thieves and outlaws, and destroyed his hermitage. Robert then returned to his original cave and remained there until he died. Various benefactors, including King John, gave him land and cows, which he used for the benefit of the poor and destitute. Monks from the Cistercian abbey of Fountains tried to claim him for their order and, when he died, to bury his body in their church, but he had made arrangements for his burial in his own chapel beside his cave. This became a place of pilgrimage, and churches were named after him. He was not officially canonized, but became the centre of a cult and was regarded as a great saint.

Robert Lawrence, St. *See* LAWRENCE.

Robert of Molesme, St (1027–1110, f.d. 29 April). Born into the nobility in Champagne, he became a monk, entering a BENEDICTINE monastery. He soon became prior, then abbot of Tonnerre. He was asked to direct the hermits at Collan and became their abbot. He took the community to Molesme, but as the community grew, it deteriorated through the wealth of some of the monks. St STEPHEN HARDING and Alberic among them suggested reform and Robert moved with them to Cîteaux in 1098, thus laying the foundations of the CISTERCIANS. Later, when Molesme had become lax, Robert was recalled to reform it and remained there for the rest of his life.

Robert of Newminster, St (c. 1110–59, f.d. 7 June). Born at Gargrave in Yorkshire, he went to Paris to study, was ordained priest, and returned to England to become parish priest of his birthplace. He founded the BENEDICTINES of Whitby and later was among the founders of Fountains Abbey in 1132. He was elected abbot of a new CISTERCIAN foundation at Newminster in Northumbria, from which grew the houses at Pipewell, Roche and Sawley. Robert was a visionary, also having encounters with the Devil. When he died, his friend St GODRIC saw his soul ascend to heaven in a ball of fire.

Roberts, St John (c. 1576–1610, f.d. 25 October). Born at Trawsynydd in Wales, he was educated at St John's College, Oxford, and the Inns of Court in London. He went to Paris and became a ROMAN CATHOLIC, entering the English College at Valladolid in 1598. He then became a monk at the BENEDICTINE monastery until 1602, when Pope Clement III initiated a mission to England. Robert, with a companion, returned to England in disguise and took part in outstanding work during the plague in London. He was arrested several times, imprisoned, and escaped, and was instrumental in founding the Benedictine monastery of St Gregory, Douai (later Downside). When he returned to

England he was again arrested and tried as 'a seducer of the people', and was condemned to be hanged, drawn and quartered at Tyburn. The night before the execution a Spanish lady gave a feast in Newgate for twenty Catholic prisoners, with Robert as the guest of honour. He was canonized in 1970 as one of the FORTY MARTYRS OF ENGLAND AND WALES.

Roch (or Roque), St. Patron of those afflicted with the plague, because 'he worked MIRACLES on the plague-stricken, while he was himself smitten with the same judgment'. He is depicted in a pilgrim's habit, lifting his dress, to display a plague-spot on his thigh, which an ANGEL is touching that he may cure it. Sometimes he is accompanied by a dog bringing bread in his mouth, in allusion to the legend that a hound brought him bread daily while he was perishing of pestilence in a forest.

His feast day, 16 August, was formerly celebrated in England as a general Harvest-Home, and styled 'the great August festival'.

Rochet. A vestment of white linen or lawn, resembling a SURPLICE but having sleeves fastened at the wrists. Used chiefly by bishops.

Rock. A symbol of solidity and strength.

> Thou art Peter, and upon this rock I will build my church; and the gates of hell shall not prevail against it.
>
> *Matt.* xvi. 18

It is the Lat. *petra*, rock, from which the name Peter is derived. *Cp.* ROCK OF AGES, below.

Rock of Ages. Christ, as the unshakeable and eternal foundation. In a marginal note to *Is.* xxvi, 4, the words 'everlasting strength' are stated to be in Hebrew 'rock of ages'. In one of his hymns Wesley wrote (1788)—

> Hell in vain against us rages;
> Can it shock
> Christ the Rock
> Of eternal Ages?
>
> *Praise by all to Christ is given*

Southey also has:

> These waters are the well of life and lo!
> The Rock of Ages, there, from whence they flow.
>
> *Pilgrimage to Waterloo*, Pt. II, iii

The well-known hymn *Rock of ages, cleft for me*, was written by Augustus Montague Toplady (1740–78) and first published in *The Gospel Magazine* (1775). One account says that he wrote it while seated by a great cleft of rock near Cheddar, Somerset; a more unlikely story is that the first verse was written on the ten of diamonds in the interval between two rubbers of whist at Bath.

Rodriguez, St Alphonsus (1533–1617, f.d. 30 October). Born in Segovia, the son of a wool merchant, he followed his father's trade, married and had two children. When the children died he entered the JESUIT ORDER as a lay brother and became the hall-porter at the college of Montesione in Majorca. He was noted for his devout life and his wisdom as a counsellor; he wrote ascetical works and was himself the subject of a poem by Gerard Manley Hopkins. He was canonized in 1888.

Roe, St Alban Bartholomew (1583–1642, f.d. 25 October). Educated at Cambridge, he was a zealous and proselytizing PROTESTANT, but when trying to convert a RECUSANT who had been imprisoned he was himself converted to ROMAN CATHOLICISM. He then entered the ENGLISH COLLEGE at DOUAI, becoming a monk at the BENEDICTINE monastery at Dieulouard, and was ordained priest in 1615. He helped in the foundation of the monastery of St Edmund in Paris, now at Wolverhampton in England. Returning to London, he was arrested and imprisoned, was released after five years and then banished, but he returned after a few months. Later he was again arrested and spent fifteen years in prison, though when transferred to Fleet Street through the influence of friends, he was able to obtain day-release and continued in his ministry. Under the Long Parliament, he was sent to Newgate, tried and sentenced to be hanged, drawn and quartered. He was canonized in 1970 as one of the FORTY MARTYRS OF ENGLAND AND WALES.

Rogation Days. Rogation Sunday is the SUNDAY before ASCENSION DAY, the Rogation days are the Monday, Tuesday, and Wednesday following Rogation Sunday. Rogation is the Latin equivalent of the Greek *litaneia*, supplication or litany (Lat. *rogatio*), and in the ROMAN CATHOLIC CHURCH on the three Rogation days 'the Litany of the Saints' is appointed to be sung by the clergy and people in public procession.

The Rogation Days used to be called *Gang Days*, from the custom of *ganging* round the country parishes to beat the bounds at this time. Similarly the weed milkwort is called *Rogation* or *Gangflower* from the custom of decorating the pole carried on such occasions with these flowers.

Roman Catholic Church. A name introduced by 'non-Catholics' for members of the CATHOLIC or Western Church under the jurisdiction of the papacy. The term is a consequence of the REFORMATION and came into use at about the end of the 16th century. *See also* POPE.

Romanus of Rouen, St (d. *c.* 640, f.d. 23 October). Educated at the court of Clotaire II, he was appointed bishop of Rouen in 630 and made the elimination of paganism his chief concern. He also devoted himself to the care of prisoners, and an interesting custom, known as the Privilege of St Romanus, was exercised by the Rouen Chapter when a condemned criminal was reprieved from death to carry the shrine of St Romanus in procession. This obtained until the French Revolution.

Romanus the Melodist, St (6th cent., f.d. 1 October). Little is known of his life except that he was a Syrian Jew from Homa and became a deacon at Beirut. His fame rests upon his hymnography, and he is regarded as the greatest and most prolific of the Byzantine hymnwriters. He originated the form known as the 'kontakion', the first being one for CHRISTMAS and others, eighty of which survive, covering the great festivals and the BIBLE.

Rome. The greatest city of the ancient world, according to legend founded in 753 BC by Romulus and named after him; but in all probability so called from Greek *rhoma* (strength), a suggestion supported by its other name Valentia (Lat. *valens*, strong). It acquired a new significance as the seat of the papacy. The 'Eternal City' was established as capital of the Papal State after 756 and became the spiritual centre of western Europe during the Middle Ages. St PAUL lived in Rome, and St PETER was traditionally the first bishop of the Roman Church. The cathedral church of the Pope is that of St JOHN Lateran. The Basilica of St Peter, the largest church in the world, is the centre of the chief papal ceremonies.

Rome penny, or **Rome scot.** The same as PETER'S PENCE.

Romuald of Ravenna, St (*c.* 950–1027, f.d. 19 June, formerly 7 February). Born into a noble family of Ravenna, he entered the CLUNIAC monastery of St Apollinare-in-Classe, having 'fled the world' after he had seen his father kill a relative in a quarrel. He studied the DESERT FATHERS and aimed to reintroduce to the West the early form of eremitical monasticism within the BENEDICTINE Order. He founded monasteries as small communities of hermits which, after his death, became known as the CAMALDOLESE or Camaldulians from the chief community in Tuscany, which survives to this day. St Romuald died at Val-di-Casto; his body remained incorrupt and was translated to Fabriano.

Ronan, St. There are various saints of this name: one a Scottish hermit of the island of North Rona where his oratory still exists; he suffered from the slanders of the women of Lewis and was told in a dream to escape them. A whale took him to North Rona where he successfully overcame the Devil's attacks on himself and his oratory.

Another St Ronan, whose feast is 1 June, was an Irish bishop who went to Brittany from Cornwall as a hermit and was said to have restored a child of the king of Brittany to life after the mother had carelessly allowed it to choke to death on bread and milk.

A third was a Scottish bishop of Kilmaronen, mentioned by BEDE as involved in the Roman–Celtic controversy over EASTER at the SYNOD of Whitby. His well at Innerleithen is the subject of a novel by Sir Walter Scott. Legend says the saint drove the Devil out of the valley, an event commemorated by the July festivities of 'St Ronan's Games' when, at the end of the games, a boy, who represents the saint, is given a pastoral staff to 'cleek the Devil'.

A fourth Ronan was reputed to be a deacon and exorcist from Caesarea. Little is known of him except that the relic of one of his arms was kept at a monastery at Canterbury. His feast day was 18 November.

Rood (connected with *rod*). The Cross of the Crucifixion; or a crucifix, especially the large one that was formerly set on the stone or timber *rood-screen* that divides the nave from the choir in many churches. This is usually richly decorated with statues, and carvings of saints, emblems, etc., and frequently surmounted by a gallery called the *rood-loft*.

> And then to see the rood-loft,
> Zo bravely zet with saints.
> PERCY: *Reliques* (*Plain Truth, and Blind Ignorance*)

Rood Day. HOLY ROOD DAY; 14 September, the EXALTATION OF THE CROSS; or 3 May, the INVENTION OF THE CROSS (*see under* CROSS).

Roque, St. *See* ROCH.

Rosalia (or **Rosalie**), **St** (13th cent.). The patron saint of Palermo, in art depicted in a cave with a CROSS and skull, or else in the act of receiving a ROSARY or chaplet of roses from the Virgin. She is said to have been carried by ANGELS to an inaccessible mountain, where she dwelt for many years in the cleft of a rock, a part of which she wore away with her knees in her devotions. A CHAPEL has been built there, with a marble statue, to commemorate the event.

Rosary (Lat. *rosarium*, rose garden, garland). The bead-roll used by Roman Catholics for keeping count of the recitation of certain prayers; also the prayers themselves. The usual modern rosary consists of five decades of ten recitations, or one-third of the complete rosary known as a *corona* or *chaplet*. The full rosary comprises 15 decades of *Aves* (Hail Marys—small beads), each preceded by a *Pater* (Our

Father—large bead), and followed by a *Gloria* (Glory be to the Father—large bead). While the first chaplet is being recited the five joyful MYSTERIES are contemplated; during the second chaplet, the five sorrowful mysteries; and during the third, the five glorious mysteries. Only one group of five mysteries is usually contemplated. Traditionally the devotion of the rosary is said to have begun with St DOMINIC early in the 13th century but this is not established. Sometimes the Venerable BEDE is credited with its introduction but quite erroneously; the idea is based upon the fanciful derivation of bead from *Beda*. *Cp*. GAUDY; PATERNOSTER.

Rose Sunday. The fourth Sunday in LENT, when the POPE blesses the GOLDEN ROSE.

Rose of Lima, St (1586–1617, f.d. 23 August, formerly 30 August). Born Isabel de Flores y del Oliver at Lima in Peru, of a Spanish family which had lost its wealth, she worked to support them. She was of a devout nature, refusing marriage, living a secluded life of extreme penance and self-torture and joining the Third Order of St DOMINIC. She experienced many visions which were subjected to medical and ecclesiastical examination, but were pronounced to be from God. She cared for the sick, Indians and slaves. Canonized in 1671, she became the first saint of the Americas and was named patron of South America and the Philippine Islands.

Rosicrucians. A secret, esoteric society which claimed to have been founded by Christian Rosenkreutz in 1459. Its teachings were based on a mystical philosophy of the nature and personality of Christ and his principles, but the existence of Rosenkreutz is now called in question, and his writings are assumed to have originated with a LUTHERAN pastor of a much later date. Rosicrucian societies are still active on a masonic basis, but with a Christian ground and symbolism. The Rose-Cross symbolizes Christ's Resurrection, Redemption and Resurrection.

Rosin Bible. *See* BIBLE, SOME SPECIALLY NAMED EDITIONS.

Rosminians. A ROMAN CATHOLIC congregation called the 'Fathers of the Institute of Charity', founded in 1828 by Antonio Rosmini, an Italian philosopher. He was appointed Superior-General and encouraged the members in all forms of charitable works.

Rota Sacra Romana. A Roman Catholic ecclesiastical court of mediaeval origin composed of auditors under the presidency of a DEAN. It was reconstituted by Pius X in 1908 and appears to take its name from the circular table originally used by the judges at Avignon. It tries cases and hears appeals from ecclesiastical tribunals.

Ruadhan (Rodan or **Ruadan), St** (d. *c*. 584, f.d. 15 April). Said to have been of royal Munster family, he was educated at Clonard under St FINNIAN and was one of the Twelve Apostles of Ireland. Nothing is known of his life, but among many legends attached to his name is one of a cursing match between the saint and the rulers of Tara which left the place ruined and deserted. Another is that, to ransom a prisoner from King Dermot, he conjured up thirty sea-green horses from the sea. He was the reputed founder and abbot of the monastery of Lothra and one of his hands was enshrined there.

Rubric (Lat. *rubrica*, red ochre or vermilion). The Romans called an ordinance or law a rubric, because it was written with vermilion.

The liturgical directions, titles, etc., in a Prayer Book are known as the *Rubrics* because these were (and sometimes still are) printed in red (*cp*. RED-LETTER DAY).

> No date prefix'd
> Directs me in the starry rubric set.
> MILTON: *Paradise Regained*, IV, 392

The directions given on formal examination papers concerning the selection of questions to be answered, etc., are called the *rubrics*.

Rue, called herb of grace, because it was employed for sprinkling holy water. Ophelia says:

> There's rue for you, and here's some for me! we may call it 'herb of grace' o' Sundays.
> SHAKESPEARE: *Hamlet*, IV, v

It also symbolizes purification and virginity.

Rufinus Tyrannius (*c*. 345–410). A theologian and presbyter born near Aquileia on the Adriatic. He became a close friend of St JEROME until they quarrelled over the doctrines of ORIGEN, which Jerome opposed. Rufinus was required to vindicate his orthodoxy, and wrote his *Apologia pro fide sua*. He was one of the monks who followed the Roman widow Melania to Palestine, at the time of the persecutions of the ARIAN Valens. At her expense he established a monastery on OLIVET, where he studied Greek theological works which he translated into Latin; he also translated the *Homilies* of Origen. The ravages of Alaric the Goth forced him and his companions to flee to Sicily.

Rule (or Regulus), St. A priest of Patrae in Achaia, who is said to have come to Scotland in the 4th century, bringing with him relics of St ANDREW, and to have founded the town and bishopric of St Andrews. The name Killrule (*Cella Reguli*) perpetuates his memory. An angel had told him to take the relics of St Andrew to an unspecified place in the north west and he went on travelling until told by the angel to stop; there he built the church of St Andrew. His feast day is kept as either 17 October or 30 March, a confusion with St Regulus of Senlis.

Rumon, St (date unknown). Said to have been a bishop of Devon, the see and the date unknown, whose relics were translated from Ruan Lanihorne, a Celtic monastery, to Tavistock. He was also reputed to have gone to Brittany, where he led a life of 'abstinence and virtue'. Legend says he was accused by a pagan woman of being a werewolf and of having eaten her child. He is patron of Tavistock and had a fair there on his feast day, 30 August. He is also patron of Romanskeigh in Devon, of Ruan Lanihorne and Ruan Major and Minor in Cornwall.

Rumwold (or **Rumbald**), **St** (? 7th cent., f.d. 3 November). An extraordinary legend of an infant saint says that the child, the offspring of the royal family of Mercia, when born immediately demanded baptism and communion, professed himself a Christian, announced his faith in the TRINITY, preached a sermon referring to the SCRIPTURES and the ATHANASIAN CREED (*see under* ATHANASIUS), specified his burial place and, announcing his impending death, died when three days old. This amazing piece of hagiography remained as a popular cult for several centuries.

Rupert of Salzburg, St (d. *c*. 710, f.d. 27 March). Possibly of Frankish or Irish family, he was one of the bishops noted for the evangelization of pagan Germany. He was bishop of Worms and Salzburg, founding a monastery at the latter and a nunnery at Nonnberg. He carried out a successful mission in Bavaria and along the Danube, where many churches were dedicated to him, and he was said to have inaugurated the salt mines near Salzburg. In art he is represented with a barrel of salt.

Russellism. Founded in the USA by Charles Taze Russell, or Pastor Russell (1852–1916), Russellism was the precursor of the JEHOVAH'S WITNESSES. Originally a CONGREGATIONALIST, Russell repudiated the doctrine of eternal punishment and maintained that Christ had returned to earth in 1874, that the MILLENNIUM, or the 'Day of Jehovah' had dawned and that the LAST JUDGEMENT would follow in 1,000 years, establishing the Kingdom on Earth. Russell published the *Watch Tower* and founded the International Bible Students' Association. His *Studies in the Scriptures* sold several millions.

Ruysbroeck, Jan van (1293–1381). A Flemish mystic, born near Ruysbroch near Brussels, he was ordained priest and later joined the AUGUSTINIANS at Groenendael, eventually becoming prior. Noted for his mystical writings, he was given the name of Doctor Ecstaticus.

S

'S. A euphemistic abbreviation of *God's,* formerly common in oaths and expletives; as *'Sdeath* (God's death), *'Sblood* (God's blood), *'Sdeins* (God's *dignes,* i.e. dignity), *'Sfoot,* etc.

> 'Sdeins, I know not what I should say to him, in the whole world! He values me at a crack'd three farthings, for aught I see.
>
> BEN JONSON *Every Man in His Humour,* II, i

S J. (*Societas Jesu*). The Society of Jesus; denoting that the priest after whose name those letters are placed is a JESUIT.

STP. (*Sacrae Theologiae Professor*). 'Professor of Sacred Theology'. 'DD'—i.e. Doctor of Divinity —is the English equivalent of 'STP'.

Sabaoth. The Bible phrase *Lord God of Sabaoth* means *Lord God of Hosts* not *of the Sabbath, Sabaoth* being Hebrew for 'armies' or 'hosts'. The epithet has been frequently misunderstood, as in the last stanza of Spenser's *Faerie Queene* (Vii, viii, 21):

> All that moveth doth in change delight:
> But thenceforth all shall rest eternally
> With him that is God of Sabaoth hight:
> O! that great Sabaoth God, grant me that
> Sabbath's sight.

Sabas, St (439–532, f.d. 5 December). Born near Caesarea of an illustrious Cappadocian family, he became a monk and a disciple of St Euthymius the Great. He retired to a cave in a cliff which could only be reached by a rope, but when he attracted a large number of disciples he converted a nearby temple for them, founded a LAURA and became a prominent figure in the growth of eastern monasticism and in the history of the Eastern ORTHODOX CHURCH. He attended missions in Constantinople and was active in combating heresies. His monastery, Mar Saba, still exists and is one of the oldest extant monasteries in the Christian world. Many legends were told of his miraculous escapes from lions and other perils in the desert. His incorrupt body was enshrined in ROME and remained there until modern times when it was translated to Mar Saba after the second VATICAN COUNCIL. His cult was confined to local calendars in the revisions of 1969.
Sabas the Goth, St (d. 372, f.d. 12 April). A church-reader at Targoviste, now in Romania, at the time of persecution of Christians by the Gothic ruler of the region, Sabas was twice arrested, refusing to escape and defying his captors. As a result he was condemned to be drowned and was tied to a pole and plunged in the river Buzau. Several others suffered at the same time for refusing to worship the gods and eat the food consecrated to them. St BASIL had the body of Sabas translated to Caesarea and he was held in great veneration in the Eastern CHURCH.

Sabbath (Heb. *shabath,* to rest). Properly, the seventh day of the week, enjoined on the ancient Hebrews by the fourth Commandment (*Exod.* xx, 8–11) as a day of rest and worship; the Christian SUNDAY, 'the Lord's Day', the first day of the week, is often inaccurately referred to as 'the Sabbath'. For Muslims, FRIDAY is the weekly day of rest.
A Sabbath Day's Journey (*Acts* i, 12) with the Jews was not to exceed the distance between the ark and the extreme end of the camp. This was 2,000 cubits, about 1,000 yards. It arose from the injunction (*Exod.* xvi, 29) against journeying on the Sabbath with that (*Jos.* iii, 4) providing for a distance of 2,000 cubits between the ark and the people when they travelled in the wilderness. As their tents were this distance from the ark, it was held that they might properly travel this distance, since the injunction could not have been intended to prevent their attendance at worship.
Sabbatarians. Those who observe the day of rest with excessive strictness, a peculiar feature of English and Scottish Puritanism enforced during the period of the Commonwealth when sport and recreation was forbidden. Some relaxation occurred after the Restoration, but the Lord's Day Observance Act of 1782 closed all places of entertainment on a SUNDAY where an admission fee was charged. A Sunday Entertainments Act, 1932, empowered local authorities to license the Sunday opening of cinemas and musical entertainments; the opening of museums, etc., was permitted. The Bill was opposed by the Lord's Day Observance Society.

Sabbatians. Members of a 4th-century NOVATIAN sect, followers of Sabbatius. They followed the Quartodeciman rule.

Sabbatical Year. One year in seven, when all the land, according to Mosaic law, was to lie fallow (*Exod.* xxiii, 10, etc.; *Lev.* xxv, 2–7; *Deut.* xv, 1–11). The term is used in universities, etc., for a specified period of freedom from academic duties, during which time a professor or lecturer is released to study or travel.

Sabellianism. The tenets of the **Sabellians**, an obscure sect founded in the 3rd century by Sabellius, a Libyan priest. Little is known of their beliefs, but they were UNITARIANS and held that the TRINITY merely expressed three relations or states of one and the same God. *See* CONFOUNDING THE PERSONS *under* PERSON.

Sabians. A semi-Christian sect of Babylonia, akin to the MANDAEANS or Christians of St John, a GNOSTIC sect which arose in the 2nd and 3rd centuries and still survives south of Baghdad.

Sacco Benedetto, or **Saco Bendito** (Ital., Sp., blessed sack, or cloak). The yellow linen robe with two crosses on it, and painted over with flames and devils, worn by those going to the stake after condemnation by the Spanish INQUISITION. *See* AUTO DA FÉ. Penitents who had been taken before the Inquisition had to wear this habit for a stated period. Those worn by Jews, sorcerers, and renegades bore a St Andrew's CROSS in red on back and front.

Sack. Friars of the Sack (Lat. *fratres saccati*). Also known as *De Penitencia*, or friars of the Penance of Jesus Christ, and so called from their sackcloth garment. They were abolished in 1274 but some remained in England until 1317.
To wear sackcloth and ashes. Metaphorically, an expression of contrition and penitence. An allusion to the Hebrew custom of wearing sackcloth and ashes as suitably humble attire for religious ceremonies, mourning, penitence, etc. The sackcloth in question was a coarse dark haircloth from which sacks were made.

> And I set my face unto the Lord God, to seek by prayer and supplications, with fasting, and sackcloth, and ashes.
> *Dan.* ix, 3

Saco Bendito. *See* SACCO BENEDETTO.

Sacrament (Lat. *sacramentum*). Originally 'a military oath' taken by the Roman soldiers not to desert their standard, turn their back on the enemy, or abandon their general. Traces of this meaning survive in early Christian usage but its present meaning comes from its employment in the Latin NEW TESTAMENT to mean 'sacred mystery'. Hence its application to BAPTISM, CONFIRMATION, the EUCHARIST, etc.
The five sacraments are Confirmation,

Penance, Orders, Matrimony, and EXTREME UNCTION. These are not counted 'Sacraments of the GOSPEL'. (*See Book of Common Prayer, Articles of Religion,* XXV.)
The seven sacraments are BAPTISM, CONFIRMATION, the EUCHARIST, PENANCE, ORDERS, MATRIMONY, and EXTREME UNCTION.
The two sacraments of the PROTESTANT Churches are BAPTISM and the Lord's Supper.
Sacramentarians. The name given by LUTHER to those who maintained that no change took place in the eucharistic elements after consecration but that the bread and wine are only the body and blood of Christ in a metaphorical sense. The name was thus applied in the 16th century to those who did not accept the REAL PRESENCE.

Sacred (Lat. *sacrare*, to consecrate). That which is consecrated or dedicated to religious use.
The Sacred City. *See* HOLY CITY.
The Sacred College. The College of Cardinals (*see under* CARDINAL).
The Sacred Heart. *See under* HEART.
The Sacred Isle, or **Holy Island.** Ireland was so called from its many SAINTS and Guernsey from its many monks. The island referred to by Moore in his *Irish Melodies* is Scattery, to which St Senanus retired and vowed no woman should set foot thereon.

> Oh, haste and leave this sacred isle,
> Unholy bark, ere morning smile.
> *St Senanus and the Lady*

Enhallow (Norse *Eyinhalga*, holy isle) is a small island in the Orkney group where cells to the Irish anchorite fathers are still said to exist. *See also* HOLY ISLAND.

Sacring Bell. From the obsolete verb to *sacre*, to consecrate, used especially of sovereigns and BISHOPS. The bell rung in churches to draw attention to the most solemn parts of the MASS. In mediaeval times it served to announce to those outside that the Mass was in progress, and for this purpose often a handbell was rung out of a side window. It is more usually called the **Sanctus bell** because it was rung at the saying of the *Sanctus* at the beginning of the CANON of the MASS (*see under* CANON), and also at the Consecration and Elevation and other moments. It is still used in the ROMAN CATHOLIC CHURCH and certain other Churches.

> He heard a little sacring bell ring to the elevation of a to-morrow mass.
> REGINALD SCOTT: *Discoverie of Witchcraft* (1584)

Sacristan. One who looks after the sacristy in a church, a room in which vestments and sacred vessels are kept; he is also responsible for preparing the altar for the celebration of the EUCHARIST and for ringing bells.

Sacy's Bible. *See* BIBLE, SOME SPECIALLY NAMED EDITIONS.

Sadducees. A Jewish party opposed to the PHAR-ISEES. They did not accept oral tradition, but only the written Law, denied the existence of ANGELS and spirits and rejected the idea of future punishments in an after-life, as well as the resurrection of the body. They were major opponents of Christ and His disciples and were involved in the events leading to His death. Substantially, they represented the interests and attitudes of the privileged and wealthy and nothing more is heard of them after the destruction of Jerusalem (AD 70).

The name is said to be from Zadok (*see* II *Sam.* viii, 17), who was high priest at the time of Solomon.

Saint. Individual saints are entered under their respective names.

The title of saint was from early Christian times applied to APOSTLES, EVANGELISTS, MARTYRS and CONFESSORS of remarkable virtue, especially martyrs. In due course the need arose for BISHOPS to intervene against local recognition of the undeserving and eventually Pope Alexander III (1159–1181) asserted the exclusive right of the Papacy to add to the roll of saints. Nowadays canonization is dependent upon a lengthy legal process where the case for the canonization of a particular person is thoroughly explored and contested. JOAN OF ARC was canonized in 1920; Sir Thomas More (1478–1535) and John Fisher (1459–1535), Bishop of Rochester, in 1935.

The Russian ORTHODOX CHURCH does not employ the complicated process of canonization used by the CONGREGATION OF RITES in ROME. Orthodox bishops had the right of local canonization until the 13th and 14th centuries, when a tendency to centralization developed and the rights were reserved for the metropolitan (later the patriarch) of Moscow. After the time of Peter the Great, canonization was only possible with the authorization of the HOLY SYNOD. There are about 385 such canonized saints.

In Christian art, saints are often depicted with a NIMBUS, AUREOLE, or glory and individual symbols by which they can be recognized. *See* SYMBOLS OF SAINTS, *below*.

Popes numbered among the saints.

From the time of St PETER to the end of the 4th century all the Popes (with a few minor and doubtful exceptions) are popularly entitled 'Saint'; since then the following are the chief of those given the honour:

Innocent I (402–17).
Leo the Great (440–61).
John I (523–6).
GREGORY THE GREAT (590–604).
Deusdedit I (615–19).
Martin I (649–54).
Leo II (682–3).
Sergius I (687–701).
Zacharias (741–52).
Paul I (757–67).
Leo III (795–816).
Paschal I (817–24).
Nicholas the Great (858–67).
Leo IX (1049–54).
Gregory VII, HILDEBRAND (1073–85).
Celestine V (1294).
Pius V (1566–72).
Pius X (1903–14).

Kings and Queens honoured as Saints.
Among them are:

Edward the Martyr (961, 975–8).
Edward the Confessor (1004, 1042–66).
Eric VIII of Sweden (1150–60).
Ethelred I, King of Wessex (866–71).
Ferdinand III of Castile and Leon (1200, 1217–52).
Louis IX of France (1215, 1226–70).
Margaret, Queen of Scotland (d. 1093), wife of Malcolm III.
Olaf II of Norway (1015–30).
Stephen I of Hungary (979, 997–1038).

Patron Saints. (1) a selected list of trades and professions with their patron saints:

Accountants, bankers, book-keepers	St MATTHEW
Actors	St GENESIUS
Advertising	St BERNADINO OF SIENA
Airmen	Our Lady of Loreto, SS TERESA of Lisieux, JOSEPH OF COPERTINO
Air Travellers	St JOSEPH OF COPERTINO
Altar Boys	St John Berchmans
Anaesthetists	St René Goupil
Architects	SS THOMAS Ap., BARBARA
Artists	St LUKE
Athletes (and Archers)	St SEBASTIAN
Authors and Journalists	St FRANCIS DE SALES
Bakers	SS ELIZABETH OF HUNGARY, NICHOLAS
Bankers	St MATTHEW
Barbers	SS COSMAS AND DAMIAN, LOUIS
Barren Women	St ANTHONY OF PADUA
Basket Makers	St Anthony the Abbot
Beggars	SS ALEXIS, GILES
Blacksmiths	St DUNSTAN
Blind	St RAPHAEL
Boatmen	St JULIAN THE HOSPITALLER
Bookbinders	St PETER CELESTINE

Bookkeepers	St MATTHEW	Headache sufferers	St TERESA of Avila
Booksellers	St JOHN OF GOD	Heart patients	St JOHN OF GOD
Brewers	SS AUGUSTINE of Hippo, LUKE, NICHOLAS OF MYRA	Hospitals	SS JOHN OF GOD, CAMILLUS DE LELLIS
Bricklayers	St STEPHEN	Hotelkeepers	St Amand
Brides	St NICHOLAS OF MYRA	Housewives	St ANNE
Broadcasters	The Archangel GABRIEL	Hunters	St HUBERT
Brushmakers	St ANTHONY	Infantrymen	St MAURICE
Builders	St Vincent Ferrer	Innkeepers and Wine merchants	St Amand
Cab-drivers	St FIACRE	Invalids	St ROCH
Cabinetmakers	St ANNE	Jewellers	St ELOI
Carpenters	St JOSEPH	Journalists	St FRANCIS DE SALES
Catechists	SS CHARLES BORROMEO, ROBERT OF BELLARMINE	Jurists	St JOHN CAPISTRANO
Charities	St VINCENT DE PAUL	Lawyers	SS IVO, GENESIUS, THOMAS MORE
Childbirth	St GERARD MAJELLA		
Children	St NICHOLAS	Learning	St AMBROSE
Choirboys	St Dominic SAVIO	Leatherworkers	SS CRISPIN AND CRISPINIAN
Church, the	St JOSEPH	Librarians	St JEROME
Clerics	The Archangel GABRIEL	Lighthousekeepers	St Venerius
Comedians	St VITUS	Locksmiths	St DUNSTAN
Cooks	SS LAWRENCE, MARTHA	Lost articles	St ANTHONY OF PADUA
Cripples	St GILES	Lovers	St VALENTINE
Dancers	St VITUS	Maidens	St CATHERINE OF ALEXANDRIA
Deaf	St FRANCIS DE SALES	Married women	St MONICA
Dentists	St APOLLONIA	Medical technicians	St ALBERT THE GREAT
Desperate situations	St JUDE	Mentally ill	St DYMPHNA
Dieticians (Medical)	St MARTHA	Messengers	The Archangel GABRIEL
Domestic Animals	St ANTHONY	Midwives	St RAYMUND NONNATUS
Domestic Servants	St ZITA	Millers	St ARNULF OF METZ
Druggists	SS COSMAS AND DAMIAN	Miners	St BARBARA
Dyers	SS MAURICE and Lydia	Missions	SS FRANCIS XAVIER, TERESA of Lisieux, LEONARD OF PORT MAURICE (parish)
Dying	St Joseph		
Earthquakes	St Emygdius		
Ecologists	St FRANCIS OF ASSISI	Mothers	St MONICA
Editors	St JOHN BOSCO	Motorcyclists	Our Lady of Grace
Emigrants	St FRANCIS XAVIER CABRINI	Motorists	SS FRANCES OF ROME, CHRISTOPHER
Engineers	St FERDINAND III		
Epileptics	SS VITUS, DYMPHNA	Mountaineers	St BERNARD OF MENTHON
Expectant Mothers	St GERARD MAJELLA	Musicians and Singers	SS GREGORY THE GREAT, CECILIA, DUNSTAN
Eye trouble	St LUCY		
Falsely accused	St RAYMOND NONNATUS	Notaries	SS MARK, LUKE
Farmers	SS GEORGE, ISIDORE	Nurses	SS CAMILLUS OF LELLIS, JOHN OF GOD, AGATHA, ALEXIS, RAPHAEL
Farriers	St JOHN THE BAPTIST		
Fathers of Families	St JOSEPH		
Firemen	St Florian	Orators	St JOHN CHRYSOSTOM
Fishermen	SS ANDREW, PETER	Orphans	St JEROME EMILIANI
Florists	SS DOROTHEA, Thérèse	Paratroopers	St MICHAEL
Foresters	St John Gualbert	Parish Priests	St JOHN VIANNEY
Founders	St BARBARA	Pawnbrokers	St NICHOLAS
Foundlings	The HOLY INNOCENTS	Pharmacists	SS COSMAS AND DAMIAN
Fullers	St Anastasius the Fuller	Philosophers	SS JUSTIN, CATHERINE of Alexandria
Gardeners	SS DOROTHEA, Adelard, Tryphon, FIACRE, PHOCAS		
		Physicians	SS PANTALEON, COSMAS AND DAMIAN, LUKE, RAPHAEL
Girls	St AGNES		
Glassworkers	St LUKE	Pilgrims	St JAMES THE GREAT
Goldsmiths and Metalworkers	SS DUNSTAN, Anastasius	Plasterers	St BARTHOLOMEW
		Poets	SS DAVID, CECILIA
Gravediggers	St ANTHONY (Ab.)	Policemen	St MICHAEL
Grocers	St MICHAEL	Postal, Radio, Telecommunications and Telephone, Telegraph	
Gunners	St BARBARA		
Hairdressers	St MARTIN DE PORRES		

and Television Workers	St GABRIEL
Preachers	SS CATHERINE of Alexandria, JOHN CHRYSOSTOM
Printers	SS JOHN OF GOD, AUGUSTINE of Hippo
Prisoners	St DISMAS
Prisoners-of-war	St LEONARD
Prisons	St Joseph Cafasso
Public Relations	St BERNADINO OF SIENA
Radiologists	St MICHAEL
Radio workers	The Archangel GABRIEL
Retreats	St IGNATIUS LOYOLA
Rheumatism	St JAMES THE GREAT
Saddlers	St CRISPIN AND CRISPIANUS
Scholars	St BRIDGET
Scientists	St ALBERT
Scouts	St GEORGE
Sculptors	St Claude
Secretaries	SS GENESIUS, Cassian
Seminarians	St CHARLES BORROMEO
Shoemakers	SS CRISPIN AND CRISPINIANUS
Silversmiths	SS DUNSTAN, Andronicus
Singers	SS Cecilia, GREGORY
Skaters	St Lidwina
Skiers	St BERNARD OF MENTHON
Skin disease	St MARCULF
Social Workers	St LOUISE DE MARILLAC
Soldiers	SS ADRIAN, GEORGE, IGNATIUS, SEBASTIAN, MARTIN OF TOURS, JOAN OF ARC
Speleologists	St BENEDICT
Stonecutters	St CLEMENT
Stonemasons	SS BARBARA, STEPHEN, Reinhold
Students	SS THOMAS AQUINAS, CATHERINE
Surgeons	SS COSMAS AND DAMIAN
Swordsmiths	St MAURICE
Tailors	St HOMOBONUS
Tax-collectors	St MATTHEW
Teachers	SS GREGORY THE GREAT, CATHERINE, JOHN THE BAPTIST DE LA SALLE
Television	St CLARE
Theologians	SS AUGUSTINE, ALPHONSUS LIGUORI
Throat sufferers	St BLAISE
Tinworkers	St JOSEPH OF ARIMATHEA
Travellers	SS ANTHONY OF PADUA, NICHOLAS, CHRISTOPHER, RAPHAEL
Vocations	St ALPHONSUS
Watchmen	St PETER OF ALCANTARA
Weavers	SS ANASTASIA, Anastasius, PAUL THE HERMIT
Widows	St PAULA
Wine-growers	St VINCENT OF SARAGOSSA
Winemerchants	St Amand
Women in labour	St ANNE
Workers	St JOSEPH
Yachtsmen	St Adjutor
Youth	St ALOYSIUS GONZAGA

(2) Some European and Commonwealth Countries with their patron saints:

Australia	Our Lady Help of Christians
Belgium	St JOSEPH
Canada	SS JOSEPH, ANNE
Czechoslovakia	SS WENCESLAS, JOHN OF NEPOMUK, PROCOPIUS
Denmark	SS Asgar, CANUTE
England	St GEORGE
France	Our Lady of the ASSUMPTION, SS JOAN OF ARC, DENYS, LOUIS, Thérèse (see TERESA). There is no official patron saint of France, those listed are recognized as patron saints by the Church.
Germany	SS BONIFACE, MICHAEL
Greece	SS NICHOLAS, ANDREW
Holland	St WILLIBRORD
Hungary	Our LADY, St STEPHEN
India	Our Lady of the ASSUMPTION
Ireland	St PATRICK
Italy	SS FRANCIS of Assisi, CATHERINE OF SIENA
New Zealand	Our Lady Help of Christians
Norway	St OLAF
Poland	Our Lady of Czestochowa, SS CASIMIR, STANISLAUS
Portugal	IMMACULATE CONCEPTION, SS FRANCIS BORGIA, ANTHONY OF PADUA, GEORGE, VINCENT OF SARAGOSSA
Russia	SS ANDREW, NICHOLAS, TERESA of Lisieux
Scotland	SS ANDREW, COLUMBA
South Africa	Our Lady of the ASSUMPTION
Spain	SS JAMES, TERESA
Sweden	SS BRIDGET, ERIK
Wales	St DAVID
West Indies	St GERTRUDE

Symbols of Saints. The symbol common to all saints is the NIMBUS which encircles the head. MARTYRS alone have the common symbols of the crown of eternal life won by their heroism and the PALM of triumph. With these is generally associated with some symbol peculiar to the individual saint, often the instrument of his martyrdom, such as the GRIDIRON of St LAWRENCE or the windlass on which the bowels were drawn from St Erasmus' body.

Saints not martyrs will be depicted with an object symbolizing their particular virtue (St AMBROSE has the beehive emblematic of eloquence) or relating to some incident in their lives (as St DUNSTAN pinching the DEVIL's nose). All saints are depicted in their proper dress, as soldiers in armour, bishops or priests in appropriate vestments, kings robed and crowned, religious in the habits of their order.

Below is a selection of some of the many symbols of saints with some of the saints to which they are applied. (*See also* APOSTLES, MARY *and entries for individual saints.*)

Alms-box: *hung round his neck*: St JOHN OF GOD

Anchor: SS Clement, FELIX, NICHOLAS

Angel(s): Singly or in their host, angels have constantly appeared to aid and protect the saints and are their companions in sacred iconography. For example: *Angel holding plough*: St ISIDORE THE FARMER;—*fish on a plate*: St Bertold;—*crosier*: St BERNARD;—*basket of flowers*: St DOROTHEA;—*bottle*: St Leontius; *Angel playing violin*: St FRANCIS OF ASSISI;—*organ*: St CECILIA; *Angel bringing monastic rule*: SS PACHOMIUS, PAPHNUTIUS;—*fish*: SS Bertold, BONIFACE, Congal; *Angel defending from lightning*: St HUGH OF LINCOLN

Anvil: SS ADRIAN, ELOI

Apple: St MALACHY; *three golden*: St NICHOLAS

Arrow(s): *as instruments of martyrdom*: SS Anastasius, CANUTE, Christina, EDMUND, Faustus, SEBASTIAN, URSULA MM.; *two, piercing heart*: St AUGUSTINE; *bunch held*: St OTTO;—*and bent bow*: St Mackesoge

Ass: SS Gerlach, GERMANUS OF AUXERRE, Philibert;—*kneeling to Blessed Sacrament*: St ANTHONY OF PADUA

Axe: *as instrument of martyrdom*: SS Anastasius, Josophat, MALCHUS, Martian, MATTHEW, MATTHIAS, Proculus, Rufus

Barge: St Bertulphus

Barn: SS Ansovinus, BRIDGET of Kildare

Barrell: SS Antonia, Bercher;—*cross in* St WILLIBRORD

Basket: SS FRANCES, Joanna, JOHN DAMASCENE;—*of bread*: SS PHILIP, Romanus;—*of flowers*: St DOROTHEA;—*of fruit*: SS Ann, DOROTHEA, ZITA;—*of roses*: St ELIZABETH OF HUNGARY

Bear: SS COLUMBA, Edmund, GALL, HUMBERT, Maximinus;—*keeping sheep*: St Florentius;—*laden with baggage*: SS Corbinian, Maximinus;—*ploughing*: St James

Beard: *obtained by prayers of* SS Galla, Paula Barbata, Wilgefortis (*see* UNCUMBER)

Bed of Iron: St FAITH

Beehive: SS AMBROSE, BERNARD, JOHN CHRYSOSTOM

Bell: SS ANTHONY THE GREAT, Gildas, Kenan;—*and fishes*: St Winwaloc; *in fish's mouth*: St Paul de Leon

Bellows: *held by devil*: St GENEVIEVE

Boar: St Emilion

Boat: SS Bertin, JUDE, MARY MAGDALENE

Boathook: St JUDE

Bodkin: SS LEGER, Simon of Trent

Book: Common attribute of Apostles, Abbots, Abbesses, Bishops etc.; specifically:—*with child Jesus standing on it*: St ANTHONY OF PADUA;—*with*

hunting horn or stag with crucifix between horns: St HUBERT;—*with wine vessel on it*: St Urban;—*in bag*: SS Antoninus, ZITA

Broom: SS Gisella, Martin of Siguenza, PETRONILLA

Bull: SS Adolphus, Regnier, Sylvester; *tossed or gored by*—; SS Blandina, Marciana, Saturninus

Calves: *two at feet*: St WALSTAN

Camel: SS Aphrodicius, Hormisdas; *bound to*: St Julian of Cilicia

Candle: St Beatrix

Cauldron: *as an instrument of martyrdom by boiling in lead, oil, pitch, water, etc.*: SS BONIFACE, CECILIA, EMILIAN, Erasmus, FELICITY, LUCY, VITUS MM.; JOHN THE APOSTLE

Chafing dish: St AGATHA

Church: A common symbol of Abbots, Abbesses, Bishops, etc., as builders of churches and monasteries

City: The attribute of a saint as protector of a particular city

Club(s) *as instrument of martyrdom*: SS BONIFACE, EWALD the White, Eusebius, FABIAN, Lambert, MAGNUS, Nicomedes, PANTELEON, VALENTINE, Vitalis MM.

Colt: St MÉDARD

Cow: SS Berlinda, BRIDGET, MODWENNA, PERPETUA

Crocodile: SS Helenus, Theodore

Cup and Serpent: *symbolizing poison detected by*: SS BENEDICT, James of Marchia, JOHN THE EVANGELIST, John a Facundo

Dagger: *as instrument of martyrdom*: SS AGNES, CANUTE, EDWARD, Irene, KILIAN, OLAF, Solange MM.

Deer: St HENRY

Devil(s): In Christian art the Devil is shown both tormenting the saints (throwing St Euphrasia down a well, disturbing the prayers of SS CUTHBERT or Madalberte, for example), and worsted by their virtue (holding a candle for St DOMINIC or seized by the nose in St DUNSTAN's pincers). The incidents are too various for separate mention.

Distaff: SS GENEVIEVE, ROSALIA

Doe: SS FRUCTUOSUS, MAMMAS, MAXIMUS OF TURIN

Dog: SS Benignus, BERNARD;—*with loaf*: St ROCH;—*with torch*: St DOMINIC

Dolphin: St Martianus;—*bearing corpse*: St ADRIAN;—*supporting*: St Calistratus

Dove: *on or over*: SS AMBROSE, BASIL, BRIDGET OF SWEDEN, CATHERINE, CATHERINE OF SIENA, Cunibert, DAVID, DUNSTAN, GREGORY THE GREAT, HILARY OF ARLES, John Columbini, Lo, Louis, MÉDARD, OSWALD, PETER OF ALCANTARA, PETER CELESTINE, SAMSON, THOMAS AQUINAS

Eagle: SS AUGUSTINE, GREGORY THE GREAT, JOHN THE EVANGELIST, PRISCA

Ear(s) of Corn: SS BRIDGET, FARA, WALBURGA

Falcon or Hawk: SS Bavo, EDWARD, JULIAN Hospitator:—*on cottage*: St OTTO

Feather: St BARBARA

Firebrand: St ANTHONY THE GREAT

Fish(es): SS ANDREW, Eanswide, GREGORY OF TOURS,

John of Burlington, RAPHAEL, SIMON. *See also* Angel, Bell, Key

Fish hooks: St ZENO

Flail: St Varus

Flower(s): SS DOROTHEA, HUGH OF LINCOLN, LOUIS OF TOULOUSE;—*in apron*: St ZITA

Fountain: *obtained by prayer*: SS Alton, Antoninus of Toulouse, Apollinaris, AUGUSTINE OF CANTERBURY, CLEMENT, EGWIN, Guntilda, HUMBERT, ISIDORE of Madrid, Julian of Mans, LEONARD, NICHOLAS OF TOLENTINO, OMER, PHILIP BENITI, RIQUIER, Servatius, Trond, VENANTIUS, WOLFGANG;—*Springing from their blood*: SS BONIFACE, Eric MM.

Frog(s): SS Huvas, Rieul, Sinorina, Ulphia

Goose: St MARTIN

Gosling: St Pharaildis

Gridiron: *as instrument of martyrdom*: SS CYPRIAN, Donatilla, Erasmus, FAITH, LAURENCE, VINCENT OF SARAGOSSA MM.

Hammer: SS ADRIAN, Reinoldus;—*and chalice*: SS Bernward, ELOI

Hare: St Albert of Siena

Harp: SS CECILIA, DUNSTAN

Hatchet: SS Adjutus, MATTHEW, MATTHIAS

Heart: SS AUGUSTINE, CATHERINE OF SIENA, FRANCIS OF SALES, JANE FRANCES;—*with sacred monogram*: SS IGNATIUS, TERESA

Hen: St Pharaildis

Hind: SS CATHERINE OF SWEDEN, GENEVIEVE of Brabant, Lupus of Sens;—*with two fawns*: St Bassian

Hoe: St ISIDORE of Madrid

Hook: *as instrument of martyrdom*: SS AGATHA, EULALIA, Felician, VINCENT OF SARAGOSSA MM.

Hops: St Arnold of Soissons

Horse: SS Barochus, Irene, Severus of Avranches

Hourglass: SS HILARION, THEODOSIUS

Ink-bottle: St JEROME

Jug or Pitcher: SS AGATHA, BEDE, BENEDICT, ELIZABETH OF PORTUGAL

Key: SS Ferdinand, Germanus of Paris, HUBERT, PETER, RAYMOND OF PANNAFORT;—*and book*: St PETRONILLA;—*and rosary*: St ZITA;—*in fish's mouth*: St EGWIN

Keys: *two*: SS HIPPOLYTUS, Maurilius, RIQUIER; *bunch of*: BVM, SS GENEVIEVE, JAMES THE GREAT, MARTHA, Nothburge

Knife: SS AGATHA, BARTHOLOMEW, CHRISTINA, EBBA, PETER THE MARTYR

Ladder: SS Emmeran, John Climacus

Ladle: St MARTHA

Lamp: SS FRANCIS, LUCY;—*and book*: St Hiltrudis

Lance or Spear: *as instrument of martyrdom*: SS BARBARA, CANUTE, Emmeran, Gerhard, GERMANUS, HIPPOLYTUS, John of Goto, Lambert, LONGINUS, MATTHIAS, OSWIN, THOMAS MM.

Lantern: SS GUDULE, HUGH, Mary of Cabeza

Leopard: *and ox, or lions*: St Marciana

Lily: SS ANTHONY OF PADUA, CAJETAN, CASIMIR, CATHERINE OF SWEDEN, CLARE, DOMINIC, JOSEPH, KENELM, PHILIP NERI, SEBASTIAN, Vincent Ferrer

Lion(s): SS ADRIAN, DOROTHEA, EUPHEMIA, GERMANUS, IGNATIUS, JEROME, MARK, PRISCA

Loom: SS ANASTASIA, GUDULE

Mason's tools: St MARINUS

Nail(s): *as instrument of martyrdom, held or piercing the body*: SS ALEXANDER, DENYS, Fausta, Gemellus, Julian of Emesa, PANTALEON, QUENTIN, Severus of Rome, WILLIAM OF NORWICH, MM.

Oar: St JUDE

Organ: St CECILIA

Ox(en): SS Blandina, Frideswide, Fursey, JULITTA, LEONARD, LUCY, LUKE, MÉDARD, OTTO

Padlock: *on lips*: St JOHN OF NEPOMUK

Pickaxe: St LEGER

Pig: St ANTHONY THE GREAT

Pilgrim's Staff: SS DOMINIC, LOUIS

Pincers: SS AGATHA, APOLLONIA, LUCY

Plough: SS Exuperius, Richard

Purse: St CYRIL OF JERUSALEM; *three*: SS BRIOC, NICHOLAS

Rats: St GERTRUDE OF NIVELLES

Raven: St BENEDICT;—*bringing food*: SS Erasmus, PAUL THE HERMIT;—*with ring in beak*: SS Ida, OSWALD

Razor: St Pamphilius

Ring: SS BARBARA, Damascus, EDWARD

Saw: SS JAMES THE LESS, SIMON

Scales: St Manous; *weighing souls in*—: St MICHAEL

Scourge: SS AMBROSE, BONIFACE, Dorotheus, GERVASE, GUTHLAC, PETER DAMIAN

Scythe: SS Guntilda, Nothburge, WALSTAN;—*and well*: St SIDWELL

Shears: SS AGATHA, Fortunatus, Marca;—*and bottle*: SS COSMAS AND DAMIAN

Shovel: *bakers'*: SS Aubert, HONORIUS

Sieve: SS BENEDICT, HIPPOLYTUS

Spade: St FIACRE

Sparrow: St DOMINIC

Spit: SS Gengulph, QUENTIN

Stag(s): SS AIDAN, EUSTACE, HUBERT, JULIAN Hospitator, OSYTH, Rieul; *ploughing with*—: SS Kenan, KENTIGERN

Star: *on or over*: SS ANASTASIA, Bernadin, BRUNO, DOMINIC, HUMBERT, NICHOLAS OF TOLENTINO, THOMAS AQUINAS

Swan(s): SS CUTHBERT, HUGH OF GRENOBLE, KENTIGERN

Sword: *as instrument of martyrdom; piercing head or body*: SS BONIFACE, EUPHEMIA, LUCY, THOMAS OF CANTERBURY;—*held*: SS AGNES, Aquila, PRISCA, CATHERINE, Irene, JAMES the Great, PAUL;—*and chalice*: St EWALD the Black;—*and club*: St Arcadius;—*and crosier or dagger*: St KILIAN;—*and hammer*: St ADRIAN;—and stone(s): SS Beztert, PANCRAS;—*and vase*: St PANTALEON;—*and wheel or book*: St CATHERINE MM.

Taper: St GUDULE

Thistle: SS Caroline, Narcissus

Tongs: SS CHRISTINA, Felician, Martina

Torch: SS AIDAN, BARBARA, DOROTHEA, Eutropia, IRENAEUS, MÉDARD

Tower: SS BARBARA, Praxedes

Trowel: SS WINNIBALD, WILLIAM OF MONTEVERGINE
Trumpet: St Vincent Ferrer
Vine: SS Elpidius, Urban, Urban of Langres
Weavers' Loom: St Severus of Ravenna
Wheel: SS CATHERINE, EUPHEMIA;—*broken*: St QUENTIN
Wolf: ST WILLIAM OF MONTEVERGINE;—*bringing child*: St Simpertus;—*bringing goose*: St VEDAST;—*stealing pig*: St BLAISE
Wolfdog: St DONATUS
Woolcomb: St BLAISE

The Island of Saints. So Ireland was called in the Middle Ages.
The Latter-day Saints. *See* MORMONS.

Sakkos. In the Eastern ORTHODOX CHURCH an embroidered vestment worn by a bishop; similar to the DALMATIC of the WESTERN CHURCH.

Salesian. A member of a ROMAN CATHOLIC order of priests and lay brothers, the Society of St Francis of Sales, founded in Turin in 1846 by St JOHN BOSCO, for the purpose of educating poor children.

Sally Army. A nickname of the SALVATION ARMY.

Salt. In Christian symbolism salt represents the elect; worth; purity; divine wisdom and strength (*Matt.* v, 13; *Mark* ix, 50; *Col.* iv, 6).
A covenant of salt (*Numb.* xviii, 19). A covenant which could not be broken. As salt was a symbol of incorruption it symbolized perpetuity.

> The Lord God of Israel gave the kingdom ... to David ... by a covenant of salt
> II *Chron.* xiii, 5

The Pillar of Salt. Lot's wife, when escaping from Sodom with her husband and daughters, looked back on the cities of SODOM AND GOMORRAH against God's command and 'She became a pillar of salt' (*Gen.* xix, 26). Our Lord, when teaching indifference to worldly affairs and material possessions, refers to the episode saying, 'Remember Lot's wife' (*Luke* xvii, 32).

Salvation Army. A religious organization founded by William Booth (1829–1912), originally a METHODIST minister. Its origins are to be found in 1865 in his Christian Mission, Whitechapel, and the movement took its present name in 1878. Booth himself became the 'General' and the 'Army' was planned on semi-military lines. The motto adopted was 'Through Blood and Fire' and the activities were directed at the poor, outcast, and destitute. The movement became world-wide, and its brass bands and open-air meetings became a familiar feature of the street scene, as did the bonnets of the Salvation Army 'lasses'. Immense good has been done by the selfless

devotion of its rank and file. It now employs 60,000 volunteers, 1,800 officers and 2,600 part-time employees. Internationally 2 million volunteers work at 14,000 outposts, running 7,100 social centres and schools in 94 countries.

Salve, Regina. An ancient antiphonal hymn recited at the end of some of the canonical hours and still widely used in Roman Catholic Churches. So called from the opening words, *Salve, regina mater misericordiae* (Hail, O Queen, Mother of Mercy).

Samaritan. A good Samaritan. A philanthropist, one who helps the poor and needy (*see Luke* x, 30–7).
The Samaritans. An organization founded by the Rev. Chad Varah of St Stephen, Walbrook, London, in 1953, to help the despairing and suicidal. It now has nearly 200 centres in the British Isles as well as some overseas. Trained volunteers give their help at any hour to those who make their needs known by telephone, letter, or by a personal visit.

Samson, St (d. 565, f.d. 28 July). Of Welsh family, he was educated by St ILLTYD in Glamorgan and ordained deacon and priest. He went to a monastery on Caldey Island, becoming first cellarer then abbot; later he retired to a hermitage near the River Severn. He then went to a monastery in Ireland, and on his return to England was consecrated bishop. In response to a vision he went first to Cornwall and then to the Channel Islands, where his name is found. He went afterwards to Brittany, founding a monastery at Dol and taking a leading part in apostolic activity, becoming one of the most noted of missioners. Miracles were told of him. In art he is depicted with a cross or staff and a book and dove.

Samthann, St (d. 739, f.d. 18 December). She was said to have been fostered by the king of Cairbre. The marriage he had arranged for her was averted by a miracle, and she became a nun at Ernaide in Donegal, moving on to Clonbroney where she became abbess. She refused large estates for her nunnery, living in poverty with only six cows to support the nuns. She was famous for her wise sayings, such as when replying to a query as to which was the best attitude to adopt for prayer, she said, 'Every position, standing, sitting or lying.' Her cult was introduced into Salzburg by St VIRGIL, an Irish bishop of that town, who had probably been educated by her.

San Benito. *See* SACCO BENEDETTO.

Sance Bell. The Sanctus bell. *See* SACRING BELL.

Sanctuary, Right of. In Anglo-Saxon England all churches and churchyards generally provided refuge for fugitives for 40 days; while permanent refuge was available at the great Liberties of Beverley, Durham, and Ripon. Sanctuary for treason was disallowed in 1486 and most of the remaining rights were severely restricted by Henry VIII. Eight cities of refuge were finally provided on the biblical model—Chester, Derby, Launceston, Northampton, Norwich, Wells, Westminster, and York. Sanctuary for criminals was abolished in 1623 and for civil offenders by acts of 1697 and 1723. These latter measures were aimed at such rookeries as Alsatia, the Savoy, the Clink, the Mint, etc.

In Scotland the most famous sanctuaries were those of the church of Wedale (Stow), near Galashiels, and that of Lesmahagow, Lanark. These were abolished at the REFORMATION. The abbey of Holyrood House remained a sanctuary for debtors until the late 19th century.

Sanctum Sanctorum. Latin for HOLY OF HOLIES.

Sanctus Bell. *See* SACRING BELL.

Sandemanians, or **Glasites.** A religious party expelled from the CHURCH OF SCOTLAND under John Glas (1695–1773) for maintaining that national churches, being 'kingdoms of this world' are unscriptural. He was suspended in 1728 and expelled in 1730. Eventually the leadership passed to his son-in-law Robert Sandeman, whence the more common name *Sandemanians.* They believe in salvation through grace and abstain from all animal food which has not been drained of blood. Love feasts (AGAPE) are held and the kiss of charity is enjoined.

Sangrail, or **Sangreal.** The Holy GRAIL. Popular etymology used to explain the word as meaning the real blood of Christ, *sang-real,* or the wine used in the LAST SUPPER; and a tradition arose that part of this wine-blood was preserved by JOSEPH OF ARIMATHEA in the Saint, or Holy Grail.

Santa Casa. *See* LORETO.

Santa Claus. A contraction of Santa Nikolaus (St NICHOLAS), the patron saint of German children. His feast-day is 6 December, and the vigil is still held in some places, but for the most part his name is now associated with Christmastide. The custom used to be for someone, on 5 December, to assume the costume of a BISHOP, and distribute small gifts to 'good children'. The present custom, introduced into England from Germany about 1840, is to put toys and other small presents into a stocking late on CHRISTMAS Eve, when the children are asleep, and when they wake on Christmas morn they find at the bedside the gifts brought by Santa Claus, who supposedly travels around in a sleigh pulled by reindeer.

Sarum Rite, or **Use.** The order of the Latin liturgy used by the majority of the churches in England and Ireland before the REFORMATION, and currently in use in some ANGLICAN churches. Its initiation was attributed to St OSMUND, bishop of Salisbury in 1078, but was more probably the work of Richard le Poore, a later bishop of Salisbury (1198–1228).

Satan, in Hebrew, means adversary or enemy, and is traditionally applied to the DEVIL, the personification of EVIL.

> To whom the Arch-enemy
> (And thence in heaven called Satan).
> MILTON: *Paradise Lost*, Bk. I, 81

He appears as the SERPENT, tempter of mankind in *Gen.* iii, 1, and the existence of Satan as the centre of evil is part of the teaching of both the OLD and NEW TESTAMENT,

> But when they have heard, Satan cometh immediately, and taketh away the word that was sown in their hearts.
> *Mark* iv, 15

Saul. Is Saul also among the prophets? (I *Sam.* x, 11). Said of one who unexpectedly bears tribute to a party or doctrine that he has hitherto vigorously assailed. At the conversion of Saul, who was afterwards called PAUL, the Jews said in substance, 'Is it possible that Saul can be a convert?'. (*Acts* ix, 21).

Sauli, St Alexander (1534–92, f.d. 11 October). Born at Milan, he entered the BARNABITE CONGREGATION and was educated at their college at Parvia, later being ordained priest and becoming Provost-General of the order. He was a noted theologian and preacher, and endowed the college with a library. He was appointed bishop of Aleria in Corsica at a time when the place was in ruins, brigandage was rife and the clergy decadent, but after his reforms and his rule of twenty years, it had been converted into a model diocese. Sauli was offered, and rejected, the sees of Tortona and Genoa, but Pope Gregory XIV insisted on his becoming bishop of Pavia. He was reputed to have gifts of prophecy and healing and was said to be able to subdue storms at sea.

Sava (or **Sabas) of Serbia, St** (1173–1236, f.d. 14 January). Born in Tirvano, the third son of Prince Stephen of Nemanya, he became a monk at Mount ATHOS in 1191. He was joined later by his father who had negotiated Serbian independence from Byzantium, and had abdicated in favour of his son Stephen II. Together at Mount Athos, father and son founded another house, called Khilandari, for Serbian monks; this became a centre for Serbian culture—religious, secular and literary—which still exists as a 'ruling monastery' there. When rivalry between his brothers reduced Serbia to anarchy, Sava left Mount Athos and returned to Sudenitsa to restore law and order. He also took his father's relics there, his father having been canonized in 1216 as St Simeon. Sava was responsible for establishing the Serbian Church as autocephalous, and became the first archbishop of the Serbs, freed from the Greek archbishop of Okhrida. Sava went on a pilgrimage to the HOLY LAND in 1230 where he built the monastery of St JOHN at Jerusalem and organized a hospice for Serbian pilgrims at Mount SINAI. He died at Tirnova, in Bulgaria, on his way home. As St Sava or Sabas he is venerated by both the ROMAN and ORTHODOX CHURCHES in Croatian and Serbian churches, and is patron saint of Serbia.

Savio, St Dominic (1842–57, f.d. 9 March). A child saint, born near Turin as one of ten children of a poor blacksmith and a seamstress, he entered the school of St JOHN BOSCO in Turin. Guided by that saint's wisdom and practical sense, the boy developed signal spiritual qualities, combined with cheerfulness and observance of discipline. He had visions, and was absorbed in prayer for hours together. One of his visions was of a bishop who brought 'light with a torch to the English people'. He died of tuberculosis at the age of fifteen, experiencing a vision of heaven.

Savonarola, Girolamo (1452–98). Born at Ferrara, he became a DOMINICAN FRIAR in 1474. He was elected prior of St MARK's convent, and gained a reputation as an eloquent preacher, a prophet and visionary, using apocalyptic language, denouncing contemporary immorality and laxity of the clergy. He led a revolt against the Medicis and founded a type of republic, but made many enemies. He was excommunicated for denouncing Pope Alexander VI in 1497, and a year later was arrested, tortured, hanged and burned for heresy. *See also* WEEPERS.

Scallop shell. The emblem of St JAMES of Compostela, adopted, says ERASMUS, because the shore of the adjacent sea abounds in them; also the emblem of the pilgrims to his shrine and of mediaeval pilgrims generally.

Give me my scallop-shell of quiet,
My staff of faith to walk upon,
My scrip of joy, immortal diet,
My bottle of salvation,
My gown of glory, hope's true gage,

And thus I'll take my pilgrimage.
SIR WALTER RALEGH: *The Pilgrimage*

Scandal (Gr. *skandalon*) means properly a pitfall or snare laid out for an enemy; hence a stumbling-block, and morally an aspersion.

In *Matt.* xiii, 41–2, we are told that the angels 'shall gather all things that offend ... and shall cast them into a furnace'; here the Greek word is *skandalon*, and *scandals* is given as an alternative in the margin; the REVISED VERSION (*see under* BIBLE, THE ENGLISH) renders the word 'all things that cause stumbling'. *Cp. also* I *Cor.* i, 23.

The Hill of Scandal. So Milton (*Paradise Lost*, I, 415) calls the Mount of Olives, because King Solomon built thereon 'an high place for Chemosh, the abomination of the children of Ammon' (I *Kings* xi, 7).

Scapegoat. Part of the ancient ritual among the Hebrews for the Day of ATONEMENT laid down by Mosaic Law (*see Lev.* xvi) was as follows: two goats were brought to the altar of the TABERNACLE and the high priest cast lots, one for the Lord, and the other for AZAZEL. The Lord's goat was sacrificed, the other was the scapegoat; and the high priest having, by confession, transferred his own sins and the sins of the people to it, it was taken to the wilderness and suffered to escape.

Scapular. A sleeveless monastic garment, hanging from the shoulders, usually almost to the feet, and sometimes having a cowl. Also two pieces of woollen cloth, joined by strings and worn by those living in the world but who are affiliated to religious orders. The wearing of this smaller scapular carries certain privileges in the ROMAN CATHOLIC CHURCH.

Scarlet Hat. A CARDINAL; from his once traditional red hat.

The Scarlet Woman, or **Scarlet Whore.** The woman seen by St JOHN in his vision 'arrayed in purple and scarlet colour', sitting 'upon a scarlet coloured beast, full of names of blasphemy, having seven heads and ten horns', 'drunken with the blood of the saints, and with the blood of the martyrs', upon whose forehead was written 'Mystery, Babylon the Great, The Mother of Harlots and Abominations of The Earth' (*Rev.* xvii, 1–6).

St John was probably referring to ROME which, at the time he was writing, was 'drunken with the blood of the saints; some controversial PROTESTANTS have applied the words to the Church of Rome, and some ROMAN CATHOLICS to the Protestant churches generally.

Schelhorn's Bible. *See* BIBLE, SOME SPECIALLY NAMED EDITIONS.

Schism, The Great. The split in the CATHOLIC CHURCH when there were rival popes at Avignon and ROME. It began in 1378 and ended in 1417. After the death of Gregory XI, the last of the AVIGNON POPES proper, Urban VI (1378–1389) alienated the French cardinals and their adherents, and they established an antipope, Clement VII, at Anagni. Clement soon retired to Avignon with his supporters, where the ANTIPOPE remained until the schism ended.

A schism is the split of a religious community into factions, breaking the unity of a church by internal dissensions and leading to the formation of independent bodies.

Scholastica, St (d. *c.* 543, f.d. 10 February). Sister of St BENEDICT and the first BENEDICTINE nun. Her convent was Plombariola near MONTE CASSINO. Brother and sister met each year at a house nearby. On the last visit Scholastica asked St Benedict to stay the night to discuss 'the joys of heaven', but he refused. She prayed for rain to delay him, and this was answered by a heavy thunderstorm which made it impossible to leave until morning. St Scholastica died three days later and St Benedict saw her soul ascend to heaven in the form of a dove. She was buried in the grave which St Benedict had prepared for himself and in which he, too, was interred later. The relics of both are under the altar of the abbey at Monte Cassino. In art St Scholastica is depicted as a nun with a crozier and crucifix and with a dove flying from her mouth.

Scholasticism. The term usually denotes the philosophy and doctrines of the mediaeval SCHOOLMEN from the 9th to the early 15th century. It was very much concerned with applying Aristotelian logic to Christian theology. On the whole, reason took second place to faith and the apparent reconciliation and harmony between the two established by St THOMAS AQUINAS in his *Summa Theologica* was undermined by DUNS SCOTUS and WILLIAM OF OCCAM. It taught men to discipline their thought and classify their knowledge. Scholasticism owed much of its decline to its own internal quibblings, verbal subtleties, and intellectual exhaustion, but it never completely lost its vitality and still attracts theologians, especially in the ROMAN CATHOLIC CHURCH. *Cp.* REALISM.

Scholia. Explanatory notes or comments, generally in the margin, of classical or ecclesiastical texts or MSS.

Schoolmen. The name given to the teachers of philosophy and theology who lectured in the ecclesiastical schools attached to certain abbeys and cathedrals as instituted by Charlemagne, and in the mediaeval universities

(*see* SCHOLASTICISM. Among the most famous are:

Flaccus Alcuin or Albinus (735–804).
Johannes Scotus ERIGENA or John the Scot (*c.* 815–*c.* 877).
Gerbert of Aurillac (*c.* 950–1003), Pope Sylvester II (999–1003).
Berengar of Tours (*c.* 998–1088).
Lanfranc (*c.* 1005–89), Archbishop of Canterbury (1070–89).
Anselm (*c.* 1033–1109), Archbishop of Canterbury (1093–1109).
Roscellinus of Compiègne (*c.* 1050–*c.* 1122).
Peter ABELARD (1079–1142).
Peter Lombard (*c.* 1100–*c.* 1160).
John of Salisbury (*c.* 1115–80).
Alain de Lille (*c.* 1128–1202).
Alexander of Hales (*c.* 1175–1245).
Albertus Magnus (*c.* 1206–80).
St Bonaventura or John of Fidanza (1221–74).
THOMAS AQUINAS (*c.* 1225–74).
Raymond Lully (*c.* 1235–1315).
Duns Scotus (*c.* 1265–1308).
William of Occam (*c.* 1280–1349).
Thomas Bradwardine (*c.* 1290–1349).
Robert Holcot (*d.* 1349).
Jean Buridan (*c.* 1300–*c.* 1368).
See also DOCTORS OF LEARNING; DUNS SCOTUS; OCCAM'S RAZOR.

Scotists. Followers of DUNS SCOTUS, who maintained the doctrine of the IMMACULATE CONCEPTION in opposition to THOMAS AQUINAS.

Scotus, Duns. *See* DUNS; SCOTISTS.

Scribe. In the NEW TESTAMENT, it means a Jewish doctor of the law, and Scribes were generally coupled with the PHARISEES as upholders of the ancient ceremonial tradition. In *Matt.* xxii, 35, we read, 'then one of them, which was a *lawyer*, asked Him... which is the great commandment in the law?' *Mark* (xii, 28) says, 'And one of the *scribes* came, and... asked him, Which is the first commandment of all?'

In the OLD TESTAMENT the word has a wider application. In II *Sam.* viii, 17, it is used in the sense of 'secretary', and again in *Jer.* xxxvi, 10, 12, 20, 21, etc. In II *Kings* xxv, 19, it applies to the military mustermaster and *Is.* xxxiii, 18, a tax-official, etc. More commonly it denotes those occupied in literary study, copying and editing of the SCRIPTURES, and especially the Law, this being akin to the New Testament usage.

Scriptorium (Lat. from *scriptus*, past part. of *scribere*, to write). A writing-room, especially the chamber set apart in the mediaeval monasteries for the copying of MSS, etc.

Scriptures, The, or **Holy Scripture** (Lat. *scriptura*, a writing). The BIBLE; hence applied allusively to the sacred writings of other creeds.

Sebastian, St. Patron SAINT of archers, martyred in 288. He was bound to a tree and shot at with arrows and finally beaten to death. As the arrows stuck in his body as pins in a pin-cushion, he was also made the patron saint of pin-makers. As he was a captain of the guard, he is the patron saint of soldiers. His feast, coupled with that of St Fabian, is kept on 20 January.

The English St Sebastian. St Edmund, the martyr-king of East Anglia (855–870) who is said to have been tied to a tree by the Danes and shot dead with arrows at Hoxne, Suffolk, because he refused to rule as a Danish vassal. His body was taken to the royal manor of Bedricsworth which came to be called St Edmund's Burgh and his remains, miraculously incorrupt, became the chief relic of the abbey of Bury St Edmunds.

Sebbi (or Sabbe), St (7th cent., f.d. 29 August). After thirty years as king of the East Saxons, he retired to a monastery, dying there shortly afterwards. He was noted for his pious works and almsgiving, and he laboured to sustain Christianity after a plague had turned many back to paganism. He was said to have built the first monastery at Westminster and to have been buried by the north wall of the old cathedral of St PAUL'S.

Second. The Second Adam. Jesus Christ.

Second Adventists. Those who believe that the Second Coming of Christ (*cp.* 1 *Thess.* iv, 15) will precede the MILLENNIUM; hence sometimes also called Premillenarians.

Sect (Lat. *secare*, to cut). A division, a body of people who, sharing the same religious opinions, have broken away from the main body to form a separate group.

Sectary. A NONCONFORMIST or Dissenter, particularly applied to those of the 17th and 18th centuries. The term can also be used for a person of extreme religious zeal.

Secular clergy. Clergy living 'in the world' as opposed to the regular clergy of the cloister, who live under a rule. In the ROMAN CATHOLIC CHURCH secular clergy take precedence over the regular clergy.

Sedilia. A set of seats, usually three in number, placed on the south side of the CHANCEL of a church, used for the clergy during intervals in a service.

See (Lat. *sedes*). The seat or throne of a BISHOP hence the town or place where the bishop's cathedral is located and from which he takes his title; and so has to be distinguished from diocese, the territory over which he has jurisdiction.

The Holy See. *See under* HOLY.

Seekers. A 17th-century puritan sect akin to the QUAKERS in their outlook who rejected the existing church and claimed to seek the true church which God would reveal in his own time. Roger Williams (*c.* 1603–83) founded Providence, New England, as a refuge for the sect.

Seiriol, St (6th cent., f.d. 1 February). He and his friend St CYBI are the principal saints of Anglesey, living on the East and West of the island. St Seiriol founded Penmon church and its dependency Ynys Seiriol (Puffin Island), and a monastery which was later revived by AUGUSTINIAN CANONS. His well and the ruins of a beehive cell still exist. In his poem *East and West*, Matthew Arnold recounts their story.

Selevan, St (? 6th cent., no feast date). He is of either Welsh or Cornish extraction. A ruined hermitage and well on the cliff of St Levan were said to be his, and he is patron saint of the district. Legend says that when fishing he caught two bream on the same hook and put them both back, but the catch was repeated three times; the third time he took them both home and found that his sister Breaga had arrived with her two children. Two fish are carved on a bench end to perpetuate the event.

Seminary. A training college for intending priests; the term is used principally among Catholics.

Semi-Pelagianism. Condemned by the Council of Orange in 529, Semi-Pelagianism was revived by OCCAM. Its followers maintained that though divine aid is necessary in living the Christian life, there must also be self-help. Believers must take responsibility and use initiative, as it is said, 'God helps those who help themselves' or, in later terms, 'Trust God but keep your powder dry.' It is necessary to seek before you can find and to knock before doors will be opened. St AUGUSTINE wrote against Semi-Pelagianism in later life, regarding it as an error of judgement rather than a heresy, because he had held such views himself in his early life. The term Semi-Pelagian was coined about 1600.

Senan of Scattery, St (d. *c.* 544, f.d. 8 March). An Irish abbot who founded monasteries at Inniscarra, Inis Mor, Mutton Island and finally Scattery Island, the houses being situated at the mouths of rivers or on islands. He was reputed to have stayed with St David in Wales.

Senan is the subject of many legends, one of which said that he read at night by the light shed by his fingers. There are numerous Irish saints of the same name.

Separatists. A name given to the BROWNISTS and Independents of the 17th century who separated from the Established Church.

September Bible. *See* BIBLE, SOME SPECIALLY NAMED EDITIONS.

Septuagesima Sunday. The third Sunday before LENT; in round numbers, 70 (in fact 64) days (Lat. *septuagesima dies*) before EASTER.

Septuagint (Lat. *septuaginta*, seventy). The most important Greek version of the OLD TESTAMENT and APOCRYPHA, so called because it was traditionally said to have been translated from the Hebrew SCRIPTURES by 72 learned Jews in the 3rd century BC, at the command of Ptolemy Philadelphus for the Alexandrian Library. They worked on the island of Pharos and completed the task in 72 days.

The name Septuagint is commonly abbreviated as LXX. It is probably the work of Jewish scholars at Alexandria working over a long period of time.

Sepulchre, The Holy. The cave outside the walls of old JERUSALEM in which the body of Christ is believed to have lain between His burial and Resurrection. The tomb is said to have been discovered by St HELENA and from at least the 4th century (*see* INVENTION OF THE CROSS *under* CROSS) the spot has been covered by a Christian Church, where today Greek, Catholic, Armenian, Syrian, and Coptic Christians have their rights of occupation.
Knights of the Holy Sepulchre. An order of military knights founded by Godfrey of Bouillon in 1099 to guard the Holy Sepulchre.

Seraphic. Seraphic Blessing. The blessing written by St FRANCIS OF ASSISI at the request of Brother Leo on Mt Alvernia in 1224. It is based on *Numbers* vi, 24: 'May the Lord bless thee and keep thee. May he show His face to thee and have mercy on thee. May he turn his countenance on thee and give thee peace. May the Lord bless thee, Brother Leo.'
The Seraphic Doctor. The Scholastic philosopher, St Bonaventura (1221–74).
The Seraphic Father, or **Saint.** St FRANCIS OF ASSISI (1182–1226); whence the FRANCISCANS are sometimes called the *Seraphic Order*.
The Seraphic Hymn. The Sanctus, 'Holy, holy, holy' (*Is.* vi, 3), which was sung by the SERAPHIM.

Seraphim. The highest of the nine choirs of ANGELS, so named from the seraphim of *Is.* vi, 2. The word is probably the same as *saraph*, a serpent, from *saraph*, to burn (in allusion to its bite); and this connection with burning suggested to early Christian interpreters that the seraphim were specially distinguished by the ardency of their zeal and love.

Seraphim is a plural form; the singular, *seraph*, was first used in English by Milton. Aabdiel was,

The flaming Seraph, fearless, though alone,
Encompassed round with foes.

Paradise Lost, V, 875

Seraphim of Sarov, St (1759–1833, f.d. 15 January, formerly 2 January, and 1 August, formerly 19 July). A noted visionary and mystic of the Russian ORTHODOX CHURCH, he was born Prokhor Moshnin, at Kursk, the son of a builder. He became a monk at Sarov, taking the name of Seraphim, and was ordained priest. He became a hermit, living in a hut in the forest, supporting himself and caring for wild animals. He is sometimes depicted with a bear. After having been savagely attacked by robbers he had to retire to a monastery for five months, but then returned to his solitary life until his health failed and he retired to a small, bare cell in the monastery. Following a vision of the VIRGIN MARY he administered to visitors, directed the nuns of Diveiev, and healed people, among them one Nicholas Motovilov whom he cured of rheumatism and other complaints. Motovilov was responsible for recording St Seraphim's teachings and visions, published some seventy years later and translated into English. There is a church dedicated to him at Walsingham. The saint was also possessed of prophetic gifts, and was said to have manifested physical phenomena, especially the 'blinding light' of spiritual illumination. He had experienced miraculous escapes as a child; at the age of seven he fell from the top of a church belfry without harm, and at ten was cured of a serious illness. At one time he was said to have spent one thousand days and nights on bare stone, engaged in prayer. He is the last of the saints of Russia canonized by the ORTHODOX CHURCH.

Serapion of Thmuis, St (*c.* 365, f.d. 21 March). An Egyptian deacon, bishop of Thmuis in the Nile Delta, he was a friend of St ANTHONY and a champion of St ATHANASIUS, opposing MANICHAEISM and ARIANISM. He composed a sacramentary which has been translated into English. There are a number of saints of the same name.

Sergius. Sergius and Bacchus, SS (d. *c.* 303, f.d. 8 October). Said to be officers of the Roman army who failed to attend sacrifices made to Juipter by the Emperor Maximian. They were

248

martyred at Resapha, in Syria, where Sergius was buried, the place being renamed Sergiopolis. It became one of the most famous centres of pilgrimage in the East and Sergius was adopted by the desert nomads as their patron saint. The cult was suppressed in the revision of 1969.

Sergius of Radonezh, St (1315–92, f.d. 25 September). Born of a noble Russian family of Rostov who were driven out by civil war, the two sons, Sergius and Stephen, became monks at the death of their parents and retired to the forest, living a simple life in touch with nature. Later they restored the monastery of the Holy Trinity which had fallen into disuse after the Tartar invasion. Disputes arose and Sergius, who had imposed communal life and prohibited begging, was replaced as superior by Stephen. He left to found other monasteries. Sergius was reinstated by the metropolitan Alexis. Later he was offered, but refused, the position of metropolitan of Moscow, but continued to be both a spiritual and political power in the land; it was said to be due to his advice and encouragement that Dimitri, Prince of Moscow, confronted and overcame the Tartars in 1380. Greatly venerated for his spiritual qualities, Sergius was also noted as a visionary and mystic and, like St SERAPHIM, manifested the aura of light. He became patron of Moscow and then of all Russia. His shrine was restored in 1945.

Serpent. The serpent is symbolical of:

(1) Wisdom. 'Be ye therefore wise as serpents, and harmless as doves' (*Matt.* x, 16).
(2) Subtlety. 'Now the serpent was more subtil than any beast of the field' (*Gen.* iii, i).
(3) The DEVIL. As the Tempter (*Gen.* iii, 1–6). In early pictures the serpent is sometimes placed under the feet of the Virgin, in allusion to the promise made to Eve after the fall (*Gen.* iii, 15).

In Christian art it is an attribute of St CECILIA, St EUPHEMIA, St PATRICK, and many other SAINTS, either because they trampled on SATAN, or because they miraculously cleared some country of snakes.

Fable has it that the cerastes (horned viper) hides in sand that it may bite the horse's foot and get the rider thrown. In allusion to this belief, Jacob says, 'Dan shall be ... an adder in the path, that biteth the horse heels, so that his rider shall fall backward' (*Gen.* xlix, 17). The Bible also tells us that the serpent stops up its ears that it may not be charmed by the charmers, 'charming never so wisely' (*Ps.* lxiii, 4).

When depicted entwining the Tree of Life, the serpent is beneficent and represents wisdom, but with the Tree of Knowledge it represents Lucifer and is malefic. The serpent raised on a pole or cross is a prototype of Christ raised on the cross, the Tree of Life for the salvation of the world; at the foot of the cross it is evil and symbolizes Christ's triumph over evil and the powers of darkness. The good serpent is seen rising from the chalice of St JOHN; the evil serpent is Satan, the dragon of the Apocalypse. Tertullian says that Christians call Christ the Good Serpent. The VIRGIN MARY crushes the head of the serpent of Eve instead of succumbing to him.

The old Serpent. SATAN.

> And he laid hold on the dragon, that old serpent, which is the Devil, and Satan, and bound him a thousand years.
>
> *Rev.* xx, 2

Server. In the WESTERN CHURCH one who assists in the sanctuary, making responses at the EUCHARIST, bringing the bread and wine to the altar and washing the hands of the celebrant.

Servites (or Servants of Mary). A ROMAN CATHOLIC order of mendicant friars founded in Florence in 1233 by seven men all of whom were canonized in 1888. The order is dedicated to preaching and missionary work, stressing the devotion to the SEVEN SORROWS of Our Lady. In 1304 St JULIANA FALCONIERI founded the order of Servite Nuns at Florence.

Servus servorum (Lat.). The slave of slaves, the drudge of a servant. *Servus servorum Dei* (the servant of the servants of God) is one of the honorific epithets of the POPE; it was first adopted by GREGORY THE GREAT (540, 540–604).

Seton, St Elizabeth. *See* ELIZABETH.

Seven. A mystic or sacred number; it is composed of four and three, which among the Pythagoreans were, and from time immemorial have been, accounted lucky numbers. Among the Babylonians, Egyptians, and other ancient peoples there were seven sacred planets; and the Hebrew verb to swear means literally 'to come under the influence of seven things'; thus seven ewe lambs figure in the oath between Abraham and Abimelech at Beersheba (*Gen.* xxi, 28), and Herodotus (III, viii) describes an Arabian oath in which seven stones are smeared with blood.

There are seven days in creation, seven days in the week, seven VIRTUES, seven divisions in the Lord's Prayer, seven sages in the life of man. Climacteric years are seven and nine with their multiples by odd numbers, and the seventh son of a seventh son was always held notable.

Among the Hebrews every seventh year was SABBATICAL, and seven times seven years was the Jubilee. The three great Jewish feasts lasted seven days, and between the first and second were seven weeks. Levitical purifications lasted seven days. The number is associated with a variety of occurrences in the OLD TESTAMENT.

In the *Apocalypse* we have SEVEN CHURCHES OF ASIA, seven candlesticks, seven stars, seven trumpets, seven spirits before the throne of God, seven horns, seven vials, seven plagues, a seven-headed monster, and the Lamb with seven eyes.

The Seven. Used of groups of seven people, especially (1) the 'men of honest report' chosen by the APOSTLES to be the first Deacons (*Acts* vi, 5), *viz.* Stephen, Philip, Prochorus, Nicanor, Timon, Parmenas, and Nicholas; (2) the SEVEN BISHOPS (*see below*); or (3) the Seven Sages of Greece.

The Seven Bishops. Archbishop Sancroft of Canterbury, and Bishops Lloyd of St Asaph, Turner of Ely, Ken of Bath and Wells, White of Peterborough, Lake of Chichester, and Trelawney of Bristol, who petitioned James II against the order to have his second Declaration of Indulgence read in every church on two successive Sundays (May 1688). James foolishly sent them to the Tower and had them-duly tried on a charge of seditious libel; they were acquitted amidst universal rejoicing. *Cf.* NON-JURORS.

> And have they fix'd the where and when? and shall
>   Trelawny die?
> Here's twenty thousand Cornish men will know the
>   reason why.
>
> *Song of the Western Men*

The Seven Champions. The mediaeval designation of the national patron SAINTS of England, Scotland, Wales, Ireland, France, Spain, and Italy. In 1590 Richard Johnson published a chap-book *The Famous History of the Seven Champions of Christendom*. In this he relates that St GEORGE of England was seven years imprisoned by the Almidor, the black king of Morocco; St DENYS of France lived seven years in the form of a hart; St JAMES of Spain was seven years dumb out of love for a fair Jewess; St Anthony of Italy, with the other champions, was enchanted into a deep sleep in the Black Castle, and was released by St George's three sons, who quenched the seven lamps by water from the enchanted fountain; St ANDREW of Scotland delivered six ladies who had lived seven years under the form of white swans; St PATRICK of Ireland was immured in a cell where he scratched his grave with his own nails; and St DAVID of Wales slept seven years in the enchanted garden of Ormandine, and was redeemed by St George.

The Seven Churches of Asia. Those mentioned in *Rev.* i, 11, viz.:

(1) Ephesus, founded by St PAUL, 57, in a ruinous state in the time of Justinian.
(2) Smyrna. Polycarp was its first bishop.
(3) Pergamos, renowned for its library.

(4) Thyatira, now called Ak-hissar (the White Castle).
(5) Sardis, now Sart, a small village.
(6) Philadelphia, now called Allah Shehr (City of God).
(7) Laodicea, now a deserted place called Eski-hissar (the Old Castle).

The Seven Deacons. In *Acts* vi, 1–6, the 'seven men of honest report, full of the Holy Ghost and wisdom' (*see* THE SEVEN). These are held to be the first deacons of the Church.

The Seven Deadly, or **Capital Sins.** Pride, Wrath, Envy, Lust, Gluttony, Avarice, Sloth.

The Seven Gifts of the Spirit, or **Holy Ghost.** Wisdom, Understanding, Counsel, Fortitude, Knowledge, Righteousness, Fear of the Lord.

The Seven Joys of Mary, or **the Virgin.** *See* MARY.

The Seven Sacraments. *See under* SACRAMENT.

The Seven Sleepers. Seven Christian youths of Ephesus, according to the legend, who fled during the Diocletian persecution (250) to a cave in Mt Celion. The cave was walled up by their pursuers and they fell asleep. In the reign of Theodosius II, some 200 years later, they awoke and one of them went into the city for provisions. They fell to sleep again, this time until the resurrection. Their names are given as Constantius, Dionysius, Joannes, Maximianus, Malchus, Martinianus, and Serapion. The legend was current in the 6th century and is referred to by Gregory of Tours.

The Seven Sorrows. *See* MARY.

The Seven Virtues. *See under* VIRTUE.

The Seven Works of Mercy. *See* MERCY.

Seven Apostles of Bulgaria, SS (9th–10th cent., f.d. 17 July, but locally also 22 and 25 November). Traditionally the first two apostles of the Bulgar people were SS CYRIL and METHODIUS who had knowledge of the Slavonic language. At the death of Methodius his place was taken by St Clement Slovensky who became a most important influence, establishing a monastery and the bishopric of Velica. He was the first Slav to become a bishop. He was succeeded by Nahum, whose works included translations into the vernacular. He is also venerated by the Russian ORTHODOX CHURCH; also venerated were Angelar and Sava.

The Seven Brothers, SS (2nd cent., f.d. 10 July). Traditionally they were the seven sons of St FELICITY, who refused to sacrifice to the pagan gods; all were martyred one by one, encouraged in their separate deaths by their mother who was the last to suffer. Their names were said to be Felix, Philip, Martial, Vitalis, Alexander, Silvanus and Januarius, but there is no historical evidence that they were either brothers or the sons of St Felicity. Their legend has similarities with that of the MACCABEES.

Their cult was confined to local calendars in the revision of 1969.

The Seven Servite Founders, SS (13th cent., f.d. 17 February). Seven Florentine men from eminent families who opposed the CATHAR heresy and the lax morality of the times; they retired to Monte Sennario as hermits and founded the SERVITES or Servants of Mary, an order of mendicant friars. They built a hermitage and church and based their lives on the rule of St AUGUSTINE and the DOMINICAN Constitution. Other centres were established in Italy and later in France, Germany and England.

Seventh-day Adventists. A sect of Adventists which grew out of a movement begun by William Miller in the United States in 1831. He preached that the present world would end about 1843. The Seventh-day Adventists adopted their name in 1860, and were formally organized from 1863. They observe Saturday as their SABBATH and insist on temperance and abstinence from alcohol, tobacco, etc., and a strict adherence to the SCRIPTURES and OLD TESTAMENT rules. Becoming a Messianic cult in the West Indies, they made great gains among Afro-Caribbean communities, but internal disputes led to breakaway groups, the chief of which is the Branch Davidians, founded in California by Victor Houteff, a Bulgarian-born Adventist who set up the Waco Community to await the Second Coming.

Seventh-day Baptists. In the USA, a group of German Baptist brethren who keep Saturday, the seventh day of the week, as their SABBATH.

Severinus Boethius, St (480–524, f.d. 23 October). Anicius Manlius Severinus Boethius was born into an eminent Christian Roman family and was early left an orphan; he was reared by Aurelius Symmachus, whose daughter he married. Boethius became a Roman statesman in the service of the Emperor Theodoric the Ostrogoth, but was martyred when he fell into disfavour. He is chiefly remembered as a scholar and philosopher, translating the Greek philosophers into Latin, writing theological works and, while in prison before his execution, writing the famous *De consolatione philosophiae.*

Severinus Noricum, St (d. 482, f.d. 8 January). A monk from the East who established himself as a missionary in Noricum (now Austria), which was dominated by Attila's Huns. Severinus founded a monastery on the Danube, near Vienna. After his death there, his monks were dispersed and took his relics to Naples where they were enshrined.

Sexagesima Sunday. The second Sunday before LENT so called because in round numbers it is 60 days (Lat. *sexagesima dies*) before EASTER.

Sexburga (or Sexburg), St (679–*c.* 700), f.d. 6 July, 17 October). Daughter of Anna, King of the East Angles, and sister of SS ETHELDREDA, ETHELBURGA and Withburga, by her marriage to King Erconbert she became mother to SS Erkengota and Ermengild. She founded a nunnery at Minster-in-Sheppey and became a nun there on her husband's death. Later she went to Ely where she followed her sister Etheldreda as abbess. Her shrine remained there until the REFORMATION. There are scenes from her life depicted at Ely Cathedral.

Sext (Lat. *sexte*, sixth). One of the CANONICAL HOURS: a service held at or near noon, i.e. the sixth hour after 6 a.m.; the service consists of a hymn, parts of PSALM 119 and a prayer.

Sexton. A minor official of the Church who takes care of the fabric and contents and can also act as bell-ringer and grave-digger.

Shakers. A sect of Adventists started by James and Jane Wardley at Manchester in 1747 who seceded from the QUAKERS, and from their excited behaviour were derisively dubbed 'Shakers'. Ann Lee, known as Mother Ann, the 'bride of the Lamb' and the 'Female Christ', soon became their acknowledged leader and the sect left for America in 1774. They practised celibacy, temperance, communal living, etc., and a few small communities still survive.

Another sect of English Shakers was founded at Battersea by Mary Anne Girling (1827–86), a farmer's daughter. The 'Children of God' settled in the New Forest but the sect petered out after Mrs Girling's death.

Shamrock. The symbol of Ireland, because it was selected by St PATRICK to illustrate to the Irish the doctrine of the TRINITY. According to the elder Pliny no serpent will touch this plant.

Sharbel, St (d. 101, f.d. 29 January). A Syrian, martyred with his sister Barbea at Edessa under Trajan. He had been a pagan high priest before his conversion to Christianity. Brother and sister were brutally tortured with hot irons before execution.

Sharbel the Maronite, St (1828–98), f.d. 24 December). Born in the village of Beqaa-Kfra in the Lebanon, he was orphaned in childhood and reared by an uncle. Hearing the call to the religious life, he entered the monastery of Our Lady of Mayfug, taking the name of the Syrian martyr Sharbel, and was ordained priest in 1859. He was noted for his delight in singing and in reading, especially the *Imitation of Christ.* He became a hermit at the hermitage of SS Peter and Paul, living in austere conditions, taking no meat, wine or fruit and sleeping on a bed of leaves. This continued for some thirty years. He died while celebrating the LITURGY. His body was found incorrupt when translated and was said to exude bloodlike fluid. The body had been buried in a chapel, but following further phenomena a new tomb was prepared in 1952 and the body was still incorrupt. Healing and miracles were reported, some among non-Christians. Sharbel was canonized in 1977.

Shaveling. Used in contempt of a young man and—especially after the REFORMATION—of a priest. At a time when the laity wore beards and moustaches the clergy were not only usually clean shaven but they also wore large shaven TONSURES.

> It maketh no matter how thou live here, so thou have the favour of the pope and his shavelings.
> JOHN BRADFORD (1510–1555): *Works*, II (*Parker Soc.*, 1853)

She. The She Bible. *See* BIBLE, SOME SPECIALLY NAMED EDITIONS.

Sheer (or Shere), Thursday. MAUNDY THURSDAY. It is generally supposed to be from M.E. *schere*, clean, i.e. free from guilt, from the custom of receiving absolution, or of cleansing the altars on this day. The *Liber Festivalis*, however, says:

> Hit is also in English tong 'Schere Thursday', for in owr elde fadur days men wold on y^t day makon scheron hem honest, and dode here hedes ond clypon here berdes and poll here hedes, ond so makon hem honest agen Estur day.

Shepherd. The Good shepherd. Jesus Christ.

> I am the good shepherd: the good shepherd giveth his life for the sheep.
> *John* x, 11

The shepherd symbolizes not only humanity and compassion but also the redemption of those gone astray. Christ is often depicted in art with a lamb on his shoulder, or holding a crook and leading the flock.

Sherwin, St Ralph (1550–81, f.d. 25 October). Born at Roddesby in Derbyshire, he was educated at Exeter College, Oxford, and was a noted scholar of Greek and Hebrew. He was converted to ROMAN CATHOLICISM and went to the ENGLISH COLLEGE of DOUAI, then on to the ENGLISH COLLEGE in ROME. He returned to England to undertake a mission but was arrested after only a few months; he was imprisoned at the Marshalsea and tortured in the Tower. He was offered his freedom and a bishopric in the CHURCH OF ENGLAND if he would recant and betray fellow Catholics; when he refused he was tried at Westminster and condemned to be hanged, drawn and quartered. He was canonized in 1970 as one of the FORTY MARTYRS OF ENGLAND AND WALES.

Shewbread. The name adopted by Tyndale, modelled on Luther's *Schaubrot*; more correctly *presence-bread*. Tyndale explains it as 'alway in the presence and sight of the Lorde'. Shrewbread denotes the 12 loaves for the 12 tribes, arranged in two piles on the table of shittim wood set beside the altar each week and when they were removed only the priest was allowed to partake of them. This ancient oblation is referred to in *Exod.* xxv, 30; *Lev.* xxiv, 5–9, etc.

Shibboleth. A test word; a catchword or principle to which members of a group adhere long after its original significance has ceased; hence a worn-out or discredited doctrine. *Shibboleth* (meaning 'ear of wheat', 'stream', or 'flood') was the word the Ephraimites could not pronounce when they were challenged at the ford on the Jordan by their pursuers, Jephthah and the Gileadites. The Ephraimites could only say *Sibboleth*, thus revealing themselves to the enemy (*see Judges* xii, 1–6).

Shorter Catechism. One of the two Catechisms (the *Larger* and *Shorter*) drawn up by the WESTMINSTER ASSEMBLY in 1647 and adopted by the English Parliament and the Scottish General Assembly. The *Shorter Catechism* proved its instructional worth and came into regular use among PRESBYTERIANS, Baptists, and later, WESLEYANS.

Shrine. Usually a casket of stone, metal or wood containing sacred relics, but the term can also be applied to any chapel, altar, tomb or place holding such sacred relics or other sacred associations.

Shrovetide. The three days just before the opening of LENT, when people went to confession and afterwards indulged in all sorts of sports and merry-making.
Shrove Tuesday. The day before ASH WEDNESDAY; 'Pancake Day'. It used to be the great 'Derby Day' of cock-fighting in England.

> Or matyr beat, like Shrovetide cocks, with bats.
> PETER PINDAR: *Subjects for Painters: Scene, The Royal Academy*, III

Si Quis (Lat., if anyone). A notice to all whom it may concern, given in the parish church before ordination that a resident means to offer himself as a candidate for HOLY ORDERS (*see under* ORDERS); and if anyone knows any just cause or impediment thereto, he is to declare the same to the BISHOP.

Sian-fu Stone, The. Discovered in North-West China in 1625, the stone is a monument set up by the NESTORIANS in AD 781 and is a valuable record of the arrival of a Christian missionary in China in 635 and of the early development of Christianity in the Far East.

Sidesman. In the CHURCH OF ENGLAND, a person elected to assist the CHURCHWARDEN at services of the church to maintain order. Originally the sidesman's function was to ensure attendance at the church services.

Sidonius Apollinaris, St (*c.* 432–82, f.d. 21 August). Caius Sollius Apollinaris Sidonius was born at Lyons, of noble family, and married Papianilla, daughter of Avitus, Emperor of the West. Sidonius was prominent in public affairs and politics, and at the same time was a scholar and ecclesiastic. Although a layman, he was appointed bishop of Avernum in Auvergne. His diplomacy saved his people from the ravages of Alaric the Goth. In the Church he introduced ROGATION DAYS. Although he wrote poems and good Latin verse, it is for his letters that he is famous, as they are an excellent reflection of the life of his times; an English translation was published in 1915. He is ranked as one of the great Gallo-Romans.

Sidwell, St Sativola (no date, f.d. 1 and 2 August). Probably of British origin and said to have lived in Devon, she was greatly venerated in Exeter. She was reported to have been beheaded by a scythe at the instigation of her stepmother. There are churches and a holy well dedicated to her and Exeter Cathedral has a stained-glass window depicting her with her emblems of the scythe and well by her.

Sigebert, St (d. 635, f.d. 27 September or 16 January). Baptized a Christian while in exile in Frankia, he returned to England as the first Christian king of East Anglia. He was a scholarly man and abdicated to become a monk, but the people forced him to leave the religious life and lead them in war against the pagan Penda of Mercia. Sigebert refused to carry weapons, only a staff, and was killed in battle. He was regarded as a martyr in the war against paganism.
Sigebert, St (631–56, f.d. 1 February). Son of King Dagobert I, he was ruler of provinces in Eastern France. He had been reared in religious traditions by Pepin of Landen and St Cunibert. He founded monasteries and churches, but died at the age of 25; his relics were kept at Nancy.

Sigfrid, St (d. *c.* 1045, f.d. 15 February). Traditionally an Englishman, a monk at Glastonbury, he went to Norway to King Olaf, carrying out a mission in Norway and Sweden and being appointed bishop of Vaxjo. He con-

verted King Olaf of Sweden, and was said to have worked also in Denmark. He was helped by his two nephews who were murdered in his absence, but Sigfrid urged forgiveness for the killers. His cult survives in Sweden and Denmark. In art he is represented in bishop's robes and holding the heads of his nephews. He is reputed to have been canonized by Pope Adrian IV.

Silas (or Silvanus), St (1st cent., f.d. 13 July ((West), 30 July (East, Greek Church). Variously called Silas or Silvanus in the NEW TESTAMENT, he was a disciple and fellow-worker of St PAUL. He took a letter from the Council of Jerusalem to Antioch (*Acts* xv), and tradition says he was the first bishop of Corinth.

Sillon. A French liberal movement in the ROMAN CATHOLIC CHURCH; it was opposed by the extreme right-wing organization 'Action française. Sillon was condemned by Pope Pius X in 1910, and Action Française in 1914, though this was not made public until 1926.

Silly is the German *selig* (blessed) and used to mean in English 'happy through being innocent'; whence the infant Jesus was termed 'the harmless silly babe', and sheep were called 'silly'. As the innocent are easily taken in by worldly cunning, the word came to signify 'gullible', 'foolish'.

Silver. Thirty pieces of silver. The sums of money that JUDAS Iscariot received from the chief priests for the betrayal of his Master (*Matt.* xxvi, 5); hence used proverbially of a bribe or 'blood-money'.

Silvester, St (d. 335, f.d. 31 December). A Roman who became Pope from 314 to 335 after Constantine had recognized Christianity by the Edict of Milan. Silvester was represented at the Council of NICAEA which dealt with the ARIAN heresy. Little is known of his life. Legend says he baptized Constantine, but this is an anachronism. In art Silvester is depicted at the baptism and he is also represented as a pope holding a small dragon in his hand or having it on a chain.

Simeon, St (f.d. 18 February), the son of Cleophas, is usually depicted as bearing in his arms the infant Jesus or receiving Him in the Temple.
Simeon the New Theologian, St (949–1022, f.d. 12 March). A Studite monk at Constantinople, he was called the New Theologian and 'the most outstanding of Byzantine mystics'. He was born in Asia Minor, of a noble family. As a disciple of Simeon the Studite he went with him to the monastery in Constantinople and later to

Simnel Cakes

St Mamas monastery where he became abbot. He was involved in conflict with the monks, who regarded his rule as too strict, and his controversy with Bishop Stephen of Nicomedia led to exile in 1009. He was restored to office later, and died in 1022. The term 'theologian' implied teaching on God and he was called the 'New Theologian' as following the teachings of the earlier theologians such as the CAPPADOCIAN FATHERS. Simeon was also influential in the use of HESYCHASM. His writings are mainly on the Divine Light and Transfiguration.

St Simeon Stylites. *See* STYLITES.

Simnel Cakes. Rich cakes formerly eaten (especially in Lancashire) on MID-LENT SUNDAY (MOTHERING SUNDAY), EASTER, and CHRISTMAS Day. They were ornamented with scallops, and were eaten at Mid-Lent in commemoration of the banquet given by Joseph to his brethren, which forms the first lesson of Mid-Lent Sunday, and the feeding of the five thousand, which forms the GOSPEL of the day.

The word *simnel* is through O.Fr. from Late Lat. *siminellus*, fine bread, Lat. *simila*, the finest wheat flour.

Simon. Simon Magus. Isidore tells us that Simon Magus died in the reign of Nero, and adds that he had proposed a dispute with PETER and PAUL, and had promised to fly up to HEAVEN. He succeeded in rising high into the air, but at the prayers of the two APOSTLES he was cast down to earth by the evil spirits who had enabled him to rise.

Milman, in his *History of Christianity* (ii) tells another story. He says that Simon offered to be buried alive, and declared that he would reappear on the third day. He was actually buried in a deep trench, 'but to this day,' says Hippolytus, 'his disciples have failed to witness his resurrection'.

Simon Stock, St (*c.* 1165–1265, f.d. 16 May). Little is known of his life, but tradition says he was born at Aylesford in Kent. He joined the CARMELITES, being among the first of the English to do so, and later was elected prior-general of the order. He founded houses in the university cities of Cambridge (1248), Oxford (1253), Paris (1260) and Bologna (1260). After a vision of the VIRGIN MARY, who promised salvation for those wearing the brown scapular of the Carmelites, there rose the SCAPULAR devotion. Although not formally canonized, his feast was approved by the HOLY SEE for the Carmelites in 1564. Simon died at Bordeaux at a great age, and his relics were enshrined at Aylesford. In art he is represented as an old man in Carmelite habit, either praying or receiving a scapular from the Virgin.

Simon, St (Zelotes) is represented with a saw in his hand, in allusion to the instrument of his martyrdom. He sometimes bears fish in his other hand, in allusion to his occupation as a fisherman. His feast day is 28 October.

Simony (from Simon Magus, *Acts* viii, 9–24). The offence of buying or selling sacred things such as positions in the Church, preferment or offices.

Simplicius, St (d. 483, f.d. 10 March). Born in Tivoli, he was pope from 468 to 483. At the time of the Council of Chalcedon he upheld the Eastern CATHOLICS against the MONOPHYSITE heretics who were supported by the Byzantine emperors. At the fall of the western Roman Empire he had also to contend with the ARIAN King Odoacer.

Sin, according to Milton, is twin keeper with Death of the gates of HELL. She sprang full-grown from the head of SATAN.

> …Woman to the waist, and fair
> But ending foul in many a scaly fold
> Voluminous and vast, a serpent armed
> With mortal sting.
>
> *Paradise Lost,* II, 650–3

Original Sin. That corruption which is born with us, and is the inheritance of all the offspring of ADAM. Theology teaches that as Adam was founder of his race, when Adam fell the taint and penalty of his disobedience passed to all posterity.

The Man of Sin (II *Thess.* ii, 3). Generally held to signify ANTICHRIST, and applied by the PURITANS to the POPE, by the FIFTH-MONARCHY MEN to Cromwell, etc.

Mortal Sins. The same as deadly sins.

The seven deadly sins. *See under* SEVEN.

Sin-eaters. Poor persons hired at funerals in olden days, to eat beside the corpse and so take upon themselves the sins of the deceased, that the soul might be delivered from PURGATORY. In Carmarthenshire the sin-eater used to rest a plate of salt on the breast of the deceased and place a piece of bread on the salt. After saying an incantation over the bread the sin-eater consumed it and with it the sins of the dead.

'Sin on' Bible. *See* BIBLE, SOME SPECIALLY NAMED EDITIONS.

Sin rent. In mediaeval England, a fine imposed upon the laity by the Church for living in sin, i.e., for concubinage. *Cp.* CRADLE CROWN.

To earn the wages of sin. To be hanged or condemned to death.

> The wages of sin is death.
>
> *Rom.* vi, 23

To sin one's mercies. To be ungrateful for the gifts of Providence.

Sinai. Mount Sinai (now Gebel Musa), in the

desert where Moses was given the TEN COM-MANDMENTS (*see* DECALOGUE), was one of the earliest regions of Christian monasticism, with a monastery dedicated to St CATHERINE of Alexandria. The Church of Sinai is a small independent body within the Eastern ORTHODOX CHURCH and is governed by the Archbishop of Sinai.

Sing. Singing bread (Fr. *pain à chanter*). An old term for the larger altar bread used in celebration of the MASS., because singing or chanting was in progress during its manufacture; also called *singing cake* and *singing loaf*.
To sing Placebo. *See* PLACEBO.

Sisterhood. A RELIGIOUS community of women. Sisters of Mercy are those engaged in nursing or caring for the needy. A sisterhood of that name was founded in Dublin in 1827.

Sisters of Charity. Founded by St VINCENT DE PAUL in 1625. After having founded the Vincentian, or Lazarist, Congregation, St Vincent was assisted by St LOUISE DE MARILLAC in founding the Sisters of Charity; they were selected girls and widows, mainly from the artisan and peasant classes. It was the first unenclosed body of nuns who were trained and devoted their lives to the sick and poor. The order started from St Louise's own home with four postulants, but spread worldwide. The sisters were to regard themselves simply as Christians devoted to the poor and the sick. 'Your convent will be the house of the sick, your cell a hired room, your chapel the parish church, your cloister the city streets or the hospital wards, your enclosure obedience, your grill the fear of God, your veil modesty.' Originally no vows were taken, but after 1642, they were taken yearly. The sisters now wear a habit of a grey wool tunic, a large white headdress similar to that of the early Breton peasant women, or a dress adapted to modern customs.

Sistine. The Sistine Chapel. The principal chapel in the VATICAN, reserved for ceremonies at which the POPE is present, so called because it was built by Pope Sixtus IV (1471–84). It is decorated with frescoes by Michelangelo and others.
Sistine Madonna, The (*Madonna di San Sisto*). The Madonna painted by Raphael (*c.* 1518) for the church of St Sixtus (San Sisto) at Piacenza; St Sixtus is shown kneeling at the right of the Virgin. The picture is now in the Royal Gallery, Dresden.

Sitha, St. *See* ZITA.

Six. The Six Articles. The so-called 'Whip with six strings', otherwise known as the 'Bloody Bill', the Statute of Six Articles passed in 1539 to secure uniformity in matters of religion. It was repealed in 1547 under Edward VI. The articles maintained (1) TRANSUBSTANTIATION; (2) the sufficiency of Communion in one kind; (3) clerical celibacy; (4) the obligation of monastic vows; (5) the propriety of private masses; (6) the necessity of auricular confession. Penalties were imposed for non-observance including death at the stake for those who spoke against transubstantiation.
The Six Points of Ritualism. Altar lights, eucharistic vestments, the mixed chalice, incense, unleavened bread, and the eastward position. So called when English Ritualists and upholders of the Oxford Movement sought to reintroduce them in the 1870s.
Six-Principle Baptists. A sect of Arminian Baptists, founded about 1639, who based their creed on the six principles enunciated in *Heb.* vi, 1–2: repentance, faith, BAPTISM, laying on of hands, the resurrection of the dead, and eternal judgement.

Sixtus II (Xystus), St (d. 258, f.d. 7 August). He was pope for one year, 257–258. He was involved in the controversy of the time on the question of the validity of baptism by heretics. Sixtus was seized, with his deacons, while preaching and celebrating the LITURGY at the catacomb of Praetextatus, and was killed immediately with the deacons.

Skoptsi (Russ. *skopets*, eunuch). A Russian sect, appearing in 1772 and led by Akulina Ivanovna, the 'Mother of God', and Blochin, 'the Christ'. They preached flagellation and were castrated to ensure celibacy. Blochin was exiled to Siberia and the movement was suppressed, but it reappeared a few years later under Selivanov, who called himself 'Tsar Christ Peter III'. When he died in 1832, it was expected that he would appear again to defeat the Antichrist, ring the Tsar Bell in Moscow, and establish the Skoptsi kingdom on earth. The cult held that Adam and Eve were created sexless and that the two halves of the apple, appearing on the human body, symbolized the woman's breasts and the man's genitals. Members of the sect fled from persecution in Russia into Romania, where they established several communities.

Smoke-farthings, smoke silver. An old church rate, the contribution of each house or hearth; also another name for PENTECOSTALS, the WHITSUNTIDE offering to the parish priest. Also called *smoke-money*, and *smoke-penny*, it appears in records as a contribution to the parochial purse as well as to the priest.

Society. Society of the Catholic Apostolate. Founded in 1835 by St Vincent PALLOTTI, it was a group of clergy and lay people working for social justice and the conversion of the world. Not all people were suited for the life of monasteries, hermitages or austerities, but could labour for the people. The society organized schools and classes for young workers of all branches.

Society of Friends. *See* QUAKERS.

Society of Jesus. *See* JESUIT.

Society of St John the Evangelist. *See* COWLEY FATHERS.

Society for Promoting Christian Knowledge. Known colloquially as the SPCK, the society was founded in 1698 by the Rev. Dr Thomas Bray, with four laymen. It is the oldest missionary society within the CHURCH OF ENGLAND and the chief agent for circulating the Church's official literature.

Society for the Propagation of the Gospel in Foreign Parts. A missionary society, known as the SPG, founded in 1701 to send ANGLICAN clergymen to British colonies in North America to convert the Red Indians. Its work later spread worldwide. In 1965 it amalgamated with the UMCA to form the United Society for the Propagation of the Gospel.

Socinianism. A form of Unitarianism (*see* UNITARIANS) which, on the one hand, does not altogether deny the supernatural character of Christ, but, on the other, goes farther than Arianism (*see* ARIANS) which, while upholding His divinity denies that He is coequal with the Father. So called from the Italian theologians Laelius Socinus (1525–62) and his nephew Faustus Socinus (1539–1604) who developed these tenets. Socinus is the latinized form of *Sozzini*.

Socrates and Stephen, SS (no date, f.d. 17 September). Said to have been early British martyrs under the Diocletian persecution, but the place of martyrdom may have been Bithynia. It is possible that a scribe changed the name to Britannia. Nothing is known of their lives.

Sodom and Gomorrah. Figuratively, any town or towns regarded as exceptional centres of vice and immorality. An allusion to the cities which God destroyed (*see Gen.* xviii, xix).

Solemn. The Solemn League and Covenant. An agreement between the English Parliament and the Scots in 1643 to strengthen their position in the struggle against Charles I. Presbyterianism was to be established in England and Ireland and the Scots undertook to provide an army in return for payment. Charles II swore to abide by the Covenant when he was crowned at Scone in 1651, but after the Restoration it became a dead letter.

See COVENANTERS.

Son. Son of God. Christ; one of the regenerate.

As many as are led by the Spirit of God, they are the sons of God.

Rom. viii, 14

Son of Man. In the GOSPELS, a title of Christ.

Song. The Songs of Degrees. Another name for the GRADUAL PSALMS.

Songs of Praise. A protestant interdenominational book of hymns of a liberal point of view, first published in 1925.

The Song of Songs. The *Song of Solomon* in the OLD TESTAMENT, also known as *Canticles*.

The Song of the Three Holy Children. An APOCRYPHAL book in the SEPTUAGINT and the VULGATE included as part of the *Book of Daniel*. It contains the prayer of Azarias and a narrative of the three Hebrews in the fiery furnace ending with the thanksgiving for their deliverance. The canticle known as the *Benedicite* is taken from this.

Sophia, Santa. The great metropolitan cathedral of the ORTHODOX CHURCH at Istanbul. It was built by Justinian (532–7), but since the capture of the city by the Turks (1453) has been used as a mosque and is now a museum. It was not dedicated to a saint named Sophia, but to the 'Logos', or Second Person of the TRINITY, called *Hagia Sophia* (Sacred Wisdom).

Sorrow. The Seven Sorrows of the Virgin. *See* MARY.

The Five Sorrowful Mysteries, the second chaplet of the ROSARY, are: the Agony in Gethsemane, the Scourging, the Crowning with Thorns, the Carrying of the Cross, the Crucifixion.

Soterology. The branch of theology concerning the doctrine of salvation through Christ's mission in the world.

Soul. The idea of the soul as the immaterial and immortal part of man surviving after death as a ghost or spirit was an ancient and widespread belief. The ancient Egyptians represented it as a bird with a human head. With Aristotle the soul is essentially the vital principle and the Neoplatonists held that it was located in the whole body and in every part. It has also been located in the blood, heart, brain, bowels, liver, kidneys, etc.

Muslims say that the souls of the faithful assume the forms of snow-white birds, and nestle under the throne of Allah until the resurrection.

All Souls' Day. 2 November, the day following ALL HALLOWS' Day, set apart by the ROMAN

CATHOLIC CHURCH for a solemn service for the repose of the departed. In England it was formerly observed by ringing the soul bell (*see* PASSING BELL *under* BELL), by making and distributing SOUL CAKES, blessing beans, etc.

Soul Cakes. Sweet cakes formerly distributed at the church door on ALL SOULS' DAY to the poor who went *a-souling*, i.e. begging for soul cakes. The words used were:

Soul, soul, for soul-cake,
Pray you, good mistress, a soul cake.

Soul-papers. Papers requesting prayers for the souls of the departed named thereon which were given away with SOUL CAKES.

South Bank religion. A journalistic label for the religious activities in the diocese of Southwark associated with Dr Arthur Mervyn Stockwood, Bishop of Southwark (1959–80), Dr John Robinson, Suffragan Bishop of Woolwich (1959–1969), author of *Honest to God* (1963), and some of their diocesan clergy. Characterized by outspokenness on moral and political issues often from a socialist angle, and energetic attempts to bring the Church into closer relation to contemporary society and its problems, South Bank religion is not without its critics and the label is often applied disparagingly by opponents. Dr Stockwood was appointed under Mr Macmillan's Tory government in 1958 and the appellation *South Bank* derives from the fact that the Southwark diocese borders on the south bank of the Thames.

That is rather the new idea inside the Church. I should definitely say you were a South Banker.

Southcottians. The followers of Joanna Southcott (1750–1814), one-time domestic servant at Exeter. Starting as a METHODIST, she became a prophetess and declared herself to be the 'woman clothed with the sun, and the moon under her feet, and upon her head a crown of twelve stars' (*Rev.* xii, 1). At the age of 64 she announced that she was to be delivered of a son, the Shiloh of *Gen.* xlix, 10:

The sceptre shall not depart from Judah, nor a lawgiver from between his feet, until Shiloh come; and unto him shall the gathering of the people be.

19 October 1814 was the date fixed for the birth, which did not take place, but the prophetess died in a trance soon afterwards and was buried in the churchyard of St John's Wood Chapel. She left a locked wooden box usually known as **Joanna Southcott's Box** which was not to be opened until a time of national crisis, and then only in the presence of all the bishops in England. Attempts were made to persuade the episcopate to open it during the Crimean War and again in World War I. It was opened in 1927 in the presence of one reluctant prelate, and found to contain a few oddments and unimportant papers, and among them a lottery ticket. It is claimed by some that the box opened was not the authentic one. *Cp.* NUNAWADING MESSIAH.

Southwell, St Robert (1561–95, f.d. 25 October). Born at Horsham-St-Faith in Norfolk of the recusant family of Sir Robert Southwell, he was educated at DOUAI and Paris by the JESUITS. He applied to join the Society at seventeen but was deemed too young; he then walked to ROME and joined there in 1578. He was ordained priest and returned to England to carry out a mission. He was arrested in 1592 and imprisoned and tortured in the Tower and Newgate. He was then tried and condemned as a priest, and was hanged, drawn and quartered. He was noted as a poet and for his acute intellect. He was canonized in 1970 as one of the FORTY MARTYRS OF ENGLAND AND WALES.

Southworth, St John (1592–1654, f.d. 25 October). Born into the recusant family at Samlesbury Hall in Lancashire, he was educated at the ENGLISH COLLEGE at DOUAI and was ordained priest in 1618. Returning to England, he carried out a mission in London and Lancashire; was arrested, imprisoned at Lancaster and condemned to death as a priest. With others, he was released at the request of Queen Henrietta Maria, but was exiled. He returned to England later and worked among recusant poor and plague victims. He was again arrested and condemned to be hanged, drawn and quartered. The Spanish ambassador bought his body, had it stitched together and embalmed; it is now in Westminster Cathedral. He was canonized in 1970 as one of the FORTY MARTYRS OF ENGLAND AND WALES.

Spanish Inquisition. *See* INQUISITION.

Speaking with Tongues. *See* TONGUE.

Speculum Humanae Salvationis (The Mirror of Human Salvation). A similar book to the BIBLIA PAUPERUM on a somewhat more extensive scale, telling pictorially the BIBLE story from the fall of Lucifer to the Redemption of Man, with explanations of each picture in Latin rhymes. Its illustrations were copied in church sculptures, wall paintings, altar-pieces and stained-glass windows. Copies of the 13th century and earlier are extant and it was one of the earliest of printed books (*c.* 1467).

Spener. *See* PIETISTS.

Spirit. Properly, the breath of life, from Lat. *spiritus* (*spirare*, to breathe, blow):

And the Lord God formed man of the dust of the

ground, and breathed into his nostrils the breath of life; and man became a living soul.

Gen. ii, 7

Hence, life or the life principle, the SOUL. In theology it is also a term for the Third Person of the TRINITY, the Holy Spirit or Holy Ghost. The Gifts of the Spirit are given in I *Corinthians* xii, 4–11. The fruits of the Spirit are: Love, Joy, Peace, resulting from the presence of the Holy Spirit.

Spital Sermons. Sermons originally preached on GOOD FRIDAY and on the following Monday, Tuesday and Wednesday from the Pulpit Cross, Spitalfields, which were attended by the Lord Mayor and Aldermen and the boys of Christ's Hospital. The pulpit was destroyed in the Civil Wars and at the Restoration the Spital Sermons were revived at St Bride's, Fleet Street. From 1797 they were delivered at Christ Church, Newgate Street and reduced to two. This church was destroyed by incendiary bombs in 1941. The one Spital Sermon is now given in the Corporation Church of St Lawrence Jewry. The boys of Christ's Hospital, Horsham, and the girls from Hertford now attend the St MATTHEW's Day service at the Church of the Holy Sepulchre without Newgate, which incorporates the former parish of Christ Church.

Sponsor (Lat. *spondere*, to make a solemn pledge). Someone who accepts responsibility (in the Church a godfather or godmother) at a child's baptism to ensure that he or she is reared in Christian beliefs. *See* GODPARENTS.

Spouse. The spouse of Jesus. St TERESA of Avila (1515–82) was given this title by some of her contemporaries.

All thy good works … shall
Weave a constellation
Of Crowns with which the King thy spouse
Shall build up thy triumphant brows.

CRASHAW: *Hymn to St Theresa* (1652)

Spy Wednesday. A name given in Ireland to the Wednesday before GOOD FRIDAY, when JUDAS bargained to become the spy of the Jewish Sanhedrin (*Matt.* xxvi, 3–5, 14–16).

Stabat Mater (Lat., The Mother was standing). The Latin hymn reciting the SEVEN SORROWS of the Virgin at the CROSS, so called from its opening words, forming part of the service during Passion week in the ROMAN CATHOLIC CHURCH. It is of unknown authorship and in addition to its traditional plainsong there are settings by Palestrina, Pergolesi, Haydn, Rossini, and others.

Stability. A vow taken by monks of the RULE of St

BENEDICTINE to remain in the same monastery for life.

Staff. *See* CROSIER.

Stag. A male deer or hart.
The Stag in Christian art. The attribute of St JULIAN Hospitaller, St Felix of Valois, and St AIDAN. When it has a crucifix between its horns it alludes to the legend of St HUBERT. When luminous it belongs to St Eustachius. The hart, or stag, symbolizes piety and religious aspiration (*Ps.* xlii); the soul thirsting after God; it also represents solitude and purity of life. As traditionally antagonistic to the SERPENT, the stag portrays Christ, or the Christian, fighting against evil.

Stalls. Fixed seats on each side of the choir of cathedrals or churches, used by the clergy or members of the choir.

Standing Fishes Bible, The. *See* BIBLE, SOME SPECIALLY NAMED EDITIONS.

Stanislaus of Cracow, St (1030–79, f.d. 11 April, formerly 7 May). Stanislaus Szczepanowsky was born into a noble family near Cracow and educated at Gnesen and Paris. He gave all his wealth to the Church and was ordained priest, later being consecrated bishop of Cracow. He was a reformer who came into conflict with the cruel and licentious King of Poland, Boleslaus II, and excommunicated him. Boleslaus then murdered Stanislaus while he was celebrating MASS. The pope laid Poland under an INTERDICT, and the king fled and died in exile in Hungary. In art the saint is represented as a bishop being hacked to pieces at the altar. He is patron of Poland, and is also revered in Lithuania, the Ukraine and Byelorussia.
Stanislaus Kostka, St. *See under* KOSTKA.

Star. In ecclesiastical art a number of SAINTS are depicted with a star; thus, St BRUNO bears one on his breast, St DOMINIC, St HUMBERT, St Peter of Alcantara, one over the head, or on the forehead, etc.
In Christianity the star represents divine guidance and favour; the birth of Christ. The Virgin Mary, as Queen of Heaven, wears a crown of stars. The twelve stars are the Twelve Tribes of Israel and the Apostles.

Staretz. Etymologically 'old man', but as used in the Russian ORTHODOX CHURCH the term carries a nuance of respect. It is usually applied to a monk who is not a priest but who is a spiritual leader and counsellor through his reputation for holiness; he can be attached to a monastery as a teacher of novices, or may have no settled abode, or be a hermit. It was said by Ivan

Kiryevsky, a follower of Macarius: 'More important than any book and all meditation is to find an orthodox staretz who can act as your guide.'

Station Days. Formerly days on which the Pope celebrated MASS at one of the Station Churches in ROME, Pope Gregory I having allocated certain churches for the Station Days.

Stations of the Cross, The. Known as the *via Calvaria* or *via Crucis*. Each station represents, by fresco, picture, or otherwise, some incident in the passage of Christ from the judgement hall to CALVARY, and at each one prayers are offered up in memory of the event represented. They are as follows:

(1) The condemnation to death.
(2) Christ is made to bear His CROSS.
(3) His first fall under the cross.
(4) The meeting with the Virgin.
(5) Simon the Cyrenean helps to carry the cross.
(6) Veronica wipes the sacred face.
(7) The second fall.
(8) Christ speaks to the daughters of Jerusalem.
(9) The third fall.
(10) Christ is stripped of His garments.
(11) The nailing to the cross.
(12) The giving up of the Spirit.
(13) Christ is taken down from the cross.
(14) The deposition in the sepulchre.

Steeple house. An old PURITAN epithet for a church.

Stephen. Stephen, St. d. *c.* 35, f.d. 26 December). The first Christian martyr—the 'protomartyr'. He was accused of blasphemy and stoned to death (*see Acts* vi–viii). The name means 'wreath' or 'crown' (Gr. *stephanos*).
The Crown of St Stephen. The crown of Hungary, this St Stephen being the first King of Hungary (975, 998–1038). He became a Christian in 985 and set out to convert his country. He was canonized in 1083 and his day is 16 August. The existing crown is probably of 13th-century origin. It was removed to the USA in 1944.
St Stephen's loaves. Stones.
Fed with St Stephen's bread. Stoned.
Stephen I, St (d. 257, f.d. 2 August (West), 7 September (East)). Of Roman birth, of the gens Julia, he succeeded Lucius I as bishop of Rome. He was involved in disputes with the NOVATIAN-ISTS in Spain and with St CYPRIAN over the question of baptism administered by heretics; he upheld the Roman tradition against the African Councils. He was said to have been martyred by being beheaded while celebrating the EUCHARIST, but the tradition is unreliable and his cult has been confined to local calendars since the revision of 1969.

Stephen Harding, St. *See* HARDING.
Stephen of Hungary, St (*c.* 935–1038, f.d. 16 August). Son of Geza, Duke of the Magyars, he succeeded his father in 997, married Gisela, sister of St HENRY II, and received the crown from Pope Silvester II, becoming the first king of Hungary. He worked to unify the kingdom and establish Christianity; he organized dioceses and founded abbeys and was regarded as a just ruler, kind and merciful. He experienced many misfortunes and difficulties before he died at Buda. His relics were enshrined there and miracles were reported at his tomb. He is regarded as a national saint and hero of Hungary.
Stephen of Muret, St (*c.* 1047–1124, f.d. 8 February). Born at Thiers in the Auvergne, of noble family, he accompanied his father on a pilgrimage to the tomb of St Nicholas of Bari. He fell ill and remained there, and was educated by Archbishop Milo. Returning to France, he renounced his inheritance and became a hermit at Muret, living in extreme austerity. Disciples joined him and he founded the GRANDMONTINES following the RULE of St BENEDICT he said its members would find only 'poverty and the cross'. The order did not spread widely but had foundations in England and France. It was suppressed at the French Revolution.

Sternold and Hopkins. The old metrical version of the Psalms that used to be bound up with the BOOK OF COMMON PRAYER and sung in churches. They were mainly the work of Thomas Sternhold (d. 1549) and John Hopkins (d. 1570). The completed version appeared in 1562.

> Mistaken choirs refuse the solemn strain
> Of ancient Sternhold.
> CRABBE: *The Borough*, III, 1. 130

Sticharion. In the Eastern ORTHODOX CHURCH, a liturgical tunic similar to the ALB of Western usage.

Stigmata. Marks developed on the body of certain persons, which correspond to some or all of the wounds received by our Saviour in His trial and crucifixion. It is a well-known psychological phenomenon and has been demonstrated in many modern instances. From Gr. *stigma*, the brand with which slaves and criminals in ancient Greece and Rome were marked; hence our verb *stigmatize*, to mark as with a brand of disgrace.

Among those who are said to have been marked with the stigmata are: (1) *Men.* St PAUL, who said 'I bear in my body the marks of the Lord Jesus' (*Gal.* vi, 17); Angelo del Paz (all the marks); Benedict of Reggio (the CROWN OF THORNS), 1602; Carlo di Saeta (the lance-wound); FRANCIS OF ASSISI (all the marks), 15 September 1224; and Nicholas of Ravenna. Francesco Forgione (1887–1968), who became a Capuchin friar in 1902 taking the name of brother Pio, is said to have received stigmata on his hands in 1902. (2) *Women*. Bianca de Gazeran; Catherine of Siena; Catharine di Raconisco (the CROWN OF THORNS), 1538; Cecilia di Nobili of Nocera, 1655; Clara di Pugny (mark of the spear), 1514; 'Estatica' of Caldaro (all the marks), 1842; Gabriella da Piezolo of Aquila (the spear-mark), 1472; Hieronyma Carvaglio (the spear-mark, which bled every Friday); Joanna Maria of the Cross; Maria Razzi of Chio (marks of the thorny crown); Maria Villani (ditto); Mary Magdalen di Pazzi; Mechtildis von Stanz; Ursula of Valencia; Veronica Giuliani (all the marks), 1694; Vincenza Ferreri of Valencia; Anna Emmerich of Dülmen, Westphalia (d. 1824); Maria von Mörl (in 1839); Louise Lateau (1868), and Anne Girling, the foundress of the English SHAKERS. Theresa Neumann, of Kounersreuth, Germany (1898–1962), received her first stigmata on the tops of her hands and feet, on GOOD FRIDAY, 1926. In subsequent years more marks appeared, on her side, shoulders, and brow. Stigmata as studied in her case, never heal and never suppurate.

Stir Up Sunday. The last SUNDAY after TRINITY. So called from the first two words of the collect: 'Stir up, we beseech thee, O Lord, the wills of thy faithful people...'. It was an old custom to stir the CHRISTMAS plum pudding on this day, hence the old schoolboy rhyme, beginning, 'Stir up, we beseech thee, the pudding in the pot.'

Stockholm Conference. *See* WORLD COUNCIL OF CHURCHES.

Stole (Lat. *stola*). An ecclesiastical vestment, also called the Orarium. Deacons wear the stole over the left shoulder like a sash. Priests normally wear it round the neck, both ends hanging loose in front. With Eucharistic vestments the ends are crossed over the chest.

Stone, St John (d. 1539, f.d. 25 October). Little is known of his life before he was ordained priest in 1538 and was a Doctor of Theology at Canterbury. He was an AUGUSTINIAN FRIAR and when others of the order took the Oath of Supremacy of the King, Stone refused. He was condemned to death by Thomas Cromwell, and was hanged, drawn and quartered at Canterbury. He was canonized in 1970 as one of the FORTY MARTYRS OF ENGLAND AND WALES.

Stool. Stool of Repentance. The cutty stool, a low stool placed in front of the pulpit in Scottish churches, on which persons who had incurred ecclesiastical censure were placed during divine service. When the service was over the penitent had to stand on the stool and receive the minister's rebuke.

Stoup. A vessel or font in churches, containing holy water.

Strain. To strain at a gnat and swallow a camel. To make much fuss about little peccadilloes, but commit offences of real magnitude. The proverb comes from *Matt.* xxiii, 24, which in Tyndale's, Coverdale's, and other early versions of the BIBLE reads *strain out*, i.e. to filter out a gnat before drinking the wine. The REVISED VERSION also adopts this form but the AUTHORIZED VERSION's rendering is *which strain at a gnat*, which was not a mistake but established usage at the time. (*See* BIBLE, THE ENGLISH.) Greene in his *Mamillia* (1583) speaks of 'straining at a gnat and letting pass an elephant'.

Student Christian Movement (SCM). Founded at a conference in Sweden in 1895, the SCM became a worldwide union of students, its aim being to win educated youth to Christianity. Its world headquarters are now at Geneva.

Sturm (or **Sturmius**), **St** (d. 779, f.d. 17 December). Born into a Bavarian Christian family, he was ordained priest and carried out a mission agmong the Saxons. He was a disciple of St BONIFACE, who appointed him as the founder of a monastery at a suitable site: he chose Fulda where he was made abbot after having journeyed to MONTE CASSINO to study the RULE of St BENEDICT. Sturm was the first German to become a Benedictine. He was greatly revered and loved by his monks, and is considered one of the great apostles to the Germans, second only to St Boniface himself.

Stylites, or **Pillar Saints.** A class of ascetics found especially in Syria, Mesopotamia, Egypt and Greece between the 5th and 10th centuries. They took up their abode on the tops of pillars, which were sometimes equipped with a small hut, from which they never descended. They take their name from St Simeon Stylites of Syria (390–459) who spent some 30 years on a pillar which was gradually increased to the height of 40 cubits. St Daniel, his most famous disciple, spent 33 years on a pillar near Constantinople. St Simeon's pillar stood on a hill on the borders of Syria and Cilicia. His fame spread beyond Syria and he was visited by large numbers of people, many of them, including visiting Arabs, being converted. It was said that for 40 years he went without food for the whole of LENT. He was famed for his teachings and miracles. His feast day is 5 January (West), and 1 September (East).

Sublapsarian, or **Infralapsarian.** A Calvinist who maintains that God devised His scheme of redemption after he had permitted the 'lapse' or fall of Adam, when He elected some to salvation and left others to run their course. The *supra*lapsarian maintains that all this was ordained by God from the foundation of the world, and therefore before the 'lapse' or fall of Adam.

Submersion. *See* BAPTISM.

Subsidiarity. A term coined by the ROMAN CATHOLIC CHURCH in the 1890s and later used by Pope Pius XI in his ENCYCLICAL of 1931, defined as 'the principle by which those in authority recognize the rights of the members of a society; and those in higher authority respect the rights of those in lower authority'.

Suffering. The Meeting for Sufferings. The standing representative committee of the Yearly Meeting of the Society of Friends, so called because originally its chief function was to relieve the sufferings imposed upon QUAKERS by distraint of TITHES and other petty persecutions.

Suffragan. An auxiliary BISHOP; one who has not a see of his own but is appointed to assist a bishop in a portion of his SEE. In relation to a METROPOLITAN or archbishop all bishops are suffragans; and they were so called because they could be summoned to a synod to give their suffrage.

Sulpicians. A ROMAN CATHOLIC order of regular priests, founded by the Abbé Olier in 1645, taking its name from its headquarters at the seminary of St SULPICE in Paris.

Sulpicius, St (d. 647, f.d. 17 January). Later called Pius, he was born into a wealthy family of Bourges, but devoted himself to the poor and good works. He was appointed bishop of Bourges and was greatly venerated and loved by his people, defending them from the tyranny of King Dagobert and his officials. The seminary of St Sulpice at Paris takes its name from him.

Sun. In Christianity the sun symbolizes God the Father, ruler and sustainer of the universe, radiating light and love. Christ is 'the Sun of Righteousness' (*Matt.* iv, 2), the LOGOS, the divine essence. The sun and moon depicted at the crucifixion portray the two natures of Christ and the powers of Nature paying homage. The sun is the abode of the Archangel MICHAEL, and the moon that of GABRIEL. In art St THOMAS AQUINAS is depicted with the sun on his breast.

Sunday (O.E. *sunnen daeg*). For centuries the first day of the week, anciently dedicated to the sun. In 1971 it became the seventh when Britain adopted the decision of the International Standardization organization to call Monday the first day.

For Christians Sunday took the place of the Jewish SABBATH; it was observed as commemorating the resurrection of Christ. In early times it was called 'the Lord's Day' (*Rev.* i, 10), the day on which Christians met 'to break bread' (*Acts* xx, 7). It became a day of rest in the time of CONSTANTINE, and people were forbidden to work. In the Middle Ages attendance at the MASS became compulsory. After the REFORMATION, PROTESTANTS imposed a strict observance of the Sabbath and in the 18th century EVANGELICAL movements ensured the closure of all places of amusement and trade. This has been relaxed in modern times.

Sunday Letters. *See* DOMINICAL LETTERS.

Sunday School. Nowadays, classes for children organized by church and chapel for a fairly short time on Sundays for religious instruction. They were first established in the 18th century to teach working class children their letters in order that they might learn to read the BIBLE, to improve their behaviour through moral instruction and to keep them off the streets all day. The movement gained considerable impetus when Robert Raikes founded his school in Gloucester in 1780 and William Fox set up the Sunday School Society in 1785. Sunday Schools became particularly strong in Wales.

Sunniva (or **Sunnifa**), **St** (10th cent., f.d. 8 July). A legendary Irish princess who, with companions, travelled to Norway via Scotland, in search of solitude and to live holy lives. They landed on Selje Island and settled in caves. One legend says they were killed by people from the mainland; another says that great rocks crashed down to block the entrances of the caves, and that later, when the caves were discovered, the body of Sunniva was found incorrupt. The legend bears similarity to that of St URSULA.

Supererogation, Works of. A theological expression for good works which are not enjoined or of obligation and therefore 'better' (Lat. *super*, over, above; *erogare*, to pay out). The phrase is commonly applied to acts performed beyond the bounds of duty.

Superior. One at the head of a religious community, or of high ecclesiastical rank.

Supremacy, Act of. An act of the English Parliament in 1534 which proclaimed the King, Henry VIII and his successors to the throne, as supreme head of the CHURCH OF ENGLAND. The act was repealed by Queen Mary but restored by Queen Elizabeth I in 1559.

Surplice. Over the *pelisse* or fur robe (Lat. *super-pellicium*, from *pellis*, skin). The white linen vestment worn by CLERGY, acolytes, choristers, etc., so fashioned for its ease of wearing over fur dress worn in northern Europe in mediaeval times. The shorter *cotta* is a development from this.

Surplice fees. The fees for marriage and burials which are the right of the incumbent of a BENEFICE.

> With tithes his barns replete he sees,
> And chuckles o'er his surplice fees
> T. WARTON: *The Progress of Discontent*, 89 (1750)

Surrogate. A substitute, in the church a clergyman or person acting as a deputy for a bishop or chancellor.

Susanna, St (3rd and 4th cent., f.d. 11 August). Incorrectly associated with St Tiburtius whose feast is on the same day, Susanna was probably a Roman martyred with three others under Diocletian. A church was dedicated to her in ROME. Her cult has been confined to this basilica since 1969.

Suso, Heinrich (*c.* 1300–66). Known as Suso of Constance, he was born at Überlingen on the shores of the Lake. His father was a von Berg, but Suso took his mother's name. He entered the monastery at Constance and was noted for his asceticism. Coming under the influence of Meister ECKHART, he became a persuasive preacher and was famed for his writings on mysticism, which he approached from both a theological and practical aspect.

Swaddlers. An early nickname for Wesleyans, and applied later by Roman Catholics to DISSENTERS and PROTESTANTS generally. Southey (*Life of Wesley*, ii) explains its origin as follows:

> It happened that Cennick, preaching on Christmas Day, took for his text these words from St Luke's Gospel: 'And this shall be a sign unto you; ye shall find the babe wrapped in swaddling clothes lying in a manger.' A Catholic who was present, and to whom the language of scripture was a novelty, thought this so ridiculous that he called the preacher a swaddler in derision, and this unmeaning word became a nickname for 'Protestant', and had all the effect of the most opprobrious appellation.

Swedenborg, Emanuel (1688–1772). Distinguished Swedish scientist and mystic, in middle life came to hold himself appointed to reveal the Lord's teachings to mankind. He taught that Christ is the one God and that the Divine Trinity was present in him. The New Jerusalem Church or New Church was set up in England in 1787 to propagate his teachings, which differ considerably from those of accepted Christianity. There are branches of the New Church in the USA, Australia, New Zealand, and in Europe. Swedenborg wrote all his works in Latin and he claimed to have witnessed the Last Judgement.

Swithbert (or Suidbert), St (*c.* 647–713, f.d. 1 March). A BENEDICTINE monk of Northumbria who, with St WILLIBRORD and companions, left England on a mission to Friesland. He returned to England to be consecrated bishop at Ripon but went back to Westphalia until driven out by the Saxon invaders. He retired to the island of Kaiserwerth in the Rhine and there founded a Benedictine monastery. He died on the island shortly afterwards, and his relics are still venerated there.

Swithin, St. If it rains on St Swithin's Day (15 July), **there will be rain for forty days.**

> St Swithin's day, gif ye do rain, for forty days it will remain;
> St Swithin's day an ye be fair, for forty days 'twill rain nae mair.

The legend is that St Swithin (or Swithun), Bishop of Winchester and adviser of Egbert of Wessex, who died in 862, desired to be buried in the churchyard of the minster, that the 'sweet rain of heaven might fall upon his grave'. At CANONIZATION, the monks thought to honour the SAINT by removing his body into the cathedral choir and fixed 15 July 971 for the ceremony, but it rained day after day for 40 days, thereby, according to some, delaying the proceedings. His shrine was destroyed during the REFORMATION and a new one was dedicated in 1962. Those who hold to this superstition ignore the fact that it is based upon the dating of the JULIAN Calendar and therefore could not hold for 40 days from the current 15 July which is based on the GREGORIAN YEAR.

The St Swithin of France is St Gervais (*see also* St MÉDARD). The rainy saint in Flanders is St Godelieve; in Germany, the SEVEN SLEEPERS have this attribute.

Sword. A symbol of martyrdom and of Christ's PASSION. The flaming sword at each gate or corner divides man from PARADISE. The sword is an emblem of the Archangel Michael and SS ADRIAN, AGNES, ALBAN, BARBARA, EUPHEMIA, JUSTINIA, MARTIN, PAUL, PETER, GEORGE of Cappadocia and JAMES THE GREAT.

The Sword of the Spirit. The Word of God (*Eph.* vi, 17). Also the name of a Roman Catholic social movement founded in 1940.

Your tongue is a double-edged sword.
Whatever you say wounds; your argument cuts
both ways. The allusion is to the double-edged
sword out of the mouth of the Son of Man—one
edge to condemn, and the other to save (*Rev.* i,
16).

Sylvestrines. A ROMAN CATHOLIC ORDER operating
under a monastic RULE of St BENEDICT. It was
founded in Italy by St Sylvester de' Gozzolini in
1231.

Synapte. A prayer in the form of a LITANY used in
the Eastern ORTHODOX CHURCHES in the LITURGY
and other services.

Synaxarion. In the Eastern ORTHODOX CHURCH, a
short history of a feast or saint read at the
ORTHROS. The books containing these accounts
are the Greater and the Lesser Synaxarions.

Synaxis. In the Eastern ORTHODOX CHURCH, a
term for a congregation in public worship, formerly used for services other than the
EUCHARIST but now including it.

Syndesmos (Gr., uniting bond). A world fellowship for ORTHODOX youth, founded in 1953,
involving youth movements and theological
students in local Eastern Orthodox Churches,
with Oriental Orthodox groups as associate
members. As the only worldwide Orthodox
association, Syndesmos covers twenty-three
countries in Europe, the Middle East, Asia,
Africa and North and Latin America. It is also
involved in the youth branch of the WORLD
COUNCIL OF CHURCHES.

Synod (Gr. *synodos*, a council). A consultative
ecclesiastical council of bishops, presided over
by an Archbishop or, if of priests, by a bishop.
In the PRESBYTERIAN CHURCH a synod acts as an
administrative body intermediate between the
General Assembly and presbyteries.

Synoptic Gospels. Those of MATTHEW, MARK, and
LUKE; so called because, taken together and
apart from that of JOHN, they form a *synopsis*
(Gr., a seeing together), i.e. a general and har-
monized account of the life of Christ.
The Synoptic Problem. The problems of the
origin and relationship of the three SYNOPTIC
GOSPELS arising from large sections of material,
and often phrasing, being common to them.
There is general agreement that MARK is the
earliest of the GOSPELS, and that it provides
much of the material for MATTHEW and LUKE.
The latter two contain material not found in
Mark (*see* 'Q'). There are varying theories
among Biblical scholars to account for this par-
allelism, etc.

Synteresis. In SCHOLASTICISM, a name given to the
knowledge of the first principles of moral
action.

Synthesist Movements. A complex mixture of
traditional tribal beliefs combined with the rites
of Christianity. Such movements occur chiefly
in Central and Southern America, the
Caribbean and Africa.

Syrian Orthodox. *See* MONOPHYSITES; JACOBITES.

T

Tabernacle (Lat. *tabernaculum*, a tent). The portable shrine instituted by MOSES during the wanderings of the Jews in the wilderness. It was divided by a veil or hanging, behind which, in the 'HOLY OF HOLIES', was the Ark. The outer division was called the Holy Place. When set up in camp the whole was surrounded by an enclosure. *See Exod.* xxv–xxxi; xxxiii, 7–10; xxxv–xl.

In Roman Catholic churches, the tabernacle is the oranmental receptacle on the High Altar, in which the vessels containing the Blessed Sacrament are reserved. The name derives from the application of the word *tabernaculum* in church ornamentation to a variety of canopied forms.

Tin Tabernacles. The name given to the corrugated iron Nonconformist chapels and other churches which were erected in the 19th and early 20th centuries to meet the needs of developing or scattered Christian communities.

Table. Archbishop Parker's Table. The table of prohibited degrees within which marriage was forbidden, published in 1563, and to be found as the *Table of Kindred and Affinity* in the BOOK OF COMMON PRAYER. Matthew Parker was Archbishop of Canterbury from 1559 to 1575 (*See* NAG'S HEAD CONSECRATION; VESTIARIAN CONTROVERSY.)

The Lord's Table. The communion table or ALTAR.

Taborites. An extreme group of HUSSITES founded by Zizka in the 15th century, taking their name from Mount Tabor near Prague; they propagated their doctrines by force but later divided, one faction joining the CATHOLICS, the other dying out.

Taizé Community. Founded in 1940 by Brother Roger, in France, during the war. At first Brother Roger gave shelter to refugees, working alone. In 1949 he was joined by others who took monastic vows in a community which united CATHOLICS, ANGLICANS and various PROTESTANTS in a 'parable of communion'. The community maintains contacts with churches, both Western and Eastern; it organizes large meetings of young people and provides retreats for priests and leaders.

Tantivy, or **Tantivy Man.** A name given Tory High churchmen in the time of James II. They were caricatured as being mounted on the CHURCH OF ENGLAND riding 'tantivy' to ROME. *To ride tantivy* is a hunting term meaning to ride at full gallop.

Tantony pig. The smallest pig of a litter, which, according to the old proverb, will follow its owner anywhere. So called in honour of St ANTHONY, who was the patron SAINT of swineherds, and is frequently represented with a little pig at his side.

Tantony is also applied to a small church bell—or to any hand bell—for there is usually a bell round the neck of St Anthony's pig or attached to the TAU CROSS (*see under* CROSS) he carries.

Tarasios (or **Tarasius), St** (d. 806, f.d. 25 February). Of patrician family at Constantinople, he was at the court of Empress Irene II. Although not ordained, he was appointed Patriarch and only accepted on condition that the iconoclastic persecution should cease. He was ordained in 784 when the second Council of NICAEA was held and approved by Pope Hadrian I. Tarasios is highly venerated in the ORTHODOX CHURCH.

Targums (Aramaic, interpretations). The name given to the various Aramaic (Chaldean) interpretations and translations of the OLD TESTAMENT, made in Babylon and Palestine when Hebrew was ceasing to be the everyday speech of the Jews. They were transmitted orally and the oldest, that of Oneklos on the PENTATEUCH, is probably of the 2nd century AD.

Tarsicius, St (3rd–4th cent., f.d. 15 August). According to an inscription written by Pope St DAMASUS, Tarsicius was carrying the HOST through the streets to Christians in prison when he was attacked by a pagan mob. He was bludgeoned to death when he refused to surrender it. It is said that he was either an acolyte or a deacon; the incident traditionally occurred on the Appian Way; it was used by Cardinal Wiseman in his novel *Fabiola*.

Tatania, St (d. *c.* 230, f.d. 12 January). Said to have been a deaconess martyred in ROME under Alexander Severus; her history bears similarities to those of SS Martina, Eustasia and Prisca. She is venerated in the Greek ORTHODOX CHURCH.

Tatwin (or Tatuini), St (d. 734, f.d. 30 July). He succeeded St Brithwald as archbishop of Canterbury in 731 while he was a monk of Bredon in Mercia. He received the PALLIUM in 733, and appointed bishops for Selsey and Lindsey. BEDE describes him as a man of learning and devout life. Two of his manuscripts survive: his *Enigmata*, or riddles, and his *Grammar*.

Tau. The letter T in Greek and the Semitic languages. Anciently it was the last letter of the Greek alphabet (as it still is of the Hebrew); and in Middle English literature the phrase *Alpha to Omega* was not infrequently rendered *Alpha to Tau*.
Tau cross. A T-shaped CROSS, especially St ANTHONY'S cross.

Tauler, Johann (*c.* 1300–61). Born at Strasbourg, he became a DOMINICAN monk. Coming under the influence of ECKHART, he became a prominent teacher of mysticism and was one of a sect of 'The Friends of God'. His mission was in preaching rather than in writing, and his sermons became famous. His outlook was practical and he devoted himself to caring for the sick during the Black Death.

Taverner's Bible. *See* BIBLE, THE ENGLISH.

Te Deum, The. So called from the opening words *Te Deum laudamus* (Thee, God, we praise). This Latin hymn was traditionally assigned to SS AMBROSE and AUGUSTINE, and was supposed to have been improvised by St Ambrose while baptizing St Augustine (386). Hence it is sometimes called 'the Ambrosian Hymn' and in some early psalters it is entitled '*Canticum Ambrosii et Augustini*'. It is now generally thought to have been written by Niceta, Bishop of Remesiana (d. *c.* 414). It is used in various offices and at MATTINS.
Te Igitur (Lat.) 'Thee therefore'. In the ROMAN CATHOLIC CHURCH, the first words of the old form of the CANON of the MASS, and consequently the name for the first section of the canon.
Oaths upon the Te Igitur. Oaths sworn on this part of the MISSAL, which were regarded as especially sacred.

Tear. To tear Christ's body. To use imprecations. The common oaths of mediaeval times were by different parts of the Lord's body; hence the preachers used to talk of 'tearing God's body by imprecations'.

Hir others been so grete and so dampnable
That it is grisly for her to heere hem swere;
Our blissed Lordes body thay to-tere.
CHAUCER: *Pardoner's Tale*, 144

Teilo, St (6th cent., f.d. 9 February). Particularly venerated in South Wales and Brittany, he was said to have been born at Penally near Tenby and to have been educated by St Dyfrig. He is also reputed to have been a companion of St DAVID and to have stayed with St SAMSON in Brittany. Teilo died at Llandaff, where he had founded a monastery. There was a legend that three places, Llandaff, Penally and Llandeilo claimed his body and that the body miraculously multiplied in the night so that each could have one.

Teinds. The Scottish term for TITHES. The custom was abolished in 1925.

Teleology (Gr. *telos*, end; *logos*, word). The doctrine of final causes; the end, that all was made to serve a divine purpose.

Temperance, The Apostle of. *See* MATTHEW.

Templars, or Knights Templar. In 1119, nine French knights bound themselves to protect pilgrims on their way to the HOLY PLACES and took monastic vows. They received the name TEMPLARS because they had their headquarters in a building on the site of the old Temple of Solomon at JERUSALEM.
    Their habit was a long white mantle ornamented with a red cross on the left shoulder. Their seal showed two knights riding on one horse, the story being that the first Master was so poor that he had to share a horse with one of his followers. Their banner, called *Le Beauseant* or *Bauceant* (an old French name for a piebald horse), was half black, half white, and charged with a red CROSS.
    Their bravery in the field was unquestionable, as was in due course the wealth and power of the Order which had houses throughout Europe, but the fall of Acre (1291) marked the ultimate failure of their efforts. Jealousy of their power and wealth rather than the internal corruption of their Order resulted in their suppression and extinction in 1312, in France accompanied by particular cruelties.
    In England the Order had its first house (*c.* 1121) near Holborn Bars, London, but it later settled on the site still called the Temple.
    At Paris, the stronghold of the Knights Templar was taken over by the Knights of St John. The old tower later became a prison where, in 1792, the royal family of France was incarcerated prior to execution and the dauphin (Louis XVII) probably died within its walls.

Ten Commandments, The. *See* DECALOGUE.

Tenebrae (Lat., darkness, gloom). In the Western Church the MATTINS and LAUDS of the following day sung on the Wednesday, Thursday, and Friday of HOLY WEEK. The lights of 15 candles are extinguished one by one at the end of each psalm, the last after the *Benedictus*. The MISERERE is then sung in darkness. This ritual goes back to the 8th century and symbolizes dramatically Christ's PASSION and Death.

Terce, Tierce. The third of the CANONICAL HOURS, between sunrise and noon; the Divine Office of that hour in CATHOLIC services, comprising hymns, psalms, readings from the BIBLE and a concluding prayer.

Teresa, St. The name of two Carmelite nuns of remarkable qualities: (1) St Teresa of Avila (1515–82) or St Teresa of Jesus, whose life combined great practical achievement with continual prayer and religious sanctity in which she reached a state of 'spiritual marriage'. She was responsible for the reform of the Carmelite Order and founded 32 convents as well as writing outstanding works on prayer and meditation. She was canonized in 1622 and in 1970 the first woman to be made a DOCTOR OF THE CHURCH. Her day is 15 October. (*See* St JOHN OF THE CROSS *under* JOHN.) (2) St Teresa of Lisieux (1873–97), a Carmelite nun, professed in 1890, who died of tuberculosis, and who is associated with miracles of healing and prophecy. Her autobiography, *L'Histoire d'une âme*, made her famous and she was canonized in 1925. She was associated with JOAN OF ARC as patroness of France in 1947 and in England she is known as 'The Little Flower'. Her feast day is 1 October.

Termagant. The name given by the Crusaders, and in mediaeval romances, to an idol or deity that the Saracens were popularly supposed to worship. He was introduced into the MORALITY PLAYS as a most violent and turbulent person in long, flowing Eastern robes, a dress that led to his acceptance as a woman, whence the name came to be applied to a shrewish, violently abusive virago. The origin of the word is uncertain.

'Twas time to counterfeit, or that hot termagant
Scot [Douglas] had paid me scot and lot too.
SHAKESPEARE: *Henry IV, Pt. 1*, V, iv

Ter-Sanctus. *See* TRISAGION.

Tertiaries. Members of 'a third order', an institution which began with the FRANCISCANS in the 13th century for lay folk who wished to strive for Christian perfection in their day-to-day life in accordance with the spirit and teaching of St FRANCIS. The system spread to other Orders such as the DOMINICANS, AUGUSTINIANS, and CARMELITES. Tertiaries are obedient to a rule and take a solemn promise. There are also Regular Tertiaries who live in communities under vows and are fully 'religious' in the technical sense. The name *Third Order* arises from the Friars and Nuns being classed as the First and Second Orders.

Tertullian (*c.* 196–212). A native of Carthage, he was the first Latin-speaking Christian writer among the FATHERS OF THE CHURCH. He showed MONTANIST sympathies but did not let their doctrines affect his theology seriously. He attacked GNOSTICISM and emphasized the importance of a full understanding of the SCRIPTURES. He is noted as a strong TRINITARIAN, defending the reality of Christ's manhood; and the resurrection of the body, and he held that post-baptismal sin is unforgivable.

Test Acts. A name given to the various Acts of Parliament designed to exclude ROMAN CATHOLICS, Protestant NONCONFORMISTS, and 'disaffected persons' from public offices, etc. They include Acts of Abjuration, Allegiance, and Supremacy, the Corporation Act, 1661, the Act of Uniformity, 1662, as well as those specifically named *Test Acts*. Those named 'Test Acts' were: (1) that of 1673 which insisted that all holders of civil and military office must be communicants of the CHURCH OF ENGLAND as well as taking the oaths of Allegiance and Supremacy; (2) that of 1678 which excluded all Roman Catholics, other than the Duke of York, from Parliament; (3) that for Scotland (1681) which made all state and municipal officials affirm their belief in the PROTESTANT faith. These Acts were repealed in 1828.

Tetragrammaton. A word of four letters, especially the Jewish name of the Deity JHVH, which the Jews never pronounced but substituted the word Adonai instead (usually rendered in the BIBLE as *Lord*). Its probable pronunciation was *Yahweh* and from the 16th century was corrupted into JEHOVAH by combining the vowels of Adonai with JHVH.

Tetrateuch. The name given to the first four books of the BIBLE.

Teutonic. Teutonic Cross. A CROSS potent, the badge of the order of TEUTONIC KNIGHTS.
Teutonic Knights. The third great military crusading Order which has its origin in the time of the Third CRUSADE. It developed from the provision of a hospital service by Germans at the siege of Acre (1190) which became the German Hospital of St Mary at JERUSALEM. It was made a Knightly Order in 1198, thenceforward confined to those of noble birth. In 1229

they began the conquest of heathen Prussia and after 1291 their contact with the East ceased. They survived as a powerful and wealthy body until their disastrous defeat by the Poles and Lithuanians at Tannenberg in 1410. The Order lingered on until its suppression in 1809, but was revived in Austria in 1840 but with Habsburg associations.

Thaumaturgus (Gr., a wonder-worker). A miracle-worker; applied to SAINTS and others who are reputed to have performed miracles, and especially Gregory, Bishop of Neo-Caesarea, called Thaumaturgus (*c.* 213–*c.* 270) whose miracles included the moving of a mountain. St BERNARD of Clairvaux (1090–1153) was called 'The Thaumaturgus of the West'.

Theatines. A ROMAN CATHOLIC order of Clerks Regular, founded in 1524 by St CAJETAN of Tiene and Pietro Caraffa, bishop of Theate and later Pope Paul IV. The chief aims of the order were: to combat existing corruption among the clergy and, in their training, to emphasize the study of the BIBLE; to restore and maintain the dignity of worship; to care for the sick; and to provide pastoral care. The order was established at ROME, but, after the city was sacked in 1527, it was moved to Naples. Cajetan later became its Superior and the order was influential in the COUNTER REFORMATION.

Thecla, St (1st cent., f.d. 23 September (West), 24 September (East)). One of the most famous saints of the 1st century, the first woman martyr. All that is known of her is from the *Acts of Paul and Thecla*, pronounced APOCRYPHAL by Pope Gelasius. According to the legend, she was born of a noble family at Iconium and was converted by St PAUL, when she visited him in prison, having bribed the jailer. She worshipped at St Paul's feet and kissed his chains. Thecla broke off her betrothal to a young man and her incensed parents were said to have blamed the saint and had him scourged. Thecla was condemned to be burnt as an example to other maidens. When youths and maidens had piled up the faggots for the fire, Thecla, looking round, saw a vision of Christ. Making the sign of the cross, she jumped into the fire, but it was quenched by an earthquake and a downpour of rain, and Thecla was freed. Other legends say that she was thrown to beasts who would not touch her, but devoured each other; or that she was tied to bulls who broke their cords and rushed off. There are numerous versions of the miraculous deliverance and of miracle-working, and a legend that she dressed as a boy and followed St Paul. Finally, a tradition said that she went to Seleucia as a solitary and died at the age of seventy-two. Her cult was suppressed in 1969.

Theist, Deist, Atheist, Agnostic. A *theist* believes there is a God who made and governs all creation; Christians, Jews, and Muslims are included among *theists*.

A *deist* believes there is a God who created all things, but does not believe in His superintendence and government. He thinks the Creator implanted in all things certain immutable laws, called the *Laws of Nature*, which act *per se*, as a watch acts without the supervision of its maker. He does not believe in the doctrine of the TRINITY, nor in a divine revelation.

The *atheist* disbelieves even the existence of a God. He thinks matter is eternal, and what we call 'creation' is the result of natural laws.

The *agnostic* believes only what is knowable. He rejects revelation and the doctrine of the Trinity as 'past human understanding'. He is neither theist, deist, nor atheist, as all these subscribe to doctrines that are incapable of scientific proof.

Theodicy (Gr. *theos*, God; *dike*, justice). The theological vindication of God's justice and goodness in the face of the existence of evil in the world.

Theodore. Theodore of Canterbury, St (602–90, f.d. 19 September, also 26 March (Canterbury)). An Asiatic Greek from Tarsus in Cilicia, he was educated there and at Athens, and then became a monk at ROME. Pope Vitalian selected him as a suitable candidate for the see of Canterbury. On the journey to England he was accompanied by St AIDAN, the latter becoming the abbot of the monastery of SS PETER and PAUL. Theodore carried out a work of unification, travelling widely, reconciling divergent factions, establishing dioceses and founding schools. Outstanding among the schools was that of Canterbury, which taught its pupils a wide range of subjects which were rarely offered, such as Greek, Latin and Roman Law, music, poetry and interpretation of the SCRIPTURES. Theodore was responsible for holding the first national council at Hereford in 672, and his work was of great importance in English history in its effect on both the Church and scholarship. He has been called the first primate of the English Church. He died at Canterbury and was buried near St AUGUSTINE; his body was translated in 1091 and was found to be incorrupt.

Theodore the Studite, St (759–826, f.d. 11 November). A noted figure in monasticism as a reformer and theologian. Born in Constantinople, he became a monk at the monastery of Studios. After ordination in 787, he entered the monastery of Saccudium where his uncle St Plato was abbot, succeeding him when his uncle resigned in his favour. Theodore was involved in controversy with the Emperor Constantine IV over his marriage, and was exiled but later re-established in the community at Studios. In the

ICONOCLAST dispute, he upheld the veneration of ICONS, and was again exiled and imprisoned. His reforms and influence in monasticism spread through the ORTHODOX CHURCH to Mount ATHOS, and on to Russia, Bulgaria and Romania. He also wrote theological and liturgical works as well as hymns, poems and epigrams.

Theodosius. Theodosius the Cenobiarch, St (423–529, f.d. 11 January). Born in Cappodocia, near Bethlehem, he founded a community which expanded rapidly with several hundred monks of various nationalities. These were divided into separate groups, each having its own church, and the patriarch of Jerusalem appointed Theodosius as head of the COENO-BITICAL communities, which were distinct from the eremitical. He was removed from office for a time on account of his strong opposition to the MONOPHYSITISM of the Emperor Anastasius, who had tried unsuccessfully to bribe him. Theodosius lived to the great age of 105 years. **Theodosius the Great** (c. 346–95). A Roman emperor who was a Christian and who was responsible for establishing Christianity as the official state religion. He called the Council of CONSTANTINOPLE in 381 and condemned ARIAN-ISM and paganism.
Theodosius of Kiev or of the Caves, St (c. 1002–74, f.d. 3 May). Theodosius Pechersky is considered to be the real founder of the LAURA of the caves of Kiev, the *Pecherskaya Lavra*, the cave monastery, immediately following St ANTHONY. He is called the St BENEDICT of Russia, as he gave monasticism its first rules. The son of a judge of Vasilkov and Kursk, he showed early piety and devotion to sacred books. His father died when the boy was only thirteen and his mother, who was a dominating woman, 'a strong woman and merely by the sound of her voice might have been taken for a man', opposed his religious life and practices. When he set out on a pilgrimage, Theodosius was captured and brought back by his mother, and kept in chains until he promised to abandon his journey. He worked for the poor and read the SCRIPTURES until, when his mother was away, he made his escape to Kiev and came to St Anthony's cave, where the saint accepted him and he received the TONSURE. He was reconciled with his mother, who was converted and took to the religious life. Later Theodosius undertook the office of HEGUMENOS and proved a model leader and a man of great compassion and generosity, leading a devout and ascetic life.

Theology. The science of the study of God and the relationship between God and his people and God and Nature. In Christianity there are various branches: natural theology deals with observation and reason; moral theology, with behaviour and ethics; dogmatic, with the formulation of dogma; mystical, with contemplation and union with God; revealed, with that which is known from divine revelation; pastoral, with the care of souls; ascetical, which deals with training and the development of Christian virtues. Theology is thus a group of sciences concerned with the investigation of beliefs and the advancement of understanding.
Theological Virtues. *See* VIRTUES.

Theophany. An appearance or manifestation of God in a visible form.

Théot, Catherine. *See under* CATHERINE.

Theotokos (Gr. *theos*, God; *tokos*, birth—the bearer of God). A term in the Eastern ORTHO-DOX CHURCH for the VIRGIN MARY, the Mother of God, 'she who brings God into the world', 'who confines within herself the unconfinable God'. The Council of Ephesus made a dogma from the word Theotokos to designate the Mother of Jesus, since Mary was not only the Mother of the flesh of Christ, but this flesh was truly the 'flesh of God, in which the Son lived and died to rise again'. However, the term was in use before the Council, appearing on a papyrus at the end of the 3rd century.

Thermarion. In the Eastern ORTHODOX CHURCH, a vessel holding the wine and warm water used for washing the ALTAR at the dedication.

Thief, The Penitent. *See* DYSMAS.

Third Order. *See* TERTIARIES.

Thirty. The Thirty-nine Articles. The *Articles* of Religion in the BOOK OF COMMON PRAYER largely defining the CHURCH OF ENGLAND's position in certain matters of dogma which were in dispute at the time. They were first issued in 1563, based on the Forty-two Articles of 1553, and revised in 1571. Clergy had to subscribe to them, but since 1865 a more general affirmation has been substituted.
Thirty-six-Line Bible. *See* BIBLE, SOME SPE-CIALLY NAMED EDITIONS.
The Thirty Years War. The wars in Germany which began in Bohemia in 1618 and were terminated by the peace of Westphalia in 1648. Traditionally regarded as a struggle initially between German PROTESTANTS and Catholics, which was exploited by foreign powers, it was more essentially part of a contest between Bourbon and Habsburg dynastic interests combined with constitutional struggles inside the Habsburg Empire waged under the cloak of religion. The idea that 'Germany' was universally devastated is largely a myth.

Thomas. St Thomas (f.d. 3 July, formerly 21

December). The Apostle who doubted (*John* xx, 25); hence the phrase, **a doubting Thomas,** applied to a sceptic.

The story told of him in the APOCRYPHAL *Acts of St Thomas* is that he was deputed to go as a missionary to India, and, on refusing, Christ appeared and sold him as a slave to an Indian prince who was visiting JERUSALEM. He was taken to India, where he baptized the prince and many others, and was finally martyred at Mylapore.

Another legend has it that Gundaphorus, an Indian king, gave him a large sum of money to build a palace. St Thomas spent it on the poor, 'thus creating a superb palace in heaven'. On account of this he is the patron SAINT of masons and architects, and his symbol is a builder's square.

Another story is that he once saw a huge beam of timber floating on the sea near the coast, and the king unsuccessfully endeavouring, with men and elephants, to haul it ashore. St Thomas desired leave to use it in building a church, and, his request being granted, he dragged it easily ashore with a piece of packthread. His relics are now said to be at Ortona in the Abruzzi.

Christians of St Thomas. According to tradition, St THOMAS founded the Christian churches of Malabar and then moved on to Mylapore (Madras), thus Christian communities were there to welcome the Portuguese when Vasco da Gama arrived in 1498. They called themselves 'Christians of St Thomas' and may be descendants of Christians converted by NESTORIAN missions, although the claim that they were evangelized by St Thomas is not entirely improbable.

Thomas Aquinas, St (*c.* 1225–74, f.d. 28 January). DOMINICAN scholastic philosopher and theologian, of outstanding authority and intellectual distinction among his contemporaries, and whose teachings have been a major influence on the doctrines of the ROMAN CATHOLIC CHURCH. He was the youngest son of Count Landulf of Aquino (midway between ROME and Naples) and became a Dominican in the face of strong family opposition. He was a pupil of Albertus Magnus and subsequently taught at Paris, ROME, Bologna and Pisa. First nicknamed the dumb ox he became *Doctor Angelicus* and 'the Fifth Doctor of the Church'. Among his many writings his *Summa Theologica* is his classic work. He drew a clear distinction between Faith and Reason and was considerably influenced by the philosophy of Aristotle. He was canonized in 1323.

Thomas of Canterbury (Becket), St (1118–70, f.d. 29 December). Thomas Becket was born in London of wealthy Norman parents and was educated at Merton Abbey and Paris. He entered the service of Theobold, archbishop of Canterbury and was sent abroad to Bolgona and Auxerre to study canon law, then appointed archdeacon of Canterbury. He became a close friend of King Henry II, who made him chancellor of England in 1155, and in 1162 archbishop of Canterbury. Prior to this appointment Thomas had led a life of luxury and extravagance as a brilliant statesman and diplomat. He had even engaged in military matters, leading troops into battle. He now relinquished his chancellorship, adopted an austere regime and gave alms to the poor. He came into conflict with the king over secular interference in ecclesiastical affairs, and the question of the powers of the state and church over clergy convicted of crimes. Becket fled to France and did not return for six years; when he did return the reconciliation was short-lived and, following rash words by the king, Becket was murdered in his cathedral by four knights. His brutal death shocked Christendom; the king did public penance and Becket was proclaimed a martyr, and was canonized. His shrine became one of the most visited, and many miracles were reported there. In art he is depicted in episcopal robes with a mitre and crozier. He kneels before his murderers and may have a sword embedded in his head.

Thomas Garnet, St. *See* GARNET.

Thomas of Hereford, St (1218–82, f.d. 2 or 3 October). Thomas Cantalupe was born at Hambledon in Buckinghamshire into a noble Norman family and was educated at Oxford and Paris. He was ordained priest when, with his father, he attended the Council of Lyons in 1245. He was chancellor of England for a short time until dismissed by King Henry III, when he returned to Oxford as professor of canon law, becoming chancellor of the University. He was appointed bishop of Hereford in 1275 and, with papal sanction, held a number of benefices in plurality, all of which he administered with great interest, efficiency and generosity. He came into conflict with John Peckham, archbishop of Canterbury and was excommunicated by him. Thomas then went to Orvieto, to the papal court, to state his case in person, but died at Montefiascone. Some of his relics were returned to Hereford, which became an important centre of pilgrimage, many miracles being reported there.

Thomas à Kempis (1379–1471). Born at Kempen, near Düsseldorf, as Thomas Hamerken, his mother kept a village school and his father was a peasant. Thomas became a monk at the AUGUSTINIAN convent of Mount St Agnes, where his brother was prior; here Thomas spent most of his life copying MSS. and writing histories, biographies, sermons and letters. He is the reputed author of one of the most famous of mystical works, *On the Imitation of Christ*.

Thomas More, St (1478–1535, f.d. 22 June, with St John FISHER). Son of a judge, More was educated at Oxford, then entered Lincoln's Inn and was called to the bar in 1501. In 1504 he entered Parliament where he became Speaker. Other offices he held were Under-Sheriff of London; envoy to Flanders; Privy Councillor and Master of Requests; High Steward of both Oxford and Cambridge Universities; and Chancellor of the Duchy of Lancaster. He was a brilliant man of letters, *Utopia* being his most noted work, a theologian, humanist and 'a gentleman of great learning' in law, art and divinity. He was also a friend of ERASMUS, Colet, FISHER, Linacre and Grocyn, and a man of great wit. At first a friend of King Henry VIII, More's integrity made it impossible for him to support the King's divorce from Catherine of Aragon and his claim to be supreme head of the Church. This led to an accusation of treason, to imprisonment in the Tower and to his execution on Tower Hill. His body was buried in the Church of St Peter ad Vincula. More, and his friend John Fisher of Rochester, were canonized in 1935.

Thomas of Villanova, St (1488–1555, f.d. 22 September). Born at Villanova, the son of a miller, he was educated at Villanueva de los Infantes and at Alcalá University. There he lectured in philosophy, and then joined the AUGUSTINIAN FRIARS at Salamanca. Following his ordination, he was appointed prior. He also lectured in moral theology at the university. He reluctantly accepted the see of Valencia and was provincial of Castile. He lived a life of great austerity and self-sacrifice, spending much of his time in prayer and experiencing ecstasies. He was also a noted preacher and wrote a number of theological treatises. His work among the people was outstanding, and he devoted much personal time and effort to the poor and sick, to orphans and every rank of the needy, including Moors who had suffered from compulsory conversion to Christianity. He was canonized in 1658, but in the revision of the calendar in 1969 his cult was restricted to particular calendars.

Thomists. Followers of St THOMAS AQUINAS (*c.* 1225–74). They were opponents of the SCOTISTS, or followers of Duns Scotus.

Thorfinn, St (d. 1285, f.d. 8 January). Little is known of his early life but that he was bishop of Hamar and was involved in the Agreement of Tonsberg in 1277 when King Magnus VI undertook to allow clerical privileges and freedom of elections. Thorfinn was exiled when the king repudiated the agreement. The saint then left for ROME to obtain support, but he fell ill and died at the CISTERCIAN abbey of Ter Doest, near Bruges. A poem written by a monk there praised Thorfinn's virtues of charity, goodness, patience and penitence.

Thorlac, St (1133–93, f.d. 23 December). The first saint of Iceland, Thorlac was born into an aristocratic family. He was ordained deacon before he was fifteen, and was a priest at eighteen. He went to Paris and Lincoln, returning to Iceland with ideas of ecclesiastical rule not yet known in his country. He was appointed bishop of Skalholt and instituted reforms, drawing up laws, eliminating simony and the marriage of the clergy. His canonization was local, in 1198, but not officially recognized. Miracles were recorded, and he was the subject of a saga.

Thorn. The Crown of Thorns. That with which Our Saviour was crowned in mockery (*Matt.* xxvii, 29); hence sometimes used of a very special affliction with which one is unjustly burdened. The crown of thorns was used as a parody on the Emperor's crown of roses.

CALVIN (*Admonitio de Reliquiis*) gives a long list of places claiming to possess one or more of the thorns which composed the Saviour's crown. *See* GLASTONBURY.

Glastonbury Thorn. *See* GLASTONBURY.

A thorn in the flesh. A source of constant irritation, annoyance, or affliction; said of objectionable and parasitical acquaintances, obnoxious conditions, etc. There was a sect of the PHARISEES which used to insert thorns in the borders of their gaberdines to prick their legs in walking and make them bleed. The phrase is taken from St PAUL's reference to some physical complaint or misfortune (II *Cor.* xii, 7).

Three Hours Service. A devotional service held on GOOD FRIDAY from noon to 3 p.m., covering the supposed hours of Christ on the cross.

Three Kings' Day. EPIPHANY or Twelfth Day, designed to commemorate the visit of the 'three kings' or Wise Men of the East to the infant Jesus. *See* MAGI.

Thrones, Principalities, and Powers. According to Dionysius the Areopagite, three of the nine orders of ANGELS. These names or their liguistic counterparts occur frequently in Jewish-Christian writings around NEW TESTAMENT times.

> The host of the heavens and all the holy ones above, and the host of God ... all the angels of power, and all the angels of principalities
>
> *Enoch* vi, 10

Thurible. A metal censer used in CATHOLIC services for burning incense. The ACOLYTE who swings the censer is called the **thurifer**.

Tiara. Anciently the turban-like head-dress worn erect by the Persian kings and turned down by lords and priests; now applied to a coronet-like head ornament, especially to the triple crown of the POPE. The latter resembles the old-style bee-hive in shape and is worn on other than liturgical occasions. It typifies the temporal or sovereign power of the Papacy and is composed of gold cloth encircled by three crowns and surmounted by a golden globe and CROSS. It is first mentioned in the early 8th century and was a kind of cap called *camelaucum*. By the 11th century, a coronet had been added to the rim with two pendants or lappets hanging down at the back. The second circlet was added by Boniface VIII (1294–1303), perhaps to symbolize both temporal and spiritual powers, and the third coronet seems to have been added either by Benedict XI (1303–4) or Clement V (1305–14). An early representation of the triple crown is in an effigy of Benedict XII (d. 1342) and its symbolism is variously interpreted. The tiara is very richly ornamented and contains 146 jewels of all colours, 11 brilliants, and 540 pearls.

Tierce. *See* TERCE.

Tikhon of Zadonsk, St (1724–83, f.d. 13 August). Born Timothy Sokolov, near Novgorod, the son of a sacristan, and reared in great poverty, he first laboured for a better-off peasant until a seminary was founded at Novgorod and his mother obtained a place for him. There he also suffered great privation, selling half his bread to buy candles to work by. He studied for fourteen years, becoming proficient in Greek, Latin, the Scriptures and patristic literature. Refusing to marry and become a well-to-do parish priest (in the ORTHODOX CHURCH marriage was a necessity for this position), he received the TONSURE and took the name of Tikhon. A year later he was ordained priest and was appointed rector of a neighbouring monastery. He was consecrated, first suffragan of Novgorod, then bishop of Voronezh. This was a difficult diocese morally and socially, with decadent clergy and a floating civil population of hunters, settlers, political rebels and religious schismatics, 'a half pagan, half barbarian region'. Tikhon made great efforts to right the wrongs, persevering in the face of opposition, until his health broke down. He resigned his see and retired to the monastery of Zadonsk, where he remained until his death, living simply, helping the people and engaged in prayer and in writing. His best-known works are: *Of True Christianity, The Spiritual Treasury; Letters from a Cell* and *Of the Truth of the Gospel*. Some of his letters are included in G. P. Fedotov's *Treasury of Russian Spirituality* (1950).

Timothy, St (d. 93, f.d. 26 January, formerly 24 January; 22 January (East)). Disciple of St Paul, accompanying him on his journeys; he was the son of a Gentile father and a Jewish mother. EUSEBIUS says that he was the first bishop of Ephesus. St PAUL wrote him two epistles which appear in the NEW TESTAMENT. He was said to have been stoned to death for refusing to observe the festival of Dionysos.

Tippet. An ANGLICAN vestment; a black scarf worn over the SURPLICE.

Tithes. One-tenth of the produce of the land given to the Church, at first voluntarily but made compulsory by the end of the 8th century. The *great* tithes were those of the major crops, the *small* consisting of lesser produce. With the growth of the parochial system, they became an important item in the income of the parson and source of friction between clergy and their parishioners. With the rise of the PURITANS and later Nonconformity a new grievance arose. Commutation of tithes began before 1600, and an attempt to commute tithes to a single rent charge was begun by an Act of 1836. Acts of 1937 and 1951 commuted them to a lump sum redeemable by instalments up to AD 2000. *See* VICAR.

Titular Bishops. The Roman Catholic dignitaries formerly known as bishops in partibus.

Titus. An alternative name for DYSMAS. Also the name of one of St PAUL's disciples to whom he wrote one of his *Epistles*. The latter is traditionally regarded as the first bishop of Crete, where he died. His head was eventually carried off by the Venetians and the skull was returned to the ORTHODOX CHURCH in Crete in 1964.

To-remain Bible. *See* BIBLE, SOME SPECIALLY NAMED EDITIONS.

Tobit. The central character of the popular story in the *Book of Tobit*, in the Old Testament APOCRYPHA. Tobit is a scrupulous and pious Jew who practised good works, but, while sleeping in his courtyard, being unclean from burying a Jew found strangled in the street, was blinded by sparrows which 'muted warm dung in his eyes'. His son Tobias was attacked on the Tigris by a fish, which leapt out of the water and which he caught at the bidding of the angel RAPHAEL, his mentor. Tobit's blindness was cured by applying to his eyes the gall of the fish. Father and son prepared to reward Azarias (Raphael), whereupon the ANGEL revealed his identity and returned to HEAVEN.

Toc H. The morse pronunciation of the letters T.H., the initials of Talbot House. The term was used in World War I, when the first Talbot House was founded, in December 1915, at Poperinghe, in memory of Gilbert Talbot, son of the Bishop of Winchester, who had been killed at Hooge in the preceding July. The Rev.

P. B. Clayton, M.C., made it a famous rest and recreation centre. In 1920, he founded a similar centre in London, also known as Toc H, which developed into an interdenominational association for Christian social service.

Toledo, Rite of. *See* MOZARAB.

Toleration Act. An Act of the English Parliament, passed in 1689, allowing freedom of worship to all PROTESTANT DISSENTERS, except UNITARIANS and ROMAN CATHOLICS.

Tongue. Confusion of tongues. According to the BIBLE (*Gen.* xi, 1–9), the people of the earth originally spoke one language and lived together. They built a city and a tower as a rallying point, but God, seeing this as the beginning of ambition, 'did confound the language of all the earth' and scattered them abroad and hence the town was called Babel. This was taken as an explanation of the diversity of languages and the dispersal of mankind and the origin of the name Babylon.

The gift of tongues. Command of foreign languages; also the power claimed by the early church and by some later mystics (as the IRVING-ITES) of conversing in and understanding unknown tongues (from the miracle at PENTECOST—*Acts* ii, 4, the implications of which are obscure).

Tonsure (Lat. *tonsura*, a shearing). The shaving of part of the head among CATHOLIC clergy became customary in the 6th and 7th centuries as a mark of the clerical state. It is not retained in such countries as Britain and the USA where it is not in accordance with custom. The western form of tonsure leaving a circle of hair around the head is supposed to symbolize the CROWN OF THORNS. The Celtic tonsure consisted of shaving off all the hair in front of a line extending over the head from ear to ear. In the East the whole head was shorn. The modern Roman Catholic tonsure varies among the different Orders and that of the secular clergy is a small circle on the crown of the head.

Torquemada, Thomas de (1420–98). Spanish DOMINICAN monk, the Grand Inquisitor of the Spanish INQUISITION, noted for his cruelty. He was reputed to have condemned some 9,000 heretics and Jews to death at the stake. He expelled the Jews from Spain in 1492.

Tortgith (or Theorigitha), St (d. 681, f.d. 26 January). A nun, a companion of St ETHELBURGBA at Barking, where she became mistress of the novices. She fell ill and was paralysed, and during her illness had a vision of St Ethelburga before the latter died. In another vision, she conversed with the saint before her own death.

Tower of Babel. *See* BABEL; CONFUSION OF TONGUES *under* TONGUE.

Tract. A short treatise or pamphlet written in colloquial language on some religious subject and distributed free as propaganda, used by both CATHOLICS and PROTESTANTS.

Tracts for the Times. A series of ninety pamphlets written by NEWMAN, PUSEY, KEBLE, Froude and other members of the Oxford Movement, giving the group the name of Tractarians.

Traditors (Lat. *tradere*, to give up). Those among the early Christian community who, when faced with persecution, gave up the SCRIPTURES or sacred vessels to the authorities and so betrayed their faith and fellow Christians.

Transept. An architectural term (from the Lat. *trans*, across; *septum*, enclosure) for the transverse portion of any building lying across the main body of that building. The transept became common in ecclesiastical architecture in the Middle Ages and almost universal in the Gothic period. The CROSS is often surmounted by a tower, spire, or dome. In a BASILICA CHURCH the transept is the transverse portion in front of the choir.

Transfiguration. The word applied to the miraculous transformation of Christ's appearance which occurred on a mountain where he was praying. It was witnessed by PETER, JAMES and JOHN and is celebrated on 6 August.

Translation. In the Church the term translation is variously applied to

a) the removal of the body of a SAINT from one place to another, usually from the place of burial to some shrine, church or monastery. Much value was set on owning such relics and the place frequently became a centre of pilgrimage. The date of the translation is often celebrated as an additional feast day.

b) to enter into spiritual rapture or ecstasy, the spirit being taken out of the body during the experience.

c) the transference of clerics from one appointment to another, in particular that of a bishop from one diocese to another.

As an example of the translation of saints: St CUTHBERT was buried at Lindisfarne in 687 and his body was enshrined there. At the Viking invasion in 875 the shrine and relics were taken away by the monks who then travelled over N. England and SW. Scotland to find a safe resting place. Finally, in 995 they reached Durham, where a church was built to house the shrine, and St Cuthbert was translated there in 999.

SS WALBURGA and WILLIBALD, sister and brother from Wessex, left England to help St BONIFACE in his mission to pagan Germany. Walburga died at Heidenheim in 779 and

Willibald at Eichstatt in 786/7. In 870 the relics of Walburga were translated to lie by those of her brother. Her feast days are thus 1 May and translation 12 October. Both shrines still exist and the famous at Walburga's oil exudes from the rock at her shrine.

Transubstantiation. A change from one substance into another. Theologically, the change of the whole substance of the bread and wine in the EUCHARIST to the body and blood of Christ, only their outward form or accidents remaining.

Trappists. Properly, the CISTERCIANS of the French abbey at Soligny La Trappe (founded 1140) after their reform and reorganization in 1664. They were absorbed by the Cistercians of the Strict Observance in 1892, to whom the name is now applied. They are noted for extreme austerity, their rule including absolute silence, a common dormitory, and no recreation.

Traskites. A sect of Puritan SABBATARIANS founded by John Trask, a Somerset man, about 1620. They believed that the law as laid down for the ancient Hebrews was to be taken literally and applied to themselves and all men. Trask was brought before the Star Chamber and pilloried. He is said to have recanted later and to have become an ANTINOMIAN, and his followers became absorbed by the SEVENTH-DAY BAPTISTS.

Treacle Bible. *See under* BIBLE, SOME SPECIALLY NAMED EDITIONS.

Treasury of the Church, Treasury of Merits, or **Satisfactions.** The theological term for the superabundant store of merits and satisfactions of Christ which were beyond the needs of the salvation of the human race. To these are added the excess of merits and satisfactions of the BVM and the SAINTS. It is by drawing on this treasury that the Church grants INDULGENCES.

Tree. The CROSS on which Our Lord was crucified is frequently spoken of in hymns and poetry as *the tree. See Acts* v, 30, '...Jesus, whom ye slew and hanged on a tree'; and I *Pet.* ii, 24, 'Who his own self bare our sins in his own body on the tree'.

The Tree of Knowledge. The tree which God planted, together with the *Tree of Life*, in the Garden of EDEN.
'But of the tree of the knowledge of good and evil, thou shalt not eat of it; for in the day that thou eatest thereof thou shalt surely die' (*Gen.* ii, 17). Eve partook of the forbidden fruit and gave some to ADAM; 'And the Lord God said, Behold, the man is become as one of us, to know good and evil; and now, lest he put forth his hand, and take also of the tree of life, and

eat, and live for ever' (*Gen.* iii, 22); and so the first man and the first woman were driven from the garden and the woes of mankind began.

The Tree of Life. While the Tree of Knowledge is dualistic with the knowledge of good and evil, the Tree of Life signifies regeneration, the return to unity, the primordial state of perfection; it transcends good and evil. Mediaeval Christian symbolism has a Tree of the Living and the Dead, bearing good and bad fruit on opposite sides, with Christ as the trunk, the unifying Tree of Life, which is also the central of the three crosses on CALVARY.

Trent, Council of. The Council was the chief instrument of the COUNTER-REFORMATION; it was held at Trent in the Austrian Tyrol, between 1545 and 1563. It was convened for the purpose of healing the breach between CATHOLICS and PROTESTANTS, and succeeded in reforming abuses and defining disputed dogmas. The doctrines agreed upon were published in 1564 as the Profession of the Tridentine Faith.

Trèves. The Holy Coat of Trèves. *See under* HOLY.

Tridentine. Related to the Council of TRENT.

Triduum Sacrum (Lat., the three sacred). The last three days in HOLY WEEK: MAUNDY THURSDAY, GOOD FRIDAY, HOLY SATURDAY.

Trine, or Triune. The method of BAPTISM which involves the baptized being immersed three times in the name of the Father, the Son and the Holy Ghost.

Trinitarians. Believers in the doctrine of the Holy TRINITY as distinct from UNITARIANS. Also, members of the Order of the Most Holy Trinity, or Mathurins, founded by St John of Matha and St Felix of Valois in 1198, concerned with the ransoming of captives and slaves and sometimes known as REDEMPTIONISTS. Their rule is an austere form of the AUGUSTINIAN.

Trinity, The. The three Persons in one God—God the Father, God the Son, and God the HOLY GHOST. *See also* CONFOUNDING THE PERSONS *under* PERSON.

And in this Trinity none is afore, or after other; none is greater, or less than another; but the whole three Persons are co-eternal together: and co-equal.
The Athanasian Creed

The term Triad was first used by Theophilus of Antioch (*c.* 180) for this concept; the term *Trinity* was introduced by Tertullian about 217 in his treatise *Adversus Praxean.*

Trinity, or Trinity Sunday. The SUNDAY next after WHITSUNDAY; widely observed as a feast in honour of the Trinity since the Middle Ages, its general observance was enjoined by Pope John XXII in 1334. The EPISTLE and GOSPEL used in the CHURCH OF ENGLAND on this day are the same as those in the Lectionary of St JEROME, and the Collect comes from the Sacramentary of St GREGORY. The Church of England followed the Sarum Use in reckoning Sundays after Trinity, the ROMAN CATHOLIC CHURCH reckons them after PENTECOST (now adopted in the ALTERNATIVE SERVICES BOOK (*see* BOOK OF COMMON PRAYER).

Triodion. In the Eastern ORTHODOX CHURCH, a liturgical book of the variable parts of the services from the fourth Sunday before LENT to EASTER Saturday.

Triptych. A painting or carving on a tablet of wood, metal or ivory, on three joined panels, usually hinged for folding, portraying some sacred theme. The side panels are usually half the width of the central panel.

Trisagion (Gr., thrice holy). A hymn in the liturgies of the Greek and Eastern Churches in which (after *Is.* v, 3) a threefold invocation to the Deity is the burden—'Holy God, Holy and Mighty, Holy and Immortal, have mercy on us.'
The name is sometimes applied to Bishop Heber's hymn for Trinity Sunday—

Holy, Holy, Holy! Lord God Almighty,
Early in the morning our song shall rise to Thee;

which is more properly called the *Ter-Sanctus*.

Triumphant, the Church. The congregation of Christians in Heaven.

Triune. *See* TRINE.

Troparion. In the Eastern ORTHODOX CHURCH, a stanza, hymn or canticle at the beginning of the LITURGY, preceding the KONTAKION.

Trump. The last trump. The final end of all things earthly; the Day of JUDGEMENT.

We shall not all sleep, but we shall all be changed, in a moment, in the twinkling of an eye, at the last trump.
I Cor. xv, 51, 52

Tulchan Bishops. Certain titular Scottish BISHOPS introduced by the PRESBYTERIANS in 1572 and whose office had ceased by 1580. A *tulchan* is a stuffed calf-skin placed under a cow that holds her milk to deceive her into yielding into the pail. The bishops were contemptuously so called because their title was but an empty one, their revenues being mainly absorbed by nobles as lay patrons.

Tunkers, Dunkers (or **Dunkards**) (Ger.,

dippers). A religious sect also known as the German Baptists, founded in Germany in 1708 by Alexander Mack. In 1719 they emigrated to Pennsylvania and spread westwards and into Canada. They reject infant baptism, the taking of oaths or bearing of arms, and practise triple immersion, the AGAPE, etc. They are now called the Church of the Brethren. The SEVENTH-DAY BAPTISTS (1728) are an offshoot.

Turin Shroud. The shroud of twill linen kept in Turin Cathedral and claimed to be that which wrapped the body of Christ after His crucifixion. The POPE agreed to radiocarbon dating in 1987 and in 1988 the Archbishop of Turin appointed the Oxford Research Laboratory for Archaeology, the Department of Physics of Arizona University and the Swiss Federal Institute of Technology at Zurich, to date the shroud, pieces of which were given to these institutes in April 1988. The results were announced on 13 October and the cloth was dated between 1260 and 1390. There is no historical evidence that it was known before the 14th century. Although not accepted by all, the general conclusion is that the shroud is a mediaeval forgery.

Twelfth Night. 5 January, the eve of the Twelfth Day after CHRISTMAS or Feast of the EPIPHANY. Formerly this was a time of great merrymaking when the Bean-King was appointed, and the celebrations and festivities seemingly derive from the Saturnalia of old Roman times which were held at the same season. By the JULIAN CALENDAR Twelfth Day is Old CHRISTMAS Day.
Shakespeare's play of this name (produced 1600–1) was so called because it was written for acting at the Twelfth Night revels.

Tyndale, William (*c.* 1492–1536). He was born on the Welsh border and studied at both Oxford and Cambridge before he was ordained. He aspired to produce an accurate translation of the BIBLE (*see under* BIBLE, THE ENGLISH) from the original Hebrew and Greek, the only translation at the time being the WYCLIF BIBLE from the Latin Vulgate, containing many inaccuracies. Unable to get support in England, he worked in Germany, first at Cologne, then at Worms and later in Antwerp where his revised NEW TESTAMENT appeared in 1534; in 1536 this was reprinted in England for Queen Anne Boleyn. Tyndale was arrested at Antwerp, imprisoned, tried as a heretic, then strangled and burnt.

Tyndale's Bible. *See* BIBLE, THE ENGLISH.

Typicon. In the Eastern ORTHODOX CHURCH, a liturgical manual of instructions for the recital of services in the ecclesiastical year.

U

Uganda Martyrs *see* LWANGA.

Ulfric (or **Wulfrid**), **St** (d. 1028, f.d. 18 January). Of English birth, he was one of the missionaries who went with St SIGFRID to Sweden and Germany. He was successful in his evangelization, but was killed by a crowd when he hacked down an image of Thor.

Ulric (or **Uldaricus**), **St** (890–973, f.d. 4 July). Of note as the first person to be recorded as canonized. He was born in Augsburg and educated at the Abbey of St Gall in Switzerland. He was appointed bishop of Augsburg in 923 and was a zealous administrator, working for the people. He was involved in ecclesiastical and secular matters, and opposed the Magyar invaders. He was canonized in 993 by Pope John XV.

Ultramontane Party. The extreme party in the Church of ROME. *Ultramontane* opinions or tendencies are those which favour the high 'Catholic' party. *Ultramontane* (beyond the mountains, i.e. the Alps) means Italy or the old Papal States. The term was first used by the French, to distinguish those who look upon the pope as the fountain of all power in the Church, in contradistinction to the Gallican school, which maintained the right of self-government by national churches.

Unam sanctam (Lat., One holy). The opening words of Boniface VIII's BULL of 1302 declaring that there was 'One holy Catholic and Apostolic Church', membership of which was necessary for salvation. It is notable for its assertion of papal claims and of the authority of the spiritual power over the temporal.

Unaneled. Unanointed; without having had extreme unction. (O.E. *ele*, oil; from Lat. *oleum*). *See* HOUSEL.

> Unhouseled, disappointed, unaneled.
> SHAKESPEARE: *Hamlet*, I, v

Unction. Anointing with oil as a religious rite of consecration, also in coronation; the rite is usually administered by a bishop or priest. In the Western and Eastern CATHOLIC CHURCHES it is used in BAPTISM and CONFIRMATION. Extreme Unction is the sacrament of anointing the sick and dying. In the NEW TESTAMENT there are accounts of anointing the sick as a healing power.

Uncumber, St (f.d. 20 July). The Portuguese St Wilgefortis, about whom little is known with any accuracy and so called according to Sir Thomas More 'because they [women] reken that for a pecke of oats she will not faile to uncumber them of their husbondys'. Traditionally, she was one of seven beautiful princesses, and wishing to lead a single life prayed that she might have a beard. The prayer was granted and she was no more cumbered with suitors, but one of them, a prince of Sicily, was so enraged that he had her crucified.

Undecimilla *See* URSULA, ST.

Unfrock. In ecclesiastical parlance, to deprive a priest of his clerical robes and reduce him to lay estate.

Uniat, or **Uniate Churches** (Lat. *unus*, one). Churches of Eastern Christendom which are in communion with ROME but retain their own rights, languages, and canon law, and differ from the ORTHODOX CHURCHES in that their priests are clean-shaven. The ICONOSTASIS doors are open at the EUCHARIST; occasional three-dimensional sacred statues occur; the Latin ROSARY is used and the words 'and the Son' are used in the creed. *See* FILIOQUE.

Unification Church. *See* MOONIES.

Unigenitus (Lat., the Only-Begotten). A Papal BULL, so called from its opening sentence *Unigenitus, Dei Filius*, issued in 1713 by Clement XI in condemnation of Quesnel's *Réflexions Morales*, which favoured Jansenism. It was a *damnatio in globo*—i.e. a condemnation of the whole book without exception. It was confirmed in 1725, but in 1730 the bull was condemned by the civil authorities of Paris and this clerical controversy died out.

Unitarians. Originally Christians who denied the existence of the TRINITY, maintaining that God existed in one person only. Many of the early heretical sects were unitarian in belief if not in name, and at the time of the REFORMATION unitarianism had numerous exponents who may be regarded as the founders of the modern movement.

In England, John Biddle (1615–1662) is generally regarded as the founding father and among the famous men who have been Unitarians are Dr Samuel Clarke, Joseph Priestley, Dr Lardner, James Martineau, Sir Edgar Bowring, and Joseph Chamberlain. Modern Unitarianism is not based on Scriptural authority, but on reason and conscience and includes AGNOSTICS and humanists among its members. There is no formal dogma or creed.

Unitas Fratrum. *See* BOHEMIAN BRETHREN.

United. United Brethren. The United Brethren in Christ, a PROTESTANT sect, was founded in the USA by Philip Otterbein (1726–1813) and Martin Boehme (1725–1812); they were its first bishops.

United Church of Canada. A PROTESTANT movement founded in 1925 to unite the METHODIST, CONGREGATIONAL and PRESBYTERIAN CHURCHES. It has a following in Canada and organizes foreign missions.

United Church of Christ. Founded in 1957 in the USA by the union of the Congregational Christian Church (*see* CONGREGATIONALISTS) with the EVANGELICAL and Reformed Church.

United Free Church of Scotland. *See* FREE CHURCHES.

United Methodists. *See* METHODISTS.

United Presbyterians. *See* PRESBYTERIANS.

United Reformed Church. The church formed in 1972 from the union of the Congregational Church of England and Wales (*see* CONGREGATIONALISTS) with the English PRESBYTERIAN Church.

United Society for Christian Literature. Formed in 1935 by the union of the RELIGIOUS TRACT SOCIETY with the Christian Literature Society for India and Africa (founded in 1858) and the Christian Literature for China (founded in 1884).

United Society for the Propagation of the Gospel. *See* SOCIETY FOR THE PROPAGATION OF THE GOSPEL IN FOREIGN PARTS.

Unity Movement. *See* WORLD COUNCIL OF CHURCHES.

Universal Doctor. Alain de Lille (*c.* 1128–1202), French theologian, so called for his varied learning.

Albertus Magnus (*c.* 1206–80), the scholastic philosopher, was also called *doctor universalis*.

Universalists. Those who believe that there is no hell or eternal punishment, but that all people will ultimately live in harmony with God, since he is goodness and love. The doctrine was

taught by the Rev. John Murray (1741–1815) in New England, and then by Hosea Ballon (1771–1852). He was originally a BAPTIST minister but had become a UNITARIAN, the two movements were virtually one.

University. Universities' Mission to Central Africa (UMCA). An ANGLICAN missionary Society founded in 1857 in response to an appeal by Dr Livingstone; it worked to abolish the slave trade which operated from Zanzibar. The mission expanded and moved to the mainland. In 1965 the UMCA merged with the Society for the Propagation of the Gospel in Foreign Parts to form the USPG (United Society for the Propagation of the Gospel).

The University Tests Act. An Act passed in 1871 abolishing in the Universities of Oxford, Cambridge, and Durham subscriptions to the Thirty-nine *Articles of Religion*, all declarations and oaths concerning religious belief, and all compulsory attendance at public worship except for those taking divinity degrees. The Act also applied to all holders of lay posts.

Unrighteous Bible, The. *See* BIBLE, SOME SPECIALLY NAMED EDITIONS.

Urban Industrial Mission (UIM), Urban Rural Mission. Inaugurated in 1961, at the third assembly of the WORLD COUNCIL OF CHURCHES, in New Delhi, the UIM was established to answer the need for 'urban industrial evangelism'. Its goal was 'to involve the total church in all continents in the ecumenical task of urban industrial evangelism', and 'in developing countries the basic aim is to try, by entering into the conflict between the power structure and its victims, to see if justice and peace can be achieved'.

Subsequent meetings were held in different countries, and in 1978 the Commission on World Mission and Evangelism was urged to bridge the gap between the 'urban' and the 'rural'. It merged the United Industrial Mission with the Urban Rural Mission as 'primarily a movement of men and women rooted in the Christian faith who are called, along with others, to the mission of God to participate in the struggle of the exploited, marginalized and oppressed for justice and liberation'.

Urbanists. *See* FRANCISCANS.

Uriel. One of the seven ARCHANGELS of rabbinical angelology, sent by God to answer the questions of Esdras (II *Esdras* iv). In Milton's *Paradise Lost* (III, 690) he is the 'Regent of the Sun', and 'sharpest-sighted spirit of all in HEAVEN'.

Ursula, St (f.d. 21 October). A 5th-century

British princess, according to legend, who went with 11,000 virgins on a pilgrimage to ROME and was massacred with all her companions by the Huns at Cologne. One explanation of the story is that *Undecimilla* (mistaken for *undecim millia*, 11,000) was one of Ursula's companions.
Ursulines. An order of nuns founded by St Angela Merici of Brescia in 1535, from their patron SAINT St URSULA. They were primarily concerned with the education of girls.

Use. A body of ritual and liturgy, a form of worship or service used in a particular church or country. There is the Roman Use of the ROMAN CATHOLIC CHURCH and the SARUM RITE (or Use) of the liturgy in the CHURCH OF ENGLAND.

Utraquists (Lat. *utraque specie,* in both kinds). HUSSITES or CALIXTINES, so called because they insisted that both elements should be administered to communicants in the EUCHARIST.

Uzziel. One of the principal ANGELS of rabbinical angelology, the name meaning 'Strength of God'. He was next in command to GABRIEL, and in Milton's *Paradise Lost* (IV, 782) is commanded by Gabriel to 'coast the south with strictest watch'.

V

Vaast, St. *See* VEDAST.

Vagantes. Priests in the Middle Ages who were not attached to any parish or order, but could roam in search of employment. They were known as 'episcopi' or 'clerici vagantes'.

Valentine, St (d. *c.* 270, f.d. 14 February). A priest of ROME who was imprisoned for succouring persecuted Christians. He became a convert and, although he is supposed to have restored the sight of the gaoler's blind daughter, he was clubbed to death. His day is 14 February, as is that of St Valentine, bishop of Terni, who was martyred a few years later. There are several other saints of this name.

The ancient custom of choosing *Valentines* has only accidental relation to either SAINT, being essentially a relic of the old Roman *Lupercalia*, or from association with the mating season of birds. It was marked by the giving of presents and nowadays by the sending of a card on which Cupids, transfixed hearts, etc., are depicted.

Chaucer refers to this in his *Assembly of Fowls* (310):

> For this was on Saint Valentine's Day,
> When ev'ry fowl cometh to choose her make,

and Shakespeare (*Midsummer Night's Dream,* IV, i) has:

> Good morrow, friends! St Valentine is past;
> Begin these wood-birds but to couple now?

Valentinians. Valentinius, an Alexandrian GNOSTIC theologian of the 2nd century, propounded a system of 'aeons', each pair consisting of a male and female element. Sophia, or Wisdom, gave birth to Achamoth, who fathered the Demiurge, or Creator, who created the world and mankind. Man proved to be an unsatisfactory degenerate, and so a redeemer was sent to the aeons in the person of Jesus Christ. His birth by the Virgin MARY was only apparent, as he had no material existence but was formed of animal and spiritual elements only. Mankind consists of people who are either material, animal or spiritual: the material are doomed to extinction; the animal may attain the world of the Demiurge; the spiritual will be united with Christ.

Vallumbrosians. A ROMAN CATHOLIC order of monks, founded in 1030 by St Gualbert, at Vallombrosa near Florence. They were an offshoot of the BENEDICTINES, but held stricter rules and practised austerities.

Vatican. The palace of the POPE; so called because it stands on the *Vaticanus Mons* (Vatican Hill) of ancient ROME, which got its name through being the headquarters of the *vaticinatores*, or soothsayers.

The Vatican City State. The area of ROME occupied by the city of the VATICAN, recognized by the LATERAN TREATY (1929) as constituting the territorial extent of the temporal power of the HOLY SEE. It consists of the Papal palace, the library, archives, and museums, the Piazza of St PETER, and contiguous buildings including a railway station, in all an area of just under a square mile. It has about 900 inhabitants and its own coinage. Certain other buildings outside the Vatican enjoy extraterritorial rights.

The Vatican Council. The twentieth OECUMENICAL COUNCIL of the ROMAN CATHOLIC CHURCH (1869–70), summoned by Pius IX and suspended when the Italians occupied ROME after the withdrawal of the French garrison. It was notable for its definition of Papal INFALLIBILITY which was limited to when the Pope speaks *ex cathedra* regarding faith or morals.

A second Vatican Council was opened by Pope John XXIII in October 1962 and concluded by Paul VI in December 1965. Among numerous controversial proposals for change, it was notably concerned with the need for Christian unity, liturgical reforms, and matters of church government. One special feature was the presence of observers from non-Roman Catholic Churches. *See* OECUMENICAL COUNCILS.

The Prisoner of the Vatican. The POPE was so called after 1870, when Pius IX retired into the VATICAN after the occupation of ROME. He proclaimed himself a prisoner for conscience's sake and his successors remained in the precincts of the Vatican until the LATERAN TREATY of 1929.

The Thunders of the Vatican. The anathemas and denunciations of the POPE.

Vaudois. *See* WALDENSIANS.

Vedast (Vaast, Gaston or **Foster), St** (d. 539,

f.d. 6 February, at Arras also 15 July and 1 October). Carried out a mission among the Franks with St REMIGIUS, and was famous as having instructed King Clovis for baptism. Vedast was appointed bishop of Arras and ruled the united sees of Arras and Cambrai, establishing the church and helping the poor. He was said to have cured a blind man, also to have taken a goose from a wolf, restoring the bird to life and giving it back to its poor owners; the incident is depicted in art and the saint is also represented with a child at his feet, or with a bear.

Veil. To take the veil. To become a nun; from the traditional head-dress of women in religious orders. The veil is a symbol of modesty and chastity and, for nuns, of spiritual marriage to Christ. In the CHURCH OF ENGLAND it is customary for female candidates to wear a white veil at CONFIRMATION. Veils are also used for covering sacred objects. In CATHOLIC practice, the cross on the altar is symbolically veiled during the period when Christ was in the tomb. The ROOD screen is the veil of the Ark of the Covenant, separating the HOLY OF HOLIES from the earthly body of the Church. Christ rending the Veil of the Temple depicted the removal of the division between Jews and Gentiles.

Venantius, St (c. 530–610, f.d. 14 December). Born near Treviso in North Italy and educated at Ravenna, he was cured of blindness and in thanksgiving made a pilgrimage to the shrine of St MARTIN OF TOURS. He settled at Poitiers and was ordained, coming to the notice of Queen St RADEGONDE, to whom he wrote poems. He became noted as a great writer, poet and hymnologist, exerting immense influence on future hymnography. He was appointed bishop of Poitiers towards the end of his life.

Venerable (Lat. *venerabilis*, worthy of honour). The title applied to archdeacons in formally addressing them ('The Venerable the Archdeacon of Barset', or 'The Venerable E. L. Brown'); and in the ROMAN CATHOLIC CHURCH, the title of one who has attained the first of the three degrees of CANONIZATION.

It belongs especially to BEDE, the monk of Jarrow, an English ecclesiastical historian (d. 735), and to William of Champeaux (d. 1121), the French scholastic philosopher and opponent of ABELARD.

Veni, Creator Spiritus. A hymn to the HOLY GHOST in the Roman breviary, probably of the 9th century and often attributed to Rabanus Maurus (d. 856), Archbishop of Mainz. It is sung at VESPERS and Terce during PENTECOST and on other occasions such as the consecration of a church or of a BISHOP. The popular

English version beginning' 'Come, Holy Ghost, our souls inspire' is by John Cosin (1594–1672), Bishop of Durham.

Veni, Sancte Spiritus (Lat., Come, Holy Spirit). A mediaeval Latin hymn, used as a sequence at PENTECOST in the ROMAN CATHOLIC CHURCH.

Venial Sin. One that does not forfeit grace. In the ROMAN CATHOLIC CHURCH sins are of two sorts, MORTAL and venial (Lat. *venia*, grace, pardon). *See Matt.* xii, 31.

Venite. Psalm 95, from its opening words *Venite, exultemus Domino*, 'O come, let us sing unto the Lord'. It is said or sung at MATTINS.

Verger. The BEADLE in a church who carries the rod or staff, which was formerly called the *verge* (Lat. *virga*, a rod). Formerly spelt 'virger' after the rod, the 'virge', carried in church processions; it is still so spelt at St Paul's Cathedral in London. Vergers are not members of the clergy, but wear cassocks when on duty.

Veronica, St (no date, f.d. 12 July). According to late mediaeval legend, a woman of JERUSALEM who handed her head-cloth to Our Lord on His way to CALVARY. He wiped His brow and returned it to the giver when it was found to bear a perfect likeness of the Saviour impressed upon it and was called *Vera-Icon* (true likeness); the woman became St *Veronica*. It is one of the relics at St Peter's, ROME. In Spanish bull-fighting the most classic movement with the cape is called the *Veronica*, the cape being swung so slowly before the face of the charging bull that it resembles St Veronica's wiping of the Holy Face.

Veronica Giuliani, St (1660–1727, f.d. 9 July). Born at Mercatello in Italy, she joined the CAPUCHIN nuns at Citta de' Castello and became novice mistress, holding the office for some thirty-four years and administering it with practical level-headedness and efficiency. Her mystical experiences were outstanding and well-attested; they included visions, prophecies and the STIGMATA. She was canonized in 1839.

Versicle. A short verse, usually from the PSALMS, said or sung antiphonically by the priest, followed by a response from the congregation or the choir.

Vesica Piscis (Lat., fish-bladder). The ovoidal frame or glory which, in the 12th century, was much used, especially in painted windows, to surround pictures of the Virgin Mary and of Our Lord. It is meant to represent a fish, from the acronym ICHTHUS. *See* ICHTHYS.

Vesperale. A book of prayers and music used at

VESPERS. In the WESTERN CHURCH it is also a cloth covering the white altar-cloth to keep it clean when no service is held.

Vespers. The sixth of the canonical hours in the Greek and Roman Churches; sometimes also used of the Evening Service in the English Church. From Lat. *vesperus*, the evening, cognate with Hesperus, Gr. *Hesperos*, the evening star.

The Fatal Vespers. 26 October 1623. A congregation of some 300 had assembled in an upper room in the residence of the French ambassador, at Blackfriars, to hear Father Drury, a JESUIT, preach. The flooring gave way, and Drury with another priest and about 100 of the congregation were killed. This accident was attributed to God's judgement against the Jesuits.

Vestiarian Controversy. The name given to the dispute about the wearing of clerical vestments raised by puritan-minded clergy in the reign of Edward VI and again in the reign of Elizabeth I. The simplest vestments such as the surplice and gown were described as the livery of ANTICHRIST. Archbishop Parker sought to enforce conformity by his *Advertisements* of 1566 ordering the wearing of the four-cornered cap, scholar's gown, and surplice, but many refused and deprivations followed. Diversity of practice remained and the controversy became merged with the puritan agitation against EPIS-COPACY.

Vestments. Liturgical garments worn by a priest when taking the services in a church; also worn by a deacon or acolyte in the act of worship. There are additional vestments for bishops and the higher orders.

Vestry (Lat. *vestiarium*, robing-room). A room in a church in which the vestments, registers, altar vessels, etc., are kept and used as a robing-room by the clergy. Some larger churches contain a priests' vestry, wardens' vestry, and choir vestry. From the habit of parishioners meeting to conduct parish business in the vestry, both the body of parishioners and the meeting were called the *Vestry*.

Up to 1894 the Vestry was the final authority in all parish matters, civil and ecclesiastical. The parish priest presided over the meeting which elected churchwardens and other parish officers and the property of the parish was usually vested in the churchwardens. The *Common Vestry* consisted of the general assembly of ratepayers and the *Select Vestry* of a body of *vestrymen* elected to represent the parish, the usual procedure in many of the larger parishes. With the passing of the Local Government Act of 1894, secular Parish Councils were elected to take over the civil administrative functions of the rural parishes and in the towns such work was subsequently transferred to Urban Councils. In 1921 ecclesiastical administration passed to the newly created Parochial Church Councils, although the meeting which elects the churchwardens is still called a *Vestry Meeting*.

Via. Via Dolorosa (Lat., Dolorous way). The route Our Lord went from the place of judgment to CALVARY, now marked by the fourteen STATIONS OF THE CROSS (*see under* CROSS).

Via Media (Lat., The Middle Way). The mean between two extremes. The Elizabethan Church Settlement of the 16th century is often so called, the CHURCH OF ENGLAND being regarded as the mean between extreme Protestantism and Roman Catholicism.

Vial. Vials of wrath. Vengeance, the execution of wrath on the wicked. The allusion is to the seven ANGELS who pour out upon the earth their vials full of wrath (*Rev.* xvi).

Vianney, St Jean-Baptist (1786–1859), f.d. 4 August). Generally known as the Curé d'Ars, he was born into a peasant family at Dardilly, near Lyons, spending his boyhood as a shepherd. He was of a devout temperament and wished to be ordained, but with little education he found the academic work difficult when he entered the seminaries of Verrières and Lyons. However, he received the TONSURE and was finally ordained in 1815. He was first appointed curate at Écully, then parish priest of Ars-en-Dombes, where he set about reforming the lax morals which obtained in the village and its environs. He became famous as a preacher and confessor, and his ministry was also noted for the manifestation of psychic phenomena, which were well examined and authenticated. They included bilocation, levitation, mind-reading, prophecy and the multiplication of food. At one time he was plagued by a poltergeist which he believed to be the work of the Devil. He worked miracles of healing, which he ascribed to St PHILOMENA, a mythical saint whose cult he established at Ars; this drew numbers of pilgrims and added to his heavy personal ministry. The Curé lived a life of extreme poverty and austerity, giving away anything bestowed on him and refusing all public recognition. His cult spread widely and he was canonized in 1925, also being made patron of parish priests.

Viaticum (Lat.). The EUCHARIST administered to the dying. The word means 'provision for a journey', and its application is obvious.

Vicar (Lat. *vicarius*, a substitute). The priest of a parish where the TITHES were appropriated in

PRE-REFORMATION times, usually to monasteries. The monastery retained the *Rectorial* or great tithes and reserved the small tithes (*Vicarial* tithes) for the incumbent. After the Dissolution such Rectorial tithes were granted to CHAPTERS, colleges, laymen, etc., known as impropriators (*see* IMPROPRIATION), who were under obligation to appoint vicars to carry out the ecclesiastical duties. The title is also given to Perpetual Curates. *Cp.* CLERICAL TITLES.

In the American Episcopal Church a vicar is head of a chapel dependent on a parish church. In the ROMAN CATHOLIC CHURCH he is an ecclesiastic representing a BISHOP.

Lay Vicar. A cathedral officer who sings those portions of the liturgy not reserved for the clergy. Formerly called a *clerk vicar*.

Vicar Apostolic. In the ROMAN CATHOLIC CHURCH, a titular BISHOP appointed to a place where no episcopate has been established, or where the succession has been established, or where the succession has been interrupted. In 1585 the English hierarchy came to an end and until 1594 Catholics came under the jurisdiction of Cardinal Allen, then that of archpriests from 1599 until 1621; but from 1623 until 1850 the Roman Catholic Church in England was governed by vicars apostolic. The term formerly denoted a bishop to whom the POPE delegated some part of his jurisdiction.

Vicar Choral. One of the minor clergy, or a layman, attached to a cathedral for singing certain portions of the service.

Vicar Forane. A priest appointed by a Roman Catholic BISHOP to exercise limited (usually disciplinary) jurisdiction in a particular part of his diocese. The office is similar to that of RURAL DEAN (*see under* DEAN). *Forane* is a form of 'foreign', hence outlying, rural.

Vicar-General. An ecclesiastical functionary assisting a BISHOP or archbishop in the exercise of his jurisdiction. In 1535 Thomas Cromwell was appointed Vicar-General to carry out Henry VIII's ecclesiastical policies.

The Vicar of Christ. A title given to the POPE, an allusion to his claim to be the representative of Christ on earth.

Vicisti, Galilaee. *See* GALILEAN.

Victorines. The 'Mystics of St Victor' was a mystical body founded by William of Champeaux in 1108 at the abbey of St Victor, near Paris. Its most noted monks were Hugh of St Victor (1096–1141), Peter Lombard (*c.* 1100–62) and Richard of St Victor, a Scotsman who died in 1173. The abbey was dissolved at the French Revolution, but the school had already declined in the later Middle Ages.

Victricius, St (d. 407, f.d. 7 August). An officer of the Roman army, he was converted to Christianity and, finding his profession incompatible with Christian teaching, he resigned. He was scourged and sentenced to death, but the sentence was not carried out. Little is known of his life until he became bishop of Rouen and carried out a successful mission among the tribes of northern Gaul and became a leader in the Church. He was a friend of St PAULINUS OF NOLA, whose letters are the main source of information on his work.

Vigil (Lat. *vigilia*, watching). A watch kept in a church or at a shrine, often with public prayer, on the eve of a festival, especially when observed as a fast and often ending with a MASS of the vigil. In 1969 the ROMAN CATHOLIC calendar abolished all vigils except that of EASTER.

Vigiliae. *See* MATTINS.

Vincent. Vincent de Paul, St (1581–1660, f.d. 27 September, formerly 19 July). Born at Ranquine (now named after him), of a peasant family, he was educated by FRANSCISCANS at Dax and at Toulouse University. He was ordained priest at the age of twenty. He was said to have been captured by pirates, but escaped and went to Paris. Although he lived among the rich his life was devoted to every branch of the poor and needy, and he organized relief for outcasts, prostitutes, convicts, orphans, the sick and the insane. For this work he founded, in 1625, the Congregation of the Mission, also called the VINCENTIANS or LAZARISTS (from the church of Saint-Lazare in Paris), and then the Congregation of the Sisters of Charity in 1633, an order of unenclosed women, now working worldwide. In art he is depicted in the habit of a sixteenth-century cleric with a knotted girdle; he either carries a child in his arms or is surrounded with Sisters of Charity. He is patron of charitable societies.

Vincent Pallotti, St (1795–1850, f.d. 22 January). Born in ROME, the son of a grocer, he was ordained priest and became a doctor of theology, teaching at the Sapienza College, and was confessor to several colleges. He founded the Society of the Catholic Apostolate and, in 1843, the Pallotti Sisters, both societies based on an apostolic role for the laity as well as the clergy. He also organized schools and evening classes on the lines of the work of JOHN BOSCO. The movement spread, not only in Italy but to the Americas and Australia, working especially among immigrants. Pallotti also took part in ecumenical movements with the Eastern ORTHODOX CHURCH. He had powers of clairvoyance and prophecy, and practised exorcism.

Vincent of Saragossa, St (d. *c.* 304, f.d. 22 January). A deacon of Saragossa, martyred during the persecution under Diocletian. He is a patron SAINT of drunkards for no apparent reason, except that he was the patron of wine-growers. An old rhyme says:

If on St Vincent's Day the sky is clear
More wine than water will crown the year.

Born at Huesca, he became the most famous of the Spanish martyrs and his cult spread widely. The style of his tortures and martyrdom appear to have been borrowed from other saints. In art he is depicted as wearing the deacon's DAL-MATIC, and holds ewers, or a book, or has a whip or a gridiron as emblems of his tortures; sometimes ravens defend his torn body.

Vincentian. A Lazarist or Lazarite, a member of the Congregation of Priests of the Mission founded (1625) by St VINCENT DE PAUL (*c.* 1581–1660).

Vine. The Rabbis say that the fiend buried a LION, a LAMB, and a hog at the foot of the first vine planted by Noah; and that hence men receive from wine ferocity, mildness, or wallowing in the mire.

In Christianity, Christ is the True Vine and his disciples are the branches (*John* xv). The vine can be portrayed as the TREE OF LIFE, and with doves resting in the branches it symbolizes souls resting in Christ in spiritual fruitfulness. Depicted with corn, the vine signifies the EUCHARIST.

Vinegar Bible, The. *See* BIBLE, SOME SPECIALLY NAMED EDITIONS.

Virgil (Virgilius or **Ferghil), St** (d. 784, f.d. 27 November). An Irish monk who set out on a pilgrimage to Palestine, but remained in Bavaria and carried out a mission there, working with St RUPERT. He was first abbot of the BENEDICTINE abbey of St Peter in Salzburg, then bishop of the city. He was famous for his conflict with St BONIFACE, who had appointed him to the see, over cosmological beliefs such as that the earth was a sphere, which shocked St Boniface. The two saints were also opposed in their attitudes to the Celtic versus Roman controversies in England in the 7th century. St Virgil is the apostle of Austria.

Virgin. The Virgin Birth. The belief that Christ had no human father and that His miraculous birth did not impair the virginity of his mother, the Blessed Virgin Mary (*see Matt.* i, 18; *Luke* i, 27–35).

Virgin Mary, The. *See* MARY.

Virtue. The Seven Virtues. Faith, Hope, Charity, Justice, Fortitude, Prudence, and Temperance. The first three are called the *supernatural, theological* or *Christian* virtues; the remaining four are Plato's *cardinal* or *natural* virtues. *Cp.* SEVEN DEADLY SINS.

Visitation, The, or **The Visitation of Our Lady.** The Blessed Virgin's visit to her cousin St Elisabeth before the birth of St JOHN THE BAPTIST (*Luke* I, 39–56). It is celebrated on 2 July.

The Order of the Visitation, or **Visitandines.** A contemplative Order for women founded by St FRANCIS of SALES and St Jane Frances de CHANTAL in 1610. They adopted a modification of the AUGUSTINIAN Rule and their chief work is now concerned with education.

Vitus, St. A Sicilian youth who was martyred with Modestus, his tutor, and Crescentia, his nurse, during the Diocletian persecution, *c.* 303.

St Vitus's Dance. In Germany in the 17th century it was believed that good health for the year could be secured by anyone who danced before a statue of St VITUS on his feast-day, 15 June. Such dancing to excess is said to have come to be confused with chorea, hence its name, *St Vitus's Dance*, the SAINT being invoked against it.

Vladimir, St (956–1015, f.d. 15 July). Venerated as the man who christianized Russia, he was descended from the legendary Rurik, Prince of Novgorod; his father was a warrior, killed in battle. Vladimir took the throne of Kiev from his elder brother Yaropolk, and carried out victorious campaigns over a wide area of White Russia. Although a grandson of St OLGA, Vladimir was reared as a pagan and had a harem of wives. When, later, he came to the aid of Basil II, emperor of Byzantium, he succeeded, after years of negotiation, in marrying the Emperor's sister Anna on condition that he became a Christian. The princess brought with her a retinue of clergy with books of devotion, relics and vestments. After Vladimir's return to Kiev he promoted Christianity ruthlessly, destroying pagan images and building churches and monasteries. The monk Jacob, in his *Eulogy*, wrote: 'The whole land of Russia was snatched from the Devil's claws and brought back to God and the true light.'

Volunteers of America. A society founded in 1896 by Bollington Booth (1859–1940), a son of General BOOTH; it followed the teachings, methods and activities of the SALVATION ARMY but, disagreeing with some of the General's policy, the Volunteers were run on more democratic lines. At Bollington Booth's death his widow, Maud Charlesworth Booth, succeeded him as commander-in-chief.

Votive Mass (Lat. *votum*, wish). A MASS celebrated by ROMAN CATHOLICS for some special occasion, such as a Nuptial Mass or an Exequial (funeral) Mass, or for the bringing of peace. Fifteen such occasions are given in the Roman Missal of 1970.

Vows (Lat. *votum*, wish). Promises taken voluntarily. Vows are taken by men and women on becoming members of a religious order; they are usually the three vows of poverty, chastity and obedience. Vows can be either 'solemn' or 'simple'. The former are not taken before the age of twenty-one by those entering an order; having taken a solemn vow the candidate cannot then marry or own property. Simple vows are taken by those first joining the congregation, they may be taken at seventeen years of age and be made perpetual later. A nun is a woman under solemn vows, a sister takes simple vows.

Vulgate, The. The Latin translation of the Bible, made about 384–404 by St JEROME, originally to establish a standard text. The first printed edition was the MAZARIN BIBLE (1456) (*see* BIBLE, SOME SPECIALLY NAMED EDITIONS). A revised edition was issued by Clement VIII in 1592 and a new edition was commissioned by Pius X in 1908. *Genesis* was published in 1926 and the work is still in progress. The name is the Lat. *editio vulgata*, the common edition sanctioned by the ROMAN CATHOLIC CHURCH.

W

Waits. A name now given to parties of singers and musicians who perform outside people's houses at CHRISTMAS-time. They derive their name from those watchmen of former times called *waits* who sounded a horn or played a tune to mark the passing hours. Waits were employed at the royal court 'to pipe the watch' and also by town corporations. The household expenses of Edward IV provide for 'A *wayte*, that nightelye from Mychelmas to Shreve Thorsdaye pipe the watche within this courte fower tymes in the somere nightes three tymes' (Rymer, *Foedera*).

Waits duly came to provide a uniformed band for their town for civic occasions, and played to the public at Christmas-time, hence the current usage. The hautboy was also called a *wayte* or *wait*, from its being their chief instrument.

> I had scarcely got into bed when a strain of music seemed to break forth in the air just below the window. I listened, and found it proceeded from a band which I concluded to be the waits from some neighboring village.
>
> IRVING: *Sketch Book* (*Christmas Eve*)

Wake. A watch or vigil. The name was early applied to the all-night watch kept in church before certain holy days and to the festival kept at the annual commemoration of the dedication of a church. In due course the festive element predominated and the name came to be associated with annual fairs and revelries held at such times. Some towns in the North country still observe local holidays called *wakes*.

In Ireland, the term denotes the watching of the body of the deceased before the funeral, and the feasting which follows, a custom formerly also common in Wales and Scotland.

Walburga (or **Walpurgis**), **St** (*c.* 710–79, f.d. 25 February, 1 May). Sister of SS WILLIBALD and WINNIBALD, she entered the double monastery at Wimborne as a nun under St Tatta. At the instigation of St BONIFACE, she joined the monks and nuns who left for his work of evangelization in Germany, and became abbess of the double monastery of Heidenheim, where she worked and died. Her relics were translated to Eichstatt, where her shrine became famous for the miraculous flow of healing oil from the rock by her tomb. As the date of her translation was 1 May, she became associated with Walpurgisnacht and was often called St Walpurgis. In art she is depicted with three ears of corn, as a protector of crops, or with crown and sceptre and a phial of the healing oil.

Waldensians, or **Waldenses.** Also known by their French name as the *Vaudois*. Followers of Peter Waldo of Lyons who sought to govern their life by the teaching of the GOSPELS and who came to be known as the 'Poor Men of Lyons'. The movement began about 1170 and papal prohibition of their preaching culminated in Waldo's EXCOMMUNICATION. Various heretical teachings followed and papal authority was completely rejected. Active persecution scattered them to other parts of France, Italy, and Spain, etc., and it continued till the late 17th century. Their doctrinal descendants still exist, principally in the Alpine Valleys of Piedmont.

> Avenge O Lord thy slaughter's Saints, whose bones
> Lie scatter'd on the Alpine mountains cold.
> MILTON: *On the Late Massacre in Piedmont* (1655)

Wall, St John (1620–79, f.d. 25 October). Born at Chingle Hall in Lancashire, of a recusant family, he was educated at the ENGLISH COLLEGE, DOUAI and the English College, ROME, where he was ordained priest. He joined the FRANCISCANS before returning to England, where he adopted the name of Marsh and carried out a mission, mainly in Warwickshire. At the time of the POPISH PLOT he was arrested and tried by the Privy Council and Titus OATES, and imprisoned in Newgate. He was then sent back to Worcester, where he was condemned for being a priest and was executed. He was canonized in 1970 as one of the FORTY MARTYRS OF ENGLAND AND WALES.

Walpole, St Henry (1558–98, f.d. 25 October). Born at Docking in Norfolk, he was educated at Norwich Grammar School, Peterhouse, Cambridge, and Gray's Inn. He was converted to ROMAN CATHOLICISM after the martyrdom of Edmund CAMPION and went to the ENGLISH COLLEGE at ROME, where he became a JESUIT. He was later ordained priest in Paris, serving as chaplain to the Spanish army in the Netherlands. He taught in seminaries in Spain and established the English College at Saint-Omer. Returning to England in 1593, he was at once arrested, accused of being a priest and sent to the Tower of London. He was severely tortured there, and then later sent to York and executed. He was canonized in 1970 as one of the FORTY MARTYRS OF ENGLAND AND WALES.

Walsingham. An ancient shrine, still a place of pilgrimage, and known as the English LORETO, also 'The Dowry of Mary'. It was founded in 1061 by the widow Richeldis de Faverches, a local noblewoman. She had received a vision of the Virgin MARY, who transported her to Nazareth and showed her the home of the ANNUNCIATION, now supposedly at Loreto. Richeldis was instructed to build a replica at Walsingham, which would be a place of healing. Two sites were marked in dew, but the builders made a mistake, choosing the wrong one. This was rectified after Richeldis had spent a night in prayer, and angels moved the building. In the 12th century, the shrine was tended by AUGUSTINIAN CANONS and, until the Reformation, the kings of England endowed the Priory and the 'King's Candle' was kept burning on the altar. Endless miracles were recorded at the shrine. The pilgrims' way from London was known as 'The Milky Way' after a relic of a vial of 'Our Lady's Milk'. The shrine was destroyed in 1538 by Henry VIII and fell into disuse, but was restored by ANGLO-CATHOLICS (*see* HIGH CHURCH) in 1897. It is now the centre of a national pilgrimage at the Spring Bank Holiday, and attracts some 10,000 pilgrims. The ANGLICAN, ROMAN CATHOLIC and ORTHODOX CHURCHES are all represented at the shrine.

Walstan, St (d. 1016, f.d. 30 May). In England, the patron saint of husbandmen. He worked as a farm labourer in Norfolk and was noted for the austerity and piety of his life and for his charity. He is usually depicted with a scythe in his hand and cattle in the background, and sometimes robed as a king. His shrine at Bawburgh was a popular cult centre for the local agricultural population; it was destroyed at the REFORMATION.

Waltheof (Waldef, Walthen or **Walden), St** (1100–60, f.d. 3 August). Son of Simon of Senlis, Earl of Huntingdon, and of Maud, whose second marriage was to King David of Scotland. Waltheof, after the death of his father, accompanied his mother to the Scottish court, where he was educated and became a friend of St AELRED. He left the court to become an AUGUSTINIAN CANON at Nostell. He was chosen as Prior of Kirkham, but later joined the CISTERCIANS as being more ascetic, and was a monk at Wardon, Bedfordshire, and at Rievaulx. In 1149 he became abbot at Melrose. Various miracles were reported of him, or at his tomb, such as

the multiplying of food and remarkable visions of Heaven and Hell. He was said to be of great cheerfulness and generosity.

Wandering Jew, The. The central figure of the widespread later-mediaeval legend which tells of a Jew who insulted or spurned Christ when he was bearing the cross to CALVARY, and was condemned to wander over the face of the earth till JUDGEMENT Day.

The usual form of the legend says that he was Ahasuerus, a cobbler, who refused to allow Christ to rest at his door, saying, 'Get off! Away with you, away!' Our Lord replied, 'Truly I go away, and that quickly, but tarry thou till I come.'

An earlier tradition has it that the Wandering Jew was Cartaphilus, the doorkeeper of the judgment hall in the service of Pontius Pilate. He struck our Lord as he led him forth, saying, 'Go on faster, Jesus'; whereupon the Man of Sorrows replied, 'I am going, but thou shalt tarry till I come again.' (*Chronicle of St Alban's Abbey*, 1228). The same Chronicle, continued by Matthew Paris, tells us that Cartaphilus was baptized by Ananias, and received the name of Joseph. At the end of every hundred years he falls into a trance, and wakes up a young man about 30.

In German legend he is associated with John Buttadaeus, seen at Antwerp in the 13th century, again in the 15th, and the third time in the 16th. His last appearance was in 1774 at Brussels. In the French version he is named Isaac Laquedom or Lakedion; another story has it that he was Salathiel ben-Sadi, who appeared and disappeared towards the close of the 16th century at Venice, in so sudden a manner as to attract the notice of all Europe; and another connects him with the Wild Huntsman.

'I'll rest, sayd hee, but thou shalt walke;'
So doth this wandring Jew
From place to place, but cannot rest
For seeing countries newe.
                    PERCY: *Reliques* (*The Wandering Jew*)

Ward, St Margaret (d. 1588, f.d. 25 October). Born at Congleton in Cheshire, she went into service in London, where she helped a priest, William Watson, escape from Bridewell prison by a rope from his cell. The rope was found to belong to Margaret, and she was arrested and tortured, but was constant in refusing to reveal the priest's hiding place. She also refused to abandon her Catholicism for the CHURCH OF ENGLAND. She was tried at the Old Bailey, condemned and executed. She was canonized in 1970 as one of the FORTY MARTYRS OF ENGLAND AND WALES.

Warden. *See* CHURCHWARDEN.

Watts, Isaac (1674–1748). English hymn-writer; pastor of the Independent Congregation at Mark Lane, London. His hymns were a strong influence in establishing the popularity of hymn-singing, particularly among NONCON-FORMISTS.

Weathercock. By a Papal enactment made in the middle of the 9th century, the figure of a cock was set up on every church steeple as the EMBLEM of St PETER. The emblem is in allusion to his denial of our Lord thrice before the cock crew twice. On the second crowing of the cock the warning of his Master flashed across his memory, and the repentant apostle 'went and wept bitterly'.

A person who is always changing his mind is, figuratively, a *weathercock*.

> Ther is no feith that may your herte embrace;
> But, as a wedercock, that turneth his face
> With every wind, ye fare.
>
> CHAUCER (?): *Balade Against Women Unconstant*

Webster, St Augustine (d. 1535, f.d. 25 October). A CARTHUSIAN monk at the Charterhouse of Sheen, he was appointed prior of Axholme in Lincolnshire. With Prior Robert LAWRENCE of Beauvale, he went to the Charterhouse in London to discuss with John HOUGHTON the Carthusian attitude to Henry VIII's religious decrees. After they had seen Thomas Cromwell they were all arrested and executed at Tyburn. With them, Webster was canonized in 1970 as one of the FORTY MARTYRS OF ENGLAND AND WALES.

Wee Frees. *See under* FREE CHURCHES.

Weep. Weepers. The derisive title (Ital. *Piagnoni*, weepers or snivellers) given to the supporters of Savonarola (1452–98) and the popular government in Florence in the 1490s, from their penitential practices and professions.
Weeping Cross. A cross set up by the roadside for penitential devotions.
The Weeping Saint. St SWITHIN, because of the tradition of forty days' rain if it rains on his day (15 July).

Wells, St Swithun (1536–91, f.d. 25 October). Born at Bambridge in Hampshire of a well-to-do family, he was a well-educated and sporting country gentleman, also a poet and musician. He married and set up a school at Monkton Farleigh, and used his home as a refuge for recusants. When priests were found celebrating MASS there the priests were arrested and executed and Wells and his wife were accused of harbouring them. They were condemned to death; the husband was executed, and Mrs Wells was kept in prison for the rest of her life.

Swithun Wells was canonized in 1970 as one of the FORTY MARTYRS OF ENGLAND AND WALES.

Wenceslas, St (*c.* 907–20, f.d. 28 September). The Bohemian martyr-prince made famous in England by the 19th-century carol *Good King Wenceslas*. He was noted for his piety and was murdered by Boleslav, his brother. He became recognized as the patron of Bohemia.

Werburga, St (d. *c.* 699, f.d. 3 February, 21 June). Daughter of King Wulfhere of Mercia and St Ermenilda, she took the veil at Ely under St Ethelfreda. She later founded monasteries at Hanbury and Weedon, and then at Trentham, where she died. Her body was translated to Chester to save it from an attack by the Danes. Her shrine at Chester was a centre of pilgrimage until destroyed by Henry VIII, though fragments of it still exist; she is patron of the city. In art she is depicted with a goose she had restored to life: a borrowed legend.

Wesley, John (1703–91), **Charles** (1707–88), **Samuel** (1766–1837). John and Charles Wesley, co-founders of the METHODIST CHURCH, were sons of the rector of Epworth, in Lincolnshire. Both studied at Oxford and were originally rigid High Churchmen; they were, with George Whitefield, members of the HOLY CLUB. John went to America as a missionary, but proved ineffective. On his return to England he was converted by the MORAVIANS and became an ardent EVANGELICAL. Charles also experienced conversion. The brothers then rode about the country preaching, largely in the open air, as the CHURCH OF ENGLAND closed its pulpits to them. They became known as Methodists, and organized Methodist societies. Charles was a noted hymn-writer, composing some 6,500 hymns of varying quality; his son Samuel became famous as an organist and composer of church and chamber music and oratorios.
Wesleyan. A member of the NONCONFORMIST church which grew out of the evangelical movement started by John Wesley (1703–91) and his associates, although there was no real break with the CHURCH OF ENGLAND until 1795. *See* METHODISTS.

West. The Western Church. The CATHOLIC CHURCH.

Westminster Assembly, The. The assembly appointed by the Long Parliament to reform the English Church. It consisted of 30 laymen and 120 clergy and met in Westminster Abbey precincts (1643–53). Its most important achievement was the WESTMINSTER CONFESSION. *See also* ERASTIANISM.
The Westminster Confession. The PRESBY-

TERIAN Confession of faith adopted by the WEST-MINSTER ASSEMBLY in 1646 and approved by Parliament in 1648. It became a standard definition of Presbyterian doctrine.

Wheel. Emblematical of St CATHERINE, who was broken on a spiked wheel.

St DONATUS bears a wheel set round with lights.

St EUPHEMIA and St WILLIGIS both carry wheels.

St QUINTIN is sometimes represented with a broken wheel at his feet.

Whig Bible, The. *See* BIBLE, SOME SPECIALLY NAMED EDITIONS.

Whip-dog Day. 18 October, St LUKE's day. Brand (*Popular Antiquities*, II) says that it is so called because a priest about to celebrate MASS on St Luke's Day happened to drop the PYX, which was snatched up by a dog.

White denotes purity, simplicity, and candour; innocence, truth, and hope. For its ecclesiastical use, symbolism, etc., *see* COLOURS.

White Canons. *See* PREMONSTRATENSIAN.

White Fathers. Members of the French Society of Missionaries of Africa established at Algiers in 1868. So called from their white tunic.

White Friars. The CARMELITES, so called from their white mantle worn over a brown habit. One of their houses founded in London on the south side of Fleet Street in 1241 gave its name to the district called *Whitefriars* or Alsatia which was long a SANCTUARY.

White Ladies. A popular name for the CISTERCIAN nuns in mediaeval England, from the colour of their habit, and for the Magdalenes. Also applied to the French Order of the Sisters of the Presentation of Mary (1796).

White Monks. The CISTERCIAN monks, whose habit was made from white wool.

White Sisters. The Congregation of the Daughters of the HOLY GHOST, founded in Brittany in 1706, so called from the colour of their habit. Also the Congregation of the Missionary Sisters of Our Lady of Africa (1869), the counterpart of the WHITE FATHERS.

A whited sepulchre. A hypocrite, especially one who conceals wickedness under a cloak of virtue.

In Biblical times, Jewish sepulchres were whitened to make them conspicuous so that passers-by might avoid ritual defilement by near approach. Thus Jesus (*Matt.* xxiii, 27) says: 'Ye are like unto whited sepulchres, which indeed appear beautiful outward, but are within full of dead men's bones, and of all uncleanness.'

White, St Eustace (d. 1591, f.d. 25 October). Born at Louth in Lincolnshire, of a good PROTESTANT family, he became a convert to ROMAN CATHOLICISM in 1584 and went to the ENGLISH COLLEGE, ROME, where he was ordained priest. He returned to England to carry out a ministry in the West Country, but was arrested at Blandford in Dorset and imprisoned at Bridewell, where he was tortured. He was condemned to death and executed at Tyburn with other Catholic priests. He was canonized in 1970 among the FORTY MARTYRS OF ENGLAND AND WALES.

Whitsunday. *White* Sunday. The seventh SUNDAY after EASTER, to commemorate the descent of the HOLY GHOST on the day of PENTECOST. It was one of the great seasons for baptism and the candidates wore white garments, hence the name.

Whitsuntide. The whole week following WHITSUNDAY.

Whitsun farthings. *See* PENTECOSTALS.

Whitsun-ale. The most important CHURCH-ALE, celebrated with much revelry.

Wicked. The Wicked Bible. *See* BIBLE, SOME SPECIALLY NAMED EDITIONS.

The Wicked Prayer Book. Printed 1686, octavo. In the Epistle for the Fourteenth Sunday after TRINITY the following passage occurs:

Now the works of the flesh are manifest, which are these, adultery, fornication, uncleanness, idolatry ... they who do such things shall inherit the kingdom of God.

('shall inherit' should be 'shall not inherit'.)

Wife-hater Bible, The. *See* BIBLE, SOME SPECIALLY NAMED EDITIONS.

Wilfrid, St (*c.* 634–700, f.d. 12 October). A Northumbrian, educated at Lindisfarne, he subsequently visited Canterbury and ROME, learning the Roman liturgy. He became Abbot of Ripon and was largely responsible for the adoption of Roman usages in preference to Celtic at the Synod of Whitby, 664. Soon afterwards he became BISHOP of York and finally of Hexham.

St Wilfrid's Needle. A narrow passage in the crypt of Ripon cathedral, built by Odo, Archbishop of Canterbury, and said to have been used to test a woman's chastity, as none but a virgin was able to squeeze through.

William. St William of Maleval (d. 1157, f.d. 10 February). A Frenchman of the 12th century who died in Tuscany. He went as a pilgrim to the HOLY LAND and on his return adopted the religious life. He was noted for his piety and asceticism and for his gifts of prayer and prophecy.

William of Malmesbury (c. 1080–1143). A monk and librarian of Malmesbury Abbey and noted chronicler and historian. Among his numerous works his two most important are his *De Gestis Regum Anglorum* (Chronicle of the Kings of England, to 1125) and *De Gestis Pontificum Anglorum* (The History of the Prelates of England, to 1122).

St William of Montevergine (d. 1142, f.d. 25 June). A 12th-century hermit of Piedmont who built himself a cell on Montevergine and subsequently founded several monasteries.

St William of Norwich (1132–44). A tanner's apprentice of Norwich, alleged to have been crucified and murdered by Jews during the PASSOVER. It was said at the time that it was part of Jewish ritual to sacrifice a Christian every year. (*See* Drayton's *Polyolbion*, song xxiv.)

William of Occam (c. 1300–c. 1349). The famous Nominalist philosopher, a native of Ockham, Surrey; also called *Doctor Invincibilis. See* OCCAM'S RAZOR.

St William of York (d. 1154). William Fitzherbert, chaplain to King Stephen and Archbishop of York (1142). He was canonized by Honorius III in 1227, largely on account of the miracles reported to have been performed at his tomb.

Willibald, St (c. 700–86/7, f.d. 7 July). Born in Wessex, he was brother of St WINNIBALD and St WALBURGA and cousin of St BONIFACE. From five years old he was educated at a monastery at Waltham, where he became a monk. He made many journeys and pilgrimages, accompanying his father St Richard to ROME and the HOLY LAND, visiting the LAURAS of the Eastern Church and staying in Constantinople. He returned to Italy and lived at the BENEDICTINE monastery of MONTE CASSINO, helping with monastic restoration and reform. He was received by Pope Gregory III who, at the request of St Boniface, sent Willibald to Germany on a mission. There he was ordained by Boniface, and appointed bishop of Eichstatt. With his brother and sister, he founded the double abbey of Heidenheim where St Walburga became abbess. Willibald was one of the most noted travellers of his time. His relics are at the cathedral of Eichstatt.

Willibrord, St (658–739, f.d. 7 November). Born in Northumberland and educated at Ripon, he went to Ireland where he trained as a missionary, going to Frisia with twelve companions. He was ordained bishop of Utrecht by Pope Sergius at the request of Pippin II. He carried out a dangerous mission among the pagans of Denmark and Heligoland. He was a notable preacher of gracious and cheerful temperament, and was said to have worked miracles. At his shrine at Echternach a ritual procession and dance takes place on Whit Tuesday.

Willigis, St (d. 1011, f.d. 2 February). Of humble family, the son of a wheelwright at Schonigen, he became a priest and was made canon of Hildesheim. He was a man of great ability in both church and state, and was appointed first chaplain, then chancellor, by Emperor Otto III. Later he was made archbishop of Mainz and vicar apostolic for Germany. He consecrated the Emperor Henry III. In art he is depicted with a wheel as an emblem of his origins; he had insisted on incorporating it in his coat of arms.

Wimple. A covering of white linen or silk for the head, neck and sides of the face, worn by women in mediaeval times, and still retained by many orders of nuns.

Winifred, or **Winefride, St** (f.d. 3 November, 22 June). Patron SAINT of North Wales and virgin martyr. According to the story she was the daughter of a Welsh chieftain and was instructed by St Beuno. Prince Caradoc made violent advances to her and she fled to the church for safety. Caradoc pursued her and struck off her head, but it was replaced on her body by St Beuno who breathed life into her again. She died a second time about 660. The miraculous healing spring of Holywell (Flintshire) gushed forth where her head had come to rest, and it became a regular resort of pilgrims and remains so to this day. In art she is depicted carrying her head and holding a palm, or with her head and axe at her feet, and a stream; she is also represented reading a book and holding a palm, symbol of martyrdom.

Winnibald, St (d. 761, f.d. 18 December). Brother of SS WILLIBALD and WALBURGA, he went with them on a pilgrimage to ROME and remained there to study for seven years before returning to England. He was then invited by St BONIFACE to join in a mission to Germany. He was ordained priest and, with his brother and sister, founded the double monastery of Heidenheim under the RULE of St BENEDICT, his sister becoming abbess. Winnibald died there and miracles were reported at his tomb.

Wise Men of the East. *See* MAGI.

Wolfgang, St (924–94, f.d. 31 October). Born in Swabia, he was educated at the BENEDICTINE abbey at Reichenau on Lake Constance. After having taught at Trier and Würzburg cathedral schools, he joined the Benedictines at Einsiedeln and was appointed headmaster of the school. He was ordained in 971 and went on a short mission to the Magyars, after which he was made bishop of Regensburg. He was a reformer of corrupt monastic institutions and was noted for his devout life, generosity, and preaching ability; he was also tutor to the Emperor Henry II. His relics at Regensburg became the centre of a cult which still continues.

Wolfram (or Wulfram), St (7th cent., f.d. 20 March, 15 October). A courtier at the court of King Dagobert, he became a monk and was appointed archbishop of Sens, but soon left his diocese to become a missionary to the Frisians. There he worked against the practice of human sacrifice. He converted King Radbod's son, but tradition says that the king asked where his ancestors were and, when told they were in hell with other heathens, he rejected Christianity and said he would rather be in hell with heroes than in heaven with a parcel of beggars. Wolfram ultimately returned to Fontenelle and died there.

Word. The Word. The SCRIPTURES; Christ as the Logos.

> In the beginning was the Word, and the Word was with God, and the Word was God.
>
> *John* i, 1

The Word, or Logos, is sacred sound, the first element in the process of manifestation.

Work. Seven Works of Mercy. *See* MERCY.

World. The world, the flesh, and the devil. 'The world' is the material things of this world as opposed to the things of the spirit; 'the flesh', sensual pleasures; 'the DEVIL', EVIL of every kind.

> From all the deceits of the world, the flesh, and the devil, Good Lord, deliver us.
>
> *The Litany (Book of Common Prayer)*

World Council of Churches (WCC). A series of oecumenical meetings in the 20th century culminated in the founding of the World Council of Churches. It had been preceded by the World Missionary Conference at Edinburgh in 1910 (the city has been called 'the birthplace of the oecumenical movement'); the International Missionary Council, Geneva (1921); the Life and Work Movement, Stockholm (1925); and the Faith and Order Movement, Lausanne (1927); also various other oecumenical conferences. All called for a united effort on the part of the churches to discuss and confront universal religious and social problems. The result was the foundation of the World Council of Churches at an assembly at Amsterdam in 1948. It included 148 churches, which involved Eastern ORTHODOX, OLD CATHOLICS, ANGLICAN and PROTESTANT denominations; 44 countries were represented by more than 1,400 delegates. The ROMAN CATHOLIC CHURCH, although regarding the movement sympathetically and sending observers to the assemblies, has not become a member.

Member churches normally have at least 25,000 followers; churches between 10,000 and 25,000 may become associate members. The WCC now lists over 3,000 churches in more than 100 countries. Its aims are practical co-operation and common study among Christian denominations, and its basis states: 'The WCC is a fellowship of churches which confess the Lord Jesus Christ as God and Saviour according to the Scriptures and therefore seek to fulfil together their common calling to the glory of the one God, Father, Son and Holy Spirit.' The word 'fellowship' in this context is traced back to a proposal made in 1920 by the Synod of the Oecumenical Patriarchate of Constantinople.

The WCC offers counsel and provides opportunities for united action in matters of common interest, but does not legislate for the churches; it discharges its functions through an Assembly, a Central Committee, an Executive Committee and other subordinate bodies; it also maintains contact with a global network of lay and study centres. Its headquarters are at Geneva.

Member churches of the WCC as of March 1995

AFRICA
African Christian Church and Schools
African Church of the Holy Spirit
African Israel Church, Nineveh
African Protestant Church (Eglise protestante africaine)
Baptist Community of Western Zaire (Eglise du Christ au Zaïre Ouest)
Church of Jesus Christ in Madagascar (Eglise de Jésus-Christ à Madagascar)
Church of Jesus Christ on Earth by His Messenger Simon Kimbangu (Eglise de Jésus-Christ sur la Terre par son Envoyé Simon Kimbangu)
Church of the Brethren in Nigeria
Church of the Lord Aladura
Church of the Province of Burundi (Eglise épiscopale du Burundi)
Church of the Province of Central Africa
Church of the Province of Kenya
Church of the Province of Nigeria
Church of the Province of Rwanda
Church of the Province of Southern Africa
Church of the Province of Tanzania
Church of the Province of the Indian Ocean
Church of the Province of West Africa
Community of Disciples of Christ (Eglise du Christ au Zaïre – Communauté des Disciples du Christ)
Community of Light (Eglise du Christ au Zaïre –

Communauté lumière)
Episcopal Baptist Community (Communauté
épiscopale baptiste en Afrique)
Episcopal Church of the Sudan
Ethiopian Evangelical Church Mekane Yesus
Ethiopian Orthodox Tewahedo Church
Evangelical Church of Cameroon (Eglise
évangélique du Gabon)
Evangelical Church of the Congo (Eglise
évangélique du Congo)
Evangelical Community (Eglise du Christ au
Zaïre – Communauté évangélique)
Evangelical Congregational Church in Angola
Evangelical Lutheran Church in Southern Africa
Evangelical Lutheran Church in Tanzania
Evangelical Lutheran Church in the Republic of
Namibia
Evangelical Lutheran Church in Zimbabwe
Evangelical Pentecostal Mission of Angola
Evangelical Presbyterian Church in South Africa
Evangelical Presbyterian Church of Togo (Eglise
évangélique presbytérienne du Togo)
Evangelical Presbyterian Church, Ghana
Lesotho Evangelical Church
Lutheran Church in Liberia
Malagasy Lutheran Church (Eglise luthérienne
malgache)
Mennonite Community (Eglise du Christ au
Zaïre – Communauté mennonite au Zaïre)
Methodist Church in Kenya
Methodist Church in Zimbabwe
Methodist Church Nigeria
Methodist Church of Southern Africa
Methodist Church Sierra Leone
Methodist Church, Ghana
Moravian Church in Southern Africa
Moravian Church in Tanzania
Presbyterian Church in Cameroon
Presbyterian Church in the Sudan
Presbyterian Church of Africa
Presbyterian Church of Cameroon (Eglise pres-
bytérienne camerounaise)
Presbyterian Church of East Africa
Presbyterian Church of Ghana
Presbyterian Church of Rwanda (Eglise pres-
bytérienne au Rwanda)
Presbyterian Church of Southern Africa
Presbyterian Community (Eglise du Christ –
Communauté presbytérienne)
Presbytery of Liberia
Protestant Church of Algeria (Eglise protestante
d'Algérie)
Protestant Methodist Church of Benin (Eglise
protestante méthodiste au Bénin)
Protestant Methodist Church, Ivory Coast
(Eglise protestante méthodiste de Côte
d'Ivoire)
Reformed Church in Zimbabwe
Reformed Church of Equatorial Guinea (Iglesia
Reformada de Guinea Ecuatorial)
Reformed Church of Zambia
Reformed Presbyterian Church in Southern Africa

Union of Baptist Churches of Cameroon (Union
des Eglises baptistes du Cameroun)
United Church of Zambia
United Congregational Church of Southern
Africa
United Evangelical Church 'Anglican
Communion in Angola'
Uniting Reformed Church in Southern Africa

ASIA
Anglican Church in Aotearoa, New Zealand and
Polynesia
Anglican Church of Australia
Associated Churches of Christ in New Zealand
Bangladesh Baptist Sangha
Baptist Union of New Zealand
Batak Christian Community Church (GPKB)
Batak Protestant Christian Church (HKBP)
Bengal–Orissa–Bihar Baptist Convention
China Christian Council
Christian Church of Central Sulawesi (GKST)
Christian Evangelical Church in Minahasa
(GMIM)
Christian Protestant Angola Church (GKPA)
Christian Protestant Church in Indonesia (GKPI)
Church of Bangladesh
Church of Ceylon
Church of Christ in China, The Hong Kong
Council
Church of Christ in Thailand
Church of North India
Church of Pakistan
Church of South India
Church of the Province of Burma
Churches of Christ in Australia
East Java Christian Church (GKJW)
Evangelical Christian Church in Halmahera
Evangelical Christian Church in Irian Jaya
Evangelical Church of Sangir Talaud (GMIST)
Evangelical Methodist Church in the Philippines
Holy Catholic Church in Japan
Indonesian Christian Church (GKI)
Indonesian Christian Church (HKI)
Japanese Orthodox Church
Javanese Christian Churches (GKJ)
Kalimantan Evangelical Church
Karo Batak Protestant Church (GBKP)
Korean Christian Church in Japan
Korean Methodist Church
Malankara Orthodox Syrian Church
Mar Thoma Syrian Church of Malabar
Methodist Church
Methodist Church in India
Methodist Church in Malaysia
Methodist Church in Singapore
Methodist Church of New Zealand
Methodist Church, Upper Burma
Myanmar Baptist Convention
Nias Protestant Christian Church (BNKP)
Pasundan Christian Church (GKP)
Philippine Episcopal Church
Philippine Independent Church

Presbyterian Church in Taiwan
Presbyterian Church in the Republic of Korea
Presbyterian Church of Aotearoa New Zealand
Presbyterian Church of Korea
Presbyterian Church of Pakistan
Protestant Christian Church in Bali (GKPB)
Protestant Church in Indonesia (GPI)
Protestant Church in Sabah
Protestant Church in South-East Sulawesi
Protestant Church in the Moluccas (GPM)
Protestant Church in Western Indonesia (GPIB)
Protestant Evangelical Church in Timor (GMIT)
Samavesam of Telugu Baptist Churches
Simalungun Protestant Christian Church (GKPS)
Toraja Church
United Church of Christ in Japan
United Church of Christ in the Philippines
United Evangelical Lutheran Churches in India
Uniting Church in Australia

CARIBBEAN
Church in the Province of the West Indies
Methodist Church in Cuba (Iglesia Metodista en Cuba)
Methodist Church in the Caribbean and the Americas
Moravian Church in Jamaica
Moravian Church in Suriname
Moravian Church, Eastern West Indies Province
Presbyterian Church in Trinidad and Tobago
Presbyterian Reformed Church in Cuba (Iglesia Presbiteriana-Reformada en Cuba)
United Church in Jamaica and the Cayman Islands
United Protestant Church

EUROPE
Armenian Apostolic Church (Eglise apostolique arménienne)
Autocephalic Orthodox Church in Poland
Baptist Union of Denmark
Baptist Union of Great Britain
Baptist Union of Hungary
Bulgarian Orthodox Church
Catholic Diocese of the Old Catholics in Germany (Katholisches Bistum der Alt-Katholiken in Deutschland)
Church in Wales
Church of England
Church of Greece
Church of Ireland
Church of Norway
Church of Scotland
Church of Sweden
Czechoslovak Hussite Church
Ecumenical Patriarchate of Constantinople
Estonian Evangelical Lutheran Church
Euro-Asiatic Federation of the Unions of Evangelical Christians-Baptists
European Continental Province of the Moravian Church (Netherlands) (Europäisch-Festländische Brüder-Unität)

Evangelical Baptist Union of Italy
Evangelical Church in Germany (Evangelische Kirche in Deutschland)
Evangelical Church of Czech Brethren
Evangelical Church of the Augsburg and Helvetic Confessions in Austria (Evangelische Kirche A.B. u. H.B. in Österreich)
Evangelical Church of the Augsburg Confession of Alsace and Lorraine (Eglise de la Confession d'Augsbourg, d'Alsace et de Lorraine)
Evangelical Church of the Augsburg Confession in Romania
Evangelical Church of the Augsburg Confession in the Slovak Republic
Evangelical Church of the Augsburg Confession in Poland
Evangelical Lutheran Church
Evangelical Lutheran Church in Denmark
Evangelical Lutheran Church of Finland
Evangelical Lutheran Church of France (Eglise évangélique luthérienne de France)
Evangelical Lutheran Church of Iceland
Evangelical Lutheran Church of Latvia
Evangelical Methodist Church of Italy
Evangelical Presbyterian Church of Portugal
Evangelical Synodal Presbyterial Church of the Augsburg Confession in Romania
Georgian Orthodox Church
Greek Evangelical Church
Latvian Evangelical Lutheran Church Abroad
Lusitanian Catholic Apostolic Evangelical Church
Lutheran Church in Hungary
Mennonite Church (Vereinigung der Deutschen Mennonitengemeinden)
Mennonite Church in the Netherlands
Methodist Church Great Britain
Methodist Church in Ireland
Mission Covenant Church of Sweden
Moravian Church in Great Britain and Ireland
Netherlands Reformed Church
Old Catholic Church of Austria (Alt-Katholische Kirche Österreichs)
Old Catholic Church of Switzerland (Christ-katholische Kirche in der Schweiz)
Old Catholic Church of the Netherlands
Old Catholic Mariavite Church in Poland
Orthodox Autocephalous Church of Albania
Orthodox Church in the Czech Republic
Orthodox Church in the Slovak Republic
Orthodox Church of Finland
Polish Catholic Church in Poland
Presbyterian Church of Wales
Reformed Christian Church in Slovakia
Reformed Christian Church in Yugoslavia
Reformed Church in Hungary
Reformed Church of Alsace and Lorraine (Eglise réformée d'Alsace et de Lorraine)
Reformed Church of France (Eglise réformée de France)
Reformed Church of Romania

Reformed Churches in the Netherlands
Remonstrant Brotherhood
Romanian Orthodox Church
Russian Orthodox Church
Scottish Congregational Church
Scottish Episcopal Church
Serbian Orthodox Church
Silesian Evangelical Church of the Augsburg Confession
Slovak Evangelical Church of the Augsburg Confession in Yugoslavia
Spanish Evangelical Church (Iglesia Evangélica Española)
Spanish Reformed Episcopal Church (Iglesia Española Reformada Episcopal)
Swiss Protestant Church Federation (Schweizerischer Evangelischer Kirchenbund)
Union of Welsh Independents
United Free Church of Scotland
United Protestant Church of Belgium (Eglise protestante unie de Belgique)
United Reformed Church of the United Kingdom
Waldensian Church

LATIN AMERICA
Baptist Association of El Salvador (Asociación Bautista de El Salvador)
Baptist Convention of Nicaragua (Convención Bautista de Nicaragua)
Bolivian Evangelical Lutheran Church (Iglesia Evangélica Luterana Boliviana)
Church of God (Iglesia de Dios)
Church of the Disciples of Christ (Iglesia de los Discípulos de Cristo)
Episcopal Anglican Church of Brazil
Evangelical Church of Lutheran Confession in Brazil
Evangelical Church of the River Plate (Iglesia Evangélica Luterana en Chile)
Evangelical Methodist Church in Bolivia (Iglesia Evangélica Metodista en Bolivia)
Evangelical Methodist Church in Uruguay (Iglesia Evangélica Metodista en el Uruguay)
Evangelical Methodist Church of Argentina (Iglesia Evangélica Metodista Argentina)
Evangelical Methodist Church of Costa Rica (Iglesia Evangélica Metodista de Costa Rica)
Free Pentecostal Mission Church of Chile (Iglesia de Misiones Pentecostales Libres de Chile)
Latin American Reformed Church
Methodist Church in Brazil
Methodist Church of Chile (Iglesia Metodista de Chile)
Methodist Church of Mexico (Iglesia Metodista de Mexico)
Methodist Church of Peru (Iglesia Metodista del Peru)
Moravian Church in Nicaragua (Iglesia Morava en Nicaragua)
Pentecostal Church of Chile (Iglesia Pentecostal de Chile)
Pentecostal Mission Church (Misión Iglesia Pentecostal)
Salvadorean Lutheran Synod (Sínodo Luterano Salvadoreño)
United Evangelical Lutheran Church (Iglesia Evangélica Luterana Unida)
United Presbyterian Church of Brazil

MIDDLE EAST
Armenian Apostolic Church
Church of Cyprus
Coptic Orthodox Church
Episcopal Church in Jerusalem and the Middle East
Greek Orthodox Patriarchate of Alexandria and All Africa
Greek Orthodox Patriarchate of Antioch and All the East (Patriarcat grec-orthodoxe d'Antioche et de tout l'Orient)
Greek Orthodox Patriarchate of Jerusalem
Holy Apostolic Catholic Assyrian Church of the East
National Evangelical Synod of Syria and Lebanon
Synod of the Evangelical Church of Iran
Synod of the Nile of the Evangelical Church
Syrian Orthodox Patriarchate of Antioch and All the East
Union of the Armenian Evangelical Churches in the Near East

NORTH AMERICA
African Methodist Episcopal Church
African Methodist Episcopal Zion Church
American Baptist Churches in the USA
Anglican Church of Canada
Canadian Yearly Meeting of the Religious Society of Friends
Christian Church (Disciples of Christ)
Christian Methodist Episcopal Church
Church of the Brethren
Estonian Evangelical Lutheran Church Abroad
Evangelical Lutheran Church in America
Evangelical Lutheran Church in Canada (Eglise évangélique luthérienne au Canada)
Friends General Conference
Friends United Meeting
Hungarian Reformed Church in America
International Council of Community Churches
International Evangelical Church
Moravian Church in America (Northern Province)
Moravian Church in America (Southern Province)
National Baptist Convention of America
National Baptist Convention, USA, Inc.
Orthodox Church in America
Polish National Catholic Church
Presbyterian Church (USA)
Presbyterian Church in Canada
Progressive National Baptist Convention, Inc.
Protestant Episcopal Church in the USA

Reformed Church in America
United Church of Canada
United Church of Christ
United Methodist Church

PACIFIC
Church of Melanesia
Congregational Christian Church in American
Samoa
Congregational Christian Church in Samoa
Cook Islands Christian Church
Evangelical Church in New Caledonia and the
Loyalty Isles (Eglise évangélique de la
Nouvelle Caledonie et aux Iles Loyauté)
Evangelical Church of French Polynesia (Eglise
évangélique de Polynésie française)
Evangelical Lutheran Church of Papua New
Guinea
Kiribati Protestant Church
Methodist Church in Fiji
Methodist Church in Samoa
Methodist Church in Tonga
Presbyterian Church of Vanuatu
Tuvalu Christian Church
United Church in Papua New Guinea and the
Solomon Islands
United Church of Christ–Congregational in the
Marshall Islands

World Evangelical Fellowship. *See* EVANGELICAL
ALLIANCE.

Worms, Concordat of. In 1122 Pope Calixtus II
and the Emperor Henry V reached an agreement settling the Investiture Controversy. The
emperor ceded the exclusive right to invest
bishops and abbots and the pope agreed that
their election should take place in the presence
of the emperor.
Worms, Diet of. An assembly of the Holy
Roman Empire (1521) at which LUTHER
appeared to defend his doctrines before the
Emperor Charles V. His teachings were condemned after he had refused to recant.
Worms, Synod of (1076). Concerned with the
Investiture Controversy, the Emperor Henry V
maintained his claims in an anti-papal statement, and was subsequently excommunicated
by Pope Gregory VII.

Worship. Literally 'worth-ship', honour, dignity,
reverence; in its highest and now usual sense,
the respect and reverence man pays to God.
At one time the word carried a sense of personal respect, as in, 'Thou shalt have worship
in the presence of them that sit at meat with
thee' (*Luke* xiv, 10), and in the marriage service
(*Book of Common Prayer*), the man says to the

woman: 'With my body I thee worship, and with
all my worldly goods I thee endow.'

Worthies, The Nine. Nine heroes—three from
the BIBLE, three from the classics, and three
from romance; or three pagans, three Jews,
and three Christians, who were bracketed
together by writers like the seven wonders of
the world. They are usually given as Hector,
Alexander, and Julius Caesar; Joshua, DAVID,
and Judas MACCABAEUS; Arthur, Charlemagne,
and Godfrey of Bouillon. Shakespeare's
Pageant of the Nine Worthies in *Love's Labour's
Lost* (V, ii) has an incomplete list of five which
includes Pompey and Hercules, who are not on
the traditional list.

> Nine worthies were they called, of different rites,
> Three Jews, three pagans, and three Christian
> Knights.
>
> DRYDEN: *The Flower and the Leaf,* 535

Wrenning Day. St Stephen's Day (26 December)
used to be so called, because it was a local custom among villagers to stone a wren to death
on that day in commemoration of the stoning of
St STEPHEN.

Wulfstan, or **Wulstan.** There are two English
saints of this name. (1) Wulfstan, Archbishop of
York (d. 1023), and formerly Bishop of
Worcester, best known for his homily in Old
English prose *Lupi Sermo ad Anglos,* etc., por-
traying the miseries of the year 1014 during the
Danish onslaught. (2) Wulfstan, Bishop of
Worcester (d. 1095), noted, in association with
Lanfranc, for suppression of the slave trade
between England and Ireland.

Wulsin, St (d. 1002, f.d. 8 January). The first
abbot of Westminster and a friend of St DUN-
STAN, who loved him like a son. He was bishop
of Sherborne in 992, introducing monasticism
there and rebuilding the church. A relic of his
is the famed Sherborne Pontifical, an outstanding example of Winchester illumination.

Wuyck's Bible. *See* BIBLE, SOME SPECIALLY NAMED
EDITIONS.

Wycliffite. A LOLLARD, a follower of Wyclif (*c.*
1320–84), who was called 'The Morning Star of
the REFORMATION'. He condemned TRANSUB-
STANTIATION, and monasticism, and held that
only the righteous have the right to dominion
and property. He attacked the Papacy and the
BISHOPS, and advocated the use of the BIBLE in
English.

X

X. X as an abbreviation stands for Christ as in Xmas. It is also the form of the CROSS of St ANDREW.

Xavier. *See* FRANCIS.

Xaverian Brothers, The. A Roman Catholic congregation founded at Bruges in 1839, concerned chiefly with the education of youth. It was founded by Theodore James Ryken who took the name Brother Francis Xavier after St FRANCIS XAVIER (1506–52), one of the earliest of the JESUITS, celebrated as the 'Apostle of the Indies' and 'the Apostle of Japan'.

Xystus, St. *See* SIXTUS II.

Y

Yahweh. *See* JEHOVAH.

Year of Our Lord. A year of the Christian era.

In the WESTERN CHURCH the liturgical year is based on the week and on the festivals, beginning on the first Sunday in ADVENT, the Sundays being numbered up to CHRISTMAS and after EPIPHANY, through LENT and after EASTER, then after WHITSUNDAY or TRINITY SUNDAY.

In the Eastern Church the year is divided into three parts: TRIODION, the ten weeks before Easter; PENTECOSTARION, the Paschal season; and the rest of the year, the OCTOECHOS.

Yew Sunday. An early name for PALM SUNDAY.

YMCA. The Young Men's Christian Association was founded in London in 1844 by George Williams, the 22-year-old son of a Somerset farmer, together with twelve other young men. They held Bible classes and prayer meetings which developed into the Association, with the goal: 'The Young Men's Christian Associations seek to unite young men who, regarding Jesus Christ as their God and Saviour according to the Holy Scriptures, desire to be his disciples in their faith and in their life, and to associate their efforts for the extension of his kingdom among young men.' The movement is PROTESTANT EVANGELICAL in persuasion and numbers some 26 million members in 96 countr es; in some parts it includes other faiths.

Yule, Yuletide. CHRISTMAS-time. O.E. *gēol,* from Icel. *jōl,* the name of a heathen festival at the winter solstice.

Yule log, or **Yule clog.** A great log of wood formerly laid across the hearth with great ceremony on Christmas Eve and lit with a brand from the previous year's log. There followed drinking and merriment.

Yves, St. *See* IVO.

YWCA. The Young Women's Christian Association followed as a companion movement to the YMCA in 1887. It began as an amalgamation of Lady Emily Kinnaird's work for the establishment of homes, rest centres, classes and lectures with Mrs Emma Robert's prayer union, and is now worldwide in its activities.

Ywi, St. *See* IWI.

Z

Zacharius, St (d. 752, f.d. 15 March (West), 5 September (East)). Born at Severino in Calabria, of Greek parentage, he was elected Pope in 741, following GREGORY III. He proved a good administrator, conciliating the Lombard Liutprand and bringing peace between the Lombards and the Greek Empire. He opposed ICONOCLASTIC policies of the Emperor Constantine Copronymus, and corresponded with St BONIFACE, encouraging his missionary work; he also supported the assumption of the Frankish crown by Pepin. He was a man of culture whose influence extended widely in Europe, as did his translation of the *Dialogues* of GREGORY THE GREAT into Greek.

Zeno, St (d. 371, f.d. 12 April). An African by birth, he was appointed bishop of Verona and was noted as a fervent pastor. He built churches, founded nunneries, was generous in almsgiving and corrected liturgical abuses. He strongly opposed the ARIAN heresy. Zeno was celebrated as an orator and his sermons, which were preserved, left a valuable history of the life of the church in his time. In art he is depicted as a dark-skinned old man in episcopal robes and mitre; a fish dangles from his crozier, denoting his love of angling. In Renaissance painting he is seen exorcizing the daughter of the Emperor Gallicenus: a demon issues from her mouth.

Zenobius, St (d. *c.* 390, f.d. 25 May). A nobleman who was converted to Christianity as a young man; he was a friend of both St AMBROSE and St DAMASUS. He became bishop of Florence and was famed for his learning, piety and austere life. Zenobius went as papal representative to Constantinople at the time of the ARIAN controversy. He was a worker of miracles, such as raising a child from the dead after it had been run over by an ox cart. He died at a great age, and when his coffin was carried to the cathedral it accidentally touched a dead tree, which at once came to life. In art he is depicted as an elderly bishop; he either holds a model of Florence or has the fleur-de-lys or a tree as an emblem. He is also represented raising the dead child or exorcizing demons.

Zephyrinus, St (d. 217, f.d. 26 August). Little is known of him but EUSEBIUS said that he excommunicated Theodotus the Cobbler and Theodotus the Money Changer who were involved in the ADOPTION controversy. His cult was suppressed in the calendar of 1969.

Zion (Heb. *Tsiyon*, a hill). Figuratively, the chosen people, the Israelites; the church of God, the kingdom of HEAVEN. The city of David stood on Mount Zion.

In *Pilgrim's Progress* Bunyan calls the Celestial City (i.e. heaven) *Mount Zion*.

Daughter of Zion. JERUSALEM or its people.

Zita, St (1218–72, f.d. 27 April). Also known as Sitha or Citha, she was born of devout but poor parents. At the age of twelve she became a servant in the household of a wealthy weaver in Lucca, remaining there all her life. She was intensely devout, spending hours in prayer and distributing food she was given to the poor. She also gave up her bed to beggars. This at first led to disputes with her employers, but later her devotion won their respect. Many miracles were recorded of her, such as angels baking the bread while she was rapt in prayer. Her relics are at Lucca, Genoa and other places. In art she is depicted with a key and rosary, or a book, or as praying at a well. In England she is known as Sitha, and invoked by domestic servants or housewives finding lost keys; she is represented in churches in Somerset, Norfolk, Devon and Oxfordshire. A chapel was built in her honour at Ely in 1456. She is patron saint of domestic servants.

Zucchetto. The small skullcap worn by Roman Catholic clergy; white for the POPE, red for a CARDINAL, purple for a BISHOP, and black for others.

Zürich. The Zürich Bible. *See* BIBLE, SOME SPECIALLY NAMED EDITIONS.

Zwickau Prophets, The. An early sect of Anabaptists at Zwickau in Saxony, who sought to establish a Christian commonwealth. *See also* ABECEDARIAN.

Zwinglian. Pertaining to the teachings of Ulrich (Huldreich) Zwingli (1484–1531), the Swiss religious reformer and minister at Zürich who ultimately rejected the papal authority and inaugurated the Swiss Reformation. He maintained that the BIBLE was the only true rule of faith. He also rejected clerical celibacy and seasons of fasting.